History in Focus

GCSE

BRITISH SOCIAL & ECONOMIC

History

BEN WALSH

JOHN MURRAY

I would like to acknowledge the consistent help and support of many colleagues, particularly Wayne Birks of Casterton Community College; Dave Perrett of Staffordshire LEA; and the editorial team at John Murray. The book is dedicated to my parents and parents-in-law for their constant support.

Ben Walsh

FOCUS TASK

Support worksheets and extra help with the focus tasks and activities in this book can be found in the Teacher's Resource Book.

Note: Some written sources have been adapted or abbreviated to make them accessible to all pupils, while faithfully preserving the sense of the original.

Words in SMALL CAPITALS are defined in the glossary on page 378.

© Ben Walsh 1997

First published in 1997
by John Murray (Publishers) Ltd
50 Albemarle Street
London W1S 4BD

Reprinted in 1999, 2000, 2002

Layouts by Fiona Webb
Illustrations by Oxford Illustrators Ltd
Cover design by John Townson/Creation
Typeset in 11/13pt Garamond Light Condensed
Colour separations by Radstock Reproductions Ltd, Midsomer Norton, Bath
Printed and bound in Great Britain by Butler & Tanner Limited

A CIP catalogue record for this book is available from the British Library.

Student's Book 0-7195-7271-1
Teacher's Resource Book 0-7195-7272-X

Contents

Acknowledgements

Thanks are due to the following for permission to reproduce copyright photographs:

Cover: *left* Hulton Getty; *centre left* Bridgeman Art Library; *centre right* Public Record Office, London; *right* Maggie Murray/Format; **p.9** *tl, tr & b* The Fotomas Index; **p.14** *tl, tr & b* Mary Evans Picture Library; **p.20** Cambridge University Collection of Air Photographs, © British Crown Copyright/MOD; **p.29** *t* Rural History Centre, University of Reading; **p.30** *l & r* Lawes Agricultural Trust; **p.31** *t* Mary Evans Picture Library, *b* Rural History Centre, University of Reading; **p.36** *t* By kind permission of The Earl of Leicester (photograph © World Microfilms Publications), *b* Copyright © British Museum; **p.43** Mary Evans Picture Library; **p.44** *t* Public Record Office, London, *b* The Fotomas Index; **p.45** *tl* By permission of The British Library, *tr* Mary Evans Picture Library, *b* Berkshire Record Office; **p.48** Mary Evans Picture Library; **p.49** Copyright © British Museum; **p.51** *t & b* Mary Evans Picture Library; **p.53** Guildhall Library, Corporation of London/Bridgeman Art Library; **p.54** Mary Evans Picture Library; **p.55** Mary Evans Picture Library; **p.56** Hulton Getty; **p.57** Mary Evans Picture Library; **p.58** Mary Evans Picture Library; **p.62** *l & r* Hulton Getty; **p.65** Mary Evans Picture Library; **p.66** Mary Evans Picture Library; **p.67** *t, c & b* The Arkwright Society; **p.69** Mary Evans Picture Library; **p.70** Manchester Public Libraries; **p.72** Mary Evans Picture Library; **p.73** *l & r* Mary Evans Picture Library; **p.79** Mary Evans Picture Library; **p.85** *t & b* Mary Evans Picture Library; **p.86** Hulton Getty; **p.88** Mary Evans Picture Library; **p.89** *tl & tr* Hulton Getty, *b* Mary Evans Picture Library; **p.93** *t* Quarry Bank Mill Trust Limited, *b* National Trust Photographic Library; **p.95** Manchester Public Libraries; **p.99** *t* Ironbridge Gorge Museum Trust, *b* Press Association/Topham; **p. 105** *t & c* Ironbridge Gorge Museum Trust, *b* Science Museum/Science & Society Picture Library; **p.107** Cyfartha Castle Museum and Art Gallery; **p.108** *l* Hulton Getty, *r* Mary Evans Picture Library; **p.110** Mary Evans Picture Library; **p.111** Sheffield City Libraries; **p.115** Mary Evans Picture Library; **p.118** Hulton Getty; **p.121** *tl, tr, bl & br* Mary Evans Picture Library; **p.122** Mary Evans Picture Library; **p.123** Public Record Office, London; **p.124** *l* Hulton Getty, *r* Mary Evans Picture Library; **p.129** Christie's, London/Bridgeman Art Library; **p.131** *l* Hulton Getty, *r* Ironbridge Gorge Museum Trust; **p.136** Mary Evans Picture Library; **p.138** Guildhall Library, Corporation of London; **p.139** *l* Hulton Getty, *r* Copyright © British Museum; **p.142** *t* Hulton Getty, *b* Mary Evans Picture Library; **p.143** Trustees of the Wedgwood Museum, Barlaston, Staffordshire; **p.144** *t* Reproduced by kind permission of Birmingham Library Services, *c & b* Black Country Museum, Dudley; **p.148** Beamish, The North of England Open Air Museum; **p.152** *b* Hulton Getty; **p.153** *tl, tr, br* Hulton Getty, *bl* National Railway Museum/Science & Society Picture Library; **p.154** *t, c & b* Mary Evans Picture Library; **p.157** *tl, tr, bl & br* Mary Evans Picture Library; **p.158** National Railway Museum/Science & Society Picture Library; **p.160** Mary Evans Picture Library; **p.162** *t & b* Hulton Getty; **p.163** Hulton Getty; **p.164** Mary Evans Picture Library; **p.165** *r* Hulton Getty; **p.166** *l* Hulton Getty, *b* Royal Holloway & Bedford New College, Surrey/Bridgeman Art Library; **p.167** National Railway Museum/ Science & Society Picture Library; **p.169** *t* Rex Features, *b* Mary Evans Picture Library; **p.170** National Railway Museum/Science & Society Picture Library; **p.177** Mary Evans Picture Library; **p.181** Mary Evans Picture Library; **p.183** *tl* Hulton Getty, *tr & b* Mary Evans Picture Library; **p.185** *t* Hulton Getty, *b* Mary Evans Picture Library; **p.186** Hulton Getty; **p.189** *t* Hulton Getty, *b* Mary Evans Picture Library; **p.190** Mary Evans Picture Library; **p.192** Wellcome Institute Library, London; **p.193** Mary Evans Picture Library; **p.199** *t* Punch, *b* Mary Evans Picture Library; **p.200** Ann Ronan/Image Select; **p.201** Mary Evans Picture Library; **p.202** *t* Mary Evans Picture Library, *b* The Fotomas Index; **p.205** Mary Evans Picture Library;

p.206 Hulton Getty; **p.207** *l & r* Reproduced by kind permission of Birmingham Library Services; **p.211** *l* Mary Evans Picture Library, *r* Amanda Knapp/Rex Features; **p.212** Hulton Getty; **p.215** National Trust Photographic Library; **p.217** Mary Evans Picture Library; **p.221** Mary Evans Picture Library; **p.222** Reproduced by courtesy of the Trustees of the William Salt Library; **p.224** Mary Evans Picture Library; **p.225** Mary Evans Picture Library; **p.227** Mary Evans Picture Library; **p.228** *tl & tr* Barnardo's Photographic Archive, *b* Mary Evans Picture Library; **p.229** *tl, tr & br* Mary Evans Picture Library, *bl* Hulton Getty; **p.230** Hulton Getty; **p.234** Hulton Getty; **p.235** *t & bl* Mary Evans Picture Library, *br* Hulton Getty; **p.236** *bl & br* Mary Evans Picture Library; **p.240** Hulton Getty; **p.242** Punch; **p.243** Hulton Getty; **p.244** Hulton Getty; **p.246** Hulton Getty; **p.247** Daily Express/Solo; **p.249** Hulton Getty; **p.255** *r* Hulton Getty; **p.258** Mary Evans Picture Library; **p.259** Mary Evans Picture Library; **p.261** *r* Hulton Getty; **p.262** Hulton Getty; **p.263** Hulton Getty; **p.264** Hulton Getty; **p.268** Communist Party Library; **p.269** The Royal Archives © Her Majesty The Queen; **p.270** Mary Evans Picture Library; **p.271** Trades Union Congress, London/Bridgeman Art Library; **p.274** By permission of the National Museum of Labour History; **p.272** By permission of the National Museum of Labour History; **p.275** *l* Mary Evans Picture Library, *r* Rural History Centre, University of Reading; **p.276** *t & b* Mary Evans Picture Library; **p.277** *t* Mary Evans Picture Library, *b* Hulton Getty; **p.278** *l* Hulton Getty, *tr* Topham Picturepoint; **p.282** *b* By permission of the National Museum of Labour History; **p.283** *l* Punch, *r* Mary Evans Picture Library; **p.284** Daily Herald; **p.285** *l & r* Hulton Getty; **p.287** Mary Evans Picture Library; **p.288** *tl* Trades Union Congress Library, *r* Mary Evans Picture Library; **p.289** Daily Herald; **p.291** *t* Mary Evans Picture Library, *b* Hulton Getty; **p.296** *l* Daily Express/Solo, *r* Topham Picturepoint; **p.298** Cartoon by Trogg, 6 May 1979, © The Observer; **p.303** *l* Museum of the Royal Pharmaceutical Society of Great Britain, *r* Wellcome Institute Library, London; **p.305** Mary Evans Picture Library; **p.306** *t* Hulton Getty, *b* Museum of the Royal Pharmaceutical Society of Great Britain; **p.308** Wellcome Institute Library, London; **p.309** *t* Ann Ronan/Image Select, *b* Wellcome Institute Library, London; **p.310** Ann Ronan/Image Select; **p.311** Institut Pasteur, Paris; **p.312** Mary Evans Picture Library; **p.313** Royal College of Surgeons, London/Bridgeman Art Library; **p.314** Wellcome Institute Library, London; **p.315** Mary Evans Picture Library; **p.316** Mary Evans Picture Library; **p.317** Hulton Getty; **p.320** Wellcome Institute Library, London; **p.321** *t & b* Mary Evans Picture Library; **p.323** The Fotomas Index; **p.327** *l & r* Glaxo Wellcome; **p.329** Glaxo Wellcome; **p.330** Glaxo Wellcome; **p.333** *l* Punch, *r* © Express Newspapers; **p.334** Public Record Office, London; **p.340** Hulton Getty; **p.341** Mary Evans Picture Library; **p.342** *l & r* Mary Evans Picture Library; **p.343** Punch; **p.344** *t* Reproduced by kind permission of Birmingham Library Services, *b* Mary Evans Picture Library; **p.348** Copyright Cheltenham Ladies' College; **p.352** Punch; **p.353** Mary Evans/ Fawcett Library; **p.354** Mary Evans/Fawcett Library; **p.356** Mary Evans Picture Library; **p.357** *l, c & r* Mary Evans/Fawcett Library; **p.358** *b* Mary Evans/Fawcett Library; **p.359** *tl* Mary Evans/Fawcett Library, *tr* Mary Evans Picture Library, *b* Popperfoto; **p.261** *t* Hulton Getty, *b* Mary Evans/Fawcett Library; **p.363** Hulton Getty; **p.365** *b* Hulton Getty; **p.366** *t* Popperfoto, *b* Imperial War Museum, London; **p.367** *t & b* Public Record Office, London; **p.368** *t* Public Record Office, London, *bl & br* Popperfoto, *bc* Hulton Getty; **p.370** Hulton Getty; **p.372** *t* Hulton Getty; **p.374** © Michael Heath, reproduced by kind permission; **p.375** *r* Popperfoto; **p.376** *t* Sally Fraser/Format, *bl* Rex Features, *br* Popperfoto; **p.377** Hulton Getty.

Every effort has been made to contact copyright holders, and the publishers apologise for any omissions which they will be pleased to rectify at the earliest opportunity.

SECTION 1

Introduction

1 Overview

1.1 *The main changes*

As you can see from Sources 1 and 2, a lot changed between 1700 and 1900. You will already have studied many of these changes in your earlier history courses. There may still be evidence of these changes in your own locality. In this book you will analyse some of these changes in detail.

SOURCE 1

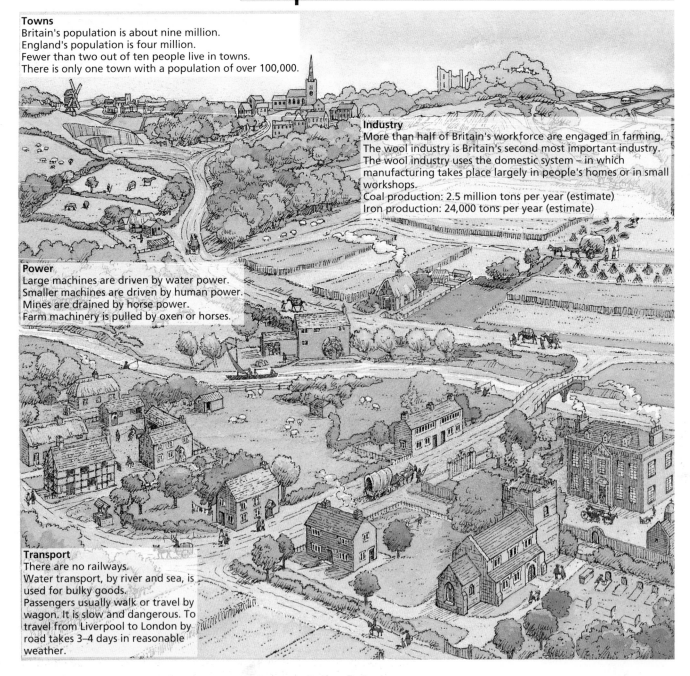

Towns
Britain's population is about nine million.
England's population is four million.
Fewer than two out of ten people live in towns.
There is only one town with a population of over 100,000.

Industry
More than half of Britain's workforce are engaged in farming.
The wool industry is Britain's second most important industry.
The wool industry uses the domestic system – in which manufacturing takes place largely in people's homes or in small workshops.
Coal production: 2.5 million tons per year (estimate)
Iron production: 24,000 tons per year (estimate)

Power
Large machines are driven by water power.
Smaller machines are driven by human power.
Mines are drained by horse power.
Farm machinery is pulled by oxen or horses.

Transport
There are no railways.
Water transport, by river and sea, is used for bulky goods.
Passengers usually walk or travel by wagon. It is slow and dangerous. To travel from Liverpool to London by road takes 3–4 days in reasonable weather.

Britain in 1700.

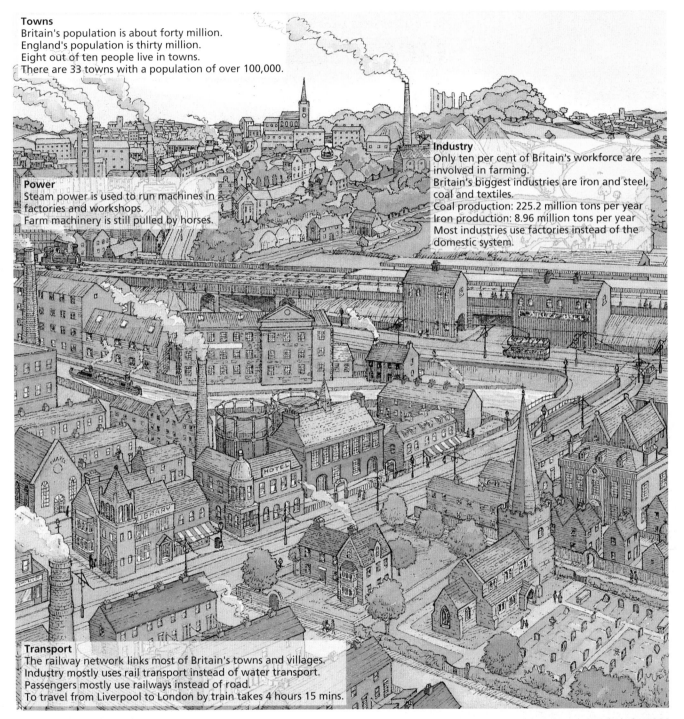

Towns
Britain's population is about forty million.
England's population is thirty million.
Eight out of ten people live in towns.
There are 33 towns with a population of over 100,000.

Power
Steam power is used to run machines in
factories and workshops.
Farm machinery is still pulled by horses.

Industry
Only ten per cent of Britain's workforce are
involved in farming.
Britain's biggest industries are iron and steel,
coal and textiles.
Coal production: 225.2 million tons per year
Iron production: 8.96 million tons per year
Most industries use factories instead of the
domestic system.

Transport
The railway network links most of Britain's towns and villages.
Industry mostly uses rail transport instead of water transport.
Passengers mostly use railways instead of road.
To travel from Liverpool to London by train takes 4 hours 15 mins.

Britain in 1900.

ACTIVITY

1 Working with a partner, discuss the differences between life in 1700
(Source 1) and in 1900 (Source 2). Draw up a list of all the changes which
appear to have taken place between 1700 and 1900.

2 Now compare life in 1900 with what you know about today. If you were
drawing a third picture for today, what changes would you show? Write
out the information you would put on today's picture.

3 The text on the pictures does not show all the changes which have
taken place. Draw up a list of other changes shown in the pictures or
which you know about from your previous study of history. You could
use a table with three columns: 1700; 1900; today.

1.2 *The main issues*

The illustration shows a reconstruction of a co-op shop at around the end of the nineteenth century. It may not look very impressive to you, but it took 200 years of industrial change and innovation to make such a shop possible. If we could walk into this shop and ask a few questions about what we see, we would soon find ourselves confronting all the main issues of Britain's social and economic history. This course will help you to understand and analyse these issues.

Economic and industrial issues

The core of this course looks at how British industry developed from 1700 to 1900.

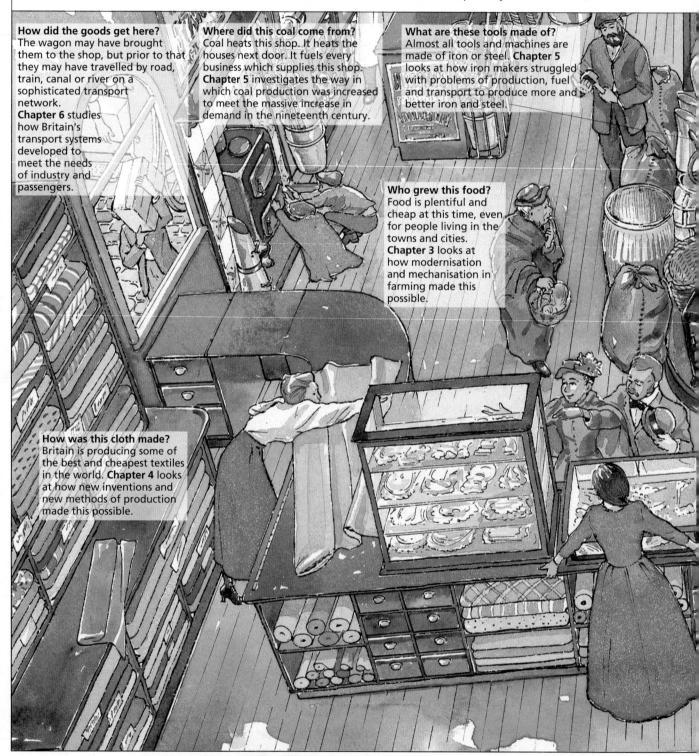

How did the goods get here?
The wagon may have brought them to the shop, but prior to that they may have travelled by road, train, canal or river on a sophisticated transport network.
Chapter 6 studies how Britain's transport systems developed to meet the needs of industry and passengers.

Where did this coal come from?
Coal heats this shop. It heats the houses next door. It fuels every business which supplies this shop. **Chapter 5** investigates the way in which coal production was increased to meet the massive increase in demand in the nineteenth century.

What are these tools made of?
Almost all tools and machines are made of iron or steel. **Chapter 5** looks at how iron makers struggled with problems of production, fuel and transport to produce more and better iron and steel.

Who grew this food?
Food is plentiful and cheap at this time, even for people living in the towns and cities. **Chapter 3** looks at how modernisation and mechanisation in farming made this possible.

How was this cloth made?
Britain is producing some of the best and cheapest textiles in the world. **Chapter 4** looks at how new inventions and new methods of production made this possible.

Social issues

The second half looks at how British society changed 1800 - the present.

What is a co-op?
Co-op is short for co-operative. The first co-operatives were set up by working-class people to help one another, and to ensure they did not get exploited by shopkeepers who charged too much or sold shoddy goods.
Chapter 10 looks at the successes and failures of working-class movements, including co-operatives and trade unions, from 1800 to the 1980s.

Which of these children are rich and which are poor?
Poverty had always been a problem both in countryside and in towns. In 1900 it still was. Britain's economic growth widened the gap between rich and poor.
Chapter 9 looks at attempts to help the poor from 1750 to the present.

Why are most of the shop assistants women?
The role of women at work and in the home has undergone many changes since the nineteenth century. Some of the changes have increased opportunities for women. Others have reduced them.
Chapter 12 investigates the changing role of women from Victorian times to the present day.

Where do these people live?
Industry drew people to towns. By 1900 80 per cent of British people lived in towns.
Chapter 8 looks at why living conditions became so bad when towns first started to grow, and how they were improved (for some) through the rest of the nineteenth century.

Why is this woman buying medicine and will it help her?
These days we would go to a doctor for medical help, but in 1900 very few people did this. Doctors were too expensive and they often were not able to help their patients.
Chapter 11 looks at how medical knowledge began to improve in the nineteenth century and why health has improved so rapidly during the twentieth.

1.3 *Chronology*

Unlike political history, which is often studied in chronological order, social and economic history is usually studied thematically. However, it will soon be obvious to you that the themes overlap with each other. They do not fall into neat packages. You will have to keep on going forwards and backwards in time, and you will have to keep on making connections between different developments. So throughout your course you will need to keep a clear chronology or time frame in mind.

You should refer to the timeline below throughout your course. It:

- summarises the main themes you will be studying.
- shows how the chapters of this book overlap chronologically and thematically.
- highlights some key political events in the period that affected social and economic history.

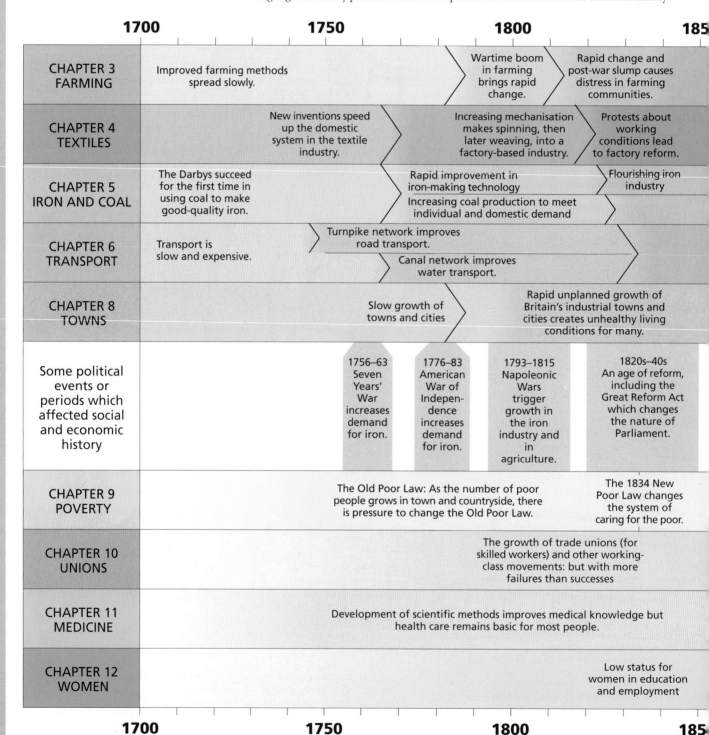

	1700	**1750**	**1800**	**185**
CHAPTER 3 FARMING	Improved farming methods spread slowly.		Wartime boom in farming brings rapid change.	Rapid change and post-war slump causes distress in farming communities.
CHAPTER 4 TEXTILES		New inventions speed up the domestic system in the textile industry.	Increasing mechanisation makes spinning, then later weaving, into a factory-based industry.	Protests about working conditions lead to factory reform.
CHAPTER 5 IRON AND COAL	The Darbys succeed for the first time in using coal to make good-quality iron.		Rapid improvement in iron-making technology / Increasing coal production to meet individual and domestic demand	Flourishing iron industry
CHAPTER 6 TRANSPORT	Transport is slow and expensive.	Turnpike network improves road transport. / Canal network improves water transport.		
CHAPTER 8 TOWNS		Slow growth of towns and cities	Rapid unplanned growth of Britain's industrial towns and cities creates unhealthy living conditions for many.	
Some political events or periods which affected social and economic history		1756–63 Seven Years' War increases demand for iron. / 1776–83 American War of Independence increases demand for iron.	1793–1815 Napoleonic Wars trigger growth in the iron industry and in agriculture.	1820s–40s An age of reform, including the Great Reform Act which changes the nature of Parliament.
CHAPTER 9 POVERTY		The Old Poor Law: As the number of poor people grows in town and countryside, there is pressure to change the Old Poor Law.		The 1834 New Poor Law changes the system of caring for the poor.
CHAPTER 10 UNIONS			The growth of trade unions (for skilled workers) and other working-class movements: but with more failures than successes	
CHAPTER 11 MEDICINE		Development of scientific methods improves medical knowledge but health care remains basic for most people.		
CHAPTER 12 WOMEN				Low status for women in education and employment
	1700	**1750**	**1800**	**185**

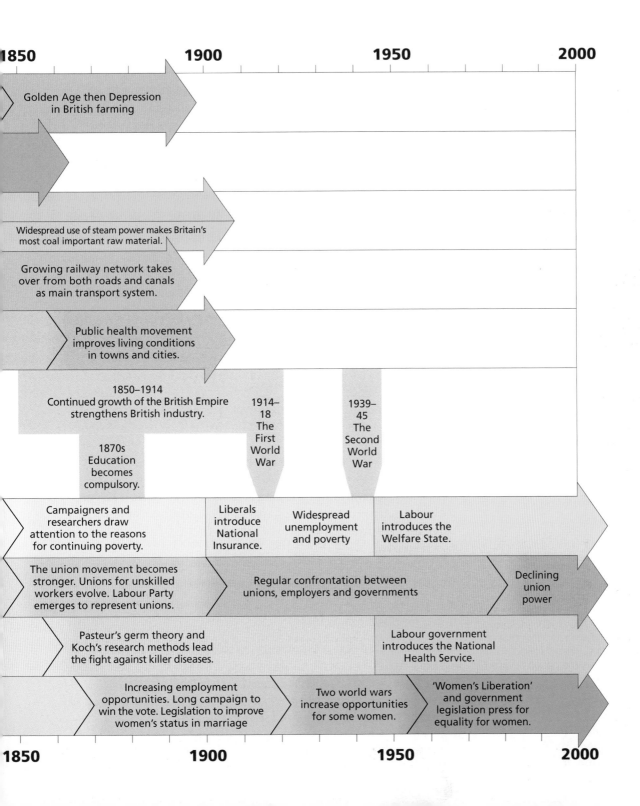

1850   1900   1950   2000

Golden Age then Depression in British farming

Widespread use of steam power makes Britain's coal most important raw material.

Growing railway network takes over from both roads and canals as main transport system.

Public health movement improves living conditions in towns and cities.

1850–1914
Continued growth of the British Empire strengthens British industry.

1914–18
The First World War

1939–45
The Second World War

1870s
Education becomes compulsory.

Campaigners and researchers draw attention to the reasons for continuing poverty.

Liberals introduce National Insurance.

Widespread unemployment and poverty

Labour introduces the Welfare State.

The union movement becomes stronger. Unions for unskilled workers evolve. Labour Party emerges to represent unions.

Regular confrontation between unions, employers and governments

Declining union power

Pasteur's germ theory and Koch's research methods lead the fight against killer diseases.

Labour government introduces the National Health Service.

Increasing employment opportunities. Long campaign to win the vote. Legislation to improve women's status in marriage

Two world wars increase opportunities for some women.

'Women's Liberation' and government legislation press for equality for women.

1850   1900   1950   2000

2 Factors behind Britain's industrial growth

FOCUS

Through pages 18–127 you will study the development of some of Britain's key industries. However, you will quickly find that certain factors appear again and again in each chapter. They are so important that they are almost 'pre-conditions' for industrial growth – that is, without them, growth would have been much slower or impossible.

In this chapter you will look at each of these factors in outline. They are:

- Britain's growing population
- Britain's overseas trade
- Coal and steam power
- Entrepreneurs and investors.

Factor 1: A growing population

From about 1700 onwards, Britain's population began to grow. No one knows exactly how quickly it grew in the eighteenth century because accurate figures were not gathered until 1801. For the eighteenth century we have to rely on estimates. However, these estimates are increasingly reliable because historians have brought together hundreds of thousands of local records such as registers of baptisms, marriages and deaths. Using modern computer methods they have been able to map out with some confidence what happened to Britain's population in the eighteenth century. As you can see from Source 1, they suggest that in the eighteenth century the growth was steady. In the nineteenth century it was very rapid indeed.

Why did Britain's population grow?

The simple answer is that the birth rate was rising (people were having more children) and the death rate was falling (see Source 2). If birth rate exceeds death rate then the population will rise. If they are equal then the population will stay the same.

Explaining why these two things were happening is much more difficult, although there are many theories.

Why did people have more children?

- Marriage registers show that men and women began to marry younger. Younger marriages tend to produce more children.
- Marriage registers also show that more people got married in total – the proportion of married people rose from 85 per cent of adults (in 1700) to 93 per cent (in 1850). More marriages meant more children.
- Written evidence from the period suggests that farm labourers became increasingly independent from their employers. In 1700 farmers and their labourers often lived in the same house. Changes in village life meant that labourers left the houses of their employers and lived in their own cottages. This extra privacy increased the incentive to start families and to have more children. It was a similar picture in the towns. Families in towns were more independent.
- As industry grew, even young children were able to earn valuable wages. This made them an 'economic asset'. It was an incentive for married couples to have more children.

Why was the death rate falling?

- Medical evidence and death certificates show that there were fewer epidemics in the late eighteenth century. For example, smallpox was one of the dreaded killer diseases – particularly of children – early in the eighteenth century. It had caused as many as 15 per cent of all deaths. By the end of the century inoculation and vaccination (see page 308) reduced this in some places to less than 2 per cent of all deaths.

SOURCE 1

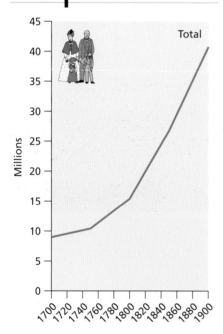

Population 1700–1900. England's population grew faster than that of Scotland or Wales. Ireland's population actually fell over the same period because of a dreadful famine (see page 51).

SOURCE 2

SOURCE 2

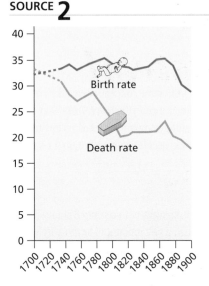

Birth and death rates 1700–1900. Remember this shows births and deaths per thousand.

1 **Look at Source 2. Which is changing fastest: birth rate or death rate?**

2 **According to the evidence in Source 2, what is the main cause of the rising population?**

- In the countryside bricks and slates increasingly replaced mud and thatch for housing. Better housing made for better health.
- Eye-witness reports from the time suggest that diet improved. This made adults healthier, which in turn produced healthier children who were more likely to survive into adulthood, and healthier adults who lived longer. Life expectancy for both men and women in 1700 was less than 40 years. By 1900 it was almost 50 for a man, and about 48 for a woman.

Why was a rising population a good thing for industry?

It increased demand

More people needed more food, so farming had to change and adapt to meet the demand. They needed more cloth, which stimulated change in the textile industries. They needed more cooking pots and more tools which stimulated the iron industry. The first major breakthrough in the iron industry came because Abraham Darby wanted to make a cheaper, mass-market cooking pot. They needed more coal to heat their homes, which stimulated the mining and the transport industries. The first major canal was built to supply the growing demand for coal to heat homes in Manchester.

It also provided workers

The population in both towns and countryside was increasing. Very soon most villages had more adults than there were jobs. The surplus young adults became miners to mine the coal, spinners and weavers to make cloth, puddlers to make iron, builders to build houses and labourers to cut canals and lay the railways. They swelled the industrial cities which grew at a phenomenal rate, particularly in the mid-nineteenth century (see Source 3).

Clearly, Britain's industrialisation was closely linked to its rising population. But... was population growth the reason why Britain industrialised? What do you think?

SOURCE 3

A 1680.

B 1728.

C 1830.

The growth of Liverpool.

FOCUS TASK

This diagram shows the basics of how population and industrialisation were linked. Re-draw the diagram and add your own notes, inserting the other elements which are mentioned on this page.

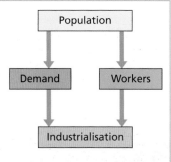

Factor 2: Overseas trade

The British Empire: a captive market!

In the eighteenth century Britain's empire began to grow fast. Some countries were taken over by British armies. Some countries were 'won' from France in the Seven Years' War (1756–63). Some were effectively taken over by British trading companies backed up by British soldiers. Others were simply settled by British people who had decided to leave Britain for a new life overseas.

> 1 **Use your own research to find out how each of the countries labelled on Source 4 became part of the British Empire.**

SOURCE 4

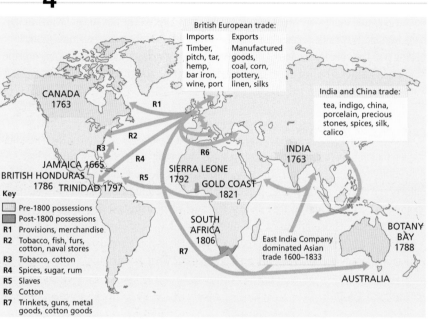

British European trade:
Imports	Exports
Timber, pitch, tar, hemp, bar iron, wine, port	Manufactured goods, coal, corn, pottery, linen, silks

India and China trade: tea, indigo, china, porcelain, precious stones, spices, silk, calico

CANADA 1763

INDIA 1763

JAMAICA 1665
BRITISH HONDURAS 1786
TRINIDAD 1797

SIERRA LEONE 1792
GOLD COAST 1821

SOUTH AFRICA 1806

BOTANY BAY 1788

East India Company dominated Asian trade 1600–1833

AUSTRALIA

Key
- ☐ Pre-1800 possessions
- ☐ Post-1800 possessions
- R1 Provisions, merchandise
- R2 Tobacco, fish, furs, cotton, naval stores
- R3 Tobacco, cotton
- R4 Spices, sugar, rum
- R5 Slaves
- R6 Cotton
- R7 Trinkets, guns, metal goods, cotton goods

The British Empire in the eighteenth century.

By the mid-eighteenth century Britain controlled a vast amount of territory in North America, the Caribbean and India. In all these areas Britain also controlled trade. Under the navigation laws, British territories had to export their goods to Britain. They could not trade with another country themselves. British merchants then re-exported these goods – such as sugar, furs and tobacco – at a profit, mainly to markets in Europe. The countries of the Empire had to buy British goods if the British told them to. India had a massive textile industry of its own until the British forced it to buy British cotton. If the British told them to, the countries of the Empire had also to sell raw materials cheaply to Britain.

The slave triangle: the money pours in!

Historians sometimes play down the importance of Britain's slave trade in this period, perhaps because the trade itself was so infamous. But it was Britain's most profitable trading enterprise in the eighteenth century and the country's industry benefited greatly from this most brutal trade (see Source 5).

The two most important ports for the slave trade were Bristol and Liverpool. Half of Liverpool's sailors were involved in it. In the 1790s Liverpool's slave trade alone made up 15 per cent of Britain's entire overseas trade. However, the slave trade had more profound importance for Britain's industry, as you can see from Source 6. The slave trade was at the centre of a triangular trade which poured money into British industry: Africa and the West Indies provided a market for British-made goods; the sale of slaves provided massive profits; the return journey provided raw materials.

In 1770 one-third of Manchester's textiles were exported to Africa and half to the West Indies. Slave-trade money founded most of Liverpool's banks, which in turn provided loans for industrialists. Processing tobacco and sugar became major British industries. Slave-trade money provided investment for railways, coal mines, cotton mills, iron foundries and steam engines. It provided work for tens of thousands of people, and spectacular wealth for some.

SOURCE 5

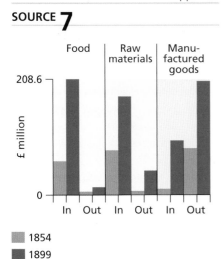

Britain's import and export trade 1750–1900. This only shows 'visible' trade. Britain's vast 'invisible earnings', such as money made by banking and insurance, don't appear on this chart. Two other features shown by this graph are the booms and slumps of the trade cycle. When exports were booming that meant plenty of work and rising wages for British workers. Slumps meant the opposite.

SOURCE 7

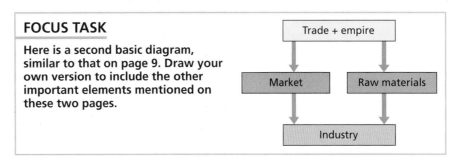

British imports and exports by category in the second half of the nineteenth century.

SOURCE 6

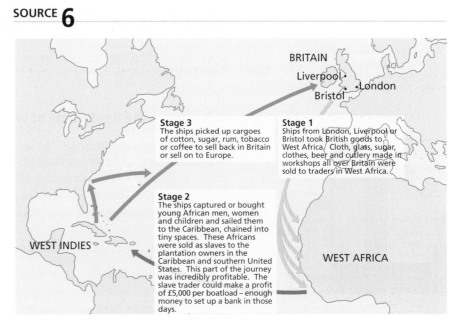

BRITAIN
Liverpool • London
Bristol

Stage 3
The ships picked up cargoes of cotton, sugar, rum, tobacco or coffee to sell back in Britain or sell on to Europe.

Stage 1
Ships from London, Liverpool or Bristol took British goods to West Africa. Cloth, glass, sugar, clothes, beer and cutlery made in workshops all over Britain were sold to traders in West Africa.

Stage 2
The ships captured or bought young African men, women and children and sailed them to the Caribbean, chained into tiny spaces. These Africans were sold as slaves to the plantation owners in the Caribbean and southern United States. This part of the journey was incredibly profitable. The slave trader could make a profit of £5,000 per boatload – enough money to set up a bank in those days.

WEST INDIES

WEST AFRICA

The slave triangle.

World trade: imports and exports keep British industry growing

As the nineteenth century dawned, British traders faced a crisis. Trade with Europe was severely disrupted by the Napoleonic Wars (see page 32) and the slave trade was banned throughout the British Empire in 1807.

So British merchants successfully developed new trade with the Middle East, the Americas and Asia for Britain's textiles, iron and other manufactured goods. As you can see from Source 5, this period saw a massive increase in British exports. The majority of Britain's cotton goods were exported. The industry could never have taken off the way it did if it had sold to the home market only, which was simply not large enough.

At the same time trade supplied British industry with raw materials such as raw cotton and pig iron.

Why was overseas trade important to British industry?

- Trade brought in immense profits which helped finance British industry.
- It provided access to markets for British goods.
- It brought in vital raw materials.

If British merchants had not been able to find markets around the world for British goods, it is hard to imagine how industrialisation could have taken place so rapidly. But was overseas trade the reason Britain industrialised? What do you think?

FOCUS TASK

Here is a second basic diagram, similar to that on page 9. Draw your own version to include the other important elements mentioned on these two pages.

Trade + empire

Market   Raw materials

Industry

Factor 3: Steam power

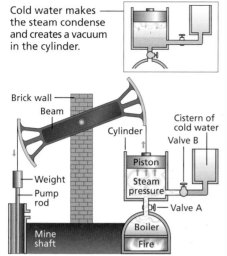

Cold water makes the steam condense and creates a vacuum in the cylinder.

Brick wall
Beam
Cylinder
Cistern of cold water
Valve B
Piston
Weight
Steam pressure
Pump rod
Valve A
Mine shaft
Boiler
Fire

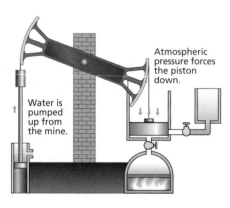

Atmospheric pressure forces the piston down.

Water is pumped up from the mine.

A How Newcomen's engine worked.

As this rod moved up and down with the beam, the operating valves opened in the correct order.

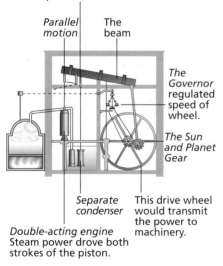

Parallel motion
The beam

The Governor regulated speed of wheel.

The Sun and Planet Gear

Separate condenser

This drive wheel would transmit the power to machinery.

Double-acting engine
Steam power drove both strokes of the piston.

B How Watt's rotary engine worked.

One of the most important features of industrialisation was the use of machinery. But machines needed power.

What were the limitations of water power?

Early factories were all water-powered. Richard Arkwright built mills near a fast-flowing stream in Derbyshire. In Cheshire the Greg family chose a site by the River Bollin for their new spinning mill in 1784. The Darby family was fortunate to find a site at Coalbrookdale which had not only the coal, iron ore and limestone needed to make iron but a stream to power the bellows for their blast furnaces. Even tiny workshops would often have their own small water wheel.

However, water power posed many problems.

- In winter the water froze.
- In summer water levels fell.
- Even at good times, water power could not drive the increasingly large machines.
- Suitable sites were running out by 1800.
- Landowners had realised the potential earnings and were charging for the rights to draw water.
- Finally, many of the water-powered sites were in hilly areas, so were awkwardly placed for recruiting workers, and for transporting raw materials to the mills and finished goods away from them.

Was steam power better?

To start with, no!

The first steam engine was developed by Thomas Savery in 1698. The first reliable engine was devised by Thomas Newcomen to pump water out of a coal mine in Staffordshire in 1712 (see Source 8A). The engine was huge and noisy. It was also inefficient – it used huge amounts of coal. However, this was not a problem for the owners of a coal mine, so Newcomen engines were soon being bought by mine owners all over the country. They remained the standard engine for draining mines until well into the nineteenth century.

In 1769 a Glasgow instrument maker, James Watt, designed an improved Newcomen steam engine (Source 8B). In 1774 Watt entered into partnership with Matthew Boulton. Together they made the Boulton and Watt engines which proved very popular in Cornish tin mines (because they used far less coal than Newcomen engines) and in ironworks to pump bellows.

So far the steam engines could only pump. In 1782 Watt and other workers at Boulton's works in Birmingham made a breakthrough. Using cogs and gears (known as sun and planet gears), they turned the up and down movement into circular or rotary movement. Here was an invention which could replace the water wheel and power machines in mills and factories. However, Boulton and Watt engines were large and expensive, and in the beginning there was not exactly a stampede to buy them. Even those who did buy one didn't trust everything to it. They preferred to use water power, keeping the steam engine as a back-up for when the water power failed them.

However, further improvements followed, and by 1800 the steam engine was becoming more common. By 1820 almost all new factories were being built to run on steam power alone. They were being sited on coalfields so that coal supply could be guaranteed. The engines were getting bigger and were powering bigger machines. And all around Britain inventors were devising new uses for the steam engine: for railway locomotives; to hammer iron; to thresh corn; to power ships...

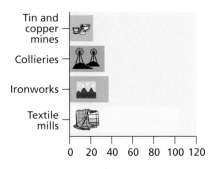

SOURCE 9

Tin and copper mines

Collieries

Ironworks

Textile mills

0 20 40 60 80 100 120

Numbers of Boulton and Watt steam engines in use 1775–1800. The four largest users.

SOURCE 11

Key
· Coal

Britain's coalfields.

SOURCE 10

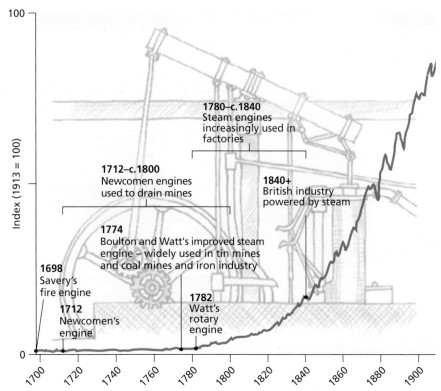

100

Index (1913 = 100)

0

1700 1720 1740 1760 1780 1800 1820 1840 1860 1880 1900

1698 Savery's fire engine

1712 Newcomen's engine

1712–c.1800 Newcomen engines used to drain mines

1774 Boulton and Watt's improved steam engine – widely used in tin mines and coal mines and iron industry

1782 Watt's rotary engine

1780–c.1840 Steam engines increasingly used in factories

1840+ British industry powered by steam

Rising industrial output 1700–1900. The figure in 1913 is taken as 100 per cent and the other years as a percentage of this. Although this index, called the Hoffman Index, has been criticised by historians, the trends shown are reliable.

What was the impact of steam power?

Steam power was just what industry needed. It was:

- Flexible. You could use it where you liked – as long as you could get coal to it the steam engine would work for you. And as you can see from Source 11, Britain had masses of coal.
- Powerful. You could think big. The biggest steam engines gave power equivalent to many water wheels.
- Reliable. Once the early teething troubles were past, steam power could work machines non-stop through freeze or drought.

It was when reliable steam power became widely available that Britain's industrial revolution really took off, as you can see from Source 10.

Clearly, Britain's industrialisation was closely linked to steam power. But... was steam power the reason why Britain industrialised? What do you think?

FOCUS TASK

Here is another basic diagram. Re-draw it so that it tells a fuller story.

Steam power

Location

Scale

Industry

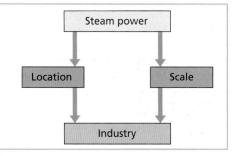

Factor 4: Entrepreneurs and investors

Entrepreneurs

Industry doesn't just happen by itself. All industrial developments come about because someone somewhere has a business idea and tries it out. If it works they make money. If it doesn't they might lose everything. But they are prepared to take that risk.

When we look back at the industrial revolution we focus on the ENTREPRENEURS or businessmen (and a few businesswomen) who succeeded. For every one who succeeded there were many who failed, but their urge to succeed, to make money, or simply to better themselves was the power driving industry in the eighteenth and nineteenth centuries.

Investors

Entrepreneurs needed money. Some used their own savings. Matthew Boulton used his wife's! Most had to borrow from investors to build factories, to build canals, to buy steam engines or to buy a patent.

Without entrepreneurs and investors the industrial revolution would have been unthinkable. But… were they the reason why Britain industrialised? What do you think?

FOCUS TASK

As you work through this book you are going to meet some of the entrepreneurs below. We have not named them, but simply located them on the timeline. Either now, or as you go through this course, try to identify who they are, what they are famous for, and what they did on the date shown on the timeline. Also try to find out where they got their money from. At the end of the course you will be able to compare their contributions to British industrial growth.

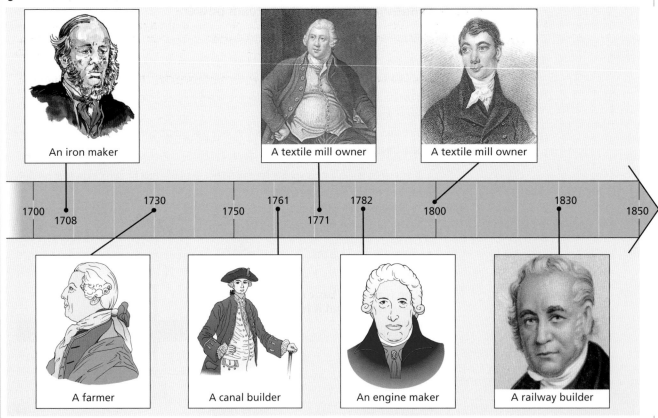

An iron maker

A textile mill owner

A textile mill owner

1700 1708 1730 1750 1761 1771 1782 1800 1830 1850

A farmer

A canal builder

An engine maker

A railway builder

Factors for growth: a summary

Industrial growth

A growing population provided:
- plenty of workers for farms or factories or mines.
- a growing home market for British goods.

Overseas trade provided:
- a world market for British goods.
- a massive amount of money coming into Britain.
- cheap raw materials from other countries.

Steam power provided:
- power to drive large machines, trains, ships, pumps, etc.
- a much more flexible source of power than water power – you could use steam power anywhere.

Entrepreneurs and investors provided:
- the readiness to take risks.
- the skill to turn good ideas into business success.
- the money to build factories, buy machinery or try out new ideas.

FOCUS TASK

You have drawn various diagrams showing how population, trade and steam power contributed to industrialisation.

Now bring them together in a final diagram of your own which also includes investment and entrepreneurs. Put industrialisation at the centre and decide how the information in your other diagrams should fit into the new one.

You will have to cut down your other diagrams to their bare essentials.

SECTION 2

Agriculture and the textile industry 1700–1900

3 The rise and fall of British agriculture

How did farmers grow more food
3.1 in the eighteenth century?

FOCUS

In 1700 the majority of British people made their living from farming, just as they had for centuries. Their methods of farming had changed little since the Middle Ages.

In the eighteenth century, however, farming began to change. As Britain's population grew and the demand for food rose, new farming methods, ideas and techniques were tried out which eventually revolutionised Britain's agriculture and changed the lives of farmers for ever. This chapter investigates why these changes took place and how they affected people in Britain.

In 3.1 you will examine how farming changed in the eighteenth century. This was a period of slow change. New methods were pioneered by some, but they did not spread widely. You will investigate:

- how the traditional 'open-field' system of farming worked.
- what new methods of farming were tried out in the eighteenth century.
- why many farmers did not adopt these ideas.

In 3.2 you will examine a period of more rapid change, from 1790 to the 1830s. The dominant feature of this period was the enclosure movement. You will investigate:

- why the number of enclosures increased after 1790.
- how enclosure affected different groups in the country.
- how rural communities responded to the many different changes that took place in this period.

Finally, in 3.3 you will study the major features of farming through the rest of the nineteenth century. You will investigate:

- what the Corn Laws were and why they were repealed in 1846.
- why British farming experienced a Golden Age in the 1850s and 1860s, followed by a great depression between 1870 and 1900.

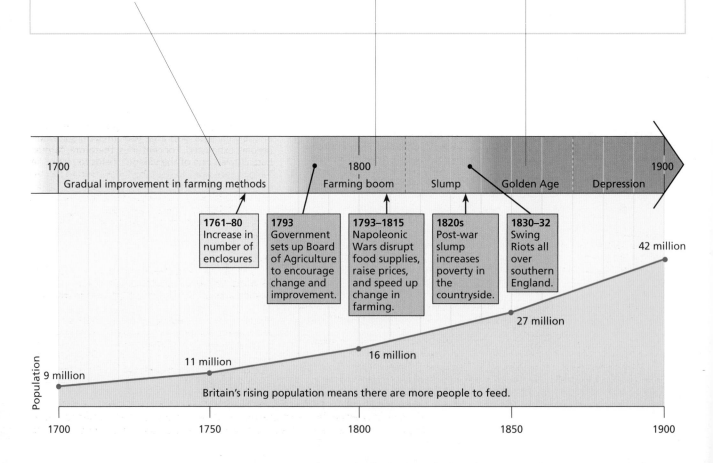

1700   Gradual improvement in farming methods   1800   Farming boom   Slump   Golden Age   Depression   1900

1761–80 Increase in number of enclosures

1793 Government sets up Board of Agriculture to encourage change and improvement.

1793–1815 Napoleonic Wars disrupt food supplies, raise prices, and speed up change in farming.

1820s Post-war slump increases poverty in the countryside.

1830–32 Swing Riots all over southern England.

Population

9 million

11 million

16 million

27 million

42 million

Britain's rising population means there are more people to feed.

1700   1750   1800   1850   1900

How did the open-field system work?

In 1700 many villages used the open-field system of farming (see Source 1). This was little changed since the Middle Ages. Each village was surrounded by a number of large fields which were divided into strips. Each farmer in the village farmed a number of strips.

SOURCE 1

Open fields
Typically there were three open fields. Each open field was divided into strips. The strips themselves may look small, but a typical strip was quite large, as you can see from Source 2. Each strip had two, three or four wide ridges.

Housing
Most villagers lived in small cottages close to the centre of the village. Many might have gardens in which they grew vegetables or kept pigs or geese. Or they might keep their animals entirely on the common land.

Tools
Farm workers largely used hand-operated tools or horse-drawn machinery.

Enclosed land
Most villages had some enclosed land. This was privately owned. It might be used to graze animals or to grow crops.

The fallow field
Experience handed down from one generation to the next told farmers that if they grew the same crop on the same land, year after year, then the soil would become exhausted. For centuries, therefore, farmers had allowed one of the village's fields to rest or lie 'fallow' each year. To help the fallow field to recover further, the villagers grazed their sheep and cattle there. The animals' manure put goodness back into the soil. If the village was near a town or city, farmers would also treat the fields with cartloads of manure from the town.

Common land
Everyone who farmed land in the village had 'common rights'. They could graze animals on the common land. The more land they farmed, the more animals they were allowed to put on the common. In most villages, common rights were determined by tradition. Few people had deeds or other legal documents such as we have today.

The common land provided for other needs: wood for fuel and for building. Farmers harvested the hay to feed the animals over the winter. They collected berries, dug peat or trapped rabbits there.

In fact some of the poorest people in the village, known as SQUATTERS, lived almost entirely on the common land. Strictly, they had no right to live there, but many squatters also worked as casual labourers at busy times, and so they were tolerated. In some villages squatters had lived on the land for generations.

Crop rotation
They would also vary the crops grown on each field each year, as the same crop grown year after year would exhaust the soil. This is a typical crop rotation:

Year 1		Year 2		Year 3	
Wheat	Barley	Barley	Fallow	Fallow	Wheat
Fallow		Wheat		Barley	

A diagram showing open-field farming. This shows a typical three-field village, but variations on this would be found elsewhere. Some villages had just two fields, others four. Some villages might have fewer strips, more pasture or more enclosed land.

Hill farms

In the eighteenth century farming in Britain varied from region to region, just as it does today. The open-field system was common in the more fertile areas of the Midlands, East Anglia and central southern England where crops could be grown (see Source 3).

In other areas, particularly in highland areas such as Cumbria, the Welsh mountains or Devon, where steep slopes and rocky terrain made it impractical to plough, the so-called 'hill farms' were organised very differently. The open field system was not used.

On a typical hill farm:

★ each farm was at the centre of its own land.
★ the small fields would be enclosed by hedges or walls.
★ most land would be used for grazing animals, particularly sheep for the wool industry, which was Britain's biggest industry after farming.
★ if the animals were to be sold they would often be taken to lower-lying pasture to be fattened up.
★ farmers grew whatever crops could be grown in the conditions – so hill farms varied very much from region to region. For example, some areas could produce rich crops of fruit, other areas vegetables.

1 Write a short (100-word) entry entitled 'Open-field Farming' for an encyclopaedia of British history. Use diagrams if you think they will help. Mention strips; common land; crop rotation; regional differences.

SOURCE 2

A photograph taken in 1953 in Padbury, Buckinghamshire, which shows the ridges. We have added the lines to show how these ridges would be combined into strips.

Source 1 might make the fields look organised, neat and tidy. However, a modern farmer would probably be struck by how 'wild' and chaotic many open fields were. There would be lots of weeds; animals might be roaming through the fields where crops were growing; the hedges would be large and rambling; the fields might be crossed by lanes or streams. The crops might look patchy. Seed was sown by hand (called 'broadcasting') and even the best sowers could not be sure of getting an even spread.

Who were the farmers?

One of the essential things for us to remember, looking back from the present day, is that when we talk about farmers in this period we are talking about almost all of rural society. Almost everyone was involved in farming in one way or another (see Factfile on page 21). Farming was an all-year-round way of life. And at busy times of year such as harvest time, it would involve entire families including women, children and old people.

SOURCE 3

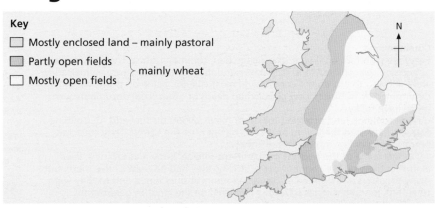

Key
☐ Mostly enclosed land – mainly pastoral
▨ Partly open fields ⎱ mainly wheat
☐ Mostly open fields ⎰

This map shows the areas where open-field farming was most common in the eighteenth century.

FACTFILE

The farmers

★ In most other countries in Europe at this time farmers owned their own small farms. However, in Britain by contrast, most farmers were TENANT FARMERS who rented their farms from the landowners (the ARISTOCRACY and the GENTRY). Some tenant farmers rented a few strips (such farmers were known as SMALLHOLDERS), whereas others ran very large farms.

★ A steward and a bailiff worked for the landowner; the steward made sure the tenant farmers paid their rent and the bailiff checked that the land was being farmed properly.

★ A few farmers owned their own land, and they were known as FREEHOLDERS (or COPYHOLDERS. The main difference between them was that copyholders' ownership rights were recorded in a copy of the Great Roll in Parliament while freeholders held their own documents of ownership, called title deeds). The largest freeholders (those with land worth more than 40 shillings per year) were also known as YEOMEN.

★ Tenant farmers employed other villagers as labourers. Labourers did not rent their own land and did not have the right to farm strips. Some labourers had full-time jobs on one farm, often with a cottage provided. Others had to move from one farm to another seeking work. At harvest time labourers were in demand and at other times there was also work like fencing and digging ditches. Others worked for tenant farmers as cowmen, shepherds, ploughmen, dairymaids or threshers.

★ Women played a vital role in the rural economy. They ran the home besides doing spinning to earn extra money and helping out on the family farm. The wives of tenant farmers supervised many tasks such as milking cows. Many farmers' wives also kept the accounts for the farm and took fresh produce to market.

2 **Read Source 4. What other items would subsistence farmers need in order to survive?**

3 **How do you think they could obtain them?**

ACTIVITY

Use the Factfile (left) to help you complete this diagram to show the structure of village society. Add notes to explain the relationships shown in the diagram.

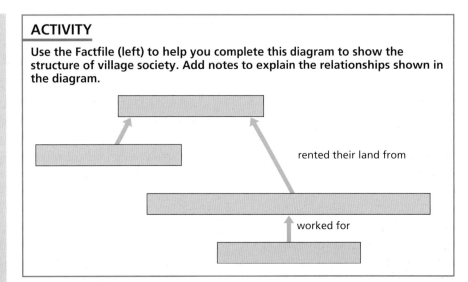

What did the subsistence farmers grow?

Subsistence farming means growing enough for your own or your village's needs. Much open-field farming at this time was subsistence farming. Source 4 shows some of the main crops grown by subsistence farmers.

SOURCE 4

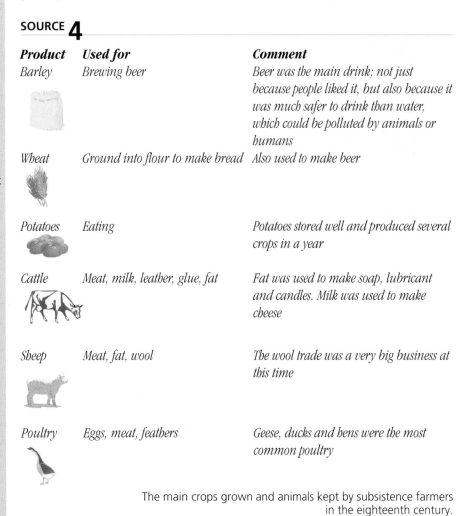

Product	Used for	Comment
Barley	Brewing beer	*Beer was the main drink; not just because people liked it, but also because it was much safer to drink than water, which could be polluted by animals or humans*
Wheat	Ground into flour to make bread	*Also used to make beer*
Potatoes	Eating	*Potatoes stored well and produced several crops in a year*
Cattle	Meat, milk, leather, glue, fat	*Fat was used to make soap, lubricant and candles. Milk was used to make cheese*
Sheep	Meat, fat, wool	*The wool trade was a very big business at this time*
Poultry	Eggs, meat, feathers	*Geese, ducks and hens were the most common poultry*

The main crops grown and animals kept by subsistence farmers in the eighteenth century.

ACTIVITY

Work with a partner to list all the advantages and disadvantages of the open-field system. Keep your lists, as you will need them later.

Was open-field farming a good system?

The answer to this has to be 'yes and no'. On the one hand the system was an effective way to organise subsistence farming. That is why it had survived for centuries. People would not have carried on with something that did not work. For generation after generation it had allowed the villagers to feed themselves and to store up enough food to see them through the winter. On the other hand there were inefficiencies about the system. The lists below summarise the main advantages and disadvantages. Look back at your lists from the activity on page 21 and compare them with the ones below.

Was it a good system? Yes!

- It allowed virtually all villagers to farm some land, or to make a living from the land.
- Land could be fairly divided. All farmers worked some high-quality land and some poorer land because all the farmers in the village had strips scattered over the open fields.
- It encouraged the villagers to work together as a community. The whole village had to make decisions about what to grow, when to plough, sow and harvest.
- It allowed equipment to be shared. Very few farmers were wealthy enough to buy their own ploughs, oxen, or horses. Under this system equipment was shared, and neighbours generally helped each other with their work, particularly around harvest time.
- It provided work for most people through the year. Even the old who could no longer work on the land could help thresh corn through the autumn. It did not matter that they worked slowly.
- In a good year it allowed some farmers to produce a surplus to sell at markets in nearby towns. The profit could be used to buy essential equipment such as tools or seed.

Was it a good system? No!

- Land was wasted. The gaps between the ridges and the space between strips, when added together, represented a large amount of under-used land.
- Farmers wasted time travelling from one of their strips to another.
- Change was difficult. All the strip farmers had to agree to any major change in farming methods.
- Diseases spread easily. A good farmer's land could be harmed by a poor farmer's mistakes. If one careless farmer let weeds grow on his strips they would quickly spread to his neighbours' strips. Disease could also spread in the same way. Similarly sick animals spread disease to healthy animals when they grazed together on the common land.
- Animal feed was a problem. There was not enough pasture to feed all the animals through the winter, so many were killed in the autumn slaughter each year.
- Very few farmers actually owned the land they worked on, so they were not very interested in improving it. It was not good economic sense to spend a lot on land which did not belong to you.
- Farmers still depended heavily on what they called 'nature's bounty'. In good years when 'nature' gave them favourable weather, or spared their crops and animals from pests and diseases, they would have enough to eat and a surplus to sell. In the bad years they might not even have enough to feed themselves.
- Subsistence farmers could in theory produce a surplus to sell in a good year. However, there was not much incentive to do so because if it was a good year for them it would probably be a good year for everyone else – so with so much surplus produce they would be unlikely to get a good price for their goods!

FOCUS TASK

A WHAT WERE THE ADVANTAGES OF THE OPEN-FIELD SYSTEM?

Work with a partner. One of you take the role of a critic of open farming, the other a defender. Role-play or write out a conversation between the critic and the defender. You will get lots of ideas from the lists above, but you can add your own ideas as well. Here are some topics for you to discuss in your role-play:

- land organisation
- the role of individual farmers
- the use of machinery
- keeping animals
- feeding the village

B WHY HAD FARMING CHANGED SO LITTLE SINCE THE MIDDLE AGES?

Here are possible reasons why farming was still run as it had been for centuries:

- Because it worked very well so there was no need to change
- Because people at the time were stupid and didn't know any better
- Because people at that time were scared of change

1   Explain which you think is the most likely reason.

2   Explain why you have rejected the others.

3   If you reject all three reasons, write your own alternative and explain why it is more likely.

Support each of your answers with information or evidence from pages 19–22.

SOURCE 5

A

TOUR

Thro' the whole ISLAND of

GREAT BRITAIN,

Divided into

Circuits or Journies.

GIVING

A Particular and Diverting Account of Whatever is Curious and worth Observation, *Viz.*

I. A Description of the Principal Cities and Towns, their Situation, Magnitude, Government, and Commerce.
II. The Customs, Manners, Speech, as also the Exercises, Diversions, and Employment of the People.
III. The Produce and Improvement of the Lands, the Trade, and Manufactures.
IV. The Sea Ports and Fortifications, the Course of Rivers, and the Inland Navigation.
V. The Publick Edifices, Seats, and Palaces of the Nobility and Gentry.

With Useful Observations upon the Whole.

Particularly fitted for the Reading of such as desire to Travel over the ISLAND.

By a GENTLEMAN.

The title page of Defoe's book, 1724.

1 Look at Source 5. What aspects of farming was Defoe interested in?

How much business farming was there in the eighteenth century?

Business farming means growing more that you need in order to sell your surplus at a profit. One of the most important sources of information we have from this period shows that there was a good deal of 'business' farming going on as early as the 1720s.

This source is a book by a man called Daniel Defoe. Defoe's most famous work was the story of Robinson Crusoe, who was shipwrecked on a desert island. He wrote a number of other adventure stories, but the most useful book (for us as historians) was written in 1724. It was called *A Tour Through the Whole Island of Great Britain*. Defoe travelled around Britain on horseback, noting down what he saw and then writing up his findings in a book.

Defoe's book is a fascinating catalogue of life in Britain in the 1720s, but his description of British farming is particularly useful. Defoe gives us a picture of a farming industry which, even in the 1720s, is beginning to specialise and is also beginning to sell its produce in the towns which are growing all over the country. The main market was the huge population of London, which dwarfed all other towns and cities at the time. However, Source 6 shows it was not the only market.

SOURCE 6

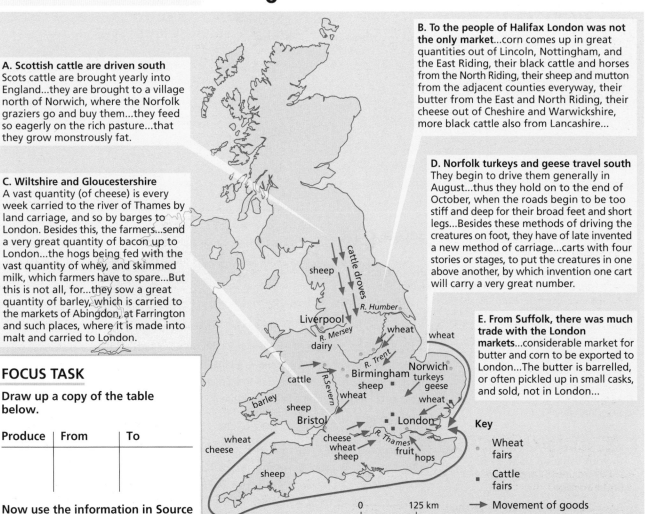

A. Scottish cattle are driven south
Scots cattle are brought yearly into England...they are brought to a village north of Norwich, where the Norfolk graziers go and buy them...they feed so eagerly on the rich pasture...that they grow monstrously fat.

C. Wiltshire and Gloucestershire
A vast quantity (of cheese) is every week carried to the river of Thames by land carriage, and so by barges to London. Besides this, the farmers...send a very great quantity of bacon up to London...the hogs being fed with the vast quantity of whey, and skimmed milk, which farmers have to spare...But this is not all, for...they sow a great quantity of barley, which is carried to the markets of Abingdon, at Farrington and such places, where it is made into malt and carried to London.

B. To the people of Halifax London was not the only market...corn comes up in great quantities out of Lincoln, Nottingham, and the East Riding, their black cattle and horses from the North Riding, their sheep and mutton from the adjacent counties everyway, their butter from the East and North Riding, their cheese out of Cheshire and Warwickshire, more black cattle also from Lancashire...

D. Norfolk turkeys and geese travel south
They begin to drive them generally in August...thus they hold on to the end of October, when the roads begin to be too stiff and deep for their broad feet and short legs...Besides these methods of driving the creatures on foot, they have of late invented a new method of carriage...carts with four stories or stages, to put the creatures in one above another, by which invention one cart will carry a very great number.

E. From Suffolk, there was much trade with the London markets...considerable market for butter and corn to be exported to London...The butter is barrelled, or often pickled up in small casks, and sold, not in London...

Map labels: sheep · cattle droves · R. Humber · Liverpool · R. Mersey · dairy · R. Trent · cattle · Birmingham · sheep · wheat · Norwich · turkeys · geese · wheat · wheat · R. Severn · barley · sheep · Bristol · wheat · cheese · cheese · wheat · sheep · London · R. Thames · fruit · hops · sheep

Key
● Wheat fairs
■ Cattle fairs
→ Movement of goods

0 — 125 km

Defoe describes Britain's farming business in the 1720s.

FOCUS TASK

Draw up a copy of the table below.

Produce	From	To

Now use the information in Source 6 to summarise what Defoe was saying about farming in the 1720s.

Case study: Farming in eighteenth-century Staffordshire

Of course, we must be careful when using Defoe's book as our only source. Defoe was a storyteller rather than a historical researcher. We cannot be sure how carefully he checked his information and we also know very little about the places which he did not visit. Take Staffordshire, for example. Defoe visited Staffordshire, travelling through it on his way from Shropshire to the Midlands. He was impressed by the Penkridge Horse Fair (see Source 8).

SOURCE 7

Staffordshire in the eighteenth century.

SOURCE 8

... for saddle horses [riding horses] ... hunters ... and racers I believe the world cannot match this fair.

Defoe describes Penkridge Horse Fair in his *Tour Through the Whole Island of Great Britain*.

He also stopped in Stafford, Lichfield and Tamworth. Stafford, he said, was growing rich through the wool trade. However, that is all that Defoe tells us about farming in Staffordshire. We have to look at other sources from the period to find out more. Sources 9 and 10 show the presence of business farming in Staffordshire.

SOURCE 9

Both Moorlands and Woodlands have goodly cattle ... From these hills and rich pastures and meadows, the great dairies are maintained that supply Uttoxeter market with such vast quantities of good butter and cheese that the cheesemongers of London have thought it worth their while to set up a factorage here ... many market days they spend no less than £500 a day ...

From *The Natural History of Staffordshire*, 1686.

1 **Read Source 9. Add another row to your table on page 23 to show business farming in Staffordshire.**

2 **How could a historian check the reliability of Daniel Defoe's descriptions of British farming?**

SOURCE 10

Key

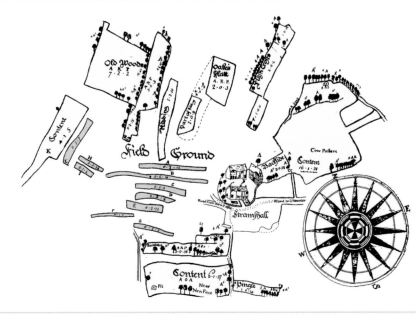

Open field strips

Enclosures

Map showing land held by Richard Mislors in the Manor of Holly Berry Hall, near Uttoxeter, 1735. Some of Richard Mislors' land has been enclosed. Much of his land is still strips in open fields. Cow pasture would be used to supply the dairies mentioned in Source 9. The numbers give the area in acres (A), rods (R) and perches (P).

If Defoe had been able to visit Staffordshire late in the eighteenth century he would have found still more interest in business farming (see Sources 11–14).

SOURCE 11

In South East Staffordshire … good grass land lets from 20 shillings to 40 shillings an acre. Most of it is used to feed cows to supply Birmingham with milk. [Birmingham was a rapidly growing industrial town.]

Arthur Young, *A Six-Month Tour Through the North of England*, 1770.

SOURCE 12

Fazeley Fair is held the first Monday after old Michaelmas [in early October]. It is the largest fair in this county, for fat cows, and lately, for sheep … with an unusual collection of bulls; chiefly offcast or aged. The buyers were butchers, from Birmingham, Wolverhampton and other manufacturing towns. The bulls were bought up chiefly for the collieries; going off in droves …

W Marshall, *The Rural Economy of the Midland Counties*, 1796.

> 3 **Make a copy of Source 7 and mark on it the main markets for Staffordshire business farmers which are described in Sources 11–14.**
>
> 4 **How are growing towns and industry affecting farming in Staffordshire?**

SOURCE 13

In the lordships of Draycott in the Moors, Dilhorne and Caverswall the open-field land produces excellent wheat and barley, as well as an abundant crop of potatoes which contributes to the comfortable support of many thousand workers in Mr Wedgwood's beehive of commercial industry, the Potteries [Stoke-on-Trent].

W Pitt, *Agriculture of Staffordshire*, 1796.

SOURCE 14

Supposing that a farmer in Staffordshire, from where immense quantities of corn are carried to Sandbach by land to be got to Manchester (for home consumption), and to Liverpool (for export), carries one ton of corn the charges will be (as much as) twenty shillings; send the same quantity of corn in a boat of his own, it would not cost him more than five shillings.

T Whitworth, *The Advantages of Inland Navigation*, 1796.
The writer is arguing the case for a canal to be built from Stafford to Sandbach to link Staffordshire farmers with their markets.

Did farming need to change?

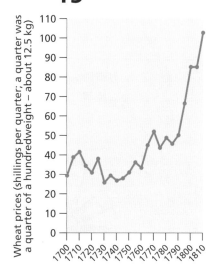

Graph showing wheat prices 1700–1810. For the poor in Britain, the price of wheat was a very important factor in their lives because it dictated the price of bread.

The increase in business farming in Staffordshire was a direct result of the growth of towns and cities. A similar pattern was repeated across the country. In towns people could not grow their own food – there was no land to do so. They wanted to buy their food. And the well-paid manufacturing jobs gave them money to do this.

As towns grew, demand for food increased, and prices rose steadily. Ambitious farmers saw that, with prices rising, they could make large profits – as long as they could increase their food production. They tried out new methods, machines and technology to improve their farms (see Source 16). However, those who were working within the open-field system had a problem.

SOURCE 16

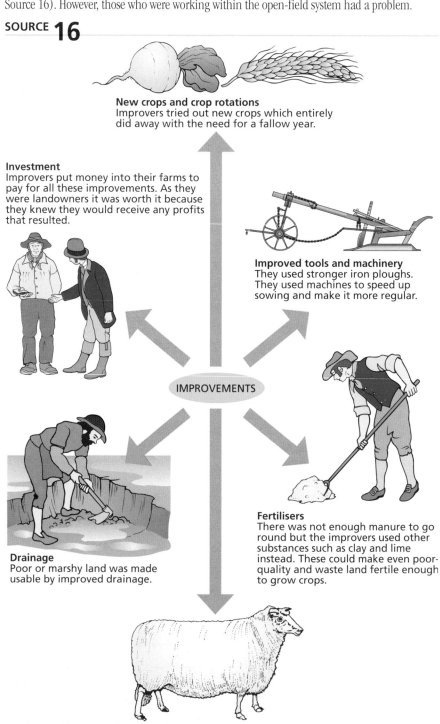

New crops and crop rotations
Improvers tried out new crops which entirely did away with the need for a fallow year.

Investment
Improvers put money into their farms to pay for all these improvements. As they were landowners it was worth it because they knew they would receive any profits that resulted.

Improved tools and machinery
They used stronger iron ploughs. They used machines to speed up sowing and make it more regular.

IMPROVEMENTS

Drainage
Poor or marshy land was made usable by improved drainage.

Fertilisers
There was not enough manure to go round but the improvers used other substances such as clay and lime instead. These could make even poor-quality and waste land fertile enough to grow crops.

Selective breeding of animals
Breeding was carefully controlled so that only the best animals with the most desirable features were used for breeding.

New farming methods and ideas in the eighteenth century. These are examined in greater detail on page 28.

1 **Look at Source 15. Write a sentence to explain how each of the following people might view the changing wheat prices:**

a) a factory worker in a town
b) a subsistence farmer in a village
c) a landowner who sees farming as a money-making business.

2 **Draw and annotate a diagram to explain how rising prices, rising population and increased business farming might be connected.**

FOCUS TASK

HAD THE OPEN-FIELD SYSTEM OUTLIVED ITS USEFULNESS BY 1790?

Copy and complete the table below.

Improvements and new farming ideas	Why these might not be adopted in an open-field system	

1 In column 1 put improvements from Source 16.
2 Decide which of the statements below to use to complete column 2. You can put more than one statement or add to the statement in column 2 by referring back to the information on page 19.
3 Leave column 3 blank as you will need it for the exercise on page 33.

Any change of crops has to be agreed by everyone. The system will not work if one farmer decides to experiment with new crops on his strip.

You can't do selective breeding when you are slaughtering most animals in the autumn, and when all animals are grazing together on common land.

Buying and transporting bulky fertilisers is very expensive. Ordinary villagers cannot afford them. Nor are they convinced they are needed.

The size of the strips of land makes it difficult to use new machinery.

Farmers cannot see the need for change. The open-field system has worked for them for centuries, so why change?

Farmers do not own the land they work on. They do not even have long leases. There is no incentive to improve their land.

All these improvements are expensive. In the hand-to-mouth existence of a subsistence farmer there is no surplus money to spend.

The system of strips means that it is not feasible to dig drainage ditches. Drainage is very expensive.

ACTIVITY

It is 1790. In the small village of Stathern in Leicestershire there is a meeting to discuss the need for change.

You are going to role-play that meeting. Half of you need to prepare arguments to support this view:

• View 1: 'The system is out of date. We simply cannot produce enough food this way.'

The other half have to find evidence to support this view:

• View 2: 'You just want to make easy money. This system has seen us through the eighteenth century, so why not the nineteenth?'

Use the information and sources on pages 26–27.

Improvers and improvements

The diagram on page 26 summarised the improvers' new methods and ideas. You are now going to investigate these new ideas in greater detail. Who came up with them? Did they work?

FOCUS TASK

WHAT NEW IDEAS WERE USED TO IMPROVE FARMING?

1   On your own copy of this diagram use the sources and information on pages 29–31 to add details of how the people mentioned improved farming.

2   Try to find evidence on pages 29–31 which suggests that each of the following improvers was successful: Townshend, Bakewell, Tull, Young.

3   Which improver do you regard as the most important? Explain your answer.

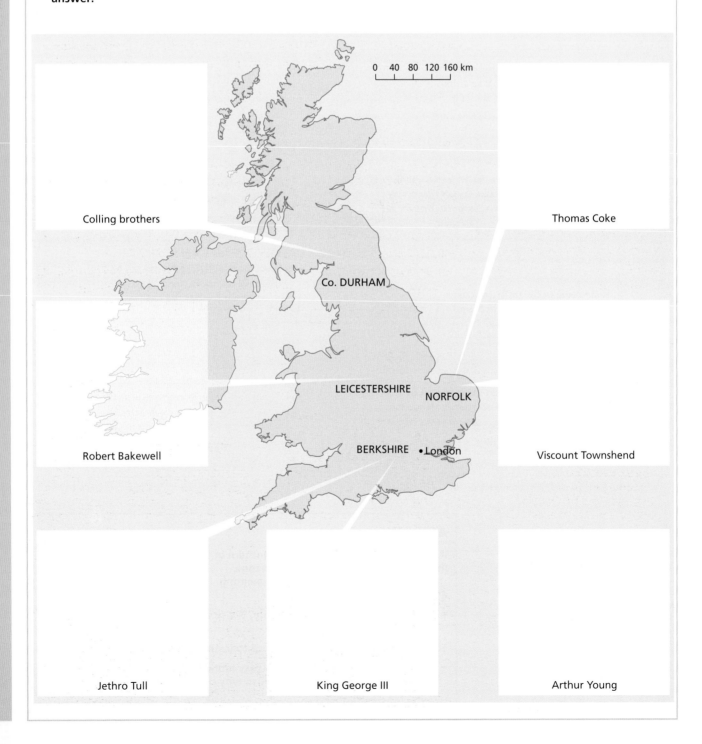

Colling brothers

Thomas Coke

Co. DURHAM

LEICESTERSHIRE

NORFOLK

Robert Bakewell

BERKSHIRE • London

Viscount Townshend

Jethro Tull

King George III

Arthur Young

0   40   80   120 160 km

New crops and new crop rotation

Norfolk was an important area for developments in farming. There were two main reasons for this. In the seventeenth century, after the English Civil War, many exiled English nobles lived in Holland, where they learnt about new techniques. Most returned to England after 1660, and many were Norfolk and Suffolk farmers. Also, East Anglia was (and still is) one of the richest farming areas in the country, which made it a good place to try new ideas.

Viscount Townshend, an important Norfolk landowner, took the lead in trying to make better use of farming land. Townshend was a nationally important figure and had been a government minister in 1714. However, after an argument with the Prime Minister in 1730 he turned his energies to farming. He promoted what became known as the Norfolk or four-course rotation of crops (wheat–turnips–barley–clover) rather than the old three-course rotation. This meant that there was no wasteful fallow land – the land was in use at all times. The turnips drew goodness from deep down in the soil, allowing the upper soil to recover. The clover added nitrogen to the soil. And both crops could be used to feed animals through the winter.

Townshend did not invent the four-course rotation and he did not introduce turnips to Britain – both had been here for a long time. Townshend's main achievement was to mix these ideas with other good business ideas. As an important landowner and former government minister people tended to take notice of his ideas. He was able to publicise them and set an example to other farmers.

Writers like Arthur Young wrote extensively about Townshend's successes.

New machinery

There were many manufacturers of agricultural machinery, particularly of ploughs. However, the most successful inventor of new machinery was Jethro Tull. Unlike other manufacturers, Tull also tried to sell a set of ideas as well as his machines. He wrote up his ideas in a book in which he criticised existing methods and tried to show how they could be improved.

Tull was particularly interested in the sowing of seeds. He criticised the method of sowing by hand and his seed drill was his most famous invention (see Source 17).

Unfortunately for Tull his ideas were not widely accepted. To begin with, Tull's seed drill did not work especially well. The iron industry in the early 1700s was still unable to make iron which was strong enough for the machine, yet light enough for horses to pull it easily. However, the greatest problem was probably that in 1730 farmers were still not very willing to change.

SOURCE **17**

It is very difficult to find a man that could sow clover tolerably. They had a habit (from which they could not be driven) to throw it once with the hand to two large strides. Thus with nine or ten pound of seed to an acre, two-thirds of the ground was unplanted, and on the rest was so thick that it did not prosper.

Jethro Tull, writing in around 1730.

SOURCE **18**

*Sow four grains in a row
One for the pigeon, one for the crow
One to rot and one to grow.*

A popular rhyme in the eighteenth century.

> 1 **Tull was not successful in spreading his ideas. How do you think Sources 17–19 help explain his lack of success?**

SOURCE **19**

A The seed drill. This is a slightly later adaptation of Tull's drill. It was almost impossible in the eighteenth century to prevent inventions being borrowed and adapted. This machine allowed seed to be spread evenly and to an exact depth.

B Tull's horse hoe.

SOURCE 20

The [land] management in this part of the country is exceedingly masterly; the soil dry and sandy, all arable … I was pleased with finding that all the dung they can raise is spread on their turnip land … They know so well the application of manure, that they buy large quantities at Manningtree from London … Kentish chalk is also purchased … with which they form composts. They feed the land with bullocks and sheep … the clover supports all the stock of the farm.

Arthur Young, *Annals of Agriculture*, 1784.

SOURCE 21

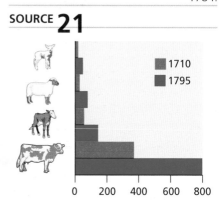

Average weight in pounds of animals sold at Smithfield market.

New fertilisers

All farmers knew the value of manure as a fertiliser for crops and they also knew that lime helped to reduce harmful acid. However, open-field farmers did not keep many animals as they were expensive to feed. A shortage of animals naturally meant a shortage of manure. Access to lime depended on where you lived. As cities grew and transport improved, both of these problems were gradually being overcome. Arthur Young described how enterprising farmers in Suffolk fertilised their land (Source 20).

Improved animals

Great advances were made during the century in selective breeding. The best-known improver was Robert Bakewell, a Leicestershire farmer. His aim was to breed bigger, more productive animals which would bring him higher prices and bigger profits. Bakewell kept very careful records on each of his animals and noted how quickly they grew, how they put on weight and how much milk they gave. Using this information he tried to mate the most productive animals with each other.

Bakewell's ideas were well received by farmers interested in the new methods. Bakewell made a lot of money from the new breed of sheep he created, called the New Leicester. The New Leicester was a barrel-shaped sheep which produced lots of fatty meat. The animal put on weight very fast and cost less to feed than other sheep. Since sheep were sold by weight, farmers were keen to breed New Leicesters.

Bakewell also helped in the breeding of the shire horse, but was less successful in breeding cattle. However, using Bakewell's ideas, the Colling brothers in County Durham produced the Durham shorthorn. The shorthorn was a very successful breed. It matured fairly quickly, but more importantly the Durham breed was good for beef and milk production.

In some ways the improvements in animal husbandry were the most spectacular successes of the eighteenth century. In the early 1700s animals were often scrawny and disease-ridden, but by 1800 they were on average much larger and healthier. They probably weren't quite as large as Source 22A suggests, but the artist was trying to make a point!

SOURCE 22

A This eighteenth-century painting shows a two-and-a-half-year-old pig. The animal supposedly weighed 300 kilos.

B The Newbus Ox. Note the feeding machine in the bottom left-hand corner of the picture.

1 In the past rich people had commissioned artists to paint portraits of their families. In the 1700s it also became fashionable for them to have paintings made of their prize animals. Why do you think the owners of the animals in Source 22 had these portraits painted?

2 Portrait painters who painted people at this time were expected to make their subjects look a little younger or more attractive than they really were. How does this affect the way you use Source 22?

3 Which of Sources 21 and 22 is more useful to an historian?

PROFILE

Arthur Young

★ Many of the sources in this chapter are written by Arthur Young. Young himself was actually a failed farmer. Like many other farmers he had tried to make the improvements he wanted, but could not afford them. Instead he travelled the country writing about what he saw.

★ From 1770 he wrote a number of books (see Source 11). In 1784 he started the *Annals of Agriculture*, a magazine for farmers. The King, George III, supported the new ideas. He even wrote some articles for Young's magazine, under the name of his shepherd Ralph Robinson.

★ In 1793, with so much interest being expressed in the new methods, the government set up a Board of Agriculture, and Arthur Young was given the job of Secretary.

★ Between 1793 and 1820 Young made further tours of Britain, looking at farming methods and encouraging farmers to take up new ideas.

★ Young's work was important in publicising new ideas. Despite this he often met with opposition and objections to new methods, and his journals describe his efforts to convince reluctant farmers to change.

---

4 **List all the different methods used by the improvers to spread their ideas.**

5 **Which people do you think each method would most effectively reach? Explain your answer.**

Enclosure

ENCLOSURE simply means taking open fields and dividing them into smaller plots which are farmed by one person. This was not a new idea. Enclosures had been created since Tudor times, but in the 1700s their numbers increased, as they made it easier for farmers to try out new ideas.

Many improvers enclosed their land so as to reduce wastage. It also meant it was easier for them to make decisions about changing the use of the land. Because enclosure brought a farmer's lands together, it was worth investing in machinery for his new farm. He would not have to transport machinery, lime, manure or seed from one strip to another. Enclosure helped farmers interested in selective breeding. It also made it worthwhile to dig drainage ditches around their fields. You will look in detail at enclosure in 3.2 (page 32).

Spreading the ideas

The ideas on pages 28–30 did not in fact spread very quickly in the eighteenth century. For every farmer who tried to copy the work of Townshend or Bakewell there were many others who were not convinced, could not afford to make changes, or who were opposed to all change. There were even more who simply never saw or heard of the new ideas. Communication in the eighteenth century was not good. People did not travel much. Many farmers could not read.

However, the improvers still tried to spread their ideas. For example, Thomas Coke (pronounced Cook) owned vast estates in Norfolk. He only let his farms out to tenants who agreed to try out the new methods and gave them long leases to allow time for the new ideas to work. He farmed one of his farms himself as a model farm. He held agricultural shows lasting three to four days at his farm at Holkham. At the shows all kinds of animals, ideas and machinery were on display.

Other farmers like Bakewell started agricultural societies to spread the ideas. These people and groups spread the word among wealthier farmers. Arthur Young (see Profile) tried to spread the word more widely and, little by little, he seems to have had some success.

Nowadays historians suggest that many of the so-called improvers were good publicists more than improvers. Coke, for example, took the credit for many improvements which were actually well under way before he took over at Holkham. He also exaggerated his achievements.

However, being able to publicise the new methods was probably just as important as making the improvements. Whether the improvers really made the improvements they claimed or not was less important than the fact that people believed they had done and were encouraged to follow suit.

SOURCE 23

A sheep-shearing festival at Woburn in 1804. This was sponsored by the Duke of Bedford who had been inspired by Coke's shows at Holkham.

3.2 *Why did farming change more quickly after 1790?*

1790–1810 were boom years for farmers. Britain was at war with France. Imports of corn were reduced. There were some poor harvests and the population was rising. As a result of these factors, food prices began to rise steeply. By the late 1790s farmers could get almost double the price for wheat that they could have got in the early 1780s. Higher prices meant farming was now a profitable business. This was a golden opportunity for business-minded farmers:

- The banks were keen to lend money to farmers who wanted to improve their land because they could see it as a profitable business.
- Farmers could afford to modernise – because the money was available and they would quickly get a return on their investment.

Furthermore, the government offered support and encouragement. In the atmosphere of war it was almost regarded as a farmer's patriotic duty to increase production.

The result was more rapid change in the countryside, for example more enclosures and more machines. Also, as farming became more of a business and less a way of life, it meant higher wages for some but increased poverty for others. Over the next 16 pages you are going to examine the reasons for, and the impact of, these changes.

How did enclosure help farmers?

As you saw on page 28 enclosure was only one of a range of measures taken by farmers trying to improve their land. Yet it was an important change because it was seen at the time as the change *on which many other improvements seemed to depend*. The view of many improvers was that you could only improve your land if you got rid of the open fields.

SOURCE 1

The benefits that would be gained from a general enclosure of common land are many. Separating dry ground from wet, and liming the rotten parts, would, with the aid of intelligent breeders, be the means of raising sheep and cattle, far superior to the present race ... It would support more stock, upon the same quantity of food, by keeping the sheep and cattle within due bounds. Their restless rambling not only treads the grass off the ground, but also takes the flesh off the bones. It would tend to preserve improved breeds from sickness ...

John Middleton of Middlesex, writing in about 1800.

SOURCE 2

There can be no question of the superior profit to the farmer by cultivating enclosures rather than open fields. In one case, he is in chains, he can make no variations according to the soil or prices or times. Whatever may be the advantages of varying the crops, he cannot change them – a mere horse in a team, he must jog along with the rest.

An article in *Annals of Agriculture*, 1800.

SOURCE 3

The common field system was admirably suited to earlier times but is absurd today when millions of acres lie waste for want of a change of system, even though famine threatens at the gate.

A writer in 1801.

1 List the improvements which Sources 1–3 say enclosure brings about.

2 Do Sources 1–3 represent objective viewpoints on the benefits of enclosure? Explain your answer.

3 Do Sources 4 and 5 agree about whether improvements are possible within the open-field system? Explain your answer.

The farmers are sensible, intelligent men, for they agree amongst themselves to sow turnips instead of fallowing on many of their lands; and also sainfoin [a plant of the clover family] by keeping off their sheep in the spring. It succeeds excellently, has been worth at one cutting £7 an acre …

Arthur Young's comments on the open-field farming he witnessed at Royston in 1785.

Now it is highly worthy of remark that the husbandry of these farmers is universally bad; their fields are in a slovenly condition, and many tracts of land that yielded good crops of corn, within 30 years, are now overrun with whins [gorse], brakes [dense bushes] and other trumpery. The farmers are a poor wretched set of people.

If it be asked, how such ill practices are to be stopped: I answer, Raise their rents. First with moderation; and if that does not bring forth industry, double them. But if you are to have a vigorous agriculture go forward, throw 15 or 20 of these farms into one, as fast as the present occupiers drop off. This is the only means in such cases to improve husbandry.

Arthur Young, *A Six-Month Tour Through the North of England*, 1770.

FOCUS TASK

WERE ENCLOSURES NECESSARY FOR FARMERS TO USE THE NEW METHODS OF FARMING?

Look back at your table on page 27. There should be a blank column 3. You are now going to fill that out. Head the column: 'Would enclosure help?' and explain in the column whether, and if so how, enclosure would help.
  Then write an answer to the focus question as follows:

1 Explain why you cannot answer this question with a 'yes' or 'no'.

2 Give examples of methods which definitely did need enclosure.

3 Give examples of methods which did not.

4 Explain which methods could work in either system.

5 Write about different areas of the country – how much regional variation was there?

6 Write a conclusion.

Try to include evidence from Sources 1–5 in your answer.

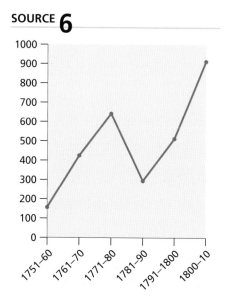

The number of parliamentary Enclosure Acts.

How did enclosure work?

There were two main ways to enclose land:

By consent (agreement)

If all the landholders in a village agreed, they could organise enclosure among themselves. These enclosures by consent were most common in the early eighteenth century.

By Parliamentary enclosure

In villages where some landowners opposed enclosure those in favour could still force it on others by Parliamentary enclosure (see page 34). In the first half of the eighteenth century there had been very few Parliamentary enclosures but the number increased from 1760. By the end of the century most enclosures were by Act of Parliament. And as you can see from Source 6, the period 1790 to 1810 saw a greater number of Parliamentary enclosures than ever before.

FACTFILE

Parliamentary enclosure

1 Local landowners

★ A meeting was held at which the owners of at least three-quarters of the land (not three-quarters of the landowners) had to agree to enclose the land of the village.

★ A petition, drawn up by the landowners, asked Parliament to pass an Act ordering all the farmers in the village to enclose their land.

★ A notice, displayed on the church door for three weeks in August or September, told the villagers that the petition was being sent to Parliament.

2 Parliament

★ A Committee of MPs, appointed by Parliament, considered the petition. Opponents of the petition could argue their case before the Committee. However, this stage was often a formality, since the MPs were all large landowners themselves and believed strongly in the benefits of enclosure.

★ Parliament, following the Committee's recommendations, passed a special Enclosure Act, and appointed three Commissioners to supervise the enclosure.

3 The Commissioners

★ The Commissioners had to find out who held the rights to particular pieces of land.

★ They interviewed villagers, asking them about the land they held and the number of animals they kept on the common.

★ They wanted, wherever possible, to see documents as proof of the right to own land and graze animals.

★ They instructed surveyors to measure and map the strips and common pasture.

★ They then drew up a new map showing how they had re-divided the land to give each farmer a compact holding.

The new map

As you can see from Source 7, the enclosure map of Stathern divided up the open fields and common land between the landowners.

In most villages the Commissioners' new map of the village kept the original boundaries of the open fields but divided up the land inside them into compact units. The new boundaries usually cut across existing strips (see Source 2 on page 20).

The common land was also parcelled up in the same way. A farmer who owned five per cent of the village land was granted five per cent of the commons after enclosure.

The new village

It might take many more months or even years to turn the new map into a new village. The new farms had to be fenced off and hedges planted on boundaries. Ditches had to be dug. On most farms new roads and new buildings were also needed.

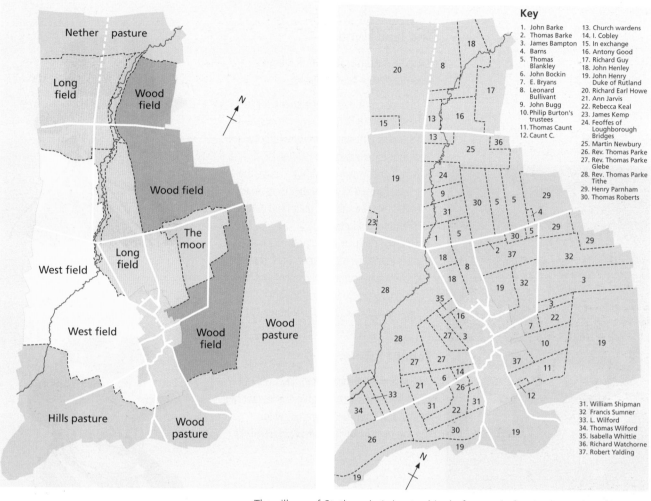

Key

1. John Barke
2. Thomas Barke
3. James Bampton
4. Barns
5. Thomas Blankley
6. John Bockin
7. E. Bryans
8. Leonard Bullivant
9. John Bugg
10. Philip Burton's trustees
11. Thomas Caunt
12. Caunt C.
13. Church wardens
14. I. Cobley
15. In exchange
16. Antony Good
17. Richard Guy
18. John Henley
19. John Henry Duke of Rutland
20. Richard Earl Howe
21. Ann Jarvis
22. Rebecca Keal
23. James Kemp
24. Feoffes of Loughborough Bridges
25. Martin Newbury
26. Rev. Thomas Parke
27. Rev. Thomas Parke Glebe
28. Rev. Thomas Parke Tithe
29. Henry Parnham
30. Thomas Roberts
31. William Shipman
32. Francis Sumner
33. L. Wilford
34. Thomas Wilford
35. Isabella Whittie
36. Richard Watchorne
37. Robert Yalding

The village of Stathern in Leicestershire before and after it was enclosed in 1792.

---

1 Compare the two maps in Source 7. Write your own detailed description of the changes made by enclosure.

The cost was shared by those who owned the land after enclosure. Many farmers built a new house on or near their enclosed land.

SOURCE **9**

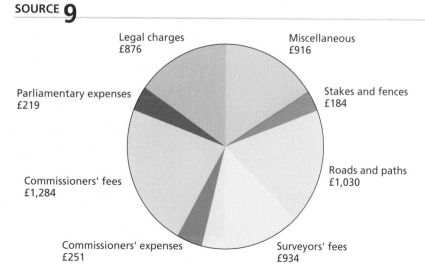

- Legal charges £876
- Miscellaneous £916
- Parliamentary expenses £219
- Stakes and fences £184
- Commissioners' fees £1,284
- Roads and paths £1,030
- Commissioners' expenses £251
- Surveyors' fees £934

The cost of the enclosure of some land in Sheffield, 1791.

SOURCE **8**

Parliamentary and legal expenses	*£8,000*
Fences and hedges	*£12,000*
New buildings and roads	*£4,000*
Total	*£24,000*
	(or £8 per acre)

The cost of the enclosure of 3,000 acres of the Fitzwilliam Estates in Northamptonshire.

Who gained from enclosure?

The landowners

It was the wealthier farmers and larger landowners who benefited most.

- High prices and soaring demand for their produce brought them large profits, and their new, efficient farms were fully capable of meeting the demand.
- Large landowners could now charge their tenant farmers much higher rents. Many found that the value of their land doubled as a result of enclosure.
- Many landowners could now afford to equip their mansions with works of art, have them decorated by leading craftsmen, and fill them with precious porcelain and high-quality furniture (see Source 10).

Tenant farmers

Tenant farmers benefited too. They did not mind the higher rents. High prices meant high profits, and loans were easy to find for improvements like machinery and fertiliser.

SOURCE 10

The state sitting room at Holkham Hall, Norfolk.

SOURCE 11

A cartoon published in 1809. The title of the cartoon was 'Farmer Giles and his wife showing off their daughter Betty to their neighbours on her return from school'. Farmer Giles meant any farmer, and in the early nineteenth century only the wealthy could send their daughters away to be educated.

1 Make a list of the evidence of wealth contained in Sources 11 and 12.

2 What is the attitude of the cartoonist in Source 11

   a) to the farmer
   b) to the daughter?

SOURCE 12

You sometimes see a pianoforte in a farmer's parlour; a servant is sometimes found and a post-chaise to carry their daughters to assemblies, the milliner's or the dancing master's. These ladies are often educated at boarding schools and the sons at the University to be made parsons …

Instead of walking, the farmers ride to market, even within short distances. Instead of going home to dinner, many of them dine at their clubs at the different inns. Many of those who do, remain after dinner to drink wine. Instead of country squires, we now have a breed of country gentleman farmers.

An observer writing in around 1800.

Some labourers

Some labourers also did well out of enclosure.

- Enclosure created an enormous amount of work in digging ditches, planting hedges and building roads.
- The more fortunate labourers even gained a new home on their master's new estate in the middle of his enclosed land.

3 In Source 13 Arthur Young lists a number of people who he believes have benefited from enclosure in Bedfordshire. Who do you think has benefited most?

SOURCE 13

The open-field farmers had been very poor and backward and against inclosure but are now converted and admit the benefit of the measure. The value of sheep's wool is greatly increased. As to the carcase, the value is more than double. The new Leicestershire is seen.

The cottagers' cows are fewer but they have allotments instead. The land now produces more corn; the farmers are coming into better circumstances; the rent is raised; the poor are better employed. On the whole, the measure has been beneficial.

Arthur Young writing about Bedfordshire, 1796.

Who lost from enclosure?

Although there were winners from enclosure, there were also many losers.

Smallholders

Many of the village's smallholders lost their way of life. Although they had rights to land in the enclosure, they simply could not afford the Commissioners' fees and expenses. If they did scrape the money together, the cost of fencing and ditches ruined them because the cost per acre of fencing a small enclosure was much higher than the cost for a larger farm. A huge number of smallholders therefore sold up all or part of their land and became wage-earning labourers. Enclosure may have created new jobs for them but these people lost their independence.

Landless labourers

Also badly hit were the squatters and the part-time labourers who had no legal rights to either the open fields or the common land. The loss of the common land was a devastating blow – to many it had been a vital part of their life. Even if the Commissioner did grant them a plot of land, it could not supply the grazing for cattle, food for pigs, pond for geese, turf, firewood and rabbits which the common land had provided. These people therefore became landless labourers. The plight of such labourers varied greatly, depending on which part of the country they were in, as you will see on pages 46–47.

SOURCE 14

I lament that I have been accessory to injuring 2000 people at the rate of 20 families per parish. Numbers, in the practice of feeding on the commons, cannot prove their rights; and many, indeed most who have allotments, have not more than an acre, which being insufficient for the man's cow, both cow and land are usually sold to the rich farmers.

A Parliamentary Commissioner speaking in 1801.

SOURCE 15

I don't want to argue about their [the Commissioners'] good intentions; poor people look at facts not intentions; and the fact is, by nineteen enclosure bills in twenty the poor are injured … It is said that the commissioners are sworn to do justice. What is that to the poor people who are left to suffer? What is that to the poor man to be told that the Houses of Parliament are very concerned about his property, while the father of the family is forced to sell his cow and his land because he can't own one without the other … The poor in these parishes say with truth, Parliament may be the protector of property: all I know is, I had a cow, and an Act of Parliament has taken it from me.

Arthur Young, writing in 1801, was dismayed by the effect of enclosure on the poor.

1 What do Sources 13–15 agree about?

2 What do they disagree about?

3 How can you explain the differences?

ACTIVITY

It is 1810. There is to be a major public debate about enclosure. The motion is: 'We believe enclosure is unfair.' Write some arguments for a speech either supporting or opposing the motion. Back up your arguments with evidence from the last seven pages.

FOCUS TASK

WHO GAINED AND WHO LOST FROM ENCLOSURE? WHY?

1 Work with a partner to place each of the characters on the right on the scale below.

2 From what each of the characters says, and from pages 32–38, draw up a list of all the factors which affected whether someone gained or lost from enclosure.

3 Which were the two most important factors in your opinion? Explain your choice.

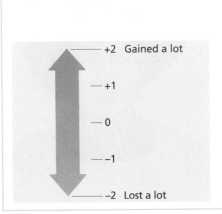

4 Look at Source 16. Explain what is meant by 'without favour or affectation or bad feeling to any person at all'.

5 If you were a smallholder whose village was about to be enclosed, would you be reassured by Source 16?

6 Would Source 17 change your mind?

7 Rewrite Source 18 as if you were explaining this viewpoint to an eighteenth-century smallholder.

8 Here are two statements:

- **The Commissioners were biased towards the rich.**
- **The Commissioners tried to be fair but the law was biased towards the rich.**

Choose the statement which you most agree with and explain your choice using evidence from the last seven pages.

Were the Commissioners biased?

The Commissioners' task was a difficult one. Enclosure was a slow process and they had to do a very thorough job. They were sometimes bitterly criticised for the way they divided up the land. The new arrangement meant that the common land was no longer available to the villagers or squatters in the way it had been, because it was divided up among the landowners. This was obviously a cause of great resentment. On the whole, however, the evidence is that most Commissioners did attempt to carry out their job fairly.

SOURCE 16

I do swear that I will fairly and honestly, according to the best of my skill and judgement, carry out the several powers and trusts reposed in me as a Commissioner by virtue of an Act of Parliament, for dividing and enclosing the lands, grounds and commons, without favour or affectation or bad feeling to any person at all.

The oath of a Commissioner for Enclosure. All Commissioners had to swear this oath as a promise that they would be fair.

SOURCE 17

December 31, 1795 At the Grange settling Kimberworth Enclosure with Lord Effingham.
January 1, 1796 Took a ride with his lordship and Rev Redhead.
February 19, 1796 Settling Draft for Upper Hallam.
February 25, 1796 Attended to Heeley Draft. Dined at the Angel with Gentlemen of the Hunt.

Diary of Arthur Elliott, Commissioner.

SOURCE 18

The conspiracy theory of Parliamentary enclosure may linger … but it is no longer a serious proposition that the enclosure commissioners were a kind of capitalist press gang.

EL Jones, *Agriculture and Economic Growth in England 1650–1815*, 1967.

FOCUS TASK

EIGHTEENTH-CENTURY FARMING: REVOLUTION OR EVOLUTION?

The changes in farming which you have studied on pages 28–39 have sometimes been called an agricultural revolution.

1 In groups, decide what the following terms mean:

a) evolution
b) revolution.

2 Look back over all of your work from pages 18–39. Decide whether you feel that the change in farming between 1700 and 1815 was revolutionary or evolutionary.

3 Write up your views in an essay explaining whether you agree or disagree with this statement: 'The period 1700–1815 was a period of enormous and rapid change in farming.'

SOURCE 19

4s 2d		Five gallons of flour
3d		Yeast and salt
1s		Bacon (1½ pounds @ 8d per pound)
1s		Tea 2d Sugar 4d Butter 4d
8d		Soap 2d Candles 3d Worsted (a yarn made from combed wool) 3d
2s 7d		Rent and fuel (plus money set aside for clothing, medical and funeral expenses)

Weekly expenditure of labourers in Barkham.

How did the poor survive?

You may be feeling a bit breathless after studying all the changes described on pages 28–39. Imagine what it must have felt like at the time. The landscape people had known was changed beyond recognition. Fences now surrounded the old common land and sliced up the great open fields. Farming became more of a business, less a way of life. New houses appeared, new crops, new animals, new machines. Of course some places carried on in the old ways. On one of his tours in 1810 Arthur Young wrote that within a day's ride on horseback he saw farming methods which were a hundred years apart. But for thousands of rural communities around Britain centuries of tradition had disappeared in a decade.

While the boom years made some people in the countryside richer, many remained very poor. Look at Source 19. It shows evidence gathered by the Reverend David Davies, Rector of Barkham in Surrey in 1787. He asked labourers in his parish how much they earned and how they spent their money. Davies found that in his village, the average weekly wage for a male farm labourer was eight shillings. Labourers' wives could earn an additional six pence per week through farm labour or work such as washing or needlework.

It is easy to assume that everyone in the country grew their own food. But as you can see from Source 19, for the landless labourer, buying food was the main expenditure. Almost half the expenditure in Source 19 is on flour for bread. Now look back at the wheat price graph on page 26. Supposing that all other prices stayed the same, then family income would have to more than double for this family just to keep pace with rising food prices. Now imagine you are sick, or old, or cannot work and have no family to support you. What then? Rising food prices would be crippling.

There were many at the time who simply could not understand how the poor managed to make ends meet.

SOURCE 20

It had always appeared to me incomprehensible, how a common farm labourer, who perhaps does not earn more than six or seven shillings a week, rears a large family, as many a one does – I desired old George Barwell, who has brought up five or six sons and daughters, to clear up the mystery.

He acknowledges that he has frequently been 'hard put to it'. He has sometimes barely had bread for his children: not a morsel for himself! having often made dinner off raw hog peas: saying, that he has taken a handful of peas, and ate them with as much satisfaction as, in general, he has eaten better dinners: adding, that they agreed with him very well, and that he was able to work upon them, as upon other food: closing his remarks with the trite maxim – breathed out with an involuntary sigh – 'Ay, no man knows what he can do, till he's put to it'.

Since his children have been grown up, and able to support themselves, the old man has saved, by the same industry and frugality which supported his family in his younger days, enough to support himself in his old age! What a credit to the species!

In 1785 William Marshall interviewed George Barwell for his book *Rural Economy of the Midland Counties*.

ACTIVITY

In pairs:
1 **A term we use today is 'quality of life'. Discuss what you think gives someone a good quality of life.**
2 **Decide whether the labourers in Sources 19 and 20 enjoyed a good quality of life.**
3 **Discuss whether you think George Barwell (Source 20) would agree with your answer.**

Attempts to help the poor

Poverty had always been common in the countryside and there had been many attempts to help the poor. Since 1722 there had been parish workhouses to give the poor shelter, food and basic clothing (see page 212). But by the 1790s the workhouse authorities were alarmed that an increasing number of workhouse residents were not the orphans, the sick or the old for which the system was intended, but labourers who simply could no longer afford to feed their families.

A new system of care was designed by magistrates in Speenhamland, Berkshire, which was quickly copied in other areas. The main change was that the poor did not have to enter the workhouse to qualify for help. Instead they could get OUTDOOR RELIEF. Those without money were given enough to buy food. Those in work but who did not earn enough to feed their families had their wages topped up. The payments were on a sliding scale – as bread prices rose, so payments rose. The system was soon copied by other parishes. The motive behind the Speenhamland system was partly to control the spiralling cost of poor relief, but partly concern for the plight of the poor. It did undoubtedly save many labouring families from starvation.

However, it did not really solve the overall problem. The poor were still poor. The Speenhamland system even created some problems of its own. Some employers deliberately kept labourers' wages low knowing that the parish would supplement them. Also, because an allowance was paid for each child, this encouraged larger families, at a time when there was already a population explosion.

But there was worse to come.

> 1 Write your own 20-word definition of the Speenhamland system to add to the historical glossary at the back of this book.

How did the post-war depression affect people in the countryside?

The improvements of 1790–1815 had been built on high food prices. These high prices had been caused mainly by the French Wars. These wars ended in 1815. There is no real surprise about what happened next. The price of wheat fell dramatically (see Source 15 on page 26) and farming went into a severe depression which affected everyone in the countryside.

Tenant farmers

Tenant farmers suffered very badly. In the boom years they had signed leases agreeing to pay high rents. Many had taken out expensive loans to pay for improvements. With food prices falling, they could not grow enough even to pay the interest on their loans, let alone pay their workers. Many went bankrupt and had to sell their land.

The smallholders who had survived enclosure were all but wiped out. Large landowners were affected too. They persuaded Parliament to ban imported corn (see page 48) but this did not keep prices high because the real problem was that British farmers themselves were now producing too much.

> 2 Draw a diagram to show how falling food prices led to bankruptcy for tenant farmers. Include these words: loans, banks, interest, expenses, income.

Labourers

The worst impact of this depression was felt by the labourers themselves. Farmers reduced labourers' wages. In 1815 average wages for a labourer were about 15 shillings per week. By 1822 they had fallen to 10 shillings. Many labourers were laid off altogether. This would have been bad enough in earlier years, but it coincided with other developments which together made labourers desperate (see page 42).

Through the 1820s and 1830s many rural families faced extreme poverty which was especially stark when contrasted with the increasing wealth of farm owners. The poor had a bad diet, poor housing, and little prospect of things ever getting better. Sources 23–25 paint a very bleak picture, but they are not untypical.

1. Loss of common land

Because of enclosure many labourers had recently lost their rights to use common land. So they had no pig to provide them with bacon and fat, no eggs from chickens and geese, and no milk from the cow they used to keep on the common.

2. Game laws

To compensate for the loss of common rights many turned to poaching rabbits, fish and game birds on the enclosed land. This so worried the landowners that game laws were changed in 1816 so that poachers faced a possible sentence of seven years' transportation to the colonies. Poachers who attacked gamekeepers could be hanged. Gamekeepers were allowed to set vicious man traps, which could trap limbs and hold a poacher until the gamekeeper came along. The injuries caused by these traps were so horrific that limbs often had to be amputated.

SOURCE 21

They hang the man and flog the woman
Who steals a goose from off the common
But a greater crime is let go loose
To steal the common from the goose.

A popular rhyme from the 1820s.

1 How would you explain the rhyme in Source 21 to a foreign visitor who heard it?

3. Mechanisation

Steam-driven threshing machines first appeared in 1786 but they were unreliable. By the 1820s they were much more effective and efficient. Labourers could not compete with steam threshing machines. Worse still, threshing had been winter work when other work was hard to find, so not only were the machines taking away work, they were doing it at the worst time of the year.

SOURCE 22

The farmer has only to light his furnace in the morning, by breakfast the steam is up, and before dinner as much grain is thrashed, cleaned and ready for sale as a dozen men could have prepared in a month.

A description of steam threshing from *Chamber's Journal.*

4. Rising population

At the same time the population in the countryside continued to rise steadily. In the boom years when labourers had more money parents had had more babies. With better diet more had survived into adulthood. Those babies were now young men and women, just at a time when work in the countryside was hard to find.

SOURCE 23

Blurton   *Labourer – windows in a shameful state. Has land to keep a cow but relets it. The cowhouse bad. Premises all in a neglected state.*

Blurton   *Widow with six lodgers – applies for the back kitchen to be rebuilt, lately fallen down. Door to be repaired.*

Blurton   *Infirm – only one room, very small and uncomfortable.*

Hanchurch   *Labourer with three children – one of four old cottages, very small and uncomfortable, there being only one bedroom to each, besides being in a wretched state of repair. They should all come down.*

Extracts from a survey of cottages near Stoke-on-Trent, in 1835.

SOURCE 25

A drawing of a labourer's cottage in the early nineteenth century.

SOURCE 26

A *The labourers' houses are beggarly in the extreme. The men and boys with dirty faces and dirty smock coats and dirty shirts. I have observed that, the richer the soil, the more miserable the labourers.*

The cause is this: the great, the big bull frog grasps all. Every inch of land is [taken] by the rich. The wretched labourer has not a stick of wood and has no place for a pig or cow to graze, or even to lie down upon. It is impossible to have an idea of anything more miserable than the state of the labourer in this part of the country.

B *Look at the miserable sheds in which the labourers reside, made of mud and straw, bits of glass without frames or hinges merely stuck in the wall. Enter them and look at the bits of chairs or stools; the wretched boards tacked together to serve for a table; the floor of pebble, broken brick or bare ground; and survey the rags on the backs of the wretched inhabitants. Wonder if you can why the jails get fuller.*

Extracts from the writings of William Cobbett, 1830. Cobbett was a well-known radical writer and speaker.

FOCUS TASK

You have been appointed by the government to report on the living conditions of the poor. Sources 19–20 and 23–26 are evidence you have gathered. Compile your report under the headings 'Housing', 'Diet' and 'Health'.

SOURCE 24

There is no difference between the lodgings of the women who labour in the fields and those who do not. The want [lack] of sufficient accommodation seems universal. Cottages generally have only two bedrooms; a great many have only one. Three or four persons commonly sleep in the same bed.

The cottages are old and in a state of decay. The floor of the room is of stone and wet and damp in the winter months. Behind the cottages the ground rises and about three yards up the elevation are the pigsties and privies. The cottages are nearly surrounded by streams of filth. It was in these cottages that a malignant typhus fever broke out two years ago which afterwards spread through the village.

The account of Alfred Austin, Poor Law Commissioner in south-west England, written in his official report to the government in 1843.

2 **Which of Sources 23–26 do you consider the most reliable for finding out about the life of the poor in the 1830s? Explain your answer with reference to the sources.**

ACTIVITY

In fours, role-play a conversation that might take place in a labourer's cottage. Four labourers (male or female) are discussing the problems in the countryside. Each of you should suggest one of these ways of dealing with the problems, and argue your case:

- **Move away from the country to find work in a nearby town**
- **Rely on handouts from the parish**
- **Emigrate to another country**
- **Scare the farmers into increasing your wages.**

You will get ideas from the text above. You can also get your teacher to help you.

SOURCE 27

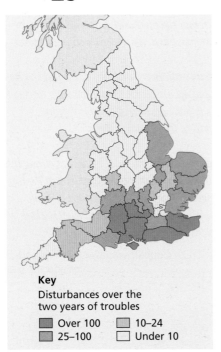

A copy of a letter sent to a farmer. The person who received it sent the note straight to the Home Secretary.

The Swing Riots 1830–32

Between 1830 and 1832 labourers all over southern and eastern England turned to violence in an attempt to solve their problems. Gangs armed with clubs or flaming torches, usually at night, attacked farmers' property. Hayricks and threshing machines were the most common targets.

SOURCE 28

Mr Ellerby had been the first to introduce the new methods. He did not believe the labourers would rise against him for he knew he was regarded as a just and kind man … One day, the villagers got together and came to [the farmer's] barns, where they set to work to destroy his new threshing machine. When he was told, he rushed out and went in hot haste to the scene. As he drew near, some person in the crowd threw a hammer at him, which struck him on the head and brought him senseless to the ground.

The memories of Caleb Bawcombe, a Wiltshire shepherd.

Many of these attacks were preceded by a threatening letter such as Source 27. Some of the letters were signed 'Captain Swing' and before long, rumours began to circulate of a mysterious Captain Swing who was organising the disturbances.

You can see from Source 29 how widespread the riots were. These were not isolated incidents and the authorities were deeply worried. Ever since the French Revolution the British government had been in constant fear of a similar revolution in Britain. At the same time there were many other 'radical' movements developing in other parts of the country. The Captain was pictured as an evil genius, stirring up the rural population in preparation for a revolution.

There was no Captain Swing of course, only desperate and angry agricultural labourers. Even so, the Swing rioters were not a disorganised mob. They caused around £120,000 in damage to property and machinery. Many Swing bands had captains, who were often respectable men, leaders of local Friendly Societies (see page 255). At the the trials, surprise was often shown at the number who were married men in their mid to late twenties. Some historians have compared these men to the weavers who made up the Luddites (page 75) or the Chartists (page 266). And these labourers eventually paid a high price for their actions. Four hundred and fifty-seven men were sentenced to transportation. Several hundred more were put in prison. Nine men were hanged, one of them for knocking off the hat of a wealthy farmer.

SOURCE 29

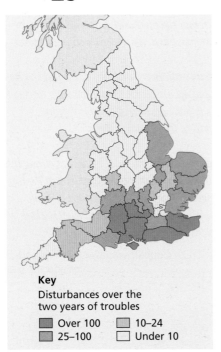

Key

Disturbances over the two years of troubles

- Over 100
- 25–100
- 10–24
- Under 10

Map showing the distribution of the Swing Riots, 1830–32.

SOURCE 30

A cartoon published at the height of the Swing Riots.

SOURCE 31

Cover of a pamphlet in which the writer allegedly expressed the views of Captain Swing.

SOURCE 32

An engraving from 1830 showing labourers in Kent setting fire to hayricks.

SOURCE 33

TO THE
Labouring Classes

THE Gentlemen, Yeomanry, Farmers, and others, having made known to you their intention of increasing your Wages to a satisfactory extent; and it having been resolved that Threshing Machines shall not be again used; it is referred to your good Sense that it will be most beneficial to your own permanent Interests to return to your usual honest occupations, and to withdraw yourselves from practices which tend to destroy the Property from whence the very means of your additional Wages are to be supplied.

Hungerford, 22nd November, 1830.

EMBERLIN AND HAROLD, PRINTERS, BOOKSELLERS, DRUGGISTS, &c. STAMP-OFFICE, MARLBOROUGH.

A magistrate's notice, published in response to the Hungerford Riots of 1830.

1 Look at Sources 30–32. Which of these are:

a) sympathetic
b) unsympathetic

to the rioters?

2 Look at Source 33. Do you think the magistrate's response to the riots was sensible?

ACTIVITY

Work in pairs.

1 You are on trial for your involvement in a Swing Riot. Write a short speech in your defence explaining why and how you got involved in the riots.

2 Swap your speech with your partner's. Now write a speech to be given by the prosecution explaining why Swing Rioters must be treated harshly.

Use Sources 27–33 in your speeches.

Why were there no Swing Riots in the north of England?

Look back at Source 28. There were almost no Swing Riots in the north of England. Why not? Thanks to a remarkable historical source we have some evidence to help answer this question.

James Caird's research

James Caird made a comprehensive study of farm labourers, which he wrote up in his book *English Agriculture 1850–51*. Caird was an excellent observer and wrote up his views thoroughly and carefully. He compared the wages of labourers in different counties. His thorough investigations allowed him to draw up a map showing how the country divided into areas of high and low labourers' wages. He carefully compared the living conditions and the diet of workers in each area. He also drew his own conclusions as to why the wages of the northern labourer were so much higher. He said: 'The influence of manufacturing enterprise is seen to add 37 per cent to the wages of the agricultural labourers of the northern counties, as compared to those of the south.'

Added to this, coal was much cheaper in the north, so labourers kept warm and ate hot food. The northern labourers had a better diet. Many observers at the time noticed that labourers in the north were able to do more work in a day.

SOURCE 34

Northern labourer
Average weekly wage 11s 6d

Southern labourer
Average weekly wage 8s 5d

SOURCE 35

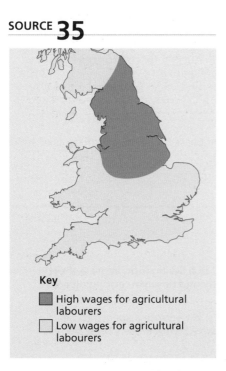

Key
■ High wages for agricultural labourers
☐ Low wages for agricultural labourers

Caird's map of the wages divide.

Caird's findings on wages.

1 Draw a diagram to show connections between the following: wages; unemployment; enclosure; poaching; threshing; war; Swing Riots.

2 The sources and text mention many differences between conditions for labourers in the north and south. Which do you think is the most significant one in explaining why there were no Swing Riots in the north of England?

3 Which do you think is the most likely explanation for why southern labourers did not move north in search of better wages?

4 Why is James Caird such a valuable source for the historian?

SOURCE 36

A Wiltshire

[For breakfast] … flour with a little butter and water 'from the tea kettle' poured over it. He takes with him to the field a piece of bread … He returns in the afternoon to a few pounds of potatoes, and possibly a little bacon, though only those who are better off can afford this. The supper very commonly consists of bread and water.

B Derbyshire

For breakfast they have porridge, then bread and cheese. They take with them to the field each man his pint of ale and as much bread and cheese as he likes. At one o'clock they have dinner which is either brawn, beef or mutton and pudding … At seven o'clock they have supper of milk porridge, then bread and cheese.

James Caird compares the diet of a southern (Wiltshire) labourer and a northern (Derbyshire) labourer.

Above all the northern labourer had more choices. If he had no work in the countryside, he could do casual work in one of the local mills, or even move to a town. Because factory wages were higher, northern farmers were forced to pay better wages if they wanted to keep their workers. They also tended to hire whole families for a whole year, whereas southern farmers hired individual labourers for weeks or even days.

In view of this the great surprise is that very few southern labourers migrated to the high-wage north. Historians are not sure why, but have suggested various reasons.

- In the south they may not have been aware that wages were high in the north. Communication was not good.
- Despite being poor they and their families simply did not want to move from where they were living.
- Travel was slow and very expensive. Their employers' goods benefited from improved transport on roads and canals, but travel for ordinary people was not really possible until the railway network grew in the 1840s.
- If a labourer moved away from his own parish he and his family would not be eligible for poor relief if he hit hard times.

FOCUS TASK

HOW DID RURAL COMMUNITIES REACT TO PROBLEMS IN FARMING?

People in rural communities faced a range of problems in the years 1815–40: falling prices; high rents; the cost of looking after the poor; mechanisation. These problems affected different people in different ways.

1 Work in groups of four. Look at these characters. Decide which of the problems most affected each character. You could choose one or two (or more) problems. You might think for some characters they were not problems at all.

Michael Cavendish, wealthy landowner

Richard Rogers, tenant farmer

Henry Standforth, smallholder

John Jenkinson, labourer

2 For each character, and the chosen problem, decide which of these options might most help them: migration; raising wages; cutting rents; violent action; buying machinery.

3 Finally, each choose one of the four characters and write a report entitled: 'Hard times and hard decisions: rural communities 1815–40'. You could organise your report in different ways:

- By people – take each individual, look at his concerns and explain his options
- By issue – who was concerned with each issue and why?
- By options – who took what action and why?

3.3 *Golden Age and depression: British farming in the nineteenth century*

It will be clear to you from pages 18–47 that farming, like all businesses, experienced cycles of prosperity and depression. Through the rest of the nineteenth century farming also became more and more dependent on factors beyond its control, such as foreign competition and transport improvements.

SOURCE 1

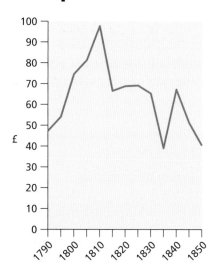

The average price of wheat after its wartime peak in the early 1800s.

Why did Parliament introduce the Corn Laws in 1815?

During the French Wars farming had become a very successful business (see page 32). This was good news for farm owners. The war kept food prices high. However, after the war ended food prices tumbled (see Source 15 on page 26).

The landowners believed that the price of wheat was dropping because cheap imports of grain from Europe had been flooding into Britain since the end of the war. The landowners were a strong group in Parliament and they proposed that Parliament introduce a Corn Law to solve the problem. The 1815 Corn Law stated that if the price of wheat fell below 80 shillings a quarter, all corn imports were banned.

The laws were intended to cover all grains. The landowners were most concerned about the price of wheat, but they were worried that if they only banned the import of wheat, people would simply switch to other crops, so they argued that all grains should be banned.

What were the arguments for the Corn Laws?

At this time the overwhelming majority of MPs were landowners and farmers and they wanted to protect their profits. Landowners argued that they and their workers faced ruin. They put forward several other arguments in favour of the laws:

SOURCE **2**

The immense quantity of foreign corn imported in the year 1814 has so overstocked the markets, that scarcely any sale can be obtained for it in many parts of the country. If corn remains at the present depressed price, it cannot be grown, the farmer cannot afford to cultivate his land, and the improvements of the country must cease; therefore the labouring poor, which was so usefully and industriously employed before, are now starving for want of employment, and the poor rates, in consequence, must be very considerably increased.

Thomas Pilley, a Lincolnshire farmer, writing to the Board of Agriculture in 1816.

Who opposed the Corn Laws?

There were two main groups in Parliament who were opposed to the Corn Laws:

Radical opponents of the Corn Laws called them a bread tax! Bread was the biggest part of a poor person's diet. They argued that the laws would hit the poorest hardest of all. The Corn Laws were subsidising the rich landowners with the hard-earned money of the poor.

Factory owners claimed that higher food prices would force them to pay higher wages. They would therefore have to lay off workers or raise prices, or both. Higher prices would be disastrous for British industry as they would harm exports. The landowners' response to this was that factory owners only wanted cheap bread so they could pay their workers starvation wages.

How did people react to the Corn Laws?

To ordinary people a law which kept food prices high was very unpopular. There was outrage from the general public who were also stirred up by pamphlets, speeches and cartoons. In Dundee over 100 shops were wrecked in riots as protesters complained about the law. In London there were three days of riots. The house of Frederick Robinson, President of the Board of Trade, was attacked and ransacked.

SOURCE **3**

An 1815 cartoon by George Cruickshank, entitled 'The Blessings of Peace'.

1 **Look at Sources 2–4. Which are for the Corn Laws and which are against? Explain your answer by referring to evidence in the sources.**

Betwixt Corn Lords and the Poor
I've not a slightest hesitation.
The people must starve to ensure
The Land its due remuneration.

A popular rhyme.

1 **How useful is Source 4 to an historian?**

2 **What evidence is there that the Corn Laws failed to achieve their aims?**

Did the Corn Laws work?

Despite all the fuss, the Corn Laws turned out to be a huge disappointment to their supporters. The price of wheat did rise to over 80 shillings in 1817 and 1818 but only because of bad weather and poor harvests. Wheat prices averaged out at around 58 shillings for the next 30 years.

By the early 1820s it was clear that foreign imports were not the real problem. Prices were actually falling because Britain's farming was now so successful that Britain itself was producing more than the market wanted. Now that farming was a business it was clear that it would be ruled by the laws of business. If you produce too much prices fall, and businesses go bust.

SOURCE **5**

Wastes have disappeared for miles and miles, giving place to houses, fences and crops … stubborn soils have been forced to bear crops … It may be safely said, not perhaps that two blades of grass now grow where only one grew before, but I am sure that five grow where four used to be!

Henry Brougham, speaking in Parliament in 1816.

SOURCE **6**

A correspondent informs me that one hundred and fifty Welsh sheep were, on 18th October, offered for 4s 6d a head [a low price] and they went away unsold … Last week, at Northampton Fair, Mr Thomas Cooper … purchased three milk cows and forty sheep for £18 16s 6d. The skins, four years ago, would have sold for more …

William Cobbett, 1821. Cobbett found that livestock farmers, as well as corn growers, were overproducing.

Why were the Corn Laws repealed in 1846?

Although they did not achieve their aims the Corn Laws remained law for 30 years. Throughout that time they caused bitter argument. They were amended in 1828. William Huskisson brought in a sliding scale rather than a simple ban on imports. Basically this meant that as corn prices fell, duties on imports rose and vice versa. Prime Minister Robert Peel had altered the sliding scale in 1842. In 1846 Peel finally repealed (abolished) the Corn Laws. Historians still disagree about why he did this. Here are three possible factors.

Factor 1: The increasing power of the industrialists

An important part of Britain's history in the nineteenth century is the struggle between the landowners (the aristocracy and gentry) and the rising middle classes (such as the factory owners). One explanation for the repeal of the Corn Laws is that by 1846 industrialists had enough influence in Parliament to challenge them.

The Anti-Corn Law League was founded in 1839 by Richard Cobden and John Bright, both factory owners from the north of England. They used the new postal service, newspapers and pamphlets to publicise their ideas. The League was probably the first truly effective pressure group.

They argued against the Corn Laws on two grounds.

- They believed in the principle of free trade – trade free of any duties, tariffs or taxes.
- They also argued that high food prices were bad for Britain. If wheat prices were allowed to drop, people would buy more meat and vegetables and have a healthier diet. Their increased disposable income (money that did not have to be spent on food) would also open new markets for industrial goods.

3 Look at Source 7. Do you think the cartoonist supports or opposes the Corn Laws?

4 What is the cartoon suggesting about the views of Prime Minister Peel?

5 Draw up a list of the Anti-Corn Law League's

a) aims
b) methods.

SOURCE 8

The bread tax is primarily levied upon the poorer classes; it is a tax, at the lowest estimate, of 40% above the price we should pay if there were a free trade in corn … The tax of 40% is, therefore, a tax of 2 shillings upon every labouring man's family earning 10 shillings a week, or 20% upon their earnings.

Richard Cobden, speaking in Parliament in 1841. Cobden was a leader of the Anti-Corn Law League and a passionate speaker.

SOURCE 9

On entering another house the doctor said, 'Look there, Sir, you can't tell whether they are boys or girls'.

Taking up a skeleton child, he said: 'Here is the way it is with them all; their legs swing and rock like the legs of a doll', and I saw that it was so in this instance.

'Sir, they have the smell of mice.'

After I had seen a great number of these miserable objects, the doctor said, 'Now, Sir, there is not a child you saw can live for a month; every one of them are in famine fever, a fever so sticky that it never leaves them.'

An eye-witness report of famine conditions in County Tipperary, Ireland.

6 In what ways is the Irish famine similar to and different from famines around the world today?

SOURCE 7

A *Punch* cartoon from 1845. The cartoon appeared the year before repeal. Cobden (on the right) is saying to Peel: 'Come along now Master Robert, do step out.' Peel replies, 'That's all very well, but you know I cannot go as fast as you do.'

Factor 2: Famine in Ireland

In 1845 a disease called blight hit the Irish potato crop. Blight affected the potato plants and the actual potatoes themselves. It spread at a terrifying rate and whole fields could be ruined in a night. In England, losing potato crops would mean hunger, but in Ireland it meant death. Reports of famine and starvation on an unprecedented scale began to reach the Prime Minister.

SOURCE 10

Charities distributing clothing in Ireland. The Irish famine was Europe's worst human disaster since the Black Death in the Middle Ages.

At the same time there were bad harvests in England in 1845–46. Starvation seemed a real possibility there too.

Peel was in a terrible position. Because of the Corn Laws, he could not import cheap corn for Ireland. In fact, because of the high prices in England, food was actually being exported from Ireland for English markets. On the other hand, Peel could not send cheap food to Ireland while English workers went hungry.

Factor 3: Peel's own views on the Corn Laws

Robert Peel was himself the son of a factory owner, even though the Conservative Party he led was mainly a landlords' party. His party pressed him to keep the Corn Laws but he was having doubts even before 1845 and did not believe foreign imports were the threat they were in 1815.

- He was worried that British farmers would become inefficient.
- He was worried that British labourers might stop eating bread and start growing potatoes, leaving them as vulnerable as the Irish.

ACTIVITY

You are Robert Peel's chief speech writer. He is about to make the most important speech of his career, explaining why he has decided that the Corn Laws must go.

Look back at pages 48–51 and prepare Peel's speech. You should provide him with information and evidence about:

- **whether farming will be ruined by repeal.**
- **the extent of the threat of foreign competition.**
- **the famine in Ireland.**
- **the food supply in England.**

The effects of the repeal

The repeal of the Corn Laws destroyed Peel's political career and split the Conservative Party. The landlords refused to support him ever again as they felt they had been betrayed.

The repeal was also too late to help the Irish people. There are no accurate figures, but at least one million died in the famine which followed. At least another million emigrated and Ireland today remains the only western European country whose population has fallen since the nineteenth century.

However, like the Laws themselves, the repeal did not have the effect people had predicted. Prices only fell a little, to a level of about 53 shillings per quarter rather than the average figure of 58 shillings between 1815 and 1846.

Why was there a Golden Age of farming from 1846 to 1870?

With the repeal of the Corn Laws some landowners predicted the collapse of British agriculture. The opposite happened. You are going to investigate why.

Inland transport

Transport inside Britain is a key factor in explaining the prosperity of agriculture in the period 1846–70. The canal network which had been developing since the eighteenth century had long been useful to farmers in getting food to the towns and cities. Farmers shipped large amounts of grain on barges, often bringing back manure for their fields. However, from the 1830s a new phenomenon entered the life of Britain – railways. The rapidly expanding railway network had a number of important effects:

- It increased the flow of people from countryside to towns, helping enlarge this market for farmers.
- It provided cheap transport for bulky produce.
- Because of its speed and reliability, farmers could send fresh produce (vegetables, milk, meat) to the towns – this brought higher profits.

FOCUS TASK

WHY DID PARLIAMENT INTRODUCE THE CORN LAWS IN 1815 AND REPEAL THEM IN 1846?

Work in groups. Your task is to prepare an outline for a schools TV programme on the Corn Laws. You can get a sheet from your teacher to help you organise your work.

You will need to work through a number of stages:

1 **Decide what kind of programme you want to make. It could be:**

- **a narrative.**
- **exploring one issue in depth (e.g. whether foreign imports were the problem).**
- **examining differing viewpoints and interpretations.**

You will have your own ideas.

2 **What evidence will you use?**

3 **What techniques will you use (e.g. interviews with experts, full-screen pictures, reconstructions)?**

4 **Plan the sequence of your programme using a storyboard. Remember that sometimes it is better to start in the middle in order to grab people's attention.**

5 **Present your ideas to the rest of the class.**

1 How does Source 11 show the prosperity of farmers in this period?

2 Write an explanation, for someone who has not read this book, about the link between farming and railways.

SOURCE 11

A painting of Smithfield Market in the nineteenth century. London was a huge market for farmers.

SOURCE 12

Cattle and sheep from the Smithfield Monday market had to leave their homes on the previous Wednesday or Thursday week. Such a long drift, particularly in hot weather, caused a great waste of meat ...

Stock now leaves on the Saturday and is in the salesmen's layers that evening, fresh for the metropolitan market on Monday morning. The cost of the rail is considerably more than the cost of the old droving charges, but against that there is the gain of 20s a head on every bullock a Norfolk farmer sends to town.

GS Read, *Recent Improvements in Norfolk Farming*, 1858.

SOURCE 13

Graziers will not have anything to do with driving cattle 100 or 150 miles ... they will get them upon the railway and convey them to market, and come back again; we allow always a man to go in charge of two wagons for the safety of the cattle themselves, and to return free.

A railway director speaking to a House of Commons Select Committee in 1846.

Population and the growth of towns

Another factor which affected the farmers favourably was the continuing rise in Britain's population. We know from the government's census returns that Britain's population grew from around 18.5 to 26 million between 1841 and 1871. In the past, this had caused problems as well as opportunities for farmers. However, more and more of this growing population were town dwellers. In 1851 for the first time in Britain's history, over half the population lived in towns. These town dwellers worked long hours in the factories and they lived in cramped accommodation – gardens and allotments were very rare indeed. Victorian factory workers had neither the time nor the opportunity to grow food. It had to be 'imported' from the countryside.

High Farming

Besides these 'external' factors farming continued to become more efficient, using new techniques and new technology. There was an explosion in publications dedicated to the new ideas, such as *Elements of Practical Agriculture* (1843) and *Organic Chemistry in its Applications to Agriculture* (1840). As always, the new discoveries took time to come into common use, but by the 1840s and 1850s farmers were fully committed to the combination of business methods and scientific practices which became known as High Farming.

SOURCE 14

The best landlords in the county are said to be capitalists from the towns, who, having purchased estates, manage them with the same attention to principles and details as gained them success in business. They drain their land thoroughly, remove useless and injurious timber, erect suitable farm buildings, and then let to good tenants on equitable terms. Nominally these rents are high; but farms provided with every facility for good cultivation can far better afford to pay a good rent, than can a dilapidated estate any rent, however apparently moderate.

James Caird, writing in *The Times* about farming in Lincolnshire.

3 According to Caird (Source 14), what benefits did the capitalists bring to farming?

SOURCE 15

Twelve years ago [in 1839] draining tiles were made by hand and cost 50 shillings per 100. Pipes have been substituted for these, made by machinery which squeezes out clay from a box exactly as macaroni is made in Italy. The cost of these pipes averages from 12 shillings to 20 shillings per 1000. The new invention has made possible drainage of land at a rate of £3–£4 per acre.

Caird writing about drainage.

SOURCE 16

Pounds of corn per acre
Plot 1 (unmanured) 923
Plot 2 (farmyard manure) 1276
Plot 3 (superphosphates) 1368

The findings of JB Lawes and JH Gilbert, published in 1851.

---

1 **The numbered points in Source 17 show the following:**

- **Byres/stables**
- **Hay ricks**
- **Saw mill**
- **Main farm building**
- **Dovecote**
- **Stock (animal) yards.**

Can you identify them?

New Model Farms

There were other important developments which helped progress in farming. The Royal Agricultural Society (founded in 1838) staged large-scale agricultural shows to publicise the new ideas. As well as the research station at Rothamstead, there was the Royal College of Agriculture at Cirencester to spread the new techniques. Prince Albert, the husband of Queen Victoria, was deeply interested in High Farming and even designed the ideal farm, which became known as the Flemish farm. Another important practitioner of High Farming was the Marquis of Bath. His farm was so up-to-date and well equipped that it became known as a model farm (see Source 17).

Drainage

Caird believed that the most important single development to make High Farming possible was drainage. During the Golden Age the price of pipes for field drainage fell dramatically, thanks to new technology.

In addition to improvements in pipe-making techniques, technology allowed farmers to dig ditches more easily, using the power of steam engines. The Duke of Northumberland spent around £1 million on his lands on drainage and other improvements. The results of improved drainage were impressive. Thousands of acres of waterlogged or badly drained land now came into cultivation, much of it in East Anglia. Machines such as Fowler's mole plough could lay pipes without disturbing the surface of the soil. Instead of doing their traditional work of pumping out water from mines, steam engines were used to pump water from waterlogged areas. Drainage was expensive, but here the government helped. The Drainage Act of 1846 allowed farmers to borrow money at low interest rates for drainage.

The appliance of science

The appliance of organic chemistry began to solve the age-old problem of keeping the land fertile. The German scientist Justus von Leibig had discovered that chemicals known as nitrates and phosphates were the most important nutrients needed by plants and crops. The best source of these chemicals was animal bones, crushed into a powder and spread on the land. Another very useful fertiliser was bird droppings (or guano). This was imported by the shipload, mainly from South America. Another important development came in 1843. A landowner called JB Lawes set up a scientific research station on his fields at Rothamstead. He experimented and noted the effects of different fertilisers on different plots of land. His greatest success was the production of superphosphates, which he made by using sulphuric acid on bones. British farming had discovered artificial fertilisers.

Scientific advances also brought new levels of efficiency to pastoral farming. Animal feeds were produced by crushing seed crops (linseed, oilseed and rape) to produce oilcake – ideal for fattening cattle. The combination of this development and artificial fertiliser meant that farmers could specialise more effectively. If their farms were not suitable for grain, they no longer had to produce it as they could buy in feed to supplement traditional staple animal foods like hay. Similarly, farmers could specialise in wheat only. With artificial fertilisers they no longer needed animal dung.

SOURCE 17

The Marquis of Bath's model farm at Longleat. This farm is a good example of the latest thinking in nineteenth-century farming.

SOURCE 18

Bullocks, pigs, sheep, each in a well-aired, well-cleaned stall. We were shown a system of byres in which the floor is a grating; beasts being fattened up there for six weeks without moving ... Steam-engines for all the work of the arable land. A narrow-gauge railway to carry their food to the animals; they eat chopped turnips, crushed beans, and 'oil cakes'. Farming in these terms is a complicated industry ... being perfected, and equipped with cleverly designed tools ... amused myself by watching the farmer's face ... the expression was cold and thoughtful. He stood in the middle of a yard in a black hat and black frock-coat, issuing orders in a flat tone of voice and few words, without a single gesture or change of expression. The most remarkable thing is, the place makes money.

H Taine, a Frenchman, observed the new methods of farming in Britain in 1862.

2 Read Source 18. Do you get the impression that Taine has seen this kind of farming before? Does he seem to be impressed? Explain your answer.

ACTIVITY

Devise an advertisement for one of the innovations described on pages 54–55.

ACTIVITY

You are a reporter in 1860. Your editor has asked you to write a 10-point 'Idiot's Guide' to High Farming. What are the points you will include?

FOCUS TASK

WHY DID FARMING EXPERIENCE A GOLDEN AGE FROM 1846 TO AROUND 1870?

Was the prosperity of the Golden Age due to

- the actions of farmers; or
- favourable circumstances beyond their control?

1 Read through pages 52–55 and complete the chart below.

Farming reasons	Non-farming reasons

2 Draw lines between factors in each of the two columns which you think are closely linked. Label these lines or draw them in different colours.

3 Explain why you have drawn each line.

Machinery

In 1851 Britain hosted the Great Exhibition at the new Crystal Palace. Amidst all of the other exhibits, the visitor would have seen a bewildering array of machines for different agricultural purposes. Soon after, a visitor to the countryside would be able to see (and hear) these machines in action. As we have seen on pages 28–29, machines were not new, but they were not common either. By 1850, steam engines were reliable enough to make it worthwhile for farmers to use them. However, very few farmers could afford to purchase this equipment and most hired contractors to carry out the jobs.

Although machines did exist for ploughing and reaping, they were not very effective. This was partly because even after enclosure, British fields were too small to make proper use of them. In fact, horse-powered reaping machines such as that invented by Patrick Bell in 1888 were simpler and more reliable. The steam engine really came into its own when it was threshing time. Although many men were still needed to feed and supervise the machine, the steam thresher was an enormous advance.

SOURCE 19

Hornsby's portable steam threshing machine. This was one of many different types of threshing machine.

Conclusion

With all of these advances and the lucrative British market, farming flourished between 1847 and 1870. Foreign competition was not as strong as farmers feared. British farmers were generally more efficient than European farmers. Also, sea transport was not yet sufficiently advanced to allow imports from further afield (the Americas or Australia). British farming was efficient and production rose by around 70 per cent in this period. Relatively little new land came into cultivation, despite the newly drained lands. At the same time, demand for farm produce was rising and farmers' labour costs were falling. From 1845 to 1870 the workforce of agricultural labourers fell by almost a third of a million. Transport costs were also falling.

The great depression in farming, 1870–1900

A changing climate – politics and the weather

From the viewpoint of British farmers, the Golden Age came to an end in around 1870. For the average town dweller, this made little difference, because there was plenty of cheap food in the shops. If you had asked a factory worker in 1879 why agriculture seemed to be in crisis, he might have pointed out that the weather in the 1870s had been very wet. More likely, he would have shrugged his shoulders – as long as there was plenty of food in the shops at prices he could afford, why should he be concerned?

Farmers, on the other hand, were extremely concerned. The weather was especially bad in 1879, but there had been a lot of poor harvests in the 1870s. The landowners pressured Parliament to set up a series of Royal Commissions to investigate the state of agriculture in 1879, and they were concerned with many factors apart from the weather. From the records and reports of these Royal Commissions, we have a very large amount of information about the factors which combined to send farming into its worst-ever depression.

SOURCE 20

A very heavy rainfall began in the early spring which continued without stopping until the end of September. Yet no flooding took place except in the lowland districts although every foot of clay on heavy soils or subsoil was both rotten and sodden, indeed filled with water …

These continuous downpours, accompanied by a damp, dank, cold atmosphere which struck a chill almost into one's bones, brought ruined crops with widespread devastation … All mechanical work in the fields was blocked by the water and the mud which often lay just below the level of the stubble of the grass.

Barley went to the dogs badly in June and on rather heavy land disappeared in July. It first turned yellow, then faded away. Wheat, instead of ripening, turned blighty and black and seemed to shrink back like the barley two months earlier …

Towards the end of September, the disastrous weather came to an end, leaving too many of us with ricks of mouldy hay; corn stacks hardly worth the threshing; our sheep folds too often wiped out or badly depleted and the farmers' bank balance seriously on the wrong side …

Mr Kendall, a Somerset farmer, writing in 1879.

SOURCE 21

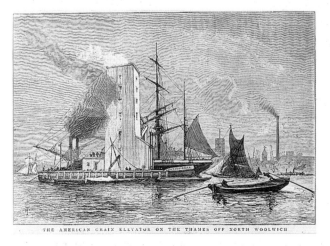

THE AMERICAN GRAIN ELEVATOR ON THE THAMES OFF NORTH WOOLWICH.

An American grain elevator on the Thames at Woolwich.

Competition from abroad

The most important factor in the depression was competition from abroad. British farmers were confident that they could compete against European imports. However, by the 1870s, farmers in the USA and Canada began to export their grain to Britain at a price which no British farmers could match. This was possible because American farming was highly efficient:

- The prairies of North America were flat, fertile plains. Fields were huge so there was a greater use of machinery.
- British farmers had small fields (even after enclosure) and the landscape was often hilly and therefore less suitable for machines.
- In 1874, 80 per cent of American grain was harvested by machine compared to only 47 per cent in Britain.
- British fields were surrounded by hedges, whereas American farmers used barbed wire – which was easier and cheaper to put up and maintain.

New developments in transport

American farmers were also helped by developments in transport technology. In the USA, the railroad companies were covering the whole of the country with a fast, efficient transport network. American hard wheat (which did not go off quickly) was moved by rail and was then transported by steamships to Britain. Before the 1870s this was not cost-effective, but the price of shipping wheat fell by over 90 per cent (33 cents to 2 cents) between 1870 and 1914.

SOURCE 22

Every line of railway that is projected in America brings an additional corn-growing area into competition with the farmer here; and you see … the cost of conveyance is so trifling. For all practical purposes, Chicago is no further distant from this country than Aberdeen is from London.

FR Leyland, owner of a major shipping line, 1881.

SOURCE 24

A CRUMB OF COMFORT.

JONATHAN. "THEY *DU* SAY WE SENT YOU THIS DARN'D WEATHER! DON'T KNOW 'BOUT THAT! ANYHOW, I GUESS WE'LL SEND YOU THE CORN!!"

FARMER BULL. "THANK'EE KINDLY, JONATHAN, BUT I'D RATHER HA' DONE WITHOUT BOTH!!!"

A *Punch* cartoon from 1879 shows Farmer Bull (England) not appreciating the weather or competition from the USA (the figure on the right).

SOURCE 23

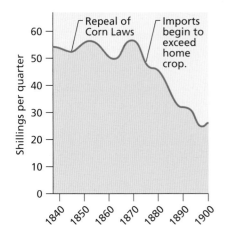

A The falling price of wheat in the later nineteenth century.

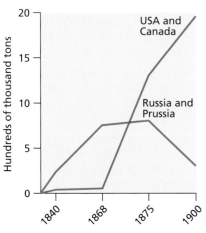

B The growth of imports in the same period.

Unfortunately for British farmers, other competitors also benefited from the same advances as American farmers. New Zealand, Australia and Argentina began to produce cheap meat and dairy produce. Cheap steamship transport, refrigerated ships and canning technology meant that the British market was flooded with imports.

SOURCE 25

An engraving from about 1885 showing London dockers unloading frozen meat from Australia. Along with tinned meat, this was a new feature of the diet of British people in the later nineteenth century.

When historians look back at the records, the picture seems extremely bleak for farming communities. The combination of competition and bad weather hurt the farmers' income, but this was not their only problem. For many farmers rents were still high, and others were paying off loans for drainage or machinery. Many fields went out of use, or were cultivated less intensively (see Source 26).

SOURCE 26

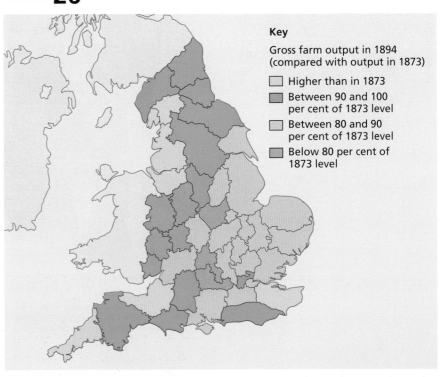

Key

Gross farm output in 1894
(compared with output in 1873)

☐ Higher than in 1873

■ Between 90 and 100
per cent of 1873 level

☐ Between 80 and 90
per cent of 1873 level

■ Below 80 per cent of
1873 level

Output of the English farming industry during the great depression.

The plight of farm labourers

The unfortunate farm labourer continued to suffer. Another 300,000 jobs were lost in farming between 1870 and 1900. Worse still, the farmers had lost much of their political power. They had enough influence to get the Royal Commission established in 1879, and in 1889 the government set up the Ministry of Agriculture. However, farming was no longer the power it used to be in Britain. In the 1880s many town dwellers and working people had the vote, and cared about cheap food more than British farmers. What government would re-introduce the Corn Laws in these circumstances? It may also be that the government suspected that the picture was not altogether bleak. Farm labourers could always leave the land for higher wages in mines and factories.

ACTIVITY

Look back at your work from the activity on page 55. You are the same journalist, now writing in 1882, and your editor wants another 10-point guide. This time the title is 'What has gone wrong with British farming?'

SOURCE 27

They nearly all went to the Welsh coalfields, where during three or four days they earned good wages, and employed the remainder of the week in spending them. A boy who was perhaps taking 6s a week at farm work would be enticed to the mines, where he receives 15s a week or more …

R Haggard, *Rural England*, 1902.

Was there a brighter picture?

Before we assume that all of the farming industry was in gloom and doom we need to look at our evidence carefully. The Royal Commission was dominated by farmers from the corn counties of the Midlands and south-east England. Of all of the witnesses called by the Commission, about three times as many came from grain-growing areas as from beef and dairy-farming areas. Many historians have therefore suggested that the grim picture painted by the Royal Commission did not apply to all of Britain's farms. Some farmers weathered the storm and even prospered from 1870 to 1900. Pastoral farmers benefited from cheap imported wheat as food for their animals. There was a growing market for fresh milk, meat and fresh vegetables, because these could still not be imported. Although small, the amount of land devoted to market gardening increased steadily in the last 30 years of the century.

SOURCE 28

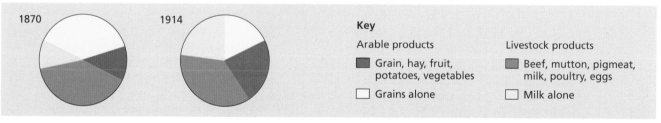

The changing pattern of agricultural produce, 1870–1914.

Despite this gleam of hope, the wheat farmers – the largest sector of British farming – suffered badly, particularly if they were unable to switch production. The great estates of the aristocracy were broken up, some of them sold off to pay mounting debts. As with earlier depressions, recovery followed in the period leading up to the First World War. As 1900 dawned, however, farming had lost its place as Britain's key business.

FOCUS TASK

WHY WAS THERE A DEPRESSION IN FARMING FROM 1870 TO 1900?

1 List the causes of the depression.

2 Which of these were unavoidable?

3 Who suffered the most from the depression, and who the least?

4 Write a letter to *The Times* on the subject of the crisis in British farming. Give three pieces of advice on what can be done to improve matters.

4 A textile industry to lead the world

4.1 How did mechanisation change the textile industry?

FOCUS

After steady growth for a couple of centuries, in the late 1700s Britain's textile industry boomed. It was the first British industry to mechanise on a large scale, the first to turn to factory production, and, after the coal industry, the first to use steam power widely. Where the textile industry led, others followed. It set the pace for the industrial revolution.

In 4.1 you will look at why Britain's textile industry changed in the late eighteenth century. You will:

- consider how the domestic system adapted to cope with the increasing demand for cloth.
- examine why in the end the domestic system was replaced by factory production.
- explore the impact of technological change on the location of the textile industry.
- investigate why some textile workers were unhappy with the introduction of new technology.

In 4.2 you will look at what life was like for workers in textile factories. You will consider:

- whether working conditions in the factories were better or worse than in the domestic system.
- why factory working conditions caused so much debate in the early eighteenth century.
- how factory workers, factory owners and Parliament tried to change working conditions.

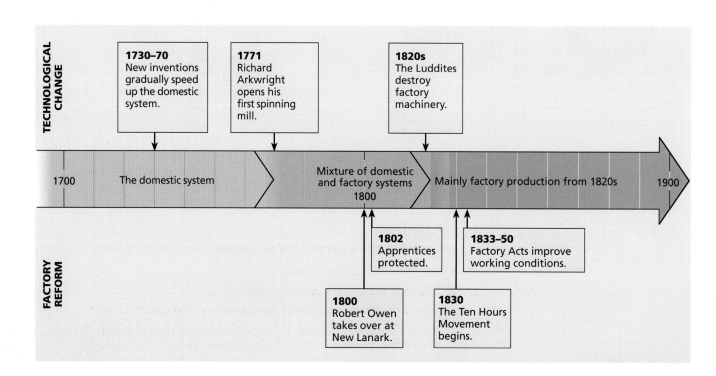

TECHNOLOGICAL CHANGE

1730–70 New inventions gradually speed up the domestic system.

1771 Richard Arkwright opens his first spinning mill.

1820s The Luddites destroy factory machinery.

1700 — The domestic system — Mixture of domestic and factory systems 1800 — Mainly factory production from 1820s — 1900

FACTORY REFORM

1802 Apprentices protected.

1833–50 Factory Acts improve working conditions.

1800 Robert Owen takes over at New Lanark.

1830 The Ten Hours Movement begins.

1 Write your own Factfile on the domestic system. It should include explanations and definitions of the following terms: cloth; fleece; carding; spinning; weaving. You could add your own illustrations and use arrows to show how the stages followed from each other. See page 20 for an example of a Factfile.

How did the domestic system work?

In 1700 the manufacture of textiles or cloth was largely carried out in people's homes. Historians have called this the 'domestic system' (domestic means simply 'in the home'). You can see from Source 1 how the system worked.

SOURCE 1

Washing and drying

The raw wool was dirty, greasy and tangled, so it had to be washed and cleaned before it could be carded.

SOURCE 2

My mother used to bat the wool in a wire sieve. It was then put in a deep round tub with a strong ley [solution] of soap. My mother put me into the tub to tread upon the cotton.

When the mug was quite full the soapsuds were poured off and each separate dollop of wool well squeezed to free it from moisture. They were then placed on the bread rack under the beams of the kitchen loft to dry.

My mother and my grandmother carded the wool by hand.

Samuel Crompton remembers his childhood. Crompton later became a famous inventor of an improved spinning machine (see page 70).

Carding and spinning

Carding means combing the tangled wool fibres into straight lines, with all the fibres going in the same direction. Once carding was complete, the wool fibres had to be spun together to form a thread or yarn. Carding and spinning were carried out by the women of the family. The spinning wheel was a simple machine and most families would own one. Mothers, daughters and sometimes grandmothers would work together, passing on the skills of the trade from generation to generation.

Weaving

Weaving was usually a man's job.

The organisation of weaving varied across the country. Sometimes the weaver wove the thread which his own family had spun. In other cases the clothier paid the spinners and took the yarn away to weavers working in his own workshops.

The weaving loom was a bulky and expensive item. So although some weavers owned their own looms, many rented one from the clothier.

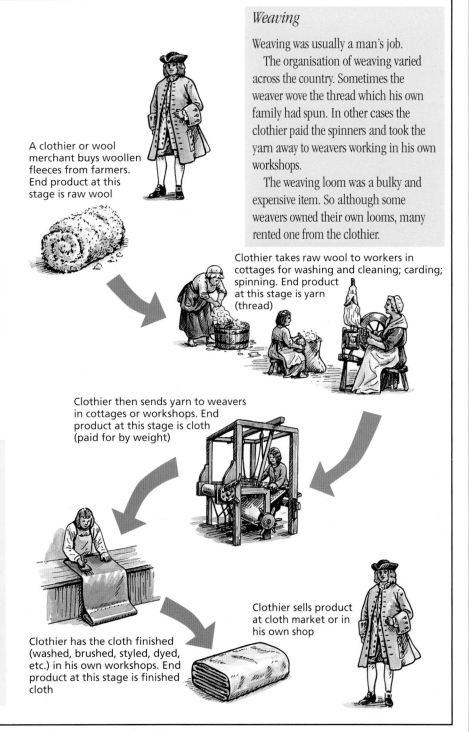

A clothier or wool merchant buys woollen fleeces from farmers. End product at this stage is raw wool

Clothier takes raw wool to workers in cottages for washing and cleaning; carding; spinning. End product at this stage is yarn (thread)

Clothier then sends yarn to weavers in cottages or workshops. End product at this stage is cloth (paid for by weight)

Clothier has the cloth finished (washed, brushed, styled, dyed, etc.) in his own workshops. End product at this stage is finished cloth

Clothier sells product at cloth market or in his own shop

The domestic system was a complex web of different people, all working for the merchant clothier. This shows how the system worked for woollen cloth – which was the main product in the early eighteenth century – but a similar pattern would be followed for other types of cloth.

How was the textile industry changing in the 1700s?

The textile industry had been growing steadily since the 1500s. The wool industry was one of Britain's biggest industries throughout that time. In hilly areas in particular, sheep farming and wool making were an important source of income for farmers. In fact in this period it would be difficult to draw a line between the farming and the textile industries. The same villagers would be involved in raising the sheep, shearing them, spinning the wool and weaving the cloth.

For example, look at Source 3 which shows an eighteenth-century farm. At the door of the farmhouse you can see a spinning wheel. If you walked through the door of the farm in Source 3 you might see a scene similar to that in Source 4.

Likewise, the weaver in Source 4 might himself be a farm worker at certain times of the year. If you asked an eighteenth-century spinner or weaver about the difference between working in farming or in the textile industry she or he would have been very puzzled!

SOURCE 4

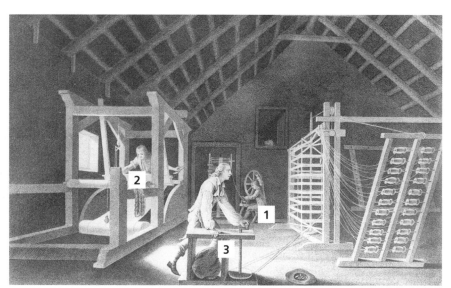

Spinning and weaving at home under the domestic system.

SOURCE 3

An engraving of a farm in the early eighteenth century.

1 **On your own copy of Source 4, explain what is happening at each of the numbered points.**

Even if cloth making was just a sideline it was still part of everyday life. By the 1700s, however, there were areas where cloth making had become an all-embracing concern, eclipsing all other economic activity. In 1724 Daniel Defoe visited the villages in the hills around Halifax in Yorkshire. In Source 5 he describes what he saw.

SOURCE 5

After we had mounted the third Hill, we found one village, hardly a House standing out of speaking distance from another … at almost every House there was a Tenter [a frame for stretching cloth] and almost on every Tenter a piece of cloth …

Wherever we pass'd any House we found a little Gutter of running Water … At every considerable House was a manufactory or Work-House and the little streams were so guided by Gutters or Pipes that none of those houses were without a River … running into and through their Work-Houses …

Among the Manufacturers' Houses are likewise scattered an infinite Number of Cottages or small dwellings, in which dwell the Workmen which are employed, the women and children of whom are always busy Carding, Spinning etc. so that no Hands being unemployed, all can gain their Bread, even from the youngest to the ancient; hardly anything above four Years old, but its hands are sufficient to itself.

From *A Tour Through the Whole Island of Great Britain*, Vol. 1 (see page 23 for details).

2 **Read Sources 5 and 6. What machinery is being used?**

3 **Do you think Defoe (Source 5) approved of what he saw?**

4 **Do Sources 5 and 6 give the same or different impressions of the domestic system? Explain your answer with reference to the sources.**

SOURCE 6

1 November 1782: A fine, frosty, clear, drafty day. Sized a warp and churned [butter] in the forenoon. In the afternoon wove five yards.

16 August 1783: I churned, sized a warp in the morning. Went to Halifax and saw two men hanged on Becon Hill, sentenced at York for rioting.

7 January 1784: Christmas holiday being over I wove five yards.

3 July 1784: I made rope shades and other jobs, got my warp dyed and sized it again and loomed part of it.

From the diary of Cornelius Ashworth, who was a handweaver near Halifax.

	Linen	Used for all manner of garments, especially shirts, shifts and also sheets
	Fustian	Made into garments such as trousers. Fustian is a mixture of cotton and wool or linen.
	Silk	Used for stockings and fancy clothing for the rich
	Wool	For all clothing, carpets and blankets
	Cotton	Used for all clothing

SOURCE 7

In 1700 the main product of the domestic system in England was woollen cloth. The only other significant product was silk. In Ireland and in Scotland there was a flourishing linen industry. Cotton was a rarity. Although cotton cloth was very desirable it was only the rich who could afford it. Cotton could not be grown in Britain due to the climate and so the small cotton industry in Britain was dependent on expensive imported raw cotton from India and, particularly in the later eighteenth century, the southern USA. It was focused around Lancaster, where the cotton could be easily imported via Liverpool.

Map showing regional specialisation of the textile industry in the early eighteenth century.

5 Look through all the pictures on pages 18–62. Make a list of all the things you can see which are made of cloth or textiles.

6 Why might demand for each of these items be growing in the 1700s?

Why did the demand for cloth grow?

In the middle of the eighteenth century the demand for cloth, particularly cotton, began to grow very fast. Historians cannot agree about the most important reasons for this, but these are the factors which they believe are important:

The growing population meant more clothes were needed.

Increasing wealth led to a demand for more and better cloth – particularly cotton cloth.

The price of cotton fell dramatically because of imports from the slave-worked plantations in the southern USA. Many more people could afford cotton goods.

How was production speeded up in the domestic system?

For cloth merchants the reasons for the growing market were not important. Their concern was whether the workers in their homes and workshops could make enough cloth to meet the rising demand.

Stage 1: Speeding up weaving

Weaving by traditional methods involved pushing the 'shuttle' (see Source 8) by hand across the weft. This worked well, but it was slow and the weaver could only make narrow strips of cloth this way.

John Kay and the flying shuttle

In 1733 a Lancashire clockmaker and weaver called John Kay invented a flying shuttle. He put a spring at each side of the loom with strings attached to the shuttle. The flying shuttle meant that wider pieces of cloth could be woven, and at a much greater speed than before.

You may be surprised to learn that Kay was not popular among his fellow weavers. They feared that Kay's invention would put them out of their jobs. In fact, Kay's house was attacked by Lancashire weavers and for a while he left the country. Nevertheless, some weavers began to use Kay's idea.

In 1760 Kay's son invented the drop box. This allowed coloured threads to be woven automatically into the cloth, so that patterned cloth could be made.

Jedediah Strutt and the stocking frame speed up knitting

Elsewhere in Britain, similar improvements were being made. In Nottinghamshire the cloth industry's main product was socks and stockings. In 1759 Jedediah Strutt invented a new stocking frame. This was a knitting machine which greatly speeded up the production of socks and stockings. More importantly, Strutt's machine was able to make the ribbed stockings which were at this time becoming fashionable.

Stage 2: Speeding up spinning

In some ways, Strutt's and Kay's inventions created new problems. Now that weavers and knitters could make more cloth, spinners could not make enough thread to keep up with them. It was estimated that five spinners were needed to supply just one weaver.

The next big breakthrough came in 1764, when James Hargreaves of Blackburn developed the spinning jenny (Source 9). The story goes that he saw a spinning wheel which had fallen over, and this gave him his idea. Whether this story is true or not, his invention was extremely important.

Using the first spinning jennies a worker in the home could spin thread from eight spindles at once. Soon the number of spindles increased. Twelve, sixteen and even twenty spindles could be worked by hand in a weaver's cottage. Like Kay, Hargreaves found that his new invention was not welcomed by workers in Lancashire. He moved with his family to Nottingham where he set up a small spinning factory.

The jenny increased speed, but it did not entirely solve the problem. It made thin thread which was rather weak. The weavers found that they could not use thread made by the jenny for both the warp and weft. They needed a stronger thread for the warp.

SOURCE 8

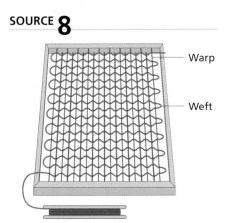

— Warp

— Weft

Warp and weft. In order to make yarn into fabric, warp and weft threads have to be woven together.

1. Can you see how a fallen spinning wheel might have given Hargreaves his idea for a spinning jenny?

2. Explain how bottlenecks in textile production were created and overcome between 1730 and 1770. Refer to: the flying shuttle; the stocking frame; the spinning jenny.

3. Why do you think Kay and Hargreaves faced opposition from other textile workers?

4. Neither Kay nor Hargreaves became wealthy from their inventions. Why do you think this was?

SOURCE 9

Cotton wool placed here and tied to spindles.

One wheel turned up to 20 spindles (operated by hand or foot).

Skilled operator drew frame of spindles back and forth.

The early spinning jenny speeded up production of yarn but it needed a skilled operator and the thread was not high quality.

These developments hardly add up to an industrial revolution but together they greatly speeded up the domestic system. All the machines were designed for use in the home or in small workshops. The numbers of people involved in textile production increased. Output grew and imports of raw cotton increased.

SOURCE 10

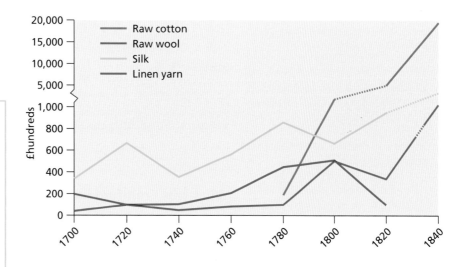

Imports of textiles into Britain 1700–1840. These are official figures, which tend to be low because there was a huge trade in smuggled goods to avoid duties. Even so they do give a good indication of trends.

FOCUS TASK

WAS THE DOMESTIC SYSTEM AN EFFECTIVE WAY OF ORGANISING PRODUCTION?

It is 1770. A merchant clothier has asked you to prepare a report on the domestic system. Your report should summarise for him:

- how the domestic system works
- regional differences
- how production has speeded up
- the problems which merchants, inventors and workers have faced in speeding up production
- what will happen if demand for cloth continues to increase.

Conclude with your own answer to the key question: 'Was the domestic system an effective way of organising production?'

Richard Arkwright and the first factories

In your report on page 65 you may have decided that the domestic system was effective or you may have concluded the opposite. There is evidence to support either conclusion and historians today are divided over the issue. However, whether it was a good system or not, over the next 50 years it was largely replaced by factory-based or mass production – for reasons which you will study over the next 14 pages.

The first cotton mill was set up by Richard Arkwright. He had an enormous impact on the development of the textile industry, so you are going to investigate his career in some detail.

An inventor and a businessman

Richard Arkwright was both an inventor and a businessman (see Profile). He knew all about the problems facing the textile industry. He could see the shortage of thread caused by the invention of Kay's flying shuttle. He also knew of Hargreaves' invention but could see that it did not entirely solve the problem. Arkwright saw the possibility of making vast amounts of money if he could solve the problem. He was friendly with John Kay and together they devised a machine which would produce thread strong enough for both warp and weft, and do it quickly. He called it the spinning frame.

Arkwright came up against the same problems as inventors before him – lack of money and opposition. But unlike the others, Arkwright was a shrewd and resourceful businessman. He had seen how the flying shuttle and spinning jenny had been widely copied, so he made sure that his machine was not unveiled until he could obtain a patent. This cost money, which he gained by entering a partnership with Jedediah Strutt, the stocking manufacturer of Derby (see page 64). Strutt provided the money to buy Arkwright a 14-year patent and to set Arkwright up in business.

Arkwright's frame was too heavy to be worked by hand in the home. He never intended it to be used at home and through his patent he prevented smaller frames being made for home use.

The first frames were powered by horses, but this did not satisfy Arkwright. In 1771 he and Strutt built their first water-powered factory at Cromford. Arkwright sent the first yarn back to Strutt in Derby and they agreed that it was of good enough quality for knitting machines.

SOURCE 11

One person will spin a thousand hanks a day so that we shall not want one-fifth of the hands [workers] I first expected ... I have made trial to spin cotton for velvet ... Richard [the mill manager] has hit upon a method to spin worsted with rollers.

Extract from a rare letter from Arkwright to Strutt, 1772.

What was Cromford like?

To observers of the late eighteenth century the Cromford mill was a marvel of efficiency and ingenuity.

SOURCE 12

An artist's impression of the Cromford mill, based on a painting from 1786.

SOURCE 13

The same mill from a different viewpoint. Note the water wheels.

1 At which points on the plan in Source 14 were the artists standing when they made Sources 12 and 13?

SOURCE 15

Weavers' houses in Cromford. Arkwright built quality housing for the workers in Cromford.

SOURCE 14

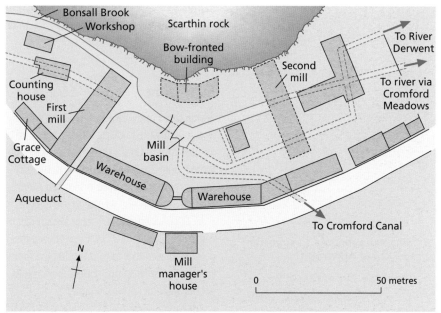

A ground plan of the mill complex.

Why Cromford?

Cromford met Arkwright's needs in two important ways:

Workers

He had a ready workforce in the wives and children of the lead miners of this upland village. Other workers moved to Cromford, mainly from Derby.

Male weavers worked in the solid cottages which Arkwright built for his workers (see Source 15). The top floors of these cottages, with their rows of windows, are where the weavers worked. At the beginning of the day the women and children left for the factory where they spun the thread which the men then wove at home.

SOURCE 16

Cotton Mill, Cromford, 10th Dec. 1771.

WANTED immediately, two Journeymen Clock-Makers, or others that underſtands Tooth and Pinion well: Alſo a Smith that can forge and file.—Likewiſe two Wood Turners that have been accuſtomed to Wheel-making, Spole-turning, &c. Weavers reſiding in this Neighbourhood, by applying at the Mill, may have good Work. There is Employment at the above Place, for Women, Children, &c. and good Wages.

N. B. A Quantity of Box Wood is wanted: Any Perſons whom the above may ſuit, will be treated with by Meſſrs. Arkwright and Co. at the Mill, or Mr. Strutt, in Derby.

Advertisement dated 10 December 1771 in the *Derby Mercury*.

Water power

It was not the workers which most attracted Arkwright to Cromford, but the power provided by the streams running down from the old lead mines in the hills above. A water wheel and complex gears could power hundreds of spindles – a vast improvement on horse power.

By bringing all his spinners together to work in one place and by using machinery and a power supply not dependent on humans or animals, Arkwright had opened the new age of factories.

Expansion

Within three years Arkwright had made enough money from selling yarn to the Nottinghamshire stocking knitters to pay off Strutt. But that still did not satisfy him. He built another mill in Cromford, probably to try out new ideas and developments as well as to make more money. He built more mills in the surrounding area. He soon expanded his business back into his native Lancashire, building a factory in Manchester. He also made money from his patent – anyone who wanted to use a water frame had to obtain a licence and pay a fee to do so.

In 1784 Arkwright sued some Manchester cotton manufacturers for copying his water frame without a licence. In court it was alleged that Arkwright had borrowed and adapted other people's ideas rather than inventing the spinning frame himself. Arkwright's machine was similar to a roller spinning machine invented in 1738 by Lewis Paul, although Paul had never got his machine to work reliably.

Arkwright therefore lost his patent in 1785. He was intensely annoyed but by this time he was already hugely successful and so was the cotton industry.

1 Read Source 16. List the jobs available at Cromford.

2 Why might Arkwright want clockmakers?

3 Why were patents so important to Richard Arkwright?

4 What do Sources 17–19 agree about?

5 What do they disagree about?

6 Why do you think the writers of Sources 17–19 disagree about Arkwright?

A genius or an exploiter?

Opinions on Arkwright both at the time and in the present day are varied. Clearly he could be a stubborn and difficult man, and he was definitely ambitious and even greedy. He was very unpopular for the way he exploited his patent. Many grumbled about Arkwright's attitude. On the other hand some praised him as a great inventor and an inspired businessman.

SOURCE 17

Arkwright has already built a great cotton works at Manchester, yet he swears it shall never be worked ... and will take cotton spinning abroad, and that he will ruin those Manchester rascals whom he has been the making of. It is agreed by all who know him that he is a tyrant ... If he had been a man of sense and reason he would not have lost his patent ... Surely you cannot think it just that any tyrant should tyrannise over so large a manufactory by false pretences.

Matthew Boulton, writing to his business partner James Watt in December 1780.

SOURCE 18

His genius for mechanics was observed ... I well remember we often had great fun with a clock he put up in his shop, which had all the appearance of being worked by the smoke of the chimney ... He was always thought clever in his peruke [wig] making business ...

Thomas Ridgeway, writing in 1799 about Arkwright as a young man in the 1750s.

SOURCE 19

The water frame was not the original idea of the man who patented it. Richard Arkwright was an unscrupulous operator who – unlike most real inventors of the period – became very rich.

EJ Hobsbawm, *Industry and Empire*, 1968.

Whatever the opinions on Arkwright, there is little doubt that he had a huge impact on the textile industry. By his death in 1792, not only had Arkwright made a fortune but he had set the textile industry on a path which would utterly change both its location and its working methods. You can see from Source 10 (page 65) the effect of the factory system on the cotton industry. Between 1780 and 1800 imports of raw cotton went up nine-fold. And although to start with these developments particularly affected the cotton industry, the wool and other textile industries would eventually follow.

ACTIVITY

SOURCE 20

Richard Arkwright.

Use the sources and information on pages 66–69 to write a 'This is Your Life' for Richard Arkwright. You should concentrate on his

• background
• talents
• contribution to the cotton industry

and include interviews with people who knew him.

Make sure that your programme is balanced and includes differing opinions on Arkwright.

Samuel Crompton and the spinning mule

1 Look at Source 22. Describe the changes it shows.
2 What effect do you think a falling price for thread would have on the textile industry?
3 How were Crompton and Arkwright
   a) similar?
   b) different?
4 Which person do you think was more important to the development of the cotton industry – Crompton or Arkwright? Explain your answer.

Arkwright may have been the most successful 'inventor' of his time but he was not the only one. Throughout the textile industry individuals were working on their own inventions or refinements of technology.

In 1779 a Lancashire weaver, Samuel Crompton, developed a cross between Arkwright's spinning frame and the spinning jenny. This was known as the mule. The jenny's thread was fine but weak, whereas Arkwright's thread was strong but coarse. Crompton's mule was able to spin fine, strong threads for both warp and weft, capable of producing cloth of the highest quality.

Crompton was not a businessman. He did not patent his machine so it was soon copied in factories across the country. The original mule had been a small hand driven machine, developed in secret by Crompton in his attic. But by 1792 other inventors had adapted the mule to be used in factories where hundreds of spindles could be supervised by unskilled workers or even children. Thus Crompton's mule was making a lot more thread than Arkwright's spinning frame, although Arkwright was the more successful businessman.

SOURCE 21

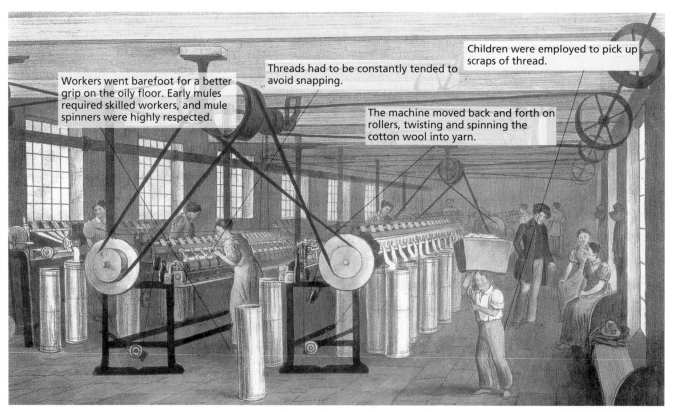

A spinning mule from the nineteenth century. Look at the number of spindles being worked by a single person.

Labels on image:
- Workers went barefoot for a better grip on the oily floor. Early mules required skilled workers, and mule spinners were highly respected.
- Threads had to be constantly tended to avoid snapping.
- Children were employed to pick up scraps of thread.
- The machine moved back and forth on rollers, twisting and spinning the cotton wool into yarn.

SOURCE 22

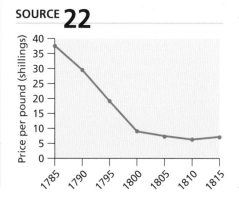

Graph showing the falling price of fine yarn. This opened up new markets at home and abroad.

A Golden Age for the handloom weavers

Spinning was now a factory industry, but weaving was not. It was a still a domestic or workshop industry. From the 1780s until about 1805 there was a golden age for handloom weavers. Manufacturers were so desperate for cloth that they paid very high wages. Many weavers emigrated from Ireland to England to join in the boom. The flood of new weavers increased throughout the period of the Napoleonic Wars.

SOURCE 23

Many weavers at that time used to walk about the street with a £5 note spread out under their hat-bands … they objected to the intrusion of any other handicraftsmen into the particular rooms in the public houses which they frequented.

Extract from *The Life and Times of Samuel Crompton*, written in 1856. He is describing the 1790s.

SOURCE 24

Fabrics made from wool or linen vanished … old loom shops were insufficient, so every lumber room, even old barns, cart-houses and out-buildings of every description, were repaired and fitted up for loom shops … New weavers' cottages rose up in every direction … The price of labour rose to five times the amount ever before experienced in this district, every family bringing home 40, 60, 80, 100 or even 120 shillings per week!

William Radcliffe, *The Origin of the New System of Manufacture*, written in 1828. He is again describing the 1790s.

FOCUS TASK

The Golden Age for the handloom weavers had many different causes and consequences.

Draw up two lists:

a) **Causes of the Golden Age.** List as many as you can.
b) **Consequences of the Golden Age.** The text and Sources 23 and 24 will help you. Use your own historical judgement as well.

Choose two causes and two consequences and explain in detail how they helped lead to, or were caused by, the Golden Age for handloom weavers.

Solving the weaving problem

Now that spinning had been mechanised so successfully the bottleneck was in weaving.

Edmund Cartwright and the power loom

The Reverend Edmund Cartwright, an Oxfordshire clergyman, decided to try to develop a machine which would solve the weaving problem. He was a clever man, but when he set out he knew very little about weaving.

Cartwright produced his first powered loom in 1785. He was excited by his new invention and opened his first weaving factory in Doncaster in 1787, and a second in Manchester in 1791. Unfortunately, Cartwright was not about to follow in Arkwright's footsteps. His loom was clumsy and unreliable. It could not match the quality of hand-woven cloth. He closed his Doncaster factory in 1793, and in 1791 his Manchester factory was closed (the same year it opened) after it was attacked and set on fire by angry handloom weavers.

However, Cartwright's career was not quite a complete failure. Other inventors and developers worked on the problem using Cartwright's design as a starting point, but trying to correct its faults. In recognition of the importance of his contribution Parliament gave him a £10,000 grant in 1809. By 1810 the first really practical power looms were in use. From the 1820s onwards they became extremely widespread.

SOURCE 25

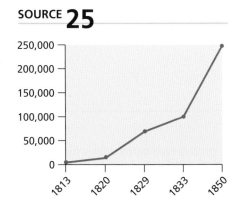

The increasing numbers of power looms, 1813–50.

Crisis for the handloom weavers

For about 20 years wages had been rising for the handloom weavers. Not surprisingly, the number of weavers had risen. The arrival of the power loom spelt disaster for the once proud and well-paid weavers. Machine-produced cloth was soon cheaper than handwoven cloth. The price of a roll of handwoven cloth in 1797 had been 29 shillings, but by 1827 it had fallen to just under 3 shillings (one-tenth of the 1797 price!).

Weavers worked 18-hour days and cut their prices to compete with the new machines, but this simply lowered their own wages. In Bolton the wages of cotton weavers fell from 25 to 15 shillings a week between 1805 and 1815. By 1818 weavers were earning less than 9 shillings.

Manufacturers now used power looms for their steady production, and only used handloom weavers on a casual basis when they had a sudden surge of demand.

SOURCE 26

Power looms in an engraving from the 1830s.

1 Machinery such as that in Source 26 was a popular subject for engravers. Why do you think this was?

2 How realistic do you think the engraving in Source 26 is? Explain your answer with reference to the source.

ACTIVITY

When did the Factory Age begin? In pairs choose two dates which could be seen as the beginning of the Factory Age and justify your choice. If you had to choose one date, which would it be and why?

The Luddites

It was a desperate situation for many weavers and caused them to take desperate measures. Groups of distressed or angry weavers lead violent attacks on machines, burnt down mills, and even attacked the mill owners themselves. Usually they first sent letters asking the mill owners to destroy the machines themselves. Some of these letters were signed 'Ned Lud' or 'King Lud' so the machine breakers were known as LUDDITES (a term which is still used today for anyone who does not like the latest technology).

What did the Luddites want?

Like the labourers involved in the Swing Riots (see page 44), the Luddites were described in pamphlets and papers as a raging mob. However, the evidence shows them as the most respectable members of the working classes. They were well organised and sometimes educated. Besides complaining about living standards, they felt that machines threatened the whole order of society. The movement worried manufacturers and government, which may explain why official reports were so bitterly anti-Luddite. Sources 27–31 will introduce you to the real Luddites, as well as to the Luddites in government reports.

SOURCE 27

A

B

Two cartoons from the time showing Luddites.

SOURCE 28

Whereas by [royal] charter, the framework Knitters are empowered to destroy all frames and engines that make articles in a fraudulent and deceitful manner … we do hereby declare to all Hosiers Lace Manufacturers and Proprietors of Frames that we will break and destroy all Frames that make the following spurious articles …[articles listed]; that do not pay regular prices heretofore agreed to the Masters and Workmen; Frames not working by the rack and rent and not paying the price regulated in 1810; Frames not marking the work according to quality; all Frames of whatsoever description the workmen of whom are not paid in the current coin of the realm will invariably be destroyed …
Given under my hand this first day of January 1812.
God protect the Trade.   *Ned Lud's Office, Sherwood Forest*

The Declaration of the Framework Knitters, 1812, from Home Office papers.

3 **From 1815 handloom weavers were caught in a downward spiral.**

   a) **Explain what is meant by a downward spiral.**
   b) **Draw a diagram showing how the weavers were affected by increased competition, falling prices and falling wages.**

1 Which of Sources 27–31 were prepared by supporters of the Luddites, and which by opponents?

2 How do they differ in their view of the Luddites?

3 According to these sources, what were
   a) the problems faced by the weavers
   b) the methods of the Luddites?

4 Do you think the Luddites' tactics were likely to succeed?

SOURCE 29

The guilty may fear, but no vengeance he aims
At the honest man's life or estate
His wrath is entirely confined to wide frames
And to those that old princes abate
These Engines of mischief were sentenced to die
By unanimous vote of the Trade;
And Ludd who can all opposition defy
Was the grand Executioner made.

And when in the work of destruction employed
He himself to no method confines
By fire and by water he gets them destroyed
For the Elements Aid his designs.
Whether Guarded by Soldiers along the Highway
Or closely secured in the room,
He shivers them up both by night and by day,
And nothing can soften their doom …

'General Ludd's Triumph' – a song.

SOURCE 30

The discontent which had thus first appeared about Nottingham, and had to some degree extended into Derbyshire and Leicestershire, had before this period been communicated to other parts of the country … in Cheshire, where anonymous letters were at the same time circulated, threatening to destroy the machinery used in the manufactures of that place, and in that and the following months attempts were made to set on fire two different manufactories … houses were plundered by persons in disguise, and a report was industriously circulated that a general rising would take place on the first of May, or early in that month … The manner in which the disaffected have carried on their proceedings, is represented as demonstrating an extraordinary degree of concert, secrecy and organisation. Their signals were well contrived and well established, and any attempt to detect and lay hold of the offenders was generally defeated.

Report of the Select Committee of the House of Lords on the 'Disturbed State of Certain Counties', printed in the *Annual Register*, 1812.

ACTIVITY

You are a weaver who has been arrested for machine breaking. Write a speech to give in court explaining:

a) the reasons that weavers are facing a crisis
b) why they have tried to destroy machinery.

SOURCE 31

A good workman, who formerly earned from six shillings to eight shillings a day, cannot now earn six shillings a week by labouring sixteen hours a day. Many manufacturers have put weavers on half work – say three shillings a week and with that miserable pittance we have to meet the needs of our hungry and naked families … a solitary meal each day of oatmeal and water is absolutely more than a man with a family of small children is able to obtain.

A statement from the Bolton weavers, February 1826.

Case study: What happened at Haslingden, Lancashire, in 1826?

Around 1800 Haslingden was a prosperous Lancashire cotton manufacturing community. As demand for cotton rose so did the number of weavers. By 1826 it was a different story. The handloom weavers were in a desperate state and there were clashes with troops in this quiet village.

There had been many such protests in the past (see page 71) but in the 1810s and 1820s these attacks became more frequent and more intense. The government at this time was very much afraid that discontent in Britain might erupt into revolution, as it had done in France. So disturbances and riots were treated very seriously.

On 26 April 1826 there were riots in Haslingden.

5 Note down the areas of agreement between Sources 32 and 33.

6 Note down the areas of disagreement.

7 Which of the differences appear to be factual?

8 Which differences appear to be interpretations of events?

9 Which version (or parts of each version) appears to be more convincing? Explain your answer.

SOURCE 32

That morning we [a crowd of handloom weavers] set off to the loom-breaking. When we had got on the road we saw horse soldiers coming towards us. There was a stop then. The soldiers came forward, their drawn swords glittering in the air. The people opened out to let the soldiers get through. Some threw their pikes over the dyke and some didn't.

When the soldiers had come into the midst of the people, the officers called out 'Halt!'. All expected that the soldiers were going to charge, but the officers made a speech to the mob and told them what the consequences would be if they persisted in what they were going to do. Some of the old fellows from the mob spoke. They said, 'What are we to do? We're starving. Are we to starve to death?'. The soldiers were fully equipped with haversacks, and they emptied their sandwiches among the crowd.

Then the soldiers left, and there was another meeting. Were the power-looms to be broken or not? Yes, it was decided, they must be broken at all costs.

From *The Reminiscences of Thomas Duckworth*, describing the events of 25 April 1826. Thomas Duckworth was a handloom weaver in Haslingden. He was 16 at the time of the riots.

SOURCE 33

At Haslingden yesterday, notwithstanding the … troop of cavalry [in the area], a mill was attacked and the machinery destroyed … This morning as early as seven o'clock … almost 3000 [people] successfully destroyed the power looms of three mills. Having been applied to [asked] most earnestly by the proprietors of two other mills for protection … the military were … placed in a position to defend a mill at Chatterton … where they were immediately assailed with volleys of stones, which placed the colonel in the necessity of ordering them to fire. Several of the mob were killed and it is to be feared from the incessant firing, which was kept up for more than a quarter of an hour, that a considerable number must have been wounded … The populace then dispersed gradually, but with the avowed intention of returning with an overbearing force. They were supplied mostly with bludgeons, clubs, etc. but no arms were observed. The obstinacy and determination of the rioters was most extraordinary, and such as I could not have credited had I not witnessed it myself.

Report for the Home Secretary written by an army officer, 26 April 1826.

ACTIVITY

Either:
Use Sources 32 and 33, and your own knowledge of this period, to write your interpretation of what you think happened at Haslingden in 1826.

Or:
In about 100 words, explain why you feel that it is not possible to piece together the events at Haslingden from these two accounts. Explain what other evidence you would need.

FOCUS TASK

HOW DID WORKERS RESPOND TO CHANGES IN THE TEXTILE INDUSTRY?

Here are three possible views that a worker might take towards changes in the textile industry.

1 What evidence can you find of each attitude in the past nine pages?

2 If you cannot find evidence of one viewpoint do you think that means no-one thought that way at the time? Explain your answer.

Thank the Lord for the arrival of these machines. I now have no trouble finding work, the wages are good and my wife and children can also earn much needed money.

These machines should be destroyed now. They have destroyed our work, our independence, our whole way of life.

Well, I suppose that there is no point in trying to fight the inevitable. Machines are here to stay so I may as well accept that my family and I are going to become factory workers.

Anatomy of a cotton mill

With the mechanisation of weaving the domestic system was largely abandoned in cotton making. The domestic system lived on in other industries and other areas but the mighty cotton industry, sometimes called 'King Cotton', was now completely dominated by factory production.

Mill owners became nationally important figures. The Greg family at Styal in Cheshire (see pages 93–96), Robert Owen at New Lanark (see pages 85–86) and Robert Peel were all respected and listened to by the government. By the 1840s Robert Peel's son (also called Robert) had risen to become Prime Minister.

The new cotton mills were the wonder of the age and they began to change the landscape of the East Midlands, Lancashire and West Yorkshire. Source 34 shows a plan of Quarry Bank Mill at Styal. Raw cotton went into the mill. Finished cloth came out. Today this seems an obvious way to organise things, but at the time it was 'revolutionary'. Many different factors came together to make such a mill possible. Let's analyse them.

SOURCE 34

Money

For the entrepreneur, the first stage was to find the money (or capital) to build the mill. The major costs were the building itself, the machinery and the power supply. Arkwright's mill in Cromford cost around £5,000 – a fortune in the 1770s.

This investment could come from various sources. Britain's banks were very wealthy and well organised in the eighteenth century, compared to those in many other countries. In many cases, entrepreneurs borrowed money from wealthy relatives. Others entered partnerships with wealthy merchants or landowners who were looking to invest profits they had made elsewhere – such as in the slave trade.

The son of a Belfast ship owner, Samuel Greg inherited his uncle Robert Hyde's fustian cloth business. At this time, Manchester clothiers were investing heavily in cotton mills, and Greg was not a man to let such opportunities slip.

Power

Factories needed power. In the early 1800s this was water power. Once the site had been found, workers were employed to build weirs and ponds to make the water supply usable.

Building materials

Each mill factory that was built gave a great boost to other industries. Brick-making, iron-making and glass-making industries all boomed during this period. Building the mills provided jobs for thousands of workers.

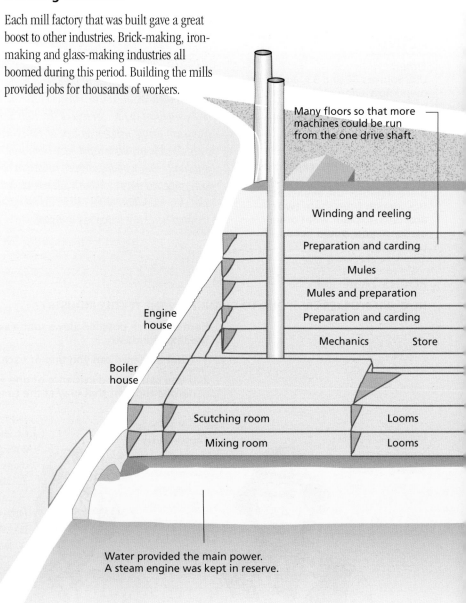

Many floors so that more machines could be run from the one drive shaft.

Winding and reeling

Preparation and carding

Mules

Mules and preparation

Preparation and carding

Mechanics   Store

Engine house

Boiler house

Scutching room   Looms

Mixing room   Looms

Water provided the main power. A steam engine was kept in reserve.

Cross-section of the Quarry Bank Mill at Styal, Cheshire, owned by the Greg family.

ACTIVITY

You are a wealthy banker in around 1800 and a young entrepreneur comes to see you to ask for financial backing to build a cotton mill.

a) What questions would you ask him?
b) What answers would encourage you to back him?

Machines

All stages of production were mechanised. Reliable machinery depended on both the skill of the inventors and the skill of the hundreds of craftsmen who built and maintained the machines.

Transport

In 1819 mill owners used road, canal and river transport to bring in their raw cotton and take away the finished cloth. However, before the coming of the railways, transport was still one of the most expensive and slowest parts of the whole cotton-making process.

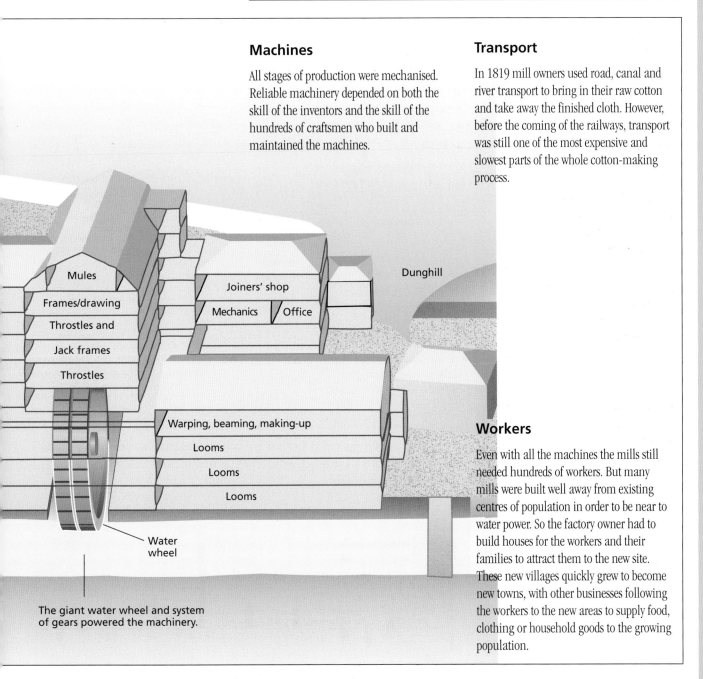

The giant water wheel and system of gears powered the machinery.

Workers

Even with all the machines the mills still needed hundreds of workers. But many mills were built well away from existing centres of population in order to be near to water power. So the factory owner had to build houses for the workers and their families to attract them to the new site. These new villages quickly grew to become new towns, with other businesses following the workers to the new areas to supply food, clothing or household goods to the growing population.

How did steam power change the location of the textile industry?

In 1800 almost all textile mills were water-powered. Although steam engines were in use in other industries by this time, they were unreliable and extremely expensive (a Boulton and Watt engine cost around £850). They also used large amounts of coal, which was difficult to transport. So there were only two Boulton and Watt engines working in cotton mills in 1800 and water power remained the key factor in choosing a mill site. Mills built at the turn of the century were concentrated around the Pennines or in central Scotland where there were plenty of fast-flowing rivers or streams.

However, by the early 1800s nearly all the best waterside sites had been taken. Improvements in coal mining and in canal transport made coal cheaper. The quality of steam engines improved to the point where they were reliable enough to run a factory.

By the 1850s, therefore, new cotton mills were largely steam-powered and the most important factor in choosing a site for a textile mill was to be near to cheap coal supplies. You can see the result in Source 35.

SOURCE 35

Key
- Woollens
- Cotton
- Silk
- Linen

◀ **A** In 1700 wool was still Britain's second biggest industry after farming. The main centres were Exeter and Norwich.

▲ **B** 1780.

▲ **C** 1850. The coalfields of Lancashire and Yorkshire had become the unrivalled centres of the textile industry.

Location of the textile industry.

A similar pattern was repeated in Scotland. Location changed from the upland areas such as Lanark (see page 85) to towns such as Paisley on the Scottish coalfields where the famous Paisley cloth was produced.

SOURCE 36

- ➡ Steam power
- ➡ Water power
- ➡ Change in number of mills

Cheshire: 16%, 35%, −21
Lancashire: 57%, 5%, +49
Yorkshire: 143%, 11%, +54
Derbyshire: 65%, 21%, −21

Change in the textile industry, 1838–50.

1 **Write a detailed description of the changes shown in Sources 35 and 36.**

The Lancashire cotton industry

The cotton industry led the way in industrialisation in England. It was centred in Lancashire. Lancashire was ideally placed for cotton production. In the days of water power it had plenty of good sites. Once steam power took over, it had plenty of coal. It had many skilled workers who had worked in the cotton industry for decades. It also had a vast supply of unskilled workers who were ready to move to the growing cotton towns from the surrounding countryside. But Lancashire had other factors in its favour as well.

Liverpool and Manchester

The port of Liverpool was the main port for imports of raw cotton from the slave-worked plantations of the southern USA. A mill in Lancashire could easily be supplied by Liverpool merchants and have the raw cotton delivered on the rapidly expanding network of canals. Liverpool was also an important port for re-exporting the finished cloth.

Nearby Manchester was a vitally important commercial centre, with its banks and stock exchange; and of course its growing population was a market for the cotton manufacturers' goods. In the early 1800s it also became an increasingly important manufacturing centre in its own right and the number of cotton mills in Manchester almost tripled between 1801 and 1851.

SOURCE 37

A steam-powered Manchester cotton mill in 1835.

Climate

One of the perpetual problems in a cotton mill was the cotton threads snapping when they became dried out. The Lancashire region had a damp climate which helped alleviate this problem.

Chemical industry

There was a long tradition of chemical manufacture along the banks of the River Mersey (in fact the giant chemicals company ICI is still there today). This gave cotton manufacturers easy access to bleaches and dyes, and workers with expertise in using them.

ACTIVITY

Either:
Prepare a leaflet explaining to potential investors the advantages of Lancashire as a site for their cotton factory.

Or:
You are a young worker in a cotton mill in Lancashire. Your father was a Luddite transported to Australia for his involvement in machine breaking in Haslingden (see pages 74–75). You have not seen your father since then. Write a letter to him explaining how you feel about the success of the Lancashire cotton industry.

The Yorkshire woollen industry

Some decades later there was a similar, if slightly slower, pattern of development in the Yorkshire woollen districts.

The wool manufacturers were slow to modernise. However, once the success of the cotton masters became clear, wool masters followed. Yorkshire manufacturers were ideally placed to follow in the footsteps of the Lancashire cotton masters. They had the same fast-flowing streams. They were also close to the Yorkshire coalfields and in their period of most rapid growth (the 1830s to the 1850s) rail transport was just starting.

By the middle of the nineteenth century the woollen industry in Yorkshire was fully industrialised. It produced around 60 per cent of Britain's wool products and exported some £10 million of goods, from woollen jackets to the saddle blankets of American cowboys. Wool never reached the same levels of production as 'King Cotton', but it was still a major industry.

SOURCE 38

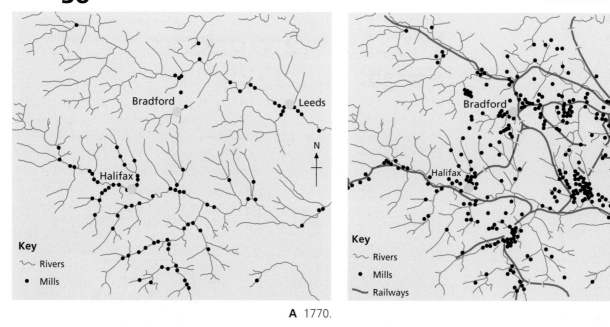

A 1770.

B 1850.

The location of Yorkshire woollen mills, showing water supplies.

FOCUS TASK

HOW DID NEW TECHNOLOGY CHANGE THE TEXTILE INDUSTRY?

1 Copy and complete the table below to show what effect new technology had on the location and working practices of the textile industry.

	Effect on location	Effect on working practices
Mechanisation		
Steam power		
Improved transport		

2 Write an essay to explain how new technology changed the textile industry. You could structure it in paragraphs like this:

- The location of the textile industry
- The decline of domestic work
- The growth of factory work.

Linen

Linen had been an important fabric in Lancashire, Scotland and Ireland. By the 1850s it was a mechanised industry, but was centred around Dundee and, particularly, Belfast. The Lancashire linen workers tended to migrate into the cotton industry. The linen industry remained strong in Ireland. For several centuries Ireland had been prevented by British government restrictions and taxes from developing any industries which might compete with those on the British mainland. However, because there was no major linen industry on the mainland the Irish linen trade was not seen as a threat.

4.2 *Factory reform: How were working conditions improved?*

The factory system undoubtedly speeded up production. Visitors to the first factories talked about them as wonders of the industrial age. However, a few decades later the cotton mills had become the subject of a bitter controversy about working conditions. Observers were appalled by the noise, heat, smell and dust of the factories. Worse still, stories circulated of child workers who were savagely beaten by the factory overseers; of tired workers maimed by unguarded machinery; of callous owners treating their workers more like slaves than employees. What had gone wrong?

By the 1820s and 1830s the controversy over 'working conditions' had become a bitter debate involving MPs, newspapers, campaign groups and government inquiries. A mass of conflicting viewpoints were expressed by supporters and opponents of the factory system. Most of the sources we have about this are biased to one side or another. It has become very difficult to tell truth from propaganda. However, as historians you are in a position to try to investigate these issues in a more balanced way.

ACTIVITY

In pairs role-play a conversation between a critic and a defender of the factory system. You can get lots of ideas from pages 81–83. The critic can use the information in the left-hand column, and the defender the information in the right-hand column.

When you have finished your role play discuss whether there was anything on which the critic and the defender agree.

What were working conditions really like?

The left-hand column below and on pages 82–83 shows some of the main criticisms of working conditions. However, as historians you also have to try to see events from the perspective of the time. The right-hand column helps you do that.

If you only looked at the left-hand column you would think that all mill owners were uncaring, callous tyrants. Some probably were. With the prospect of getting rich many mill owners did exploit their workers. However, you must try to see working conditions from the employer's point of view as well.

1. Working hours were very long

Criticism

Shifts of 12 hours for all workers – men, women and children – were common. In busy times it was not unheard of for workers to be at the mill on shifts of 18 hours, six days a week. Source 1 shows you a typical day for a child factory worker.

SOURCE 1

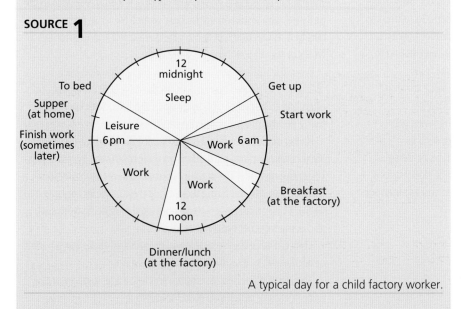

A typical day for a child factory worker.

Employer's defence

Most employers had invested large amounts in their mills.

They believed they had to keep their factories running for as long as possible in order to make a profit. They could not afford to run their mills only when their workers felt like working.

Many factory owners were also devout Christians, who disapproved of idleness and believed in the value of hard work. Hard work was good for people.

2. Workers' jobs were insecure

If the mill went though a bad patch workers could be fired and not taken on again until trade improved.

The employer's view was that jobs were always dependent on a factory doing well. If all jobs were guaranteed businesses would go bankrupt.

To compensate for insecurity, factory work was better paid than working in the domestic system or as a farm labourer, which were the two main alternatives available.

Significantly there was never a shortage of workers – people wanted factory work.

3. The mills were dangerous and unhealthy

There were whirling belts, grinding gears and wheels, which were open and unguarded. An unfortunate worker could easily lose all or part of a finger if he or she lost concentration while tending to the machines. The machines were also very noisy.

The atmosphere was smelly and hot. Factory windows were kept tightly shut. In some parts of the factory the air was thick with cotton dust. Carders got 'carder's cough'.

A hot and humid atmosphere was ideal for cotton making.

The windows had to be kept closed in the spinning rooms as any pollution that came in through the windows could harm the delicate threads.

Machinery in these early factories was quite erratic. It was constantly breaking down. It had to be easily accessible to be quickly repaired.

4. Child labour was widespread

Children as young as six or seven worked in the mills. Most of these children were brought to the mill by their parents to work alongside them. Others were PAUPER APPRENTICES.

Pauper apprentices were orphans who were in effect 'owned' by the mill owner. They lived in the mills or near them. In return for board and lodging from the mill owner the apprentices signed an 'indenture', an agreement which meant that they were bound to work at the mill until they became adults. In some mills apprentices were badly treated. They worked the same very long hours as adults for little pay. They received no education.

Children were particularly at risk from the long hours because the work they did was boring and repetitive. Work such as replacing bobbins, piecing together snapped threads or oiling mechanisms required great concentration but little skill. On long shifts of 12 hours it was very difficult to keep alert enough to avoid accidents.

Children had always worked for their parents in the domestic system, so little had changed. It was mostly the parents who brought the children anyway! Employers would also argue that the pauper apprentice system was offering a valuable service to the parishes, who would otherwise have to care for these orphan children. It was much better to give them a job and a skill than to let them stay in a workhouse somewhere.

From the mill owners' point of view there was often little alternative to pauper apprentices. In the days of water power, mills often had to be placed well away up in the hills. With no workers living nearby, pauper apprentices fulfilled a need.

It also made economic sense to employ children. Children were ideal cotton workers, particularly in their main jobs as scavengers (cleaning up under the machines) or as piecers (watching for snapped threads and fixing them while the machines continued to work). Their small fingers were well suited to delicate work such as piecing together broken threads.

They did what they were told – particularly if there was a parent or adult there to discipline them if they did not!

They were also cheap to employ and low wages kept down the price of cotton, which was good for everyone.

Clocks, hooters and bells dominated the lives of factory workers and they were not allowed to leave the room without permission from the factory overseer. Even talking, singing and whistling were banned, and an enormous number of offences could be punished by fines.

In the domestic system workers had been used to taking days off, then working harder the rest of the week to catch up. Now they needed discipline. In the early days of the factory system the need to fit in with rules or different working methods was a severe shock.

Factories fined workers for lateness and absence, mainly because it was a huge problem. Reports on factory work in South Wales show that workers skipped off about 20 per cent of their working time. Workers who were paid at the end of the month often stayed away for a third of the time in the two weeks after they were paid!

SOURCE 3

I found the utmost distaste on the part of the men, to any regular hours or regular habits … The men themselves were considerably dissatisfied, because they could not go in and out as they pleased, and have what holidays they pleased, and go on just as they had been used to do [when they worked at home].

R Cookson giving evidence to a Parliamentary Commission in 1806.

SOURCE 2

RULES TO BE OBSERVED By the Hands Employed in THIS MILL.

RULE 1. All the Overlookers shall be on the premises first and last.
2. Any Person coming too late shall be fined as follows:—for 5 minutes 2d, 10 minutes 4d, and 15 minutes 6d, &c.
3. For any Bobbins found on the floor 1d for each Bobbin.
4. For single Drawing, Slubbing, or Roving 2d for each single end.
5. For Waste on the floor 2d.
6. For any Oil wasted or spilled on the floor 2d each offence, besides paying for the value of the Oil.
7. For any broken Bobbins, they shall be paid for according to their value, and if there is any difficulty in ascertaining the guilty party, the same shall be paid for by the whole using such Bobbins.
8. Any person neglecting to Oil at the proper times shall be fined 2d.
9. Any person leaving their Work and found Talking with any of the other workpeople shall be fined 2d for each offence.
10. For every Oath or insolent language, 3d for the first offence, and if repeated they shall be dismissed.
11. The Machinery shall be swept and cleaned down every meal time.
12. All persons in our employ shall serve Four Weeks' Notice before leaving their employ; but L. WHITAKER & SONS, shall and will turn any person off without notice being given.
13. If two persons are known to be in one Necessary together they shall be fined 3d each; and if any Man or Boy go into the Women's Necessary he shall be instantly dismissed.
14. Any person wilfully or negligently breaking the Machinery, damaging the Brushes, making too much Waste, &c., they shall pay for the same to its full value.
15. Any person hanging anything on the Gas Pendants will be fined 2d.
16. The Masters would recommend that all their workpeople Wash themselves every morning, but they shall Wash themselves at least twice every week, Monday Morning and Thursday morning; and any found not washed will be fined 3d for each offence.
17. The Grinders, Drawers, Slubbers and Rovers shall sweep at least eight times in the day as follows, in the Morning at 7½, 9½, 11 and 12; and in the Afternoon at 1½, 2½, 3½, 4½ and 5½ o'clock; and to notice the Board hung up, when the black side is turned that is the time to sweep, and only quarter of an hour will be allowed for sweeping. The Spinners shall sweep as follows, in the Morning at 7½, 10 and 12; in the Afternoon at 3 and 5½ o'clock. Any neglecting to sweep at the time will be fined 2d for each offence.
18. Any persons found Smoking on the premises will be instantly dismissed.
19. Any person found away from their usual place of work, except for necessary purposes, or Talking with any one out of their own Alley will be fined 2d for each offence.
20. Any person bringing dirty Bobbins will be fined 1d for each Bobbin.
21. Any person wilfully damaging this Notice will be dismissed.

The Overlookers are strictly enjoined to attend to these Rules, and they will be responsible to the Masters for the Workpeople observing them.

WATER-FOOT MILL, NEAR HASLINGDEN,
SEPTEMBER, 1851.

J. Read, Printer, and Bookbinder, Haslingden.

Rules from Water Foot Mill near Haslingden, Lancashire, 1851.

1 Read Source 2. Divide the rules into four lists:

   a) Those designed to ensure cleanliness
   b) Those designed to prevent fire
   c) Those designed to keep machinery running smoothly
   d) Those designed to preserve the moral standards of the workers.

2 Which rules cannot be put into any of these lists? What is the purpose of each of these rules?

3 Judging by the punishments for each offence, what do the employers regard as the most serious offences?

4 Why do you think these offences were regarded as being so serious?

1 What are the advantages of the domestic system according to Sources 4 and 5?

2 How does it differ from the factory system?

3 Write a paragraph to send to the writer of Source 4 explaining how far you agree with her representation of the domestic system.

4 Which of the 'down' side and 'up' side features of the domestic system do you think an ordinary worker in the domestic system would think most important?

FOCUS TASK

HOW DID THE FACTORY SYSTEM CHANGE WORKING CONDITIONS?

It is 1832. You are aged 15, the eldest of five children in a family of cotton-mill workers. Your family had previously been working in the domestic system. You moved to Styal from the Cheshire countryside to work in the mill shown on page 76. Your family wages have doubled as a result.

Someone investigating working conditions in the factory interviews you about how things have changed for you and your family.

You are going to answer this question in a balanced way. You should mention:

- the work you did in the countryside (agricultural work and domestic spinning and weaving).
- the working conditions in the domestic system.
- how factory work is different.
- the working conditions in the factory.
- what is the biggest change.
- whether you regret moving.

You can present your work as either

a) a series of interview questions and answers; or
b) a letter to the inspector.

Were factories worse than the domestic system?

The factory system was undoubtedly very different from the domestic system, but it is debatable whether conditions were so much worse. We assume they were because even by the 1830s the domestic system was being presented in a very idealised way by critics of the factory system.

SOURCE 4

Down to 1800 the majority of workers laboured in their own homes. The spinning wheel was to be found in almost every house. These were the golden times of manufacturing. By the work carried out under a man's roof he retained his respectability and earned enough not only to live comfortably, but also to rent a few acres of land.

Written by P Gaskell in 1833.

SOURCE 5

[In the domestic system] children grew up in fresh country air. If they could help parents it was only occasionally. Of eight or twelve hours' work for them, there was no question.

From Friedrich Engels, *The Condition of the Working Class in England*, 1845. Engels was a savage critic of the factories and their owners.

However, this is not the whole picture of what the domestic system was really like. Historians now suggest that there were definitely two sides to the domestic system.

The 'down' side to the domestic system

Exploitation. The relationship between the merchant and his workers could be difficult and even exploitative. There were often disputes over the price to be paid for finished work, and its quality. It was not uncommon for clothiers to pay with goods instead of money – the weavers had little choice in the matter. They had no power over the clothier. There were always plenty of other workers he could employ.

Insecurity. Domestic work was also insecure. Income depended on the worker's health and on the state of the cloth trade. Weavers were not paid if they could not finish their work because of illness, for example. When business was slack, the clothier could simply stop sending work to his outworkers. The clothier generally had enough money to tide him over, but for the domestic worker slumps in business meant hunger and hardship.

Child labour. Children worked as soon as they were able to do so and their parents could be as harsh as any factory overseer.

Long hours. In the domestic system hours could be long, particularly when there was a major batch of work to be done.

Boring work. Even the argument that workers in the domestic system were skilled craftsmen and craftswomen taking pride in their work does not really stand up. Many jobs in the domestic system were also dull, repetitive and unskilled.

The 'up' side to the domestic system

Independence. The workers were indeed able to control their own working environment and their own time. There was a tradition of Saint Monday – taking Monday off, often to get over a hangover, then catching up through the week.

Safety. The machinery was human-powered, and much safer.

Control. The workers controlled the speed at which the machinery worked rather than it controlling them.

Robert Owen

★ Born in Wales in 1771.
★ Worked his way up from draper's shop assistant to mill owner.
★ In 1800 he took over the mills at New Lanark, in Scotland.
★ He made many improvements, including building comfortable houses and providing education and shops for his employees.
★ In 1819 he persuaded Parliament to pass a Factory Act to improve conditions in the mills. However, because of the opposition of other factory owners it did not go as far as he wanted.
★ In 1824 he went to the USA to set up a new company called New Harmony. It was not a success.
★ He returned to Britain in 1829 and helped set up one of the first national trade unions which fought for better pay for workers.
★ Until his death in 1858 Owen wrote about and gave lectures on his ideas.

How were Robert Owen's mills different?

Robert Owen was one of the leaders of the factory reform movement. Yet surprisingly this most powerful critic of textile mills was himself a very successful mill owner. However, Robert Owen's mills at New Lanark were different from other mills. They were not just a successful business, they were also a social experiment. He treated his workers well, educated them and encouraged them to better themselves. Owen believed strongly that if all mills were run this way then not only would the workers be more fulfilled but profits would increase. He wrote books about his experiment and spoke at meetings all over Britain. Between 1815 and 1825 over 10,000 people visited his mills and marvelled at what he had achieved. New Lanark had a good reputation even before Owen took it over, as Source 6 shows. He was determined to make further improvements.

SOURCE 6

Four hundred children are fed, clothed and educated… The rest live with their parents in neat, comfortable homes, receiving wages for their labour. The health and the happiness on the faces of these children shows that the owner of the Lanark Mills has remembered kindness in the midst of making his money. The rules here to protect the health and happiness of the workers are very different from most factories in this country, which are mostly full of disease. To the honour of the founder of New Lanark, out of the 3,000 children who have worked in these mills only 14 have died and not one has suffered punishment for crime.

From *The Gentleman's Magazine*, 1796, reporting on the mills at New Lanark.

SOURCE 7

The Governing Principle of Manufacturing and Commerce … is immediate money gain, to which everything else has to give way. All are trained to buy cheap and sell dear. To succeed in this art, they acquire [a spirit of deception], destructive of that open, honest sincerity, without which man cannot make others happy, nor enjoy happiness himself.

But the effects of this principle, above all else, unchecked, are the more worrying on the working class employed in the operative parts of the industry; for these branches are more or less harmful to the health and morals of adults. Parents do not hesitate to sacrifice the well being of their children by putting them to unsuitable work.

Written by Robert Owen in *Observations on the Effects of the Manufacturing System*, 1815.

SOURCE 8

Robert Owen's school at New Lanark. Compared to other schools at the time, the education in this school was very good.

SOURCE 9

Owen's complex of mills at New Lanark was the largest textile operation in Britain.

SOURCE 10

The practice of employing children in the mills, of six, seven, and eight years of age, was discontinued ... The child was removed from the erroneous treatment of the yet untaught and untrained parents ... The children were taught reading, writing, and arithmetic, without expense to their parents ... Children are trained in the institution for forming their character without any punishment ... The character of man is, without a single exception, always performed on him.

Robert Owen, *A New View of Society*, 1813.

1 **What were Robert Owen's aims at New Lanark? Use all the sources in your answer.**

2 **How do you think Robert Owen would justify the actions in Source 10 to the parents of the children concerned?**

3 **What do you think Sources 8 and 11 would have done for Owen's reputation in Britain?**

4 **Which of Sources 6–11 is most useful for telling you about**

   a) **what life was really like for workers in Owen's mills.**

   b) **what people who visited Lanark thought of the mills?**

SOURCE 11

Commission: At what age do you take children into your mills?
Owen: At ten and upwards.
Commission: What are the regular hours of labour per day, exclusive of meal times?
Owen: Ten hours and three quarters.
Commission: What time do you allow for meals?
Owen: Three quarters of an hour for dinner, and half an hour for breakfast.
Commission: Why do you not employ children at an earlier age?
Owen: Because I believe it would be injurious to the children, and not beneficial to the proprietors.
Commission: What reason have you to suppose it is injurious to the children ... to be employed at an earlier age?
Owen: The evidence of very strong facts.
Commission: What are these facts?
Owen: [In 1808] I found that there were 500 children [at New Lanark] who had been taken from poor-houses, chiefly in Edinburgh, those children were generally from the age of five and six to seven and eight ... The hours of work at that time were 13, inclusive of meal times, and an hour and a half was allowed for meals. I very soon discovered that although those children were very well-fed, well-clothed, well-lodged and very great care taken of them when out of the mills, their growth and their minds were clearly injured by being employed at those ages within the cotton mills for 11 and a half hours per day. It is true that those children, because of being so well-fed and clothed and lodged, looked fresh ... yet their limbs were generally deformed, their growth was stunted. Although one of the best school-masters upon the old plan was engaged to instruct those children every night, in general they made but a slow progress, even in learning the common alphabet.

Robert Owen giving evidence to a Parliamentary Commission in 1816.

Who were the reformers?

The campaign for factory reform began well before 1800. The leading figures in the early days were Robert Owen and Robert Peel. Like Owen, Peel came from a mill-owning family. He would later become Prime Minister.

However, the reform movement attracted many others who were drawn to the campaign for a range of reasons:

1. Some were radicals who believed that the factory system showed the evils of capitalism and the workers needed organising to fight against exploitation.
2. Some wanted reform for simple humanitarian reasons.
3. Others believed that factories damaged the 'moral ethic' of society. Mills divided families, put boys and girls together when they should be kept apart and encouraged too much independence in women.
4. Some reformers believed that better conditions made better business sense as happy workers were more productive.
5. The campaign to reform the factories also has to be seen as part of a wider struggle between the landowners (the aristocracy) and industrialists (the rising middle classes) over who would be most influential in Britain. You will have read in Chapter 3 how industrialists campaigned for the repeal of the Corn Laws. The campaign for factory reform gave landowners the opportunity to fight back.

It was an unlikely alliance, but they mounted a strong and increasingly effective campaign.

FOCUS TASK

HOW DID LEGISLATION AFFECT WORKING CONDITIONS?

Draw up a table like this. As you work through pages 87–92 fill it out. In the first column list each stage of the campaign. In the second column summarise what it achieved. In the third column reach your own judgement as to how important this part of the campaign was in improving working conditions.

Stage	What it achieved	How important?

Stage 1: Protecting pauper apprentices

In 1802 the reformers managed to get Parliament to pass the Health and Morals of Apprentices Act because they were deeply troubled by the way in which some cotton mills were abusing the apprentice system. The Act

- banned night work.
- set a maximum 12-hour shift.
- made education for apprentices compulsory.

However, any factory owner who wished to ignore the law found it very easy to do so because there was no police force or body of inspectors to enforce it. Local Justices of the Peace were usually unqualified or uninterested or, in many cases, friends of the mill owners.

By 1820 the system of pauper apprentices was in decline anyway. They were too expensive to keep. As the population rose the mill owners could cut their costs by using ordinary workers rather than pauper apprentices. One of the last owners to use apprentices was Robert Hyde Greg (see page 93), owner of several mills including those in Styal, in Cheshire. Even so Greg estimated that apprentices cost four and a half pence more per week to employ than ordinary workers.

Stage 2: The Ten Hours Movement

In 1830 a new campaigner added his powerful voice to the case for reform. Richard Oastler was a Huddersfield land agent. Along with John Fielden MP, he started a Short Time Committee which later became the Ten Hours Movement. Soon such committees had been set up in Lancashire, Yorkshire and Glasgow.

Oastler was a determined man and a powerful speaker and campaigner. Source 13 is a typical piece of his campaigning. In 1830 the anti-slavery movement was at its strongest and Oastler drew a controversial comparison between the situation of the slave and the situation of the factory worker.

For two years Oastler and his supporters campaigned solidly for the working day to be reduced to 10 hours. MPs John Fielden and Michael Sadler made sure that the issue of factory working conditions was continually raised in Parliament. The Ten Hours Movement also gained a particularly powerful ally in Lord Shaftesbury (known at this time as Lord Ashley). He was a landowner, and a reformer.

The Ten Hours Movement was well organised and widely supported. Cleverly, the campaigners concentrated their attention on the treatment of children in factories. They particularly focused on the fate of the pauper apprentices. Both sides knew that if conditions were improved for children, then they would also improve for adult workers.

SOURCE 12

'English Factory Slaves', a cartoon by Cruickshank from the early nineteenth century.

1 Source 13 caused a sensation when it was published. Why do you think this was?

2 What similarities are there between the messages of Sources 12 and 13?

SOURCE 13

The very streets that receive the [leaflets] of the Anti-Slavery society are every morning met by the tears of innocent victims … who are compelled (not by the cart whips of the negro slave drivers) but by the dread of the equally appalling thong or strap of the overlooker, to hasten, half dressed but not (even) half fed, to those magazines [strongholds] of British Infantile Slavery – the woollen mills in the town and neighbourhood of Bradford!!!

A letter from Oastler to the *Leeds Mercury*, 1830. Bradford was the constituency of William Wilberforce, who had fought strongly for the abolition of slavery.

SOURCE 14

They reached the mill about half past five. Blincoe heard a burning sound … and smelt the fumes of oil with which the axles of the twenty thousand wheels and spindles were bathed. The moment he entered the doors, the noise appalled him, and the stench seemed intolerable.

The first task allotted to him was to pick up the loose cotton that fell upon the floor. Apparently nothing could be easier, and he set with diligence, although much terrified by the whirling motion and noise of the machinery, and not a little affected by the dust and flue [fragments of thread floating in the air] with which he was half suffocated. Unused to the stench he soon felt sick, and by constantly stooping, his back ached. Blincoe took the liberty to sit down: but this attitude, he soon found, was strictly forbidden.

Extract from *The Memoirs of Robert Blincoe, An Orphan Boy* by John Brown (c. 1840).

SOURCE 15

A sketch of pauper apprentices eating from a trough. This scene was allegedly based on a true incident in which starving apprentices were so hungry that they stole food from the pigs' trough.

SOURCE 16

A

The ceaseless whirring of the million hissing wheels, the scents that reek around. All this is terrible but what the eye brings home to the heart is hundreds of helpless children, [whose] lean and distorted limbs, dim hollow eyes … give each tiny, trembling, unelastic form, a look of premature old age.

Abridged extract and illustration from Frances Trollope's novel, *The Adventures of Michael Armstrong, Factory Boy* (1840). Michael goes to work in the factory at the age of six and throughout the story he experiences all of the worst features of factory work. It seems likely that Frances Trollope based her book on the story of Robert Blincoe (Source 14).

B

SOURCE 17

One of them gave a calculation of the miles a child had to walk in a day in minding the spinning machine, it amounted to twenty-five! … if the distance that [the child] has to walk to and from home be thrown in, it makes, not infrequently, a distance of thirty miles.

In *The Curse of the Factory System* John Fielden describes a meeting with Manchester workers in 1836.

SOURCE 18

An engraving showing the treatment and working conditions of children in the mills.

3 List the criticisms of the mills made in Sources 12–18.

4 Which of Sources 12–18 do you think would be most useful to the Ten Hours Movement? Explain your choice.

Stage 3: The Royal Commission

The influence, wealth and connections of these campaigners whipped up a storm of protest which could not be ignored, and Parliament set up Royal Commissions to investigate the conditions of Britain's factories. Between 1831 and 1832 the Commissioners spoke to hundreds of witnesses, owners, workers, overseers and children. The evidence they amassed was shocking. It confirmed that working conditions in some mills were every bit as bad as the critics had said. However, historians today are sure that to some extent the investigations were stage-managed. Sadler, who was a leading supporter of factory reform, was also organising the commission. He arranged the timetable of the inquiry so that the owners could not present their case properly or get it published. Some of the witnesses were rather suspect. One weaver who had first given evidence to Parliament in 1803 was called out again and again whenever the commission needed him.

As you look at Sources 19 and 20 bear this in mind.

SOURCE 19

Question: At what time, in the brisk time, did those girls go to the mill?

Answer: In brisk time, for about six weeks they have gone at three o'clock in the morning, and ended at ten or nearly half past at night.

Q: What intervals for rest and refreshment were allowed during those nineteen hours of labour?

A: Breakfast a quarter of an hour, dinner half an hour and drinking a quarter of an hour.

Q: Had you not great difficulty in awakening your children to this excessive labour?

A: Yes; in the early time we had to take them up asleep and shake them when we got them on the floor to dress them, before we could get them off to their work; but not so in the common hours.

Q: What time did you get them up in the morning?

A: In general at two o'clock to dress them.

Q: So that they had not above four hours of sleep at this time?

A: No, they had not.

Q: The usual hours of work were from six in the morning till half past eight at night?

A: Yes.

Q: Did this excessive term of labour cause much cruelty also?

A: Yes, with being so much fatigued the strap was frequently used.

Evidence given by Samuel Coulson to the Parliamentary Commission on the Factory Children's Labour, 1831–32.

SOURCE 20

Q: Do you live at Bradford?

A: Yes.

Q: Are you the overlooker of Mr. John Wood?

A: I am.

Q: Will you have the goodness to state the present hours of working in your factory?

A: Our present hours are from six till seven.

Q: With what intervals for rest and refreshment?

A: Half an hour for breakfast and forty minutes for dinner.

Q: Do you believe that the children can endure the labour you have been describing without injury?

A: No I do not.

Q: When your hands [employees] have been employed for some time, do you see any alteration in their appearance?

A: In the course of a few weeks I see a paleness in their faces, and they grow spiritless and tired.

Q: Have you remarked the cases of deformity are very common in Bradford?

A: They are very common. I have the names of, I think, about two hundred families I have visited myself that have deformed children, and I have taken particular care not to put down one single case where it might have happened by accident, but only those whom I judge to have been thrown crooked by the practice of piecening.

Evidence given by John Hall to the Parliamentary Commission on the Factory Children's Labour, 1831–32.

1 **How do the working days described in Sources 19 and 20 compare with that shown in Source 1 on page 81?**

2 **How do you think the conditions in Sources 19 and 20 would have affected the health of the workers?**

Stage 4: The 1833 Factory Act

The Royal Commission led directly to the 1833 Factory Act.

Hours of work

Children under 9 years old not to work in textile mills

Children aged 9 to 13 to work no more than 9 hours

Young people aged 14 to 18 to work no more than 12 hours

No one under 18 to do night work

Government inspectors

Four inspectors were appointed by the government to make sure that factory owners were keeping the law.

In some ways the 1833 Factory Act was a breakthrough:

- For the first time it reduced working hours for all children and forced employers to provide education for their child workers.
- Previous legislation had suffered because it could not be enforced. It was an important part of this Act that Parliament appointed inspectors to check the law was being followed.
- Even more important, the LAISSEZ-FAIRE attitude (where things are left alone to 'sort themselves out' – that is, factory owners were allowed to do what they wanted) had finally been defeated. Now that Parliament agreed it was its job to control working conditions, other reforms could follow.

In other ways the 1833 Act did not succeed at all:

- Only four inspectors were appointed and they had thousands of mills to supervise. One inspector died from overwork.
- The inspectors faced opposition from mill owners, local magistrates and doctors. Magistrates were sometimes mill owners themselves, or were of the same class as the owners, owning businesses related to the mills. Doctors saw little or no value in the work required of them, and resented being under the inspectors' control. They also found themselves unpopular with parents, who were angry at losing the wages their children could earn. They all made it difficult for the inspectors to do their work.
- Without birth certificates it was often impossible to tell the age of a child. Parents who wanted their children to work could easily get around the law. Some mill owners did not know how old their workers were. Even a law-abiding mill owner like Robert Hyde Greg found himself convicted of 12 offences in the first year of the Act.
- Very few mill owners provided a quality education.
- The fines for breaking the law were so small that mill owners were prepared to pay them in order to keep their mills running.

So the Act was not perfect, but it was an important step. Three years later it was strengthened when registration of births, marriages and deaths became compulsory. It now became easier to check the age of workers.

SOURCE 21

As to the conclusions I have come to from the working of my … mill … for 11 hours instead of 12 hours each day … I am quite satisfied that both as much yarn and cotton may be produced at quite as low a cost in 11 as in 12 hours … It is my intention to make a further reduction to 10 and a half hours, without the slightest fear of suffering loss … I find the hands work with greater energy and spirit; they are more cheerful and happy … About 20 years ago … we had about 30 young women in our Manchester warehouse. I requested that they would work 12 hours [a day] instead of 11. At the end of the week, I found that they had not a mere trifle more work done; but supposing there was some incidental cause of this I requested that they worked 13 hours [a day] the following week, at the end of which they had produced less instead of more work. They were exhausted and making bad work and little of it. Since then I have been an advocate of shorter hours of labour.

From a letter written by a Lancashire mill owner in 1845.

Stage 5: The 1844 Factory Act

The campaign continued. And the next success came in 1844.

> **Hours of work**
> Children aged 8 to 13 to work no more than $6\frac{1}{2}$ hours
> Young people aged 14 to 18 and women to work no more than 12 hours
> Children of 8 allowed to work in mills, but hours cut for children under 13 and for women
>
> **Safety precautions**
> Machinery to be fenced in

1 **Which law was the most important in terms of**

a) changing attitudes
b) improving conditions?

Explain your choices.

Stage 6: The Ten Hours Bill or the 1847 Factory Act

The Ten Hours Movement continued its campaign, gathering evidence from factory owners such as that in Source 21.

The Ten Hours Movement finally achieved its aim in 1847 when the Ten Hours Bill became law. The 10 hours limit did not apply to men – only to women. The thinking was that the male workers would also enjoy a 10-hour day because their female and child colleagues would not be able to help them once their shifts ended. However, employers used relays of women and child workers to get round the Act and men worked the same long hours as before.

> **Hours of work**
> Young people and women to work no more than 10 hours

Stage 7: The 1850 Act

The 1850 Act prohibited the use of relays of women and young people. It increased permissible hours to $10\frac{1}{2}$ per day, but it set the limits of the working day as 6am to 6pm or 7am to 7pm, with one and a half hours for breaks. All workers in the textile mills now had a $10\frac{1}{2}$-hour day.

Why did the Acts limit the working hours of women?

There were a range of motives among the campaigners. For some of them, Lord Shaftesbury included, a prime motive was the protection of family life. He believed that factory work was disruptive of family life, made women less likely to attend to their domestic duties, and made them too independent. In one Parliamentary debate he argued that women would not obey their husbands if they had jobs where they were doing the same work as men; they would not do their domestic chores, but would say to their husbands 'If I work I will also have the amusement'. Many other reformers had a similar moral aim in their campaigning.

SOURCE 22

It is dirty, unroofed, ill ventilated, with machinery not boxed in, and passages so narrow that they could hardly be defined. It seemed more to be a receptacle of demons than the workplace of industrious human beings.

The appearance and language of the workers, both men and women, proved the state of demoralisation which exists here … It was painful to find in the eating and sleeping room of such a nest of profligates [immoral people], two or three young females without a parent or relation in the neighbourhood to look after their conduct …

Description of a mill in Kincardineshire, Scotland.

SOURCE 23

The children – those who survive – grow to girlhood. Those who have the choice prefer the life of a factory girl to that of a servant – and they are not wrong. They have comparative freedom and work only at stated hours, but they learn to be independent, selfish and impatient of their duties as women. The unmarried girl becomes the wife and mother. What is the training that has fitted her for the working man's wife? [They have been] prevented from learning needlework or those habits of cleanliness, neatness and order, without which they cannot, when they have the charge of families of their own, [make the most of] their husband's earnings or give their homes any degree of comfort.

A Jameson, *Memoirs and Essays*, published in 1846.

FOCUS TASK

1 **Sources 13–23 illustrate the arguments and aims of the different types of reformers. Find one source which you think belongs to each of the following categories:**

a) **Radicals who believed that working people needed protection against exploitation**
b) **Humanitarians who wanted reform so people would have better lives**
c) **Moralists who believed factories damaged the 'morals' of workers**
d) **Entrepreneurs who believed that reform would make workers more productive.**

2 **Using all of Sources 13–23 list the different:**

a) **techniques; and**
b) **arguments**

being used for factory reform.

Who opposed factory reform and why?

Opponents of factory reform fell into two main groups.

Some opposed factory reform because they thought the government should not interfere. Whilst they disliked what they heard about the factories, they did not see it as Parliament's job to interfere with the freedom of the individual. This viewpoint was known as *laissez faire*.

The other group was the factory owners themselves. Not all owners opposed reform, as you have already seen, but many did. They were accused of putting their own profits before the health and safety of their workers. However, it is important to explore the views of the factory owners in the context of the 1830s and 1840s. To do this we will look at the arguments against factory reform put forward by Robert Hyde Greg.

Case study: Robert Hyde Greg of Quarry Bank Mill, Styal

Quarry Bank Mill was a family business. It had been built by Samuel Greg (Robert's father) in 1783–84 on the banks of the fast-flowing River Boll near the village of Styal in Cheshire. Samuel Greg was a shrewd businessman. His mill was very successful. The family set up other mills in Lancashire and by the 1830s was known throughout the country.

As the business expanded Greg became desperate for workers, partly because Styal was such an isolated location. He found the workers he needed from workhouses in Liverpool, nearby Stoke-on-Trent, and even from as far away as Buckinghamshire.

Wages at Quarry Bank Mill were lower than those in nearby Manchester and working hours were the standard 12 hours. However, Samuel Greg and his family gained a reputation as kind and fair employers. They built quality housing for their workers. They provided fresh food from the Greg estates at reasonable prices. The Gregs' shop was eventually turned over to the workers and run as a co-operative. Adult workers had a small sum taken from their wages as a form of sickness insurance, to tide them over if they fell ill and could not work. The apprentice house at the mill was large and, for the time, conditions were good. The children received a basic education and attended church every week. One apprentice, James Henshall, rose through the ranks to become mill manager in 1847. Relations between the workers and the Gregs seem to have been extremely good and there was only one strike between 1834 and 1846.

Robert Hyde Greg.

SOURCE 24

Bedlow, December 4th 1834
Gentlemen
We who sign this letter are the paupers of the parish of Bedlow. We have asked the magistrate at West Wycombe to order the overseers of the poor to give us more relief. They told us that the overseers have no more money …

Gentlemen, we have looked for work in vain. We have gone here and there and found none. Times used to be better for us before Bedlow enclosed … We therefore humbly entreat you that you will visit our parish without delay …

A letter sent out on behalf of the poor by the Poor Law Commissioners of Bedlow, Bucks, to anyone who might come and take away the excess poor to work in their mills. Greg was a known employer and received a copy of this 'circular'. Greg was asked to visit the parish to look at potential employees.

SOURCE 25

Reconstruction drawing of the apprentice house at Styal. In comparison with some other mills, apprentices at Styal were well treated.

1 As a 'fair' employer you might expect Greg to be in favour of factory reform. What does Source 26 suggest about his attitude to the Commission, when he was called to give evidence?

SOURCE 26

Q: Do the spinners ever ill treat the piecers?

A: They do not, for the overlooker takes them up if they do it: spinners have been suspended from their employment for a week or two for beating the piecers.

Q: Are the piecers all paid by the spinners?

A: Yes.

Q: Who pays the scavengers?

A: The master.

Q: Are the children in your mill taught at night schools or Sunday schools?

A: Both.

Q: Every night in the week?

A: About three nights in the week.

Q: During what hours?

A: From half past seven to a little after nine.

Q: But is a factory child at school all these hours?

A: They are mostly grown up lads at these schools; a very few young ones go to these night schools.

Q: Are not the lads too tired to pay attention to learning at these night schools?

A: I think not: there is no compulsion; it is a matter of choice with them, and the desire of their parents.

Q: Can most of the workmen read and write?

A: Yes; we have proved by demonstration.

Q: It is said that workmen are unwilling to give evidence to this commission on the Ten Hours Bill from fear of the masters. Do you feel that fear well grounded as respects the generality of masters?

A: I am not aware of any intimidation being used; but can only speak as respects my own master.

Q: Is there any convenience to enable the workmen to wash themselves, or to change their clothing, on entering or leaving the factory?

A: There is, if they wish to do.

Q: Do you think that, if the hours of labour were reduced, the work would be diminished in the same proportion?

A: Not exactly so, but nearly so.

Q: Why not exactly so?

A: These are very nice points; the difference in proportion would not be much.

Q: Is the mill fire-proof?

A: Yes; the mills are more healthy for the hands when built upon that principle.

Q: Why?

A: For several reasons: first, they are of a more regular atmosphere; they are cleanlier kept than other mills can be; other mills are boarded; fire-proof mills are all covered with tiles.

Q: Do you find it pleasanter to work in fire-proof mills than others?

A: Yes, for the reasons just given.

Q: Why do the hands work without shoes and stockings?

A: It is the spinners who only work so; the tiles are so slippery, you stick better.

Q: Do the tiles ever injure feet?

A: They are not liable to injure the feet one half so much as boarded floors.

Robert Hyde Greg's evidence to the Commissioners.

Although he was a 'fair' employer Greg was opposed to the Ten Hours Bill. In 1837 he published a pamphlet called *The Factory Question of the 10 Hours Bill* giving his reasons. Here are some extracts from this document.

SOURCE 27

It is time, that in the factories, we are no longer shocked by the sight of children of very tender age, and if we find any under 13 years we have the satisfaction of knowing they only work 8 hours daily; some alteration has also been made in the general hours of work; but, on the other hand, it may be enquired also, where are the children who have been discharged from the mills? Are they, for whose protection … the provisions of the present law were enacted and enforced … in a better physical and mental condition than they were before? Or, has the object of legislation failed in their case as in so many similar ones and the parties been injured whom it was intended to benefit.

Extract from Part 1, *The Factory Question of the 10 Hours Bill*, on the alleged effects of the 1833 Act, according to Greg.

SOURCE 28

We cannot help remarking upon the general unfairness of the phraseology and assumptions of the enemies of the [factory] system. Thus, all the workers in the mills are spoken of as being children, all children spoken of as delicate or, as being infants of tender years … All the employment is spoken of as severe and unremitting labour, and all the unpleasant or injurious circumstances, in [different industries and in different places] are represented, most absurdly, as being all present at one time and one spot, upon one person … a child of tender years and delicate constitution.

Extract from Part 2 (see Source 26).

As you can see, Greg felt strongly about factory reforms. He went on to argue that reduced hours would cut production and raise prices. This would hurt the population as a whole and also damage Britain's cotton export trade.

Greg also made the perfectly fair point that the poor health of factory workers was as much due to where they lived as where they worked. He amassed large amounts of evidence to show that factory workers were no more prone to illness than miners or workers in other industries.

Greg was certainly trying to protect his own interests and those of other mill owners. In 1844 he founded the Central Committee of the Association of Mill Owners. However, Greg also acted on the principles he believed in. He believed passionately in free trade and was a prominent supporter of the Anti-Corn Law League (see page 50). He also genuinely believed in *laissez faire*. In his view, government attempts to solve social and economic problems usually ended up causing as many problems as they solved. Certainly there were many who completely agreed with Greg, and like him they resented being portrayed as heartless monsters with no care for their workers.

There was, however, one controversy which slightly damaged the reputation of Robert Hyde Greg as a fair employer and brought him into conflict with the Ten Hours Movement.

In 1835 a number of Greg's apprentices left Styal, without permission, to visit family in Liverpool. One of these, Esther Price, repeated this offence in 1836 and as a punishment she was confined with the threat of having her hair cut off. She was very frustrated and resentful about this. She was eager to leave Styal as quickly as possible. As a result of the incident Greg was visited by a gentleman named Mr Turner who was a Liverpool parish official and a member of Manchester's Short Hours Committee. He was accompanied by a man by the name of John Doherty.

SOURCE 29

Esther Price's baptismal certificate. Most people were unconcerned about certificates and did not have one. Esther went to great lengths to get hers to prove her age so that she could get out of Styal and go back to Liverpool.

Two years later, in 1838, an anonymous pamphlet attacking factory owners appeared. The pamphlet directly attacked Robert Hyde Greg and raised some of the details of Esther's case. It seems likely that John Doherty wrote it. For one thing we know he printed it, and it is also likely he had a grudge against Robert Greg – as a magistrate. Above all, however, the pamphlet was designed to answer Greg's pamphlet on Factory Reform (Sources 27 and 28).

SOURCE 30

They said there were some bad reports about the mill, that many left the place and would not stay. Bower said that few left and they were generally glad enough to come back again … He had worked for 35 years under Mr Greg and did not think there was any better master.

Report of the words of a mill worker, L Bower, who spoke to the Royal Commission on Factory Conditions in 1842.

1 How can you tell that the Gregs were successful?

2 What evidence suggests that the Gregs were good employers?

3 Do you think Esther Price was a one off? Explain your answer.

FOCUS TASK

THE CASE AGAINST FACTORY REFORM

1 Read through pages 89–92 and the case study of Robert Hyde Greg.

2 Work in groups. Each group take one of Sources 26–28. For each source decide the following.

   a) What points does Greg make?
   b) Do they seem reasonable?
   c) Is he making points from his own view?
   d) Does any other evidence in this chapter support what he says?

3 Prepare notes for a class debate on the following topic: 'The opponents of factory reform were only acting in self-interest.'

FOCUS TASK

WHY HAD CONDITIONS IN THE TEXTILE INDUSTRY IMPROVED BY 1850?

Historians have pointed out that the Factory Acts had a limited effect. However, many mills were forced to introduce new measures to improve working conditions. Why did this happen? Look at the following views:

- Conditions improved because of the good example set by employers like Robert Owen.
- Conditions improved because of the campaigning of the Ten Hours Movement, and individuals like Lord Shaftesbury and Richard Oastler.
- Conditions improved because treating workers well made good business sense.
- Conditions improved because legislation forced mill owners to improve them.

1 Copy the following chart.

View	Supporting evidence	Do you trust this evidence?

2 Gather evidence which supports each of the views and write it into column 2 of your table. In column 3 explain how far you trust this evidence.

3 Compare your findings with others in a small group. Produce a version of the table which you can all agree on.

4 Now use your work to write an answer to this question: Were conditions in factories improved by the work of individuals or by legislation?
   You should organise your answers in paragraphs:

   1 Your overall view
   2 The work of individuals
   3 How this work improved conditions
   4 How legislation improved conditions
   5 How the work of individuals and legislation were linked
   6 Your conclusion.

SECTION 3

Iron, coal and transport 1700–1900

5 The industrial revolution in iron and coal 1700–1900

5.1 Why was the iron industry so important to Britain's industrial revolution?

> **FOCUS**
>
> Coal and iron were closely linked. So as Britain entered its machine age both the iron and coal industries grew enormously. They fed off each other's success and contributed to each other's growth.
>
> In 5.1 of this chapter you will investigate:
>
> - why the demand for iron rose in the eighteenth century.
> - how the Darby family in Coalbrookdale improved iron making.
> - how later iron makers tried to improve further on the Darbys' techniques.
>
> In 5.2 you will explore:
>
> - how coal mining developed so that production was increased.
> - why the government brought in laws to control working conditions in the coal mines.
> - how changes in the coal and iron industries triggered improvements in Britain's transport systems.
>
> In 5.3 you will study:
>
> - how the steel industry evolved from 1850 to 1900.

The development of the coal and iron industries are closely related. This timeline gives you an overview of the main events you will be studying on pages 98–127.

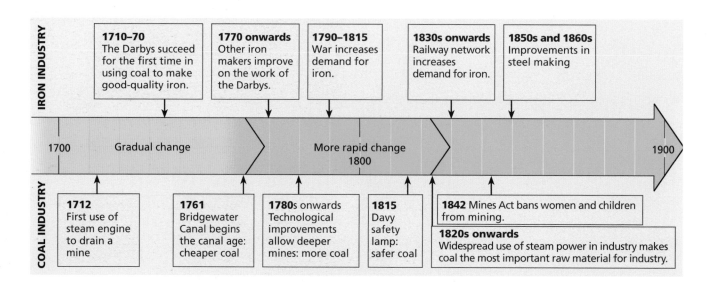

IRON INDUSTRY

1710–70
The Darbys succeed for the first time in using coal to make good-quality iron.

1770 onwards
Other iron makers improve on the work of the Darbys.

1790–1815
War increases demand for iron.

1830s onwards
Railway network increases demand for iron.

1850s and 1860s
Improvements in steel making

1700 — Gradual change — More rapid change 1800 — 1900

COAL INDUSTRY

1712
First use of steam engine to drain a mine

1761
Bridgewater Canal begins the canal age: cheaper coal

1780s onwards
Technological improvements allow deeper mines: more coal

1815
Davy safety lamp: safer coal

1842 Mines Act bans women and children from mining.

1820s onwards
Widespread use of steam power in industry makes coal the most important raw material for industry.

The iron bridge

SOURCE 1

The iron bridge across the River Severn, built in 1779.

SOURCE 2

The concrete and steel Queen Elizabeth II Bridge at Dartford, built across the Thames in 1991.

Both these bridges caused a sensation when they were built. It's easy for us to see why Source 2 might do so – it was the largest single-span bridge ever built, and cost £86 million. But Source 1? It might seem a fairly ordinary bridge to you, but people came from all over the world to see it. They painted pictures of it. They made replicas of it. They talked about it as one of the miracles of the modern age! What was so special about it?

To answer that question you will need to look back 80 years before it was built, to when the British iron industry was facing a crisis.

SOURCE 3

1775 41 tons

451 tons
1776

453 tons
1777

689 tons
1779

1,221 tons
1781

Effect of the American War of Independence on cannon production at Rotherham Ironworks.

---

1 **On your own copy of Source 4 add notes to explain other factors which might increase the demand for iron.**

Rising demand for iron

In 1700 iron was a very important material. For hundreds of years it had been used to make weapons, tools, chains, pots, pans, knives, nails, hinges, horseshoes: the list is endless. It was as important to everyday life as plastic is today. Look at almost any picture of people at home or at work in this period and you will see something made of iron.

Britain needs more iron!

In the eighteenth century the demand for iron was increasing. One reason for this will be familiar from your study of earlier chapters – the growing population. More people needed more iron goods. However, in the case of iron there were other particularly important factors, which are summarised in Source 4.

Britain needs more high-quality iron!

Iron was used in two main ways. Cast iron – iron which is cast into shape in a mould – does not need to be of high quality. But wrought iron (iron which can be hammered into shape) does. If it is not, it will simply break. As you will see from Source 4, the demand for this high-quality iron was increasing.

SOURCE 4

War

As Britain grew as a world power, it became involved in numerous wars. Britain was heavily involved in the Seven Years' War from 1756 to 1763, then even more so in the American War of Independence (1776–83) and the Napoleonic Wars (1793–1815). Britain fought these wars on land and sea. The wars meant a huge increase in demand for iron for weapons, carts, buckles – any number of items. A large part of the iron needed was for cannon – for both the army and the navy (see Source 3).

Mechanisation

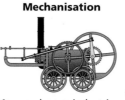

More and more industries were using machines. Machines were built using iron frames. Small machines needed bolts, springs, catches and locks. Large machines like steam engines required tons of iron. Iron was also needed for the new buildings to house the machines.

RISING DEMAND FOR IRON

Trade

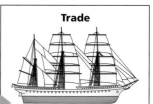

Britain's overseas trade, particularly in guns and tools, was growing steadily. This was helped by the fact that the British government prevented Britain's colonies from setting up their own industries, so that British manufacturers could sell them their goods instead.

Population

The population was growing. Pots, pans, knives and forks were needed by the millions.

Farming

Improvements in agriculture created demand for quality iron to make better tools and machines.

Rising demand for iron in the eighteenth century.

2 Use Sources 5 and 6 to write a short Factfile entitled 'Iron production in the early eighteenth century'. It should list the main features in a way that makes it easy for someone to revise. You can see an example of a Factfile on page 20.

Why was the iron industry facing a crisis?

Source 5 shows you how iron was made. Source 6 shows you some of the problems facing the industry in the early eighteenth century.

SOURCE 5

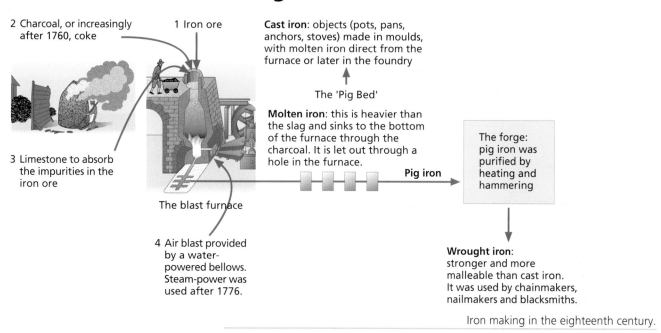

2 Charcoal, or increasingly after 1760, coke

1 Iron ore

3 Limestone to absorb the impurities in the iron ore

The blast furnace

4 Air blast provided by a water-powered bellows. Steam-power was used after 1776.

Cast iron: objects (pots, pans, anchors, stoves) made in moulds, with molten iron direct from the furnace or later in the foundry

The 'Pig Bed'

Molten iron: this is heavier than the slag and sinks to the bottom of the furnace through the charcoal. It is let out through a hole in the furnace.

Pig iron

The forge: pig iron was purified by heating and hammering

Wrought iron: stronger and more malleable than cast iron. It was used by chainmakers, nailmakers and blacksmiths.

Iron making in the eighteenth century.

SOURCE 6

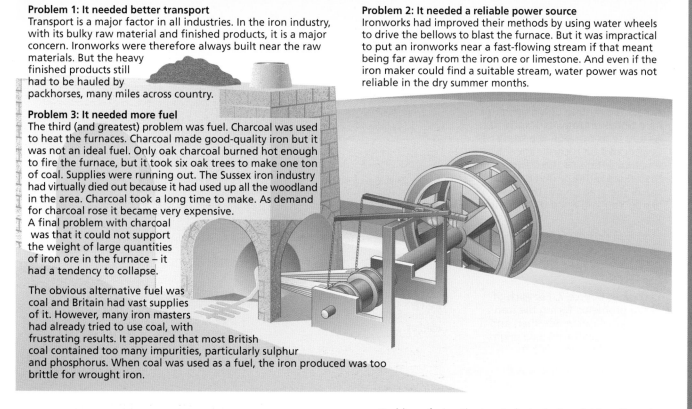

Problem 1: It needed better transport
Transport is a major factor in all industries. In the iron industry, with its bulky raw material and finished products, it is a major concern. Ironworks were therefore always built near the raw materials. But the heavy finished products still had to be hauled by packhorses, many miles across country.

Problem 3: It needed more fuel
The third (and greatest) problem was fuel. Charcoal was used to heat the furnaces. Charcoal made good-quality iron but it was not an ideal fuel. Only oak charcoal burned hot enough to fire the furnace, but it took six oak trees to make one ton of coal. Supplies were running out. The Sussex iron industry had virtually died out because it had used up all the woodland in the area. Charcoal took a long time to make. As demand for charcoal rose it became very expensive.
A final problem with charcoal was that it could not support the weight of large quantities of iron ore in the furnace – it had a tendency to collapse.

The obvious alternative fuel was coal and Britain had vast supplies of it. However, many iron masters had already tried to use coal, with frustrating results. It appeared that most British coal contained too many impurities, particularly sulphur and phosphorus. When coal was used as a fuel, the iron produced was too brittle for wrought iron.

Problem 2: It needed a reliable power source
Ironworks had improved their methods by using water wheels to drive the bellows to blast the furnace. But it was impractical to put an ironworks near a fast-flowing stream if that meant being far away from the iron ore or limestone. And even if the iron maker could find a suitable stream, water power was not reliable in the dry summer months.

Problems facing the iron industry in the eighteenth century.

Could the British iron industry meet the growing demand?

The short answer is no! If the industry was to meet the growing demand, it needed to solve the problems in Source 6. It was far from doing so. In 1700 half of Britain's iron was imported. By 1740 two-thirds were imported. At that time, Sheffield, which was Britain's most important centre for making high-quality iron goods, relied almost completely on imported iron.

However, in the end, rising demand is usually a good thing for industry. You've already seen how rising demand led to changes and improvements in farming and textiles. Exactly the same was about to happen in the iron industry.

The Darbys of Coalbrookdale

To see how the iron industry solved its problems you are going to focus on a remarkable family of iron makers, the Darbys of Coalbrookdale. Other iron manufacturers were also hard at work in this period, but it was the Darbys who led the way. The story begins at the start of the century with the first Abraham Darby.

Abraham Darby I

Abraham Darby I was born in 1677 in the Midlands. As a Quaker, Darby and all his family were barred from certain professions, particularly government administration. Because of this, and the fact that they were well educated, many Quakers went into business with great success. Darby's first job was in the malt mills in Birmingham, where he first came across the process of making coke. In the malt industry, coal was heated to produce coke, before it was used to dry malt (for brewing). This removed many unpleasant gases from the coal which would harm the malt.

In 1699 Darby moved to Bristol and rose to become a partner in a brass foundry. Here he learnt about the metal trade and in 1707 developed a method for casting iron pots and patented the idea. Like Richard Arkwright (see page 66) Darby could see the business potential of his idea, so in 1708 he rented a disused furnace at Coalbrookdale in Shropshire where he started mass-producing cheap cast-iron pots. He guessed correctly that such pots would sell very well to the growing population who could not afford expensive brass pots.

SOURCE 7

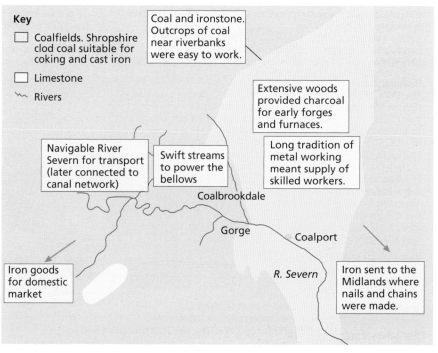

Key
- ☐ Coalfields. Shropshire clod coal suitable for coking and cast iron
- ☐ Limestone
- ∿ Rivers

Coal and ironstone. Outcrops of coal near riverbanks were easy to work.

Extensive woods provided charcoal for early forges and furnaces.

Navigable River Severn for transport (later connected to canal network)

Swift streams to power the bellows

Long tradition of metal working meant supply of skilled workers.

Coalbrookdale

Gorge

Coalport

R. Severn

Iron goods for domestic market

Iron sent to the Midlands where nails and chains were made.

Coalbrookdale in the eighteenth century. Abraham Darby found that Coalbrookdale had many advantages, including privacy to test new ideas.

FOCUS TASK

IRON MAKING AT COALBROOKDALE

Across the middle of a page, draw up a timeline from 1675 to 1850. As you read through the study of Coalbrookdale record above the timeline details of the Darbys, and their discoveries or inventions. Leave the area below the line blank. You will need it for a later task.

1 Look at Source 7. For each of the problems facing the iron makers explain whether, and if so how, Coalbrookdale might help Darby overcome it.

2 Which do you think was the most important advantage of Coalbrookdale for Abraham Darby?

Of course, Darby soon found the same problems with the supply of charcoal (the fuel used in blast furnaces) as other manufacturers. The local woods would not keep his furnaces going for long. However, as Source 8 describes, he found an answer.

SOURCE 8

About the year 1709 he came into Shropshire to Coalbrookdale and with the other partners took a lease of the works. Here he cast iron goods in and out of the blast furnace that he blowed with wood charcoal …

Sometime later he suggested that it might be possible to smelt the iron from the ore in the blast furnace with coal. He first tried with raw coal as it came out of the mines, but it did not work. He [was] not discouraged, had the coal cooked into cinder [coke], as is done for drying malt, and then succeeded …

Abiah Darby, about her father-in-law Abraham Darby I.

Darby's discovery was an important technological advance, but it was not exactly a breakthrough. The iron produced by Darby's new method was fine for casting pots, but not for most other uses and it was certainly not suitable for wrought iron. However, that was not Darby's concern. It was good enough for his cooking pots which he could now mass-produce. He was in business and the Coalbrookdale Company was soon making pots for Britain, America and the world.

Richard Ford

Abraham Darby I died in 1717 when his son, Abraham II, was only six. The works were managed by Richard Ford until the second Abraham Darby took over in 1738. Ford did not make any major changes, but the company began making cast-iron cylinders for steam engines.

Abraham Darby II

Abraham Darby II took over the business in 1738. He borrowed heavily to improve the works at Coalbrookdale.

- He bought a Newcomen steam engine in 1742 to pump water back into the feeder pond for the water wheel. Before this recycling process, the furnaces had been idle for three and sometimes four months of the year, because of water shortages.
- He built six new blast furnaces and built special ovens for coking coal.
- He bought up the local coal mines and iron-ore quarries.
- He built a horse-powered tramway from the mines to the furnaces. One horse could now pull twenty times as much as it had done before.
- He developed an important new market making cast-iron boilers for steam engines being produced in Birmingham.

However, his most notable achievement was to improve the quality of coke iron. Abraham Darby I had been happy with the product, as it allowed him to make his pots. However, it still needed to be reheated and beaten several times until it was pure enough to be used for wrought iron. This took so long that the forges still preferred to use charcoal iron. In the 1750s Darby II saw times were changing, and that there was potential for the Coalbrookdale Company if they could make coke iron.

A number of factors came together to allow Darby to make the breakthrough. Demand for iron was rising because of war. The price of charcoal was spiralling. By 1760 it was £3 per ton more expensive than coke. More important still was Darby's perseverance. He continually experimented with different cooking methods, blast pressure and a different balance of ingredients in the blast furnace. His wife Abiah reported that he once worked on this non-stop without sleep for a whole week. Finally he believed he had got the quality he wanted. He took samples to his forges. They agreed. This was good enough to be used as wrought iron.

Over the next 20 years the company made huge profits selling pig iron to wrought-iron manufacturers. Darby could sell as much iron as he could produce.

3 **Darby was not the only person who knew about coke being used in brewing. Why do you think he was the first to use coke successfully in making iron?**

SOURCE 10

For the conveyance of coal and iron to different parts of the works, and to the River Severn, wooden rails had been in use, which from the great weights carried upon them, were liable to give way and break occasionally, causing loss of time and interruption to business, and great expense in repairing them.

It occurred to us that the inconveniences could be lessened by the use of cast iron. We tried it at first with great caution, but found it to answer so well, that very soon all of the railways were made with iron. We did not attempt to secure by patent the advantage of this invention, and the use of cast iron in the construction of railways was afterwards generally adopted.

A letter from Richard Reynolds.

1 **How was the success of the Darbys similar to and different from Richard Arkwright's (see page 66)? Think about:**
   - **inventions**
   - **patents**
   - **investment**
   - **workers**
   - **power**
   - **advertising.**

ACTIVITY

It is 1790. Design a logo for the Darbys' company. It should show one of their important achievements.

SOURCE 9

Had not these discoveries been made, our iron trade would have dwindled away, for woods [suitable for making] charcoal became very scarce and the owners raised the price exceedingly high. But as pit coal is introduced in its stead the demand for wood charcoal is much lessened, and in a few years' time I expect will set its use aside.

Edited extract from the memoirs of Abiah Darby, wife of Abraham Darby II, written in the 1770s.

Richard Reynolds

Richard Reynolds was Abraham Darby II's son-in-law and ran the company from Darby II's death in 1763 until Abraham Darby III took over in 1768. Reynolds improved the works by linking the forges and furnaces with a railway made of cast-iron rails in 1767.

Abraham Darby III

By the time Abraham Darby III took over the works, the problem of producing coke iron was solved. However, Darby III continued to improve the business. To attract good workers he bought local farms to supply them with food. He paid higher wages than in other industries and built better houses for the workers.

However, Darby III's greatest work was to promote Coalbrookdale iron. He managed to show the world that Coalbrookdale iron was a strong and versatile material with many different uses. His most spectacular success was the iron bridge in Source 1. Fifty years earlier an iron bridge like this would have been impossible. Coke iron was too weak and charcoal iron too expensive. But in 50 years iron making had improved so much that now iron could be used not only for bridges, but to make boats, steam engines and wheels. The iron bridge became a symbol of the Darbys' success and a symbol of the new age of iron. It was the best advertisement his company could have had and it made the Coalbrookdale Company internationally famous.

The Darby business went from strength to strength. Soon there was a great demand for goods made by the company which had built the iron bridge.

SOURCE 11

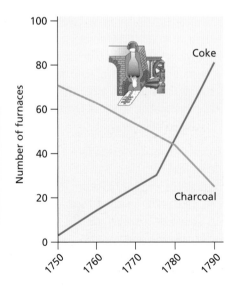
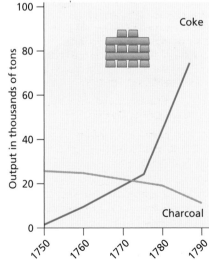

Charcoal and coke production 1750–90.

2 Look at the two paintings in Source 12. Write a detailed description of what is happening in each picture.

3 Many artists came to Coalbrookdale to paint the iron industry. Why do you think this was?

4 Do Sources 12A, 12B and 13 give similar impressions of iron making at Coalbrookdale? Which do you think gives the most accurate impression? Explain your answer.

SOURCE **12**

A

B   The Darby ironworks at Coalbrookdale.
A was painted in 1758 by George Perry (who owned a nearby ironworks) and T Vivares.   **B** was painted in 1777 by William Williams, a local artist.

SOURCE **13**

Furnaces in the Severn Gorge near Coalbrookdale, painted by Philippe de Loutherbourg, who was famous as a scenery painter for London theatres. These furnaces were run by one of the Darbys' rivals. The fire and smoke were particularly spectacular at night. Many famous paintings of this period feature magnificent sunsets and it seems likely that the amount of smoke put into the atmosphere by these new industries was partly responsible for the effect.

FOCUS TASK

HOW WAS IRON PRODUCTION IMPROVED IN THE EIGHTEENTH CENTURY?

The Darbys and their partners improved methods of iron production at Coalbrookdale throughout the eighteenth century. You are going to consider if any one development was more important than others.

1 List the improvements made by each of the Darbys.

2 For each one explain how it improved iron production at Coalbrookdale.

3 For each development give it a score out of ten for how important it was in improving iron production.

4 Would you regard any of the developments as a breakthrough? Write a paragraph to explain your answer.

5 Now write a paragraph explaining which improvement you think was the most important. You might think two are equally important.

FOCUS TASK

Look at your Coalbrookdale timeline from the task on page 102. You are now going to complete it. Use the area below the line to summarise the other developments described on pages 106–108.

How did iron-making technology improve after the Darbys?

The Coalbrookdale study treats the Darbys as if they were the whole iron industry. Of course they were not. Their success drew other iron makers to Shropshire. In 1788 Shropshire was the main iron-producing area, but it still produced only one-third of Britain's iron. The methods tried out by the Darbys were also being tried out by others. In fact, by the late eighteenth century technology had moved on quickly from the Darbys' achievements. You are now going to examine how iron making was improved by other individuals.

John Wilkinson

John Wilkinson was an iron maker. He had a number of ironworks and casting shops in the Midlands, including one in Coalbrookdale.

Wilkinson greatly improved casting methods. In 1774 he invented a cannon lathe which could make a cannon by boring accurately down the centre of a block of iron. With war against the American colonies and then the French in the period 1776–1815, this invention made his business very successful.

Wilkinson's cannon lathe was also turned to more peaceful uses to make the Boulton and Watt steam engine possible (see below). The steam engine needed a very accurately bored cylinder. Wilkinson's lathe was the only one accurate enough for the engine's cylinders.

Soon Wilkinson was developing new markets. In 1788 he supplied the city of Paris with 40 miles of iron pipes for its water supplies. He also built an iron boat which he successfully tried out on the River Severn. He even made himself an iron coffin, although he was too fat to use it when he died!

Boulton and Watt

Boulton and Watt were not iron makers. But their steam engine had a massive impact on iron making. Using Wilkinson's lathe, their improved steam engine (first used in 1776) quickly replaced water power as the means of blasting a furnace.

The Cranages

In a conventional furnace the coke was mixed with the iron. In 1766 the Cranages invented their reverbatory furnace. This kept the coke separate from the iron ore (see Source 14) which greatly reduced the impurities. However, the really important thing about the reverbatory furnace was that it made possible the next improvement – the puddling process.

Henry Cort

Henry Cort owned a forge near Portsmouth and had an important contract to supply the navy with cannon. Despite the success of the Darbys in improving coke iron he still could not get enough good-quality pig iron. He had either to take time heating and hammering poor-quality pig iron, or to import high-quality iron. So he experimented with ways of making coke iron purer.

In 1784 he introduced his PUDDLING and rolling method. He used the reverbatory furnace but stirred (puddled) the molten iron as it cooked. He discovered that if this stirring was done skilfully then it could bring all the impurities to the surface where they were burned off. He then rolled the hot iron to purify it further.

Cannon lathe improves casting

1 John Wilkinson was known as 'Iron-mad Wilkinson'. Explain why.

Steam power replaces water power

Reverbatory furnace keeps coke and iron apart

Puddling makes purer iron

SOURCE 14

The reverbatory furnace

A Front elevation

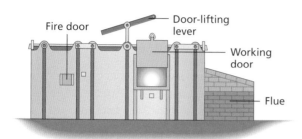

B Cross-section from front

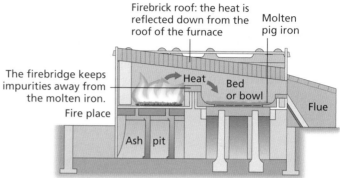

Puddling
Puddling was a highly skilled job. Despite the intense heat of the furnace, the puddler had to watch the molten pig iron constantly. He stirred the iron so that the impurities were burned off. The puddler had to judge when the iron was ready to be removed from the furnace. When it was he used long tongs to twist the molten iron in the furnace into a large glowing ball of white-hot metal. The ball was then hammered to remove any further impurities.

Rolling
The hot iron was now ready to be rolled. Rolling was not a new process but Cort's contribution was to create rollers of different shapes. This meant that the iron would cool as bars, sheet iron or whatever shape was needed for the next stage of the process.

Improvements in the iron industry.

2 **Why was Cort's puddling and rolling process so important?**

> **Iron making on a grand scale**

Richard Crawshay

Despite his invention Cort's business remained small. The real benefit of the puddling process was to other iron makers such as Richard Crawshay of South Wales who adopted Cort's methods on a massive scale. Crawshay built enormous furnaces and rolling mills. He turned iron making from a small-scale into a large-scale business able to cope with the escalating demand. He built his own canal to connect his ironworks with the sea.

By 1812 the Cyfartha works employed 2,000 people and was producing 10,000 tons of iron a year. By the 1830s there were 191 blast furnaces in the South Wales valleys. Merthyr Tydfil was the centre of the industry, specialising in producing rails for the growing railway network. It had been a small village in 1750. By the 1830s it was an unplanned town with a population of more than 100,000 and some of the worst workers' housing of any industrial town in Britain.

SOURCE 15

The rolling mills at Crawshay's Cyfartha works; a painting by Penry Williams, 1825.

ACTIVITY

Work in pairs. Devise 10 Mastermind-style quiz questions about the individuals and inventions mentioned here. Swap questions with another pair and see how many you can get right, without looking at this book.

Hot blast reduces fuel consumption

Steam hammer shapes iron more easily

James Neilson

In 1829 James Neilson tried out a hot air blast in his furnaces in Scotland. A large oven heated air before it was blasted into the furnaces. The effect was remarkable. The furnace temperature rose to 600 °F (315 °C) and three times more iron was produced with the same amount of coke.

James Nasmyth

In the same year, 1829, also in Scotland, James Nasmyth invented a steam-powered hammer for working wrought iron. It was immensely powerful but it was also very accurate and easy to control. Nasmyth boasted that his hammer could be set to shape a four-ton engine part or to crack an egg.

SOURCE 16

A

B

A James Nasmyth pictured with his steam hammer in 1856.
B Steam hammers soon became much larger and played a key role in making rails for Britain's rapidly growing railway network.

1   Read Source 17. From the information on pages 106–108 give names to each of the processes or pieces of equipment the bemused observer is describing.

FOCUS TASK

HOW HAD THE IRON INDUSTRY ADVANCED SINCE THE DARBYS?

In the nineteenth century people were keen on competitions and prizes. Imagine they have set up the Iron Technology Awards. Nominations are invited in the following categories:

a)   **The individual who has contributed most to the iron industry**
b)   **The invention which has saved most money**
c)   **The invention which has contributed most to improving the quality of iron.**

Who would you nominate? Choose a winner for each category and explain why you chose them.

SOURCE 17

Among the massive piles of brickwork flames crawl upward from the main furnaces … The mouth of each of these furnaces is near ten feet [three metres] in diameter …

The air blast is driven by two powerful steam engines through the main furnaces … I have listened to a storm on the Atlantic, I have stood on the Table Rock at Niagara Falls, yet never did I hear so terrific or so stunning a din.

Athletic men bathed in sweat, naked from the waist upwards … some with long bars stirring the fused metal through the door of the furnace … By raking backwards and forwards and stirring around and about they manage to weld together a shapeless mass … This, by a simultaneous effort of two men with massive tongs, was dragged out of the furnace along the paved floor – a snowball in shape.

Now subjected to the blows of a heavy hammer (at least four tons) … the men managed to heave the mass round and round at every rise of the hammer. Its every fall sounded like a mallet on a cotton bag …

They pass the slab several times between a pair of weighty cylinders … which get closer and closer as the plate gets thinner.

A description of an ironworks in the 1830/40s.

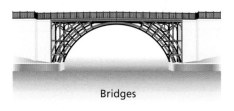

Machines

Weapons

Railways

Shipping

Bridges

Building

Tools

Pipes and chains

Domestic

The main uses of iron in the nineteenth century.

What was the iron industry like in the 1840s?

As you can see from Source 19, demand for oron grew phenomenally in the nineteenth century. One important reason for this was the growth of the railway network. Fifteen per cent of Britain's iron output went into rails alone. Source 18 summarises some of the other main reasons for the surge in demand.

Once an industry gets going improvements come thick and fast. It becomes impossible to list them all. All over the country individual iron makers were devising new techniques to improve iron making. For example, in the 1830s they discovered that round blast furnaces were 30 per cent more efficient than traditional square ones; in the 1840s they found a way of recycling the hot furnace gases to heat the blast. The list could go on and on.

What was clear, however, was that these developments changed the iron industry.

Scale changed. The Darbys had worked with furnaces just a few metres high. Crawshay's were monsters more than five times the size. The Darbys employed a few hundred people, Crawshay 2,000. Crawshay produced 10,000 tons of iron a year, almost as much as the entire British iron industry had produced a century before.

The entire iron-making process was **mechanised**. Not just the blast, but the hammer and the rolling mills were powered by vast steam engines.

SOURCE **19**

1740 County	No of furnaces (charcoal)	Iron production in tons
Staffordshire	2	1,000
Shropshire	6	2,100
Wales	9	2,550
Scotland	No figures	No figures
Rest of UK	42	11,700

1788 County	No of furnaces (charcoal + coke)	Iron production in tons
Staffordshire	9	6,900
Shropshire	24	24,900
Wales	20	15,500
Scotland	8	7,000
Rest of UK	24	14,000

1823 County	No of furnaces (all coke)	Iron production in tons
Staffordshire	84	133,590
Shropshire	38	57,923
Wales	72	192,325
Scotland	22	24,500
Rest of UK	43	43,728

1841 County	No of furnaces (all coke)	Iron production in tons
Staffordshire	129	532,120
Shropshire	Not known	81,287
Wales	123	418,030
Scotland	62	270,920
Rest of UK	47	85,194

From a Staffordshire Mining Commission report, 1841. The report looked back at iron production over the previous hundred years.

Location changed, as you can see from Sources 19 and 22. In the past ironworks had been by streams near to iron ore. Now they were all on or near coalfields. Coal was now the most important raw material for the ironworks. It heated the furnaces; it fired the steam engines.

The area to the north and west of Birmingham became an important centre of iron making during the industrial revolution. Towns like Wolverhampton and Dudley, which were on the canal network and had easy access to cheap coal, grew rapidly. The coal mines of Staffordshire supplied the energy and the 'Black Country' (so called because of the smokey air) supplied the workers and the finished products, particularly chains, nails and other small but essential goods. The city of Birmingham was becoming a manufacturing and commercial giant and its population was an important market for the local manufacturers. All of these factors meant that the area relied on canals as a cheap, efficient and reliable means of transporting heavy raw materials and finished products around the Midlands and beyond.

SOURCE 20

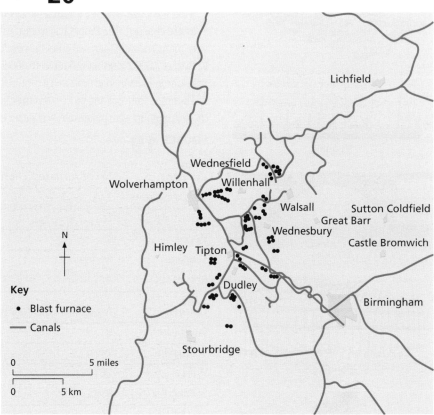

The canal network of the West Midlands in 1826.

SOURCE 21

West Bromwich ironworks in around 1830.

1 **Look at Source 20. Which canal route could you use to transport**

a) **chains from Wolverhampton to Liverpool**

b) **iron bars for building a factory from Dudley to Manchester**

c) **an iron cylinder for a steam engine from Birmingham to London?**

You may need to refer to an atlas or Source 35 on page 143.

SOURCE 22

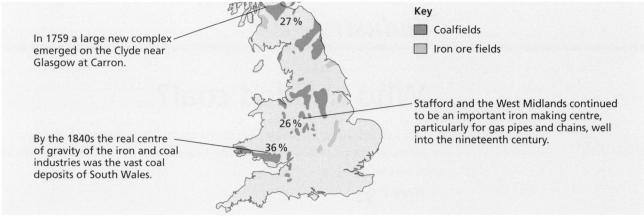

In 1759 a large new complex emerged on the Clyde near Glasgow at Carron.

By the 1840s the real centre of gravity of the iron and coal industries was the vast coal deposits of South Wales.

Stafford and the West Midlands continued to be an important iron making centre, particularly for gas pipes and chains, well into the nineteenth century.

27%
26%
36%

Key
- Coalfields
- Iron ore fields

The changing location of the iron industry, 1740–1840.

2 Write your own detailed description of the changes shown in Source 22. Include your own explanation of what factors caused the change in location.

SOURCE 23

All the works seem to be conducted upon the old plans of 40 years ago … Great fortunes have been made here – no wonder, they had formerly no opposition … I imagine that now they are doing little good … I imagine never more will they do much good, for the minerals [coal and iron ore] now lie at considerable distance. To make these works do equally to the Staffordshire and Welsh people they must be entirely rebuilt from the very foundations.

Written by a visitor to Coalbrookdale in 1815.

3 Read Source 23. Look again at your timeline. Add information about Coalbrookdale in 1815.

4 Why was Coalbrookdale in decline by 1815? Write an explanation under these headings: methods, competition, raw materials.

What happened to Coalbrookdale?

In 1815 a visitor wrote Source 23 about the once-proud Coalbrookdale.

FOCUS TASK

SOURCE 24

To IRONMASTERS, and Manufacturers of Steam-Engines, Boilers, Castings, Rails, Bar Iron, &c., &c.

MILTON IRON WORKS.

TO BE LET, for a term of 21 Years, and may be entered upon the First of October next, all those Old-established Iron-Works, called "THE MILTON IRON-WORKS," situate near to the Elseecar Coal-Field and the Tankersley Park Ironstone Grounds, and at a convenient distance from the Manufacturing Towns of Sheffield, Rotherham, and Barnsley, in the County of York. The Works consist of—

TWO BLAST FURNACES, with every requisite Appendage :—

FORGE and MILL, with Puddling and other Furnaces, Chafery for Drawing Uses, Rolling and Slitting Mills, &c., capable of Manufacturing from 90 to 100 Tons of Finished Iron per Week :—

FOUNDRY, with Pits, Drying Stoves, and every requisite Apparatus for making Engine Work, and Castings of every description, to the extent of 100 Tons per Week :—

ENGINE-FITTING SHOPS, with Lathes, Boring and Planing Machines, Boiler Makers' and Smiths' Shops, and every requisite for carrying on Engine and Railway Work to a large extent :—

Together with an ample supply of ELSECAR COALS, and TANKERSLEY PARK and SWALLOW-WOOD IRON-STONE, on terms to be agreed upon.

The Works possess at present excellent Canal and River Communication, and will shortly have the advantage of the South Yorkshire Railway.

N.B.—Although the Owner of the Works would not absolutely restrain the Lessees from making and Manufacturing Hot Blast Iron, yet he would prefer treating with parties who would undertake to make and manufacture Cold Blast Iron only.

For further Particulars, apply to **Mr. NEWMAN**, of Darley Hall, near Barnsley ; or Mr. WOODHOUSE, of Overseal, near Ashby-de-la-Zouch.

Darley Hall, near Barnsley, 15th June, 1848.

An advertisement for Milton Ironworks in Yorkshire, 1848.

1 Read Source 24. Is Milton Ironworks well equipped by the standards of the 1840s?

2 How much iron could Milton produce per year?

3 The advertisement lists many good points of the Milton works. Choose three which you think are its greatest strengths.

4 You are the manager of a Coalbrookdale works in 1848. The owners of the company are thinking of closing in Coalbrookdale (see Source 23) and buying the lease on Milton Ironworks (Source 24), with you as the new manager. Write a letter advising them whether they should do so. Give reasons for your advice.

5.2 *Growth and change in the coal industry*

Who needed coal?

As with the iron industry the demand for coal rose dramatically in the second half of the eighteenth century. As you can see from Source 1, supplying the iron industry was an important part of this demand.

SOURCE 1

Salt

The salt industry was a major industry in Britain. In the days before refrigeration salting was the main method of preserving food. Salt was also increasingly important as a raw material in the chemical, bleaching and dyeing industries.

Domestic use

The rising population increased the domestic market for coal. Coal was used for heating in homes and for washing and cooking.

Steam power

As the Lancashire and Yorkshire textile mills turned to steam power (see pages 79–80) demand for coal escalated. Newcomen steam engines (or fire engines as they were called) were enormous mechanical giants which devoured coal. Although the later Boulton and Watt engines used less coal there were more of them and the result was the same – more steam engines in use meant that more coal was needed.

Other industries

A wide range of other industries which needed heat, such as brickmaking, pottery making, soap making and brewing, were stimulated by the growing population. Each of these increased its use of coal. The bleaching and dyeing industries also used large amounts of coal, and these trades were stimulated by the rapidly expanding textile industries.

Key

☐ Salt production

☐ Iron industry

☐ Domestic use

☐ Export

☐ Other industrial uses

▨ Colliery use and waste

☐ Gas

Iron

The new coke furnaces being introduced in the iron industry swallowed up eight tons of coal for every ton of iron they produced. The new steam engines being introduced in the ironworks also used much coal.

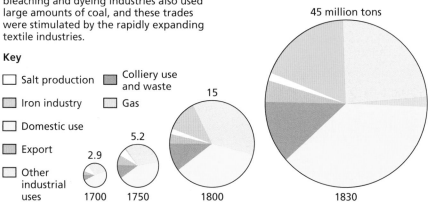

45 million tons

15

5.2

2.9

1700   1750   1800   1830

Coal production and consumption, 1700–1830.

FOCUS TASK

WHY DID THE DEMAND FOR COAL INCREASE?

On your own copy of this diagram, summarise the reasons why the demand for coal increased.

Industrial demand

Domestic demand

How was production increased?

In 1700 coal was mined using traditional and rather inefficient techniques, such as adit mining and bell pits (see Source 2). As demand grew, these methods had to change.

SOURCE 2

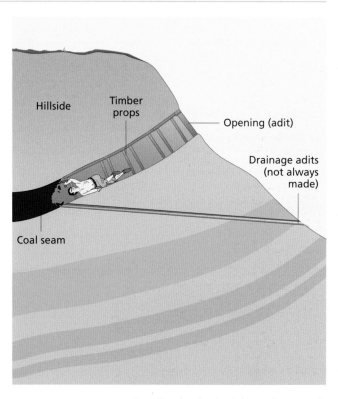

A Bell-pit mine (early eighteenth century).

B Adit mine (early eighteenth century).

SOURCE 3

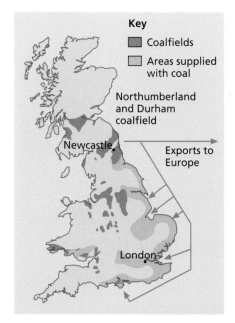

Britain's coal trade in around 1750.

Phase 1: Sink more pits

At first, the growing demand was met by sinking new pits and developing existing pits close to the source of demand for coal. You saw on pages 80 and 111 how local mines developed in the Midlands to supply the new iron industry and in Lancashire and Yorkshire to supply the textile industries. These used the traditional methods – usually bell pits or adit mines (see Source 2). They were often family businesses run in a similar way to the domestic system of the textile industry (see page 61). Men would hew out the coal. Women and children would help carry the coal out of the mine. The more coal they mined the more they could earn.

Phase 2: Improve transport

These coalfields expanded to serve their local markets, domestic and industrial. However, it was not really economically viable to transport coal further than about 10 miles. The only cheap way to move bulky coal at this time was by river or sea. London and the east coast of Britain were served by the Northumberland and Durham coalfield. Some other areas could get their coal by river. However, many could not.

In the 1770s inland water transport began to improve rapidly. Canals were built to link together the main navigable rivers (see page 145). This made it easier and cheaper to supply the industrial areas of northern England. The most important new venture was the Bridgewater Canal (see Factfile on page 118).

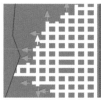 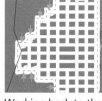

Working out from the shafts, pillars of coal are left.

Working back to the shafts, removing the pillars.

Pillar and chamber mine (mid- to late-eighteenth century).

Phase 3: Dig deeper mines

Few eighteenth-century mines were more than 60 metres below ground although there were some notable exceptions: the Kinnel mine in Scotland reached 130 metres and one pit in Whitehaven on the Cumbrian coast was 280 metres deep. However, by 1750 most of the easily accessible surface coal had long since disappeared. To keep pace with demand the mines became deeper and more complex, as you can see from Sources 4 and 5.

In the eighteenth century mining had been a small business. Many adit or bell-pit mines would be worked by one or two individuals and their families. As demand grew, mining became very big business. Only the rich could afford the investment to sink a mine hundreds of metres deep and buy steam engines, winding gear and other equipment needed to run a mine. So many miners left their own small pits and went to work for a mine owner. Some of the largest pits employed thousands of people.

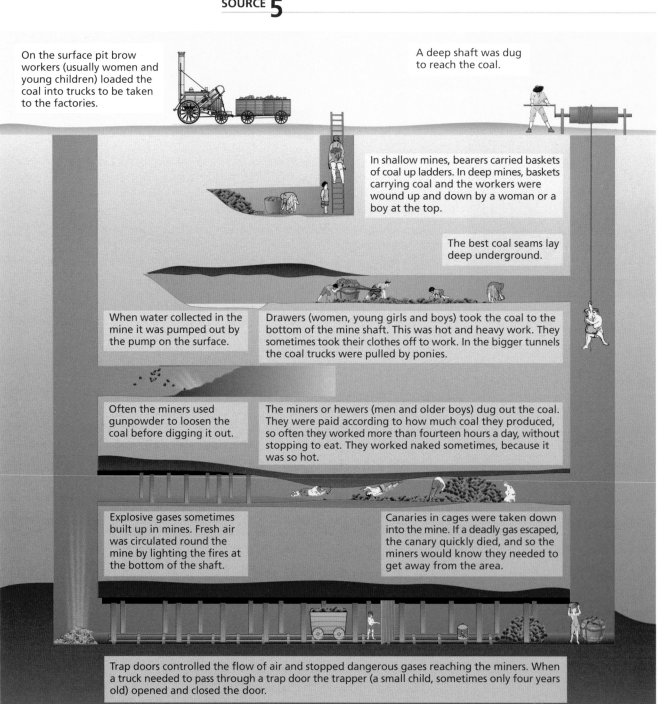

On the surface pit brow workers (usually women and young children) loaded the coal into trucks to be taken to the factories.

A deep shaft was dug to reach the coal.

In shallow mines, bearers carried baskets of coal up ladders. In deep mines, baskets carrying coal and the workers were wound up and down by a woman or a boy at the top.

The best coal seams lay deep underground.

When water collected in the mine it was pumped out by the pump on the surface.

Drawers (women, young girls and boys) took the coal to the bottom of the mine shaft. This was hot and heavy work. They sometimes took their clothes off to work. In the bigger tunnels the coal trucks were pulled by ponies.

Often the miners used gunpowder to loosen the coal before digging it out.

The miners or hewers (men and older boys) dug out the coal. They were paid according to how much coal they produced, so often they worked more than fourteen hours a day, without stopping to eat. They worked naked sometimes, because it was so hot.

Explosive gases sometimes built up in mines. Fresh air was circulated round the mine by lighting the fires at the bottom of the shaft.

Canaries in cages were taken down into the mine. If a deadly gas escaped, the canary quickly died, and so the miners would know they needed to get away from the area.

Trap doors controlled the flow of air and stopped dangerous gases reaching the miners. When a truck needed to pass through a trap door the trapper (a small child, sometimes only four years old) opened and closed the door.

A modern artist's reconstruction of a deep coal mine in the early 1800s.

How did technology improve mining?

As coal mines became deeper a wide range of new problems arose, some of them deadly. Below ground miners faced four major difficulties: drainage, ventilation, lighting and transport. In this section we will look at how new technology helped miners to tackle these problems.

Drainage

All miners had to cope with the problem of drainage. The early adit mines had used drainage shafts or adits (see Source 2). These were time-consuming to dig but took the water out of the mine effectively. (Bell pits had no means of drainage other than by hauling the water out in buckets.)

In deep-shaft mines the same idea was used. Shafts were dug to take the water to the lowest point in the mine where the water from the other shafts would collect. However, this collected water had to be brought up to the surface and tipped away. Sometimes this was done by using buckets on ropes. Whatever the method, it was a laborious, time-consuming and costly process.

These early processes usually relied on horse power. A horse walked around a winding mechanism called a horse gin (see Source 7). This system always had flaws: horses needed a lot of feed and they got tired. However, in deep mines it did not work at all. The horses were simply not strong enough to raise vast chains and buckets from a shaft many metres deep.

The steam engine developed by Thomas Newcomen (see page 12) was therefore a breakthrough for mine drainage. It could drain deep mines. It used huge amounts of coal, but in a coal mine this was not seen as a particular problem!

Between 1733 and 1775 the number of Newcomen engines rose from 78 to just under 400. In 1800 many Newcomen engines were still fully operational, although they were gradually being replaced by the more efficient Boulton and Watt engines. Whatever the engine, steam power solved the drainage problem.

FOCUS TASK

On your own copy of Source 5, make notes to illustrate each of the problems and solutions described on pages 115–18.

SOURCE 6

The iron chain is stiffened with knobs of cloth seldom more than 9 feet apart. The chain is turned round by a wheel 2 to 3 foot in diameter furnished with iron spikes to keep steady the chain so that it may rise through a wooden [shaft] 3, 4 or 5 inches above [the water] and from 12 to 22 feet long, and by means of the knobs bring it up with a stream of water.

An eighteenth-century writer describes the rag-and-chain-pump method.

1 **Read Source 6. Draw a sketch to show the process being described.**

2 **How is Source 8 an improvement on Source 7?**

3 **Is it fair to say that the Newcomen engine was a breakthrough?**

A horse gin. In the early eighteenth century this was a common method of lowering miners and raising coal as well as draining water.

SOURCE 7

SOURCE 8

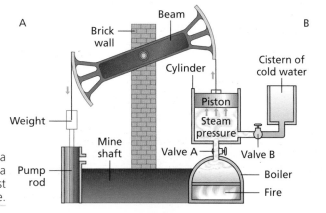

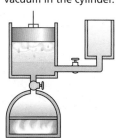
Cold water condenses the steam and creates a vacuum in the cylinder.

How the Newcomen engine drained a mine. The mine shaft was, in effect, a well. It was always sunk to the lowest point of the mine.

Ventilation

For miners, ventilation was a matter of life or death. On 25 May 1812 a gigantic blast ripped through Felling Colliery in the north-east of England.

SOURCE 9

On Monday afternoon, one of the most terrible accidents on record in the history of collieries took place at Felling, near Gateshead, in the mine belonging to Mr Brandling, which was the admiration of the district for the excellence of its air and arrangements. Nearly the whole of the workmen were below, the 2nd set having gone down before the 1st had come up, when a double blast of hydrogen gas took place, and set the mine on fire, forcing up such a volume of smoke as darkened the air to a considerable distance, and scattered an immense quantity of small coal from the upcast shaft. In the calamity, 93 men and boys perished, 86 of whom are still in the mine – which continues unapproachable. The few men who were saved happened to be working in a distant part of the colliery, to which the fury of the explosion did not reach.

From the *Newcastle Courant*, 30 May 1812.

The explosion was probably caused by a flame igniting a pocket of methane gas, also known as fire damp. It wrecked the winding gear, which made rescue difficult as a horse gin had to be used instead. The miners not killed by the blast were suffocated by the poisonous fumes given off by the burning coal, as the mine was now on fire. There were many more minor explosions of this type each year.

The answer to fire damp and other poisonous gases (mainly carbon monoxide or choke damp) was ventilation. As Source 10 shows, simple ventilation systems made use of convection currents. From about 1760 systems of trap doors made sure that fresh air followed a particular route and reached all parts of the mine (Source 10B).

SOURCE 10

1

A The burning coals cause the hot air to rise up the ventilation shaft.

B A draught of fresh air comes down into the mine through the main downshaft.

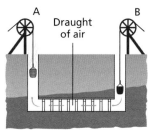

2

Trap doors or barriers controlled the flow of the fresh air so that it reached all parts of the mine. When trucks of coal needed to pass through, the trap doors were opened by small boys.

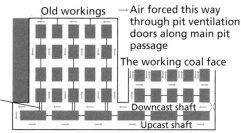

Methods of ventilation in coal mines.

However, any system that involved a fire carried risk, since methane could be carried out with the fresh air and explode when it reached the fire. Dangerous gases continued to be one of the miners' greatest hazards until well into the nineteenth century. The first system of ventilation which did not involve a flame was the steam-powered fan developed by John Buddle in 1807, but it was the late 1860s before this device became common.

Lighting

Lighting a mine was one thing, doing so in safety was another matter. From 1730 miners used steel mills, devices to create showers of sparks, to test for methane before they lit their lamps. You can imagine how dangerous this was.

The problem of safe lighting was not solved until Sir Humphrey Davy developed his safety lamp in 1815. By surrounding the flame with a wire mesh the lamp prevented fire damp from reaching its ignition temperature. George Stephenson produced a similar lamp known as the Geordie lamp.

> **1** How far was the problem of ventilation solved in the eighteenth century? Explain your answer carefully.

SOURCE 11

Question: What is the deepest pit you know?

Answer: The deepest pit I am acquainted with as a working pit is 180 fathoms [328 metres] of shaft, but they do go deeper.

Q: Do you think that the particular accidents by explosion, which you have described, have been much lessened by the introduction of Sir Humphrey Davy's safety lamp?

A: They have, I conceive. If we had not had the Davy lamp, these mines could not now have been in existence at all; for the only substitute we had, and that was not a safe one, was what we called steel mills. They were completely superseded by the Davy lamp of the simplest construction; it costs only about 5 or 6 shillings … this lamp introduced quite a new era in coal mining, as so many collieries are now in existence, the old collieries have been reopened, producing the best coals, which must have lain dormant but for the introduction of the Davy lamp.

An extract from evidence presented to the Select Committee of the House of Lords on the state of the coal trade in 1829.

SOURCE 12

ACTIVITY

You are a London reporter in about 1800. You have just spent two weeks with miners in the north-east of England, researching an article entitled: *Gas: The Miners' Invisible Enemy.* Write your article, explaining the enemy and how it can be fought.

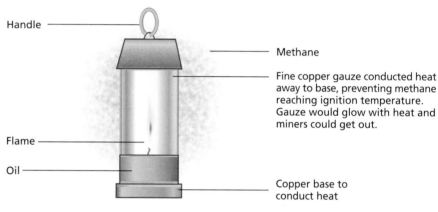

Handle

Methane

Fine copper gauze conducted heat away to base, preventing methane reaching ignition temperature. Gauze would glow with heat and miners could get out.

Flame

Oil

Copper base to conduct heat

How the Davy lamp worked.

SOURCE 13

I accompanied Mr Stephenson and Mr Wood down the A pit at Killingworth Colliery to try Mr Stephenson's first safety lamp. I told Mr Stephenson that if the lamp should deceive him we should be severely burned, but Mr Stephenson should insist on the trial which was very much against my desire. So I went out of the way at a distance and left Mr Stephenson to himself, but we soon heard that the lamp had answered his expectations with safety. Since that time I have been many times with Mr Stephenson trying his different lamps.

John Moody describes an early trial of George Stephenson's safety lamp, in around 1815.

Other safety measures

Through the nineteenth century various measures were introduced to improve safety. One ever-present danger was of ropes snapping under the strain as they pulled coal or miners out of a mine. This danger was greatly reduced in the 1830s with the introduction of wire cables. Also in the 1830s pit cages and guide rails in shafts improved the safety and efficiency of this aspect of mining.

2 In what ways could the Davy lamp be seen as a breakthrough?

3 Was it more or less important to coal-mining than the Newcomen engine? Explain your answer.

Underground transport

As pits became larger the distances from the coal deposits to the surface became greater and greater. Since coal was heavy and bulky this presented a real problem. For much of the eighteenth century, and indeed up to 1842, transporting coal underground was by human muscle power. Corves (wooden tubs) of coal were pushed or pulled from the coal face to the shaft by women or young boys. More efficient pits used wooden, then later iron, rails. This speeded up the process and by about 1800 many pits were using wheeled trolleys on rails, pulled by pit ponies when there was room, and by humans when there wasn't.

Getting the coal to the surface was another problem. The horse gin was used but an average horse gin could raise only 100 tons of coal in a day. The Newcomen engine was no good for this because it only gave up and down movement.

In 1781 the crucial development came with the invention of the 'sun and planet' gearing system. This created rotary movement. Steam engines could now wind ropes round and round rather than simply pumping up and down. Not surprisingly, this development was eagerly taken up – about 130 of these engines were in service by 1800.

SOURCE 14

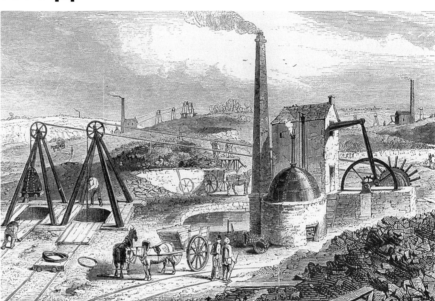

An engine drawing coal at a pithead in Staffordshire in the early nineteenth century.

Surface transport

Steam power also transformed the transport of coal away from the pithead. Canals (see the Factfile on the Bridgewater Canal) and horse-drawn railways (see page 103) had been in use for this purpose for some time. In the 1820s George Stephenson built the first steam-powered railway from the coalfields near Darlington to Stockton. Stockton was a busy port which sent coal from the South Durham coalfield to all parts of the country. Until the 1820s the coal was carried by road, and this was proving to be expensive and inefficient. The mine owners at first decided to build a canal to link Stockton and Darlington. However, the terrain was not ideally suited to canal building and the new technology of steam-powered railways seemed a tempting alternative. George Stephenson had shown his talents in surveying and building railways in local collieries and his son had an established reputation as a designer and builder of locomotives. Together they built the line and the locomotives which ran on it. Although passengers did travel on the line, its primary purpose was to transport coal.

FACTFILE

The Bridgewater Canal

The growing town of Manchester suffered from high coal prices in the 1750s. Coal was easily produced in many mines on the Lancashire coalfield. What put the price up was transporting it by packhorse and road. Coal was heavy and bulky – it took a lot of effort to move it anywhere. The Duke of Bridgewater had plenty of coal in his mine at Worsley. He sank his money into the building of a canal from his mines to Manchester, which almost ruined him. However, when the Duke's coal reached Manchester in 1761 he was able to sell it at half the price of other coal. Very soon he recouped the investment and was making large profits. He even extended the canal to Runcorn. (See page 141 for more details.)

ACTIVITY

Design an advertisement for one of the technological developments or inventions on pages 113–19.

Your advertisement has got to convince some very hard-headed businessmen, so include drawings and diagrams to show how your chosen piece of technology works.

Then write about the benefits of your chosen product, for example how it has:

- improved safety.
- saved money.
- increased efficiency.
- increased output.

SOURCE 15

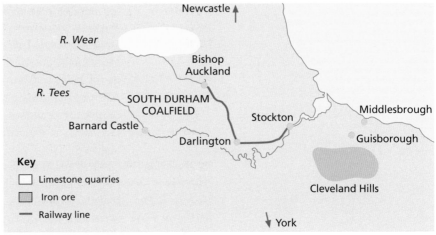

The Stockton and Darlington Railway, built to carry coal.

SOURCE 16

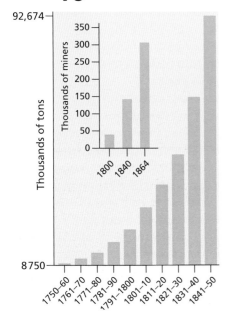

Coal mined and numbers of miners, 1750–1850.

SOURCE 18

The coal trade was greatly affected by the technological changes which occurred in many industries during the industrial revolution, but mining itself did not undergo a revolution … Increased production of coal was achieved … largely by human labour, and at the cost of much suffering. Until 1842 women and children were employed underground in many mines for the heavy haulage jobs. They pushed or pulled corves and wagons loaded with coal up inclined planes, sometimes in narrow seams where it was impossible to stand upright. Long hours were worked in conditions of great discomfort and considerable danger.

Written by historian RN Rundle in 1973.

The human achievement

By the 1830s almost all the country was within reach of affordable and abundant coal, as you can see from Source 16. You have seen that new technology had played a central part in this, but it was not the whole story as you can see from Sources 17 and 18.

SOURCE 17

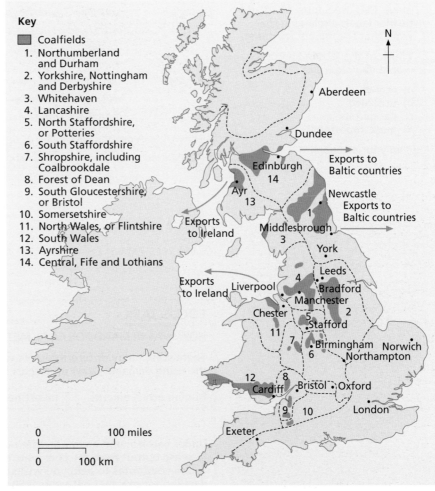

Britain's coalfields in the 1830s, showing the areas normally supplied by each coalfield before the coming of the railways.

SOURCE 19

The viewer	Site manager responsible to the owner of the mine
The overman	Foreman or overseer of the pit
The deputy	Set the timbers and pillars which supported the roof of the mine, cleared the passageways of any eruption of gas or fall of stone, and organised the collapsing of the excavated areas of the mine
The onsetter	Supervised the loading of coal at the bottom of the shaft into baskets to be raised to the surface
The crane onsetter	Responsible for the loading of the coal from the putters' baskets into the wagons
The craneman	Operated the crane which lifted the coal
The hewer	Dug the coal out of the seams
The horse keeper	Looked after the horses
The wagon driver	Drove the horse wagons from the end of the inclined plane, along the outer passageway to the bottom of the shaft
The lampkeeper	Maintained the lamps. It is likely that these were oil lamps. Even though the first safety lamps were developed at about this time their use was not yet fully established
The wasteman	Maintained those parts of the mine which had been abandoned. He made and repaired the timber pillars which supported the roof and kept the airways open through the wastes
The putter	A young child who pushed, pulled and carried coal. The youngest and smallest putters pulled baskets of coal through the narrow passageways. Older children of about 15 years pushed and pulled the coal in small carts, each cart holding several wicker baskets of coal
The trapper	Trap doors, made from wood, were placed across the passageways in order to divert the current of clean air through the proper channels of the mine. Each trap door was attended by a boy of seven or eight who would pull a string to open the door for passing coal carts
The shifter	Very often an old man who supervised the changes of shifts. In between shifts he helped with the repair and maintenance of the mine: building traps, heightening the roof, stowing away equipment

A modern description of the different workers in Felling Colliery and their responsibilities in the early nineteenth century.

1 On your own copy of Source 5 (page 114) use Source 19 to add further labels explaining the work that the miners are doing.

2 Which of the jobs in Source 19 would you regard as

a) skilled
b) unskilled
c) dangerous
d) most important?

Explain your answers.

FOCUS TASK

HOW WAS DEMAND FOR COAL MET?

There were many different factors which allowed the coal industry to meet the rising demand. Draw up a chart like this:

Human achievements	Investment	Technology	Transport

Under each column heading write notes explaining how that factor helped increase output from the coal industry.

Use your notes to help you write an essay entitled 'How was rising demand for coal met between 1750 and 1825?'. Write a paragraph on each factor, then in a concluding paragraph explain which factor you think was most important.

3 What would each of the workers in Source 20 be called if they worked in Felling Colliery (Source 19)?

4 Which job in Source 20 would you
   a) most
   b) least like to do?

   Explain your choice.

Why did Parliament pass the Mines Act?

In the 1830s Lord Shaftesbury and others had successfully campaigned for a Factory Act to control working conditions in the textile mills (see page 90). After their success Lord Shaftesbury pushed for a similar investigation into conditions in the mines. In 1840 Parliament set up an inquiry. It reported back in 1842. Lord Shaftesbury had learned from the campaigns for the Factory Act that the most effective way to achieve change was to shock the public and MPs. Sources 20 and 22 are from his report.

SOURCE 20

A

B Children being winched down into a mine.

C

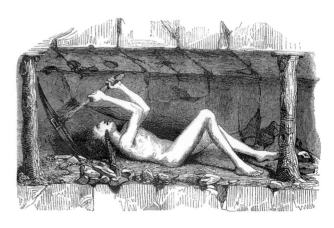

D In some mines coal seams were often less than a metre in depth, which meant very cramped working conditions.

Illustrations from the 1842 Report of the Royal Commission by Lord Shaftesbury. Readers were appalled at the scenes shown, but mine owners claimed that the report presented a distorted picture.

1 Compare the working conditions in Sources 20 and 21. Why do you think that Lord Shaftesbury did not include Source 21 in his report?

2 Source 22 mixes facts and opinions very freely. On your own copy underline in one colour words or phrases which report *factual conditions*; in another colour underline words or phrases which express the writer's *opinion* on conditions in the mines.

3 Does Source 22 tell you more about the conditions in the mines or about the opinions of the writers? Explain your answer.

Bradley mine in Staffordshire was fortunate in having a very deep seam of coal which was relatively easy to get at.

A *I have often been shocked in contemplating the hideous and anything but human appearance of these men, who are generally found in a state of bestial nakedness, lying their whole length on the uneven floor, and supporting their heads upon a board or short crutch; or sitting upon one heel balancing in their persons by extending the other. Black and filthy as they are in their low, dark, heated and dismal chambers, they look like a race fallen from the common stock. It did not much surprise me to be told that old age came prematurely upon them: indeed the careworn countenances, the grey hair and furrowed brows I met with were sufficient indications of that fact.*

B *The children that excite the greatest pity are those who stand behind the doors to open and shut them: they are called trappers, who are in darkness, solitude and stillness as of night, and eke out a miserable existence for the smallest of wages. I can never forget the first unfortunate creature I met with: it was a boy of about eight years old, who looked at me as I passed with an expression the most abject and idiotic – like a thing, a creeping thing, peculiar to the place. On approaching and speaking to him he shrank trembling and frightened into a corner.*

C Evidence given by Betty Harris, a 37-year-old mine worker.

I have a belt round my waist, and a chain passing between my legs and I go on hands and feet. The road is steep and we have to hold by a rope … The pit is very wet where I work and the water comes over our clog tops sometimes … I am not as strong as I was and cannot stand my work as well as I used to. I have drawn till I have had the skin off me; the belt and chain is worse when we are in the family way.

D *I found assembled around the fire a group of men, boys and girls … The girls as well as the boys stark naked down to the waist … and trousers supported by their hips … In the Flockton and Thornhill pits the system is even more indecent; for though the girls are clothed, at least three-fourths of the men for whom they 'hurry' work stark naked.*

Extracts from the 1842 report, Parliamentary Papers.

4 Compare Sources 19, 20, 21 and 22. Which is most useful as a source of information about conditions in the mines? Explain your choice.

5 'The 1842 Mines Act was based on moral outrage rather than concern about conditions.' Do you agree?

The opponents of reform criticised the report and the way it was put together (see Source 23) but the report was a massive success for Lord Shaftesbury. His nineteenth-century middle-class audience was deeply shocked. The thought of young boys trapped in the dark for long days was a cause for concern. Worse still was the employment of women as human packhorses.

The report played up the immorality of half-naked women and sometimes naked men working together in the mines. However, it seems that the reformers, largely middle-class men used to the idea that women should be helpless creatures, in the home rather than at work, were as much shocked by the independence and 'maleness' of women workers as by their working conditions.

6 Do you think that Sources 20–22 taken together give you a reliable view of conditions in the mines? Explain your answer with reference to Source 23.

7 Using everything you have found out about the mines from pages 113–23 write an extra paragraph for Shaftesbury's report, giving a balanced description of working conditions in the mines.

SOURCE 23

The way in which the commissioners collected the evidence talking to artful boys and ignorant young girls – and putting answers into their mouths – was most unfair. The manner in which the report was accompanied by pictures of a disgusting and obscene character was designed to excite people's feelings, not help them form a reasoned judgement. The trapper's job is not dull and boring. He is not kept in darkness all the time he is in the pit. The trapper is usually happy and cheerful and passes his time cutting sticks, making models of windmills and drawing figures in chalk on his door.

The pit owner Lord Londonderry.

Furthermore, of around 150,000 miners, only about 5–6,000 were women. Modern efficient pits did not employ women and children in the dreadful conditions described in the report. There were no women at all in the Northumberland and Durham and Midlands coalfields.

What was the impact of the Mines Act?

The Mines Act was passed in 1842. It became illegal for women and children under the age of 10 to be employed underground in the mines. The Act also made sure inspectors could visit the mine at any time. However, the Mines Act said nothing about men's hours or working conditions.

There were further Acts after the 1842 Act:

8 How would each of the Acts from 1843 to 1872 improve safety in the mines?

1843	No worker under the age of 15 was to be left in charge of the winding gear
1850	Strengthened the powers of the inspectors by allowing them to go underground (see Source 26)
1855	Laws controlling ventilation passed
1862	Single-shaft mines made illegal
1860	Boys under 12 not allowed underground unless they could read and write
1872	Mine managers had to hold a certificate qualifying them for the job.

Among the workers' unions there was some support for banning women workers. They felt women were taking men's jobs. But the Act was not popular among women workers themselves, who lost a wage and were being treated in the same way as children. Many women continued to work above ground in the mines (see Sources 24 and 25).

SOURCE 24

A pit bank girl photographed in the late nineteenth century.

SOURCE 26

In April 1849 Robert Smith, mineral agent of Blaenavon Colliery, went down the pit. He turned out 70 women and girls, as many as 20 … being no more than 11 or 12 years of age. He has no doubt that since then many have gone back from time to time. He gave notice that he would fine any man employing them again, and he has fined seven or eight from 5s to 10s each.

Inspector's report on a South Wales mine, 1850.

SOURCE 25

In all parts of the coal districts where women had been employed complaints were numerous of the hardships that the Act had occasioned to elder females, widows, orphan daughters of a mature age, families where there were no sons to aid a father who was old and ailing; and other similar cases.

Mining Commissioners' report, 1844.

FOCUS TASK

WHAT WAS THE IMPACT OF LEGISLATION ON COAL MINING?

It is 1850. The famous humanitarian Robert Owen (see page 85) has asked you to inform him about the Mines Act and how it has improved conditions in the mines.
    Write a letter to Owen that explains:

- the poor conditions revealed in the report.
- the improvements made by the Act.
- the problems which have not been tackled.

Finally, compare the impact of the Mines Act with that of the Factory Acts on textile mills (Owen would know all about these).

Why did the iron and coal industries bring about change in transport?

Throughout this chapter there have been references to transport improvements. Iron and coal, as bulky heavy materials, were much more difficult to transport than textiles or farm produce. These two industries were therefore much more dependent on transport, and they brought about many improvements to transport. You will investigate this in more detail in Chapter 6.

FOCUS TASK

HOW DID CHANGES IN THE IRON AND COAL INDUSTRIES AFFECT TRANSPORT?

The Bridgewater Canal (page 118)

Canals in the West Midlands (page 110)

The Stockton and Darlington Railway (pages 118–19)

1   Make notes to show how the needs of the iron and coal industries stimulated each of the improvements shown.

2   Many aspects of the industrial revolution follow a similar pattern. Improvements take place because:

   a) there is a need.
   b) there is money.
   c) there is technology.
   d) there is an individual to take advantage of it.

   Look at the improvements in the diagram and explain:

   • why iron and coal created a need for improved transport.
   • why there was money to invest.
   • how technology in iron and coal helped improve transport.
   • the role of individuals in improving transport.

5.3 *How did the steel industry change between 1850 and 1900?*

Cast iron and wrought iron were too brittle and inflexible to stand up to the stress and strains put on them by larger trains, boats and other machinery being designed and built by engineers like Isambard Kingdom Brunel. In fact, when Brunel designed the giant steamship *The Great Eastern* he gave specific instructions that no cast iron should be used anywhere on the boat. He preferred steel. Steel is an ALLOY made by mixing iron with other metals to make it harder, stronger and more flexible than pure iron.

In the second half of the nineteenth century, as the trains, boats and machines being made by British industry became larger, demand for steel began to increase. Unfortunately, steel was extremely difficult to make and very expensive. However, the new demand stimulated action and three important developments met the need. As you have seen with other developments, this in turn meant that steel became cheaper and other uses were found for it, which in turn created further demand. For example, in the second half of the nineteenth century surgery advanced greatly and a new business developed in making steel surgical instruments. These had the huge advantage of being strong and easy to sterilise by boiling. There were many other applications for steel in building, engineering and tool making, so let us look at how the problems of making steel were overcome.

> **1 Why would it have been impossible to make Brunel's ship with iron?**

Development 1: The Bessemer converter

In 1856 inventor and engineer Henry Bessemer developed a machine to convert iron into steel. Bessemer experienced the problems with ordinary iron while working on the design of gun barrels at the time of the Crimean War (1854–56). After much thought, trial and experimentation Bessemer came up with the converter shown in Source 1.

SOURCE 1

1 Molten iron is poured in.

2 Heated air is forced in through holes in its base for 20 minutes. This combines with impurities in the iron and burns them away.

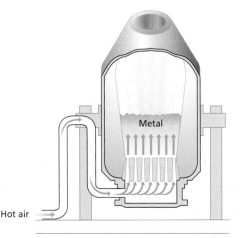

Metal

Hot air

3 Manganese or carbon is added, and mixed in.

4 Molten steel is poured out.

How steel was made using a Bessemer converter.

The converter was not an instant success. Many manufacturers found that the steel was brittle. The problem was that most British iron ores contained phosphorus, except those around Barrow-in-Furness in Cumbria. Bessemer set up his own steelworks in Sheffield using these Cumberland (haematite) ores. Until well into the next century Sheffield continued a proud tradition of steel making in specialist areas, particularly in cutlery. The Sheffield armaments and engineering firm Vickers began using steel for guns and shells in 1890. Gradually, other manufacturers took up Bessemer's converter. One important development was the establishment of a steel plant in Crewe in 1863. This plant was owned by the London and North Western Railway and used Bessemer technology to produce rails. The railways were the major users of Bessemer steel. The Midland Railway Company found that on one busy section of track, steel rails lasted over 10 years. Iron rails had needed to be changed every six months. Not surprisingly, Barrow became an important steel centre, and by 1872 there were 17 Bessemer converters operating in the town. Barrow was 15 times larger in 1881 than it had been in 1861.

Development 2: The Siemens open-hearth furnace

A German scientist called Friedrich Siemens devised an open-hearth furnace that was very efficient and not as complex a method of making steel as the Bessemer method. Source 2 shows how the furnace worked. The open-hearth furnace was slower than the Bessemer converter, but it had many other advantages. One of the most important was the ability to melt down scrap and pig iron to make higher-quality steel than had been possible before.

SOURCE 2

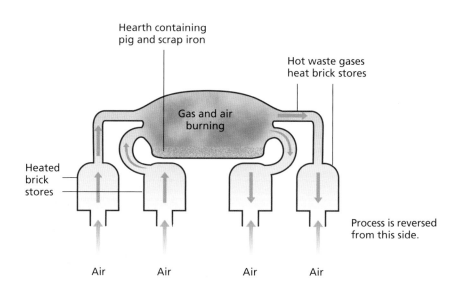

Siemens open-hearth furnace – the alternative to the Bessemer method.

The major market for open-hearth steel was shipbuilding. At the giant shipyards on the River Clyde in Scotland, steel ships replaced wooden ones over a period of 10 years (1877–87). Shipbuilding became one of Britain's most successful industries. Open-hearth steel was also strong and flexible enough for building projects like the Forth Bridge, opened in 1890.

Development 3: Gilchrist Thomas and the dolomite process

Steel making is a two-stage process. The first stage still involved the smelting of the iron in the blast furnace. In the late 1870s Sidney Gilchrist Thomas, along with his cousin who was a chemist at an ironworks, found a way of improving this first stage. Gilchrist Thomas used a type of limestone called dolomite in the blast furnaces which he discovered removed more phosphorus from the iron than other forms of limestone. Unfortunately, using dolomite required expensive conversion to furnaces. As British firms were slow to do this, the steel industries in Germany and the USA began to move ahead of Britain's.

The only area where Gilchrist Thomas's dolomite methods were adopted successfully on a large scale was in Middlesbrough. They got their dolomite from the Pennines. They got their coal from the Durham coalfield and they had plenty of iron ore in the surrounding hills.

1 Look back at your own copy of Source 22 on page 111. Mark on it the main steel-producing areas.

2 Are they in the same places or in different places from the iron and coal areas?

3 Write notes around your map to explain why:

   a) Middlesbrough
   b) Sheffield
   c) Barrow

   were good places to make steel.

4 How did the following factors affect development in the steel industry:

   a) War
   b) Transport improvements
   c) Technological changes?

FOCUS TASK

HOW DID THE STEEL INDUSTRY CHANGE?

It is 1880. You work at the Bolckow and Vaughan Steelworks in Middlesbrough. It is a very successful company which uses the Gilchrist Thomas method of blasting with dolomite, followed by steel making in Bessemer converters. You have been asked to escort some visitors round the works.

   Write notes to remind yourself of the key features that you will need to explain to your visitors. Use the following headings:

- **The uses of steel and why demand for it has increased**
- **The difficulties people have faced in producing steel**
- **The different solutions to the problem before Gilchrist Thomas**
- **Why the Gilchrist Thomas method was such an improvement.**

   You could write out your notes as a handout with diagrams for your visitors.

6 Transport changes 1700–1900

6.1 How did road and water transport improve in the eighteenth century?

ROAD	WATER	
1700		
Poorly kept roads are the main type of land transport.	Improved rivers (navigations) and coastal shipping are the main types of water transport.	
1750		
1750s and 1760s Turnpike boom	**1761** Bridgewater Canal	
		RAILWAY
Golden Age of coaching 1800	**1790s** Canal mania	
Coaching declines in importance because of the growth of the railway network.	Canals decline in importance because of the growth of the railway network.	**1830** Opening of the Liverpool and Manchester Railway
		1840s Railway mania
1850		
1900		

FOCUS

In 1700 Britain's transport system had improved very little since the Middle Ages. Road transport was very poor indeed. It was faster to travel from London to Edinburgh by sea than on land. However, the century from 1750 to 1850 saw rapid improvement. First road transport, then water transport were transformed as a network of turnpikes and canals criss-crossed the country. Finally, from the 1830s onwards, a comprehensive network of railways was built to link every major city and town in Britain. In this chapter you will investigate the causes and consequences of these rapid changes.

6.1 examines improvements in road and water transport up to 1840. You will:

* investigate whether road and water transport were really as bad in the 1700s as they are often made out to be.
* examine the factors which made it possible to improve roads, and build many canals, by the end of the eighteenth century.
* consider how significant the new roads and canals were to Britain's industrial development.

6.2 investigates the emergence of railways from 1825 onwards. You will:

* examine the fierce arguments for and against the building of railways in the 1820s and 1830s, using the Liverpool and Manchester Railway as an example.
* investigate how the railway network developed and changed after 1840.
* consider the economic and social impact of railways.

The developments in different transport networks overlap with each other. The timeline on the left should help you keep the different changes in perspective and relate them to the industrial changes you have already studied.

What was road transport like in the early 1700s?

Road transport in the early eighteenth century was slow, expensive and dangerous. Source 1 shows the different methods of road transport available.

The roads themselves were in poor condition. To a modern observer many would seem to be nothing more than dirt tracks. In summer these might just cope with the many wagons and coaches which passed over them. In winter they declined badly as the huge iron-rimmed wheels mangled the unmade road surfaces. There were frequent accidents. Passengers on horseback could make reasonable progress because they could cut through fields and keep to the sides of roads, but for bulky goods road transport was very impractical. Heavy or bulky goods were usually transported by water. They were only transported by road when there was no alternative.

SOURCE 1

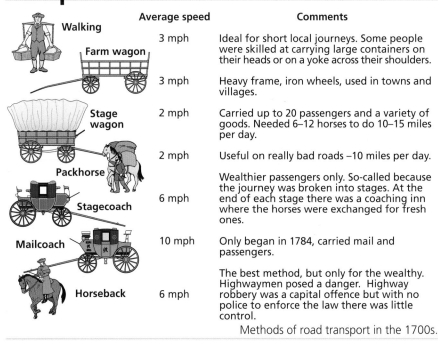

	Average speed	Comments
Walking	3 mph	Ideal for short local journeys. Some people were skilled at carrying large containers on their heads or on a yoke across their shoulders.
Farm wagon	3 mph	Heavy frame, iron wheels, used in towns and villages.
Stage wagon	2 mph	Carried up to 20 passengers and a variety of goods. Needed 6–12 horses to do 10–15 miles per day.
Packhorse	2 mph	Useful on really bad roads –10 miles per day.
Stagecoach	6 mph	Wealthier passengers only. So-called because the journey was broken into stages. At the end of each stage there was a coaching inn where the horses were exchanged for fresh ones.
Mailcoach	10 mph	Only began in 1784, carried mail and passengers.
Horseback	6 mph	The best method, but only for the wealthy. Highwaymen posed a danger. Highway robbery was a capital offence but with no police to enforce the law there was little control.

Methods of road transport in the 1700s.

1 Which of the forms of transport in Source 1 can you see in Source 2?

2 Which form of transport do you think was most dangerous? Explain your choice.

SOURCE 2

A road in the early eighteenth century. Muddy tracks like this constituted much of Britain's network.

SOURCE 3

This day an inquest was held at Ingatestone on the body of Richard Aimes, when it appeared that the deceased was thrown from his horse, a little on the side of Ingatestone, into a ditch, and was suffocated by mud and filth.

From the *Ipswich Journal*, 18 March 1769.

What attempts had been made to improve the roads?

Despite the perils of road travel some of the roads were very busy. One of the popular myths about this period is that travel was so difficult that no one ever bothered to go anywhere. It is true that the average person would not travel far. Many people never travelled more than 10–20 miles from their birthplace in their entire life. However, evidence from the period suggests there was a lot of *local traffic* on these roads. Travellers reported roads where there was an almost constant stream of stagecoaches, market traders, hay wagons, packhorses or pedestrians.

With so many people travelling you would have thought that there would be every reason to improve the roads. Some attempts had been made.

Road repairs by the parish councils

The government was concerned about the state of the roads. Way back in the sixteenth century the Statute for Mending the Highways had made local parish councils responsible for maintaining and repairing all roads in their locality. All members of the parish had to spend four (later increased to six) days per year working on the repair of the roads. This still applied in the 1700s. In practice, however, the work was not taken seriously and at worst it was deeply resented. Many thought they were doing such work only for the benefit of people passing through the parish. Even when locals could be bullied or persuaded to come out and work, the local (unpaid) parish surveyor was frequently not qualified for the work.

SOURCE 4

The [road repairers] make a holiday of it, lounge about and generally waste their time. As they are in no danger of being turned out of their work, they stand in no awe of the surveyor. It is a common saying that if a drop of sweat should happen to fall from any of them, it would probably wash away the road!

From *The Complete Farmer*, 1787.

SOURCE 5

[The roads are]… so very much destroyed by the great carriage of salt, iron, coal and other wares, that they are almost impassable, several carts and wagons having been there broke, the goods spoiled and many horses lost, and the inhabitants unable to repair them.

Merchants and traders of Droitwich, 1706.

Presumably it is these rather inadequate repairs to which Arthur Young refers in Source 10.

George Wade: road repairs by the army

One organisation which saw the risks attached to such poor roads was the army. Some roads in the north of England and southern Scotland were therefore improved by the army under General George Wade between 1726 and 1737. As commander of the army he believed he could only prevent an uprising in the border country if he could quickly move troops to trouble spots. He built good roads, some of them up to 10 metres wide, strongly founded on layers of stone. However, although these roads helped the army, they did not serve the areas of main population in either England or Scotland and had little effect on the main road network.

Turnpike trusts

It was clear to many that the parishes lacked both the skill and the money to keep up the roads. In 1663 a new idea was tried. Local magistrates in Hampshire received permission from Parliament to set up a turnpike trust. They were allowed to take over a stretch of road, improve it, and most importantly charge people tolls to use it. The idea worked. Their road was used by local traffic and by travellers passing through on their way to London. The tolls helped pay for the upkeep of the road. The turnpikes had arrived. By 1750 there were 143 turnpike trusts in Britain, controlling 3,400 miles of road.

Turnpike trusts were usually run by local magistrates. They were non-profit making, but local businessmen and farmers were usually prepared to invest in them because they improved their own trade.

Turnpikes greatly improved the quality of the roads in Britain in the early part of the century. Foreign visitors often commented upon their high quality. Daniel Defoe (see page 23), who travelled the entire country, largely on horseback, was an enthusiastic supporter of turnpikes (see Source 6).

SOURCE 6

A From London through this whole country towards Ipswich and Harwich… roads were formerly deep, in times of flood dangerous and at other times, in winter, scarcely passable; they are now so firm, so safe, so easy to travellers and carriages as well as cattle, that no road in England can be said to equal them.

B The benefit of the turnpikes now appears to be so great and the people in all places so sensible of it, that it is incredible what effect it has already had on the trade in the counties where it is more completely finished; even the cost of carriage of goods is reduced, in some places 6d per hundredweight, in some places 12d.

C The soil of all the Midland part of England is of deep stiff clay… The number of horses killed by the excess of labour in these heavy ways has been such a charge to the county that building new roads, as the Romans did of old, seems a much easier expense.

Daniel Defoe writing about the turnpike roads in 1726.

---

1 Read Source 6. List Defoe's reasons for thinking turnpikes are a good idea.

SOURCE 7

BRAYDON LANE GATE

A Table of the Tolls to be Taken at this Gate, By order of the Trustees of this District of Road, and under the authority of the Act of 4th, Geo. 1th, Cap. 95

For every Horse, Mule, Ass, Ox, or other Beast drawing any Waggon, Wain, Cart, except a Cart upon springs or any Cart drawn by one Horse or two Oxen only or other such Carriage, having the Fellies of the Wheels of less breadth or gauge than four and a half inches from side to side at the Bottoms or Soles thereof, the Sum of _____ 6d

For every Horse, Mule, Ass, Ox, or other Beast drawing any Waggon, Wain, Cart, except any Cart drawn by one Horse or two Oxen only or other such Carriage having the Fellies of the Wheels thereof of the breadth or gauge of four and a half inches and less than six inches, at the bottom or Soles, the Sum of 5d

Tolls displayed on a turnpike near Swindon.

---

2 Who had to pay most to use this turnpike (Source 7)?

3 Why do you think they had to pay more?

SOURCE 8

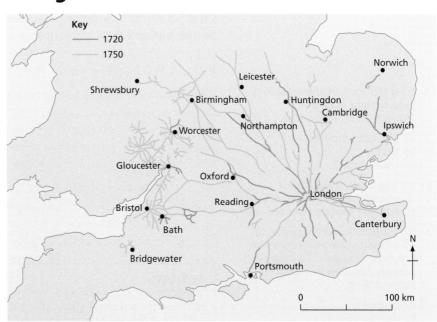

At each end of the turnpikes were toll gates. The tolls varied according to what goods you were carrying. Money from the tolls was supposed to be spent on the upkeep of the road. This eighteenth-century toll house stands at the Ironbridge Museum in Shropshire.

SOURCE 9

Key
— 1720
— 1750

Norwich
Leicester
Shrewsbury
Birmingham · Huntingdon
Cambridge
Worcester · Northampton
Ipswich
Gloucester
Oxford
London
Reading
Bristol
Canterbury
Bath
N
Bridgewater
Portsmouth

0   100 km

The growth of turnpike roads in the first half of the eighteenth century.

---

4 Which of the different measures taken to improve the roads was the most significant in your opinion? Explain your answer.

Why had there not been more improvement?

The turnpikes seemed like a good idea to Defoe (Source 6). They may seem like a good idea to you. However, one must put the growth of turnpikes into perspective. There may have been 3,400 miles of turnpike road but that was a tiny proportion (just three per cent) of Britain's 100,000 miles of roads.

What's more, the growth of the turnpike network was haphazard and slow. On average only 40 new miles of turnpike road were built each year between 1663 and 1750. And these were usually short stretches of road, so travelling long distances tended to involve a large number of tolls. The turnpikes were also disconnected from each other; as soon as you left the turnpike you could easily find yourself on the kind of roads described in Source 10.

Anyone wanting to set up a turnpike faced an uphill struggle:

- Setting up a turnpike was a lengthy and expensive business. You had to get an Act of Parliament. You had to raise a lot of money, and recruit skilled surveyors and workers.
- There was also much opposition to turnpikes. Travellers who had formerly used the roads for free objected to having to pay for the privilege. There were anti-turnpike riots in Bristol in 1749, and in Leeds in 1753 several people were shot in a protest against turnpike roads, although these were extreme cases.

Finally, there were some turnpikes which actually did very little to improve the roads! Some trusts were corrupt. Members of the trusts misused the money and very little was put into improving the roads. Other incompetent trusts sometimes hired inexperienced surveyors who built low-quality roads. The Acts which set up the turnpikes did not specify that trusts had to use qualified engineers to keep the roads in good repair.

The net result of these problems was that in the mid-eighteenth century Britain had an unreliable road network. It was improving, but only in patches.

SOURCE 10

A On the road from Chorley to Wigan, 1770.

I know not how to describe this infernal road. To look at a map, and perceive that it is a principal one, not only to some towns, but even to whole counties, one would naturally conclude it to be at least decent, but let me most seriously caution all travellers, who may accidentally purpose to travel this terrible county, to avoid it as they would the devil; for a thousand to one they break their necks or their limbs by overthrows or breakings down. They will here meet with ruts which I have actually measured four feet [1.2 metres] down, and floating with mud only from a wet summer; what therefore must it be after winter? The only mending it receives in places is the tumbling in of some loose stones, which serve no other purpose than jolting the carriage in the most intolerable manner.

B On the road from Billericay to Tilbury, 1772.

It is for near twelve miles so narrow that a mouse cannot pass by any carriage… the ruts are of an incredible depth … to add to all the infamous circumstances which concur to plague the traveller, I must not forget eternally meeting with chalk wagons; themselves frequently stuck fast, till a collection of them are in the same situation, and 20 or 30 horses may be tacked to each, to draw them out one by one.

Accounts written by Arthur Young, adviser to the government on agriculture (see Profile on page 31).

1 **How did each of these factors help or hold back the improvement of roads:**

   a) **The government**
   b) **War**
   c) **Local trade?**

2 **Do you trust what Arthur Young says about the roads in Source 10? Explain your answer.**

3 **On page 134 you are going to be writing your own report on Britain's transport. To help you prepare for it make notes summarising**

   a) **problems**
   b) **improvements in road transport.**

ACTIVITY

Write your own short story, set in the eighteenth century, about someone who has a disastrous road journey. Some good things could happen too. Base your story on Sources 1–10.

Why did industrialists prefer water transport?

If at all possible businessmen and merchants sent their goods by river. For bulky items like pig iron, coal or limestone, roads were just not practical. Waterways were much cheaper and more reliable, and not much slower. The cost of transporting one ton of goods from Liverpool to Manchester in 1750 was 12 shillings by river but £2 by road.

Coastal shipping

The most important coastal route was from the north-east of England to London. This was dominated by the coal trade. But thousands of other goods ranging from horse feed to roofing slate were carried by ships all around the coast of Britain. Coalbrookdale's iron goods bound for north-west England actually travelled from Coalbrookdale down the River Severn to Bristol and then by sea round the coast of Wales to Chester, a 300-mile round trip, rather than trying to go overland to Chester, which was just 60 miles away.

SOURCE **11**

Six or eight men, by the help of water carriage, can carry and bring back in the same time the same quantity of goods between London and Edinburgh, as 50 broad-wheeled wagons, attended by 100 men and drawn by 400 horses.

Adam Smith, *The Wealth of Nations*, 1776.

Rivers and navigations

Rivers were essential to Britain's trade. By 1700 most major rivers had been extensively improved. They had been widened or deepened. Low bridges or fords had been removed. Long loops had been straightened out by cuts. To pass around weirs, locks had been built. Such improved rivers were known as 'navigations'.

SOURCE **13**

By... navigable rivers the merchants of Lynn supply about six counties wholly and three counties in part with their goods, especially wine and coal... all heavy goods are brought... by water carriage from London, and other parts, first to the port of Lynn, and then in barges up the Ouse, from the Ouse into the Cam.

Daniel Defoe writing about East Anglia, 1726.

However, even after improvement, many rivers were far from ideal:

- There were still hidden sandbanks or treacherous currents.
- In winter rivers could flood. In summer water levels could fall so that boats had to sail with smaller cargoes or not at all.
- Wind power was unreliable except on the largest rivers, so boats had to be towed by horses. Some landowners refused to allow tow paths on their land.
- Boatmen competed with millers for water. Most mill owners filled their ponds by drawing water from rivers. Boats could be held up for days until the mill owner opened the sluice gates to allow the river level to rise.
- You still needed road transport to get goods to and from the riverside. Sometimes this link journey and the loading and unloading could take as long as the water journey.

4 Explain why the owners of Coalbrookdale chose such a long route for their goods rather than a shorter one.

5 Did river transport solve all the problems of transporting goods? Explain your answer.

SOURCE **12**

Key
— Navigable waterways

The main coastal and river waterways in the eighteenth century.

FOCUS TASK

HOW EFFECTIVE WAS BRITAIN'S TRANSPORT SYSTEM IN THE EARLY EIGHTEENTH CENTURY?

Britain's industry depended on transport in two obvious ways – for raw materials and for transporting finished goods. You have already come across many examples of this in earlier chapters.

You have been asked by a group of industrialists to prepare a report on the state of Britain's transport system in the middle of the eighteenth century. Use the information on pages 129–34 to write your report. You should mention:

- **the problems in road transport.**
- **the problems in water transport.**
- **improvements which have been made in each type of transport.**
- **whether these improvements are adequate to serve Britain's growing industries.**

You can add drawings or diagrams if you think it will help.

SOURCE 14

It seems to me that the men who thought up the idea of the navigation had no idea how much trade was likely to be carried on the rivers. Their plan was on too small a scale. The water is not deep enough and several of the lock gates have been laid too high... The designers were not aware that millers like to draw [water for] their ponds. The navigation has always been under difficulties for these reasons.

John Smeaton, engineer, writing in 1771 about the rivers Aire and Calder 70 years after their improvement.

SOURCE 15

By reasons of frequent and long stoppages in the said rivers, Aire and Calder, the passage of wares, merchandise, wool, corn, coal and other goods is delayed. Many embezzlements occur which are chiefly attributed to the vessels being detained so long in their passage.

A complaint about security on the rivers Aire and Calder in around 1770.

Canals

In the south-west the business community provided the first glimpse of the answer to this problem. In 1698 the city of Exeter agreed to pay the huge sum of between £5,000 and £6,000 for the building of a canal that would allow sea-going ships to dock in the city itself. The canal was completed in 1701 and its effect on Exeter's trade was dramatic. However, the cost and the technical problems made others cautious about following Exeter's example. The cost of the Exeter canal was way beyond what any individual businessman would risk, and the technical problems were very great. By the middle of the century the Exeter canal was badly silted up and traffic was declining.

ACTIVITY

This chart shows various transport needs which you have come across in previous chapters. Copy and complete the table showing the best form of transport for each item and the reason you have chosen it. You will need to use Sources 9 and 12 and your wider knowledge.

Item	From	To	Purpose	Suggested transport	Reason for choosing it
Coal	Newcastle	London	Domestic heating		
Iron ore	Shropshire countryside	Coalbrookdale	Making iron		
Bricks	Nottingham	Sheffield	Building		
China clay	Cornwall	Stoke	Making pottery		
Pottery goods	Stoke	Birmingham	Domestic use		
Raw cotton	Liverpool	Manchester	Spinning		
Woollen fleeces	Yorkshire countryside	Leeds	Spinning		
Slate	Wales	Bristol	Roofing for houses		
Passenger	Edinburgh	Glasgow	On a tour of Britain		
Letters	Exeter	London	Company reporting to investors		
Linen	Belfast	Liverpool	Export to Europe		

How was road transport improved?

The years 1750–1770 were the period of most rapid increase in turnpike mileage. An average of 580 miles of turnpike road were added each year, as you can see from Source 16.

SOURCE 16

1663

NO TURNPIKES

1750

1770

1836

143 ROADS 3,400 MILES

500 ROADS 15,000 MILES

1000 ROADS 22,000 MILES

The turnpike boom.

There were many reasons for this boom.

Turnpikes had increasing support from the government. For example, in 1753 Parliament passed an Act requiring wide wheels on wagons specifically to protect the turnpike roads from damage caused by narrow, iron-rimmed wheels.

Industrialists increasingly supported the setting up of turnpikes. In the areas surrounding Stoke-on-Trent the pottery manufacturer Josiah Wedgwood eagerly supported the development of a network of turnpike roads. Using the turnpikes he set up the first team of travelling salesmen to sell his pottery goods from town to town. As a wealthy manufacturer, he had the money and the influence to give others the confidence to invest in trusts. We see a similar picture in Shropshire, where the Darbys and John Wilkinson became trustees in turnpikes. In Cheshire, Lancashire and Yorkshire textile merchants were only too glad to see turnpike roads replace the wretched packhorse trails for their growing trade. You can see how the support of important men like these was important in getting the trusts set up. These men gained directly from better transport and the cost to them was limited. Most turnpikes paid for themselves from tolls.

The technology of road building improved, which led to increased transport, which led to more turnpikes, which led to further improvements… and so on.

Three road builders

Early turnpikes had not always been well built. As the network grew, different techniques of road building were tried out. Professional road builders and surveyors became respected individuals.

Thomas Telford

Telford is one of history's greatest civil engineers and was a widely admired and respected figure in his day. He built over 1,000 miles of road although road building was only one of his accomplishments.

His roads were famed for their quality. His methods differed from Metcalf's and McAdam's in that he used a deeper layer of hard stones on a basis of heavy, tapered foundation stones. There was a thin surface of gravel.

Probably his greatest achievement was the London to Holyhead road, the main route to Ireland. The road took a total of 11 years to complete and included the spectacular Menai Suspension Bridge which still carries local traffic today.

Telford also built two canals, and 1,000 bridges as well as lighthouses, harbours and docks. He built roads in Shropshire for the iron industry in the 1780s. He brought many of Scotland's roads up to standard between 1802 and 1815.

SOURCE 17

Telford's Menai Suspension Bridge, opened in 1826. The story is told that when the middle section of the bridge was raised into place, Telford could not bear to watch.

SOURCE 18

If the hill be cut away, it is walled a few feet up, and then sloped and the slope turfed; if there be no slope a shelf must be left, so that no rubbish may come down upon the road, and on the hillside back drains are cut out... The road is made as nearly perfect as possible. After the foundation has been laid, the workmen are told to throw out every stone that is bigger than a hen's egg.

Robert Southey, a famous poet and a friend of Telford.

John Metcalf

Born in 1717, John Metcalf was a road builder from 1755 until his retirement in 1792. Known as 'Blind Jack of Knaresboro' because he had lost his sight through smallpox at the age of six, he built over 180 miles of road. Much of this was in the difficult Pennine countryside of Lancashire and Yorkshire.

Metcalf brought a careful, well-planned approach to road building, as well as uncanny instincts. One story tells of him feeling the presence of an old Roman road many feet underground.

Metcalf built temporary housing for his workers near the site of the road and set up stables and stores of stone. He believed that foundations were vital, and built up his roads in layers. On boggy ground he laid down heather as a first layer. He gave his roads a convex surface, topped with a thick layer of gravel and drainage ditches alongside.

John Loudon McAdam

John McAdam was a Scot, although most of his roads were built in the south and west of England. While he admired Telford's thoroughness, he did not believe that all of Telford's measures were necessary. He felt that if the soil was dry to begin with, then a firm foundation with stone chippings to make the surface watertight would be perfectly adequate. McAdam insisted on the importance of a camber or slope and a drain to allow water to run off the road.

McAdam was more an improver of roads than a builder. He also saw the need to reduce the number of trusts and to produce larger single stretches of road. More than 30 different trusts sought out his advice and he was responsible for many thousands of miles of 'macadamised' road. Because his methods were cheap as well as effective, most trusts adopted McAdam's roads. In recognition of his contribution Parliament granted him £10,000 in 1825.

The merits of the roads built by Telford and McAdam have been hotly debated ever since. It was because McAdam's were cheaper that his method was eventually adopted widely. He gave his name to the term 'tarmac' or 'macadamised', used by the road builders of today.

SOURCE 19

It is in reality to Mr McAdam that we owe it all. The roads in England, within a few years, have been remodelled upon principles of Roman science. From mere beds of rivers and systems of ruts, they have been improved universally to the condition and appearance of gravel walks in private parks.

Thomas de Quincey, nineteenth-century author.

ACTIVITY

SOURCE 20

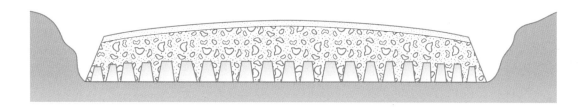

A

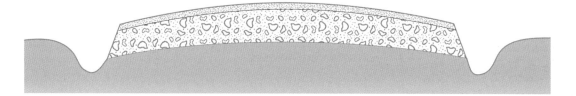

B

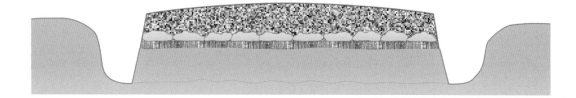

C

Three methods of road building.

1   Look at Source 20. Use the information about each individual to decide which of illustrations A, B and C shows

   a) Telford's
   b) Metcalf's
   c) McAdam's

   technique.

2   On your own copy of Source 20 add notes to explain the features of each method.

3   Whose contribution to road building was most important – Metcalf's, Telford's or McAdam's? Explain your view.

4   Write a profile of your chosen road builder.

What were the effects of the improved roads?

The new roads had a huge impact on Britain.

A national network

In 1750 the network of turnpike roads had been patchy. By 1770 there was something approaching a national network. The quality of the roads was still variable and the number of tollgates quite daunting (the London to Edinburgh stagecoach had to pay at over 200 tollgates) but the new roads gradually strengthened links between cities that had previously seen little communication with each other. The journey time from London to Edinburgh was halved between 1750 and 1780.

Equally importantly, the turnpikes gradually linked together to form local networks, although the vast majority of local roads were never developed as turnpikes.

Haulage businesses

This network of roads created new businesses. The Pickford family opened their road haulage business and became a large company offering long-distance haulage all over the country. The company survives to this day, specialising in removals. The local networks of turnpikes helped create many smaller-scale transport businesses. In 1832 in Leeds there were 163 haulage carriers but only 32 of these carried goods long distances. By 1835 there were about 14,000 different haulage services operating across the country.

The postal service

As early as 1754 a theatre manager in Bath, John Palmer, had set up a private mail coach service. With the growth of the road network the idea was soon adopted by the Post Office and replaced the mounted post boys who had previously delivered the mail.

SOURCE 21

The Bristol Coach meets the London coaches from Birmingham, Liverpool, Warrington, Lancaster, Chester and Kendal at Coventry; the Worcester Coach at Moreton, and the Gloucester and Oxford Coaches at Cirencester – by which passengers and parcels will be forwarded to the above places, with utmost care and expedition…

Jackson's *Oxford Journal*, August 1772.

SOURCE 22

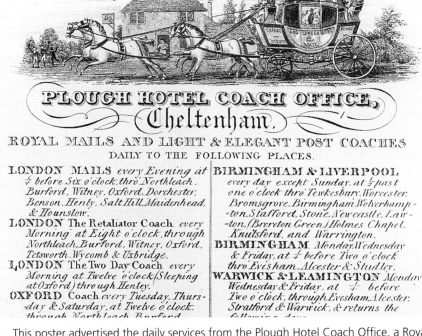

This poster advertised the daily services from the Plough Hotel Coach Office, a Royal Mail coaching house in Cheltenham.

SOURCE 23

Map showing mail coach routes in 1800. These were all on turnpikes.

SOURCE 24

The Devonport mail coach in the 1820s. This advanced coach had iron springs to cushion passengers from the worst of the bumps on the roads.

SOURCE 25

I rode… on a very dangerous outside seat behind, backwards. We were four upon it, and it was too short for much of this number… It was very necessary to keep my eyes open, for the least drowsiness and I should have dropped headlong.

Miss Weeton's journey, 1824.

Passenger transport

Stagecoach travel greatly increased in popularity from the 1780s. There were soon enough turnpike roads built and enough demand for travel to support a large number of companies. By 1835 there were 700 mail-coach routes and over 3,000 ordinary stagecoach routes. This period became known as the Golden Age of coaching. There was fierce competition between the coach-operating companies who offered improved comfort and increased speed.

As the roads began to improve, so did the design of the coaches. The original coaches were simply boxes suspended on leather straps, but later versions had wrought-iron springs which protected passengers from the worst of the bumps in the road. Even so, a coach trip could still be a hair-raising experience.

Increased speed

Stagecoach companies began to compete for passengers on the major routes, particularly to and from London. Speed was a greater selling point than comfort. Good drivers became minor celebrities. The new mail coaches were the fastest coaches of all. To protect the coach from highwaymen each mail coach had armed guards who had strict instructions not to let the coach stop except at official stages. Mail coaches did not pay the tolls and the guard was provided with a horn to warn the tollkeeper to open the turnpike and allow the mail through. Not surprisingly, coach companies competed with each other to operate a mail service.

The coach companies also competed on price. However, coach travel was never cheap, which ever company you chose. As well as the fare, passengers tipped the driver and guard. On long trips food and lodging at the coaching inns had to be paid for. So coach travel was only ever for the wealthy. It was too time-consuming and expensive for the great majority of the population.

SOURCE 26

A cartoon by Rowlandson about the hazards of coach travel.

ACTIVITY

The author of Source 25 has just got off the coach and you have met her at the stage. Convince her of the merits of road travel. You could either role-play this in pairs or write down your arguments. Include details from the sources and text on pages 135–39 in your arguments.

Benefits to industry

For heavy industries such as coal and iron the new roads were a lot less significant than the growth of canals which was taking place at the same time (see page 134). Even so, there was a benefit. On better roads larger carts could carry greater loads with fewer horses (see Source 27). So where the roads were the only option, for example when unloading a river barge and transporting the goods to their final destination, turnpikes made such local transport both quicker and more reliable.

For farmers fresh food was easier to transport to the major markets, particularly London. The turnpikes also made it easier for farmers to introduce the new methods you studied in Chapter 3 as the roads gave them better access to lime and manure. For lighter industries such as textiles the turnpikes were much more valuable. The journey from the cotton city Manchester to the cotton port Liverpool took just three hours by road (as against 36 hours by river). There were 22 regular passenger coach services every day between the two cities. The road was always busy with carts and wagons, although as a result it was often in a bad state of repair.

SOURCE **27**

One person took 180 kg

One person took 1–2 tonnes

Two people took 50 tonnes

Changes in the transport industry.

SOURCE **28**

[In 1778] The heavy goods passing through Leicester for London and the South, and on the great northern routes to Leeds and Manchester, did not require more than about one wagon a day each way… one weekly wagon to and fro served Coventry, Warwick, Birmingham and so on to Bristol and the West of England.

[In 1828] At present there are two wagons, two vans and two fly boats daily to London, the same number not only extend the connection to Leeds and Manchester, but by means of canal to the ports of Liverpool and Hull. There are at least six weekly wagons to Birmingham.

A man from Leicester describes road transport in the city.

ACTIVITY

Design a poster advertising one of the services mentioned on pages 138–40. Think about:

- **what kind of person would use the service.**
- **how you could make the service appeal to that kind of person.**

FOCUS TASK

WHY DID ROAD TRANSPORT IMPROVE BETWEEN 1750 AND 1840?

Many different factors are responsible for an improvement as wide-ranging as that described above.

1. **Work with a partner to list all the different factors which made the improvements to the road system possible. Think about: the work of individuals; technology; government actions. Make as long a list of factors as possible. Use these to compile a class list.**

2. **On your own choose two or three of these factors which you think are particularly important and write a paragraph to explain why you have chosen each one.**

How did canals improve water transport?

While the turnpikes were transforming road transport, canals were doing the same for water transport. The story of the canal revolution begins in the north-west of England.

The Sankey Brook Canal

In the 1750s Liverpool could not get enough coal for domestic and industrial use. The price of coal was rising and discouraging industry. The council of Liverpool commissioned the engineer Henry Berry to develop the Sankey Brook into a canal. The work lasted from 1754 to 1757. Like the Exeter canal (see page 134) it was a long and expensive venture but its effect on Liverpool's industry was remarkable. The price of coal fell and a range of heavy goods, particularly stone for building, became easily available.

The Bridgewater Canal

At the same time as the Liverpool council was investing in the Sankey Brook Canal a rich landowner, the Duke of Bridgewater, was hatching plans for a canal of his own to supply coal to the growing town of Manchester. The Bridgewater Canal was a much bigger project than either the Exeter or Sankey Brook canals. Many regard it as the first really major canal so it is worth investigating its story in detail.

Origins

The story goes that the Duke of Bridgewater was devastated by an unhappy love affair. In order to forget his troubles he threw himself wholeheartedly into his business interests. Like Liverpool, the growing town of Manchester suffered from high coal prices in the 1750s. The Duke owned coal mines with plenty of coal less than 10 miles away, but the high cost of transport made his coal expensive in Manchester. He was granted permission by Parliament to build a canal to transport the coal.

Building the canal

The canal was only six miles long, but the canal builders had to overcome various problems. It took two years to build and cost the Duke £200,000.

Water supply
The first problem was water for the canal. This was solved by the Duke's estate manager, John Gilbert. He pointed out that by digging a sough (an outlet channel) from the Duke's mines at Worsley he would not only supply the canal with water but also drain the mine. In the end the completed canal actually went directly into the mine, making transporting the coal even easier.

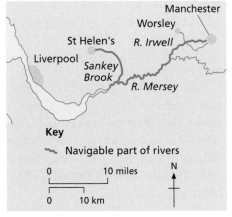

Key

〰️ Navigable part of rivers

0 ——— 10 miles

0 ——— 10 km

N ↑

Crossing the Irwell
Brindley and the Duke were determined that the canal would run on the same level for its full distance and would not require the building of locks. The problem was that the canal had to cross the River Irwell. The solution to the problem was the Barton Aqueduct. It was breathtakingly ambitious and stories say that Brindley could not look when the aqueduct first opened. Observers were impressed with the canal generally, but as a feat of engineering the Barton Aqueduct left them in awe.

Making the canal waterproof
The next problem was keeping the water in the canal – leaks and soaking into the soil made it difficult to keep the level high. This was solved by James Brindley, the engineer taken on to build the canal. Brindley used puddled clay (clay mixed with water) to line the canal and seal it effectively.

SOURCE 29

At Barton Bridge Brindley has erected a navigable canal in the air; for it is as high as the top of trees. Whilst I was surveying it with a mixture of wonder and delight, four barges passed me in a matter of three minutes, two of them chained together, and dragged by two horses, who went on the terrace of the canal, whereon, I durst hardly venture to walk as I almost trembled to behold the large River Irwell beneath me.

The Annual Register, 1763.

1 **In what ways was the Bridgewater Canal a breakthrough for canal building?**

2 **Explain why the writer of Source 29 is so impressed.**

PROFILE

James Brindley

★ Born 1716 at Thronsett near Chapel-en-le-Frith.
★ As a young man he was apprenticed to a millwright.
★ Soon showed a talent for engineering. In 1752 he developed a water-powered engine for draining a coal mine.
★ His plans for a silk mill, along with other successful projects, impressed the Duke of Bridgewater who took him on to build his canal.
★ Brindley was an unorthodox engineer. He never learned to read and write and rarely even used diagrams.
★ When faced with especially difficult problems he retired to bed to think through the problem.
★ He died in 1772, having built 365 miles of canals.

SOURCE 30

The Barton Aqueduct on the Bridgewater Canal.

The impact of the canal

The canal was carrying coal to Manchester by the summer of 1761. The Duke was soon raking in huge profits on his coal. He could now sell it at half the price of his competitors and still make a healthy profit. By 1767 Brindley had extended the canal for him 16 miles in the other direction to link it to the Mersey at Runcorn (see Source 34). This meant that the Duke of Bridgewater now controlled an entirely new water route from Liverpool to Manchester. He could charge tolls for other people to use the canal and he could sell cheap coal in both Liverpool and Manchester, the two fastest-growing towns in the country. The Duke's business gamble had paid off on a grand scale.

However, the more profound impact of the canal was on the way people thought about canals. The whole canal, but the Barton Aqueduct in particular, were spectacular symbols that physical problems which appeared to be insurmountable could be overcome.

The Duke's profits were an equally powerful reminder of the profits that awaited the bold investor. Financing the canal had almost ruined the Duke. Not many individuals could raise £200,000 in the first place, still less risk that huge sum. But the Duke had succeeded and all around the industrial areas, wherever coal was needed, businessmen began to make plans for their own canals.

The creation of a network

Brindley found himself showered with offers of work. By 1772 he was adviser to over ten different canal companies in the north-west, Staffordshire and the Midlands.

Brindley was more than just a canal builder. He understood that canals could only realise their full potential if they were linked to each other. Brindley's vision was of a 'silver cross' of canals which would link the Trent, the Mersey, the Severn and the Thames.

Others shared his vision, notably the pottery entrepreneur Josiah Wedgwood. Wedgwood became chairman of the Grand Trunk Canal Company in 1766 (also known as the Trent and Mersey Canal). His pottery business used massive amounts of raw materials: coal in firing the pottery kilns and coal in making the pottery. He also knew that canals would ensure smoother and safer transport than roads for the delicate pottery goods. With Wedgwood's support and energy the Grand Trunk was finished in 1777. It ran right alongside his own pottery works (see Source 34)!

Other canals followed, supported by other businessmen, such as John Wilkinson (page 106). The Staffordshire and Worcester Canal was completed in 1772. It linked Bristol, Birmingham and Wolverhampton with Liverpool and the north-west. The Thames and Severn Canal was built between 1783 and 1789. When the Oxford Canal was finally completed in 1790 the first stages of the canal network were complete. Barges could travel from the Mersey to the Thames with no need to unload onto land transport.

SOURCE 31

Key

☐ Salt mines

☐ Coalfields

〰 Navigable part of rivers

S Salt refinery

1 First Bridgewater Canal 1764

2 Second Bridgewater Canal 1776

3 Trent and Mersey (Grand Trunk Canal) 1778

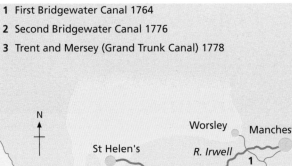

Brindley's first canals served the transport needs of the expanding industries of the north-west and Staffordshire.

SOURCE 32

The present price of carriage of clay and flint for pottery in Staffordshire which is 15 shillings per ton will be reduced by this Grand Trunk Canal to 2 shillings… the carriage and freight of the earthenware in return will be reduced from 28 shillings to about 12 shillings, which must greatly increase the exportation of that manufacture from this port.

Extract from a letter from Wedgwood, August 1765, written while he was in Liverpool.

SOURCE 33

Key

— Navigable rivers

⊥⊥⊥ Canals

⊥⊥⊥ Canals of the 'silver cross'

The canal and river network in the early nineteenth century showing Brindley's silver cross.

SOURCE 34

Josiah Wedgwood's works at Etruria on the banks of the Trent and Mersey Canal in the late eighteenth century.

3 Compare Source 33 with Source 12 on page 133. How will the silver cross help the national network?

4 Explain why Wedgwood was so keen on canals. Refer to Sources 31 and 33 in your answer.

5 Why was it such an advantage to a business to build on the banks of a canal?

Fantastic profits

The canals attracted investors for two main reasons. They wanted an efficient transport system. However, they also wanted to profit directly from the canal.

The Birmingham Canal Company was formed in 1767 and its first shares were sold at £140 each. The investors were largely Midlands businessmen. The canal reached the coal mines of Staffordshire in 1769 and the price of coal in Birmingham fell from 15 shillings to 4 shillings a ton. Midlands industry was kick-started as mine owners increased production and industry (especially the metal trade) gained access to cheap fuel. The canal made huge profits. The original £140 shares were worth £370 in 1782. Ten years later their value was an amazing £1,170. At its peak the Birmingham Canal Company, carried 8.5 million tons of cargo per year.

ACTIVITY

You are chair of a company which wants to build an extension to part of the Birmingham Canal. Use Sources 35–37 and your wider knowledge to write a prospectus. The aim of your prospectus is to encourage investors to buy shares in a new canal.

Crescent Wharf in the centre of Birmingham, early in the nineteenth century.

Parkes' chain works near Dudley. The heavy industry of this area invested heavily in, and depended on, the canals.

The Patent Borax soap works, Birmingham. This company built its own branch of the canal direct to its works.

ACTIVITY

The canals were a popular subject for engravers, as you can see from Sources 34 and 35–37. Choose one of these sources and write a description in the style of Source 29. Think about what would most impress an observer of the time about your picture.

Swap your description with a partner and see if they can work out which picture you have described.

SOURCE **38**

Canals are chiefly used for the following purposes: 1st for conveying the produce of the mines to the sea shore. 2nd conveying fuel and raw materials to some manufacturing towns and districts, and exporting the manufactured goods. 3rd conveying groceries and merchant goods for the consumption of the district through which the canal passes.

Thomas Telford.

1 **Telford (Source 38) has put the uses of canals in what he thinks is their order of importance. Do you agree with him?**

Canal mania!

Profits like those of the Birmingham Canal Company soon attracted other investors. This was just as well. The only way to pay the huge up-front costs of building a canal was by forming a canal company and selling shares to investors. Once the canal was up and running the shareholders received dividends – a share of the profits made by the canal. Forty-two canals were financed in this way between 1791 and 1794. The estimated cost of these 42 canals was £6 million.

The fantastic profits of the early canals had clouded people's business judgement, however. Some of this new round of canals were ill-advised. They were built in rural areas of the south of England, away from areas of industrial development, and with little or no chance of making a profit.

Others, however, increased the reach of the network around Birmingham and the Midlands and promoted the further development of heavy industry. Wherever coal was needed, canals were likely to succeed. It is no surprise therefore that the most enthusiastic investors in canals were usually the owners of collieries and ironworks.

The network grows

Canals continued to be built over the next 40 years.

- The Grand Junction Canal was completed in 1805. It was a more direct link between the Midland network and London. It took barge traffic directly into London, avoiding the Thames.
- The Rochdale and Huddersfield canals carried traffic across the Pennines, but capacity was increased by the mighty Leeds–Liverpool Canal, begun in 1770 and finally completed in 1816.
- In Scotland the Forth–Clyde Canal opened in 1790.
- The north of Scotland was linked by Thomas Telford's Caledonian Canal, built between 1822 and 1840.
- Telford also built the Ellesmere Canal linking the Midlands with north Wales, opened in 1803, and the Birmingham and Liverpool Junction Canal in 1835. In between he found time to complete a survey for the Gotha Canal in Sweden in 1808.

By 1850 Birmingham had more miles of canals than Venice. The canal network as a whole covered over 4,000 miles.

Technical achievements

The building of the canals allowed Britain's great engineers to show their genius. Brindley's early canals had tended to follow contours to avoid locks. This was cheaper but it meant twisting canals and longer journey times.

Brindley's Grand Trunk Canal, on the other hand, had to negotiate rises and falls of 395 feet [120 metres]. The canal contained 75 locks, five aqueducts and five tunnels. The most impressive feature was the Harecastle Tunnel, over one and a half miles long and cut mainly through solid rock.

Nineteenth-century engineers like Smeaton, Rennie and Telford learned from and improved on Brindley's methods. Telford's second and superior Harecastle Tunnel took a fraction of the time to build.

What was the impact of canals?

Canals changed the lives of thousands of people, directly or indirectly, especially those who lived and worked in the towns.

Impact... on towns

Canals brought cheap coal, fresh food, building materials and innumerable other products into the towns. By carrying human refuse out of the town canals provided farmers with a valuable source of manure for their fields.

SOURCE 39

The cottage, instead of being covered with miserable thatch, is now secured with a substantial covering of tiles or slate, brought from the distant hills of Wales or Cumberland. The fields, which before were barren, are now drained, and, by the assistance of manure, conveyed on the canal toll-free, are clothed with a beautiful verdure. Places which rarely knew the use of coal are plentifully supplied with that essential article upon reasonable terms: and what is still of greater public utility, the monopolisers of corn are prevented from exercising their infamous trade.

Thomas Pennant, *A Journey from London to Chester*, 1789.

... on jobs

The canals also created thousands of jobs in their construction. Building the canals required the services of thousands of labourers. They became known as the navigators or NAVVIES (see page 157). These extraordinary men could shift as much as 20 tons of earth in a day with only picks and shovels and wheelbarrows. The canals also needed skilled engineers, bricklayers, masons, carpenters and surveyors, but they could not have been built without the navvies.

Once the canals were built they kept thousands in work. As many as 50,000 people worked on or with the canal boats by the 1840s. As well as boatmen there were wharfmen. They unloaded the cargoes as they arrived and loaded the empty barges.

... on the cost of transporting goods

The cost of transporting goods fell steadily. When the Grand Trunk Canal was opened, freight rates from Manchester to Lichfield fell from four pounds to one pound a ton. Manufacturers could strike deals with hauliers and gain favourable contracts. Many large businesses had their own canal wharves and some operated their own fleets of boats. The Pickford company built special fly boats. These were pulled by two horses, which were changed regularly, and could reach speeds of 10 miles per hour. Some canal boats carried passengers but canals could not really compete with stagecoaches, and the vast majority of their business was in goods.

SOURCE 40

Thomas Coleman loads daily for Liverpool, Manchester and Chester. From Liverpool goods can be shipped to Lancashire and Cumberland ports, Glasgow, Ireland or North Wales. Boats also load for Gainsborough and Hull, for Sheffield, Lincolnshire, the East and West Ridings, Newcastle, Edinburgh and eastern Scotland.

Advertisement in the *Birmingham Gazette*, September 1811.

... on the geography of Britain

Canals created new towns, the most spectacular example being Stourport. When Brindley wanted to take the Grand Trunk Canal through one Shropshire village he was told they did not want his 'stinking ditch'. He thus took the canal to Stourport, turning it into a thriving town.

… on financial services

Since the process of financing canals was extremely important, techniques for raising investments and for managing companies, shares and dividends were developed.

The Oxford Canal paid dividends in the range of 30 per cent a year for a period of 30 years to its investors. In 1825 the 10 most successful canals were paying an average dividend of 27.5 per cent a year. Since profits were so great there was soon a new group of people who were prepared to invest in other transport projects.

… on industry

Historians generally agree that it is hard to overstate the importance of canals to the growth of British industry. Without canals industry would have been stalled because of the shortage of coal. Out of 165 Acts of Parliament passed for canal building up to 1803, 137 served mines or ironworks. As industry mechanised and steam power became all important industry's appetite for coal rose rapidly.

SOURCE 41

In the last analysis… it is inappropriate to judge the contribution of canals to British economic growth in terms of the rewards they yielded to their shareholders. What mattered was that the coal got to the consumers at a reasonable price, that the iron foundries and potteries could reduce costs, that the factory worker could warm his family in winter and still have some money left to buy the products of British industry, and that the bread and cheese eating labourers of southern England could have cooked meals occasionally. In these terms the Canal Age made a massive contribution to the first industrial revolution.

Phyllis Deane, *The First Industrial Revolution*, 1965.

1 Source 41 lists the impact of canals. Rearrange the effects in order of importance to Britain's industrial revolution.

2 Write a paragraph to explain your order.

FOCUS TASK

WHAT FACTORS MADE THE CANAL NETWORK POSSIBLE?

'The key factor in establishing the canal network was the creation of canal companies issuing share certificates. All other factors are secondary.' Do you agree with this statement?
  Explain your answer in paragraphs:

• Why and how shares were important (remember to say what evidence there is)
• Other factors that were important (e.g. labour, market, engineers, industrial growth)
• Finish with a conclusion which explains whether you agree with the statement and why/why not.

FOCUS TASK

HOW DID IMPROVEMENTS IN TRANSPORT HELP INDUSTRY?

Your local newspaper has asked you to write an article about how road and canal transport changed between 1760 and 1840. You must write three sections:

• Key developments
• The importance of those developments to industry
• Local examples which provide evidence to support your views.

You can use the evidence on pages 135–47. You can also use information from your local area if you have it.

6.2 *How did the railway network change Britain?*

Where was the first railway?

There is much debate about which was the first railway. Rails had been in use for a long time before the nineteenth century. Source 2 summarises early developments in railway transport.

SOURCE 1

An early railway on the Northumberland and Durham coalfield, 1773. By the early nineteenth century such railways were common throughout the coal and iron industry. There were 300 miles of track. When the gradient was uphill the horse would pull from the front. When it was downhill it would act as a brake from behind. Here the coal is being taken to the riverside. In the background you can see the river barges being loaded with coal.

SOURCE 2

1604   *First recorded use of wooden tracks – Derbyshire coalfield*

1767   *First use of iron rails – Coalbrookdale ironworks*

1801   *First steam-driven road vehicle – the Puffing Devil, built by Richard Trevithick in Cornwall*

1801   *First railway open to the public – Surrey iron railway*

1804   *First steam-driven railway locomotive – Pen-y-darren in Wales, built by Richard Trevithick. The experiment fails as the engine is too heavy for the rails*

1807   *First passenger railway – Oystermouth, South Wales*

1809   *First use of stationary steam engine to tow wagons – Northumberland*

1813   *First steam locomotive in Northumberland – the Puffing Billy*

1814   *First Stephenson steam locomotive – Killingworth in Northumberland*

1823   *Twenty steam locomotives in use on colliery lines all over Britain*

Developments in railway transport before 1825.

The Stockton and Darlington – the first modern railway!

Any of these early developments could be claimed to be the first railway because it all depends on what you mean by railway. Historians now tend to talk in terms of the 'first modern railway', by which they mean a railway open to the public, using a moving rather than a stationary engine, running on fixed iron rails over a long distance. By these criteria the Stockton and Darlington, built between 1821 and 1825, is often regarded as the first modern railway. You have already investigated this railway on page 118.

- It took paying passengers.
- It carried toll-paying freight.
- It required an Act of Parliament since it crossed many people's land.
- It used steam locomotives.
- It travelled between two towns.
- It was built by the Stephensons, who would go on to build some of the most important new railways of the nineteenth century.

1 **Which of the features of the Stockton and Darlington listed above do you regard as the most important innovations?**

The Liverpool and Manchester: the first inter-city railway!

While the Stockton and Darlington is generally thought of as the first modern railway, the Liverpool and Manchester is usually thought of as the first really major railway – because it linked the two most important cities of the industrial revolution. You are going to explore the building of this railway in detail.

Origins

Liverpool and Manchester were the two main centres of the industrial revolution. They were already connected by the Bridgewater Canal (see page 141), but by the 1820s the two cities were keen to explore alternatives. The canal was slow. Merchants claimed it sometimes took longer for raw cotton to travel from Liverpool to Manchester than from the USA to Liverpool! It was also very expensive. Because the canal was better than the other options available, the tolls charged had risen steadily over the years. The cities had outgrown the canal. Liverpool's trade had doubled in 20 years. The cotton trade between the two cities was doubling every 10 years. Both cities had a growing need for coal, for farm produce, a better and swifter mail and parcel service, and a better passenger service. There was no doubt in the minds of the merchants and industrialists that a railway would help meet all these needs.

Planning the railway

In 1822 merchants and factory owners got together to form a Provisional Committee to plan the railway. In 1824 they formed the Liverpool and Manchester Railway Company and sold £300,000 worth of shares to eager investors.

They were impressed with the work of Stephenson on the Stockton and Darlington line and in 1824, even before Stephenson had completed the Stockton and Darlington Railway, he had started to survey a line for the route between Liverpool and Manchester.

In 1824 they issued a prospectus. This was a weighty document which laid out in detail the reasons for a railway. Source 3 is an extract from this.

1 **Work with a partner. On your own copy of Source 3 underline any words or phrases you do not understand. Use a dictionary to work out the meaning together.**

2 **Some words are used in a different way from how they would be used today. Mark those and discuss how the use of the word differs from today.**

3 **Add subheadings to summarise the main point of each paragraph.**

4 **Divide the points made in the prospectus into**

   a) **positive points about the railway**
   b) **negative points about canals.**

5 **Bearing in mind the nature of this document, should we simply accept all of these points?**

6 **Which do you think is the most powerful argument for the railway?**

7 **For each petitioner explain why they might oppose the railway.**

SOURCE 3

The Committee think it right to state concisely the grounds upon which they rest their claims to public encouragement and support.

The importance to a commercial state, of a safe and cheap mode of transit, for merchandise, from one part of the country to another, will be readily acknowledged. This was the plea upon the first introduction of canals; it was for the public advantage; and although the [canals] interfered with existing and inferior modes, and were opposed to the feelings and prejudices of landholders, the great principle of the public good prevailed, and experience has justified the decision.

It is upon the same principle that rail roads are now proposed, as a means of transport manifestly superior to existing modes… the rail road scheme holds out to the public not only a cheaper but faster conveyance than any yet established…

It will afford a stimulus to the productive industry of the country, [its value] can be fully understood only by those who are aware how seriously commerce may be impeded by petty restrictions, and how commercial enterprise is encouraged and promoted by fair competition and free trade.

The Committee are aware that it will not immediately be understood by the public how the proprietors of a rail road, requiring an invested capital of £400,000, can afford to carry goods [so much cheaper] than the present canal companies. But the problem is easily solved… It is not that the water companies have not been able to carry goods on more reasonable terms, but that, in their monopoly, they have not thought proper to do so. Against the most arbitrary exactions the public have hitherto had no protection, and against the continuance of the evil they have but one security – it is competition that is wanted…

But it is not altogether on account of the exorbitant charges of the water carriers that a rail road is desirable. The present canal establishments are inadequate to the great aim, namely, the regular and punctual conveyance of goods at all periods and seasons. In summer time there is frequently a deficiency of water, obliging boats to go only half loaded, and thus occasioning great inconvenience and delay; while in winter they are sometimes locked up with frosts for weeks together, to the hindrance of business. From these impediments a rail road would be altogether exempt.

There is still another ground of objection to the present system of carriage by canals, namely, the pilferage… for which the privacy of so circuitous and slow a passage affords so many facilities. A conveyance by railway, effected in a few hours, and where every delay must be accounted for, may be expected to possess much of the publicity and consequent safety of the King's highways.

Extract from the prospectus of the Liverpool and Manchester Railway Company, 1824.

Why was the plan rejected?

In 1825 the survey was complete, the money was raised, the costs worked out, and the company put its plan to Parliament. It was rejected!

Looking back from today the advantages of rail transport may be obvious to you, but at the time there was a powerful group of people who feared and opposed the growth of the railway network. They obstructed the survey (see Source 4) and countered the arguments of the Railway Committee (see Source 5). Many also sent petitions to Parliament objecting to the proposed railway including:

- The Earls of Derby and Sefton who owned land which the railway would cross
- The Duke of Bridgewater who owned the Bridgewater Canal
- Many smaller landowners along the proposed line
- The Leeds and Liverpool Canal Company
- Barton Road Turnpike Trustees
- The shareholders in the Bridgewater Canal
- The Mersey and Irwell Navigation Company

PROFILE

George Stephenson

- ★ Born at Wylam near Newcastle in 1781.
- ★ His father looked after the engines at a colliery in the north-east.
- ★ Worked in collieries and rose to become a fireman. Saved his wages to pay for his own education at night school.
- ★ By 1812 he had become the engine wright at Killingworth colliery and in 1814 he built his first steam locomotive.
- ★ In 1815 he invented the Geordie Lamp – a safety device for coal miners (see page 117).
- ★ As well as locomotives he surveyed and built railways on colliery sites.
- ★ In 1821 he was appointed to build the Stockton and Darlington Railway.
- ★ In 1824 he was approached to build the Liverpool and Manchester Railway.
- ★ In the 1830s he built railways all over the north of England and the Midlands.
- ★ He died in 1848.

8 Read Source 5. How does it affect your view of Source 3?

9 Read Source 6. In your own words, explain the attitude of *The Times* towards the argument.

10 Were the supporters and opponents of the railway equally powerful? Explain your answer.

SOURCE 4

We have had a sad work with Lord Derby, Lord Sefton and Bradshaw the canal proprietor, whose ground we go through with the projected railway. Their ground is blockaded on every side to prevent us getting on with the survey. Bradshaw fires guns in the night to prevent the surveyors coming through in the dark. We are to have a field day next week. The Liverpool Railway Company are determined to force a survey through if possible. Lord Sefton says he will have 100 men to stop us. The company thinks those great men have no right to stop our survey. It is the Farmers only who have a right to complain, and charging damages for trespass is all they can do.

A letter from George Stephenson to Edward Pease, 1824.

SOURCE 5

The vessels at present employed upon several canals between Manchester and Liverpool are capable of carrying with ease a much larger quantity of goods every week than has ever been stated by the promoters of the Bill.

Vessels can be loaded and discharged with much greater ease and expedition at the wharves of the carriers, than can be possibly the case from the railway.

The rates charged by the carrier are much overstated by the promoters of the Bill.

From the petition of the Mersey and Irwell Navigation Company.

Turnpike trusts, canal companies, coaching companies and coaching inn landlords certainly had good reason to be concerned. They could all see the railway would harm their businesses if, as it promised to be, the railway was cheaper, quicker and more popular than either the roads or the canals.

Opponents said that Stephenson's survey was flawed, although given the conditions of the survey, this was hardly surprising. They said that he had not really worked out a practical route and that his plans to cross the boggy area of Chat Moss would not work. They also claimed that there would be chaos at the Liverpool end of the line, where it entered a heavily built-up area.

These were genuine concerns; however, some arguments were less plausible. Some people simply objected to the use of steam engines; the dirty, fiery locomotives were contrasted to stately canal boats. Many believed that the human body could not stand the strain of travelling at speed. Opponents claimed that steam locomotives would ruin hunting and scare grazing cattle as they passed; that flying sparks or exploding boilers would burn crops and even farm buildings as they passed; that smoke from the steam engine would harm vegetation and invade the houses of people who lived near the line in Manchester or Liverpool; and that the noise and vibration would cause pregnant women to miscarry.

It is hard to be sure how much of this 'environmental' opposition was genuine and how much was stirred up by landowners who were basically trying to improve the price of their land. The more trouble they stirred up the more likely it was that the railway builders would pay a higher price for their land.

The Times (Source 6) pleaded that the bill be debated rationally, but at that time Parliament was dominated by landowning interests. The cities of Manchester and Liverpool, although they were the fastest-growing cities in the land, did not have one MP to speak for them in Parliament.

It was not difficult for the landowners on page 150 to persuade Parliament to reject the bill.

SOURCE 6

Canals superseded to a large extent the means of transport previously employed: if railroads are found better than canals, the latter must, in their turn, give way. The question, in short, reduces itself to this – can transport be best effected by canals or rail-roads? If by the former, the parties interested in them have nothing to fear from competition – if by the latter, the public must and ought to have the benefit of it.

The Times newspaper, commenting on the proposed railway, 1824.

A second attempt

The company was not going to give in, of course. It submitted a revised plan, adjusting its route so it did not run through the land of the Earls of Sefton and Derby. It left open the question of whether steam locomotives or horses would be used. It proposed a tunnel into Liverpool. It also offered canal owners an opportunity to invest in the railway themselves. It increased the compensation offered to landowners and the following year its revised plans got through Parliament with very little opposition.

Building the railway

The building of the railway was supervised by George Stephenson with the help of his son Robert. The Stephensons were building in the same countryside as Brindley when he built the Bridgewater Canal (see page 141). It is therefore not surprising that some similarly spectacular feats of engineering were needed to get the line through.

Chat Moss

The most serious obstacle was the swampy area known as Chat Moss near Leigh in Lancashire. Stephenson lay awake at night struggling with the problem until, like most great individuals, he hit upon a solution which borrowed from predecessors and added some ideas of his own.

SOURCE 7

No engineer in his senses would go through Chat Moss… The surface of the moss is a skirt of long grass tough enough to enable you to walk upon it, about half a leg deep. In the centre, where the railroad is to cross, it is all pulp from the top to the depth of 34 feet [10.4 metres]; at 34 feet there is a vein of 4 or 6 inches [10 or 15 centimetres] of clay, below that there are 2 or 3 feet [60 centimetres to a metre] of quicksand; and the bottom of that is hard clay, which keeps all the water in.

Francis Giles, giving evidence to Parliament in 1824.

Stephenson solved the problem by floating the track on a 'raft'. He tipped thousands of tons of soil and rubble on to the moss. Then, taking a tip from the road builder John Metcalf, he used wooden hurdles woven with heather to form a raft. The sand and gravel were laid over this, and finally the sleepers and tracks.

SOURCE 8

Navvies laying Stephenson's 'rafts' on the line over Chat Moss.

SOURCE 9

The completed track over Chat Moss.

Sankey Brook

Stephenson had to cross a wide valley at Great Sankey near Warrington. Inspired by Brindley's and Telford's aqueducts he designed the magnificent Sankey Viaduct.

SOURCE 10

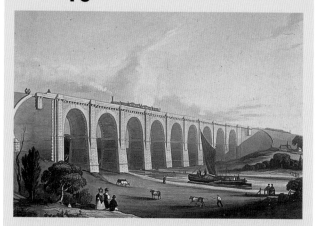

The Sankey Viaduct on the Liverpool and Manchester Railway.

The Edgehill Tunnel

Finally, the railway needed a one and a quarter mile tunnel into Liverpool.

SOURCE 11

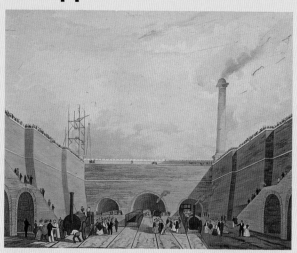

The entrance to the Edgehill Tunnel.

SOURCE 12

The route of the Liverpool and Manchester Railway, showing some of the physical obstacles to be overcome.

Olive Mount

As the railroad approached Liverpool, it faced a huge outcrop of rock known as Olive Mount. As trains come into Lime Street Station today, they still pass through the immense cutting dynamited and smoothed by Stephenson's navvies.

SOURCE 13

A

B

Two views of the Olive Mount cutting on the Liverpool and Manchester line.

1 Use Source 7 to draw a cross-section sketch of Chat Moss.

2 Add Stephenson's solution to the cross-section.

3 The two pictures in Source 13 show the same cutting.

   a) How do they differ?
   b) Why do you think they differ?
   c) Do you think one is more accurate than the other?

4 Compare Sources 9–11 and 13. Which do you think is the greatest achievement and why?

5 Do you think Stephenson would have agreed with you?

1 **Compare the portraits of Robert Owen, James Brindley and George and Robert Stephenson (pages 85, 142, 151 and below). What are the similarities and differences?**

SOURCE 14

The Rocket, designed by George Stephenson and winner of the Rainhill trials.

FACTFILE

Robert Stephenson

★ Born at Willington Quay near Newcastle, 1803, only son of George Stephenson.
★ Apprenticed as a coalviewer at Killingworth.
★ In 1822 his father sent him to Edinburgh University for six months to study engineering.
★ In 1823 helped his father survey the Stockton and Darlington Railway.
★ Spent three years building railways in South America.
★ He built the Britannia Bridge (see page 157) and many other bridges in the UK and abroad.
★ Became an MP in 1847.
★ Died in 1859 and was buried in Westminster Abbey.

The Rainhill trials

The company was persuaded by George Stephenson that they should use steam locomotives. The question now was, which locomotive? The company announced a competition to build a suitable locomotive, and all the entrants were called to a grand trial at Rainhill in October 1829.

A crowd of more than 10,000 turned out to watch as the engines had to make 20 timed runs of almost two miles pulling three tons for every ton of their own weight.

Four locomotives entered:

- Brandreth's Cyclopede, a heavy lumbering giant of a machine that blew up early in the trials.
- The Novelty by Braithwaite and Ericsson – which was lightweight and fast and quickly became the crowd's favourite.
- The Sanspareil ('without equal'), built by Timothy Hackworth, one of the Stephensons' rivals as engine builders in the north-east.
- The Stephensons' Rocket, built at Robert Stephenson's engineering works in Newcastle.

After some early competition from the Novelty, the Rocket eventually came through, covering the course in six and a half hours, including stops. The prize was £500, but more important for the Stephensons was that it established them as the premier engine builders as the railway boom began.

The impact of the railway

Trials and exhibition rides took place through 1830 leading to the grand official opening on 15 September 1830. Despite the fact that William Huskisson, President of the Board of Trade, and a guest of honour at the opening, was killed by a passing locomotive as he stepped onto the track, the railway received a rapturous reception.

SOURCE 15

Betley Hall, 20th June, 1830
My dear Lord
David Hodgson, my Quaker friend, was at the trial of the Liverpool Manchester Rail Road and went at the rate of 27 miles an hour, faster than human beings ever before moved upon the face of the earth. He describes the motion as perfectly easy, so much so that you could almost read or write. London will ere long be connected with Dublin thro' Liverpool, Edinburgh and Glasgow – Carlisle, Lancaster, Preston and Manchester, Birmingham and so on. This great line, which I call the backbone of England, will help the whole length of Staffordshire – if we are not ninnies enough by obstacles to throw it in some other direction. [Owning] property close to such a line of communication must have unknown advantages. You are 10 years younger than I am and may live to see all this put in action.

George Tollet, a businessman of Betley in Staffordshire writing to Lord Stafford.

SOURCE 16

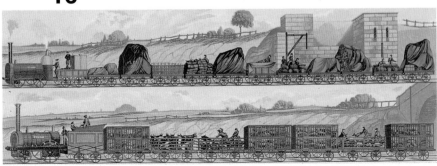

Goods being carried on the Liverpool and Manchester line in the 1830s.

2 What does Tollet (Source 15) mean by the 'backbone of England'?

3 How can you tell he was impressed by railways?

4 Look at Source 16. What is being carried?

5 Use Sources 15–19 to list all the different changes brought about by the building of the Liverpool and Manchester Railway.

6 Which of the changes in your list do you think would be most significant?

SOURCE 17

All the coaches bar one have ceased running. The mail all travels by the railway, at a saving of two thirds the expense. The locomotives travel in safety after dark. The canals have reduced their rates 30%. The saving to manufacturers in Manchester in the transporting of cotton alone has been £20,000 per year. The railway pays between 3000 and 4000 pounds per year in local rates. Coal pits have been sunk and factories established on the line, giving great employment to the poor. Transport of milk and garden produce is easier. Residents along the line can use the railway to attend their business in Manchester and Liverpool with ease and little expense. The value of land on the line has gone up because of the railway. It is much sought after for building.

The *Annual Register*, 1832, describing the impact of the Liverpool and Manchester Railway.

SOURCE 18

	Coach	Rail	Canal
Passengers			
Passengers per day	688	1070	
Fares	10s/5s	5s/3s 6d	
Journey time	4 hours	1 ¾ hours	
Goods			
Cost of goods per ton		10s	15s
Time taken		2 hours	20 hours

The *Annual Register's* comparison of rail, coach and canal transport in 1832.

SOURCE 19

Parliamentary reform must follow soon after the opening of this railway. A million persons will pass over it in the course of this year, and see the hitherto unseen village of Newton; and they must be convinced of the absurdity of it sending two members to Parliament, whilst Manchester sends none.

A traveller writing about the opening of the Liverpool and Manchester line in 1830. Parliamentary reform did indeed follow two years later.

FOCUS TASK

THE LIVERPOOL AND MANCHESTER RAILWAY

Having looked in depth at the Liverpool and Manchester Railway you are now going to try to consider it through the eyes of people at the time. Choose one of the characters below and write two diary entries which they might have written:

a) during the planning or building of the railway; and

b) in 1832, two years after the opening of the Liverpool and Manchester Railway.

CHARACTERS

- **Mr Gladstone**
A Liverpool merchant who imports cotton to sell to factories in Manchester.

- **Lord Sefton**
A landowner on the route of the line.

- **John Williams**
Owner of a general store in Manchester selling mainly hardware and food.

- **Millie Gardner**
A working-class woman in Liverpool. Her husband is a casual labourer on Liverpool docks. She looks after their three children and earns extra money by taking in washing and ironing.

Before you write your diary entries think about how your character might have been affected by the various stages of the planning and building of the railway.

- Would they have been interested in the initial arguments about the building of the railway?
- Would they have been affected by the process of building the railway?
- How might the railway have affected their lives once it was fully operational?

The railway boom

The Liverpool and Manchester Railway was an impressive technical achievement. Its profits were equally impressive. Just as the Bridgewater Canal had attracted many businessmen to invest in canals in the 1760s, so the Liverpool and Manchester attracted many to railways. There was a rush to invest in the 1830s, followed by an even greater boom in the 1840s.

In 1838 Liverpool, Manchester and London were linked when the Grand Junction Railway reached the Liverpool and Manchester. The Birmingham to London line opened the same year. London was linked with the port of Southampton in 1840 and Brunel's Great Western joined Bristol and London in 1841. Queen Victoria pronounced herself a devotee of railway travel after her first trip in 1842. In the early 1840s London also gained links to Brighton and to France through Dover. The Great Northern linked London to Doncaster, and the Midland linked Manchester to Leeds. By 1852 £300 million had been invested in the railways. The main frame of the national network was complete with over 8,000 miles of track.

> **1** Using only the information in Sources 20 and 21, explain what is meant by the term 'railway boom'.

SOURCE 20

Britain's railway network in 1852. After this time many more miles of track were laid. These were mainly branch lines, connecting lines or additional tracks on existing lines.

SOURCE 21

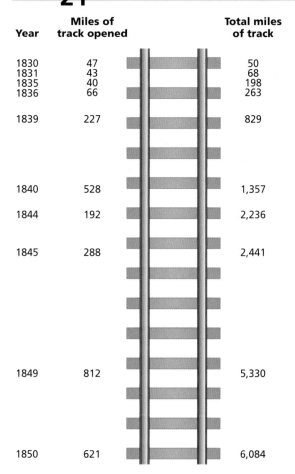

Year	Miles of track opened	Total miles of track
1830	47	50
1831	43	68
1835	40	198
1836	66	263
1839	227	829
1840	528	1,357
1844	192	2,236
1845	288	2,441
1849	812	5,330
1850	621	6,084

Miles of railway track opened, 1830–1850.

The engineers

Each new railway needed a skilled engineer. Following the success of the Liverpool and Manchester the Stephensons were much in demand. They built the London to Birmingham route and later the London to Holyhead. Over the Menai Straits, Robert Stephenson built the Britannia Railway Bridge (see Source 22). The bridge continues to carry today's much faster and heavier trains.

The other key figure of the 1830s and 1840s was Isambard Kingdom Brunel. Brunel built the Great Western line, including the equally impressive Saltash Bridge over the Tamar near Plymouth. It was 300 yards (274 metres) long, and had to be high enough to allow the tall masted ships to pass underneath.

You will find out more about the influence and rivalry of these two great railway builders on page 162.

SOURCE 22

A

B

C
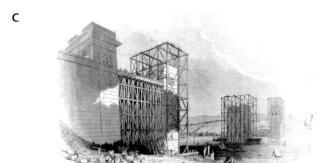

D
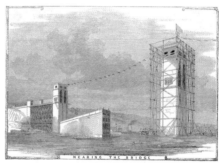

NEARING THE BRIDGE

The stages of building the Britannia Bridge.

You will find out more about the influence and rivalry of these two great railway builders on page 162.

ACTIVITY

Match these captions to the four stages of building the Britannia Bridge in Source 22.

a) The basic frame of the bridge
b) Building the metal tubes which would carry the trains
c) Floating the tubes out on to the river to be hauled into place
d) The finished bridge

The navvies

However spectacular they appear, these engineering achievements represented only a tiny part of the effort of building the railways. By far the greatest part of the work in building railways was simply moving earth and stone. This was the work of the navvies. Where the track met rising ground the navvies dug cuttings – by hand. Where the ground sank they built it up with embankments – by hand. Where the line met solid rock they dug tunnels – by hand.

SOURCE 23

The tunnel is nearly two miles long and is ventilated by six shafts. It contains over 30 million bricks and cost 100 lives. For two and a half years, the tunnel required a ton of gunpowder and a ton of candles every week.

Brunel's son describes the work on the Box Tunnel on the London to Bristol line.

The name 'navvy' comes from navigator. The navvy had first appeared in the improving of waterways or navigations. They had been the powerhouse behind the building of canals. The railway builders found in the navvies a tough, skilled and ready workforce.

Navvies worked in gangs and each gang developed a tremendous bond of loyalty. They were more highly paid than ordinary labourers but they also faced much greater risks. Accidents and deaths were common, especially on dangerous projects like tunnels which involved blasting (see Source 23).

Many navvies were migrant workers from Ireland or Scotland. Others were local men. The migrant navvies lived on the edge of society. As they travelled they built their own shanty towns and their womenfolk and families travelled with them. To some in Victorian society they appeared as terrifying savages. There is much evidence that when navvies were in an area there was crime and trouble. In one alarming incident the small town of Penrith in Cumbria was the centre of a huge disturbance. Around 2,000 navvies, roughly equal numbers of Scots, English and Irish, were working on the Lancaster to Carlisle line in 1842. This created a tense rivalry which exploded into violent riots lasting over two days. The disturbances were so serious that the local militia had to be called out.

SOURCE 24

Navvies building a cutting at Tring on the London to Birmingham line, 1837.

1 **What does Source 25 tell us about the navvies?**

2 **Are Sources 23–25 more useful to a historian taken together than separately? Explain your answer.**

3 **'The great engineers received the credit, but the real heroes of the Railway Age were the navvies.' Do you agree?**

SOURCE 25

The canals and the bridges,
The embankments and cuts,
They blasted and dug with
Their sweat and guts.
They never drank water
But whiskey by pints,
And the shanty towns rang
With their songs and their fights.

CHORUS:
Navigator, navigator, rise up and be strong,
The morning is here, and there is work to be done.
Take your pride and your shovel and the old dynamite,
For to shift a few tons of this earth we delight.

They died in their hundreds
With no signs about where,
Save the brass in the pockets
Of the entrepreneur.
By landslide and rock blast
They got buried so deep,
That in death if not life
They'll have peace while they sleep.

CHORUS (repeat)
Their mark on this land
Made with barrow and spade,
A way for a commerce
Where vast fortunes were made.
The supply of an empire
Where the sun never sets,
Which is now deep in darkness
But the railway's there yet.

A folk song about the navvies.

Did opposition to the railways disappear?

The growth of the railways did not go unchecked. The Liverpool and Manchester Railway had also set a pattern of protest against them. There were five main groups who tended to oppose the development of the railways:

1. Landowners

Railway Acts could force landowners to sell land, even if they did not wish to. In a country where property was seen as almost sacred, many viewed this as a deeply disturbing development.

On the other hand, many landowners protested against the railway simply to bump up the price of their land. The London to Birmingham line cost £6,300 per mile. One landowner on this line received £30,000 for a small strip of land – more than his whole estate was worth. What was more, he gained a similar deal for a different strip soon after with a rival company! The Duke of Bedford was so ashamed of the artificially inflated price he had been paid for his land that he returned £150,000 of it to the railway company.

2. Canal investors

The canals had been the success story of the previous generation. Many people still had massive amounts of money tied up in the canals and stood to lose badly. The Liverpool and Manchester Railway had forced the Bridgewater Canal to cut its tolls by one-third, yet the canal still lost traffic. Other canal owners faced similar problems, as you can see from Source 27.

There was some dirty competition between the railway companies and canal companies. Canal owners pulled strings to prevent railways being built. Railway companies would buy one stretch of canal and either close it or charge exorbitant tolls, having the effect of ruining the rest of the canal. The best solution would have been a co-operative approach, but that was not in the spirit of the Victorian period.

SOURCE 26

The following case… is submitted by him to Members Of Parliament, with an appeal to them as landowners and Gentlemen not to allow so cruel an invasion of property… The railway would totally destroy the view from the mansion, would cut up and ruin the most beautiful part of the park, and would render the place comparatively worthless as a residence!…

The present railway is not the least wanted: it would pass through a purely agricultural district, which is already approached by the main lines… The project has entirely originated with speculators, for their own individual gain; very few, if any, of the landowners or residents on the proposed line being proprietors.

Sir Charles Wolseley of Wolseley Hall, Staffordshire, opposes the Stafford and Rugby Railway Bill, 1841.

> **4 Do you think that Sir Charles Wolseley (Source 26) is a genuine protester or simply trying to raise the price of his land? Explain your answer with reference to the source.**

SOURCE 27

… it is proposed to convert the Ellesmere and Chester Canal into a railway… if it be stopped up and converted into a railway under the management… of the London and Birmingham and Grand Junction Railway Companies, a monopoly in railway traffic will be created, and competition destroyed…

Works have been established on the banks of the canal… and no railway can be built which will afford equal accommodation to the coal and iron trade…

Traders not being permitted the uninterrupted use of the Railroad at all times, innumerable obstacles may be thrown in their way; whereas the boats navigating the canals being their property… no such obstacles can arise. The railway companies, being carriers themselves, have furthermore a direct interest in keeping other carriers off the line.

An expenditure to a very considerable amount has been made by the coal and iron masters… for more conveniently carrying on their trade by means of water communication, which will be entirely useless if the canals be stopped up.

A public statement by the Staffordshire coal and iron masters against railway developments, 1846. Rather like a modern press release, this statement was intended to be printed widely in all the newspapers.

3. Farmers

Some farmers stood to benefit greatly from the new railways. Others lost out. Farmers near to growing cities complained that railways brought them into competition with other farmers further away. Before the railways fresh food could not be transported great distances. This meant that any town or city had to get its food from local farmers. Railways meant that cities like London could gain daily access to livestock and other produce from all over the country.

4. Moralists

Some opposed the railways on moral grounds.

The Duke of Wellington was uneasy about the possible impact of allowing the masses to travel. If people could travel far they would come into contact with 'corrupting influences'.

Oxford University and Eton College forbade railways to come near because they might bring the corrupting influence to them. The towns of Northampton and Stafford both turned down the opportunity to become railway centres for similar reasons.

The navvies who built the railways were famous for being coarse and hard-living. Some people feared the effect the navvies could have on the morals of people in their locality.

5. Environmentalists

The popular magazine *John Bull* led an environmental campaign saying that railways ruined the beauty of the countryside and that embankments would destroy drainage and water tables. However, in the nineteenth century environmental issues did not inspire anything like as much interest as they do today.

1 **Which of the five groups do you think would be most active in protesting against a new railway today?**

2 **Do you think the opponents of the railways were simply motivated by self-interest? Support your answer with evidence from pages 150–60.**

Who provided the money?

Building a railway was a very expensive venture. Yet there was no shortage of people queuing up to invest. Britain was extremely prosperous in this period. Many small investors had money which before this time would have been saved for a rainy day. People were aware how many investors had got rich through the canal boom. They did not want to be left behind. The potential profits from railway investment encouraged people to invest and even to speculate.

What's more, the canal boom had created a whole new area of expertise in financing such major projects which would now be turned to financing the railway network.

SOURCE **28**

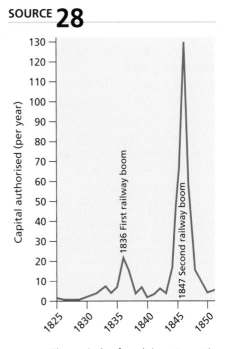

The periods of peak investment in railways.

SOURCE **29**

A cartoon from 1845 entitled *The Railway Juggernaut*. People are worshipping the locomotive which is labelled 'Speculation'.

3 Explain the message of Source 29 in your own words.

4 Is railway mania an accurate term for the developments in this period? Refer to Sources 28–30 in your answer.

SOURCE **30**

The gambling on railways was as common outside London as in the capital. In Leeds it absolutely raged. In no town were more taken in by double dealing… The streets near the stock exchange were blocked by people…The lawyer sold the property of his client to meet his losses. The physician put his life savings and the well being of his family at risk.

John Francis, journalist and publisher of the journal *Athenaeum*, commenting on the railway mania, 1851.

How did Parliament control the growth of the railways?

There had been a big change in Parliament between the time when canals were introduced in the 1760s and 1770s and when the railways were introduced in the 1830s and 1840s.

Parliament itself had been reformed to be more representative. In 1832 the new industrial towns such as Manchester had got their first MPs. You have already seen how Parliament passed new laws to control factories and ban women and children from coal mining. Fifty years earlier the attitude of Parliament had been *laissez-faire* – don't get involved. In the 1840s MPs knew they had to get involved – and especially in something as major, fast-growing and as complex as the railways.

Parliament was in favour of railways, but the rapid expansion of the network raised many problems which needed to be sorted out if the network was to flourish.

Problem: ensuring fair competition and fair pricing

The government was all in favour of competition. Competition with canals was one of the main reasons that Parliament had agreed to the building of railways. Competition, they argued, kept prices down. But how do you guarantee competition on the railways?

Solution

To start with, Parliament wanted the lines to operate like canals: anyone could put a vehicle on them and pay a toll. Fairly soon, however, it was realised that this was not practical. Instead they would try to control the railways to ensure fair competition with the canals and the road networks. They carefully controlled the railway operation of a new postal service.

The 1844 Railway Act also forced companies to provide one 'subsidised' train per day, running the length of the line and charging just one penny per mile. These so-called 'parliamentary trains' were unpopular with the railway owners, who often laid on the worst and slowest trains, but they did offer the opportunity of accessible transport to the masses and they were still faster than stagecoaches.

Problem: co-ordinating the different parts of the network

Railways posed other problems which had not affected canals. With the canal network it had not mattered that different companies owned different stretches. As boats passed from one canal to another they simply paid another toll. This did not slow them down much and speed had never been the main asset of canals anyway.

On the railways, however, multiple ownership posed a real problem. Even on a short journey trains might travel on lines owned by a myriad of companies. Passengers and businesses had to book tickets with many different companies, all using different systems of charging. This was awkward and slow, yet railways were supposed to be speedy and convenient.

Solution

In 1842 the government set up the Railway Clearing House to co-ordinate trains travelling on several companies' lines and to standardise fares.

Later it backed moves by individuals to amalgamate small companies into larger groups.

Isambard Kingdom Brunel

★ Born 1806 in Portsmouth, son of a French engineer.
★ 1821 Studied in Paris.
★ 1823 Joined his father's firm, where he helped to plan the first tunnel under the Thames.
★ Designed the Clifton Suspension Bridge 1829–31.
★ In 1833 he became engineer to the Great Western Railway.
★ In 1838 he designed the *Great Western* steamer, the first steamship to cross the Atlantic.
★ Built many bridges, tunnels and laid hundreds of miles of track.
★ 1853–58 He also built and designed the *Great Eastern*, at the time the largest ship ever built.
★ He died in 1859.

1 **Compare the picture of Brunel with the portraits you studied on page 154. How is this portrait different?**

2 **Look at the two sides in the debate about gauges:**
   a) **What were the advantages of Brunel's broad gauge?**
   b) **What were the advantages of the narrow gauge?**

3 **After taking all of the circumstances into account, do you think the government made the right decision over gauges? Explain your answer.**

4 **What was Parliament's most important contribution to the development of the railway system?**

Problem: the gauge

The most extreme example of the problem of co-ordinating the different companies was the question of gauge sizes (i.e. the width of the rails). Most railways were built using the four foot eight and a half inch [1.4 metres] gauge used by George Stephenson. However, Brunel had built the Great Western using a gauge of seven feet [2.1 metres]. As the network grew, engineers, businessmen and the government became concerned about the possibility of non-matching gauges.

Problem: safety

The railways travelled at undreamed-of speeds. There were accidents – as you have already read, William Huskisson, President of the Board of Trade and a member of the government, was killed on the opening day of the Liverpool and Manchester. In 1848 around 200 people were killed on the railways. Not all companies took good care of their passengers. Some passengers failed to take care of themselves – they just did not realise the power and speed of trains. Many were killed jumping off moving trains. Some of the accidents were horrific.

SOURCE 31

A picture of a railway crash at Kentish Town in 1861.

Solution

Brunel demanded a trial. The trial proved that the wider gauge was superior and supported heavier trains at higher speeds. Despite this, the government opted to make Stephenson's narrow gauge the standard. There were two reasons for this. First, there were many more miles of narrow gauge track in 1846. Secondly, the wider gauge could easily be converted by laying a third rail inside the existing broad gauge, whereas converting to Brunel's wide gauge would have meant relaying most of the 3,000 miles of track in Britain.

Solution

In 1840 the Board of Trade appointed safety inspectors and investigated accidents. Then in 1844 William Gladstone sponsored the Railway Act which allowed the government to take control of any company which failed to meet regulations. It banned open wagons for carrying passengers.

In the 1860s block signalling was introduced – only one train was allowed onto a block of track. Signals at either end of the block prevented other trains entering that stretch of track.

The government pressurised train operators to install brakes on all carriages rather than just the hand-operated guard's brake at the rear of the train. The expense made companies unwilling and it was only legislation in 1899 that made railway operators fit continuous brakes.

George Hudson – the railway king

5 What is the cartoonist trying to say in Source 32?

6 Did Hudson do more good than harm? Explain your answer.

One man who made a rather double-edged contribution to the growth of the railway system was a York draper called George Hudson.

To Hudson and others it was soon clear that large companies were more efficient and profitable than small ones. Hudson used an inheritance of £30,000 to buy shares in a railroad from Leeds to York. The venture paid off and Hudson made money on his investment.

He saw the potential benefit of amalgamation. By merging smaller companies they could cut their costs, become more efficient and make larger profits. Soon Hudson was buying shares in other railroads, and convincing others to invest in his ventures or loan him money.

In 1844 he merged the three Midlands companies to form the Midlands Railway. Soon after he created the North Eastern Railway. Hudson became known as the Railway King, and even became an MP in 1846.

SOURCE 32

KING HUDSON'S LEVEE.

A *Punch* cartoon showing William Hudson, the Railway King, November 1845. Look closely at the people who are kneeling before Hudson.

Two years later Hudson's career hit the rocks. His business methods worried the government and in 1848 his accounts were closely examined. He was found to have tricked investors by exaggerating the profitability of companies he wanted them to invest in. He was accused of bribing witnesses to lie to parliamentary inquiries. He had used money invested in one company to pay dividends to shareholders in other companies. Many thousands of pounds had disappeared from his companies in suspicious circumstances. Hudson himself fled to France but was eventually arrested and spent a short time in prison. His companies collapsed and many small investors lost their savings.

Despite Hudson's dishonesty, his ideas were basically sound, and the process of amalgamation continued. By 1852 the four giants who were to dominate the second half of the century had appeared. These were the London and North Eastern Railway (LNER), the London and North Western (LNWR), the Midland, and the Great Western (GWR) – see Source 20 on page 156.

FOCUS TASK

WHAT MADE THE DEVELOPMENT OF THE RAILWAY NETWORK POSSIBLE?

Various factors helped to create an effective railway network. For example:

- Engineering skill
- The strength of the navvies
- Lessons learned from canal building
- Investment
- Government control.

1 Add other factors to this list if you think there are any we have missed.

2 Use the information and evidence on pages 148–63 to explain how each factor was important in the development of the network.

3 Which factors were most important in
   a) building the railways
   b) financing the railways
   c) regulating or controlling the railways?

   Explain why you have chosen these factors above others.

4 Draw a diagram to show how all the factors you have listed are connected to each other.

What was it like to travel on a train in the mid-nineteenth century?

Unlike canals, railways immediately attracted passenger traffic. Unlike the coaches, from the start they attracted poor as well as rich passengers.

In the early years of railway travel passengers were divided into first, second and third class. First-class passengers travelled in comfort and style, but most railway companies were not terribly concerned, in the early years, about the comfort and security of the third-class passengers. You can draw your own conclusions from Source 34.

SOURCE 33

The growth of passenger travel on the railways, 1842–97.

SOURCE 34

A First-class travel in 1831.

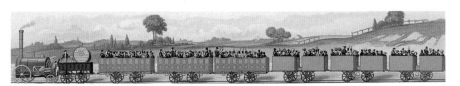

B Third-class travel in the 1840s.

SOURCE 35

You skim along like magic.

The coaches in no way differ from those which go with horses except that the inside is divided into six seats by elbows, and numbered so that you take your place by number and get as far from the steam engine as you can.

At Newton, we met the train (as it is called, not coach or coaches) coming from Manchester to Liverpool. We then took this machine which had no open parts but complete handsome coaches in succession (but forming only one machine) each coach having a separate name, for instance the Hero, March of Intellect etc.

As a style of convenience I cannot imagine anything to exceed it, if you could wholly free yourself from the idea of being blown to Hell or Hurled into the air in a thousand pieces.

John Dalton of Suffolk describes travelling on the Liverpool and Manchester, October 1831.

SOURCE 36

The traffic during Whitsun break [end of May holiday] has been limited to a certain extent by the weather, which is very unfavourable. Not withstanding, the number of passengers was very great, amounting to 52,279 – the receipts being more than £1500 – larger portions of the passengers now being conveyed in open goods wagons.

Report of the South Staffordshire Railway Company, 1851.

1 **What has most impressed John Dalton (Source 35) about travelling on the railways?**

2 **Is he travelling first, second or third class?**

The government passed the 1844 Railways Act partly to protect third-class passengers. The Act insisted that these passengers should travel in covered rather than open wagons. Despite this, Source 34 shows open carriages being used, probably for passengers on the parliamentary trains (see page 161).

SOURCE 37

Male passengers have sometimes been assaulted and robbed, and females insulted… And this has been most frequently the case when there have been only two occupants in the carriage. In going through a tunnel therefore, it is as well to have the hands and arms ready disposed for defence, so that in the event of the attack, the assailant may be instantly beaten back or restrained.

The Railway Traveller's Handy Book, 1862.

Government legislation probably made conditions more bearable, but there is a good deal of evidence that train travel was an uncomfortable process in the 1850s and 1860s. *The Railway Traveller's Handy Book* (see Source 37), published in 1862, advised travellers to wear overcoats at all times in the year and to carry a rug to keep out the cold. The guide also recommended special spectacles to protect those sitting by windows from smoke and ash. It warned third-class travellers of cramped conditions and poor ventilation. Travellers on the parliamentary trains were warned to expect a trip of 100 miles to take all day.

Attacks (see Source 37) may have been rare, but other discomforts were part of everyday travel. There were no lavatories on trains until the late 1870s, and then only for the first-class passengers. At the so-called 'refreshment stops' passengers were given the grand total of 10 minutes to relieve themselves, buy and consume refreshments and reclaim their seats. These refreshment stops gave cartoonists great amusement.

SOURCE 38

A cartoon showing the rush at the 10-minute stop.

SOURCE 39

A cartoon about refreshment rooms.

At interchange stations travellers changing from one company's train to another could find themselves in a chaotic jumble of tickets, inspectors, fellow travellers and luggage. To add to the confusion, stations and trains usually operated on London Time. For stations far from London the difference between station and local time could be as much as 10 minutes. These time differences had not mattered in the days of slower travel, but in the increasingly carefully timed railway timetable, 10-minute differences could lead to chaos. In later years 'railway time' was introduced to standardise time all over Britain. In the early years companies were reluctant to publish timetables anticipating arrival times at given destinations, although these were common by the 1850s.

ACTIVITY

1 **Imagine John Dalton (Source 35) travels again in the 1870s from Suffolk to Liverpool via London and his journey does not go very well. Imagine all the things that could go wrong and write a letter in which he describes his terrible journey.**

2 **Compare the letter with your story from page 132. Are there any similarities?**

SOURCE 40

A Pullman car interior.

Improvement

From the 1870s the numbers of ordinary working people using trains led the Midland Company to improve its third-class carriages. In 1875 the second class/third class distinction was removed – third-class carriages were upgraded to second class. The other companies were forced to follow Midland's lead in order to keep their customers.

First-class travel also improved. In 1873 the first sleeper car appeared, followed in 1876 by the luxurious Pullman cars – the most exclusive form of travel in the late nineteenth century (see Source 40). The 1880s saw trains with dining cars and even heated carriages. In 1892 the familiar corridor train became standard, and toilets at the end of the carriages were no longer a novelty.

SOURCE 41

This painting by William Powell Frith shows Paddington station in 1862. Frith was an extremely successful painter in commercial terms and was well known for his large paintings vividly depicting scenes like the one shown here. Other artists felt that his style was rather vulgar. This has become one of the most famous images of the nineteenth-century railways. It is used in almost all books about railway transport in this period.

ACTIVITY

With a partner study Source 41. Discuss whether the travellers are rich or poor. Are they arriving or leaving? Work out as much as you can about what is going on in the picture, then write your own description of it. Conclude with your own ideas as to whether this is a realistic portrayal of the railways and whether it is a good illustration of the railways to use in a school textbook.

FOCUS TASK

HOW DID PASSENGER TRAVEL IMPROVE IN THE NINETEENTH CENTURY?

You are the compiler of *The Railway Traveller's Handy Book* (see Source 37).

1 Write at least three entries giving up-to-date advice and information to the traveller of the 1890s.

2 Add an appendix for the 1899 'end of century' edition explaining how conditions at the end of the century compare with conditions on the first trains in the 1830s.

How did the growth of the railway network affect Britain's economy?

The railways themselves became a major industry. Building the railways and the stations needed thousands of navvies, carpenters and bricklayers. Making the engines and coaches kept dozens of engineering works in business throughout the century. Running and maintaining the railways needed drivers, guards, clerks, station masters, signalmen. The numbers of permanent staff directly employed by railway companies (i.e. excluding those in related industries) rose steadily through the century: 47,000 in 1847; 112,000 by 1860; 275,000 by 1873. Britain's railway network was largely complete by the end of the century but the railway industry still grew, building railways in many other countries all around the world.

The railways had what economists called a 'multiplier' effect. As they grew, other industries grew with them. For example, stations, bridges and embankments were built of bricks so the brick industry grew. In 1845 alone the railway industry used 745 million bricks! In the same way the building of stations and carriages stimulated the timber, leather, glass and rubber industries. The railways created whole towns such as Crewe, Ashford (Kent) and Swindon (which before the railway was a tiny village, but once it became a railway centre grew to a town of 100,000 people).

There was also a massive set of service industries which grew up around the railway network. Hoteliers set up lodging houses or restaurants to cater for the travellers. Taxis and buses were introduced to ferry travellers to and from stations. Publishers produced railway books, maps, timetables and magazines. The first travel agencies appeared (see page 170).

The list is endless. Almost no area of British industry was untouched by the railway revolution. The diagram on the next page summarises the main effects of the railways on industry, trade and commerce.

SOURCE 42

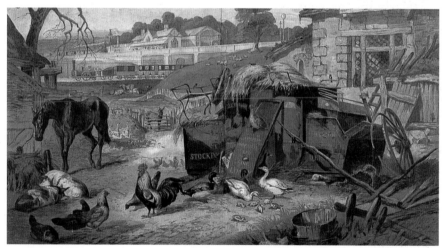

A painting by the Leighton Brothers from around 1845.

SOURCE 43

There were crowds of people and mountains of goods departing and arriving, scores upon scores of times every day.

Night and day, the conquering engines rumbled at their distant work, gliding like tame dragons into the corners grooved out for them. They stood bubbling and trembling, making the walls quake, as if they were shivering with the secret knowledge of great powers within them and strong purposes not yet achieved.

Extract from *Dombey and Son*, by Charles Dickens.

1 **What do you think was the message of the artists who painted Source 42?**

2 **Read Source 43. What do you think Charles Dickens means by 'great powers and strong purposes'?**

A national market

Before the railways most trade was fairly local. The turnpikes and canals had started to help businesses to sell their goods more widely, but the railways were the breakthrough. They created the possibility of a national market. They made it practical to transport fresh food long distances. Ports such as Grimsby and Lowestoft specialised in getting fresh fish onto the night train in time for London's morning market. Farmers in the West Country discovered an important market in London for fresh milk.

All over the country shopkeepers and markets responded to the opportunity this created. The shopkeeper could now order goods from anywhere, either on his own initiative or in response to a request from a customer. Britain's high streets were transformed.

Iron and coal

The effect of railway expansion on the iron and coal industries was particularly dramatic. The railways became the main customer of the iron and coal industries. Historians estimate that in the 1840s, 15 per cent of all iron production was used in making rails, and that was only for the tracks. Engines, wheels, carriages and trucks also used enormous amounts of iron. The engines themselves burned coal, of course. In 1850 the railways used one million tons of coal. That's at least 2 per cent of the entire national output.

Canal transport

To start with, railways affected the canal industry less dramatically than they affected the road industry. The railways offered quick and reliable transport, but in many industries speed was less important than price and reliability, so canals could still compete. Canals reduced their tolls: for example, canal tolls from Hull to Manchester were reduced by half when the railway was built. Twenty years after the opening of the Liverpool and Manchester line, twice as much freight still travelled between the cities by canal as by rail. Even in 1870 half of London's coal still arrived by water rather than railway.

However, as the rail network improved later in the century, canals competed less and less effectively. In 1850 railways carried as many goods as the canals. By 1898 the railways carried 10 times as much!

Road transport

The railways had a disastrous effect on the turnpike roads and coaching companies. In 1836 turnpikes between Birmingham and London had generated £38,000. In 1839, one year after the opening of the London to Birmingham railway, they earned £16,000.

The railways brought a swift end to the Golden Age of coaching. They forced many coaching companies and coaching inns out of business (see Source 41).

On the other hand, railways could not deliver to the door. One historian has said that without road transport, railways were like 'stranded whales'. While railways may have killed the national coaching trade they generally increased local traffic.

Business methods

Railways helped change business methods. They brought a new dimension to business travelling. The travelling salesman, an idea pioneered by Wedgwood (see page 135) became part of every company's team. One businessman in 1830 talked of how railways, by halving travelling times between destinations, effectively doubled the business time of salesmen and managers.

The railway boom also gave Britain a generation of skilful managers, businessmen and bankers with experience in financing and funding large amalgamated companies. It is no coincidence that Britain made a healthy profit in giving advice and financial services in this period.

1 Compare the impact of railways on jobs with the impact of canals (see page 146). Which had the greater impact?

ACTIVITY

It is 1900. Some schoolchildren are doing a local history project. They interview a retired railway worker who has worked on the railways for 50 years about how railways changed business. Reconstruct this interview.

What was the social impact of the railway network?

No development in the nineteenth century had as great an impact on ordinary life in Britain as the railway network. One writer described it like this:

SOURCE 44

Your railroad starts the new era, and we of a certain age belong to the new time and the old one… We elderly people have lived in that pre-railroad world, which has passed into Limbo and vanished from under us. I tell you it was firm under our feet once, and not long ago. They have raised those railroad embankments up, and shut off the old world that was behind them.

The novelist William Thackeray, 1860.

This is quite a claim! Let's see if it can be supported by the evidence.

The new era of mass travel

Historians do agree that the railways brought about a great change in ordinary life in Britain.

Before railways only the rich could afford the time or money to travel long distances. With the advent of the railways ordinary people could afford to travel. It increased what is known as 'mobility'. Increased mobility triggered a whole series of 'social' changes which combined into a social revolution. Increased mobility allowed people more choice over where they could live; where they could work; where they could go on holiday. It affected what they could eat; where they could shop. It even affected how some people thought.

One nation?

Before the transport revolution different regions in Britain had been fairly separate. The roads and canals had started to bring them together – the railways speeded the process. The railways shrank Britain. Most parts of the country could be reached in less than a day's journey. 'Railway time' was adopted as standard throughout the country. The railways linked distant places. Trade between cities and regions brought people closer together. One very specific example of how the railways helped unite different parts of Britain was that they made national daily newspapers possible. Before the railway boom it sometimes took days for news to get from one region to another. Now everyone around the country could read the same papers on the same day. Newspapers kept them informed about events at home and abroad. Even the actions of their MPs at Westminster could be watched over and discussed. National campaigns could now be effectively mounted. The Anti-Corn Law League was able to use the railways in its campaigning activity.

Commuting and the suburbs

On the other hand, the railways also increased some divisions in society. They helped create the suburbs. The nineteenth-century city was a fairly awful place to live, but if that was where industry and commerce was, people had no choice but to live there. However, when the railways arrived it became practical for those who could afford it to commute into town for work and retreat out of the town again at the end of the day. Only the middle classes and more prosperous tradesmen could afford to commute every day, but an increasing number moved out of the polluted, cramped and often dangerous environment of the inner cities into the rapidly growing suburbs which grew up along the railway lines out of all the major industrial cities.

The railways helped separate out the middle classes (who moved to the suburbs) from the poor (who stayed in the towns) and thus intensified some of the social divisions already affecting British society. Middle-class commuters could ride on high viaducts over slum areas of Britain's cities, getting a bird's-eye view of urban poverty. But they did not need to mingle with it.

The urban landscape

Embankments, bridges and cuttings, and looming viaducts sliced through the urban landscape. Hundreds of steam trains added to the air pollution which was part of everyday life. Some were affected more directly still. Railways were invariably built through the poorest areas of housing as this land was cheaper for the railway company to buy. Tens of thousands of people were displaced to make way for new railways.

SOURCE 45

The poor are displaced, but they are not removed. They are shovelled out of one side of the parish, only to render more overcrowded the stifling apartments in another part… You may pull down their wretched homes: they must find others, and make their new dwellings more crowded than their old ones. The tailor, shoemaker and other workmen are in much the same position. It is making a mockery to speak of the suburbs to them.

The Times, commenting on railway building, 1861.

> **2 Look at Source 46. Why do you think stations were built in such grand style?**

SOURCE 46

St Pancras station in London, built in 1868.

SOURCE 47

The centre of Leeds in 1868, showing the area taken up by the railway companies. The railway companies were then, and still are today, among the major urban landowners.

1 Use the map in Source 19 (page 156) and an atlas to work out which of the resorts named on the right might appeal to workers on day trips from: Liverpool, Manchester, Leeds, London.

Excursions and package holidays

The railways helped create modern tourism.

In 1851 thousands of people made a railway trip to the Great Exhibition in London, including many who had never travelled on a train before and many who had never been to London. It firmly established in people's minds that 'outings' were possible. It became increasingly common for city dwellers to take day trips to towns such as Blackpool, Llandudno, Windermere, Scarborough and Brighton. Railway companies laid on special trains for such day trips.

The travel entrepreneur Thomas Cook fully understood the potential of the railways. By organising large bookings of tickets he was able to buy seats on trains at a discount price. This meant that he could then offer excursions to popular resorts at reasonable prices but still make a profit. His first excursion was a temperance trip (transporting temperance or anti-alcohol campaigners to a meeting) from Loughborough to Leicester in 1841. This was only one market, however. Soon he began to offer a 'complete package' including rail travel to a seaside resort and lodgings at the resort. The package tour was born. The Isle of Wight became an important package holiday destination in the 1860s. By the end of the century many working people looked forward to holidays by the seaside each year.

SOURCE 48

A poster advertising trips to the Great Exhibition, 1851.

Fresh food and shopping

The economic changes you looked at on page 167 also had their effect on ordinary people's lives – for example the railways brought fresh food into the towns and transformed the retail trade.

SOURCE 49

In the grey mist of the morning… we see a large portion of the supply of the London markets disgorged by these night trains. Fish, flesh and food, Aylesbury butter and dairy-fed pork, apples, cabbages and cucumbers… No sooner do these disappear than at ten minutes' interval arrive other trains with Manchester packs and bales, Liverpool cotton, American provisions, Worcester gloves, Kidderminster carpets, Birmingham and Staffordshire Hardware, crates of pottery from north Staffordshire… which have to be delivered in the city before the hour for the general commencement of business.

Railway News, December 1864, reporting from London.

2 Why do you think the writer of Source 49 was so enthusiastic about the railways?

ACTIVITY

Prepare a panel for an exhibition on Victorian railways. Your panel is on 'How the Victorians felt about the railways'. You can choose two pictures and two written sources which show nineteenth-century attitudes to the railways. Use pages 148–71 or other books in your research. Explain your choice of sources.

Towns   Leisure

Jobs   Politics

Shopping   Social
                       divisions

FOCUS TASK

WHAT WERE THE SOCIAL AND ECONOMIC EFFECTS OF THE RAILWAYS?

1 On your own copy of the diagram on the left find one or two examples of how that aspect of life was affected by the railways.

2 Draw lines between the linked effects and explain why you think they are linked.

3 Now you are going to think about Thackeray's statement in Source 44. Use the evidence on pages 167–71 and your completed chart above to explain why Thackeray might feel like this.

4 In small groups discuss whether you agree or disagree with this statement: 'The railways had far more impact on ordinary people than any other development in the period 1700–1900'.

7 Review: Two centuries of change

Agriculture: The main changes

From	To
Open fields and common land	Enclosure
Human power and horse power	Still mainly human and horse power, but steam power is used for some specialised jobs such as threshing
Subsistence farming	Business farming
Relying on 'nature's bounty'	Perfecting nature by scientific farming
Most people involved in farming	Farming being just one of Britain's many industries
Farming being Britain's main industry	Farming being Britain's main industry
Growing food for your own locality	Growing food for a national or international market

Textiles: The main changes

From	To
The domestic system	The factory system
Wool	'King Cotton'
The south and east of England	The coalfields of the north of England
Human power	Steam power
Uncontrolled working conditions	Government-controlled working conditions

Iron: The main changes

From	To
Charcoal iron	Coke iron
Water-powered blast	Steam-powered blast
South of England	Midlands and South Wales
Small-scale production	Large-scale production
Low-quality iron	High-quality iron
Slow transport by wagon	Fast transport by railway

Coal: The main changes

From

Small-scale mining of surface coal

Women and children involved in mining

Low demand: wood and charcoal were Britain's main fuel

A labour-intensive industry – coal hewed by hand

Transport by river and sea

To

Large-scale mining of deep seams

Women and children banned from mines

High demand: coal was Britain's main fuel

Still a labour-intensive industry – coal still hewed by hand

Transport by coach and railway

Transport: The main changes

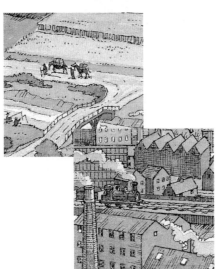

From

Poor, unmade roads

Rivers, navigations and coastal shipping

Horse-powered tramways in coal mines

Twelve days London to Edinburgh

Horse and wind power

To

Carefully engineered turnpikes

Canals

A national network of steam-powered railways

Nine hours London to Edinburgh

Steam power

FOCUS TASK

This review diagram shows some of the main changes you have studied in Sections 2 and 3 of this book.

Use it to make your own summary chart, using your own words, explaining what you feel were the most important changes between 1700 and 1900.

Factors for change

In Chapter 2 you read about various factors which were important in stimulating and influencing the patterns of change in Britain as it industrialised.

These appear and re-appear regularly throughout pages 18–171. Now it is time to step back and look at them again.

FOCUS TASK

A Copy the following table.
Fill it out to show the connections between each factor and the changes you have studied in farming, textiles, iron, coal and transport. You may not be able to fill out every box.

B These are not the only factors which brought about change. Other factors were also important. For example, war helped bring about change in some of these areas. Use the fifth column to note connections between war and the changes in some of these areas.

C Transport is shown as a row in your table – because it was something that changed during the period. It could equally well be a column because it was also a factor for change in other areas. Use the final column of your table to explain how transport was connected to changes in farming, textiles, iron or coal.

	The growing population	Overseas trade	Steam power	Entrepreneurs and investors		
Farming						
The textile industry						
Iron						
Coal						
Transport						

D Look back at page 14. Which of the entrepreneurs do you think made the most significant contribution to Britain's industrial growth? Explain your choice.

SECTION 4

Urbanisation 1750–1900

What were the causes and consequences of rapid urban growth?

8.1 Why did towns grow?

FOCUS

Most of Britain's towns and cities grew rapidly in the nineteenth century. This growth brought opportunities and prosperity to some. It also brought squalor and poor health to others.

In 8.1:

- You will examine reasons why towns grew so quickly in the nineteenth century.
- You will investigate why living conditions were so appalling in some of Britain's growing towns.
- You will reach your own conclusions on whether living conditions in the towns were better or worse than those in the countryside.

In 8.2 you will examine the public health movement:

- You will investigate how people tried to improve conditions in the towns.
- You will consider reasons why it took such a long time to improve living conditions.

Population change

You have already read a lot about population change and the growth of towns. Sources 1–4 are a reminder of the main changes.

SOURCE 1

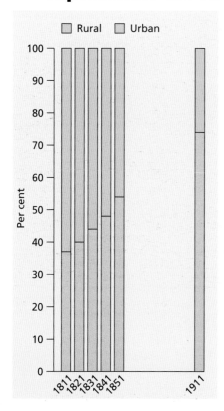

The shift of population, 1811–1911.

SOURCE 2

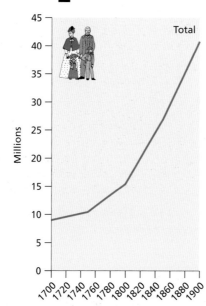

Population growth in the UK, 1700–1900. The figures for the eighteenth century are estimates.

177

WHAT WERE THE CAUSES AND CONSEQUENCES OF RAPID URBAN GROWTH?

SOURCE 3

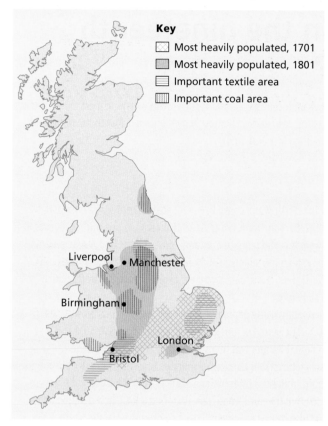

Key

⊠ Most heavily populated, 1701
▨ Most heavily populated, 1801
▤ Important textile area
▥ Important coal area

Liverpool • Manchester
Birmingham •
London •
Bristol •

A The changing distribution of Britain's population, 1701–1801.

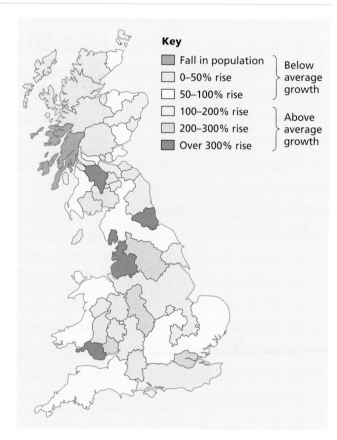

Key

▨ Fall in population   ⎫ Below
☐ 0–50% rise   ⎬ average
☐ 50–100% rise   ⎭ growth
☐ 100–200% rise   ⎫ Above
▧ 200–300% rise   ⎬ average
▨ Over 300% rise   ⎭ growth

B Population growth, 1801–71.
By 1801 the most heavily populated areas were on the great coalfields.

SOURCE 4

City	1801	1851	1901
London	959	2,362	4,536
Liverpool	82	376	704
Glasgow	77	329	776
Birmingham	71	233	523
Manchester	70	303	645
Edinburgh	66	160	317
Bristol	61	137	339
Leeds	53	172	429
Sheffield	46	135	407
Newcastle	33	88	247
Stoke-on-Trent	83	84	215
Oldham	22	72	137
Brighton	7	70	123
Norwich	36	68	114
Aberdeen	27	72	154

The population growth (in thousands) of 15 British towns, 1801–1901.

SOURCE 5

'The March of Bricks and Mortar', a cartoon by George Cruikshank, 1829.

ACTIVITY

Write a 100-word explanation of Source 5, using both the data in Sources 1–4 and your wider knowledge.

SOURCE 6

The location of Bangor and Bradford.

Why did towns grow so rapidly in the nineteenth century?

Most towns grew in the nineteenth century. For many the growth was quite spectacular. You are going to look at two contrasting case studies: Bangor (which grew ten-fold in the nineteenth century) and Bradford (which grew twenty-fold).

Bangor

Bangor is a small town on the North Wales coast. In the nineteenth century its busy port exported millions of tons of Welsh slate for roofing. In 1821 there were one million houses in Britain, but by 1851 there were two and a quarter million. Most of these had a slate roof, and the port of Bangor was one of the main suppliers of roofing slate. Thousands of Liverpool houses were roofed with Welsh slate. It was said that every capital city in the world had at least one building with a Welsh slate roof.

Source 7 shows Bangor's steadily rising population; the only pause in this growth was a typhus epidemic in the 1890s. The period of greatest growth was in the 1830s and 1840s – despite the fact that in that period Bangor was hit by a deadly epidemic of cholera.

Source 8 is an 1851 census return from Bangor. You can see that at 19 Foundry Street none of the Williams family were born in Bangor itself. We can also see from the variety of places in which the children were born that the family had moved around a lot. Their neighbours in number 20, the Joneses, had also moved to Bangor. They had once lived in the North Wales countryside. They also spent some time in Liverpool before moving to Bangor. Both of these families would have moved to Bangor to work, possibly because they were attracted by better wages. The Joneses and their lodgers were involved in shipping as riggers or sailors, probably associated with the booming slate trade.

Just around the corner, in 1 Water Street, were the Irish McGever family. They appear to have been a poorer household than the other two, with two residents existing by begging. In the years after the Irish famine (see page 51) Britain's cities received many Irish immigrants, escaping the desperate suffering and poverty in Ireland. We see that the McGevers had three visitors in the house when census officials called. It is likely that such visitors were themselves intending to settle, either in Bangor or another town, perhaps in England.

SOURCE 7

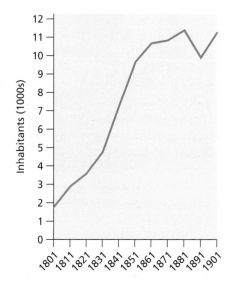

Bangor's population, 1801–1901. The hiccup in 1891 was caused by a severe outbreak of typhus fever.

179

WHAT WERE THE CAUSES AND CONSEQUENCES OF RAPID URBAN GROWTH?

SOURCE 8

Name of street or road	Name of each person in house	Relation to head of household	Condition	Age of males	Age of females	Rank or occupation	Place of birth
19 Foundry St	Elizabeth Williams	head	widow		37	Dressmaker	Angelsea Pentraeth
	Ellen Williams	dau			9	Scholar	Llangefni (Ang.)
	Jane Williams	dau			8	Scholar	Derwen, Denbighshire
	Ann Williams	dau			6		Brecknock, Merthyr
20 Foundry St	Humphrey Jones	head	mar	60		Rigger of vessels	Caernarvonshire
	Jane Jones	wife			52		Ang. Llanfair
	Jane Jones	dau			17		Lancs. Liverpool
	Richard Jones	son		14		Scholar	Lancs. Liverpool
	William Jones	lodger	widow	80		Mariner	Caerns. Bangor
	John Lewis	lodger	unm	20		Mariner	Caerns. Bangor
1 Water St	Andrew McGever	head	wid	56		Pauper, hawker of fish and former agric labourer	Ireland
	Mary McGever	dau	mar		22	Hawker of drapery	Ireland
	Thomas McGever	son	unm	19		Mariner	Ireland
	Patrick McGever	son	unm	17			Ireland
	Brigit McGever	dau			14		Ireland
	John Morris	visitor	unm	21		Rag and bone dealer	Ireland
	Brigit Gillin	visitor	wid		40	Beggar, former agric labourer's wife	Ireland
	Cath. Gillin	visitor	unm		20	Beggar	Ireland

Information on three houses in Bangor from the 1851 census.

ACTIVITY

On your own copy of an outline map of North Wales mark the places where each of the people mentioned in Source 8 were born; the distance of these places from Bangor; and the different moves made by the Williams and Jones families.

SOURCE 9

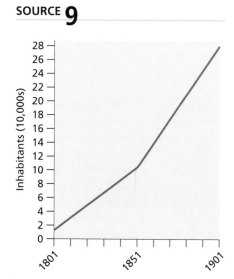

The growth of Bradford's population according to census data.

Bradford

Bradford lies 150 miles away from Bangor, on the Yorkshire side of the Pennines. It was a centre of the textile industry.

Source 9 shows that Bradford's population rose even more dramatically than Bangor's. Bradford really took off with the coming of steam power to the woollen industry. It had easy access to coal and after 1820 the number of woollen mills grew very quickly: in 1834 Bradford had 39 mills; in 1841, 83; in 1851 there were 153. Some of these new mills were in Bradford itself, others were in the surrounding villages.

Each mill needed hundreds of workers. People walked to work, so they had to live nearby. As you can see from Source 11, these 'mini settlements' around each mill soon merged to become conurbations and eventually the outlying villages were swallowed up into the growing town.

This new work in turn attracted others to the towns. In 1851 there were over 30,000 mill workers in Bradford, making it by far the biggest single category of worker. However, many more worked elsewhere, some in trades related to wool, for example servicing machines, dyeing cloth or as tailors. Others worked in unrelated occupations, servicing the growing town. In the 1851 census 25 other occupations are listed including teachers, domestic servants, builders and shoemakers. There were over 2,300 shopkeepers. There were hundreds of inns and ale houses to sell drink to the workers. Thousands of builders were kept busy meeting the desperate demand for new housing.

SOURCE 10

Address	Name of each person in house	Relation to head of family	Condition	Age of males	Age of females	Rank, profession or occupation	Where born
20 Green Air Place	Catherine Ward	head	widow		50		Ireland
	Mary Ann Ward	dau	unm		28	Minds wool-combing machine	Ireland
	Bridget Baines	dau	mar		18	Minds wool-combing machine	Ireland
	Ann Croker	dau	unm		14	Piecer, worsted	Ireland
	Joseph Baines	son	mar	19		Wool comber	Bradford
	William Quinlan	lodger	mar	30		Glazier	Ireland
	Bridget Quinlan	lodger	mar		28		Ireland
	Robert Quinlan	lodger		7			
19 Green Air Place	James Hill	head	mar	48		Basket maker	Aylesbury, Bucks
	Ann Hill	wife	mar		45		Hemel Hempstead, Herts
	Frances Hill	dau	unm		19	Power loom weaver, worsted	Banbury
	Elizabeth Hill	dau	unm		14	Piecer	Leeds
19A Green Air Place	John McKenna	head	mar	27		Wool comber	Ireland
	Ellen McKenna	wife	mar		21	Minds combing machine	Ireland
	Ann Finnigan	sister-in-law	unm		19	Minds combing machine	Ireland
18 Green Air Place	Jonathan Dobson	head	mar	56		Basket maker	Bradford
	Mary Dobson	wife	mar		36		Bradford
	Robert Dobson	son	mar	26		Wool comber	Bradford
	Sarah Ann Dobson	dau	mar		25	Power loom weaver, worsted	Bradford

Information on four homes in Bradford from the 1851 census.

1 Write your own account of the inhabitants of Green Air Place in Bradford (Source 10) in a similar style to the description of Foundry and Water Streets on page 178.

SOURCE 11

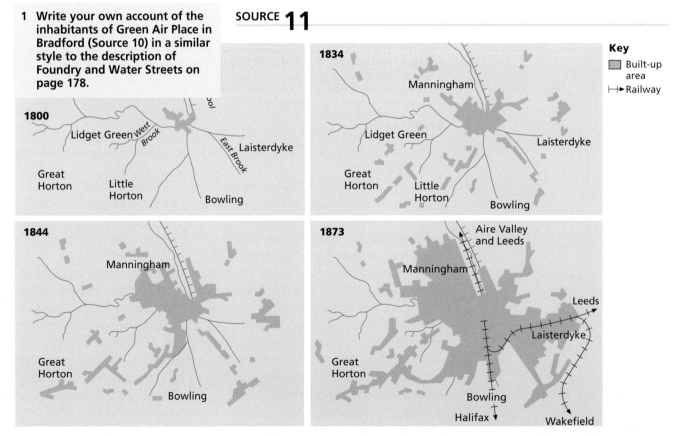

The growth of Bradford, 1800–73.

SOURCE **12**

181

WHAT WERE THE CAUSES AND CONSEQUENCES OF RAPID URBAN GROWTH?

Bradford in the nineteenth century.

2 Why is census data valuable to historians?

3 Much old census material is now going onto computer databases. How will this help historians?

ACTIVITY

Imagine you were born in Little Horton (see Source 11) in around 1800. You are now 75 years of age and are talking to your grandchildren about the changes you have seen. How would you explain the changes to them? Use Source 12 in your answer.

4 On your own copy of Source 12 label the following: a quarry; a woollen mill; a factory chimney; a church; workers' housing; the town hall; the railway.

5 Do you think Source 12 shows Bradford in 1800, 1834, 1844, or 1873? Explain your answer with reference to Source 11.

6 What evidence is there of the impact of canals and the railways on the growth of Bradford?

7 Would you agree that Sources 9–12 are more useful taken together than separately? Explain your answer.

FOCUS TASK

WHY DID TOWNS GROW SO RAPIDLY IN THE NINETEENTH CENTURY?

Work in groups.
  Here is a list of factors which contributed to urban growth. Can you find evidence in Sources 7–13 for each of these factors in:

a) Bangor; and
b) Bradford?

• The need of key industries for workers
• Immigration from Ireland
• Immigration from the countryside
• Jobs in supporting trades or professions
• Improved transport

You can add other factors to the list if you think they are also important.

182

WHAT WERE THE CAUSES AND CONSEQUENCES OF RAPID URBAN GROWTH?

Did other towns follow the same pattern?

Census data for other growing towns shows a similar pattern:

Young people migrated to towns for money or jobs.
Many people – particularly between the ages of 15 and 25 – moved to towns as it was becoming increasingly difficult to get work in the countryside. The population of the countryside was growing, and there were not enough farming jobs to go round. Besides, farming jobs were badly paid. So it was the obvious thing to travel to the local towns to work in the docks, workshops, forges or mills – depending on the area's speciality.

Such migration was not limited to industrial areas. Even the older towns such as Norwich or Exeter, which were not industrial centres, grew in this period. However, without the opportunities provided by industry their growth was much slower.

Most migrated locally. Some migrated long distances.
Most migrants did not move far – usually just to the nearest town, ten or twenty miles away. Such local migration swelled the population of London by around 300,000 between 1831 and 1841. After the railway boom of the 1840s longer-distance migration became more common. By 1851 there were 100,000 Irish migrants in London alone. The really massive growth of towns occurred when railways made transport in and around towns easier and cheap.

Each new migrant drew others into the towns.
Inward migration had a 'multiplier' effect. Each new person in a town needed food, housing and clothing. The majority of the town's population would be involved in supplying such services. Even in the towns of Lancashire only one in three workers worked in a cotton mill.

Migrants married earlier and had larger families.
The evidence also suggests that young people in towns married earlier than they would have done in the country. They also had larger families. This all increased the rate of growth of the urban population. This was further encouraged by the fact that children as young as five years old would bring in wages.

1 Historians refer to 'push' and 'pull' factors in studying migration. From pages 178–81 make a list of push factors (things which make people want to leave where they are) and pull factors (things which attract people to where they are going) which caused people to move from the country to the towns.

SOURCE **13**

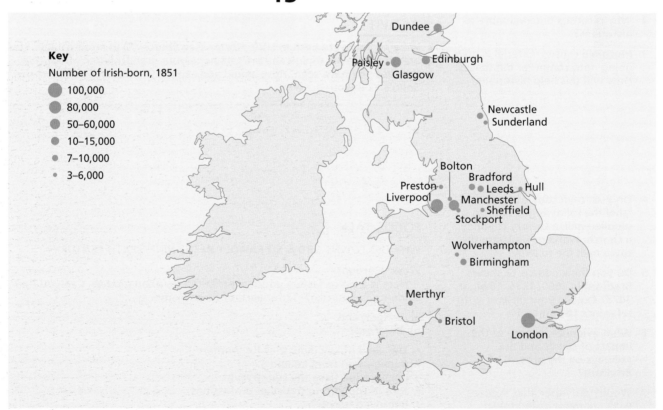

Key

Number of Irish-born, 1851

- 100,000
- 80,000
- 50–60,000
- 10–15,000
- 7–10,000
- 3–6,000

Dundee
Paisley
Glasgow
Edinburgh
Newcastle
Sunderland
Bolton
Preston
Liverpool
Bradford
Leeds
Hull
Manchester
Sheffield
Stockport
Wolverhampton
Birmingham
Merthyr
Bristol
London

Irish settlement in Britain. This map shows the 20 largest Irish settlements in Britain based on the 1851 census.

Rich and poor in the growing towns

The rapid rise in population led to a desperate housing shortage.

A rich family could afford a large detached house such as Source 14A, preferably set on a hill, away from the smells and pollution that hung over every urban area.

A middle-class family could afford a terraced house such as Source 14B, with its own garden, plus quite often an attic room for their servant to live in.

The poor, however, could only afford to live in run-down or poorly built houses, in the least desirable areas of the town (see Source 14C for example).

Poor-quality housing would be made worse by chronic overcrowding. You might find a family of six living in a single room, and then on top of that taking in lodgers to help pay their rent. In the early nineteenth century, in the booming iron-making town of Merthyr Tydfil, 20 people would lodge in one ill-ventilated cellar.

SOURCE 14

A

B

C

Housing for rich and poor.

184

WHAT WERE THE CAUSES AND CONSEQUENCES OF RAPID URBAN GROWTH?

Housing for the poor

The poor formed the vast majority of the urban population, so on the next eight pages you are going to investigate their living conditions in more detail. Why were living conditions so awful, and what were the consequences of this for people's health?

SOURCE 15

Typical back-to-back housing in a Victorian town.

Unplanned growth

Urban growth led to a frenzy of building. The number of houses in Britain doubled between 1800 and 1851. Most new houses were built as cheaply and quickly as possible. Landlords' and builders' main consideration was to make profits from high rents, not to build value-for-money housing or ensure the health and welfare of the inhabitants. Little thought was given to drainage, sewage, water supply, or pavements on the street. Local councils had very little power to interfere with building work. There were no building regulations. In any case, many did not believe it was the councils' responsibility to worry about such matters.

Back to back

To pack in as many houses as possible, as cheaply as possible, builders built back to back. Sources 15 and 16 show terraces of back-to-back housing. These were common in towns in the Midlands and the north of England. In Nottingham over 7,000 such houses were built. Most have now been cleared but some are still standing in Leeds and other industrial cities.

1 **Look at Source 15. Can you see why such housing was cheap to build?**

185

WHAT WERE THE CAUSES AND CONSEQUENCES OF RAPID URBAN GROWTH?

2 Look at Source 17. How many new dwellings have been built in the garden of the old house?

Courts

Most back-to-backs were built as courts, with housing surrounding a central courtyard on three sides, with a single access to the main street. Sometimes the entrance to the court was very narrow. With the demand for housing so high, houses were built on any plot of land which a builder or landlord could buy. For example, they found that they could fit whole terraces of back-to-back housing in the gardens of older houses.

SOURCE 16

A court in Glasgow, photographed in 1868. The single exit to the street is marked. The height of these buildings made the problem of ventilation worse.

SOURCE 17

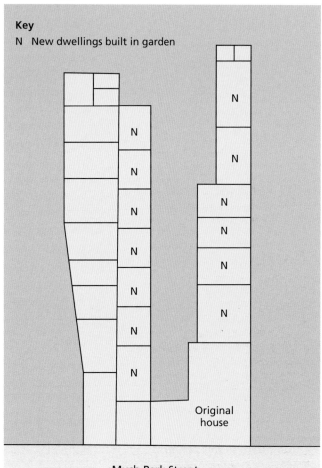

Plan of a new court in Much Park Street, Coventry.

SOURCE 18

This narrow alley was the only access to these houses in Yorkshire.

SOURCE 19

Courts and Cul-de-sacs exist everywhere … in one cul-de-sac in Leeds there are 34 houses, and in ordinary times dwell in these houses 340 persons, 10 to every house. The name of this place is Boot and Shoe Yard, from whence the commissioners removed, in the days of cholera, 75 cartloads of manure which had been untouched for years.

To build the largest number of cottages on the smallest possible space seems to have been the original view of the speculators. Thus neighbourhoods have arisen in which there is neither water nor privies.

From *An Inquiry into the State and Conditions of the Town of Leeds* by Robert Baker, published in 1842.

Tenements

In some cities builders built tenements of five or six storeys (see Source 16). This allowed them to get more people into a space.

SOURCE 20

Jo lives – that is to say, Jo has not yet died – in a ruinous place, known to the like of him by the name of Tom-all-Alone's. It is a bleak, dilapidated street, avoided by all decent people; where the crazy houses were seized upon, when their decay was far advanced, by some bold vagrants, who, after establishing their own possession, took to letting them out in lodgings.

Now, these tumbling tenements contain, by night, a swarm of misery. As on the ruined human wretch, vermin parasites appear, so, these ruined shelters have bred a crowd of foul existence that crawls in and out of gaps in walls and boards; and coils itself to sleep, in maggot numbers, where the rain drips in; and comes and goes, fetching and carrying fever, and sowing more evil in its every footprint than Lord Coodle and Sir Thomas Doodle, and the Duke of Foodle, and all the fine gentlemen in office, down to Zoodle, shall set right in five hundred years.

Twice, lately, there has been a crash and a cloud of dust, like the springing of a mine, in Tom-all-Alone's; and, each time, a house has fallen. These accidents have made a paragraph in the newspapers, and have filled a bed or two in the nearest hospital. The gaps remain, and there are not unpopular lodgings among the rubbish. As several more houses are nearly ready to go, the next crash in Tom-all-Alone's may be expected to be a good one.

An extract from the novel *Bleak House* by Charles Dickens, 1853. Dickens is describing the living conditions of Jo, a street sweeper. Dickens was a careful observer of city life, although he also tried to shock his readers.

Cellars

The poorest of the poor lived in the cellars of the back-to-backs or tenements. The worst city for these cellar dwellings was probably Liverpool, where in 1840 around 40,000 people lived in cellars.

SOURCE 21

These houses are the last refuge between poverty and death. Below the miserable dwellings are the rows of cellars to which a sunken corridor leads. Twelve to fifteen human beings are crowded into each of these damp holes.

Alexis de Tocqueville, *Journeys to England and Ireland*. De Tocqueville was a French nobleman who visited Manchester in 1835.

1 **Which of the houses shown or described in Sources 14–21 would you least like to live in? Explain your choice.**

2 **Source 20 comes from a novel. Do you think it is useful as evidence about housing conditions in this period?**

3 **Which of Sources 14–21 do you think gives the most reliable information about housing conditions at this time?**

ACTIVITY

Work in groups.
Discuss Source 22 together. Think about who the characters are, why they chose to live where they do, and what might happen if they are evicted. Try to see the situation from the different points of view of each of the individuals involved.
Now role-play or write out a scene which shows what might have happened next.

SOURCE 22

A bailiff prepares to evict a family from their cellar dwelling for non-payment of rent in the 1830s.

187

WHAT WERE THE CAUSES AND CONSEQUENCES OF RAPID URBAN GROWTH?

Poor housing = bad health

Such bad housing posed many threats to health.

Damp

Housing for the poor was often 'jerry-built' (badly built). The foundations were shallow. There were no cavity walls or damp courses. The floors were boards over flagstones laid on bare earth. Builders often skimped on slates for the roofs of these houses. Without a proper overlap, rain soon found its way through these roofs. Houses were usually damp and infested with mould.

Poor ventilation

Houses were built so close together that it was virtually impossible for air to circulate. The windows (if any) were kept tightly shut to keep out the smell of the refuse outside. Damp and poor ventilation are notoriously bad for chest infections.

Overcrowding

Families with four or more children were crammed into one or perhaps two rooms. Families shared beds or had none at all and despite these conditions they still took in lodgers to help pay the rent (see Source 8 on page 179). Any infection could quickly be passed on to all the others in the dwelling.

> 4 Look at Source 23, and work out possible sleeping arrangements for the five families.

SOURCE 23

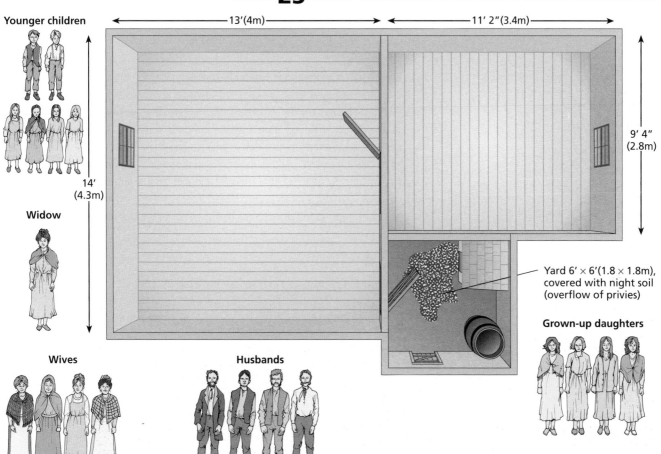

Drawn from London Statistical Society information, 1848. Five families shared this accommodation. There was a widow with three grown-up daughters, a married couple with a grown-up daughter, and three married couples with two young children each.

Food

Cooking facilities were minimal. Food could not be stored hygienically so it was easily infected.

Water supply

Very few houses had piped water. Page 189 opposite shows how the poor could get water. Often that water was polluted and carried disease.

Personal hygiene

With water in such short supply, washing – of clothing or bodies – was not a priority. Many diseases were carried by body lice or by bacteria living on bodies or in dirty clothing.

Refuse collection

There was often no effective system for collecting rubbish. There was usually enough room to push a barrow through the entrance to a court to collect refuse, but not always. Refuse could spread many infections. Some town dwellers also kept pigs in the yards, just as they had always done in the country. This added to the smell.

Sewage and sanitation

The biggest health problem of all was that houses were built without sewers or toilets. Most courts had a privy, shared among a number of houses. A privy was a wooden shed. Inside the shed was a wooden seat and below the seat was a cesspit.

The cesspits were a major cause of infection and illness.

- They were not lined, so infection could seep out of them into the water supply.
- They were not emptied often enough. In wet weather they sometimes overflowed. Reports from the time tell of courts awash with human sewage. One vicar attending a dying man in a rain storm described how the cesspit used by 13 cottages overflowed and ran through the cottage between his feet and the bed of the dying man, as he prayed over him.
- The job of emptying 'night soil' from cesspits was done by nightmen. The job of the nightmen was not one that inspired care or pride, as Source 24 shows.
- Even when the cesspits were emptied, there was still the problem of what to do with the contents. Enterprising 'muck majors' collected and sold them to farmers to spread on the fields, but this was rarely enough to clear streets. Most was simply piled up to rot or to be washed away by rain, all too often finding its way back into the water supply.

SOURCE 24

Many of the privies are damaged and rendered useless by the nightmen wilfully breaking up the floors and seats to get the soil out; they will pull down one side of the bog hole that their work may be done with more ease. In this way they cause considerable damage to property, and it is too often left in the same state for a considerable time, and the place becomes an open mass of filth from daily accumulation.

Dr Rishton, Town Surveyor, Liverpool, 1845.

1 **Draw up your own chart to summarise the threats to health posed by bad housing.**

Problem	Why this was a threat to health

189

WHAT WERE THE CAUSES AND CONSEQUENCES OF RAPID URBAN GROWTH?

Where did the poor get their water?

Local rivers or streams

The poor inhabitants of Jacob's Island, Bermondsey in London (Source 25) effectively lived on a swamp. They filled buckets of water from their stream, but as the picture shows, it was this stream which received the refuse from the privies of the area.

Rain water

Rain water could be collected in large tubs or butts at the bottom of downpipes. This would often be polluted by soot and smoke, or by refuse thrown into the butts. Thankfully, the gruesome problem described in Source 26 was probably a particularly extreme case.

Wells

There were similar problems if people drew their water from wells. Overflowing pools of refuse and seepage from privies could easily contaminate the wells.

The water companies

Most people were supplied by the water companies. They pumped water to standpipes set up in the streets or in the courts.

In London, the worst of these companies simply pumped water direct from the Thames. The water supply was not constant. Sometimes water was only available for two hours a day. When the water did come on there was a scramble to fill as many buckets, cans or jars as possible. Not all towns were as bad as this. For example, Nottingham had some of the worst housing in the country, but the Trent Water Company supplied some of the highest-quality water in any town in Britain.

SOURCE 25

Jacob's Island, Bermondsey, in around 1850. The wooden shacks on the bank of the river are privies.

SOURCE 26

A family living in Bondgate had been using the water from one of the rain butts for some weeks, and finding it exceedingly offensive, the vessel was examined, when the source of contamination was found to be the decomposing body of a child which had been saturating there for more than a month!

Report from the Darlington Local Board of Health, 1851.

SOURCE 27

An engraving from 1862 showing a queue for water.

SOURCE 28

Leeds is very ill supplied with that most needful element, water, by its public water works, which were established more than forty years ago and adapted to the size of the town at that time ... only 12,000 people receive water from the water works.
A population upwards of 60,000 have no water supply except from wells and rainwater ... the water is raised from the river near Leeds Bridge ... Its quality is very indifferent.

Leeds Directory, 1834.

2 **Was fresh water supply a more or less serious problem than sanitation? Explain your answer.**

Other threats to health

Poor housing was only one of the problems. Step outside the court and into the street. What do you find?

Many streets were unpaved and were simply mud and dirt alleys. Some streets had an open drain running through the centre. Only a severe rain storm would clear these streets of filth and refuse, and even then it was only effective if the area had a 'good fall' (was on a slope).

Take a deep breath. If the smell does not overwhelm you then the air pollution might! Thousands of chimneys of forges, workshops, factories and domestic fires were belching smoke all day every day. Many of London's landmarks were black with soot by the mid-nineteenth century. When there was a good wind the pollution was wafted away. When the air was still and the pressure high the smog settled over the town and literally choked those with delicate chests.

SOURCE 29

Sheffield is one of the dirtiest and smoky towns I ever saw. There are a quantity of small forges without tall chimneys. One cannot be long in the town without experiencing the necessary inhalation of soot, which accumulates in the lungs, and its baneful effects are experienced by all who are not accustomed to it. There are, however, numbers of persons in Sheffield who think the smoke is healthy.

JC Symons, writing about Sheffield in a letter, 1843. The pollution described came from domestic coal fires as well as industry.

> 1 Read Source 29. Why might people think the smoke is healthy?

SOURCE 30

Air pollution in the iron-making town of Barrow-in-Furness, in Cumbria. This engraving was made in around 1840.

ACTIVITY

Design a poster to make people aware of the health hazards they face on coming to towns. Use Sources 15–30. Remember that many people cannot read, so it must have a visual impact.

FOCUS TASK

DID TOWN DWELLERS MAKE THEIR OWN LIVING CONDITIONS WORSE?

SOURCE 31

Beyond Hirael is Garth, a pretty spot but upon which a number of ill-built, close and undrained cottages have sprung up. I found them in a filthy condition, and affording a proof how little is the advantage of healthy position and good fall where those who built houses will not supply the ordinary means of cleanliness. Catherine Griffiths pays seven pound per annum rent for upper rooms and a smithy. The house is dark and close, it has no back premises at all – they throw soil and ashes into the stable behind and the river, but she would gladly pay 2d a week for water if it were brought in. Several others said the same.

Report to the General Board of Health on the Borough of Bangor in 1851.

SOURCE 32

It is a disorderly collection of tall, three or four storied houses, with narrow, crooked, filthy streets. A vegetable market is held in the streets, baskets with vegetables and fruits, naturally all bad and hardly fit to use … and from these, as well as the fish dealers' stalls, arises a horrible smell. The houses are occupied from cellar to garret … and their appearance is such that no human being could possibly wish to live in them. But all this is nothing compared with the narrow courts and alleys between the streets, entered by covered passages between the houses, in which the filth and the tottering ruin surpass all description. Scarcely a whole window pane can be found, the walls are crumbling, doorposts and window frames loose and broken, doors of old boards nailed together … Heaps of garbage and ashes lie in all direction, and the foul liquids emptied before the doors gather in stinking pools.

Friedrich Engels, *The Conditions of the Working Classes in England in 1844*. Engels was a bitter critic of the conditions the poor lived in. Here he describes a London slum.

SOURCE 33

Portobello-lane. This I found in a most filthy state from top to bottom, there being in it at the time about twenty cartloads of filth. Adjoining this lane was a common receptacle for all manner of filths and manure, which was allowed to run into a cottage. Next to this is called the 'Barrackyard'; this was also in one of the most filthy states that ever I saw anywhere, there being a well, covered over for the last 20 years, and a very large and offensive middenstead [dung heap]; it was swarming with pigs in a filthy state; the dwellings were most unwholesome, wanting paving, draining, air, light and water; the back part of these houses was also in a very bad state, there being a sewer choked up by the railway company, and they have also built high fences close to the windows. These remarks also apply to a row of houses in the lane in a most unhealthy state, there being in some of them two feet of water under the floors and sometimes above them.

An extract from a health inspector's report on Monkwearmouth, Sunderland, 1849.

1   Study Sources 31–33 carefully, then copy and complete this table.

Place	Problems caused mainly by residents	Problems caused by others

2   For each source, explain how reliable you think it is.

3   Now use these sources and other information on pages 184–90 to argue either:

   a) that landlords were responsible for poor living conditions; or
   b) that town dwellers made their own living conditions worse.

WHAT WERE THE CAUSES AND CONSEQUENCES OF RAPID URBAN GROWTH?

192

WHAT WERE THE CAUSES AND CONSEQUENCES OF RAPID URBAN GROWTH?

1 For each of the diseases in Source 35, explain how living conditions in the towns could make the problem worse.

2 What do you think the person in Source 34 is suffering from?

3 'Ignorance was much more of a health hazard than any disease.' Do you agree?

SOURCE **34**

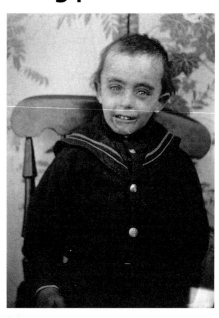

4 How does Source 35 help explain the findings described in Source 36?

A health disaster

These problems combined to produce a health disaster. Disease had long been associated with living in towns: many of the diseases in Source 35 had been present since the Middle Ages or before. However, overcrowding and poor sanitation made them even more of a problem.

SOURCE **35**

Disease	Causes	Comments
Smallpox	Contact with an infected person	Began to die out in the nineteenth century due to vaccination. There were outbreaks in the towns during the 1830s
Typhus fever	A virus carried by lice	Overcrowding, poverty and poor hygiene were responsible for several typhus epidemics in the nineteenth century
Cholera	Polluted water supply	Small organisms attack the intestine and the victim cannot keep any food or water down. Death caused by dehydration
Scrofula	Contact with a victim	Very unpleasant skin disease
Tuberculosis	Contact with infected person	Attacked the lungs – victim usually wasted away. The largest killer of the nineteenth century
Typhoid	Contaminated water or food	Spread through bad sanitation, unhygienic conditions or polluted water
Diphtheria	Polluted water	Similar to typhoid
Influenza	Spread through coughing and sneezing	Affected all ages, particularly the weak. There were regular flu epidemics throughout the nineteenth century.

Some killer diseases of the nineteenth century.

SOURCE **36**

Of all who are born of the labouring classes in Manchester more than 57% die before they attain 5 years of age … In Liverpool where the conditions of the dwellings are reported to be the worst – there the chances of life are still lower than in Manchester or Leeds. In Liverpool, of the deaths which occurred amongst the labouring classes, 62% were under 5 years of age. For Birmingham where there are many manufactories but where the drainage is comparatively good, the proportion of mortality was, in 1838, 1 in 49, whilst in Liverpool it was 1 in 31.

Edwin Chadwick, *Report on the Sanitary Conditions of the Labouring Population*, 1842.

ACTIVITY

You are going to design your own 'snakes and ladders'-style board game to show what might happen to someone from the country who has come to live in a town.

1 Use all the information about housing and health on pages 184–92 to compile a list of things which might go right and things which might go wrong. These are supposed to be real events, so for each item add a page or source reference where you can find evidence to support it.

2 Then make up your board. At the top of each snake put things that could go wrong. Put the worst things at the top of the longest snakes. At the bottom of each ladder put things which might go right. Put the best things at the bottom of the longest ladders.

Town versus countryside

The awful conditions in the towns might lead you to ask: why did people want to come and live there? Here are some possible explanations:

- They did not know how awful conditions were until they arrived there.
- They were prepared to tolerate such conditions for the sake of earning better wages.
- The bad conditions in the towns have in fact been greatly exaggerated and most people could find better housing than that described on pages 184–90.
- They did not worry because they were used to awful conditions in the countryside as well (see Source 37).

SOURCE 37

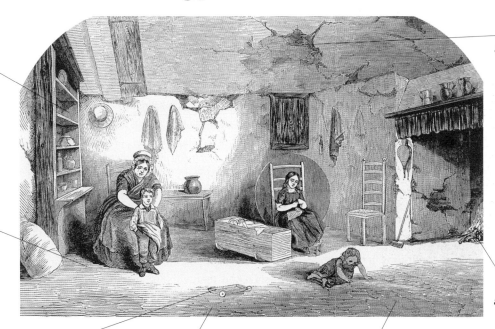

Few possessions. Rural workers were poorer than town workers and were more vulnerable to periods of unemployment.

Many cottages were damp and unhealthy. Stone walls caused condensation in winter, leading to damp and mould.

No water supply or sanitation. Some rural housing was like this until well into the twentieth century. Water came from wells or even streams.

Cold. Town dwellers had easier access to cheap fuel.

Opportunities for leisure were fewer than in towns.

Most rural cottages had only one room. Some families shared accommodation with their animals.

Floor of packed earth, dirty and dusty – no floorboards. A potential health hazard.

This interior of a cottage in Dorset in 1846 shows the conditions in which many agricultural workers lived.

FOCUS TASK

HOW DID CONDITIONS IN THE COUNTRYSIDE COMPARE WITH CONDITIONS IN THE TOWNS?

1 From your study of Chapter 3 you already know quite a lot about conditions in the countryside. Source 37 will remind you. You can also look back at pages 40–59. What evidence is there to support the view that conditions in the countryside were bad?

2 Now look back at pages 178–92. Choose one picture and one written source which you think show similarly poor living conditions in the towns. Explain your choice.

3 Do you think living conditions were worse in the countryside or in the towns? Explain your answer

with reference to the sources you have chosen for question 2. You can answer in paragraphs:

- The evidence that living conditions in the countryside were poor
- The wider picture of what life was like in the countryside (refer to Source 37 and pages 40–59)
- The evidence that living conditions in the towns were poor
- The wider picture in the towns
- Your conclusion

4 Under 'Town versus countryside' above there is a list of possible explanations for people moving to towns despite poor living conditions. Which explanation do you find most convincing?

194

WHAT WERE THE CAUSES AND CONSEQUENCES OF RAPID URBAN GROWTH?

Why didn't the councils try to solve these problems?

To a modern observer it might appear that councils simply did not care about the conditions in their towns. To some extent this harsh judgement is justified, but it is important to look at this problem from the perspective of the time.

- As you saw on page 193, many people had been used to poor living conditions in the countryside. Likewise, poor conditions in the towns were nothing new. There had been squalor and filth in towns since medieval times. People saw it as a part of urban life.

- All members of the councils were rich citizens elected by other rich citizens. The overriding concern of most councils and officials was to keep the level of local rates (taxes) under control. Providing new pavements, sewers and water supplies would inevitably lead to increased rates.

- Local authorities were nothing like the councils we have today. Many local authorities had few paid employees; and they had even fewer who had relevant experience. Local justices had the power to make and enforce local regulations, but very few had the knowledge and technical experience to draw up regulations which would be effective in dealing with building methods, drainage and sanitation.

- There were too many different organisations involved. In London, for example, there were nine water companies. When authorities for paving, sewage and general hygiene were taken into account, London had over 300 different authorities to co-ordinate.

- While some towns were run by justices, others were run by municipal corporations. These often contained the worst examples of uncaring and corrupt local government. These corporations appointed themselves and in some towns positions had become virtually hereditary. Some of the councillors actually owned water companies or were landlords of poor properties.

- We should not underestimate the importance of attitudes. Many local councillors, and indeed MPs, believed strongly in the doctrine of laissez faire and the freedom of the individual. It was the responsibility of the individual to better himself or herself, not the responsibility of local or national government. There was also a strong suspicion that if the poor saved their money and drank less gin they would be more careful about the conditions in which they lived. It was often pointed out that those who suffered the most from disease were beggars and drunkards.

- Perhaps the greatest problem was ignorance. Understanding of the causes of disease was at an early stage. People instinctively knew that dirt was associated with disease, but they didn't know what the link was. They believed bad smells (MIASMA) spread disease.

- Although the most appalling slums were often within walking distance of the well-to-do areas, the wealthy never saw them. Before the 1830s the living conditions of the poor were simply not an issue. If you look at the dates of the written sources on pages 184–91 you will see that they are nearly all after 1830. In 8.2 you will investigate why people got worried about conditions in the towns after 1830.

FOCUS TASK

WHY DID THE GROWTH OF TOWNS LEAD TO SUCH TERRIBLE CONDITIONS?

A local history museum is to be set up in the nearest town or city to you. The trustees of the museum have asked you for an exhibition panel on urban living conditions in the first half of the nineteenth century.

You can either prepare your panel on the general picture in Britain or concentrate on conditions in one town or area. Whichever you choose your exhibition panel should contain:

1 Two to four visual sources, including details of their PROVENANCE

2 Two to four written sources (a maximum of 200 words in total), again including details of provenance

3 A commentary from you (250–300 words) explaining why you have chosen your sources.
   Remember that your aim is to tell visitors about

   - the speed of growth of towns.
   - the effectiveness (or otherwise) of local authorities.
   - attitudes at the time – of government and ordinary people.
   - living conditions.
   - health hazards.
   - other problems.

ACTIVITY

Here is the start of a conversation which might have taken place between councillors in the early 1800s. Either write a continuation of their conversation or role-play it with a partner. You will need to base your arguments on the text above. Think about what someone at the time would have thought or said. What measures might they have thought of taking? Why might those measures have been difficult to put into practice?

We've got to do something to clean up our town. Conditions are awful.

That's dangerous talk. Think of the cost. Leave people to sort out their own problems.

195

WHAT WERE THE CAUSES AND CONSEQUENCES OF RAPID URBAN GROWTH?

8.2 *The public health movement: How were living conditions in the towns improved?*

1 Draw your own timeline from 1830 to 1900. As you read through pages 195–203 summarise on your timeline the events which led to improvement.

You are now going to turn your attention to what is known as the public health movement. Public health measures are action taken by governments or councils to improve health. As you saw on page 194, until the 1830s there was little action being taken. What action there was was local and unco-ordinated. Source 1 is typical.

The same factors which allowed towns to become so unhealthy in the first place also made improvement difficult. There were many who opposed health reforms; there were others who did not care; still more thought it was none of their business.

Some towns had applied to Parliament for an Improvement Act which allowed them to set up boards for lighting, drainage or sewage, but most had not – for all the reasons outlined on page 194. Then in 1832 a new visitor arrived in Britain ... cholera!

1832: Cholera shocks people into action

The first recorded victim of cholera was William Sproat, who died on 28 October 1831, in the filthy slums near the Sunderland docks. It required several doctors with experience in India to recognise the new killer was cholera.

By 1832 cholera had spread to most towns in Britain. In the epidemic of 1831–32 at least 32,000 deaths were officially recorded, and the number of unrecorded deaths will never be known.

SOURCE 1

Streets Cleaning, &c.&c.

Bradford.

November 3d, 1801.

THE Inhabitants are hereby informed, that unless the STREETS are regularly swept, every FRIDAY, and TUESDAY, proper Persons will be appointed to sweep and clean them. Also to remove all Dirt Heaps, Middens, and other Offensive Matter, in all the Back-Lanes, and Alleys, in and about the Town.

This Measure is adopted with a View to Cleanliness folely.—It having been judged one Step necessary towards checking the Progress of the present Fever.

With the same Intentions, the Poor are also informed, that they will be furnished with Quick Lime, *gratis*, at the Work-house, for the Purpose of White-Washing their Houses. That being known by repeated Experiments, and indeed general Practice, to be a most powerful Means of destroying Contagion.

| Jos. Hellings, John Oddy, | Constables. | W. Smithson, J. Wilkinson, | Overseers. |
| W. Garnett, R. Crosley, | Churchwardens. | John Blesard, James Cousin, | Surveyors. |

A notice issued by the town officials of Bradford, November 1801. *Gratis* means free.

SOURCE 2

I visited William Sproat on October 26th. We found him in a low, damp cellar, near the fish quay. He had only been ill a few hours. He was vomiting fluid tinged with blood. He was passing rice-like water. His body was cold, his eyes sunken. He had a pulse of 90 and was very weak. He was given brandy, opium and a hot bath but he fell into a coma and died.

Doctor's report on William Sproat, 1831.

SOURCE 3

Area	Population in 1831	Cases of cholera	Deaths by cholera	Widows by cholera	Orphans by cholera	First reported case in 1832
Bilston	14,492	2,250	750	150	400	4th of 9th
Darlaston	6,667	220	68	10	60	13th of 9th
Dudley	23, 043	1,224	227			23rd of 6th
Kingswinford	15,156	263	87	7	19	30th of 6th
Sedley	20,557	1,452	404	80	533	15th of 6th
Walsall	15,066	346	85			13th of 8th
Wednesbury	8,437	285	95	30	40	9th of 8th
West Bromwich	15,527	297	62			15th of 7th
Wolverhampton	24,732	565	193			8th of 8th
Wednesfield	1,879	1				7th of 8th
Willenhall	5,328	42	8	5		7th of 8th

The impact of cholera in the Midlands, 1832, based on medical records and census data.

People in towns had lived with all the diseases described in Source 35 (page 192) for years. Cholera never killed as many people as tuberculosis or diphtheria. But cholera horrified people, for several reasons:

- Partly it was the **suffering** of its victims. They were racked with vomiting and cramps. They turned blue–black and died in agony, usually within 36 hours.
- More frightening still was the **speed** at which the disease spread. For example, you can trace its rapid progress around the Midlands in the final column of Source 3.
- But most frightening of all, to the rich, was that **cholera affected rich and poor**. Other diseases seemed to be diseases of poverty. This one could as easily strike a rich family as a poor one.

How did people try to tackle cholera?

The reason cholera spreads so fast is that it is transmitted through infected water. Germs from the excreta of infected people spread from the privies to the water supply. Once a water supply is infected, anyone using that supply can catch the germs. However, in 1832 no one knew that. Some thought cholera was a punishment from God. Others believed that it was spread through touch. The most common theory among medical experts was that it was spread by bad air (called 'miasma') from all the decaying rubbish and sewage in the streets. Experts were sure that squalor and filth allowed cholera to thrive. These theories produced a range of measures to combat the disease.

Cholera hospitals were set up. The streets were cleaned. Houses were lime-washed and barrels of sulphuric acid placed in courts to try and remove the smell. Local regulations were even brought in to force people to open windows.

In response to the crisis of cholera, Parliament set up a Central Board of Health, and towns were encouraged (but not forced) to set up local boards and to take measures such as cleaning the streets and removing dung heaps. Cholera hospitals were set up and some areas tried to institute quarantines. These powers came into operation in areas where the death rate was 23 per 1,000 or greater. Boards could also appoint inspectors to make sure that houses were built with drains and lavatories. They could supply water if no water company existed (levying a rate) or check on the quality of supply of existing water companies.

In many towns these measures were taken reluctantly, and with much grumbling about interference from the central government and about the cost. Abattoirs, dyeing plants, chemical factories and a host of other businesses dumped their effluent into rivers – they were not keen on expensive alternatives to the removal of waste. Similarly, if local authorities were to cleanse the towns this would mean a rise in the rates in order to employ workers to do this. The cost of brick sewers was enormous and building them was an extremely complex job.

As a result, the improvements were short-lived. The cholera epidemic had passed by 1833. As the memory of cholera faded, boards were dissolved. In 1835 there had been over 200 boards of health. By 1840, although many of them still operated, it is doubtful how effective they really were.

1832: The Great Reform Act

In 1832 the Great Reform Act (see page 264) changed the way that the country was represented. For the first time the large new industrial towns were able to elect MPs. Some of these MPs were keen supporters of moves to clean up the towns. Others were opposed because they saw how much it would cost the towns. However, the key point is that the combined effects of the Great Reform Act and the cholera epidemic of 1832 made living conditions in towns a major political issue.

SOURCE 4

...That, with a view of checking and preventing as far as possible the further extension or spreading of the Disease, called Cholera, into these Towns and Neighbourhoods, all Parish-Officers, Constables, Peace-Officers, and others, are enjoined and required to prevent all Beggars, Vagrants, Trampers and Persons of suspected characters, and especially those coming from Newcastle, Gateshead, and other infected Places, from having any communication or intercourse with the Inhabitants of the said Towns: and that they do arrest and detain all Persons who shall be found committing acts of Vagrancy, by begging, or otherwise: and do bring them, as soon as may be, before one or more Magistrates, in order that they may be examined, and dealt with according to the Law.

A notice in Sunderland, 4 January 1832.

1 From the evidence in Source 4, what did the authorities in Sunderland believe caused cholera?

2 Would their measures help fight cholera?

1842: Edwin Chadwick reports on conditions in the towns

There was one outstanding individual who was deeply interested in public health and also had the personality to take on the opponents of reform. His name was Edwin Chadwick. Chadwick had been a Poor Law commissioner. He had already brought about great changes in the way the poor were treated by his work on the Poor Law Amendment Act of 1834 (see page 219). In his investigations into poverty he had become interested in the links between health and living conditions. Like most people of his time he was a firm believer in the miasma theory of disease and believed that cleanliness and drainage were crucial to improving health.

He began to research this question and soon came up with some interesting conclusions and some shocking evidence.

Chadwick's report: the four main points

- Disease killed more citizens than any wars.
- Parliament should pass and enforce laws to make drainage and sanitation effective.
- These measures should be funded from local rates and small increases in rents.
- Bad conditions led to immoral behaviour, not the other way around.

Chadwick's report quoted hundreds of examples to support his conclusions. One of the most famous pieces of evidence was his comparison of age at death in the countryside with age at death in towns (see Source 5 below). This was powerful proof that urban living conditions were more hazardous to health than rural conditions. He pointed out that the quality of housing in the countryside was often worse than in the towns and that rural poverty contributed to poor diet and bad health. Despite this, the poorest farm labourer could expect to live longer than a prosperous Liverpool solicitor. He would almost certainly live a lot longer than a factory worker in the same city – possibly twice as long.

SOURCE 5

Average age of death in Liverpool (urban) and Rutland (rural area) in 1840. These statistics were gathered by Chadwick for his report.

When he published his report in 1842 it stirred up great controversy. Chadwick had learned from Lord Shaftesbury's mines report (see pages 121–23) that shock tactics were one way of getting Parliament to act, so he filled the report with harrowing descriptions of poverty and illness. Some of the doctors and officials who helped him compile the report refused to be named in it. The report sold 20,000 copies. A further 10,000 were given away.

3 Why do you think Chadwick's report sold so many copies?

1844: Parliament reports on the health of towns

Despite its impact the report did not lead to immediate action. It was seen as Chadwick's own document, rather than a government report, which robbed it of some authority. However, the report was so detailed and well argued that it could not be ignored. The Home Secretary Sir James Graham was forced to set up the Health of Towns Commission to investigate Chadwick's findings officially.

The commission interviewed doctors, Poor Law officials, engineers and architects. Officially, Chadwick was not involved in the commission, but in fact he was the guiding force. He chose the witnesses and he supervised the inspections and interviews.

SOURCE 6

I persuaded the commissioners to go and see the conditions for themselves. My annual holidays were taken up in visiting some of the worst parts of some of the worst towns. Dr Playfair has been knocked up by it and is seriously ill. Mr Smith has dysentery. At Bristol Sir Henry de la Beche had to stand at the end of an alley and vomit while Dr Playfair was looking at overflowing privies.

Edwin Chadwick, 1844.

When the commission published its report in 1844, it largely repeated Chadwick's findings. This was the signal for some very active campaigning:

- In 1844 the Health of Towns Association was formed, including the future Lord Shaftesbury. This organisation used posters and the press to keep the issue of public health at the top of the political agenda. It was partly successful in its campaign.
- In 1847 a Public Health Bill was put to Parliament. However, it was defeated by opponents to reform, who became known as the 'Dirty Party'.
- In 1847 Liverpool used its Public Health Board to appoint a medical officer of health. Manchester and Glasgow followed this lead and began to take a series of small-scale but important measures. Working-class homes were provided with ash pails and, more importantly, councils took on workers to collect the refuse daily.

ACTIVITY

Read Source 6 carefully. Use this source and pages 195–97 to write the personal diary entries of either Dr Playfair, Mr Smith or Sir Henry. As well as describing the conditions they saw, think about their own feelings, whether they supported or opposed Chadwick's reforms at the start, and whether what they have seen has changed their views.

1 Why do you think the reformers called their opponents the Dirty Party?

2 If the local council were advertising for a chief inspector of health, what qualities would they look for?

1848: The Public Health Act

In 1848 cholera returned to Britain. Once again the dreaded disease helped the public health movement. With cholera raging the Dirty Party dropped their objections. The Public Health Act was passed.

Provisions of the Act

1 A general Board of Health was set up. The members were leading reformers, and Lord Shaftesbury and Chadwick himself were commissioners.

2 Any town could set up a board of health if 10 per cent of the ratepayers wanted one. If the death rate reached 23 in a thousand, a town had to have a board.

3 Local boards had powers to: appoint officials; connect older houses to sewers; make sure new housing had drainage; supply water or supervise existing water companies; provide public parks; inspect slaughter houses; and levy a local rate to pay for measures.

199

WHAT WERE THE CAUSES AND CONSEQUENCES OF RAPID URBAN GROWTH?

Was the Act effective? Yes!

Chadwick soon set to work. The Board of Health tried to work with the local boards wherever possible. With the cholera epidemic of 1848–49 killing over 50,000 people there was much interest in health measures. Among the greatest successes of the Board was a new network of sewers. The Board recommended glazed earthenware pipes for new sewage systems. These were more hygienic than brick and were also cheaper. Between 1848 and 1856, 2,500 miles of new sewer pipes were laid.

Equally important, public health issues were kept in the public eye.

SOURCE 7

THE WATER THAT JOHN DRINKS.

This is the water that JOHN drinks.

These are the fish that float in the ink-
-y stream of the Thames with its cento of stink,
That supplies the water that JOHN drinks.

This is the sewer, from cesspool and sink,
that feeds the fish that float in the ink-
-y stream of the Thames with its cento of stink,
That supplies the water that JOHN drinks.

This is the Thames with its cento of stink,
That supplies the water that JOHN drinks.

A cartoon from *Punch* magazine, October 1849. Although it was a humorous magazine, *Punch* tackled major issues of the time.

SOURCE 8

3 **Look at Sources 7 and 8. Are these cartoons supporting or opposing public health reform? Explain your answer.**

A cartoon from 1852 entitled 'A Court for King Cholera'. Notice the signs offering beds and lodgings for travellers. Also, look at the many threats to health shown in the drawing.

200

WHAT WERE THE CAUSES AND CONSEQUENCES OF RAPID URBAN GROWTH?

1   Look at Source 9. Is this a fair portrayal of local councillors? Explain your answer.

2   Does this cartoon provide evidence of opposition to public health reforms?

SOURCE 10

My impression is that the miasma chemically infects exposed water, and the poorer classes using such water are consequently the greatest sufferers.

From a letter written to the Board of Health in 1848.

SOURCE 11

We prefer to take our chance with Cholera and the rest than be bullied into health. There is nothing a man so hates as being cleaned against his will, or having his floors swept, his walls whitewashed, his pet dungheaps cleared away, or his thatch forced to give way to slate, all at the command of a sanitary bumbailiff. It is a positive fact that many have died of a good washing. All this shows extreme tenderness with which purification should advance. Not so thought Mr Chadwick ... till mankind began to fear a deluge of soap and water ... It was a perpetual Saturday night, and Master John Bull Britain was scrubbed till the tears came into his eyes, his teeth chattered, and his fists clenched themselves with worry and pain.

A leading article from *The Times*, 1854. The Public Health Act was passed in 1848 but it met with opposition. *The Times* here rejoices at the end of the Act in 1854.

3   Read Sources 11–13. What evidence is there of personal dislike of Chadwick?

4   What were the Board's achievements?

5   What were the Board's failings?

Was the Act effective? No!

However, Chadwick was disappointed by the limited powers of the new board. It was a PERMISSIVE Act rather than a compulsory one. It *allowed* local authorities to act, but it did not *force* them to clean up their towns. It did not hold authority in London. Many local authorities refused to set up local boards. By 1853 only one-sixth of the population was covered by a board, although that was still more than before, of course. Other authorities refused to form boards or to spend money on improvements, if they had formed boards at all.

SOURCE 9

SANATORY MEASURES.
Lord Morpeth Throwing Pearls before ———— Aldermen.

A cartoon from 1848. Lord Morpeth (the Home Secretary) is offering various measures to local councillors (the pigs) which will give them powers to cleanse their towns.

Some measures were resisted by the very people they were designed to help. People in towns did not like being forced to remove dung heaps or being told that the pigs they kept in their courtyards were a health hazard.

There were also some unfortunate incidents in the Board's six-year existence. In 1852 a serious outbreak of typhus fever in Croydon was traced to the new earthenware pipes. The truth was that the contractor had not laid the pipes properly, but it was Chadwick who got the blame. The new sewer pipes were too thin, and were easily blocked.

Chadwick also made mistakes. After the cholera epidemic of 1832 people had begun to draw a link between water supply and cholera outbreaks, even though they did not understand correctly what the link was (see Source 10). Chadwick was not convinced by such arguments, and in an attempt to combat cholera ordered all of London's rubbish and sewage to be flushed into the Thames. This polluted it still further. It is easy to see Chadwick's problems. Lack of medical knowledge was a major obstacle to health reform, and theories on cholera were plentiful. He could not have acted on all of them. However, such mistakes undermined the reputation of the Board of Health.

There was significant personal opposition to Chadwick himself. He was a difficult man and made enemies. He had little time for the medical profession and was quick to criticise engineers and architects. He also threatened some powerful interest groups – particularly the water companies, but also businesses which had to clean up their methods.

201

WHAT WERE THE CAUSES AND CONSEQUENCES OF RAPID URBAN GROWTH?

PROFILE
Edwin Chadwick

★ Born 1801 near Manchester.
★ Trained as a barrister and earned his living as a writer.
★ First important article was on poverty in 1828.
★ Deeply interested in social reform. Also interested in laissez faire ideas.
★ Responsible for the reform of the Poor Law in 1834 (see pages 219–21).
★ Shifted his energies to public health in 1838.
★ Produced the ground-breaking *Report on the Sanitary Conditions of the Labouring Population* in 1842.
★ Became a member of the Health of Towns Association in 1844.
★ Heavily influenced the Royal Commission on Large Towns in 1844, although technically not involved.
★ In 1848 became the commissioner of the new Public Health Board.
★ Always a controversial and sometimes a difficult person, he achieved great things and also made mistakes, upsetting many important people and groups.
★ in 1854 he was forced to resign as Public Health Commissioner and the Board was not renewed.

ACTIVITY

Draw up a story strip detailing the career of Edwin Chadwick. Use the Profile and the information in the text above to help you.

SOURCE 12

Our enemies include the civil engineers, because we have selected able men, who have carried into effect new principles, and at a less salary. The college of Physicians, because of our success at dealing with the Cholera, when we proved that many a Poor Law Medical Officer knew more than all the flash and fashionable doctors of London. Then come the water companies for we devised a method of supply, which together replaced them. The commissioners of Sewers, for our plans and principles were the reverse of theirs; they hated us with pure hatred.

Lord Shaftesbury's diary, August 1853.

SOURCE 13

Having stated as what he regarded as Mr Chadwick's merits, he would not disguise that, like many other ardent reformers, Mr Chadwick often, in his zeal for change, overlooked or disregarded the objections and repugnance with which his views were received by others … It was very probable that Mr Chadwick had not observed towards these persons the most conciliatory tone.

Report of a speech by Lord John Russell, July 1854.

The Board of Health is dismantled

In 1854 Chadwick's opponents finally got the better of him. When the Act came up for review in 1854 Chadwick was voted out and forced to retire. The Board itself was dissolved in 1858.

Despite this failure it had made considerable progress and the Board created a climate which was favourable to future reformers.

FOCUS TASK

WHY WAS PUBLIC HEALTH REFORM AN UPHILL STRUGGLE?

This diagram shows factors which held back public health reform.

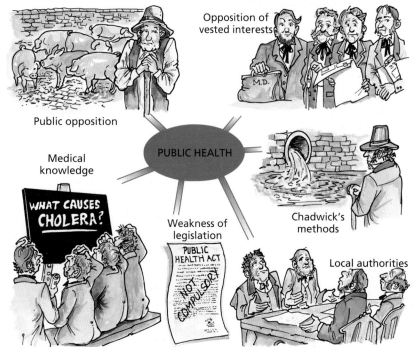

1 Draw your own diagram.
2 For each factor:
   a) Explain how it slowed the progress of public health.
   b) Find evidence to support what you say.
3 Explain how any of the factors were linked to each other.

What factors led to the Public Health Act of 1875?

1854: The work of John Snow

John Snow was a London doctor who was very interested in cholera. With others he had worked out a link between cholera and water supply and had conducted his own meticulous research. When a severe outbreak of cholera hit the Broad Street area of central London in 1854 he visited all infected houses in the area. He made a careful analysis of what water supply they were using. He also visited houses in the same area which had not been affected. He discovered:

- that all the infected houses got their water from a single water pump.
- that a local brewery which had not been affected by cholera never used that pump because it had its own water supply.
- that a woman living a long way from the area who had died of cholera always had water from the Broad Street pump sent to her as she liked its taste.

He got permission to remove the handle of the Broad Street pump. There were no more cases of cholera. The pump was dug out and it was found that a cesspool just one metre from the pump had a cracked lining so its contents were leaking into the water supply.

Snow published his findings the same year. They focused the public health debate on water supply.

A From *Punch*. It was called 'A Drop of London Water'. Since the development of an improved microscope in the 1830s the study of micro-organisms had become popular in the scientific community, although the link between microbes and disease had not yet been identified.

SOURCE 14

SALUS POPULI SUPREMA LEX.

Time, Mid-day.   Tide, Low Water at London Br.

Devilish thick !
yes, here I stick !
It makes me Sick !

What torrents of filth come from
that Walbrook Sewer !!

Sewer ! why there are 130 such !

Oh' never mind any nastiness goes down
here in the Borough.

What do they drink that !

Prodigious !

"Tell it not in Gath."

Give us Clean Water !

Give us pure Water !

We shall all have the Cholera

give us clean water

Give us Clean water

SOURCE OF THE SOUTHWARK WATER WORKS

Hail long-expected days
That Thames's glory to the stars shall raise.

George Cruikshank fecit.

B By Cruikshank. The Southwark Water Works supplied much of south London with water. Most of London's sewers emptied into the Thames near the Southwark Water Works inlet.

203

WHAT WERE THE CAUSES AND CONSEQUENCES OF RAPID URBAN GROWTH?

1855: Dr John Simon becomes chief medical adviser

The central government realised that it had to work with local authorities to improve conditions. Learning the lessons from Chadwick's time, the government appointed Dr John Simon as chief medical adviser. Simon was able to achieve important results. He introduced tough regulations which effectively made smallpox vaccination compulsory.

1858: The Great Stink

In 1858 London suffered what was to become known as the 'Great Stink'. It was a hot summer and the filthy River Thames smelt so bad that Parliament was suspended. The Great Stink convinced people that the issue of sanitation had to be addressed, and steps were taken to improve London's sewage system. By 1865 London's sewage, although still dumped in the river, was being dumped downstream, away from the city.

The builders learnt from Chadwick's mistakes. The new sewers were very large. They could not easily be blocked.

1860: A Royal Commission

A Royal Commission in 1860 found that conditions in many towns were as bad as ever.

1866: More cholera!

A cholera outbreak in 1865–66 killed 20,000. This allowed Simon to push through a Sanitary Act in 1866 which said that all local authorities should have a Board of Health.

1867: Working-class men get the vote

Urban working men gained the vote in 1867, which meant that politicians took social reform even more seriously.

1861–72: The causes of disease are identified

Alongside these other developments, understanding of disease advanced in leaps and bounds. In 1861 in France Louis Pasteur published his germ theory, which for the first time proved a link between germs and disease. Pasteur's work triggered more research by other scientists and doctors. By 1872 Robert Koch had discovered the specific germ which caused cholera.

The Public Health Act of 1875

John Simon's most important achievement was to write and force through the Public Health Act of 1875. There were two key aspects of this Act.

- Firstly, the Act brought together all the previous measures into one law. This was a great help to the local authorities who wished to carry out improvements.
- Secondly, the Act was compulsory. By law local authorities now had to provide clean water, proper drainage and sewers, and appoint a medical officer of health. In 1870 there were only 50 medical officers of health; by 1880 there were more than 1,200.

Also in 1875, the Food and Drugs Act clamped down on practices such as watering down milk. The Act allowed local authorities to appoint analysts to check the quality of food and drugs.

---

1 Was the Great Stink the real point, or did it simply focus people's minds on a bigger issue?

2 How was the 1875 Public Health Act different from the 1848 Act?

3 List the factors which led to the passing of the 1875 Act.

4 Choose two factors which you think are particularly important and explain your choice.

FOCUS TASK

Compare John Simon's achievements with Chadwick's. Which of these two men achieved the most?

You could use a diagram like this to help you:

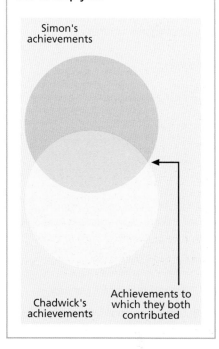

Simon's achievements

Chadwick's achievements

Achievements to which they both contributed

204

WHAT WERE THE CAUSES AND CONSEQUENCES OF RAPID URBAN GROWTH?

The work of other improvers

Alongside the story of public health improvement there is another story of individuals doing what they could to improve the health of ordinary people in towns. They are exceptions, but they are important exceptions and their influence increased as public health became more and more of an issue through the century.

Some of them operated out of a sense of idealism or PHILANTHROPY – that is, they wished to help those less fortunate than themselves. Others believed that healthy, well-housed workers were more efficient and effective.

Case study 1: Lord Mostyn and the Llandudno Improvement Act 1854

Llandudno lies 20 miles along the coast from Bangor (see Sources 7 and 8 on pages 178 and 179) in North Wales. It is on the main route from London to Holyhead (the main port for Ireland).

The land was owned by Lord Mostyn, who wanted to establish Llandudno as a holiday resort for the well to do, and as a stopping place for travellers to Ireland. He was particularly keen to capitalise on the new railway being built along the North Wales coast. As the owner of the land he could make profits by selling or renting property in the new town.

Because he wanted to attract visitors he was anxious that his new town should be free of disease and filth and should not be afflicted by cholera, as Bangor had been. You can see his plans in Sources 15–17. Lord Mostyn was extremely strict about enforcing the regulations.

His plan worked. By the 1880s Llandudno had become a thriving holiday resort. Its wide streets and the open feel of the town were very attractive to Victorian visitors.

Lord Mostyn's motive was to protect his business investment, but his strict regulations also brought the benefit of a healthy and clean environment.

SOURCE 15

Plan of Llandudno in 1849, showing the proposed plots of land for development.

SOURCE 16

New Streets
No new street shall be made without the consent of the vendor in writing. Principal streets to be no less than 36 feet [11 metres] wide, with a clear space for the bed of the street of no less than 24 feet [7.3 metres] in width

Back Streets
To be no less than 18 feet [5.5 metres] wide

Courts
No courts or courts of houses will be permitted to be erected for habitation

Cellars
No cellar shall be let as a distinct and separate habitation

Passages
At the back or side of houses not to be less than 4 feet [1.2 metres] wide

Ashpits
Must be in connection with every house

Coal Vaults
Not to be made without consent of the vendor

Size of Rooms and Height of Storeys
No house shall be built which shall not have at least 144 feet [43.9 metres] [square] [of clear wall space not attached to another property], superficial, clear – not less than 8 feet [2.4 metres] in height – no bedroom less than 7 feet 6 in [2.3 metres], save in attics. Cellars used as kitchens shall be not less than 7 feet [2.1 metres] in height

Size of Windows
In rooms for habitation, not less than 5 feet 6in [1.7 metres] in height, 3 feet wide.

Building regulations, Llandudno, 1854.

205

WHAT WERE THE CAUSES AND CONSEQUENCES OF RAPID URBAN GROWTH?

1 Choose what you think are the three most important laws and regulations in Sources 16 and 17 and explain your choice.

2 What evidence is there that Lord Mostyn's surveyors had learned lessons from other towns?

SOURCE 17

That it shall not be lawful to let separately, except as a warehouse or storehouse, or suffer to be occupied as a dwelling house any room or building which, or any part of which, is or shall be directly over any privy or cesspool, unless the same privy or cesspool shall have fitted up in connection with it a water closet, with an adequate and constant supply of water, to the satisfaction of the commissioner; and any person who shall build any house contrary to this provision, or who shall let separately (except as aforesaid) or who shall knowingly suffer to be occupied as a dwelling house, any room or building within the limits of the Act, contrary to this provision, shall be liable to a penalty not exceeding 40 shillings, and a further penalty not exceeding 10 shillings for every day during which such house shall continue contrary to this provision, or such a room or building shall be so occupied after conviction of the first offence.

A clause from the Improvement Act, 1854.

Case study 2: George Peabody and the Peabody Trust

The Peabody Trust was a charity providing housing for working people. The trust was named after (and funded by) the wealthy American merchant and philanthropist George Peabody, who came to London to live in 1837. The trust built American-style apartment blocks which were a great improvement on slum conditions.

SOURCE 18

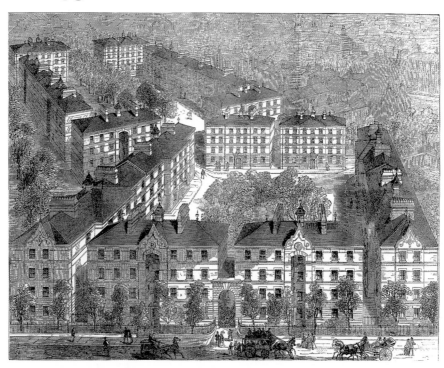

Peabody Trust apartment blocks. The first Peabody housing was built in 1869. Although rather grim-looking, the apartments were well built and maintained. They also had full water and sanitation facilities, as well as windows and balconies.

These apartments were very popular, but there were not enough of them to solve the general housing problem. The rents were also too high for the poorest workers.

SOURCE 19

Model housing in Saltaire.

FOCUS TASK

1 Copy this chart:

Case study	What improvement?	Who was the housing for?	Motive of improver

2 Fill out the chart as fully as you can for the three case studies.

3 Which do you think was the most significant achievement? Explain your answer.

Case study 3: Titus Salt and Saltaire

The most unusual and impressive experiments were those of employers who built whole model villages for their workers.

Sir Titus Salt had built a spinning mill near Bradford in 1834. He was a very religious man, but he was also a successful businessman, and became an influential local figure. He was mayor of Bradford in 1848 and an MP from 1859 to 1861.

In 1853 he built Saltaire, a village of 800 houses, for the workers in his Bradford textile mills. It consisted of well-built, well-planned cottages, with piped gas, water and a WC.

Other improvers

Similar principles were employed by the chocolate manufacturer George Cadbury at Bournville, Birmingham and by Joseph Rowntree at Earswick near York. The Lever family at Port Sunlight also created a model town with all the houses arranged around open green spaces. Of course, only the workers and their families could live in these model villages and towns.

These employers enjoyed national reputations and became famous for the quality of housing they provided for their workers. Their motives were predominantly philanthropic, but there were definite practical advantages to providing quality housing for workers.

How did councils improve housing?

The focus of the public health movement through the nineteenth century was on water supply and sanitation. Improving these services was a major achievement. However, in the 1870s the crisis in housing with which this chapter began still remained. This was a much more difficult problem to deal with. It is possible to relay sewers and run new water supplies if the money and the will are there. It is quite another thing to demolish poor housing and replace it with modern housing.

207

WHAT WERE THE CAUSES AND CONSEQUENCES OF RAPID URBAN GROWTH?

Although their achievements were impressive, people like Mostyn, Peabody or Salt did little to help the great mass of the poor. However, they did help to guide the bodies who could help the poor – the large local authorities. By the Artisans Dwellings Acts of 1868 and 1875, they were empowered to improve their towns. The 1868 Act (Torren's Act) gave local councils the power to buy and demolish a house if the landlord refused to improve it. The improvers had shown it was much more practical to improve housing if you were starting from scratch, and the 1875 Act (Cross's Act) allowed councils to clear whole districts. Both Acts were permissive rather than compulsory and the cost of reconstruction dismayed most councils.

Joseph Chamberlain

The radical Mayor of Birmingham, Joseph Chamberlain, was an exception. He took up these powers with enthusiasm. Between 1872 and 1876 Chamberlain bought almost 40 acres of slum housing in the centre of Birmingham, cleared it and replaced it with Corporation Street (see Source 21B). It was a tremendous achievement and a tribute to Chamberlain's abilities and energy. Eighty years later Corporation Street was still a gleaming monument to his work. On the other hand, the poor evicted from the Gullet (see Source 21A) may have been less impressed with Chamberlain. No official arrangements were made to re-house them, and the needs of the poor were certainly not the only thing in Chamberlain's mind. The majority of Birmingham's slums remained untouched.

1 **What do you think motivated Chamberlain in his attempts to improve housing in the centre of Birmingham?**

2 **Look back at your chart from page 206. Add a further row to summarise the work of Joseph Chamberlain.**

SOURCE **20**

I think I have now almost completed my municipal programme … The town will be parked, paved, assized, marketed, gas and watered and improved – all as a result of three years' active work.

Joseph Chamberlain, 1876.

SOURCE **21**

A

B

Housing around the Gullet (**A**) was replaced by Corporation Street (**B**).

208

WHAT WERE THE CAUSES AND CONSEQUENCES OF RAPID URBAN GROWTH?

How much did living conditions in towns improve?

The cost of Chamberlain's work had been enormous. It scared off many other authorities who might have followed his example. However, from the 1870s onwards some councils, particularly in London and Liverpool, began clearing some slums and building council flats for the people evicted.

New housing was also built to increasingly higher standards. Building regulations were drawn up and enforced. However, better housing is nearly always more expensive to build, so this particularly benefited the skilled workers or tradesmen who could afford the higher rents of the new and better houses or even to buy their own houses.

Overcrowding in towns was also eased by the coming of the railways, as the middle classes moved out of the towns into the suburbs (see page 169).

So although the situation was improving in the late nineteenth century you must keep these improvements in perspective.

The better-off workers enjoyed improved conditions and the fortunate few lived in model housing. For the majority, however, slums were still common and two world wars would pass before government really tackled the housing question. In 1889 Charles Booth undertook a major study of living conditions of the poor in East London and found conditions every bit as bad as those in Sources 6 and 8 on pages 198 and 199. When the government wanted to recruit men for the Boer War in 1899, it was alarmed to find that almost half of the potential recruits were unfit for service. This triggered a government inquiry into the health of the poor that found the housing in many areas and for many people was still unhealthy and in need of major reform. Well into the twentieth century urban housing was still a major problem and some would say it has remained so to this day.

FOCUS TASK

WHY HAD CONDITIONS IMPROVED IN TOWNS BY 1900?

The Times newspaper commented that disasters were usually the greatest incentive to reform:

> Cholera is the best of all sanitary reformers. It overlooks no mistake and pardons no oversight.

You are going to write an essay explaining how far you agree with this statement. To get yourself started:

1 Look back at the text and sources on pages 195–208 and list all the evidence to support the statement.

2 Now look at each of the following factors, and alongside each one find an example of it influencing the public health movement.

- The work of individuals
- Extension of voting rights
- Scientific research

3 Add any other factors which you think were important.

4 Look at the two Public Health Acts. Explain how any of the three factors above helped bring that movement about.

5 Decide for yourself whether either of these important Acts would have been introduced if it hadn't been for cholera.

6 Now you are ready to write your essay, with paragraphs as follows:

- Begin, as usual, by explaining what the question is about.
- Explain the evidence to support the view.
- Outline how other factors played a part.
- Describe how these factors together helped to bring about two important Public Health Acts.
- Finally, reach your own conclusion as to the importance of cholera.

SECTION 5

Responses to economic and social change

9

Poverty 1815–1990

9.1 The introduction of the new Poor Law

FOCUS

Poverty had always been a problem in Britain, but in the nineteenth century it became one of the government's major concerns. As the number of poor people rose, the cost of looking after them also increased. There was intense debate about how to help the poor.

9.1 looks at poverty in the early nineteenth century. You will:

- examine how poverty was dealt with before 1834.
- look at the causes and consequences of the introduction of the new Poor Law in 1834.

9.2 covers poverty in the late nineteenth century and up to 1914. You will:

- investigate changing attitudes to poverty in this period.
- look at the work of individuals and governments to help the poor.

9.3 covers the period from 1918 until 1939. You will:

- look at the problem of poverty between the world wars.
- examine the situation in different parts of Britain during this period.

9.4 examines the Welfare State. You will:

- study the setting up of the Welfare State.
- see how far poverty has been defeated in the 1990s.

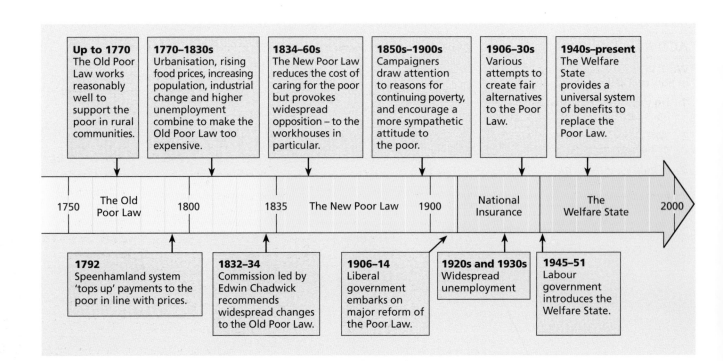

Up to 1770 The Old Poor Law works reasonably well to support the poor in rural communities.

1770–1830s Urbanisation, rising food prices, increasing population, industrial change and higher unemployment combine to make the Old Poor Law too expensive.

1834–60s The New Poor Law reduces the cost of caring for the poor but provokes widespread opposition – to the workhouses in particular.

1850s–1900s Campaigners draw attention to reasons for continuing poverty, and encourage a more sympathetic attitude to the poor.

1906–30s Various attempts to create fair alternatives to the Poor Law.

1940s–present The Welfare State provides a universal system of benefits to replace the Poor Law.

1750 — The Old Poor Law — 1800 — 1835 — The New Poor Law — 1900 — National Insurance — The Welfare State — 2000

1792 Speenhamland system 'tops up' payments to the poor in line with prices.

1832–34 Commission led by Edwin Chadwick recommends widespread changes to the Old Poor Law.

1906–14 Liberal government embarks on major reform of the Poor Law.

1920s and 1930s Widespread unemployment

1945–51 Labour government introduces the Welfare State.

What is the best way to help the poor?

Society has always found it hard to make up its mind about the best way to help the poor. Is it better to give them money, or to force them to do something about their own situation? Look at Source 1.

SOURCE 1

A

HOMELESS! HELPLESS! HOPELESS!

B

People begging in the street. **A** is an illustration from 1866, **B** a photograph from the 1990s.

ACTIVITY

Work in pairs. Discuss the pictures in Source 1 with your partner.

1 Do you regard the people in each picture as poor?

2 What would be the best way of helping each person?

3 Would people in the nineteenth century have agreed with you?

Opinions on poverty in the early nineteenth century

In the early nineteenth century, most political and industrial leaders (who were important because they were the ones whose decisions most affected poor people) would have accepted the statements shown in Source 2.

SOURCE 2

The poor must learn to help themselves. If you help the poor it makes them depend on you and turns them into scroungers.

Poverty is necessary. Poverty is not an evil. It is acceptable and even desirable. Without poverty, people have no incentive to work to better themselves. So without poverty landowners and businesses have no labourers.

There is a difference between being poor and being a pauper. A few people are genuinely unable to improve their situation because they are too old, too sick or too young to work. They are paupers. They need help.

Opinions on poverty in the early 1800s.

How were the poor dealt with under the old Poor Law?

The old Poor Law had been set up in the time of Queen Elizabeth I, in 1601. This law made the local PARISH responsible for looking after its own paupers (see Source 3). All landowners in the parish paid 'poor rates'. These ratepayers also took it in turns to act as unpaid Overseers of the Poor.

The old Poor Law distinguished between two types of poor people, as follows. **The deserving poor** were people whose circumstances made them poor and who could do nothing about it. The law specified that they should be housed in a poorhouse or workhouse. In theory, the parish supplied tools and raw materials, and the inmates of the workhouse then carried out useful work such as making candles or weaving baskets.

In many cases, however, it made more sense to provide people with OUTDOOR RELIEF — food, clothing and medical care in their own homes — than to make them enter the workhouse. This was commonly done, although strictly speaking outdoor relief was not allowed under the Poor Law.

SOURCE 3

The poor and helpless persons in each parish shall be given relief from that which each rate payer shall of their charity give weekly; and the same relief shall be gathered in every parish by collectors and handed out to the poor; for none shall openly go or sit begging.

The 1601 Poor Law.

SOURCE 4

An eighteenth-century playing card showing busy paupers in a workhouse.

SOURCE 5

Half a pound of butter and sugar for Old King	*4 ½d*
Gave him more in his illness	*1s 6d*
Paid the clerk's fee for burying King	*2s 6d*
Mary Mason for a coat	*6s 5d*
4 shirts for workhouse boy	*8s 9d*
Coffin for Old King	*7s 6d*

Poor Law accounts from Patshull, Staffordshire, 1744.

1 **What were the aims of the old Poor Law?**

2 **Does the old Poor Law strike you as harsh?**

3 **What kind of relief is described in each of Sources 4–5?**

4 **Why do you think many parishes did not follow the law but allowed outdoor relief?**

5 **What activities can you see happening in Source 4?**

6 **What impression does it give you of the workhouses in the eighteenth century?**

The idle poor were people who were able to work but did not want to. It was believed that they were poor because they did not try hard enough to better themselves. Under the Poor Law they were supposed to be sent to a House of Correction, where they would be given hard work and a poor diet. However, in many parishes no such place existed. Most Overseers realised that there were very few poor who would not (as opposed to could not) work.

SOURCE 6

Main factors

Old age

Loss of breadwinner in the family

Illness or injury

Low wages or high prices

WHAT MADE PEOPLE POOR?

Subsidiary factors

Changes in working methods

A bad period for trade

Bad harvests

Reasons for poverty.

Improvements to the old Poor Law

On the whole, the system worked well in most areas until the 1750s. The parish usually covered a single village, so the Overseers and the paupers knew each other and each other's families. The spirit of the 1601 Act was observed, even if it was not followed exactly. Old and sick people in the parish were cared for with outdoor relief, and orphans were looked after until they could be apprenticed to a tradesman. However, some problems emerged and action was taken to solve them.

The Settlement Act, 1622

One problem with the old Poor Law was what to do about poor people in a parish who originally came from other parishes. The Settlement Act of 1622 allowed parishes to send away paupers from elsewhere after 40 days, unless the pauper had a note from his or her 'home' parish agreeing to pay back any money spent.

1 Read Source 7. Do you think Thomas Whitworth looked forward to his turn as Overseer?

2 Why would Overseers want to send away paupers from other parishes?

3 Pregnant women suffered especially harshly under the Settlement Act. Can you work out why?

4 Bearing in mind what you know about population change and the industrial revolution, why would you expect the Settlement Act to cause increasing problems from 1750 onwards?

ACTIVITY

Write your own Factfile on the old Poor Law. Include definitions of the terms 'deserving poor', 'idle poor', 'pauper', 'outdoor relief', 'workhouse', 'parish' and 'The Settlement Act'.

SOURCE 7

Dear Sir

A man of the name of Richard Ball belonging to your Parish is in a very distressed situation, his wife is helpless, and himself lame, and not able to work and the family is absolutely starving for want of provisions. There's no one will trust him with anything. He came to me last night, I gave him 2 shillings. He said he was with you on Monday you gave him 3 shillings and that is all the family have had to subsist on since. You said you would see them in a few days. I hope you will consider their case; and either come over and see what a situation they are in or send me a note to advance them a little money or they will be lost.
Your humble servant
Thomas Whitworth, Overseer

A letter from one Overseer to another, 1817.

The Workhouse Act, 1722

It was relatively easy for parishes to take the action described and shown in Sources 5, 6 and 7. Overseers had a more serious problem when it came to able-bodied labourers who simply could not find any work. The aim was to provide work for the able-bodied poor, but it was usually a shortage of work which drove such people to ask for relief in the first place. In 1722, a Workhouse Act said that parishes must build workhouses. However, even after this Act most parishes still preferred outdoor relief: it was cheaper than a workhouse, and if a labourer continued to live at home it was easier for him or her to do any occasional work that came along. Some people also thought it was wrong that workhouse inmates made cheap items such as mops or brushes, because it was unfair competition for traders in those businesses.

The old Poor Law under pressure

By the end of the eighteenth century, the system of poor relief was coming under increasing pressure. The rising population meant there were more mouths to feed. In the north, the new cotton mills were taking away the livelihood of spinners and weavers. Food prices were rising faster than wages, so even people in work were often unable to feed their families. The economy was suffering ever more extreme booms and slumps, which meant that almost any worker – even a skilled tradesman – could suddenly be out of work.

To cope with these increased demands, the government and the parishes tried a range of measures.

Gilbert's Act, 1782

In 1782, the government passed Gilbert's Act. This Act allowed parishes to join together into unions to build workhouses, to make the cost more affordable. These workhouses would be for the old, the sick and children. The Act also officially allowed outdoor relief, recognising that most parishes were already giving this in any case. Poor Law Guardians were to administer it. In practice, this Act made little difference. Few parishes formed unions, and the cost of taking care of the poor continued to rise.

The 'roundsmen' system

Some parishes tried to solve the problem of the able-bodied poor by using the 'roundsmen' system. Labourers were given tickets by the Poor Law Guardians, and then went round local farmers looking for work. If they were offered work, the parish council paid some or all of their wages for that day.

5 Look back at Source 6. Which of the factors shown were becoming more important as causes of poverty in the late eighteenth century?

The Speenhamland system, 1792

Another problem in the 1790s was that food prices were increasing rapidly, but the wages paid to labourers in work were lagging far behind. The parishes and the government knew that this was exactly the problem that had triggered the French Revolution. If people cannot afford even to buy bread, they become desperate, and this could cause disaster for the authorities.

In many parishes, an allowance system was developed to top up the wages of casual labourers so that they could feed themselves and their families. The best-known example of this was the Speenhamland system (see page 41). Payments under this system rose in line with bread prices.

In the short term, this system probably did help to avoid widespread riots and disturbances. However, in the longer term the system made labourers worse off. Firstly, it damaged their sense of pride and self-respect. Also, farmers were tempted to keep wages low because they knew that they would be topped up by the parish. Critics of the system argued that allowances paid for children encouraged people to marry early and have more children (see Source 8), even though the growing population was already a problem.

The system also meant that the parish had little control over the rising cost. As the price of wheat rose during the French wars (see page 32), so did the number of people seeking poor relief. The total cost of poor relief was less than £2 million before the war. In 1812, with wheat prices at their highest, it cost £8.8 million.

By the 1830s, as you saw on page 44, there were an increasing number of riots among the rural poor all over southern England. The Poor Law did not even seem to be able to keep the peace.

Pauper apprentices

It had always been a common practice for orphans in the care of a parish to be apprenticed to a local craftsman to learn a trade. The orphan would live with and work for the craftsman. With the growth of textile mills it became increasingly common in the late nineteenth century for poor children to be sent to the mills as pauper apprentices. For the local overseers this was an attractive way of offloading some of their growing responsibilities. For the mill owner they were a useful supply of cheap labour. However, as you saw on pages 87–89, the treatment of pauper apprentices was bitterly criticised by factory reformers.

FOCUS TASK

HOW WERE THE POOR TREATED UNDER THE OLD POOR LAW?

Use the information and sources in this section to choose answers to each of the following questions. Whichever answer you choose, be ready to justify your choice with a reasoned answer and supporting evidence.

1 Was the old Poor Law fair or unfair to 'paupers'?

2 Was the old Poor Law fair or unfair to the 'able-bodied poor'?

3 Were attempts to improve the old Poor Law successful or unsuccessful?

SOURCE 9

A reconstruction drawing of the apprentice house at Styal in 1830. The apprentices at Styal were better looked after than those in many other mills.

A Royal Commission

With the cost of poor relief rising and the law being criticised on all sides, the government felt that action was needed. In 1832, eight commissioners were appointed to investigate how effective the Poor Law was and whether it needed reform.

The Commission was headed by the economist Nassau Senior. However, most of the 'leg work' of gathering and sorting information, which took two years, was carried out by 26 assistant commissioners. These officials visited over 3,000 parishes across the country.

The most prominent of these assistant commissioners was Edwin Chadwick, whom you have already come across in Chapter 8. Chadwick was a former lawyer and journalist. He impressed the commissioners with the enormous amount of evidence he collected from his allotted areas in London and Berkshire. It was Chadwick and Nassau Senior who wrote most of the Commission's 300-page report.

The final report contained a devastating attack on the old Poor Law and proposed radical new measures. It concluded that the old Poor Law encouraged idleness and discouraged paupers from improving themselves. It had to be replaced with a system which made even the lowest-paid employment preferable to being a pauper. The Commission's findings are shown below.

1. Cost

Everyone knew that the old Poor Law was expensive, but the Commission spelled it out in detail.

SOURCE 10

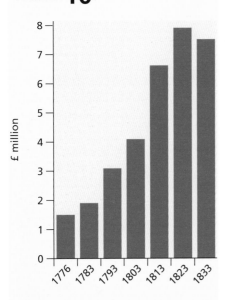

The cost of poor relief 1776–1833.

2. Inefficiency

The old Poor Law's use of the parish system was inefficient. Britain in 1830 was very different from Britain in the time of Queen Elizabeth I, when the old law was passed. Parishes were too small to operate efficiently, and their officials were unpaid amateurs.

SOURCE 11

As a body I found annual overseers wholly incompetent ... either from the interference of private occupations, or from want of experience and skill; but most frequently from both these causes. Their object is to get through the year with as little unpopularity and trouble as possible.

An assistant commissioner's views on the Overseers in North Wales.

3. Inconsistency

The report also pointed out that the old Poor Law was not being consistently applied. The old system had already been altered in many areas, and the labour rate or roundsmen system were being used instead. In many parishes workhouses were non-existent.

4. Allowances

The commissioners felt that allowance systems encouraged paupers to continue 'on the parish' and removed incentives to find work. The Speenhamland system came under fierce attack because of the way in which it discouraged individuals from trying to better themselves. If they worked hard to earn more money, labourers simply received less relief.

SOURCE 12

First the labourer becomes more steady and diligent; next, the more efficient labour makes the return to the farmer's capital larger, and the consequent increase of the fund for the employment of labour enables and induces the capitalist to give better wages.

An extract from the report expressing the commissioners' views on the effect of withdrawing relief.

SOURCE 13

The magistrates do a great deal of harm by their scales of allowance. For instance, a man by the name of Robert Smith is now on the road, only works half what he ought to do, has 11 shillings by order of the magistrates and has five children living in the house with him, some of whom work, and he gets their wages. He ... says he will not try to get work anywhere else, as he cannot have such good masters anywhere as the magistrates.

Written by a Derbyshire Overseer in 1831.

1 **For each recommendation explain how it would help deal with the findings of the report.**

Recommendations of the Commission

- There should be one system of poor relief for the whole country.
- Outdoor relief for the able-bodied should be ended.
- Parishes should join together to form unions. These unions would be able to run large workhouses, which could cope with the paupers, old and sick of the parishes.
- Paupers should receive relief only if they and their families were prepared to enter a workhouse. If not, they would receive no relief. This became known as the 'workhouse test'.
- Workhouses should be run on a harsh regime. Conditions in the workhouses should be so tough that only the truly desperate would enter them.

5. Workhouses

Comfortable workhouses also came in for criticism. They took away the incentive for the poor to work.

SOURCE 14

… in by far the greater number of cases, it is a large almshouse, in which the young are trained in idleness, ignorance and vice; the able bodied maintained in sluggish sensual indolence … and the whole body of inmates subsisted on food for exceeding both in kind and in amount, not merely the diet of the independent labourer, but that of the majority of the persons who contribute to their support.

An extract from the report of the Royal Commission of 1834 on workhouses.

SOURCE 15

The parish workhouse at St James's, London, in the early nineteenth century; it was criticised for being too comfortable.

SOURCE 16

… a room full of sturdy labourers in hobnailed boots and smock frocks, sitting round a stove with their faces half roasted … they never rose from their seats and had generally an overfed, mutinous and insubordinate appearance.

Assistant commissioner Sir Francis Head describing a workhouse he found in Kent.

There was no shortage of evidence and opinion to draw on. Almost everyone had something to say about the old Poor Law. However, the commissioners were particularly influenced by the work of the Reverend Thomas Malthus on population and Jeremy Bentham's views on individual rights.

Thomas Malthus

Malthus believed that population controlled itself by means of certain checks, including war, disease and starvation. He argued that poor relief kept the population too high, and that wages were too low because of overpopulation. Malthus also had a very low opinion of the working class.

SOURCE 17

The labouring poor always live hand to mouth. Their wants of the moment are all they think about and they seldom think of the future. All they have above their needs of the moment goes, generally speaking, to the ale house. The poor laws of England may therefore be said to lessen both the power and the will to save among the common people and thus to weaken the incentive to soberness and hard work, and hence to happiness.

Thomas Malthus, *Essay on Population*, 1797.

Both Edwin Chadwick and Nassau Senior largely agreed with the views of Malthus.

SOURCE 18

There is no employment for me in my own parish: there is abundance in the next. Yet if I offer to go there, I am driven away. Why? Because I might become unable to work one of these days, and so must not work while I am able. I am thrown upon one parish now, for fear I should fall upon another, 40 or 50 years hence. At this rate how is work ever to get done? If a man is not poor he won't work: and if he is poor, the laws won't let him.

Written by Jeremy Bentham in 1823.

Jeremy Bentham

Bentham believed that individuals should be allowed to sort out their own problems. In this way, according to Bentham, the greatest possible number of people would gain the greatest amount of happiness. These ideas became known as Utilitarianism. Chadwick and other Utilitarians agreed with Bentham that paupers' troubles would be solved only through their own efforts. The duty of the state and the government was to encourage individuals to make these efforts and also to remove any obstacles which would stop them doing so.

The report in hindsight

Historians have criticised the report and its authors for not presenting a balanced view.

The report described abuses which were taking place under the old Poor Law and mentioned countless examples of poor relief encouraging idleness. They pointed out that disturbances like the Swing Riots (see page 44) took place in areas where most outdoor relief was given. This was seen as proof that outdoor relief made labourers lazy and disrespectful. However, the report glossed over evidence that rural labourers' wages were not keeping pace with rising prices.

Nor did it consider the causes of poverty in depth. Although the overall cost of poor relief was rising, it tended to rise and fall with changing economic conditions, but the Commission ignored this. Radicals such as Robert Owen and Richard Cobden argued that poverty was caused by unfair sharing out of wealth, or lack of jobs, but the Commission had very little time for such views.

Their critics claim that the Poor Law commissioners knew what they were going to say before the investigations took place. All they needed was the right evidence to prove their case.

1 Write 25-word definitions of:
   a) Malthusian views.
   b) Utilitarian views.

ACTIVITY

1 **Put yourself in the shoes of Edwin Chadwick. Prepare a two-minute presentation to the government about your proposals.**

2 **Historians have claimed that the report was a very one-sided view of the old Poor Law. Prepare a two-minute presentation to balance Chadwick's.**

FOCUS TASK

WHY WAS THE POOR LAW UNDER ATTACK BY 1834?

1 Read these statements carefully:

- The Poor Law was collapsing under the strain of changing economic conditions in the period 1800–30.
- The Poor Law simply encouraged idle labourers to live comfortable lives without working, supported by the ratepayers.
- Workhouses before 1834 were too comfortable and actually encouraged pauperism.
- Disturbances like the Swing Riots were the desperate attempts of starving labourers to preserve their own livelihood.

2 Look back over pages 214–18. For each statement:
   a) Decide whether this view was generally held by influential people in 1834.
   b) Find one or two examples to show that you are correct.

3 Now consider each statement from the viewpoint of a modern historian.
   a) Would the modern historian agree with the view?
   b) Briefly explain your answer.

You may find it helpful to refer to pages 40–47 of Chapter 3 on rural poverty.

The new Poor Law: the Poor Law Amendment Act, 1834

In 1834, most of the Commission's recommendations were written into a new Act of Parliament. The Act dealt with general points. For example, parishes were to be grouped into unions, each of which had to provide a workhouse. Local Boards of Guardians would be elected from among the ratepayers to supervise the workhouses. However, issues such as the workhouse regime and how to abolish outdoor relief were not discussed in Parliament. To sort out the details, the government set up a Central Poor Law Commission, headed by three commissioners, one of whom was George Nicholls. Chadwick was made Secretary to the Commissioners.

SOURCE 19

Terms of the Act	The thinking behind it	Change from the old Poor Law?
One system of poor relief	Poor relief would become cheaper and more efficient because poor law officials would have to follow strict rules – there would be no local exceptions.	Yes
Abolition of outdoor relief	If the poor were inside the workhouse they could not cheat the ratepayer by taking on extra work. Also, the segregation of the workhouse meant that labourers too poor to support their families would not have more children, as they had supposedly done under the Speenhamland system.	Yes
The workhouse test	This would make people think twice about whether they really were so poor that they could not support themselves. They would only be allowed into the workhouse if they were worse off than the poorest-paid labourer.	Yes
Care of sick, old and orphans	Anyone truly unable to look after themselves would be taken into the workhouse.	No

A summary of the changes brought about by the new Poor Law.

FOCUS TASK

WHAT WERE THE MAIN CHANGES IN THE NEW POOR LAW?

1 Work in pairs or small groups. Look back at Sources 3–5 on page 212. Using Source 19 and the information in this section, decide which of the measures and actions described in Source 5 would be allowed under the new regulations.

2 Imagine it is 1834 and you are Thomas Whitworth (from Source 7). You are once again asked for help by Richard Ball, whose problems are almost identical to what they were in 1817. Explain to Richard what choices are open to him. You could present this as a dialogue between the two, with Richard pleading his case and Thomas explaining the new rules.

Putting the Act into operation

It was up to Chadwick and the commissioners to see that these ideas were carried out around the country.

Success in the south

Chadwick began where the problems were greatest – in the rural south. He made good progress: by 1838 over 13,000 parishes had been joined to form 573 unions. By 1839 there were around 700 unions, and about 350 new workhouses were either completed or under construction. The poor bitterly resented the new arrangements, but on the whole Chadwick had the support of the local ratepayers. It was also fortunate that on the whole harvests were good and wages and prices were reasonable in the mid 1830s.

The cost of poor relief began to fall dramatically. In some parishes, it dropped by a half or even two thirds. On a national scale, the cost of poor relief fell by around one third by 1850. A second report commissioned in 1836 seemed to show that the Act was a success and that everything was going according to plan.

SOURCE 20

In the parish of Hitchin in Hertfordshire, a well-managed parish where an increase was confidently predicted, the poor rates in 1835, before the formation of the Union, amounted to £1716; after the Union they were reduced to £496.

The parish of Hitchin described in the 1836 Report.

SOURCE 21

People who never could be made to work before have become good labourers, and do not express any dissatisfaction with the measure. In most parishes the moral character of the poor is improving: there is a readiness to be more orderly and well behaved … The great body of labouring poor throughout the Union have become reconciled to it; the workhouse is held in great dread …

A report on the Market Harborough Poor Law Union, 1836.

Problems in the north

The successes in the south were not matched when the assistant commissioners tried to establish the new system in the industrial north in 1837. Here they came up against some daunting problems. By 1837, industry had gone into one of its periodic slumps. The Poor Law officials began their work at a time when the need for relief was rising.

Also, the problem of pauperism was different in the north. There was relatively little long-term unemployment, but labourers were laid off for short periods when trade was slow. In these conditions, outdoor relief to tide over workers between jobs was exactly what was needed, yet that was just what the assistant commissioners wanted to abolish. They faced great opposition from the poor.

Despite this, the assistant commissioners might have succeeded if the local middle classes had supported them. However, in most industrial towns the officials and magistrates felt that workhouses were expensive and the wrong answer. In towns, many ratepayers were shopkeepers, who did not want to see potential customers locked up in a workhouse.

In this climate, the assistant commissioners found it increasingly difficult and dangerous to carry out their task. Some were attacked. In Stockport, a full-scale riot broke out in 1842, and the workhouse was stormed and ransacked.

SOURCE 22

On Monday last Mr John Banks, the Relieving Officer of Kirkheaton, presented himself before the Guardians of the Huddersfield Union in a most desperate plight, his clothes hanging in tatters and his head and face greatly disfigured. It appears that the deluded populace of this district had been on the look out for him for three days, threatening his life if he durst commence his duties under the new law.

From *The Times*, April 1839.

1 Write a 100-word article to go with Source 23, explaining why the New Poor Law has faced such opposition in the north of England.

SOURCE 23

A scene from the *London Illustrated News* showing the Stockport riots, 1842.

The new workhouses

The new workhouses were the central feature of the Act. The basic aim was for conditions in the workhouses to be so harsh that only the truly desperate would enter them. This became known as the 'principle of less eligibility': life in a workhouse should be less comfortable than life outside the workhouse.

Edwin Chadwick had a fairly clear idea of how to achieve this aim. He wanted not appalling conditions, but a tough regime. In his research for the commission, Chadwick had been impressed by the workhouse run by John Nicholls, the Overseer of the Poor in Southwell, Nottinghamshire. At Southwell, diet was adequate but plain and sparse, all inmates worked hard and had to follow strict discipline, and families were split up into dormitories for males and females, with husbands and wives, parents and children separated.

Chadwick's proposals included plans for buildings, suggested diets and sample codes of discipline. Paupers would have to wear workhouse uniforms. The work would be dull but compulsory: anyone who refused to work while in a workhouse could be imprisoned. Workhouses were to be large, grim buildings, built to look like prisons.

Even the process of obtaining relief was made deliberately off-putting. The old Poor Law had been run locally. Officials and paupers usually knew each other, and Overseers often made special allowance for a pauper's individual circumstances. In the new Poor Law, these local customs were replaced by central regulations. Someone needing relief would approach the Relieving Officer, a paid official. This officer would have hundreds of paupers to deal with across the parishes in his union and would deal with every pauper 'by the book'.

SOURCE 24

If paupers are made miserable, paupers will needs decline in multitude. It is a secret known to all rat catchers.

Thomas Carlyle commenting on the principles of the new Poor Law in 1834. Carlyle was a successful and respected historian and writer.

FOCUS TASK

1 Study Sources 25–29. Explain how each one helps to put Chadwick's ideas into practice.

2 Which feature of the new workhouse do you think would be most unpopular with the inmates?

SOURCE 25

Date	25 March to 29 September	29 September to 25 March
Time of rising	5.45 a.m.	6.45 a.m.
Interval for breakfast	6.30–7.00 a.m.	7.30–8.00 a.m.
Time for work	7.00–12.00 a.m.	8.00–12.00 a.m.
Interval for dinner	12.00–1.00 p.m.	12.00–1.00 p.m.
Time for work	1.00–6.00 p.m.	1.00–6.00 p.m.
Interval for supper	6.00–7.00 p.m.	6.00–7.00 p.m.
Time for going to bed	8.00 p.m.	8.00 p.m.

Typical workhouse timetable. Paupers would also say prayers before breakfast and supper. They had to do a hard day's work – this was usually picking oakum (unpicking old ships' ropes) or crushing stones. Another common job was crushing animal bones for fertiliser.

SOURCE 26

DIETARY for able-bodied Men and Women.

		BREAKFAST		DINNER			SUPPER			
		Bread.	Gruel.	Cooked Meat with Vegetables.*	Potatoes	Soup with Vegetables.*	Suet Pudding.	Bread.	Cheese.	Broth Thickened
		oz.	Pints.	oz.	Pints.	Pints.	oz.	oz.	oz.	Pints.
Sunday	Men	7	1½	6	—	—	—	5	—	1½
	Women	6	1½	5	—	—	—	4	—	1½
Monday	Men	7	1½	—	—	1½	—	6	2	—
	Women	6	1½	—	—	1½	—	5	2	—
Tuesday	Men	7	1½	—	—	—	14	6	2	—
	Women	6	1½	—	—	—	12	5	2	—
Wednesday	Men	7	1½	6	—	—	—	5	—	1½
	Women	6	1½	5	—	—	—	4	—	1½
Thursday	Men	7	1½	—	—	1½ } Pea Soup.	—	6	2	—
	Women	6	1½	—	—	1½ }	—	5	2	—
Friday	Men	7	1½	—	2	—	—	6	2	—
	Women	6	1½	—	2	—	—	5	2	—
Saturday	Men	7	1½	—	—	—	14	6	2	—
	Women	6	1½	—	—	—	12	5	2	—

OLD PEOPLE of 60 Years of Age and upwards, may be allowed 1oz. of Tea, 7oz. of Sugar, and 5oz. of Butter per Week, in lieu of Gruel for Breakfast, if deemed expedient to make this change.

CHILDREN under Nine Years of Age to be allowed Bread and Milk for their Breakfast and Supper, or Gruel when Milk cannot be obtained, also such proportions of the Dinner Diet as may be requisite for their respective ages.

CHILDREN above Nine Years of Age to be allowed the same quantities as Women.

SICK to be Dieted as directed by the Medical Officer.

"SOUP" made in the proportion of One Pound of Beef or Mutton to One Gallon of Water, with Vegetables.

"PEAS SOUP" made in the proportion of One Pound of Beef or Mutton and One Pint of Peas to One Gallon of Water.

*The VEGETABLES are EXTRA, and not included in the above specified.

The week's diet at Stafford Union Workhouse.

SOURCE 27

Any pauper who shall neglect to observe such of the regulations herein contained as are applicable to and binding on him;

Or who shall make any noise when silence is ordered to be kept;

Or shall use obscene or profane language;

Or shall by work or deed insult or revile any person

Or shall threaten to strike or assault any person;

Or shall not duly cleanse his person;

Or shall refuse or neglect to work, after having been required to do so;

Or shall pretend sickness;

Or shall play at cards or other game of chance;

Or shall enter or attempt to enter, without permission, the ward or yard appropriated to any class of paupers other than that to which he belongs;

Or shall misbehave in going to, at or returning from public worship out of the workhouse, or at prayers in the workhouse;

Or shall return after the appointed time of absence, when allowed to quit the workhouse temporarily;

Or shall wilfully disobey any lawful order of any officer of the workhouse;

Shall be deemed DISORDERLY.

It shall be lawful for the master of the workhouse, with or without the direction of the Board of Guardians to punish any disorderly pauper by substituting, during a time not greater than forty-eight hours, for his or her dinner, as prescribed by the dietary, a meal consisting of eight ounces of bread, or one pound of cooked potatoes, and also by withholding from him, during the same period, all butter, cheese, tea, sugar or broth, which such pauper would otherwise receive at any meal during the time aforesaid.

The rules of the workhouse, from the commissioners' regulations.

SOURCE 28

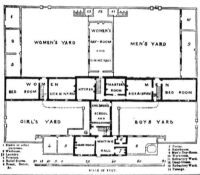

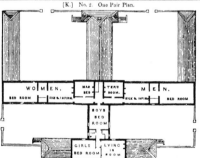

This plan was for a workhouse of 200 inmates. It was included in the commissioners' report as an example of how a workhouse should appear.

SOURCE 29

The paupers, so far as the workhouse admits thereof, shall be classed as follows, subject nevertheless to such arrangements as the Board of Guardians may deem necessary with regard to persons labouring under any disease of body or mind, or for the further sub-division of any such classes:

Class 1 Men infirm through age or any other cause.

Class 2 Able-bodied men, and youths above the age of 15 years.

Class 3 Boys above the age of 7 years, and under that of 15.

Class 4 Women infirm through age or any other cause.

Class 5 Able-bodied women, and girls above the age of 15 years.

Class 6 Girls above the age of 7 years and under that of 15.

Class 7 Children under 7 years of age.

To each class shall be assigned that ward or separate building and yard which may be best fitted for the reception of such class, and each class of paupers shall remain therein, without communication with those of any other class.

Classes of pauper defined by the Act.

What were the workhouses really like?

From the start the workhouses were the most emotive issue surrounding the New Poor Law. They also presented an easy target for the Law's opponents. Cartoons, speeches, newspaper articles and novels described the horrors of the workhouses. Pamphlets, broadsheets and demonstrations attacked the commissioners as 'tyrants'. The workhouses were called 'Bastilles' after the dungeon used by the kings of France before the French Revolution. Charles Dickens' immensely successful novel *Oliver Twist* painted an extremely bleak picture of life in the workhouse, and particularly of the treatment of orphans (see Source 30).

Much protest focused around the treatment of children in the workhouses. They were harshly disciplined and very badly fed, and in some places stories were told of pauper children fighting over the kitchen scraps. The Act said that children were to receive education, but many reports by the commissioners show that education was either very poor or non-existent.

Orphans were particularly badly treated. If possible, they were sold as apprentices to tradesmen, but all too often this meant working as climbing boys (apprentices to chimney sweeps), where they suffered even worse abuses.

Another problem was that because families were forced to enter the workhouse and were then split up, many of them lost their homes forever. Too often, the Act had the effect of permanently breaking up family life.

There were also serious problems in the treatment of old people under the new Act. Respectable old people who had worked hard all their lives had received outdoor relief before 1834, but with the new Poor Law they had to enter a workhouse. Married couples who had been together for decades were suddenly separated.

SOURCE 30

The members of the Board were very wise men … so they established the rule that all poor should have the alternative of being starved by a gradual process in the house or by a quick one out of it.

An extract and illustration from *Oliver Twist* by Charles Dickens, written in 1838.

SOURCE 32

What, Sir, is the principle of the new Poor Law? The condition imposed upon Englishmen by the accursed law is that man shall give up his liberty to save his life. That, before he shall eat a piece of bread he shall go into prison, under circumstances which I shall speak of hereafter. In prison he shall enjoy his right to live, but it shall be at the expense of that liberty, without which life itself becomes a burden and a curse.

Written by a radical campaigner, Richard Oastler, in 1838.

SOURCE 31

We youngsters were roughly disrobed, roughly and coldly washed, and roughly attired in rough clothes, our under garments being all covered up by a rough linen pinafore. Then we parted amid bitter cries, the young ones being taken one way and the parents (separated too) taken as well to different regions in that merciful establishment.

We might have committed some unnameable crime, or carried some dreadful infection …

I was hungry, but that bread! that greasy water! those few lumps of something which would have made a tiger's teeth ache to break the fibres of! the strangeness, the repulsiveness, and the loneliness, made my heart turn over, and I turned over what I could not eat to those near me, who devoured voraciously all I could spare.

In the afternoon we had our school work to do, and as I could read well I had no trouble with such lessons as were given. But if some of the other lads had had heads made of leather stuffed with hay they could not have got more knocks! …

Tea and supper by a wise economy were joined together. The new Poor Law was to be economical if anything, even to the least quantity of food a growing boy's stomach could do with. But supper time came. What would it bring? That was the question for me. It brought a hunch of bread and a jug of skilly. I had heard of workhouse skilly but had never before seen it. I had had poor food before this, but never any so offensively poor as this. By what rare culinary-making nausea and bottomless fatuousness it could be made so sickening I never could make out. Simple meal and water, however small the amount of meal, honestly boiled, would be palatable. But this decoction of meal and water and mustiness and fustiness was most revolting to any healthy taste. It might have been boiled in old clothes, which had been worn upon sweating bodies for three-score years and ten. That workhouse skilly was the vilest compound I ever tasted.

Life at Chell Workhouse in Staffordshire, 1840. The writer entered the workhouse as a child.

1 **Read Source 32. What does the writer really think of 'The members of the Board'? Explain your answer carefully.**

The Commission's own evidence

The assistant commissioners were able to visit unions only twice a year, so supervision was minimal. When they did visit, they found that conditions were much worse than had been intended by the commissioners. Before 1834, many workhouse masters had been petty and cruel, and living conditions unhygienic and unhealthy. In too many cases this continued after the Act was passed. Corruption was common. For example, in 1836 in Stoke on Trent, the assistant commissioner found that the workhouse master was also the main supplier of food to the workhouse. The more poor people there were in his workhouse, the more money he made. At the same time, the commissioner also found that the quality of the food was very bad.

The Andover scandal

In 1845, a serious scandal broke. The workhouse in Andover had a reputation for treating its inmates badly. When Parliament investigated conditions in this workhouse, there was outrage. The men worked by crushing old bones for fertiliser, but they were so hungry that they had been eating the marrow from these decaying remains.

SOURCE 33

'The Milk of Poor Law Kindness', a cartoon from *Punch* magazine published in 1843.

2 Explain how the following features of Source 33 make it an effective attack on the Poor Law:
  • The devil figure
  • The angel
  • The child
  • The mother
  • The background.

3 Do you think that the commissioners would be pleased by the evidence of poor conditions in workhouses?

4 Sources 30–33 were all created by critics of the workhouses. Explain carefully how you can use such sources to find out about workhouses under the New Poor Law.

ACTIVITY

Work in pairs.
  One of you is a supporter of the new workhouses, the other is a critic.
  Supporter: You are to write a letter to your friend, who is a critic, convincing him or her that the New Poor Law is a good thing. Think carefully about which are the best sources to support your views and how you can use those sources. Then write your letter.
  Critic: You are to write a letter to your pro-Poor Law friend. Think carefully about which sources will support your views and how you can use them, then write your letter.
  Compare your letters and discuss:

1 Which is the most convincing?

2 Why do you think it is more convincing than the other one?

Changes to the new Poor Law

By 1841, even the commissioners were beginning to realise that the principles of the 1834 Act were not entirely workable.

Less eligibility

Perhaps the greatest problem was the principle of less eligibility. The starvation and squalor suffered by out-of-work labourers in town or countryside were appalling. The problem then was how to make the workhouses even worse. In fact, it was not possible without having the sort of workhouse seen in Andover.

Applying the principle also created some stupid policies for example: Under the new Poor Law, officials were not allowed to give widows a few pence to send their children to school, because this would give them an advantage over children who were not paupers. Even though this would have been a sensible way to help the family work their way out of poverty.

Outdoor relief

Between 1841 and 1842, the Guardians in rural areas were given special orders which allowed them to provide outdoor relief. Technically, this was supposed to be only in exceptional cases, but in practice outdoor relief was already being given all over the country. The new measure simply formalised what was already happening.

For urban areas, the commissioners issued the Outdoor Labour Test Order in October 1842. The labour test effectively replaced the workhouse test. Labourers could now receive outdoor relief, although they still had to earn it by doing hard tasks such as crushing stones. The need for this type of measure was undeniable: in hard times, there were often not enough spaces in the workhouse for all of the paupers in these areas.

Cost

It was becoming clear that workhouses were too expensive. The overall costs of poor relief had fallen, but this was because the dread of the workhouse meant that there were fewer claimants. For those who did go on relief, outdoor relief was more cost-effective. In one London parish it cost 4s 8d a week to keep a pauper in the workhouse, compared with 2s 3d for outdoor relief.

By 1846, there were an estimated 1.3 million paupers, but only 0.2 million were in the workhouses. These were almost exclusively the old and the sick: the rest were on outdoor relief. In 1847, the commissioners were replaced by a Poor Law Board, supervised by a minister in Parliament.

In the late 1840s and 1850s, the demand for poor relief fell as a result of an upturn in the economy and the general prosperity created by the expansion of the railways. The main aspects of the new system remained, however, and reforming the Poor Law was an ongoing theme for many decades to come, as you will see from pages 232–37.

FOCUS TASK

WAS THE NEW POOR LAW SUCCESSFUL?

1 It is 1856. You are an important Victorian business leader and also a magistrate in London. You worked closely with Edwin Chadwick in the 1830s in the setting up of the 1834 Act and approve of his ideas. In your morning post you receive a request for a reference for Edwin Chadwick for an important post overseas. Write this reference, explaining why you think his work on the Poor Law makes him the man for the job. You could mention:

- the problems of the old Poor Law as they were seen (cost, settlement, idleness and so on).
- Chadwick's ideas and the people who influenced him.
- the measures taken to deal with the problems (workhouses, workhouse tests, banning outdoor relief and so on).

You might also want to mention the criticisms of the Act and why you feel they were wrong.

2 The people thinking of appointing Chadwick are not sure. They decide to get in touch with one of his opponents, Richard Oastler (see Source 32). Write a letter from Richard Oastler explaining your views on Chadwick and the new Poor Law. It could mention:

- the conditions in workhouses.
- why the Act was unworkable.
- its failure to get rid of outdoor relief.

3 When you have completed these pieces of work, draw up a table of key points to help with revision in the future. Alternatively, you might find it useful to do this before tackling 1 and 2 above.

Problem	Action of Poor Law	Success or failure

How and why did attitudes to the poor change?

In the later part of the nineteenth century, the attitude of governments and the ruling classes towards the poor began to change. However, the pace of this change was slow, and it took many years before any real action was taken. Various factors contributed to these changing attitudes.

The poor help themselves

In the second half of the nineteenth century more and more working people were influenced by the idea of self-help. Many working people joined FRIENDLY SOCIETIES, for insurance against hard times and the dreaded workhouse. In this sense, Chadwick's Poor Law had worked! The co-operative movement (see page 264) also began to prosper in the second half of the nineteenth century. In 1869, the Charity Organisation Society was founded, with the aim of helping the deserving poor to help themselves.

New views on poverty

At the same time, a number of journalists, investigators and campaigners began to bring the awful conditions in which the poor lived to people's attention. They did this through investigative reports and articles, which were written purely descriptively, without moral judgements. Middle-class Victorians were used to reading moral lectures about the poor and how they drank away all their money. These writers were different: they did not hold the poor responsible for being poor.

The motives of these campaigners varied widely. Some, such as the SOCIALIST Beatrice Webb or the trade unionist Ben Tillett, had political aims. Others were motivated by religion, such as William and Catherine Booth and Dr Barnardo. Some campaigners felt a social responsibility for the poor.

Henry Mayhew

One of the first of these campaigners was the journalist Henry Mayhew, who investigated the conditions of women workers in the sweated clothing trade. Between 1849 and 1851, Mayhew's reports on sweated labour in London appeared in the *Morning Chronicle*.

'Sweated labour' basically meant exploitation of workers. The women described by Mayhew worked very long hours for extremely low pay, sometimes in their own homes and sometimes in filthy and insanitary workshops. Although Mayhew concentrated on the clothing trade, sweated labour was found in many other industries. It continued to be a major problem until well into the twentieth century.

Mayhew did not confine his efforts to this problem. He went on to collect evidence on the treatment of criminals, on trade unions, on poverty and on social issues in general.

Henry Mayhew

SOURCE 1

At one of the docks alone I found 1823 stomachs would be deprived of food by the mere chopping of the breeze ... That the sustenance of thousands of families should be as fickle as the very breeze itself ... was a climax of misery and wretchedness that I could not have imagined to exist.

Mayhew made the point in the 1860s that earnings of dockers could be drastically cut by unfavourable winds delaying a ship.

1 How was Mayhew out of step with popular opinion in the 1850s?

SOURCE 2

I cannot earn more than 4s 6d to 5s per week – let me sit from eight in the morning till ten every night; and out of that I shall have to pay 1s 6d for trimmings; and 6d candles every week; so altogether I earn about 3s in the six days. But I don't earn that, for there's the firing you must have to press the work and that will be 9d a week ... so my clear earnings are a bit more than 2s.

Mayhew describes in the *Morning Chronicle* how a sweated worker earned a living in the clothing trade.

Dr Barnardo

Dr Barnardo was a member of the upper middle class. He was training to become a MISSIONARY doctor abroad, when one evening he stumbled across young paupers in the doorway of a church hall and realised that his true mission lay in inner-city London. In 1867, he opened a hostel for destitute children, and in 1870 the first Dr Barnardo's home for orphaned children opened. The emphasis of the home was on caring for the children and then training and educating them. Discipline was strict, but the children were never blamed for their situation. Most Barnardo's children became labourers or domestic servants, but many were sent to Canada to work on farms.

A photograph of some boys admitted to Barnardo's home in around 1880.

1 How was Henry Mayhew's work
   a) different from
   b) similar to

the work of Doctor Barnado?

Very often the hall of the hotel would be inconveniently crowded with young men, for the most part well grown, stalwart, muscular fellows, bronzed and bearded and altogether so changed that I usually quite failed to recognise in them the puny, half starved, homeless waifs that had come under my care in England, 12, 15 or 20 years before.

Dr Barnardo's description of his last visit to Canada in 1900.

Arnold Toynbee

Arnold Toynbee was a writer and historian. He was the first to use the term 'industrial revolution' to describe the changes that occurred in the nineteenth century. Toynbee believed that the working classes had been harmed by the industrial revolution. He also felt that the middle classes had betrayed the working classes. They had taken over the leadership of the country from the aristocracy, but they had refused to take up the caring role which the aristocracy had previously fulfilled.

Samuel Barnett

Barnett, a close friend of Toynbee, was an Anglican clergyman. Toynbee died in 1883, and in his memory Barnett founded Toynbee Hall in the East End of London, where he ran lectures on social conditions. Barnett also helped to organise the University Settlement Movement, which brought young, better-off men into contact with the dreadful conditions suffered by the poor. This movement gave future reformers like William Beveridge (see page 247) and Clement Attlee their first contact with poverty.

Andrew Mearns

In 1883, a NONCONFORMIST minister, Andrew Mearns, published a pamphlet called *The Bitter Cry of Outcast London*. Mearns pointed out that attendances at church and chapel were falling. He believed that the reason was that the church was irrelevant to most working people. His description of their living conditions – filthy housing, sweated labour, disease and squalor – showed that little had changed since Chadwick's report on urban poverty 40 years before.

Samuel Barnett

2 Why do you think religious organisations took a lead in changing attitudes to the poor?

William and Catherine Booth: the Salvation Army

William and Catherine Booth were missionaries with a difference. They set up a number of MISSION halls in poor areas. By 1878, the Booths had 45 branches, and they renamed their mission the Salvation Army. It was organised just like an army, but its war was on sin and poverty.

William Booth came to the conclusion that young girls were forced into prostitution by poverty, rather than as a result of moral corruption. He published a shocking pamphlet called *In Darkest England and the Way Out*. One of the points he made which really hit home was that horses in London generally received kinder treatment than many of the capital's poor. The pamphlet resulted in donations of £100,000, which the Booths used to set up a small match factory as well as shelters and soup kitchens. The activities of the Salvation Army brought Booth into conflict with organisations which believed in self-help, but he was not worried about this.

SOURCE 5

Living conditions of a poor family at the turn of the century.

SOURCE 6

Class A: The lowest class – loafers, criminals, occasional labourers – 1.25 per cent

Class B: Very poor – casual work, widows and deserted women – 11.25 per cent

Class C: Poor – casual workers, vulnerable to trade conditions – 8 per cent

Class D: Poor – casual and low paid regular workers – 14 .5 per cent

Classes E and F: Regular and reasonably paid working classes

Classes G and H: Middle and upper classes

Figures from Charles Booth's *Life and Labour of the People of London*, 1889–1901.

3 What was the most important aspect of Charles Booth's work?

Charles Booth

Charles Booth (no direct relation to William and Catherine Booth) was a successful businessman, the owner of a Liverpool shipping line which opened a London office in 1880. Like many wealthy men of the period, he had a strong sense of responsibility and a desire to put something back into society in return for his own personal success.

Booth became interested in social issues as a result of his wife's friendship with the socialist Beatrice Webb. He attended Barnett's lectures at Toynbee Hall on a regular basis, and also read the alarming pamphlets and reports about poverty in London. However, he had a sneaking suspicion that the reports were exaggerated by groups such as the Social Democratic Federation to increase sympathy for the poor and support for themselves.

Over the following 19 years, Booth collected masses of information on poverty in London. His findings dismayed him almost from the start. He had been right to think that the estimates about poverty were wrong, but he had not expected them to be underestimates! Like other investigators before him, he found the most appalling conditions and grinding poverty.

Because Booth was a respectable businessman who had set out to show the reports were exaggerated, he was taken more seriously than other campaigners. Also, he took care to avoid sensational reporting and concentrated on finding out the scale of the problem. The first of his 17 books, published in 1889, claimed that the idle, criminal or undeserving poor made up only about 1 per cent of the population. It also showed that about 30 per cent of London's population lived below the poverty line, unable to afford decent food, clothing and accommodation. Most importantly of all, he said that the problem was mainly the result of low wages, casual work, trade depressions and old age or illness.

SOURCE 7

Mr Booth's report is more valuable than an ocean of sensational writing.

From the *Morning Post*.

Seebohm Rowntree

Booth's findings were backed up by the work of Seebohm Rowntree in York. The Rowntree family had become wealthy making chocolate and had a reputation as caring employers. Using the most up-to-date scientific knowledge, Rowntree showed that in York 27 per cent of the population lived below the poverty line. He showed that the poor suffered from a cycle of poverty which hit hardest in infancy, then when the individual married and had children, and then when old age came. The lives of these unfortunate people were harsh and extremely precarious: an illness or downturn in trade could spell disaster.

SOURCE 8

Unemployment or partial employment: 5 per cent

Death of wage earner: 10 per cent

Illness or old age of wage earner: 5 per cent

Low wages: 22 per cent

Large family: 52 per cent

Other: 6 per cent

Seebohm Rowntree's findings on the causes of poverty.

SOURCE 9

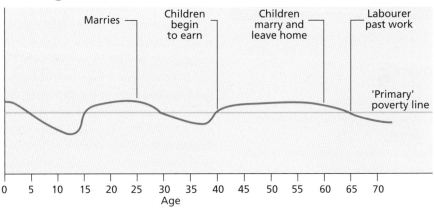

Rowntree's Poverty Line.

SOURCE 10

A family living on [the poverty line] must never spend a penny on railway fare or omnibus. They must never go into the country unless they walk … They must never contribute anything to their church or chapel, or give any help to a neighbour which costs them money. They cannot save … The children must have no pocket money … The father must smoke no tobacco … The mother must never buy any pretty clothes … Should a child fall ill it must be attended by the parish doctor … Finally, the wage earner must never be absent from his work for a single day.

An extract from Rowntree's book *Poverty*.

1 Did Rowntree's findings build on Charles Booth's work, or simply repeat it in another town? Explain your answer.

How important were these campaigners?

It is hard to decide exactly how much influence these campaigners had on the lives of the poor. On the one hand, it would be easy to argue that they achieved very little. Terrible poverty and appalling living conditions continued until well into the twentieth century. Governments did not attempt to find a wide-ranging solution to the problem of poverty until after the Second World War. On the other hand, future reformers such as Winston Churchill and David Lloyd George were deeply affected by the work of Booth and Rowntree. You will look at the importance of this on page 232.

FOCUS TASK

HOW DID THE WORK OF INDIVIDUALS CHANGE ATTITUDES TO THE POOR?

Henry Mayhew
1812–1887

Dr Barnardo
1845–1905

Samuel Barnett
1844–1913

Catherine Booth
1829–1880

William Booth
1829–1912

Charles Booth
1840–1916

Seebohm Rowntree
1871–1954

Use the information and sources to create your own 'Hall of Fame' of social reformers. Your tasks are to decide how the exhibits should be arranged and to write the information plaques about each reformer.
 The information plaque for each reformer should mention:

- Name
- Date of birth and death
- Interest in social reform
- Important views and ideas
- Contribution made
- Importance in your view (% mark)

You can organise the Hall of Fame in two ways, either chronologically or in order of importance. Explain your choice.

Why did the Liberal governments of 1906–1914 try to help the poor?

Booth and Rowntree showed that most poverty was a result of economic conditions and not moral failings. However, the government in the 1890s was not convinced that it needed to act on the problem. Then in 1906 a Liberal government came to power in a landslide election victory. The Liberals did not focus on WELFARE reforms during the election campaign, but once they were in power they treated the problem of poverty very seriously. Between 1906 and 1914, they introduced the most ambitious and most expensive series of welfare measures ever taken. Why was this?

The influence of individuals

Without doubt, one important factor was the influence of the Liberal politician David Lloyd George. Lloyd George came from a humble background in a Welsh village. He hated the English upper classes and sympathised with the ordinary people. He was also a very able politician, and by 1908 he had risen to the post of Chancellor of the Exchequer.

Another key figure was Winston Churchill. He had been a leading Conservative, but switched sides in 1906 when the Liberals started their welfare reforms, supposedly because he supported them, although his enemies said it was because he did not want to be in the party of opposition. In 1908, Churchill became President of the Board of Trade.

These two and other leading Liberals had read the work of Booth and Rowntree and felt that poverty needed to be tackled. They were aware of the contrast between Britain's vast wealth, including its overseas empire and magnificent navy, and its squalid urban slums.

The Boer War

SOURCE 11

I see little glory in an Empire which can rule the waves and is unable to flush its own sewers.

From a speech by Winston Churchill, 1899.

Between 1899 and 1902, Britain was at war to defend its lands in Southern Africa. Half of the recruits who volunteered to go and fight were found to be unfit for service because of ill health. In some poor areas of Britain, 60 per cent were unfit. The potential recruits were so badly fed that they had not grown properly. The army had to lower its minimum height for a soldier in order to find enough infantrymen.

This was alarming for a government which needed to be able to call up a strong army at short notice. A government Committee on Physical Deterioration was set up to investigate the issue, and its recommendations influenced the Liberal programme of reform.

Industrial decline

Britain's military strength was not the only concern. From 1870 onwards, Britain's position as the world's leading industrial power was being challenged by the USA and Germany. Lloyd George was extremely impressed with the programme of welfare packages introduced by the German Chancellor Bismarck. Germany's rapid development appeared to be closely linked to its healthier, better-educated and therefore more efficient workforce.

The rise of socialism

Finally, the Liberals saw welfare reforms as a way of fighting socialism. If the working classes were healthier and happier, there would be less support for the type of revolutionary socialist movements that were troubling France, Germany and Russia at this time. It was also hoped that reforms would undermine support for the new Labour Party. This was only small in 1906, with 29 seats in Parliament. The Liberals hoped to keep it that way.

SOURCE 12

What are the real causes of poverty among the industrial classes? Old age, bad health, the death of the breadwinner and unemployment due either to the running down of industries or to depressions in trade. When Bismarck was strengthening the German Empire, one of his first tasks was to set up a scheme which insured German workers and their families against the worst evils arising from the accidents of life. And a superb scheme it is. It has saved a huge amount of human misery among thousands of people.

Lloyd George speaking in 1890.

SOURCE 13

The country that spent £250 million to avenge an insult levelled at her pride by an old Dutch farmer [the Boer War] is not ashamed to see her children walking the streets hungry and in rags.

Lloyd George speaking in around 1906.

FOCUS TASK

WHY DID THE LIBERALS EMBARK ON A PROGRAMME OF WELFARE REFORMS?

1 The text on page 232 suggests some possible reasons why the Liberals started their welfare reform programme:

- **Military needs**
- **Industrial needs**
- **Social conscience**
- **Fear of Socialism**
- **International rivalry**

Explain how each one helped influence the Liberals.

2 Write a short speech for either Winston Churchill or Lloyd George explaining why the Liberals need to introduce welfare reforms. You will be addressing a hostile audience who think that welfare reforms are expensive and who still believe in self-help. Choose three of the points above which you think your audience will find important and use them to present your case. You can get ideas from Sources 11–13.

What did the poor gain from the Liberal reforms of 1906–1914?

The system that the Liberals were replacing was still essentially the same as in the nineteenth century.

FOCUS TASK

WHAT HELP WAS GIVEN TO THE POOR?

As you read the next two pages, fill in your own copy of this table.

Group	How helped before Liberal reforms	Measures taken by the Liberals to tackle this problem	How this reform helped	Limitations of the reforms
Children	No real system – some charities helped poor families with children; orphans looked after in workhouses			
The old	Charities; families; the workhouse			
The sick	Charities; families; the workhouse			
The unemployed or underemployed	Outdoor relief; voluntary labour exchanges			

1. Children

The Liberals began their programme of reforms almost as soon as they came to power. In 1906, an Act was passed which allowed (but did not force) local authorities to provide free school meals. The new law meant that children would eat at least one decent meal per day. In a single year, 14 million meals were served up, most of which were free.

In 1907, attention was turned to medical care. Many parents were not able to afford proper treatment. Now, every local education authority had to set up a school medical service. At first, the service provided only regular medical checks, but from 1912 this was extended to provide treatment in school clinics as well.

Another Act of 1908, the Children and Young Persons Act, was inspired by a terrible social evil. In the past, insurance companies had paid out money to parents on the death of their young children, even in suspicious circumstances, with predictable results. The Act gave children special status as protected persons, and their parents could now be prosecuted for neglect. It also made it illegal to insure a child's life. The Act set up special courts to deal with child crime, and special homes or Borstals to house young offenders so that they did not need to be sent to adult prisons.

1 **Describe the main differences between the two labour exchanges in Sources 16 and 17.**

2 **Can you find any evidence in these reforms that old ideas about poverty were still present?**

3 **Leading Liberals described these measures as 'a lifebelt against poverty', and 'a net over the abyss'. What do you think they meant?**

4 **Which of these reforms would you say was the most radical measure? Explain your choice.**

2. The old

Pensions were not new: for some time, people had been encouraged to pay money into private or local pension funds. In Lloyd George's first Budget as Chancellor of the Exchequer, he introduced a government-funded old-age pension. Old people over 70 with no other income would receive five shillings per week. Couples would receive 7s 6d. It was hardly a generous measure, but the effect on the elderly poor was enormous. Many old people had been dependent on poor relief. Some still lived with the threat of the workhouse. In both town and countryside, life was transformed for many retired labourers. Their pension made them independent for life! In the first year, some 650,000 old people collected their pensions. The number of people claiming outdoor relief fell by over 80,000.

SOURCE 14

Old people collecting their pensions at a London post office on 1 January 1909.

As well as helping thousands of old people, the Act established new and important principles. Firstly, it was non-contributory. In other words, people received it without having paid anything towards a pension fund. Secondly, poverty was being tackled by direct funding from the government, rather than local rates. It was a small measure but a big step.

SOURCE 15

... now we want to go on living forever, because we give them [his son's family] the 10 shillings a week, and it pays them to have us along with them. I never thought we should be able to pay the boy back for all his goodness to me and the missus.

An old man talks about his pension in 1912.

3. The unemployed

Booth and Rowntree had shown how great a problem unemployment and underemployment (irregular work) could be. Labour exchanges run by volunteers had existed for some time. Here, workers could sign on to a register when they were unemployed, and they could find out about available work. In 1909, the government set up its own labour exchanges as part of its campaign against unemployment.

SOURCE 16

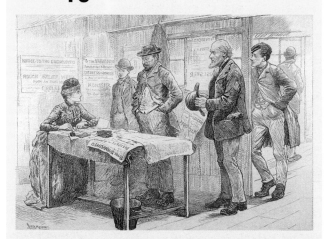

A voluntary labour exchange in Chelsea in 1887.

SOURCE 17

The government labour exchange at Camberwell Green, February 1910.

SOURCE 18

Nothing wearies more than walking about hunting for employment which is not to be had. It is far harder than real work. The uncertainty, the despair, when you reach a place only to discover that the journey is fruitless. I've known a man to say: 'Which way shall I go today?' Having no earthly idea which way to take, he tosses up a button. If the button comes down on one side he treks east; if on the other, he treks west.

Written by William Crooks, a working man who later became an MP.

4. Workers: the National Insurance Act

The really important measure was the NATIONAL INSURANCE Act of 1911. Insurance was not a new idea. It had been the basis of the friendly society, for two centuries or more. But Lloyd George's scheme went far beyond any of these private schemes.

Sick pay

The first part of the Act dealt with health insurance. All men and women in lower-paid manual and clerical jobs earning under £160 per year had to join. They then had to pay 4d out of each week's wages. Each payment earned them a 'stamp' on their card. The employer added 3d worth of stamps and the government a further 2d. Liberal posters talked of workers getting 9d or 4d. The money went to a friendly society of the worker's choice.

In return, the worker received up to 26 weeks of sick pay at 10 shillings a week from the friendly society. There was also free medical care for the insured worker. It was an important boost for low-paid workers, but it did not solve all their problems. The families of workers were not entitled to free treatment, and widows did not receive pensions.

SOURCE 19

THE DAWN OF HOPE.

Mr. LLOYD GEORGE'S National Health Insurance Bill provides for the insurance of the Worker in case of Sickness.

Support the Liberal Government
in their policy of
SOCIAL REFORM.

A Liberal election poster from 1911.

Unemployment benefit

The second part of the Act dealt with unemployment and underemployment. In trades such as building, shipbuilding and engineering, occasional unemployment was common. To cover this, the Act required a further contribution of 2½d per week from the worker, supplemented by 2½d from the employer and 1⅔d from the government. Again, these paid for 'stamps' on the worker's card. During times of unemployment, a worker would receive seven shillings per week for up to 15 weeks. Again, it was not much, certainly not enough to support a working man and his family. This was deliberate, because the government wanted to encourage careful saving and did not want workers to 'sit back and enjoy' the benefits. The old attitudes were not entirely gone.

Reactions to the reforms

The reforms were controversial and caused enormous opposition. Conservatives opposed the cost and the idea of the 'nanny state'. Doctors were not convinced about health insurance. The friendly societies and insurance companies prevented National Insurance benefits being given to widows. Some workers resented the deductions from their wages.

SOURCE 20

THE BIG DOG AND THE LITTLE ONE.

LORD HALSBURY: I don't think much of that paltry little thing—it's a mockery of a dog.

AGED PENSIONER: Well, my lord, 'tis only a little 'un, but 'tis a wunnerful comfort to me. Us bain't all blessed wi' big 'uns!

A cartoon from a Liberal Party leaflet, February 1909. Lord Halsbury had criticised the pension for being too small. As a former Conservative Lord Chancellor, his own pension was £5,000.

SOURCE 21

RICH FARE.

THE GIANT LLOYD-GEORGESTER: "FEE, FI, FO, FAT, I SMELL THE BLOOD OF A PLUTOCRAT; BE HE ALIVE OR BE HE DEAD, I'LL GRIND HIS BONES TO MAKE MY BREAD."

Lloyd George is shown in this 1909 *Punch* cartoon as a giant preparing to force the rich to give some of their wealth to the less well-off.

SOURCE 22

THE PHILANTHROPIC HIGHWAYMAN.

Mr. LLOYD-GEORGE: "I'LL MAKE 'EM PITY THE AGED POOR!"

Lloyd George as a highwayman, a *Punch* cartoon from 1909. Note the motor cars (a new symbol of wealth) approaching from the distance.

The reforms were one cause of a major constitutional crisis which ended with the reduction of the power of the House of Lords. Lloyd George said that the upper classes inherited much of their wealth and did little work to earn what they had, so they should pay for social reforms to help those who did work and suffered poverty.

SOURCE 23

There can be no doubt that taken as a whole the Liberal reforms constitute an impressive body of social legislation, the greatest ever passed by any one government up to that time … a radical new plan of campaign had been developed to meet the most urgent social needs of the working classes, and to do so outside the Poor Law System.

Written by the historian Eric Hopkins in *A Social History of the English Working Classes*, 1979.

SOURCE 24

… though the principle of social services according to need rather than ability to pay is commonplace today, in the very early 1900s it appeared revolutionary; 50 years earlier … such a proposal would have been unthinkable.

By the historian RN Rundle.

---

1 Choose one of the cartoons in Sources 20–22 and explain its message.

2 What do Sources 21 and 22 agree about?

3 What do they disagree about?

4 Which of Sources 23 and 24 do you think would have most pleased Lloyd George? Explain your choice.

FOCUS TASK

HOW EFFECTIVELY DID THE LIBERALS HELP THE POOR?

You should now have filled in a chart showing all the Liberal reforms. Use it to help you write an essay: 'How effectively did the Liberals help the poor?' You can organise your essay in paragraphs:

- Introduction: for example, why help was needed
- The Liberals' record on children
- Their record on the old
- Their record on the sick
- Their record on the unemployed
- Your conclusion: which group was helped the most or the least; whether the group that most needed help received most help.

FOCUS TASK

WHO HELPED THE POOR MOST?

1 Working in groups, look back over all your work in Parts 1 and 2 of this chapter.

   a) Half of your group should compile evidence of individuals helping the poor between 1834 and 1914.

   b) The other half should compile evidence of governments or local authorities helping the poor over the same period.

2 When you have finished your research, write up the main evidence on a scales diagram like this.

WHO HELPED THE POOR MOST?

Contribution of individuals

Contribution of governments

3 Now, as a group, decide which way the scales would tip. Don't just think about the quantity of evidence in each pan. Think about its importance in helping the poor. For example, you might think a single government action which helped the poor would outweigh all the work of individuals. Or the action of a single individual in changing attitudes might outweigh all the help given by governments. Whatever answer you arrive at, be ready to justify it with evidence and a reasoned argument.

4 Finally, write a report of about 150–200 words explaining why it was difficult to decide which way the scales should tip.

9.3 *Why was there so much poverty in the 1920s and 1930s?*

The 1911 National Insurance Act turned out to be the last major reform by the Liberals, although they had not planned it that way. In 1914, thoughts of social reform were swept away by the Great War. However, the appalling sacrifices and the incredible heroism of British men in the First World War brought changes in attitude. Before the war ended, Lloyd George spoke of providing homes fit for heroes. People hoped a better Britain might rise from the ashes of war. Sadly, this was not to be. The First World War had so damaged Britain's economy that the country plunged into a post-war slump from which some would say it never recovered.

George Orwell (see Source 1) was a political journalist as well as a novelist. In 1936, he was commissioned to explore conditions in the industrial regions of Lancashire and Yorkshire. His book, *The Road to Wigan Pier*, was a series of devastating descriptions of conditions in the major industries and of the miseries of unemployment. Source 2 shows that, in Orwell's view, unemployment and poverty were even worse than official figures suggested.

SOURCE 1

It seemed that nobody was anxious to pay me £2000 a year for sitting among streamlined office furniture and dictating letters to a platinum blonde. I was discovering what three quarters of the blokes who'd been officers were discovering – that from a financial point of view we'd been better off in the army than we were ever likely to be again. We'd suddenly changed from gentlemen holding His Majesty's Commission into miserable out of works whom nobody wanted. My ideas soon sank from £2000 a year to three or four pounds a week.

A character in a novel, *Coming Up for Air* (1939) by George Orwell, describes the post-war years.

SOURCE 2

A Labour Exchange officer told me that to get at the real number of people living on (not drawing) the dole, you have got to multiply the official figures by something over three … in addition, there are great numbers of people who are in work but … are not drawing anything that can be described as a living wage. Allow for these and their dependants … and you get an underfed population of well over 10 millions.

From *The Road to Wigan Pier* by George Orwell.

Problems in Britain's industries

Although it was not recognised at the time, Britain's economy had for a long time had problems which economists call structural weaknesses.

One main structural weakness was that too much money and too many jobs were tied up in a small number of large STAPLE INDUSTRIES – coal, iron and steel, shipbuilding and textiles. This meant that even small changes in these industries during the 1920s and 1930s had a disastrous effect on a vast number of ordinary working people and even on the whole economy.

The second weakness was that Britain had lagged behind in the use of technology and new methods of production, particularly in these core industries. It could not compete with similar industries in other countries.

In the 1920s, each of these key industries went into decline.

Coal

The coal industry, employing almost nine per cent of the total British workforce, found its sales declining in the 1920s after centuries of increasing production. Oil and electricity were replacing coal as the preferred fuels for transport and industry. The age of steam was ending.

For the miners, this meant lower wages or unemployment.

SOURCE 3

When a quarter of a million miners are unemployed, it is part of the order of things that Alf Smith, a miner living in the back streets of Newcastle, should be out of work. Alf Smith is merely one of the quarter million, a statistical unit. But no human being finds it easy to regard himself as a statistical unit. So long as Bert Jones across the street is still at work, Alf Smith is bound to feel himself dishonoured and a failure.

From *The Road to Wigan Pier* by George Orwell.

Iron and steel

Britain's iron and steel industries were in almost as bad a situation as coal. Throughout the 1920s, these industries were badly hit by foreign competition. Steel plants in Japan, Scandinavia and the USA were much larger and used more up-to-date equipment.

The industry did better in the 1930s. The British Iron and Steel Federation created larger mills and took older ones out of production. This helped the industry to become competitive, but it was of little comfort to the working people in the iron and steel areas. The new, efficient plants required fewer workers.

Shipbuilding

Another of Britain's staple industries, shipbuilding, also suffered. Again, competition from Scandinavia and Japan hit hard, and for the same reasons. There were too many small, uneconomical shipyards in Britain. Shipyard owners began closing smaller yards in an effort to become more efficient. During the 1930s, this did help the shipbuilding industry to become more competitive, but it was again at the expense of the working people. When the Jarrow shipyard closed, it left some 70 per cent of the men without a job.

SOURCE 4

Just after the Armistice, I was sent to look after some German prisoners of war. They had a certain look, these prisoners of war. Most of them had been captured two or three years before. It was a strained, greyish, faintly decomposed look. I did not expect to see that kind of face again for a long time; but I was wrong. I have seen a lot of those faces on this journey. They belong to unemployed men.

The writer and broadcaster JB Priestley travelled through England in 1933. Here he describes what he saw in the North East.

Cotton

The cotton industry relied on exports, particularly to Africa and Asia. During the war, little or no shipping was available to take cotton abroad. The result was that other countries took over the markets from British firms. The Japanese were particularly successful, adapting British technology to electrically powered machines.

Britain also lost most of its huge market in India. One reason for this was that India itself was beginning to produce cotton in factories. Another was that the Indians boycotted British cotton goods as part of their campaign for independence.

SOURCE 5

The tragic word round there [the cotton mills in Blackburn], I soon discovered is dhootie … A dhootie is the loin cloth of India … and it is also the name of the cheap cotton fabric from which these loin cloths are made … This fabric was manufactured in the town and surrounding district on a scale equal to the needs of the gigantic Indian population. So colossal was the output that Blackburn was the greatest weaving town in the world …That trade is almost finished.

JB Priestley was proud of his northern 'roots'. Here he discusses Blackburn in 1933.

ACTIVITY

Two workers from different industries meet at a union meeting in the 1930s. They talk about their problems. Choose one industry each. Write or role-play a dialogue that they might have had which begins with one of them saying, 'We've suffered worse than anybody else.' You can get plenty of ideas from the text, but you can also do your own research.

SOURCE **6**

I KNOW 3 TRADES
I SPEAK 3 LANGUAGES
FOUGHT FOR 3 YEARS
HAVE 3 CHILDREN
AND NO WORK FOR
3 MONTHS
BUT I ONLY WANT
ONE JOB

Even skilled workers found themselves on the dole as traditional industries struggled.

1 **What do you think would be the greatest problem facing someone who lost their job in the 1920s or 1930s?**

FOCUS TASK

WHY WAS UNEMPLOYMENT SUCH A PROBLEM IN THE 1920S AND 1930S?

It is 1935. You are one of a team which has been commissioned to investigate this question. Your job is to plan a two-minute presentation on the structural problems in Britain's economy and how they have caused poverty. Your presentation should mention:

- problems in particular industries.
- main reasons for problems (e.g. competition).
- how working people have been affected.

Your presentation could make use of statistics and flow charts or similar diagrams to show how events are connected.

The Great Depression

In 1929, the Wall Street Crash in America dragged the entire world economy, including Britain's, into a prolonged and deep depression. Britain's decline was not as marked as that of some other countries, but only because it was already in a bad state in the first place. The existing problems were intensified: British exports, already falling in the 1920s, fell by half in the 1930s, while unemployment tripled.

SOURCE **7**

	Coal	*Iron*	*Cotton*
	Total output of coal in UK (millions of tonnes)	*Output of pig iron in UK (millions of tonnes)*	*Exports from UK (millions of metres)*
1873	*131*	*7*	*3,186*
1897	*205*	*9*	*4,382*
1913	*292*	*10*	*6,469*
1929	*261*	*8*	*3,443*
1938	*231*	*7*	*1,324*

Declining industrial output in Britain.

Unemployment

SOURCE **8**

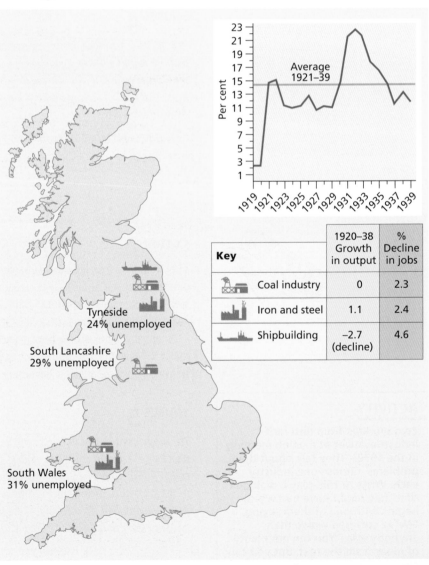

Tyneside
24% unemployed

South Lancashire
29% unemployed

South Wales
31% unemployed

Key		1920–38 Growth in output	% Decline in jobs
	Coal industry	0	2.3
	Iron and steel	1.1	2.4
	Shipbuilding	−2.7 (decline)	4.6

Unemployment in industrial areas in the 1920s and 1930s.

Did all of Britain suffer equally in the 1920s and 1930s?

The picture was bleak in the areas of the traditional industries (see Source 8), but in other parts of the country, where the newer industries were located, there was a different story.

2 Look at Source 8. In around 50 words describe the regional pattern of unemployment it shows.

3 How are Sources 9 and 10 useful to an historian who is trying to build up a detailed picture of Britain's economy in the 1930s?

SOURCE 9

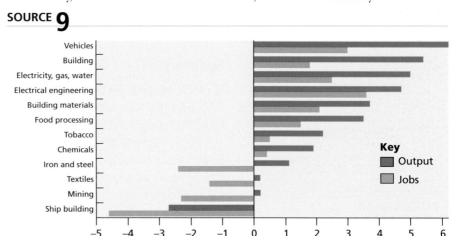

Average annual % growth or decrease of output and jobs in various industries, 1920-38.

Electricity

The introduction of the wonderful new source of energy, electricity, created thousands of new jobs. In 1926, the government set up the Central Electricity Board to run the National Grid. By 1938, two out of three homes were on mains electricity, and this stimulated demand for electrical goods. Electric cookers, irons and vacuum cleaners sold in their hundreds of thousands. The jobs created were in the Midlands and, in particular, the South East.

Chemicals

The chemical industry also saw rapid and important changes during this period. Chemical fertiliser manufacture, photography and glass making all became important areas of employment. The boom in house building between the wars created an increased demand for paint, which was also made by chemical companies. At the same time, a new material, plastic, began to revolutionise the production of everyday items such as light fittings.

The government encouraged amalgamation, the joining together of smaller companies to form large super-corporations. The largest was Imperial Chemical Industries (ICI). Another large company was Unilever, which was formed in 1926 by the joining of Lever Brothers with a Dutch group of companies.

SOURCE 10

... we could work any hours we liked. So I worked all the hours I could. I had £7 17s 10d wages, and I was only a boy of 17. Two pounds was a week's wages for a bus driver.

A Coventry car worker describing his work in the 1930s.

The motor industry

Probably the most successful industry of the period was the motor industry, based in the Midlands. The number of cars in the country rose from 30,000 in 1920 to two million in 1939. The Morris and Austin plants at Oxford and Dagenham employed thousands of workers. Britain became the most successful car-building country in Europe, partly because its winding roads made American imports unsuitable.

1 Draw up two lists, one giving the features of the 'old industries', the other the features of the 'new industries'. Use the text and sources to help you.

2 Why was the growth of new industries of little help to those who were being laid off from the old ones?

Aviation

The aircraft industry developed rapidly after the Great War. The main growth was in the USA, but British business saw the possibilities as well. Again, the government encouraged amalgamation, with Imperial Airways Ltd being formed in 1924. A new company, British Airways, was set up in 1935, and in 1939 the two companies joined to form the British Overseas Airways Corporation (BOAC).

Jobs were also created in the aircraft building industry. Large manufacturers such as De Havilland, Handley Page and Rolls Royce became established employers, again mainly in the Midlands and South East, but also around Bristol in the South West.

Summary

As a whole, prosperity and living standards for the majority of the population rose during the 1920s and 1930s. Many workers simply moved from the old industries to the new ones. However, the new industries were different from the old ones in several important ways.

Firstly, the new industries were concentrated in the Midlands and the South East, away from the old industrial heartlands. They also produced goods mainly for the home market, rather than for export, and as a result companies stayed fairly small. They were never able to fill the gaps in employment left by the declining traditional industries. The new industries relied on new methods of production and new technologies. This meant they employed far fewer workers than the staple industries, with more skilled work and less heavy manual labour.

Finally, the new industries created new ways of working. Many companies employed women part-time, rather than providing full-time jobs for men. Retailing and food packaging, which grew hugely between the wars, were good examples of the new type of work. The food packaging industry and a redundant shipyard riveter had little to offer each other.

SOURCE 11

Only six per cent of the Deptford unemployed were long-term unemployed, but 63 per cent in the Rhondda … Among every 1000 workers, four in Deptford, but 280 in Rhondda have failed to get a job for at least a year … The difference between a prosperous and a depressed area is thus not in the neighbourhood of 1:7 but 1:70: One long-term unemployed man to seventy.

A government report, 1938.

FOCUS TASK

DID ALL AREAS OF BRITAIN SUFFER DURING THE 1920S AND 1930S?

Add an extra section to your presentation in the Focus Task on page 240, explaining that not all areas were suffering during this period. You may wish to mention points such as:

- new industries.
- signs of prosperity (e.g. air travel, car ownership).
- how these new industries affected employment.

SOURCE 12

THE MOUNTAINEER.

Ratepayer (to the Premier). "I KNOW YOU'RE ALWAYS KEEN ON MOUNTAINS, SIR. HAVE YOU NOTICED THIS ONE?"

A *Punch* cartoon published soon after the war.

How did governments react to the problem of poverty between the wars?

Lloyd George was still Prime Minister when the Great War ended, and remained there until 1922. Neither he nor any of the major political parties were ready for the economic miseries which were to follow the war.

The Liberal Government introduces 'the dole'

Until this point, National Insurance had been based on 'insured benefit'. This meant that a worker's benefits were in proportion to the 'stamps' he or she had paid (see page 235). When their 'stamps' had been used up, the unemployed had to rely on poor relief. The post-war slump threatened to throw hundreds of thousands of Britain's war heroes onto poor relief.

The Liberal government responded to the immediate crisis by extending the National Insurance scheme so that the unemployed received benefit for 32 weeks instead of 15, after which they would have to seek poor relief under the Poor Law. These extended benefits were officially called 'public assistance', although most people called them 'the dole'. However, the government underestimated the problem. The new scheme had been designed for short-term unemployment: the aim was to tide workers over the worst. In reality, much unemployment was long-term.

In the 1930s, the problem of unemployment became even worse. In 1929, the Labour Party won a general election and formed the first ever Labour government. With the Wall Street Crash causing economic depression throughout the world, it was a dreadful time to take over the running of the troubled economy.

Even before the depression, it was clear to the Labour Prime Minister, Ramsay Macdonald, that 'dole' payments would not be enough to fend off poverty. Now he was faced with the prospect of millions of workers relying on Poor Law outdoor relief, paid for by local ratepayers who were themselves hard pressed.

The dole is reduced

To deal with the crisis, Macdonald formed a National Government of Labour, Conservative and Liberal MPs. This COALITION government had to make cuts in its spending to keep the country solvent through these hard times. The National Government cut the pay of civil servants and teachers. Insured workers had their benefits cut by 10 per cent. Many Labour MPs disagreed with this policy and split with Macdonald.

The means test

An even more controversial new rule said that in order to qualify for the dole a worker had to pass a means test. This meant that officials from the Public Assistance Committee (PAC) made a thorough investigation into the unemployed person's finances, including every detail of the family's income and savings. If an unemployed man's son had a paper round or his wife had a few pounds saved in the post office, he had to declare this money. His 'dole' would then be reduced.

Many called the means test humiliating. Workers felt that they were due the dole by rights. If their families were able to earn a little money on the side, that should be allowed.

However, it was the intrusiveness of the means test, and the insensitive manner of some of the officials who carried it out, that caused most resentment. For example, a man who was drawing dole might buy his child a gift. If the 'means test man' got to hear about it, he would call to check how this had been paid for. Did the man have some undeclared income? Mistrust and suspicion were the order of the day. Lying behind it all was the old suspicion from the days of the Poor Law that poor people were basically scroungers. It seemed the old attitudes still lived on after all!

SOURCE 13

The Means Test is very strictly enforced, and you are liable to be refused relief at the slightest hint that you are getting money from another source. Dock labourers, for instance, who are generally hired by the half day, have to sign on at a Labour Exchange twice daily; if they fail to do so it is assumed that they have been working and their dole is reduced correspondingly.

George Orwell, *The Road to Wigan Pier*.

SOURCE 14

This photograph shows clashes between police and demonstrators protesting about the means test in London in 1932.

3 Why do you think the government thought the means test was necessary?

4 Do you think the fact that the means test caused such resentment means that it was effective or that it was ineffective?

The Unemployment Assistance Board

In 1936, the Unemployment Assistance Board took over the running of labour exchanges, the dole and dreaded means test. The UAB also set up training schemes and provided help to people who wanted to move to another area to find work. Older unemployed men were sometimes given allotments where they could grow vegetables or raise poultry and rabbits. The means test remained, but by all accounts it was less severe than it had been under the PAC.

SOURCE 15

Unemployed men on a training scheme funded by the government in the 1930s.

The Special Areas Act

In 1934, the government identified South Wales, Tyneside, West Cumberland and Scotland as areas with special needs. Government money was invested in projects such as the new steelworks in Ebbw Vale. The Act's success was limited, however, because the level of investment was not high enough.

It was not until the very late 1930s that the shadow of unemployment lifted from Britain, and then it was only because the government was spending money on building weapons in preparation for war.

SOURCE 16

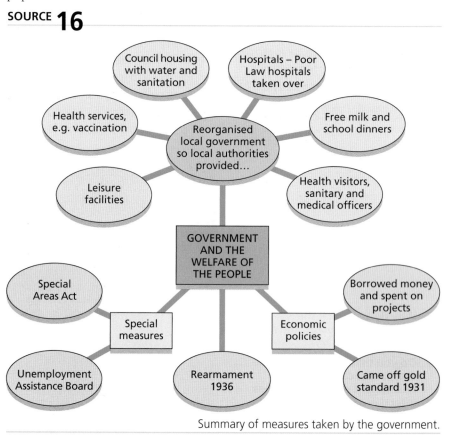

Summary of measures taken by the government.

FOCUS TASK

HOW DID GOVERNMENTS REACT TO ECONOMIC DEPRESSION?

'Government action in the 1930s showed that the spirit of the 1834 Poor Law was still alive.' Do you agree?

Look carefully at the government's actions in the 1920s and 1930s. For each measure, note down:

- what it was.
- its aims.
- how it was paid for.
- whether it showed the spirit of 1834 (self-help, no government funding, weeding out the undeserving poor).

You might find it helpful to use a table with the following headings:

- Measure/date
- Aim
- How it worked
- How paid for?
- Effects
- Spirit of 1834?

How did the poor react to their problems in the 1930s?

Some of the best evidence about the thoughts and feelings of ordinary people during this period was produced by the writers JB Priestley, Walter Greenwood and George Orwell. You have come across two of these earlier in this section (see Sources 1–5 and 13). Orwell and other writers described the problems of malnutrition, particularly among the children of families hit by unemployment. Both Orwell and Priestley commented that by the mid to late 1930s the boring, depressing and fruitless search for work was taking a terrible psychological toll on the unemployed. Government schemes and local charities provided allotments and social clubs, but for once-proud workers used to the challenge of a disciplined working day and to good wages these were no substitute.

SOURCE 17

A dozen or so rows of chairs … were quickly occupied the instant the men rushed in. Those coming later lounged against the wall. When one of those seated was called to the counter, his immediate neighbour took his seat. The remainder … all moved up a place … the queue waiting for chairs often stretching into the yard. The proceedings had come to be known as 'musical chairs'.

A description of a labour exchange in *Love on the Dole*, a play by Walter Greenwood, 1933.

SOURCE 18

So you have whole populations settling down, as it were, to a lifetime on the PAC. And what I think is admirable … is that they have managed to do it without going spiritually to pieces … they realise that losing your job does not mean that you cease to be a human being … Families are impoverished, but the family system has not broken up … Instead of raging against their destiny they have made things tolerable by lowering their standards … You can't get much meat for threepence, but you can get a lot of fish and chips … you can wring 40 cups of tea out of a quarter-pound packet.

George Orwell, *The Road to Wigan Pier*.

SOURCE 19

By the time the North of England is an industrial ruin, we shall be able to beat the world at table tennis.

Written by JB Priestley in 1933.

1 **In Source 19, Priestley's comment is ironic. What does he mean?**

2 **Look at Sources 17–19. Choose five words which you think best describe the attitude of the poor to the sufferings of the 1930s.**

3 **Which do you think was more damaging to an unemployed person in the 1930s: the direct effects of poverty (less food, few luxuries) or the psychological effects? Explain your answer with reference to Sources 17–19.**

Despite the widespread problems faced by the poor in the 1930s, there was relatively little organised protest. Why was this? Historians have come up with different explanations for this.

The dole

Despite the failings of government action, few people actually starved to death as a result of unemployment. The dole was intended to keep the unemployed alive, and it did exactly that. In fact, if people were careful, they could even afford an occasional treat on very rare occasions. It is tempting to wonder what would have happened 100 years earlier if there had been three million people unemployed and no national system of relief. Would there have been mass starvation or even revolution?

The failure of the General Strike in 1926

In the 1920s, conflict between working-class organisations and the government led to the General Strike (see page 286). The failure of the strike weakened the trade union movement, reducing its influence. In the 1930s, it tended to focus on representing its members – those who were still in work – rather than trying to deal with the needs of those who were out of work.

SOURCE 20

During the last 15 years Jarrow has passed through a period of industrial depression without parallel in the town's history. Its shipyard is closed. Its steelworks have been denied the right to re-open. Where formerly 8000 people, many of them skilled workers, were employed, only 100 men are now employed on a temporary scheme.

Part of the Jarrow marchers' petition, 1937.

1 Read Source 22. Why would the police be concerned about the march?

The Jarrow march

One of the most notable exceptions was the Jarrow march of 1937. You have already seen the devastating impact of unemployment on Jarrow (see page 239). In October of that year, 200 men, chosen from hundreds of volunteers, began a 300-mile march on foot to London to present a petition to the Prime Minister, Stanley Baldwin.

SOURCE 21

The Jarrow marchers following their MP Ellen Wilkinson, who can be seen at the front. They are arriving in Luton after 250 miles of their walk.

The radical Labour MP Ellen Wilkinson led the march and presented the petition to Parliament on 2 November. The government was asked why it could not give orders for naval ships to be built at Jarrow, but no answer was given. The marchers returned to Jarrow by train, empty-handed. To add insult to injury, the UAB officials in Jarrow had docked their dole because they had not been available for work. However, new engineering and ship-breaking work did become available in Jarrow in the later 1930s.

SOURCE 22

The march throughout the Metropolitan Police District was well organised, and the men well disciplined. The general public were sympathetic and generous and the demonstration was kept free from political propaganda. During the marchers' stay in London their conduct was exemplary and no incident occurred necessitating police action.

A Special Branch report on the Jarrow march, 1937.

Despite their treatment, the marchers achieved one of their aims – to raise public awareness of the effects of unemployment on working people. Many historians believe that the march had an impact on the civil servants and MPs who in the early 1940s set about planning the next phase in the war against poverty – the setting up of the Welfare State.

FOCUS TASK

HOW DID THE POOR REACT TO THEIR SITUATION IN THE 1930S?

Work in groups. Your task is to prepare a radio broadcast on the arrival of the Jarrow marchers in London on 1 November 1937. You are going to use this broadcast as a way to describe the different ways in which the poor reacted to their poverty in the 1930s.
  Plan your broadcast using a flow chart. Radio broadcasts always try to begin with something which interests the listeners. The arrival of the marchers might be a good point to begin with.
  Your broadcast should explain:

- **why the marchers are marching.**
- **what has happened to Jarrow.**
- **how other areas have suffered.**
- **how unemployment has affected the poor.**
- **the aims of the marchers.**
- **reactions to them.**

9.4 *Has poverty been wiped out since the Second World War?*

The Beveridge Report

Do you know what this week's bestselling book is? If not, it would be a sensible guess to suggest that it is a crime novel, or a spy thriller. In December 1942, the bestselling item was a report on social insurance by William Beveridge. This may seem odd, until you think back to the misery of the 1930s. Beveridge's report set out some hard facts and some radical ideas. As a result of it, he has been seen as the father of the WELFARE STATE, even though he himself disliked the term.

Sir William Beveridge was the ideal man to plan what the future of welfare after the Second World War should be. He was a civil servant who had worked on the Liberal National Insurance Act of 1911 (see page 235). In fact, his job in 1942 was to take a long, hard look at National Insurance, which had become rather fragmented. However, Beveridge, a very shrewd man, made a much wider investigation into poverty, health and welfare in general (see Factfile). In doing so, he took his political masters by surprise, and by publishing the report he created a groundswell of public opinion which politicians could hardly ignore.

FACTFILE

The Beveridge Report

★ Beveridge identified five great social evils which plagued ordinary working people. These were want, disease, ignorance, squalor and idleness.

★ He recommended new principles upon which the relief of poverty was to be based. The core principle was universality. This would replace the principle of less eligibility, the means test and insured benefit, which, Beveridge argued, had caused confusion and humiliation. They had even discouraged people from claiming.

★ The main changes recommended by Beveridge were:
• The differences between insured benefit and public assistance would be scrapped.
• There would be no means test.
• The National Insurance scheme would be run by the government (not the insurance companies).
• There would be a flat rate contribution and everyone would be entitled to a flat rate benefit.
• The flat rate benefit paid out to unemployed or sick workers would be high enough and last long enough that there would be no need for public assistance.
• In order to relieve poverty, there would have to be extra benefits which provided for children and for health care.

SOURCE **1**

RIGHT TURN

A cartoon by David Low published in the *Daily Express* in 1942. Low was a strong supporter of the Beveridge Report.

SOURCE 2

Ministers should, in my view, be careful not to raise false hopes, as was done last time by speeches about 'homes fit for heroes' etc. The broad masses of the people face the hardships of life undaunted but they are liable to get very angry if they feel they have been gulled or cheated.

Prime Minister Winston Churchill speaking in January 1943.

SOURCE 3

In spite of the social services, the interruption or cessation of earnings frequently meant privation and suffering; and the actual earnings of the lower-paid workers were commonly insufficient for the needs of families with more than a limited number of children. Yet these social surveys showed that 'the total resources of the community were sufficient to make want needless' and that 'want was a needless scandal due to not taking the trouble to prevent it'.

On the basis of the diagnosis of want Sir William Beveridge specifies two main requirements. The abolition of poverty calls both for greatly improved provision against interruption and loss of earning power, and for the adjustment of incomes, in periods of earning as well as during interruptions in earning, to family needs. Under the first head it is proposed to improve the present schemes of social insurance in three directions – by extending their scope to cover those who are now excluded, by covering risks which are now excluded, and by raising standards of benefit. Under the second head a system of children's allowances, starting with the second dependent child in every family, is recommended …

Plainly it is too early to pass judgement on every detail of Sir William Beveridge's proposals. They will call for further examination here. What can be said, however, at once is that the report is a momentous document which should and must exercise a profound and immediate influence on the direction of social change in Britain. Some modifications in detail may prove necessary or unavoidable, but the central proposals of the report must surely be accepted as the basis of government action.

An article on the Beveridge Report published in *The Times* in 1942.

1 Read Source 3 carefully. *The Times* newspaper was always regarded as a supporter of self-help. Does this quote suggest a change of attitude?

2 On your own copy of Source 4, add notes to summarise in your own words the main points of the Beveridge Report.

SOURCE 4

Family allowances

Free health care

THE BEVERIDGE REPORT

MAIN PROPOSALS

Cost met by the government

National Insurance covering everyone from the cradle to the grave

Flat rate benefits for the unemployed and the sick

The new look of government policy on poverty.

How did Labour create the Welfare State between 1945 and 1951?

The first of Beveridge's proposals came into effect before the war ended. In 1944, a Ministry of National Insurance was set up in Newcastle. In June 1945, the Conservative government passed the Family Allowances Act. This gave every family five shillings per child per week. However, this amount was lower than Beveridge had proposed and did not apply to the first child.

In July 1945, a general election produced a landslide victory for the Labour Party under Clement Attlee. Attlee had campaigned hard during the election for the creation of a welfare state to implement all of the Beveridge proposals.

However, Attlee and other Labour MPs were not only campaigning against the caution of the Conservative government. They were also haunted by the record of the their own Labour Party in the 1930s. They felt that by being over-cautious then Ramsay Macdonald had let down his party and working people.

In 1945, Labour had their largest ever majority in Parliament and massive support from the British people. It was time for radical action.

National Insurance

The first measure was the National Insurance Act of 1946. The old National Insurance system was dismantled, and National Insurance now became compulsory for all workers except married women (who had the option to pay it). Different types of workers paid different levels of contribution according to their age, but most people paid 4s 11d a week, a fairly substantial sum. In return, workers received benefits for 'interruption of earnings' as a result of illness, unemployment or old age. As an extension to the scheme, the Industrial Injuries Act gave compensation to people injured at work or the families of those killed.

No benefits were given to strikers, as this was seen as the responsibility of the unions. Also, benefit could be withheld if someone refused a job found for them by a labour exchange.

Older people were paid a state pension on reaching the age of 65 (men) or 60 (women). In practice, older workers were encouraged to carry on working, and two thirds of men decided to do so rather than take up their pension. A death grant gave widows much-needed help with funeral expenses when their husband died.

National Insurance also provided maternity benefits. Mothers received a lump sum on the birth of each child. If they had been paying National Insurance, they received an allowance for 18 weeks.

The NI system formed the basis of state systems for the relief of poverty which are still in place today.

SOURCE 5

The Question is asked – Can we afford it? Supposing the answer is 'No', what does this mean? It means that the sum total of the goods produced and the services rendered by the people of this country is not sufficient to provide for all our people at all times, in sickness, in health, in youth and in age, the very modest standard of life that is represented by the sums of money set out in the Second Schedule to this Bill. I cannot believe that our national productivity is so slow, that our willingness to work is so feeble or that we can submit to the world that the masses of our people must be condemned to penury.

Clement Attlee speaking about the National Insurance Bill in 1946.

SOURCE 6

An employment exchange.

3 Write your own 15-word definition of the term 'the Welfare State'.

All the benefits applied only to insured workers. Those who were not working, and so not paying National Insurance contributions, were covered by the National Assistance Board (NAB), set up in 1948. The Board took over from the old Unemployment Assistance Board. Claimants were still interviewed to see what kind of help they needed, but their family's earnings were not considered. The means test was dead.

Some of Beveridge's proposals were altered or not taken up. For example, the benefit provided was not based on a national minimum standard of living. Instead, the government fixed a benefit rate and promised to review it every five years. It felt that a rate which constantly changed with prices would be too complicated to calculate.

Beveridge had proposed benefits for divorced women and women looking after elderly parents. He also suggested sickness benefit for housewives. These measures were not included.

Other measures

The Labour government also tackled some of the other evils which Beveridge identified. In 1948, it set up the National Health Service (see page 332). This was, in its way, just as radical a measure as National Insurance.

The government also continued the slum clearances effectively begun by German bombing during the war, and began a huge house-building programme.

The issue of the long-term decline of the core industries was tackled by NATIONALISING industries such as coal mining, shipbuilding and iron and steel. The government hoped to be able to plan the operation of these industries for the benefit of the country as a whole: this would include preserving jobs and so preventing unemployment.

FOCUS TASK

WAS THE BEVERIDGE REPORT REVOLUTIONARY?

This chart summarises the main features of poor relief between 1834 and the 1940s. It is not yet complete.

1   Copy the incomplete chart into your own book.

2   Fill out the first three columns by referring back to the pages suggested.

3   Use the information on pages 249–50 to complete the final column.

4   Use the information to help you write an essay entitled 'Was the Beveridge Report revolutionary?'.

Issues	1834 Poor Law (page 219)	1911 Liberal Reforms (pages 232–35)	1920s and 1930s (pages 242–44)	The Welfare State
Who qualified for poor relief?				
What benefits were available to the poor?				
Who paid for poor relief?				
What was the attitude to the poor?				

Has the Welfare State solved the problem of poverty?

The costs of these measures began to rise dramatically, causing disagreements between Labour MPs. Labour lost the election of 1951, and the new Conservative government criticised many Labour measures. It reversed some of them: for example, the coal industry was sold back to private owners. However, the Conservatives had no plans to touch Labour's Welfare State.

The 1950s were relatively prosperous years. The Welfare State seemed to be working, but the main worry was old people. In 1950, the campaigner Seebohm Rowntree (at the age of 79) published his last report on conditions in York. He found that in York the major cause of poverty was now old age. Beveridge himself admitted in 1953 that a quarter of people on retirement or widow's pensions were having to go to the NAB for extra help. However, in general there was an optimistic spirit during this decade.

In the 1960s, by contrast, poverty seemed to be 'rediscovered' in Britain. As with the Booth and Rowntree reports of the 1880s and 1890s, new research by the government and academics showed that poverty was alive and well. One important factor was that prices rose steadily during the 1950s and 1960s. A government report published in 1966 suggested that 166,000 families were living in poverty – mainly owing to the low wages of the father. Many old and unemployed people were also struggling as increases in their pensions and benefits lagged far behind price rises. The researcher Peter Townsend used Rowntree's methods to calculate that in the 1960s six to nine per cent of the population were in poverty and up to 28 per cent were on the POVERTY LINE. In 1965, the Child Poverty Action Group was formed, in response to a claim that 720,000 children were living in poverty.

Over the next 20 years, poverty became an overriding concern of governments. In 1968, the government created the Department of Health and Social Security (DHSS), a huge organisation which took over from the old NAB and many other bodies. The DHSS introduced supplementary benefits to top up the other benefits people were receiving. Although this stopped people falling into absolute poverty, many thousands lived only just above the new unofficial poverty line.

Beveridge had always assumed that the ill or unemployed would be helped by their families. However, from the 1960s onwards Britain saw a rising number of divorces, and many single parents were unable to call on an extended family. In 1971, Family Income Supplement was introduced (later to become Family Credit). FIS provided grants towards essential items such as cookers, and children from poor families were also entitled to free school meals. This benefit was a break with the principle of universality, because it targeted low-income families.

Welfare costs continued to rise rapidly. Today, the social security budget is the single largest item of government spending. Between 1951 and 1980, the number of people receiving either National Assistance or Supplementary Benefit rose from 1.5 million to 3.3 million.

Redefining poverty

In Edwin Chadwick's time, the definition of poverty was an inability to stay alive without help. The Poor Law aimed simply to make the difference between life and death.

In the late nineteenth century, Rowntree developed the idea of the poverty line, the level of income below which poor people could not afford the basic essentials of life.

By the time of the Beveridge Report, poverty was seen much more as a low quality of life. Part of the aim of the Welfare State was to enable the poor to buy small luxuries such as radio licences. Source 7 shows how the purposes of benefits had changed.

SOURCE 7

The poor must be able to keep themselves reasonably fed, and well enough dressed to keep their self respect and attend interviews for jobs. Their homes must be reasonably warm; their children should not feel shamed by the quality of their clothing, the family must be able to visit relatives, read newspapers, retain their TV sets …

Supplementary Benefit Commission report, 1978.

1 Do you agree with Source 7 about the purposes of benefit?

FOCUS TASK

1 Despite the massive rise in the cost of benefits, research shows that millions of pounds' worth of benefits to which people are entitled are not claimed. Why do you think this is?

2 By 1979, the Welfare State had helped to redistribute the country's wealth. In 1951, the poorest 20 per cent of households received less than 1 per cent of the country's income. By 1979, they were receiving 9 per cent. Do you think this is a good thing?

3 Would

a) Edwin Chadwick
b) David Lloyd George
c) Clement Attlee

have agreed with you? Explain your answers carefully.

Has the Welfare State succeeded or failed?

The Welfare State has not removed poverty – there are still many poor people – but that does not necessarily mean that it has failed.

Some commentators see the Welfare State as a great success. They point to the rising numbers of people helped by it, and to the increasing expectations of it, as shown in Source 7, as evidence that the scheme is working. They also claim that rising costs are not a failure of welfare but a sign of its success: poverty has always been a problem, so tackling it effectively will always be expensive. They point out that the Welfare State has effectively redistributed income from the rich to the poor.

Others say that despite all the money spent on it the Welfare State has failed. It has left the basic problem of poverty largely untouched. The poor are still poor, and people are still trapped in their poverty, unable to improve their situation even with benefits.

Some people believe, as Chadwick and his nineteenth-century colleagues did, that such a comprehensive welfare system has in fact taken away people's desire to improve their own situation. Margaret Thatcher, leader of the Conservative government which was elected in 1979, criticised the Welfare State. Her view was that it was 'the nanny state', which by setting out to care for everyone destroyed their motivation to work. The Conservatives felt that it should not be an aim of government to redistribute wealth to the poor. Instead, they tried to create an economic climate in which the poor could become richer by their own efforts. Most famously, Thatcher called for a return to what she called 'Victorian values'. She said that in the nineteenth century people had 'great self-reliance', and she wanted to help people rediscover that.

FOCUS TASK

HAS THE WELFARE STATE SUCCEEDED?

1   Here are four possible views on the Welfare State. For each one suggest what evidence the speaker could use to justify their view.

The Welfare State has stamped out the extreme poverty which was common in the nineteenth century...

The Welfare State has failed because it has not done enough...

The Welfare State has changed attitudes to poverty...

The Welfare State has failed because it has tried to do too much...

2   *Either:*

A Use the arguments you have worked out in 1 for a class debate.

Or:

B   Bring your findings together in an essay on the topic 'Has the Welfare State succeeded or failed?'. This should look at the achievements of the Welfare State in a balanced way. Organise your answer in paragraphs:

- Why the question is controversial and arouses strong opinions. You could refer to the long debate going back to the nineteenth century over what causes poverty and how best to solve the problem of poverty.
- Why the Welfare State has failed to stamp out poverty.
- In what ways the Welfare State has succeeded in its fight against poverty.

10 Trade unions and working-class movements 1800–1990

10.1 Working-class movements 1800–1850

> ### FOCUS
>
> As industry changed in the nineteenth and twentieth centuries, workers discovered that they were often stronger and safer if they joined together in societies or unions.
>
> In 10.1 you will study the period 1800–1850. You will:
>
> - investigate early working-class movements.
> - examine how governments reacted to early trade unions.
> - study the successes and failures of working-class movements such as Chartism and New Model Unions.
>
> 10.2 covers the period 1850–1900. You will:
>
> - look at the development of trade unions for unskilled workers.
> - see how governments reacted to these new unions and how the Labour Party evolved.
>
> In 10.3 you will look at trade unions in the twentieth century. You will:
>
> - investigate the events of the General Strike.
> - examine the role and attitude of trade unions from the General Strike until the present.

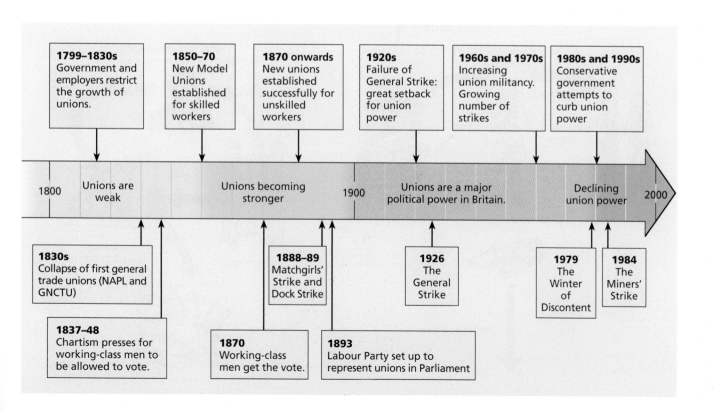

The weavers' dilemma

It is 1726. William Pike is a West Country cloth merchant. He announces to the local weavers that he is going to cut the price he pays them for their cloth. What should the weavers do? These are the options:

- Each weaver could decide individually whether or not to work for William Pike's new wages.
- All the weavers employed by William Pike could agree to refuse to work for him if he reduces wages.
- All the weavers in the district could form a trade club. Then even those who do not currently work for William Pike will refuse to work for his low wages.

The weavers chose the third option. All the members of the trade club refused to work for William Pike, and he had to give in and pay the higher rates. Such disputes were common in the eighteenth century, but such outcomes were not: trade clubs usually lost, and employers usually won. The law was on the side of the employers, as were the governments of the day. Disputes sometimes turned to violence. Even if trade clubs managed to settle the problem for which they had been formed, they usually withered away again after the fuss had died down.

This chapter charts the way in which working people increasingly succeeded in protecting their interests by joining together in collective action. It also charts the changing relationship between such workers' unions, their employers and the government.

1 What would be the result for the weavers of a cut in their wages?

2 What are the advantages and disadvantages of each option?

3 From your study of industrialisation, explain how

a) machinery
b) factory work
c) trade cycles

changed the position of workers.

4 The capitalist is the person who provides or borrows the capital to get an industry going. Give examples from any of the industries you have studied in Chapters 3–6.

How was work changing in the eighteenth century?

Before industrialisation, work had been based on handicrafts which took years to learn. The individual craftsman was at the centre of the working process. Machinery was hand operated.

After industrialisation, the machine was increasingly central. Work became less skilled: in fact, many machines in the spinning mills could be operated by children.

This resulted in increasing separation of the employers from the employees. Also, trade cycles – economic booms and slumps – made the workers more vulnerable to unemployment and wage reductions at certain times.

SOURCE 1

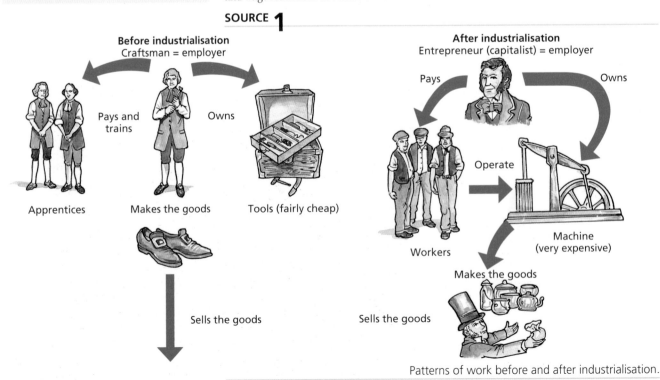

Patterns of work before and after industrialisation.

Working-class movements around 1800

In 1800, there were several types of organisation run by and for working people. As you will see from the descriptions below, there tended to be overlaps in the way these organisations worked.

Friendly societies

Friendly societies were set up to help workers put money aside for hard times. The society collected money from each member. It then paid out a certain sum to members who were unemployed or unable to work because they were sick or injured. It also made sure that they were given a proper funeral. (Having a 'pauper's funeral' was the greatest fear of most working-class people.)

One such society, the Society of Journeymen (unskilled) Shoemakers, was set up in 1780 in a parish near the Tower of London. Members paid 2s 6d as an entrance fee and then a subscription of 1s 3d every month. If the box held more than £20, a sick member received seven shillings per week. If funds fell below £20, then he received four shillings. The Society would contribute £7 to a member's funeral and £5 for that of his wife.

> **5** Why do you think friendly societies were given this name?

Trade clubs (also called trade societies)

Trade clubs were set up by well-paid, skilled handicraft workers such as weavers, carpenters, tailors, printers or hatmakers. A trade club aimed to protect its members' wages.

- It restricted entry to the trade: people wanting to learn it had to undergo long apprenticeships. Some trade clubs admitted only the children of existing tradesmen.
- It set minimum rates and maximum working hours for members, so that no member could undercut another member by working longer hours or charging less.
- It helped unemployed members to find work, and even supplied food and lodging to members who were travelling to a new area to look for work.
- It also acted as a friendly society for its members (see above).
- It might take employers to court and even send petitions to Parliament.
- It might organise strikes for higher wages, and members might refuse to work for a merchant who had started using new machinery or who was selling poor-quality goods.
- It also acted as a social club.

SOURCE 2

A membership ticket for a shearmen's club.

SOURCE 3

An illustration from a list of regulations drawn up by the Felt Makers' Company, 1820. (Felt makers finished off hats.) The man in the centre is looking for work.

FOCUS TASK

WHAT WAS THE PURPOSE OF EARLY WORKING-CLASS MOVEMENTS?

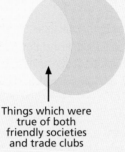

Things which were true of friendly societies only

Things which were true of trade clubs only

Things which were true of both friendly societies and trade clubs

Copy this diagram. Add notes to show the connections between trade clubs and friendly societies.

Are there more similarities than differences between friendly societies and trade clubs?

SOURCE 4

We have a general spirit of combination amongst all sorts of labourers and skilled workers who are opposed to all legal control. The introduction of machinery to replace hand labour in weaving is a cause of particular disgust and jealousy.

A letter from Manchester magistrates to the Home Secretary, 1791.

1 **What is the attitude of the writer of Source 4 towards combinations?**

Combinations

As traditional working methods came under greater pressure as a result of the industrial revolution, local trade clubs did not have the necessary power to protect their members. In the second half of the nineteenth century, trade clubs increasingly joined together or co-operated with other clubs in a particular area to protect their members. These became known at the time as 'combinations of workers'. The main difference between a combination and a trade club was that a combination had a wider membership. Even so, combinations still generally represented skilled workers rather than the mass of factory workers or agricultural labourers.

Gradually, the term 'trade union' became used instead of combination, trade club and trade society.

How strong were these organisations?

In the 1790s, these organisations were small and weak. A single trade club rarely had more than 500 members. They were usually confined to a small area and represented the workers in one trade. Nor did they have much money. With prices rising faster than wages, members could afford only small subscriptions.

Strike action was not effective. With the growing population and the increasing mobility of workers, employers usually had no trouble replacing any workers who went on strike.

Why did the government pass the Combination Acts in 1799?

Although the unions were quite weak, British governments were extremely hostile and suspicious towards them. Why was this?

In the late eighteenth century, Britain was going through social and industrial changes that no British government, and indeed no other country, had ever seen before. Rioting was the most common form of protest. The government saw every organised movement as a potential threat to peace and the established system, and felt that its duty was to crush it.

This feeling was made stronger by the events of the French Revolution, which began in 1789. By 1793, England was at war with France, and the government was deeply concerned about revolutionaries within Britain. A mutiny in the British navy in 1797 and a rebellion in Ireland in 1798 increased the government's worries.

At the same time, interest in politics was growing among skilled workers. In 1792, a RADICAL writer, Tom Paine, who had been very active in the American Revolution, returned to Britain and published *The Rights of Man*, a book which called for a fairer system of voting.

War also brought economic strains. Food prices rose, and combinations of workers pressed their employers for higher wages. In the past, employers had often asked Parliament to regulate or restrict combinations in individual trades. For example, this had already happened in the paper trade. When the master millwrights of London asked for help in 1799, they found Parliament especially ready to listen.

The Combination Acts

When the millwrights' petition was heard, Parliament was keen to act, and measures were proposed to regulate the mill workers' combinations. As Source 5 shows, however, some MPs, such as William Wilberforce, were anxious to go even further. They suggested that a more general Act should be passed, to deal with all combinations of workers. Later campaigners bitterly criticised Wilberforce as a hypocrite for fighting to free black slaves while repressing English working people.

SOURCE 5

8 April: Sir John Anderson brought up a report of a Select Committee to whom the Petition of master millwrights was referred. The substance of the report was that there existed among the journeymen millwrights, within certain districts in and about the metropolis, a combination which was dangerous to the public, and which the masters had not sufficient power to repress.

The report being read, Sir John Anderson moved 'that leave be given to bring in a Bill to prevent unlawful combinations of workmen employed in the millwright business, and to enable the magistrates to regulate their wages with certain limits'.

Mr Wilberforce said that he did not object to the principle of this motion ... but he [asked] whether it might not be advisable to extend the principle of this motion, and make it general against all combinations of workmen. These combinations he regarded as a general disease in our society.

17 June: Mr Chancellor Pitt said it was his intention to provide a remedy to an evil of very considerable magnitude; he meant that of unlawful combination among workmen in general – a practice which had become much too general, and was likely, if not checked, to produce very serious mischief. He could not state particularly the nature of the Bill which he intended to move for leave to bring in; but it would be modelled in some respect on that of the Bill for regulating the conduct of the paper manufacturers ... He then moved that leave be given to bring in a Bill to prevent unlawful combinations of workmen.

Report of a debate in the House of Commons, 1799.

The first Act was passed in 1799 and then modified in 1800. These Acts' main aim was to break up gatherings of workers and to allow swift trials of strikers so that the ringleaders could be dealt with quickly. The penalties for breaking the new laws were light by the standards of 1800. However, employers (who included many MPs) were happy because the Combination Acts made strikes difficult. The government was content to see organisations of working men, potential revolutionaries in their eyes, banned.

The Acts certainly restricted the ability of trade clubs to combine. However, there has been some debate among historians as to just how damaging they were to the movement. Some historians have suggested that general economic conditions were much more of a problem for trade unions than the Combination Acts. Look at the different views expressed in Sources 6 and 7.

SOURCE 6

... it is now felt that the effect of the Combination Acts is easily exaggerated ... The Acts ... made prosecution easier, but in fact few prosecutions took place. Malcolm Thomis [another historian] has shown that in Nottingham, for example, at least 50 illegal unions existed during the years of the Acts, at least 15 strikes took place, but there were no more than five prosecutions.

Written by the historian Trevor May in *An Economic and Social History of Britain, 1760–1970*.

> 2 **Were the Combination Acts really intended to restrict trade unions? Explain your answer.**

SOURCE 7

Attempts have been made to argue that the effect of the Combination Acts was small. The reasons put forward are ... that the Acts did not apply to Scotland, that most recorded cases were, as before, taken to the High Courts under existing laws, and that many unions undoubtedly continued to exist. But these objections do not stand up to serious examination ... The Scottish judges ... re-interpreted the ... Law so as to hold all combinations illegal ... The intention of the Act was to make combination an offence that could be dealt with summarily [very quickly] in order that strikes might be broken. The proceedings of courts of summary jurisdiction were not recorded [which means that there may or may not have been a lot of prosecutions] ... It is certainly true ... that unions continued to exist. Some of them did so by resorting to methods of great secrecy and, occasionally, intimidation. Others were shattered and driven out of existence. In fact, their life or death depended on the caprice of the magistracy.

GDH Cole and R Postgate, *The Common People, 1746–1946*. First published in 1938, this book has been criticised by other historians for being too much on the side of the working class.

ACTIVITY

Prepare a short presentation entitled 'The controversy over the Combination Acts'. Your aim is to simplify the arguments and explain:

- **what the controversy is.**
- **ways in which Sources 6 and 7 agree.**
- **how and why they disagree.**
- **what your view is.**

How did the government deal with the radicals?

The Combination Acts did not destroy the working-class organisations. They also failed to destroy protest.

The post-war slump caused great hardship, yet in the midst of this Parliament passed the Corn Laws (see page 48) which made food more expensive. Working people felt powerless to fight the government as only a few rich people had the right to vote, and so the workers had no say in how the country was run. There were powerful calls for change from a small group of men known as RADICALS.

One of the most outspoken radicals was Henry 'Orator' Hunt, MP for Preston. He spoke about the need for reform at meetings attended by thousands of people. Late in 1816, a meeting at Spa Fields in London ended in a riot. Early in 1817, unemployed cotton workers began to march to London to demand the vote. These 'Blanketeers' (they carried blankets to sleep under) were stopped by soldiers in Cheshire. At this point, the government took strong action. Radical publications were banned and many radicals were put in prison.

Peterloo

The protests went on, however. In 1819, a huge crowd gathered to hear Hunt speak at St Peter's Fields near Manchester. Magistrates were concerned and decided to arrest Hunt, with tragic results. Inexperienced troops and local yeomanry went into the crowd, killing 11 members of the public and injuring 400. Was this just an unfortunate incident? Some historians have wondered whether the local yeomanry and magistrates were trying to take revenge on people they suspected were Luddites or Luddite supporters. The events caused bitter criticism of the government, and came to be called the Battle of Peterloo – a sarcastic reference to Waterloo.

1 Write your own definition of the term 'radical', using examples.

2 From your study of Chapters 3–6, find one other example of a radical.

SOURCE 8

I saw the main body proceeding toward St Peter's Fields, and never saw a gayer spectacle … The 'marching order' of which so much was said afterwards was what we see now in the procession of Sunday School children … Our company laughed at the fears of the magistrates and the remark was, that if the men intended mischief they would not have brought their wives, their sisters or their children with them.

The recollections of a member of the crowd, 1851.

FOCUS TASK

1 Why was Peterloo such a disaster for the government?

2 Which is the most powerful comment on Peterloo, Source 9 or Source 10? Explain your choice.

SOURCE 9

An illustration published soon after the Peterloo incident.

An interpretation of events at Peterloo by Cruikshank, a famous cartoonist, 1819.

It is difficult to know exactly what happened. According to the radicals the meeting was an orderly march; the marchers were wearing their Sunday best, and there were many women and children present. However, it seems that the magistrates were alarmed by the size of the crowd. The yeomanry were ordered to disperse it in an orderly fashion, but it quickly got out of control and chaos followed. Each side blamed the other, not surprisingly. It seems most likely that, although the crowd was good-humoured, the magistrates could not believe that it would remain that way, especially given Hunt's revolutionary ideas. When the yeomanry were asked to move in, they probably took to their task with greater zeal than was required. The government remained quiet about the whole episode, mainly because of a lack of knowledge, and realising that whatever they said would be greeted with outrage.

The government's response: the Six Acts

None of this criticism deflected the government, however, and it passed the Six Acts in 1819, giving magistrates the power to ban meetings and marches. The Acts also limited the freedom of the press. The campaign for working men to be given the vote was, for now, crushed. You will pick up the story again on page 266.

The Trade Unions Act, 1825

By 1824 the government was convinced that trade unions were no longer a threat, and they repealed the Combination Acts. However, as soon as the Acts were repealed, a wave of strikes broke out all over the country. Parliament quickly passed the Trade Unions Act in 1825. This allowed trade unions, as they were now known, to exist, but effectively banned strikes, picketing or the intimidation of any workers who did not go on strike.

FOCUS TASK

WORKING-CLASS MOVEMENTS 1800–1825

William Cobbett was an MP and journalist, well known for supporting radical causes and for highlighting injustice to ordinary people. He was a supporter of extending the right to vote to more people and his views were put forward in his newspaper, the *Political Register*. You will have come across Cobbett when you looked at enclosure in Chapter 3.

Your task is now to write an article for William Cobbett's *Political Register*. You have a number of aims:

- To explain why the Combination Acts were passed then repealed
- To explain why they were repealed
- To explain whether you feel working-class movements have made real progress in the years 1800–1825
- To look ahead to the future.

Were unions getting stronger or weaker, 1825–50?

The period 1825–50 was an extremely active one for many different reform movements. The Ten Hours Movement campaigned for factory reform (see page 88), while the Chartists campaigned for reform of Parliament (see page 26). Many trade union leaders were active in all these movements.

The NAPL: the first national union

In 1829, there was a disastrously unsuccessful spinners' strike in the mills in and around Manchester. Many workers' leaders felt that for trade unions to succeed they had to be much larger and organised nationally. Delegates from unions in the spinning trade met on the Isle of Man, and established the Grand General Union of All Operative Spinners. The leader of this national union was John Doherty, who was the head of the Lancashire spinners. You may remember his clashes with the mill owner Robert Hyde Greg, described on page 95.

For Doherty, the spinners' union was only a beginning. The following year he founded a general union in Manchester, which he called the National Association for the Protection of Labour (NAPL). Doherty's aim was to bring together many different types of worker, and over 20 trades were represented at the first meeting, including potters, miners and builders. Around 150 societies had affiliated to the NAPL by 1831. In January of that year, the NAPL launched its own newspaper, the *Voice of the People*. It claimed that the union had 100,000 members.

SOURCE 11

Resolved: 1 That the miserable condition to which, by repeated and unnecessary reductions of wages, the working people of this country are reduced, urges upon this meeting the necessity of adopting some means for preventing such reductions and securing to the workman a just and adequate reward for his labour.

An extract from the resolutions of the NAPL, 1830.

However, the union had overestimated its strength. Early in 1831, the Lancashire spinners went on strike against a cut in wages. The idea was that other members of the NAPL would also strike in support. However, the different trades within the NAPL were reluctant to support strikers in another trade, and even spinners from other regions were less than enthusiastic in their support. In March 1831, the strike collapsed. Soon afterwards, the secretary ran off with the union's funds. By the next year, the NAPL had broken up into regional unions. Doherty had tried to achieve too much too quickly. He had tried to act before the union had built up enough funds and before workers really felt ready to be part of a national union.

Attitudes to the unions

At around the same time as the NAPL rose and fell, a national union of builders (the Operative Builders' Union) was set up. Unfortunately, it too went the same way.

These unions were probably too large and too radical to survive. For one thing, their size alarmed the ruling classes and employers. What was more, they did not simply try to protect their members. They also argued that Britain's whole economic system was unfair and unjust, and that working people needed more protection from employers and from booms and slumps in trade. In doing so, they soon generated bitter hostility. Source 12 shows how the trade union movement was ridiculed, but Source 13 portrays the fears which unions raised in some sections of society.

SOURCE **12**

A

B

Anti-trade-union cartoons.
A is from 1830: note the empty box.
B was published in 1834, the year in which the GNCTU began.

1 What do Sources 12–13 tell us about the unions?

SOURCE **13**

On combinations of all kinds among manufacturing journeymen, we have spoken so earnestly on many previous occasions, that we shall not now add much. Every man, if he please, is at liberty to desist from working when he thinks his wages inadequate; but he has no right to menace or drag others from their work.

The workmen who engage in these combinations to raise by voluntary strikes, or by ruffian intimidation, the rate of wages, proceed on the erroneous supposition, either that the master manufacturers are realising enormous profits at their expense, or that, by demanding higher wages, they can compel the public, foreign or domestic, to purchase the productions of their labour at a higher price. On either hypothesis they are completely wrong, and their leaders, who preach such doctrines, are only doing all they can to render them the victims of a mischievous delusion.

From *The Times*, 1833. *The Times* usually sided with the government and employers.

Robert Owen

Doherty and the NAPL were not the only ones who challenged the existing system. The most important was the cotton mill owner Robert Owen. You read on page 85 how Owen became famous for making very large profits while still treating his workers unusually well. However, Owen was much more than a kind mill owner. He was an idealist and a radical thinker, who believed that Britain's entire economy and society needed to change. He wrote over 100 books, articles and pamphlets setting out his views, but the best summary of his ideas was contained in his book *A New View of Society*. He said that 'Men should work to produce happiness for all, not to make profits for a few. Co-operation, not competition, is a better way of running industry and society.'

For many years, Owen's ideas were well received, even at the highest levels. He was able to convince Parliament to investigate working conditions in 1802 and 1816. In the 1820s, however, his wealthy and powerful friends became concerned that some of his ideas were too radical.

In 1825, Owen went to the USA to found a new co-operative community called New Harmony. This venture failed, which pleased his critics. He returned to Britain in 1829, somewhat disillusioned and poorer, but was soon back at work.

The National Equitable Labour Exchange

Owen believed that merchants and shopkeepers set the price of goods at unnecessarily high levels. In 1832, he opened a National Equitable Labour Exchange, with branches around the country. Workers brought goods they had made to these shops and in return received a labour note – credit for the work they had put into the item. With the labour note, the worker could then buy something which another worker had brought in. In this way, for example, a weaver might exchange some cloth for a pair of shoes. The exchanges were not a great success, and two years later began to shut down. They were not able to attract enough members, and many of the goods ended up more expensive than in ordinary shops.

SOURCE 14

A labour note from one of Owen's exchanges, 1833.

SOURCE 15

We the undersigned do hereby declare that we are not members of a trade union; that we do not and will not pay towards the support of any such association.
Signed

The 'document'.

1 **Make lists of the strengths and weaknesses of the GNCTU.**

2 **How did it compare with the NAPL?**

The Grand National Consolidated Trades Union

Owen was encouraged and impressed by the NAPL and Operative Builders' Union, despite the fact that they had failed. In January 1834, he brought together workers from various trades in the Grand National Consolidated Trades Union. The GNCTU was very large: by June 1834, it had over half a million members. Membership was only 3d per week.

The union would support members on strike in any trade. The aim was also to set up a network of labour exchanges. Most importantly, Owen intended to organise a general strike to change the existing system: he called this a national holiday.

Unfortunately for Owen, his members were not really ready for such ambitious plans. In Derby, silk weavers had been in dispute with employers since November 1833. Like the NAPL before it, the GNCTU was unable to mobilise the support of other trades, and the weavers returned to work in March 1834. Employers in many industries forced their workers to sign 'the document' (Source 15). Such hostility caused many workers to leave the union.

The Tolpuddle Martyrs

The government was worried by the growing membership of the GNCTU. It wanted an opportunity to scare the union. This came when a Dorset landowner wrote to the Home Secretary, Lord Melbourne, in 1834. He complained that local labourers in the village of Tolpuddle had 'combined', preventing him from cutting their wages. The men belonged to the GNCTU and were led by a local Methodist preacher, George Loveless.

Although trade unions were no longer illegal, the government found a reason to arrest some of the labourers. Because of intimidation by employers and the fact that workers could not read or write, unions often used rituals and oaths to introduce members to the union and get them to pledge their loyalty. Under an Act of 1797, such secret oaths were illegal. Such an oath had been used by George Loveless to swear in the Tolpuddle labourers.

SOURCE 16

John Lock: James Brine asked me if I would go to Tolpuddle with him ... others joined us as we were going along. One of them asked if there would not be something to pay, and one said there would be one shilling to pay on entering and one penny a week after. We all went to Thomas Standsfield's house into a room upstairs. John Standsfield came to the door of the room. I saw James Loveless and George Loveless go along the passage. One of the men asked if we were ready. We said, yes. One of them said, 'Then bind your eyes', and we took out handkerchiefs and bound over our eyes ... Someone then read a paper ... After that we were asked to kneel down which we did. Then there was some more reading; I don't know what it was about. It seemed to be out of some part of the Bible. We were told to kiss the book ... The others said we were as brothers ...

Evidence from the trial of the Tolpuddle Martyrs.

Six of the union members were arrested. George Loveless made a dignified speech at his trial. The labourers' lawyer pointed out the flimsy nature of the charges (see Source 17), but as Source 18 shows everyone knew that the real issue was not the oath but membership of a union which the authorities wanted to suppress.

SOURCE 17

As to the oath ... [there was only] the evidence of two stupid witnesses who told them [the jury] that at a certain meeting where they had chosen voluntarily to bind themselves, some words were uttered by someone whom they did not know, about something they did not understand, but in which they recollected the words 'eternity' and 'soul', for what purpose introduced they could not imagine.

The labourers' defence lawyer made this point.

SOURCE 18

The formal charge against them was that of administering and being bound by secret and therefore, unlawful, oaths; whereas the real guilt ... was the forming of a dangerous Union, to force up, by various forms of intimidation and restraint, the rates of labourers' wages.

From *The Times*, 1 April 1834.

A success for the government or the union?

Loveless and his colleagues were convicted and transported to Australia. Such harsh treatment had its desired effect. Many workers, particularly vulnerable rural labourers, were intimidated into leaving or not joining the union. The GNCTU itself collapsed in 1835.

However, some historians have argued that the case in fact did more to advance the cause of trade unionism than to harm it. The labourers became immortalised as the Tolpuddle Martyrs. (A martyr is someone who dies for a cause, usually a religious belief). The GNCTU organised a massive demonstration in London (Source 19). There was a public outcry against the harshness of the sentence for such a trivial offence. The case of the Tolpuddle men galvanised and united trade unionists as never before. Rallies, speeches and petitions all expressed outrage at the treatment of the men. The injustice of the punishment seemed to be proved when the 'martyrs' were pardoned and brought back to England after two years. Five of the six emigrated to Canada, but Loveless remained in England.

SOURCE 19

An illustration from the *Pioneer*, a working-class magazine, in 1834. It shows a rally at Copenhagen Fields, London, organised by the GNCTU, in protest against the treatment of the Tolpuddle Martyrs. The event was a huge affair, but it went off peacefully, with processions and speeches by Chartist leaders.

3 The 'martyrs' did not serve the full term of their sentence. Does this change your view of these events?

4 It has been argued that there was no case against the Tolpuddle men, and that they were victims of the government's desire to clamp down on unions. Do you agree? Explain your answer with reference to Sources 16–18.

Why did the GNCTU collapse?

Despite Owen's optimism and its apparent strength, the GNCTU had many weaknesses. The membership was made up of the more radical workers. Members of the more well-established craft unions – potters, builders, spinners and clothiers – who were better educated and better off, did not join. Like other unions, the GNCTU was short of funds, but local branches squandered money on pointless local strikes instead of focusing on central issues. Its actions were badly co-ordinated, partly because communications between different areas of the country at that time were just not good enough to run an effective national union. Many potential leaders preferred to put their energy into the Ten Hours Movement and Chartism, which were also active at this time.

Owen also overestimated the willingness of the working classes to co-operate. He had believed that all workers shared a common bond, but in fact he found there was very little working-class unity. Spinners in Lancashire felt little loyalty towards spinners in Nottingham and even less towards carpenters in Yorkshire.

The Miners' Association

The failure of the GNCTU showed how difficult it was to set up and maintain a general union, but it did not kill off the union movement. Other large unions were set up, within single industries. The Miners' Association of Great Britain was one of the more successful and solid unions. However, as Source 20 shows, by 1850 such a union was no match for the government or employers.

Co-operatives

If the picture seems rather gloomy, there was one important success story of the period. In the 1830s and 1840s, workers, sometimes with the encouragement of their employers, began to form co-operatives. The national co-operative movement (the origin of today's Co-op stores) began in Rochdale in 1844. In that year, 28 Rochdale 'pioneers' saved up money to buy a shop and sell quality goods to the poor at reasonable prices.

SOURCE 20

There was no eagerness for a strike, for there were no defensive resources … The tommy shops would close … There were no co-operative societies … The union had no reserve funds … In 1844 the men left their work in April; and immediate steps were taken to fill the place left vacant. Men were brought from Wales … under much better terms … Then came the evictions. The coal owners are the proprietors of the cottages in which the pit men live …

Just as the cause might be, it was not at that time destined to prevail … The mine owners won 'hands down' … by treating the men as if they did not exist.

From a biography of Thomas Burt, a miners leader and one of the first working-class MPs. His experience as a miner led him to become an MP.

SOURCE 21

A photograph of some of the original 'Rochdale Pioneers'.

1 **How did the employers treat the workers?**

2 **What advantages did the employers have?**

3 **Can you find examples of other similar situations on pages 54–64?**

Anyone could join the Co-op after paying a small deposit. No credit was allowed, but the profits made by the stores were divided between the members of the society. The more a customer spent, the more he or she received as a dividend; this could be cashed in or left as savings. From this humble beginning grew up a huge and successful movement. Co-ops sold clothing and numerous other articles (see page 4). They bought or rented land and employed members to farm it. Co-ops paid for social clubs and adult education classes. By 1850 there were 130 co-operatives and by 1870 there were close to 1,000.

FOCUS TASK

WHY WERE THE EARLY TRADE UNIONS WEAK?

Government actions

Opposition of employers

Why were early trade unions weak?

Economic conditions

Attitudes of workers

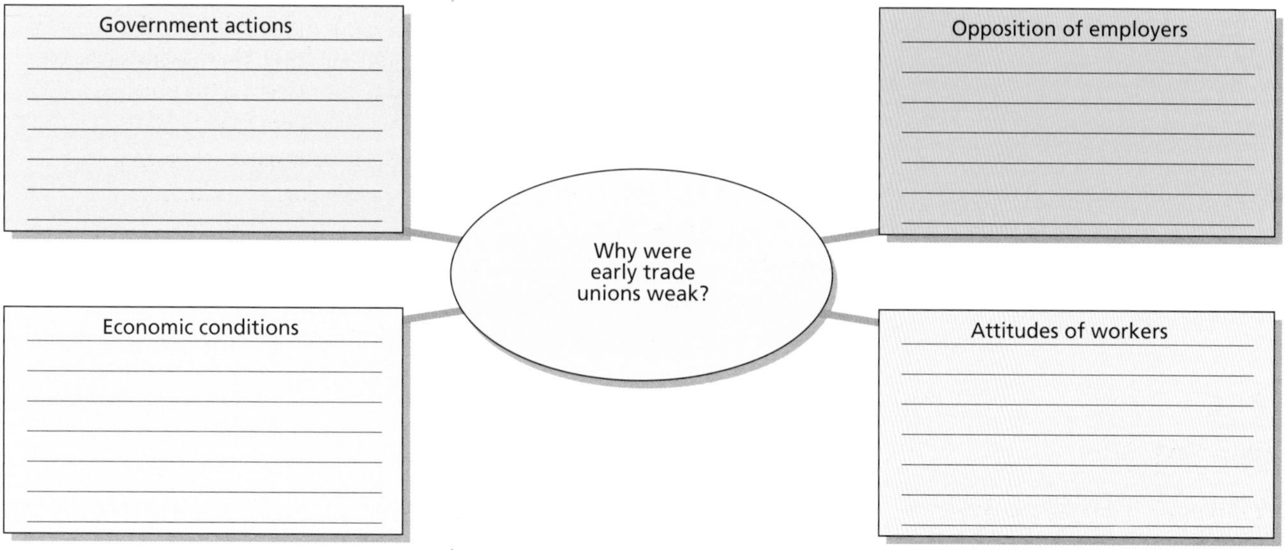

1 On your own copy of this diagram, add notes to summarise how each of these factors contributed to making early unions weak:

- Government actions
- The opposition of employers
- Economic conditions
- The attitudes of the workers themselves

2 What evidence is there that the union movement was getting stronger in the period 1825–30?

FOCUS TASK

HOW DID THE GOVERNMENT REACT TO EARLY WORKING-CLASS MOVEMENTS?

1 Here is a headline which might have appeared in William Cobbett's *Political Register* in 1834.

> # SHAMEFUL VERDICT ON TOLPUDDLE MARTYRS
>
> ## Government continues its relentless persecution of working-class movements

Write the article to accompany this headline, explaining how the Tolpuddle verdict fits into the pattern of government action since 1800. Mention:

- the Combination Acts.
- radicalism.
- Peterloo.
- the GNCTU and the Tolpuddle Martyrs.

Remember that you are presenting a one-sided view.

2 Now write a letter from Lord Melbourne to the *Political Register* complaining about how one-sided the article was. You should mention:

- the threats to security.
- the true impact of the Combination Acts.

PROFILE

Feargus O'Connor

★ Born in 1794 in Dublin.
★ Studied at Trinity College and became a lawyer.
★ Became MP for Cork in 1832.
★ He was never a very stable character, and was prone to violent outbursts.
★ A fiery speaker, he was dedicated to improving the condition of the working classes in England. He became involved in northern England in 1835.
★ He founded the *Northern Star* newspaper in 1837.
★ It was never clear whether he was really prepared to use force or whether he just talked about it to frighten the government.
★ In 1847 he became MP for Nottingham.
★ He presented the huge Chartist petition to Parliament in 1848.
★ After this failure he became unstable. By 1852 he was described as being insane.
★ Died in 1855.

SOURCE 23

GRAND PROCESSION ON MONDAY NEXT,

O'CONNOR

THE UNFLINCHING ADVOCATE

All Persons wishing to join the PROCESSION, and to do honor to that unjustly persecuted FRIEND OF THE PEOPLE! are informed that the DARLASTON & WALSALL ASSOCIATIONS will meet the BILSTON and WOLVERHAMPTON Associations

A poster publicising one of O'Connor's meetings. He was a powerful speaker.

1 Do you think each demand in Source 22 is reasonable?

2 Who would have agreed with you in the 1830s?

Why did the Chartists fail?

One of the largest working-class movements of this period was Chartism, named after the People's Charter in which its aims were set out. It was a true mass movement, which appeared to have a great deal of promise. Even so, it too collapsed and failed. The timeline on the left summarises the main phases of the Chartist movement.

The origins of Chartism

In 1832, Parliament passed the Parliamentary Reform Act. Many working men had been involved in the campaign for greater democracy that led up to the Act, but only farmers and some middle-class men were given the vote. To add to this disappointment, the Poor Law Amendment Act of 1834 brought a new horror into the lives of working people: the workhouse (see pages 219–25).

The north: Feargus O'Connor

One radical leader in the North of England, Feargus O'Connor, was outraged by the Act. He argued that only if working men had the vote would they be treated fairly. He spread his ideas in his newspaper, the *Northern Star*.

The south: William Lovett

In 1834, a cabinet maker in London called William Lovett founded the London Working Men's Association. He had the support of the well-known radical activist Francis Place and six radical MPs. The LWMA believed in 'moral force' or peaceful forms of protest. In 1836 it set out its aims in the six points of the People's Charter (see Source 22).

SOURCE 22

The Six Points OF THE PEOPLE'S CHARTER.

1. A VOTE for every man twenty-one years of age, of sound mind, and not undergoing punishment for crime.

2. THE BALLOT.—To protect the elector in the exercise of his vote.

3. No PROPERTY QUALIFICATION for Members of Parliament—thus enabling the constituencies to return the man of their choice, be he rich or poor.

4. PAYMENT OF MEMBERS, thus enabling an honest tradesman, working man, or other person, to serve a constituency, when taken from his business to attend to the interests of the country.

5. EQUAL CONSTITUENCIES, securing the same amount of representation for the same number of electors, instead of allowing small constituencies to swamp the votes of large ones.

6. ANNUAL PARLIAMENTS, thus presenting the most effectual check to bribery and intimidation, since though a constituency might be bought once in seven years (even with the ballot), no purse could buy a constituency (under a system of universal suffrage) in each ensuing twelvemonth; and since members, when elected for a year only, would not be able to defy and betray their constituents as now.

A handbill produced by Chartists, detailing the six points of the Charter. Printers often had a reputation as political radicals, and many supported the movement by creating items such as these. The second point is calling for voting in secret.

A divided movement

In 1838 the northern and southern movements came together, and the Chartist movement was born. It was agreed that the first action would be to gather signatures for a petition to Parliament, asking it to accept the Charter. Also, Chartists would set up their own Chartist Convention, which would effectively be an extra Parliament. If the Charter was rejected, there would be a general strike.

The movement was a curious mixture right from the start. The moderates were clear that Chartism was about the right to vote, and that this in turn would bring better wages, shorter hours and other improvements for working people (see Sources 24–25). However, many Chartists joined the movement for other reasons. Some wanted to protest about the New Poor Law. Others opposed currency reforms or Robert Peel's new police force.

Support for the movement was patchy. The strongest support came from skilled workers in the textile and metal industries, whose way of life was being destroyed by industrialisation. The large towns and cities did have Chartist movements, but they tended to be more moderate.

The most serious division, however, was over methods. Lovett and pro-Chartist MPs advocated moral force, and also placed an emphasis on education, bettering oneself and a Christian spirit. This side of the movement became known as New Move Chartism. O'Connor was deeply critical of New Move Chartism. He could not see anything Christian about a society which treated working people so badly. O'Connor was a fiery radical, and was quite prepared to upset the government by talking about physical force.

A movement like Chartism had little hope of success in the Britain of the 1840s. Moderates such as Thomas Attwood and Lovett had some chance of getting MPs and the middle classes, who had recently been given the vote themselves, to be sympathetic. However, O'Connor's huge meetings and raging speeches alienated them. More importantly, neither wing of the movement was sufficiently well organised to put real pressure on the government.

3 You are a journalist covering the Chartist Convention. Write a short article (up to 100 words) summarising the prospects for the movement.

ACTIVITY

1 Which of Sources 24–28 do you think were written or spoken by the following people?

- **William Lovett**, a moderate Chartist leader
- **Feargus O'Connor**, a radical Chartist leader
- The *Northern Star*, a radical Chartist newspaper
- The *Manchester and Salford Advertiser*, a moderate pro-Chartist newspaper
- **Thomas Attwood**, a radical MP and Chartist supporter, presenting a Chartist petition to Parliament

Explain your choice with reference to the sources.

2 What do Sources 24–28 agree about?

3 What do they disagree about?

SOURCE 24

The question … is a knife and fork question, a bread and meat question … every working man in the land has a right to a good coat on his back, a good hat on his head, a good roof for the shelter of his household, a good dinner upon his table, no more work than will keep him in the enjoyment of plenty, and all the blessings of life that reasonable men could desire. Chartism means better wages, shorter hours of labour, comfort, independence, happiness …

SOURCE 25

[Chartists] … only sought a fair day's wages for a fair day's work; and that if they [Parliament] could not give them that, and food and clothing for their families, they then said they would put forward any means which the law allowed, to change the representation of that House.

SOURCE 26

Universal suffrage there shall be – or our tyrants will find to their cost that we will have universal misery. We will make our country one vast howling wilderness of desolation and destruction rather than the tyrants shall carry out their infernal system … Believe me, there is no argument like the sword and the musket [gun] is unanswerable.

SOURCE 27

My desire is to try moral force as long as possible but I would have you remember that it is better to die free men than to live as slaves. Physical force is treason only when it fails; it is glorious freedom when it is successful.

SOURCE 28

The whole physical force agitation is harmful and injurious to the movement. Muskets are not what are wanted, but education and schooling of the working people … O'Connor wants to take everything by the storm, and to pass the Charter into law within a year. All this hurry and haste, this bluster and menace of armed opposition can only lead to … the destruction of Chartism …

[Napier invited Chartist leaders to a gunnery demonstration and said] … he would never allow them to charge him with their pikes, or even march 10 miles, without mauling them with cannons and musketry, and charging them with cavalry when they dispersed to seek food; finally, that the country would rise on them and they would be destroyed in three days.

From the *Life and Opinions* of Sir Charles Napier.

Patrolled all last night. Saw the Chartist sentinels in the streets; we knew they were armed with pistols, but I advised the magistrates not to meddle with them. Seizing these men could do no good; it would not stop Chartism if they were all hanged, and they offered no violence; why starve their wretched families and worry them with a long imprisonment?

From Napier's diary, January 1840.

1 **Read Sources 29 and 30. Use them to describe General Napier's attitude towards the Chartists.**

The first petition

The first Chartist petition in May 1839 had 1.3 million signatures on it, but Parliament rejected it by 235 votes to 46. The government prepared for trouble, and handled the events which followed very effectively. In contrast, the response of the Chartists was a shambles. After the petition was rejected, the Convention called for the general strike to begin, as planned, but this was soon abandoned. Thousands of Chartists were already out of work as business was bad.

The government arrested Lovett in July of 1839, and put General Napier in charge of controlling the Chartists in northern England. Napier was a sensible man and sympathetic to the Chartists. However, he had no time for rebellion, and convinced O'Connor that any attempt at violence would be disastrous for the Chartists.

The Newport Rising

There was some isolated fighting in various places, but the most serious incident was the Newport Rising. This was a chaotic affair, involving around 1,000 miners led by John Frost. It was easily broken up by a small number of troops, and 14 Chartists were killed. It was violent enough, however, for Chartism to be branded an extreme movement worthy of suspicion.

A drawing showing the Newport Rising of 1839.

The second petition

From 1840 onwards, Feargus O'Connor began to dominate the Chartist movement, and founded the National Charter Association. By 1842, its 48,000 members had put together another petition with over three million signatures. However, Parliament rejected it again, and strikes and riots followed. These became caught up with local disputes in the North and Midlands which became known as the Plug Plots (because steam engines in factories were vandalised by having their plugs removed). The rioters did great damage, but they failed to influence Parliament.

Lovett abandoned Chartism to work in adult education, and from 1844 until 1847 O'Connor also forgot Chartism. He established a National Land Company, whose aim was to provide small plots of land for craft workers who did not wish to work in factories. He raised about £90,000 from shareholders, who then entered a lottery. Winners were allocated the first plots of land bought. The scheme was enthusiastically supported, but it collapsed in 1849, almost bankrupting O'Connor himself.

Although Chartism appeared to many to be a progressive party, these two developments showed how out of touch it was. The National Land Company and the Plug Riots looked back to an age that was fast disappearing – an age of domestic industry before factories and mechanisation.

ACTIVITY

Write a speech by Feargus O'Connor responding to the criticisms in Source 33.

2 Do you think the Chartists were badly organised? Give evidence to support your answer.

3 How did the following events harm the Chartists?

  • The failure of the National Land Company
  • The third petition
  • The Plug Riots

  Give evidence to support your answer.

4 How were the problems facing the Chartists similar to and different from the problems facing Robert Owen's GNCTU?

FOCUS TASK

WHY DID CHARTISM FAIL?

1 Copy the diagram below into your book and complete it by adding:

  a) factors which contributed to the failure.
  b) reasons why each factor contributed to the failure.
  c) evidence of how each factor contributed to the failure.

2 Make lists of all the factors under the following headings:

  • Actions of the Chartists
  • Factors outside their control

3 Why did Chartism fail? You could structure your answer like this:

  • Explain how Chartism's own actions contributed to its failure.
  • Explain how opposition to Chartism contributed to its failure.
  • Give your own view as to which was more important: Chartist actions, or opposition to the Chartists.

The third petition

Hard times in 1847–48 gave Chartism one last lease of life. By this time, O'Connor was MP for Nottingham. In 1848, the National Charter Association presented a third petition to Parliament. To coincide with this, O'Connor organised a massive meeting at Kennington; estimates of the crowd varied from the government's figure of 15,000 to O'Connor's of 500,000. The government mobilised thousands of troops and constables to prevent the crowd marching on the Houses of Parliament. Although Parliament did receive the petition, it threw it out, and with this failure, O'Connor was finally silenced.

SOURCE 32

An early photograph, showing the Kennington Chartist rally in 1848. Estimates of the number of people at the rally varied hugely.

SOURCE 33

The Honourable Member for Nottingham stated that 5,706,000 names were attached to the petition. On the most careful examination of the number of signatures, this has been found to be 1,975,496. On many sheets the signatures are in one and the same handwriting. The Committee also observed the names of famous people who can hardly be supposed to agree with the charter's aims: among which occurs the name of Her Majesty as 'Victoria Rex', April First, Cheeks the Marine, Robert Peel and the Duke of Wellington. The Committee also noted a number of names which are clearly made up, such as 'No Cheese', 'Pug Nose', 'Flat Nose'.

Report of the House of Commons on the Chartist petition, 1848.

Why did the Chartists fail?

Of the six points of the original Charter, the only demand which is not in place today is that for annual elections. The Chartists also succeeded in mobilising millions of working-class men and women. However, judged against its own objectives, the movement failed.

After the third petition was thrown out, Chartism disappeared from the political scene. There still seemed to be no possibility of working men being given the vote. Rising prosperity in the 1840s made workers less interested in the movement. Other organisations such as the Anti-Corn Law League and the Ten Hours Movement seemed to offer more hope of success, and because they appeared less extreme than the Chartists they attracted the more moderate reformers.

10.2 *Was the union movement more successful from 1850 to 1900?*

What were the new model unions?

The failures of working-class movements during the period 1800–1850 had at least taught their leaders what made for a successful (and unsuccessful) organisation. They recognised that governments and employers were more sympathetic towards respectable organisations such as friendly societies than they were to radical political movements such as the Chartists.

During the same period, however, the more moderate unions grew and prospered. Their members were skilled, often well-paid workers. They placed a high value on education and encouraged their members to better themselves through adult education. These ideas fitted in very well with the self-help philosophy held by most middle-class politicians.

By the late 1840s, when railways had made efficient communications possible, and the postal service had improved, these unions became truly national. They became known as 'new model unions'.

The Amalgamated Society of Engineers

The first new model union was the Amalgamated Society of Engineers, led by William Allen, which was founded in 1851. The ASE included skilled workers such as engineers, machine operators and millwrights – the essential workforce of the industrial and railway age. Subscription rates were high – a shilling a week – but the benefits it paid out were generous. It had a central office in London and full-time paid officials. Wherever possible, the ASE avoided confrontation with employers: its leaders believed that in the long run strikes hurt workers more than employers.

The example of the ASE was followed by the Amalgamated Society of Carpenters and Joiners, formed in 1860 and led by Robert Applegarth.

SOURCE 1

A *Punch* cartoon from 1852. The title was 'Effects of the strike on the capitalist and on the working man'.

---

1 **Look at Source 1. Would the new model unions agree with this cartoon? Explain your answer.**

SOURCE 2

The trade emblem of the ASE. Many unions had such emblems, which showed what the union stood for.

SOURCE 3

Under no circumstances will any branch be allowed to strike without first obtaining the sanction of the council, whether it be for a new privilege or against an encroachment of existing ones. He [any prospective member] must be healthy, have worked for five years at the trade, be a good workman, of steady habits, of good moral character, and not more than 45 years of age. He is seconded by some member who also knows him well. He then fills in the following form [and pays 3d for a copy of the rules] … He pays 2s 6d, which is called 'proposition money', and waits for enquiries to be made respecting his character and abilities … If he is rejected his money is handed back to him; if he is accepted he pays his second 2s 6d … and he pays 1s a week from that time, and 3d per quarter to a benevolent fund.

The benefits are as follows: Donation benefit for 12 weeks, 10 shillings per week; and another 12 weeks, 6 shillings per week … tool benefit to any amount of loss … £5; sick benefit for 26 weeks, 12 shillings per week, and then 6 shillings a week so long as his illness continues; funeral benefit £12 … accident benefit £100 … The emigration benefit is £6, and there are benevolent grants, according to circumstances, in cases of distress.

Robert Applegarth, Secretary of the Amalgamated Society of Carpenters and Joiners, explains the rules of his union.

ACTIVITY

You are a member of the ASE, and you are telling some new members about your badge (Source 2). Explain what it shows and what it tells you about the aims, methods and beliefs of the ASE.

The London Trades Council

New model unions were not typical, and did not represent all workers, since only about 15 per cent of workers were skilled. However, the new model unions did much for the whole trade union movement. In the 1860s, Allen, Applegarth and the leaders of the bricklayers', shoemakers' and iron founders' unions formed the London Trades Council. The LTC became known as the Junta (from the Spanish word for a council), and came to represent trade union opinion nationally. It carried out disciplined and peaceful campaigns: for example, it worked successfully for a change to the Master and Servant Law, which had effectively made it an imprisonable offence to strike. Its moderate methods were one factor in persuading the Conservative leader Benjamin Disraeli to pass the 1867 Reform Act, which finally gave some urban working men the vote. However, in the late 1860s this new leadership was severely tested.

Problems for the unions

Trade booms and slumps were by now a regular feature of Britain's economic climate. In the 1866–67 slump, the unions were blamed for pushing up wages and so preventing British industry from competing with overseas manufacturers. This enmity towards the unions formed the background to the Hornby v. Close court case in 1867.

Hornby v. Close

In 1867, the Boilermakers' Union sued an official for money he owed it. However, in what is known as the 'Hornby versus Close case', the judge ruled that trade unions' funds were not protected by law, because trade unions were illegal organisations since they acted in 'restraint of trade'. This was a major setback for the unions, but there was worse to come.

2 How were the new model unions different from the GNCTU (see pages 262–63)?

The Sheffield outrages

In 1866, members of cutlers' unions in Sheffield attacked workers who refused to join the unions. The violence resulted in two murders and one man's house being blown up with gelignite. The 'Sheffield outrages' led the government to set up a Royal Commission to investigate the whole question of trade unions.

The Royal Commission

The leaders of the LTC were anxious that the unions should be represented fairly on the Commission. Because of the reputation it had gained through its peaceful campaigning, the LTC was allowed to nominate Robert Applegarth as a member of the Commission.

Applegarth and Allen both gave evidence to the Commission, as well. As a result of their work, the Commission concluded that the Sheffield outrages were not representative examples of trade unions. In 1871, the Trade Union Act was passed: this gave legal protection to union funds.

The TUC

Not all unions were happy with the policies of the Junta, which many saw as too moderate. The Manchester and Salford Trades Council was made up of several unions. In 1869 they saw the need for unions to come together and discuss important issues relating to wages, conditions and trade union issues generally. The Junta chose not to attend, but most other unions were represented at this Congress, which then became annual and evolved into the TUC. By the early 1870s, the TUC represented over a million workers and was an accepted part of the industrial scene.

1 **What was the most significant achievement of the new model unions during the 1860s? Explain your choice.**

SOURCE 4

PROPOSED CONGRESS OF TRADES COUNCILS

AND OTHER

Federations of Trades Societies.

MANCHESTER, FEBRUARY 21st, 1868.

FELLOW-UNIONISTS,

The Manchester and Salford Trades Council having recently taken into their serious consideration the present aspect of Trades Unions, and the profound ignorance which prevails in the public mind with reference to their operations and principles, together with the probability of an attempt being made by the Legislature, during the present session of Parliament, to introduce a measure detrimental to the interests of such Societies, beg most respectfully to suggest the propriety of holding in Manchester, as the main centre of industry in the provinces, a Congress of the Representatives of Trades Councils and other similar Federations of Trades Societies. By confining the Congress to such bodies it is conceived that a deal of expense will be saved, as Trades will thus be represented collectively; whilst there will be a better opportunity afforded of selecting the most intelligent and efficient exponents of our principles.

It is proposed that the Congress shall assume the character of the annual meetings of the British Association for the Advancement of Science and the Social Science Association, in the transactions of which Societies the artizan class are almost entirely excluded; and that papers, previously carefully prepared, shall be laid before the Congress on the various subjects which at the present time affect Trades Societies, each paper to be followed by discussion upon the points advanced, with a view of the merits and demerits of each question being thoroughly ventilated through the medium of the public press. It is further suggested that the subjects treated upon shall include the following :—

1.—Trades Unions an absolute necessity.
2.—Trades Unions and Political Economy.
3.—The Effect of Trades Unions on Foreign Competition.
4.—Regulation of the Hours of Labour.
5.—Limitation of Apprentices.
6.—Technical Education.
7.—Arbitration and Courts of Conciliation.
8.—Co-operation.
9.—The present Inequality of the Law in regard to Conspiracy, Intimidation, Picketing, Coercion, &c.
10.—Factory Acts Extension Bill, 1867: the necessity of Compulsory Inspection, and its application to all places where Women and Children are employed.
11.—The present Royal Commission on Trades Unions: how far worthy of the confidence of the Trades Union interest.
12.—The necessity of an Annual Congress of Trade Representatives from the various centres of industry.

All Trades Councils and other Federations of Trades are respectfully solicited to intimate their adhesion to this project on or before the 6th of April next, together with a notification of the subject of the paper that each body will undertake to prepare; after which date all information as to place of meeting, &c., will be supplied.

A circular sent out to all unions, inviting them to the first congress in Manchester in 1869. The Junta unions did not attend this meeting.

FOCUS TASK

WERE NEW MODEL UNIONS MORE SUCCESSFUL THAN EARLIER UNIONS?

1 Read through pages 270–72. Make two lists, one showing the challenges faced by new model unions and the other giving their achievements.

2 Now look back at pages 255–64 and your own work. Make a list showing the achievements of one of the following and the obstacles it faced:

• Trade clubs of the early 1800s
• The NAPL
• The GNCTU

3 In pairs or small groups, decide whether you feel that the new model unions were more successful than these earlier unions.

2 List four examples of:
   a) skilled work.
   b) unskilled work.

3 List the factors which contributed to the growth of the new unions.

4 Explain how each factor helped.

5 Source 7 is very critical of unions. Does that mean that they were not doing a good job for their members?

What were new unions?

New unions were unions for unskilled workers. This was the most obvious contrast between the new unions and the new model unions. Unions for unskilled workers had existed earlier in the century, but the term 'new union' was applied to the many unskilled workers' unions set up after 1870.

The first new union was the Tea Operatives' and General Labourers' Association, founded in 1870. Perhaps the most ambitious of the new unions was Joseph Arch's Agricultural Labourers' Union, formed in Warwickshire in 1872 (see the case study on page 275). During the 1870s, unions were also set up for rail workers and gas workers, and there was also a specialist women's union.

How did new unions differ from new model unions?

Most workers were not eligible to join the new model unions. They were not skilled workers, and were not sufficiently well paid to afford the high subscription rates for the new model unions.

As MECHANISATION continued, the number of unskilled workers in Britain was growing faster than the number of skilled workers. The new unions had much lower subscriptions: for example, gas workers paid 2d a week. They tended to represent whole industries (such as coal, farming or the docks) rather than specialist crafts.

Because their members did not have a craft, the new unions were not concerned with professional standards. They also focused much less on providing benefits and more on fighting for higher wages and against unemployment. The leaders of the new unions had little time for the idea of bettering oneself through education. They felt that poverty, unemployment and safety at work were more pressing issues. These unions were much more inclined to strike than new model unions, partly because striking was the only really effective weapon they had.

The new unions were much more openly political in their aims. Certainly, many of the leaders of new unions were influenced by the socialist writer Karl Marx. Some of these leaders were men of outstanding ability, such as Ben Tillett and Tom Mann (see page 274). Encouraged by the fact that some working men could now vote, new unions campaigned for Parliament to pass laws to protect employment, guarantee wage levels and limit the working day to eight hours. The introduction of elementary education in 1870 meant that more unskilled workers could read, which helped make them more aware of their own rights and of political issues.

SOURCE 5

I do not believe in having sick pay, out of work pay, and a number of other pays; we desire to prevent as much sickness and men being out of work. They way to accomplish this, is firstly to organise, then reduce your hours of labour or work, that will prevent illness and members being out of employment.

Will Thorne, leader of the Gas Workers' Union, speaking in 1889.

SOURCE 6

A great number of them [new model union leaders] looked like respectable city gentlemen; wore very good coats, large watch chains, and high hats ... Amongst the 'new' delegates not a single one wore a tall hat. They looked workmen; they were workmen.

John Burns, a Social Democratic Federation member, describing the 1890 Trades Union Congress.

SOURCE 7

Trade unions have made the operative class suspicious and discontented, by teaching them that their employers are deceiving and oppressing them. That they have stepped in between the employers and the employed, and prevented the association of interest that both instinctively desire. That they have taught them to consider the employer's loss their gain. They deny the undoubted rights of employers and employed to make their own terms. They seek to make every trade a close one by limiting the numbers employed in it. That they advocate coercion and even terrorism in support of their policy.

From *Capital and Labour*, a pamphlet published by Manchester Chamber of Commerce, 1867.

SOURCE 8

The working man's skill and labour are his capital. They may be considered so much goods or merchandise, whose price varies with the supply and demand. No artificial means can raise or lower wages.

From GH Smith, *Outlines of Political Economy*, 1866.

SOURCE 9

The manufacturer aims primarily at producing, by means of the labour he has stolen from others, profits. That is the wealth that is produced over and above the wages of his workmen. We must get rid of this system.

Written by William Morris, leader of the Socialist League, in 1885.

SOURCE 10

The true union policy of aggression seems entirely lost sight of; in fact the average unionist of today is a man with fossilised intellect ... supporting a policy that plays into the hands of the capitalist exploiter.

An extract from a pamphlet by Tom Mann, one of the dockers' leaders, 1886.

SOURCE 11

A railway union banner from about 1900.

1 **Which of Sources 4–11 would leaders of the new model unions:**

   a) **agree with?**
   b) **disagree with?**

2 **Which of Sources 4–11 best illustrates that the new unions were more radical than the new model unions?**

FOCUS TASK

HOW DID NEW UNIONS DIFFER FROM NEW MODEL UNIONS?

1 Copy and complete this table, comparing the new unions with the new model unions.

	New unions	New model unions
Membership		
Leaders		
Political views		
Aims		
Actions		

2 Use your table to write an entry for an encyclopaedia of British history explaining the difference between the new unions and the new model unions for people who might find this confusing. Choose two pictures to illustrate your article.

Joseph Arch and the National Agricultural Labourers' Union

Agricultural labourers were probably the most downtrodden of all unskilled labourers. Their wages were low, even when business was good. When times were hard, they faced grinding poverty, the humiliating trip to charity soup kitchens, or worst of all the workhouse. The farm labourers were ready for action, and Joseph Arch offered them leadership.

SOURCE 12

After the harvest of 1871 had been reaped and the winter had set in, the sufferings of the men became cruel and by 1872 there seemed to be two doors open to them. One ... led to a life of degradation in the workhouse; the other ... to the grave. Their poverty had fallen to starvation point and was past all bearing. They saw that if they were to rise out of their miserable state, they must force open a door of escape for themselves. Oppression and hunger and misery made them desperate, and desperation was the mother of the union ...

From Joseph Arch's memoirs, *Joseph Arch, the Story of His Life, by Himself*, 1898.

SOURCE 13

[The aim was] to elevate the social position of the farm labourers of the country by assisting them to increase their wages; to lessen the number of ordinary working hours; to improve their habitations; to provide them with gardens or allotments; and to assist deserving and suitable labourers to migrate or emigrate.

From Joseph Arch's memoirs.

Within weeks of Joseph Arch setting up the NALU in 1871, it had over 100,000 members. However, farmers and landowners joined forces to smash the new union. In 1874, employers held a lock-out, refusing to employ any labourers who were members of the NALU. Because many labourers lived in 'tied cottages', which came with their jobs, they could be thrown out of their homes if they were sacked, and so many union members were evicted (see Source 15). In Suffolk, 600 NALU members went on strike against the lock-outs and evictions, but by the time the action collapsed NALU membership was down to around 20,000.

The union did not have the funds to fight wealthy farmers. What was more, British farming entered a serious depression in the 1870s (see page 56), which meant there were fewer jobs for farm workers. In these circumstances, NALU virtually collapsed and did not revive until the 1890s.

On the positive side, wages for farm labourers did rise a little. Joseph Arch himself became an MP and spent much time helping farm labourers emigrate to Canada, America and Australia, where farm labourers were better paid and could more easily buy their own land.

SOURCE 14

Joseph Arch talks to farm labourers by torchlight at a night-time meeting. Meetings were often held in secret at night for fear of victimisation from landowners.

SOURCE 15

Dorset farm labourers evicted in 1874 for membership of the NALU.

ACTIVITY

1 Summarise the aims of the NALU in five key words.

2 Create a union banner in the style of Source 11 for the NALU using your five key words.

---

3 Why do you think the NALU failed in the 1870s?

Breakthrough for new unionism, 1888–89

The depressed economy of the 1870s weakened many of the new unions, as well as the NALU, and their successes were very limited. In the late 1880s, however, business began to pick up. As workers found their services in greater demand, their unions began to apply pressure for better terms and conditions. Between the 1880s and 1914, the new unions experienced very rapid growth.

The London match girls' strike, 1888

The conditions in many workplaces were terrible, but not many workers put up with worse conditions than the women in the Bryant and May match factory in the East End of London. There were two main types of job, and both were badly paid. The workers who made matchboxes, many of whom worked from home, earned 2¼d for making 144 boxes. The women who made the matches were even worse off. They earned about 1d per hour dipping matches into phosphorous. Not only were they subject to strict discipline from the foreman, but they also tended to suffer from a horrible form of cancer known as 'phossy jaw'.

SOURCE 16

Emma Harris had pain in her upper and lower jaws. Her throat glands were swollen and painful, her gums inflamed. Her teeth became loose and started to fall out. She was operated on twice. Fear prevented her from going back to hospital to have a third operation and a false jaw and teeth put in.

A description of phossy jaw.

In 1888, the socialist and feminist writer Annie Besant (see Profile) brought these conditions into the public eye in a magazine article called *White Slavery in London*. She demanded a boycott of Bryant and May matches. The match girls came out on strike.

It is important to realise what a huge risk this strike was. While the women were on strike, they would be earning nothing. They stood a strong chance of losing their jobs for good, just as many agricultural labourers had.

However, they had powerful friends in Annie Besant and the Liberal MP Charles Bradlaugh. Besant convinced them that a strike was the best way to make the most of the public sympathy generated by her articles. The strikers raised money from collections and from donations from other trade unionists. This went towards strike pay for the workers.

SOURCE 18

If we ever worked in our lives, we worked during that fortnight. We asked for money and it came pouring in. We made sure the girls received strike pay, got Mr Bradlaugh to ask questions in Parliament, stirred up constituencies in which shareholders were members.

From the diary of Annie Besant.

Annie Besant campaigned hard for official support from the leaders of other unions. Finally, the London Trades Council agreed to act as referees in the dispute, and after three weeks Bryant and May gave in. The match workers were given higher wages and improved working conditions. They also set up their own Matchmakers' Union.

SOURCE 17

A photograph of Bryant and May match workers in 1888.

1 **What were the main successes of the match girls' strike?**

2 **Why did they win?**

SOURCE 19

Gas works in the Old Kent Road, London. This illustration from 1891 gives a good impression of the smoke, heat and fumes endured by gas workers.

The gas workers' strike, 1889

Encouraged by the match girls' success, the gas workers, led by Will Thorne, went on strike to reduce their 12-hour shifts to eight hours. The strike was a success, and by 1890 the union had 20,000 members and more than 50 branches.

The London dock strike, 1889

Most dockers were casual labourers. The skilled workers on the docks, the stevedores, who loaded and unloaded ships, had a strong union and were well paid, but it was a very different story for the casual workers. They lined up at the beginning of each day, and foremen would pick men from the crowd. In some cases, men were herded into a shed with iron bars known as 'the cage'. Most ended up disappointed. With so many men desperate for work to feed themselves and their families, struggles were inevitable. Even when they had work, wages were poor, at about 5d per hour. The working conditions were also extremely hazardous, and accidents were common. What was worse, being picked might mean only a few hours' work. If so, the unfortunate docker then had to rejoin the others, often waiting all day in all weathers in the hope of work.

SOURCE 20

At the 'cage', so termed because of the stout iron bars made to protect the 'caller on', men ravening for food fought like madmen for the ticket [the voucher the men got for a half day's work which they then took to receive their pay from the cashier]… coats, flesh and even ears, were torn off, men were crushed to death in the struggle … The strong literally threw themselves over the heads of their fellows, and battled with kick and curse through the kicking, punching, cursing crowd to the rails of the cage, which held them like rats – mad, human rats, who saw food in the ticket…

From *A Brief History of the Dockers' Union*, by the dockers' leader, Ben Tillett.

SOURCE 21

Waiting for work on the docks. The men in bowler hats are the foremen. Why do you think the police were needed?

Because they were mainly casual workers, the dockers were difficult to organise into a union. However, they were convinced by the success of the match girls and the gas workers. Ben Tillett was already leader of the small Tea Operatives' and General Labourers' Association. With the help of other leading unionists – Tom McCarthy, Tom Mann and John Burns – Tillett led the dockers to a hard-fought victory over the employers. They demanded 6d per hour (the 'dockers' tanner'), a guaranteed minimum of four hours' work, and only two 'call-ons' in a day.

The strikers had the sympathy of the public. They picketed all the London docks, allowing no strike breakers in. They organised large but orderly marches through the city, collecting funds and raising support. Soon, the world's largest port was at a standstill, and food began to rot in the ships and warehouses. Even so, the dockers kept going only because of a grant of £30,000 from trade unionists in Australia. After five weeks, the Catholic Cardinal Manning negotiated an agreement between the two sides, and the dockers got their tanner. It was a great victory.

PROFILE

Ben Tillett

★ Born in 1860 in Bristol.
★ Worked as a brickmaker, bootmaker, sailor and docker.
★ He took up the challenge of organising the dock workers after being told it was impossible because of their casual status.
★ He led the successful dock strike in 1889.
★ In 1896 he was expelled from Hamburg and Antwerp for supporting dock strikes there.
★ He also led the London transport workers' strike of 1911.
★ He was a Labour MP 1917–24 and 1929–31.

SOURCE 22

SOUTH SIDE
CENTRAL STRIKE COMMITTEE,
SAYES COURT, DEPTFORD.

SEPTEMBER 10, 1889.

GENERAL MANIFESTO.

Owing to the fact that the demands of the Corn Porters, Deal Porters, Granary Men, General Steam Navigation Men, Permanent Men and General Labourers on the South Side have been misrepresented, the above Committee have decided to issue this Manifesto, stating the demands of the various sections now on Strike, and pledge themselves to support each section in obtaining their demands.

DEAL PORTERS of the Surrey Commercial Docks have already placed their demands before the Directors.

LUMPERS (Outside) demand the following Rates, viz:—1. 10d. per standard for Deals. 2. 11d. per stand. for all Goods rating from 2 x 4 to 2½ x 7, or for rough boards. 3. 1s. per std. for plain boards. Working day from 7 a.m. to 5 p.m., and that no man leave the "Red Lion" corner before 6.45 a.m. Overtime at the rate of 6d. per hour extra from 5 p.m. including meal times.

STEVEDORES (Inside) demand 8d. per hour from 7 a.m. to 5 p.m. 1s. per hour overtime. Overtime to commence from 5 p.m. to 7 a.m. Pay to commence from leaving "Red Lion" corner. Meal times to be paid for. Holidays & Meal times double pay, and that the Rules of the United Stevedores Protection League be acceded to in every particular.

OVERSIDE CORN PORTERS (S.C.D.) demand 15s.3d. per 100 qrs. for Oats. Heavy labour 17s.4d. per 100 qrs. manual, or with use of Steam 16s.1d. All overtime after 6 p.m. to be paid at the rate of ¼d. per qr. extra.

QUAY CORN PORTERS (S. C. D.) demand the return of Standard prices previous to March 1889, which had been in operation for 17 years.

TRIMMERS AND GENERAL LABOURERS demand 6d. per hour from 7 a.m. to 6 p.m. and 8d. per hour Overtime; Meal times as usual; and not to be taken on for less than 4 hours.

WEIGHERS & WAREHOUSEMEN demand to be reinstated in their former positions without distinction.

BERMONDSEY AND ROTHERHITHE WALL CORN PORTERS demand: 1. Permanent Men 30s. per week. 2. Casual Men 5s.10d. per day and 8d. per hour Overtime; Overtime to commence at 6 p.m. Meal times as usual.

GENERAL STEAM NAVIGATION MEN demand:—1. Wharf Men, 6d. per hour from 6 a.m. to 5 p.m and 8d. per hour Overtime. 2. In the Stream, 7d. per hour ordinary time, 9d. per hour Overtime. 3. In the Dock, 8d. per hour ordinary time, 1s. per hour Overtime.

MAUDSLEY'S ENGINEER'S MEN. Those receiving 21s. per week now demand 24s. and those receiving 24s. per week demand 26s.

ASHBY'S, LTD., CEMENT WORKS demand 6d. per ton landing Coals and Chalk. General Labourers 10% rise of wages all round, this making up for a reduction made 3 years ago.

GENERAL LABOURERS, TELEGRAPH CONSTRUCTION demand 4s. per day from 8 a.m. to 5 p.m., time and a quarter for first 2 hours Overtime, and if later, time and a half for all Overtime. No work to be done in Meal Hours.

Signed on behalf of the Central Committee, Wade Arms,
BEN. TILLETT,
JOHN BURNS,
TOM MANN,
H. H. CHAMPION,
JAS. TOOMEY.

Signed on behalf of the South side Committee,
JAS. SULLIVAN
CHAS. H
HUGH J

side to be sent to Mr. HUGH BRO   Central Strike Committee, Sayes Court.

The demands of the dockers, set out in their manifesto.

SOURCE 23

A painting of a procession of dockers through London. The unusual banners, along with the orderly behaviour of the strikers, did much good for their cause. They also collected precious funds from passers-by.

SOURCE 24

A bitter cartoon from the Australian trade union paper the *Australian Bulletin*, 1889. The title of the cartoon is 'The Secret of England's Greatness: 5d per hour'.

SOURCE 25

Suddenly the big contribution of £30,000 came from Australia in one lump, and put a new face on the whole matter. The men and the leaders were immensely encouraged; the employers, who really had a very bad case, were proportionally depressed. It at once became possible to carry on the strike for a little time longer.

From *Further Reminiscences* by HM Hyndman, founder of the Social Democratic Federation.

---

1 What were the similarities and differences between the victories of the dockers and the match workers? Think about:

- **support.**
- **finance.**
- **publicity.**
- **their case.**
- **the economic climate.**
- **organisation.**

---

2 Write your own explanation of the pattern shown in Source 27.

SOURCE 26

Expenditure: Food tickets, £21,369; Fares and post £200; Pickets £1251; Bands £936; Printing and stationery £165; Legal expenses £350; Hire of halls £196; Contribution to other striking unions £10,234; Other £8271; Total £42,999

Income: Public (by post) £10,661; Public (street collections) £1071; British trade unions £4234; European trade unions £78; American trade unions £29; Australian trade unions £30,423; Benefit concert £31; Total £46,526.

The financial balance sheet of the strike fund, 1889.

A pattern of growth

The whole union movement grew as a result of these successes. For example, membership of the Railway Servants' union rose from 12,000 to 30,000 between 1888 and 1891. The NALU gained a new lease of life. The total membership of the trade union movement doubled, and by the end of the century there were around 120,000 women trade unionists.

However, a pattern of labour relations seemed to be setting in. When economic conditions were good and unemployment was low, unions would prosper and advance. When they were bad and unemployment was high, workers tended to leave their unions, either because they were unemployed or because they were frightened of losing their jobs, and the unions would suffer and decline.

As economic conditions became worse in the 1890s, employers began to strike back. The gas workers' and dockers' unions collapsed in the early 1890s, and the NALU closed completely in 1896. Even the ASE suffered a major defeat in 1898.

However, despite these setbacks, overall union membership continued to grow, and there was no doubt that trade unions were now an essential part of Britain's economic and political life. The victories of the new unions had shown that unskilled workers could unionise and, if conditions were favourable, succeed.

SOURCE 27

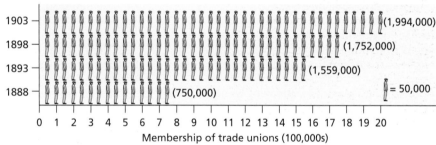

1903	(1,994,000)
1898	(1,752,000)
1893	(1,559,000)
1888	(750,000)

= 50,000

0 1 2 3 4 5 6 7 8 9 10 11 12 13 14 15 16 17 18 19 20
Membership of trade unions (100,000s)

Trade union membership.

FOCUS TASK

HOW DID NEW UNIONISM BENEFIT UNSKILLED WORKERS?

1 Look back over pages 276–79. Copy and complete the table below.

Achievements of new unionism

Event/action	Did it improve pay/ conditions? If so, how?	Did it strengthen the union movement? If so, how?

2 Discuss this question in groups:

- **Is it fair to say that the farm labourers', match girls' and dockers' actions were of more benefit to new unions generally than to the workers in those trades themselves?**

3 Write up your conclusions in two or three paragraphs.

How successful were Parliament and the courts in limiting the power of trade unions?

The growth of trade unions worried employers and the government. As you saw on page 272, the government appointed a Royal Commission to investigate trade unions in 1867. The result was a series of court cases, Acts and measures which attempted to clarify where trade unions belonged in Victorian Britain. These are shown in the Factfile below.

FACTFILE

Legal moves against the unions

★ 1867

Hornby v. Close

The Boilermakers' Union tried to sue an official for £24 he owed it. The judge ruled that trade unions were illegal, but not criminal organisations. This meant that their funds were not protected by law.

After this, the TUC led a campaign for legal protection for union funds.

★ 1871

Trade Union Act

This Act of Parliament, drawn up by the Liberal Prime Minister William Gladstone, gave legal status to unions and legal protection to their funds.

Criminal Law Amendment Act

Passed by Parliament at the same time, this Act restricted picketing. It was resented by unions, and unsympathetic judges used it to sentence gas workers to harsh prison sentences in 1872. The judge ruled that strikers had broken their contracts with employers. Breaking a contract was a civil offence for employers, but a criminal offence for employees.

The trade unions campaigned and lobbied Parliament against this Act. Despite this, 12 women farm workers were imprisoned for intimidating strike breakers. The TUC made use of the fact that working men now had the right to vote and lobby MPs by appointing a Parliamentary Committee.

★ 1875

Conspiracy and Protection of Property Act

This replaced Gladstone's 1871 Act. It allowed peaceful picketing.

Employers and Workmen Act

This made breach of contract a civil offence for employer and employee.

★ 1896

Lyons v. Wilkins

Lyons was a manufacturer of leather goods.

Although there had been no violence in a dispute between him and the Fancy Leather Workers' Trade Society, he gained a court injunction which prevented picketing of his premises.

London Building Trades Federation

The London Building Trades Federation had to pay damages to a firm which it had put it on a blacklist of unfair employers.

As a result, the unions complained that judges were not neutral, but favoured employers. Certainly, the legal position of unions, and what they were able to do, was very unclear.

★ 1900

The Taff Vale Judgement

This was a much more serious blow to trade unions. In 1900, the Amalgamated Society of Railway Servants went on strike on the Taff Vale Railway in South Wales. The Railway sued the union for its losses during the strike, and the union was ordered to pay £23,000. This was potentially disastrous. If it became an established principle, the weapon of strike action would be effectively lost.

The TUC realised that the law had to be changed, and that meant the unions needed a voice in Parliament. Many unions joined the Labour Representation Committee (see page 282). They also used their campaigning skills, and the further extension of the electorate in 1884, to pressurise the existing parties. In 1906, the new Liberal government passed the Trades Disputes Act. The main clause in this Act was that unions were not liable for losses caused by strike action.

★ 1903

The Osborne Case

In 1903, the TUC agreed to help pay the expenses of Labour MPs by a levy on members. A Liberal supporter, railwayman WV Osborne, objected to this practice, and in 1909 the House of Lords gave its judgement. It ruled that trade unions were not political organisations, and were therefore not entitled to raise a political fund. It was a major blow to the new Labour Party, and 16 Labour MPs lost their source of income.

The TUC and Labour Party continued to campaign for another change in the law. This was achieved with the 1913 Trades Union Act. The Act allowed unions to raise a political levy, but only if the majority of members approved. Any member who did not wish to pay the levy could 'contract out', although few did.

FOCUS TASK

+5 Step forward for the unions	
+4	
+3	
+2	
+1	
0	
-1	
-2	
-3	
-4	
-5 Step back for the unions	

HOW SUCCESSFUL WERE PARLIAMENT AND THE COURTS IN CURBING THE UNIONS' POWER?

1 Score each judgement in the Factfile on a scale of –5 to +5 according to whether it is a setback for the unions or a step forward.

2 Write a paragraph explaining how events in the Factfile fit each of these two views:
   - 'The period 1871–1913 shows trade unions gaining the upper hand over hostile courts and Parliament.'
   - 'The period 1871–1913 was a desperate struggle for survival for the unions. They constantly had to fight unfavourable judgements, and it took years to reverse each one.'

3 Now write a third paragraph, which begins with your own view.

How successful was the early Labour Party?

You have come across several mentions of the Labour Party in this chapter. Where did it fit into the story of trade unions, and what did it achieve by 1914?

In the early nineteenth century, many working men were involved in protest movements such as Chartism. But they could not be members of Parliament, nor belong to the main political parties (the Conservatives and Liberals). No political party in Parliament would have welcomed an ordinary working man as a member, and no working man would have thought it worth joining even if he had been allowed to. Members of the main parties were all middle and upper class.

However, trade unions, friendly societies and co-operatives had created a body of well-educated, able and politically active working men. In 1867, the Reform Act doubled the electorate to about two million men (mostly householders in the towns), and this was extended to two out of three working men by the Reform Act of 1884. Whom would these newly 'enfranchised' men choose to vote for: one of the existing parties, or a party of their own? Among working-class leaders there were three different groups claiming their loyalty.

Henry Broadhurst and the Lib-Labs

After the 1884 Reform Act, three working men were elected to Parliament. They voted with the Liberals and became known as Lib-Lab MPs (short for Liberal/Labour). Henry Broadhurst was the first working man to become a government minister. He was intensely loyal to the Liberal leader, Gladstone, and felt that there was no need for a working-class party because Lib-Lab MPs could influence the Liberals if action was needed.

Keir Hardie and the Socialists

At the 1887 TUC conference, the leader of the Scottish miners, Keir Hardie, attacked Broadhurst. Hardie believed there was a real need for a separate party for working men. Soon afterwards, Hardie stood (unsuccessfully) as an independent candidate against the Liberals in a Scottish by-election.

SOURCE 28

The state itself is neither capitalist nor anti-capitalist. When the workers get sense enough to stop sending capitalists, and send socialists drawn from their own ranks to represent them, then the state becomes your servant, and not the servant of the capitalists.

From one of Keir Hardie's election speeches.

1 **Explain the main differences between the views of Keir Hardie and Henry Broadhurst.**

A May Day edition of *Justice*, the SDF Paper, 1896.

PROFILE

Keir Hardie

★ Born 1856 in Holytown, Lanarkshire.
★ Worked from childhood in a coal mine.
★ As a young man, he became interested in trade unions and tried to organise the miners into a union.
★ He was sacked and moved to Cumnock after threats and intimidation.
★ Became a campaigning journalist.
★ He first stood as an MP in 1888, but was defeated.
★ He was MP for West Ham 1892–95 and Merthyr Tydfil 1900–1915.
★ Began and edited the *Labour Leader* newspaper.
★ A committed pacifist, even when this was not a popular policy, he lost his seat for opposing the Boer War.

The Social Democratic Federation

Hardie's views were close to the views of the Social Democratic Federation (SDF). Its members were influenced by the ideas of Karl Marx. In Marx's view, there would always be a class struggle between workers and capitalists, until the workers finally overthrew the system and set up a state run by and for workers.

Some members of the SDF were moderates. They included the Fabian Society, which believed in peaceful campaigning and gradual improvements in conditions for the working classes. This approach was nicknamed 'gas and water socialism' because of its focus on supplying essential services such as gas, water and sanitation.

However, much of the SDF was more inclined to radical action. Its members included dockers' leaders such as Tom Mann (see page 278). It had its own newspaper and led demonstrations. SDF members and other socialists played an important role in the victories of the new unions in 1888 and 1889.

The Independent Labour Party

Something or someone was needed to bring these different strands together, and that someone was Keir Hardie.

In the 1892 general election, Hardie was voted in as MP for West Ham, in London. He refused to call himself a Liberal, as the other working-class MPs had done, and he also insisted on wearing the clothes of a working man in Parliament. Hardie criticised both the main parties for ignoring the working classes. In 1893, he called a conference in Bradford, a town where he knew there was a great deal of support for his views. A number of socialists and trade unionists came together to form the Independent Labour Party.

However, in their first general election, in 1895, all 28 ILP candidates lost, including Hardie. They were more successful in local elections. In London, ILP councillors were active in council house programmes as Poor Law Guardians. In Bradford, Margaret MacMillan was elected onto the School Board.

Relations between the Liberals and trade unions were becoming strained by the the late 1890s. In 1899, the ILP finally persuaded the TUC to back a workers' party, which it had refused to do for years. One reason for this decision was that the ASRS (Amalgamated Society of Railway Servants) decided that unions needed special representation in Parliament. The ASRS suspected that Liberal MPs were unwilling to support them because many of them owned shares in railways.

The new Labour Representation Committee (LRC) was set up in 1900. However, union support for it was lukewarm: only 12 unions joined it. It was a compromise, and there were many arguments about its aims and methods. The hard work of Hardie and its secretary, Ramsay Macdonald, kept it going, and it managed to win two seats in the 1901 General Election.

The Taff Vale Judgement of 1900 (see page 280) was a turning point. Faced with the threat to their funds, more unions joined the LRC. By 1903, the LRC could claim to represent eight million trade unionists. Ramsay Macdonald promised the Liberals that if they did not stand against LRC candidates at the election, LRC members who were elected to Parliament would support the Liberals. As a result, LRC candidates won 29 seats in the 1906 election, and the organisation changed its name to the Labour Party.

As you have read, the Liberals passed the Trades Disputes Act in 1906 to reverse the Taff Vale decision. However, it would be wrong to think that the Labour Party was 'calling the shots'. The Liberals had a large majority in the Commons in 1906, and did not need Labour's support. When the Osborne judgement hit the unions in 1909, it took four years of hard work to get it reversed. In fairness, this was not only because the Labour Party was weak or the unions were unpopular. By 1913, civil war seemed likely in Ireland, and by 1914 an even greater conflict – the Great War – was looming. Parliament was deeply concerned by unions and industrial relations, but there were other pressing matters as well.

FOCUS TASK

WAS THE LABOUR PARTY A REAL OR A POTENTIAL FORCE IN BRITISH POLITICAL LIFE BY 1914?

1 Look at Sources 30–35 carefully and then copy and complete this chart.

Source	Suggests Labour was a real or potential force?	Reason	Can it be accepted at face value?	Conclusion

2 Was the Labour Party a real or a potential force in British political life by 1914? Base your answer on what you have written in your chart.

SOURCE 30

A cartoon published in 1906 while Parliament was debating the Trade Disputes Bill. The man is Prime Minister Asquith. The passing of the Trade Disputes Act was the first time Labour's influence was seen in Parliament.

SOURCE 31

FORCED FELLOWSHIP.

A *Punch* cartoon, 'Socialism and Liberalism', from 1909. The artist, Bernard Partridge, was not particularly sympathetic towards socialism. The man on the left is saying 'Any objection to my company, guvnor? I'm going your way – and further.'

SOURCE 32

The party quickly developed a large number of local speakers. Many young men who were Nonconformist local preachers were attracted to the movement by the ethical [moral] appeal of socialism … The movement was something new in politics. It was politics inspired by idealism.

Written in 1900 by Philip Snowdon (later to become a Labour Chancellor of the Exchequer) on the Labour Party in Yorkshire.

SOURCE 33

The growth of the Labour Party astounded contemporaries. In 1900 63,000 men voted Labour and returned two Labour MPs … In 1906 323,000 men did so and 29 Labour MPs took their seats in the Commons, a number which was increased to 42 in the second election of 1910. After 1911 the Labour Party even had its own newspaper, the Daily Herald.

From RN Rundle, *Britain's Economic and Social Development, 1700–1977.*

SOURCE 34

Under Ramsay Macdonald's care the Labour Party in these years [1900–1914] had been building up a solid political machine in the constituencies. By 1914 it had become a formidable force …

From RB Jones, *Economic and Social History of England.*

SOURCE 35

The past 21 years have been years of progress, [but] we are only at the beginning. The emancipation of the worker has still to be achieved.

From a speech by Keir Hardie, 1914.

10.3 *Have unions caused more conflict or harmony in the twentieth century?*

The period 1900–1914 was a time of increasing conflict in British industry, when there were large numbers of particularly hard-fought strikes. The worst incidents were in the coal and shipbuilding industries. Troops were called in to deal with strikers in South Wales in 1910, and in 1911 there were deaths during a strike by dockers and transport workers.

Whose fault was this? If you had asked most middle-class British people this question in 1914, they would have had little doubt: trade unions caused the trouble. They would point to the changes in the union movement (see below) and say that the unions were becoming too powerful and were harming Britain.

However, if you had asked union supporters, they would have argued that it was the government and employers who caused the trouble: working people were only fighting for survival. For example, between 1900 and 1914, wages did not rise as quickly as prices. By 1914, a miner's wage packet was worth only 90 per cent of his 1900 wage.

In 1914, it looked to many people as if Britain was in crisis. The outbreak of war in August 1914 solved the crisis in the short term, but the core issues were not resolved.

Changes in the union movement, 1900–1914

SOURCE **1**

> 1 What impression does Source 1 give you of
>
> a) the capitalist?
> b) the workers?

Master Baker: Give us this day workmen pure in heart, meek in spirit, as soft and pliable as the dough they daily punch; and punish the wickedness of the agitators who want them to 'rise.

A cartoon from the pro-union newspaper the *Daily Herald* in 1913. The fat wealthy capitalist became a feature of trade union cartoons after the First World War.

During this period, and in particular between 1910 and 1914, trade union membership rose quite substantially. In addition, from 1910 onwards, some of the main unions began to amalgamate to form giant industry-wide unions. In 1910, the dockers and seamen formed the National Transport Workers' Federation (NTWF). In 1912, four different railway unions came together to form the National Union of Railwaymen (NUR). The third, and most radical, of these giant unions was the Miners' Federation.

Syndicalism

At this time, a new movement called syndicalism was gaining strength in France and the USA. The idea of syndicalism was to create large, powerful unions, and then to destroy the government by means of a general strike. This was something totally new for trade unions, and it scared the government. The syndicalist leader James Connolly brought violence to the streets of Dublin in 1913 as his Citizen Army fought against police and troops (see Source 3). However, in reality, few British unionists were syndicalists.

Alliances

In 1913, the Triple Alliance was formed between the transport, railway and miners' unions. This meant that if one union went on strike, the other two would also do so. It seems likely that most unionists saw this merely as an effective tactic. However, the government saw it as syndicalist and potentially revolutionary.

SOURCE 2

Ben Tillett, the dockers' leader, talking to strikers at Tower Hill in London, 1912. This was one of many strikes around the country in the years leading up to 1914.

SOURCE 3

The Dublin lock-out, 1913. Employers at Dublin's docks and railways sacked all the strikers and locked them out of work, employing non-union labour. The result was extensive rioting and street fighting.

ACTIVITY

Choose either Source 2 or Source 3. Write two captions to go with it: a caption that might have appeared in an anti-union newspaper, and a caption that might have appeared in a pro-union newspaper.

   Then write a paragraph to explain why people in 1910–1914 had such different views of the union movement.

Why was there a General Strike in 1926?

The First World War did not solve any of these problems; it simply put them off for a few years. Some problems were even made worse. You are now going to investigate the events which led to the General Strike of 1926.

Industry during the First World War

During the war, the government took over the running of major industries, including transport and coal (see below). Union leaders and employers sat together on Whitley Councils, which were set up to advise the government on how to run these industries.

Post-war strikes

By the end of the war, the unions seemed strong. The police and railwaymen held successful strikes in 1918 and 1919. By 1920, there were over eight million trade unionists. An enormous new union, the Transport and General Workers' Union, was set up in 1921, under a very able leader called Ernest Bevin. Many observers wondered whether the unions' new strength would lead to a clash with the government. If it did, it was likely to start in the coal industry.

The coal industry

Although other energy sources were beginning to emerge, British industry still relied on coal. This was why coal mining was one of the areas controlled by the government during the war. Between 1914 and 1918, wages, hours and safety improved, and at the end of the war miners wanted to keep the advantages they had gained. Sir John Sankey led a Commission to investigate this issue in 1919. It recommended that NATIONALISATION should continue, but the Prime Minister, Lloyd George, refused. The mine owners were influential and powerful, and in addition the Prime Minister was not anxious for the government to take control of an industry which had serious problems. He returned the mines to the mine owners in 1921.

SOURCE 4

Even on the evidence already given, the present system of ownership and working in the coal industry stands condemned and some other system must be substituted for it, either nationalism or a method of unification by national purchase and/or joint control.

From the report of the Sankey Commission.

SOURCE 5

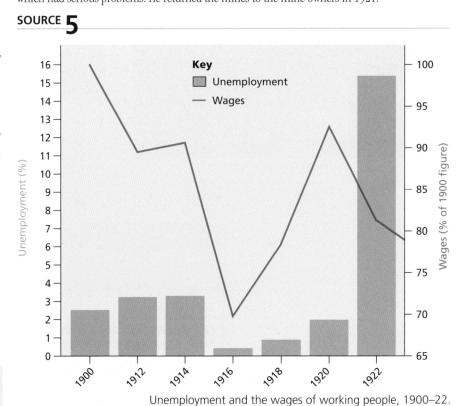

Unemployment and the wages of working people, 1900–22.

---

1 What factors put the unions in a strong position after the war?

2 What were the causes and the results of Black Friday?

'Black Friday': miners' wages reduced

By 1921, the British coal industry was under pressure from foreign competition. To reduce costs, the mine owners proposed a cut in wages and an extended working day. The miners refused to accept these measures. They came out on strike, and called on the Triple Alliance for support. Unfortunately for the miners, the railwaymen and transport workers felt that the miners should have tried harder to negotiate. After initially agreeing to support the miners, they withdrew their support on 15 April 1921. This became known as 'Black Friday'. The miners continued with a bitter strike, but were eventually forced to accept the wage cut and go back to work.

The post-war slump

Between 1921 and 1925, relations between the Labour Party and the trade union movement on the one hand and the government and employers on the other hand steadily deteriorated. The situation was made worse by the fact that many areas of British industry went through a disastrous slump in the years after the war. British industry had lost many of its markets to American and Japanese competition during the war. The industries which were particularly hard hit were the old 'staple' industries such as shipbuilding, coal and textiles, which were large employers. These industries relied heavily on export markets that were rapidly disappearing.

Employers were trying to cut costs as much as possible, and in their view the place to start was with wage rates. Like the miners before them, dockers, rail workers, builders and many others all had to take wage cuts.

To defend their members, unions drew closer together. In 1921, Ernest Bevin of the Transport and General Workers' Union convinced the Trades Union Congress (TUC) to create a General Council. Its role was to co-ordinate a large-scale strike if this became necessary.

SOURCE 6

THE PROBLEM-PICTURE OF 1921.
HOW TO MAKE THE TAIL WAG.

A 1921 cartoon about the Triple Alliance, by Bernard Partridge. (In ancient mythology, a three-headed dog guarded the gates of hell.)

3 What is Source 6 saying about the Triple Alliance?

Hardening attitudes

Other factors hardened attitudes on all sides. The rise of the Labour Party worried employers. (It won 191 seats in Parliament in the 1923 general election, and formed a short-lived government.) There was also a suspicion that organisations such as the TUC were dangerously radical or even revolutionary. In 1920, London dockers refused to load a ship with arms that were being sent by the UK government to the anti-communist forces in Russia. In 1924, AJ Cook, a self-confessed syndicalist, became the leader of the miners. In the same year, the *Daily Mail* published the 'Zinoviev letter', which seemed to suggest that Labour was in league with Russian Communists. The letter was in fact a forgery, but some Conservative politicians genuinely believed that the unions were influenced or even inspired by Communists. William Joynson-Hicks, the Home Secretary, was a strong supporter of this view.

In 1925, Britain went back onto the gold standard. This was a way of protecting the value of the pound against foreign currency, particularly the dollar. However, it tended to depress the economy and made British exports more expensive. This in turn made the rising unemployment of the 1920s worse (see pages 238–40).

SOURCE 7

[The miners] are the victims of the economic juggernaut. They represent in the flesh the 'fundamental adjustments' engineered by the Treasury and the Bank of England to satisfy the impatience of the City … They are the 'moderate sacrifice' still necessary to ensure the stability of the gold standard.

The economist JM Keynes criticises the decision to go on the gold standard.

'Red Friday': subsidies for mine owners

In the summer of 1925, attention shifted back to the coal industry. On 30 June 1925, the mine owners gave a month's notice that the workers' existing conditions would end. A new offer was made, involving a further cut in wages and an extra hour added to the working day. The miners' leader was firm in his view: 'Not a penny off the pay, not a minute on the day'. A lock-out seemed likely, but this time the Triple Alliance held together. It threatened a complete embargo on all production or transportation of coal, which would have brought the country to a standstill.

The TUC certainly wanted to help the miners, but it also wanted to involve the government in the dispute, in the hope that this would help to bring about a lasting settlement. This plan was a partial success. The Prime Minister, Stanley Baldwin, agreed to pay mine owners a SUBSIDY, which would stop the wage cut.

This success became known as Red Friday. However, the agreement was only for nine months, and the government took no responsibility for the running of the mines. It seemed likely that conflict would arise again once the subsidy ended. In another attempt to buy time, Baldwin also set up the Samuel Commission to study the coal industry and report back.

In the meanwhile, the government set up the Organisation for the Maintenance of Supplies (OMS). This established a force of volunteers who would drive trains, buses and so on in the event of a strike. The OMS also collected stores of food and fuel.

As 1925 moved into 1926, the tension increased between the government and the mine owners on one side and the unions on the other side.

SOURCE 9

We want nationalisation. First, for the sake of economic security, and secondly, because we want safety. Under private ownership our men are murdered. Safety is not the first consideration, but the last … Sixty per cent of the accidents are preventable. Explosions ought to be a thing of the past … the men who run the mines run them from London simply for profit, and safety is the last consideration.

AJ Cook, Secretary of the Miners' Federation, speaking in 1925.

SOURCE 10

It would be possible to say without exaggeration that the miners' [union] leaders were the stupidest men in England, if we had not had frequent occasion to meet the mine owners.

A comment by a government minister, Lord Birkenhead.

SOURCE 8

A cartoon entitled 'The subsidised mine owner, poor beggar'. It appeared in 1925 in the trade union paper *Unity*.

SOURCE 11

A cartoon from 1925 criticising the miners' leader, AJ Cook. Cook came in for a real battering in the anti-union press.

SOURCE 12

A PRETTY PENNY IN THE SLOT.

MASTER STANLEY BALDWIN. "COME ON, UNCLE, FORK OUT; IT'S WELL WORTH IT."
JOHN BULL. "ALL RIGHT, MY BOY, I'LL TAKE YOUR WORD FOR IT. BUT ONLY THIS ONCE, MIND."

A *Punch* cartoon by Bernard Partridge from 1925. The small boy is the Prime Minister, Stanley Baldwin, and the adult is John Bull, representing Britain.

SOURCE 13

The danger was not over. Sooner or later this question had got to be fought out by the people of the land. Was England to be governed by Parliament and the Cabinet or by a handful of trade union leaders?

Written by Sir William Joynson Hicks, the Home Secretary.

The outbreak of the General Strike

The Samuel Commission made its report in March 1926. It recommended small wage cuts but not longer hours.

This was not acceptable to either the miners or the employers. The TUC considered limited industrial action – an embargo on moving coal. However, the railway and transport unions complained that this would fall solely on them: any proof of solidarity must be more widespread. The other unions agreed, and thus, in the opinion of some historians, 'stumbled towards' a general strike.

The TUC General Council threatened a strike of key workers on 3 May. Printers at the *Daily Mail* refused to print a leading article criticising the TUC written for the newspaper (Source 15). For the government, the action by the *Daily Mail* printers was the last straw. All negotiations with the TUC were broken off, and the General Strike began on 4 May.

SOURCE 14

A cartoon in the workers' paper, the *Daily Herald*, in 1925. It appears to show what AJ Cook thought of Parliament. Many TUC leaders were deeply concerned by any words or actions which suggested that unions were threatening democracy.

SOURCE 15

A General Strike is not an industrial dispute. It is a revolutionary movement intended to inflict suffering upon the great mass of innocent persons in the community and thereby to put forcible constraint upon the Government. It is a movement which can only succeed by destroying the Government and subverting the rights and liberties of the people.

The leading article written for the *Daily Mail* on 3 May 1926, which printers refused to print, triggering the strike.

1 Look back at the six cartoons on pages 284–89. Select the one that you think is the cleverest. Explain your choice.

2 Explain why you think the unions and bosses were favourite subjects for cartoonists in this period.

FOCUS TASK

WHAT FACTORS LED TO THE GENERAL STRIKE OF 1926?

1 The table lists a number of factors which led up to the General Strike. Copy the table.

   a) In the first column, note down evidence from pages 286–89 that each factor played a part in causing the General Strike.
   b) In the second column, explain, in your own words, how each factor led to the strike.

	Evidence	Explanation
Wages and conditions in the coal industry		
Economic conditions after the war		
Desire for nationalisation		
The Triple Alliance		
Government fear of union power		
Gold standard		
Syndicalism		
Fear of communism		

2 Many historians say that the unions stumbled into this strike rather than planning it.

   a) What do they mean by this?
   b) What evidence is there to support this view?

SOURCE 16

The General Council of the TUC wishes to emphasise the fact that this is an industrial dispute. It expects every member taking part to be exemplary in his conduct and not to give any opportunity for police interference.

A radio broadcast by the TUC, May 1926.

The course of the strike

The strike was not particularly well organised, but it was amazingly well supported. Strikers from the Triple Alliance industries were joined by workers in building, shipbuilding, printing, electricity, steel and many others. Around 80 per cent of the TUC's 10 million members joined the strike. There is a day-by-day account of the strike in the Factfile which starts below.

During the strike, the TUC published a newspaper called the *British Worker*. This gave details of the solidarity of the strike, and also criticised the actions of the government; it accused Winston Churchill, in particular, of trying to provoke violence. The TUC stressed that its aims were industrial. It had not called out essential workers in health or sanitation, for example, and it offered to help distribute essential supplies.

The government, in contrast, took every opportunity to claim that the unions were trying to change the way in which Britain was governed. It refused to negotiate with the TUC, but put all its energies into 'breaking' the strike.

The OMS mobilised around 30,000 volunteers: many middle-class men achieved lifelong ambitions to drive buses or trains! Troops were obvious on the streets, and supplies were transported in convoys escorted by armoured cars and attended by special constables. These officials were particularly resented by the strikers, who felt that they were politically motivated. They were often ex-soldiers and not from the local area. They were not respected or trusted like the regular police officers and reacted accordingly. The strikers also resented the fact that the special constables were well paid; they received £2 6s 3d per week, while miners had been locked out for refusing £1 11s 7½d. However, there was very little violence, considering the size of the strike, although some property was damaged and there were over 1,000 arrests.

The emergency systems put into place by the government managed to keep the country working. Although it was a long way from 'business as usual', Britain was in no way brought to its knees. The General Strike was called off after only nine days, although the miners stayed out on strike for another six months.

ACTIVITY 1

Using the Factfile, work out what each of the photographs on the page opposite shows and when and where it might have been taken.

ACTIVITY 2

Suggest how either photo could be used:

a) **by the *British Gazette* to show the fragility of the strike.**
b) **by the *British Worker* to show the solidarity of the strike.**

FACTFILE

A diary of the General Strike

★ **Day 1: Tuesday 4 May**
On the whole, there was good humour and good order. London's transport system was almost at a complete standstill. Thousands of commuters tried to catch the few buses which did run, driven by non-union labour. The great majority walked. The only news service available to the public was on BBC radio, as the printers were all on strike. Volunteers joined in with the distribution of food and other essential supplies by the army, and this went smoothly.

In Parliament the Budget was passed with virtually no debate at all. This was unheard-of, but the explanation was simple. Opposition leaders wanted to get through this business to discuss the General Strike. The Prince of Wales came back from Paris to listen to the debate. He continued to take a keen interest in events.

★ **Day 2: Wednesday 5 May**
Both sides managed to publish their first newspaper. The strikers brought out the *British Worker*, which highlighted the solidarity of the strike but also stressed that it was purely industrial. The government published the *British Gazette*, edited by Winston Churchill. It ridiculed the strikers and stated that their aim was to overturn democracy. It seems that the general public found this publication distasteful because it was so extreme, and treated anything it said with great suspicion.

An attempt to run trams in London was abandoned when a large hostile crowd formed to prevent it: the trams were too easy a target. However, trams did run in most other towns during the strike. Using emergency powers, the government was able to get some trains moving with military staff. A number of London buses also ran, with a police escort and a wire mesh to protect the drivers from missiles. Some buses were attacked in London. In Leeds and Nottingham there was crowd trouble but nothing serious.

Hyde Park in London was closed off and used as the centre for the distribution of milk to the capital.

★ **Day 3: Thursday 6 May**
A skeleton service began to run on the London Underground, manned by volunteers. Eighty buses also ran, but nearly 50 of them were damaged. The government took stronger measures to protect the buses and also any workers who had refused to strike. The railway companies announced that over 1,700 trains had run.

There were disturbances in Edinburgh, where civilians and five policemen were hurt. There was also some violence in Leeds, Aberdeen and various parts of London.

★ **Day 4: Friday 7 May**
A government statement announced that the situation was becoming more intense, that the strikers planned to disrupt the temporary transport networks, and that 50,000 special constables were to be taken on in London. It also admitted that there had been no trouble

up to this point. The statement also claimed that the TUC was attempting to starve the country, and that there had been widespread intimidation of volunteers and non-strikers.

The Archbishop of Canterbury appealed to the government and strikers to return to peace negotiations. The appeal was not broadcast by the BBC until 11 May, and it was not reported in the *British Gazette* at all.

About 2,400 trains ran.

★ Day 5: Saturday 8 May

Prime Minister Stanley Baldwin spoke on the BBC. He again accused the unions of threatening democracy. He also said that the government was not attacking the living standards of workers. The TUC replied that while the PM appealed for the strike to end he did not appeal for the mine owners to end their lock-outs. Russian trade unions sent the TUC a large cheque, but the TUC returned it.

After several lorries had been prevented from leaving the docks in London, the first military convoy was used. It was two miles long and contained 16 armoured cars. There was no violence and relatively little ill-feeling. American observers commented that even minor strikes in the USA caused more violence than this General Strike.

Many shops and businesses usually open on Saturdays did not open.

★ Day 6: Sunday 9 May

Being Sunday, it was a quiet day across the country. Many strikers marched to church. Clergymen appealed for an end to the strike. The Catholic Cardinal Bourne called the strike a sin, and some Labour MPs protested about this.

The government announced that there had been a small but steady stream of strikers going back to work, although to most observers there was little sign of the strike weakening. The Home Secretary appealed for recruits for a new Civil Constabulary Reserve to keep order, and many people volunteered.

★ Day 7: Monday 10 May

Sir Herbert Samuel tried to negotiate a settlement behind the scenes, but the government made it clear that he was not acting officially but on his own behalf. Some sources suggested that the government tried to discourage him.

The government restated its pledge to protect workers who had not gone out on strike, or who had returned to work, from victimisation. It also claimed that the flow of people going back to work was increasing, but this was denied by the TUC.

The government was becoming increasingly confident in the success of its emergency supply services. Some 3,677 trains ran. The Manchester Ship Canal was closed to shipments of wheat, as flour employees came out on strike.

SOURCE 17

SOURCE 18

★ Day 8: Tuesday 11 May

Rumours of an imminent peace were everywhere. The TUC called a special meeting to discuss the strike and their tactics. However, it also called the engineering and shipbuilding workers out on strike, and refused a request from the print unions to allow some newspapers to be printed.

A court action was brought by the National Sailors' Union and the Firemen's' Union to prevent TUC officials calling the members of these unions out on strike. This led to a judgement by Justice Astbury that the General Strike was illegal. The judgement also said that those involved in a general strike were not protected by the 1906 Trades Disputes Act (which said that unions were not liable for losses suffered by employers).

Sir John Simon, speaking for the Liberals in Parliament, proposed a peace plan. It was dismissed in the *British Gazette*.

In terms of violent disturbance, the country was still mainly quiet. However, in Glasgow there was some serious trouble. Police announced that in the course of the strike Glasgow police had made some 300–400 arrests. ➡

FACTFILE CONTINUED

★ **Day 9: Wednesday 12 May**
At midday, the TUC representative went to Downing Street and announced that the strike was being called off. The reasons given for the end of the strike by the TUC were not clear. The *Daily News* suggested that it was a combination of the following factors:

- A realisation that the General Strike was a blunt and ineffective weapon, and must fail sooner or later.
- The Astbury judgement that the strike was illegal.
- A shortage of strike funds in certain unions, and a reluctance on the part of the banks to grant overdrafts for continuing strike pay in a dispute which had been ruled as an illegal one.
- A fear that large numbers of strikers might begin to stream back to work and bring an inglorious end to the demonstration of solidarity.
- A genuine and deep-rooted desire on the part of the members of the TUC not to extend an intolerable situation.

Rumours floated around that the government was planning drastic action. Labour journals suggested that there were plans to arrest the leaders of the TUC and to confiscate union funds. The TUC simply said that it accepted Sir Herbert Samuel's proposals for a settlement. The government quickly repeated its statement that Samuel had no official role as a negotiator.

Prime Minister Baldwin called the end of the strike a victory for common sense. The King sent a special telegram pleading for an end to any bitterness and saying that there should be no victimisation.

AJ Cook and the miners refused to accept the call to peace.

Why was the strike called off?

Many strikers were deeply disappointed when the strike was called off, and the miners certainly felt that they had been betrayed. There was no doubt that the main point of the strike, to preserve the miners' pay and conditions, was not achieved. So why was it called off?

The government always viewed the strike as a test of strength between itself and the unions as to who was going to run the country. Having presented it in this way, it could not afford to lose! It was determined to win the dispute, whatever the cost, and refused every offer to negotiate with the strikers.

The TUC leaders could see that the government was never going to give in. Many officials in the TUC had been nervous about the strike from the beginning. They were concerned that radicals might cause violent confrontation and that the TUC's good name might be tarred. They also considered that it was wiser deliberately to stop the strike early than for it to collapse as people drifted back to work.

SOURCE 19

We felt ashamed. But I was of the opinion that if it had gone on another week it would have been hopeless, it was crumbling. Before the end of the strike I was really worried about keeping my men out. Looking at my own trade, I don't think we were sufficiently organised, not more than 70 per cent, and men were going back to work.

Written by a district organiser of the Painters' Union.

SOURCE 20

Every day that the strike proceeded the control and the authority of that dispute was passing out of the hands of responsible executives into the hands of men who had no authority, no control and were wrecking the movement from one end to the other.

Written by Charles Duke of the General and Municipal Workers' Union, 1926.

FOCUS TASK

WAS THE GENERAL STRIKE A POLITICAL OR AN INDUSTRIAL DISPUTE?

1 Look through the sources on pages 286–92 for:
   - one or more sources that present the strike as a political dispute (a dispute over how the government ran the country).
   - one or more sources that present it as an industrial dispute (a dispute over working conditions or pay in a single industry).
   - one or more sources that suggest a combination of the two.

   Summarise the point of your chosen source(s) and note who made or wrote it and when.

2 Which of the sources do you find most convincing?

3 Finally, write three paragraphs to explain whether, in your opinion, the General Strike was a political or an industrial dispute. Include:
   - evidence to suggest it was a political dispute.
   - evidence to suggest it was an industrial dispute.
   - your own view on whether it was a political or industrial dispute.

1 What reasons do Sources 19 and 20 give for the strike being called off?

2 Does the fact that it was called off without resolving the issue of miners' pay mean it had failed?

FOCUS TASK

WHY DID THE GENERAL STRIKE FAIL?

Work in threes.

1 Choose one of these characters each and write their explanation of why the General Strike failed.

- A member of the Conservative Cabinet
- A moderate member of the TUC General Council
- A radical like AJ Cook

2 Compare your explanations. Do they agree about anything?

How did the failure of the General Strike affect the trade union movement?

For the miners, the failure of the strike was disastrous. They stayed out on strike for a further six months. Eventually, hunger drove them back to work. They had to accept longer hours, lower pay and other terms to suit individual mine owners. There was victimisation of strikers, and the employers took the opportunity to get rid of workers whom they saw as potential troublemakers. This also happened in other industries, such as the railways.

SOURCE 22

The bosses knew which men they wanted and which they would never have back. They treated us like pigs. The best unionists didn't get back. The cripples got the sack too. Only those that wouldn't make trouble stood a chance.

A description by a South Wales coal miner.

The longer-term effects of the strike on unions were drastic. In 1927, Parliament passed a new Trades Disputes Act. This Act made strikes in sympathy or support of workers in other trades illegal, effectively crippling the Triple Alliance. It placed severe restrictions on PICKETING. Union members now had to make a positive decision to pay money into a union's political fund, a reversal of the Act of 1913 (see page 280).

Trade union membership fell by about 1.5 million over the next seven years, although this was mainly a result of the terrible unemployment in the 1930s following the Wall Street Crash (see page 240).

Unions in new industries such as electronics and car manufacture grew, but these were moderate unions, more like the new model unions of the nineteenth century. Employers such as Austin Motors would only tolerate skilled workers' unions in their factories.

The Labour Party too gained little from the General Strike, because weakened unions meant a weakened party. In the aftermath of the strike some unionists turned to the Communist Party and Labour activists spent valuable time fighting with the Communists for the support of union members. Despite the setbacks Labour was able to form its first government as early as 1929. However, the worldwide economic depression swept away any plans Labour had for creating a brave new world. In fact the severe measures adopted by Ramsay Macdonald as a response to the Depression split the party, and most Labour MPs lost their seats in 1931. From 1929 to 1935 Macdonald and a few Labour ministers led a National Government of mainly Conservative MPs. Labour did not take office again until 1945.

FOCUS TASK

HOW DID THE FAILURE OF THE GENERAL STRIKE AFFECT THE UNIONS?

It is 1928, two years on from the General Strike. You have been asked by union leaders to prepare a balanced assessment of the General Strike. They want a document in three sections:

- Damage caused to the union movement
- Benefits to the union movement
- Lessons to be learned by the union movement

You can write paragraphs or short notes under each heading. You may find that some sections are longer than others.

Why did unions become more militant in the 1960s and 1970s?

During the Second World War, unions co-operated closely with the government, just as they had in the First World War. A former union leader, Ernest Bevin, became Minister of Labour in 1940. The links between the Labour Party and the trade unions gave both politicians and union leaders valuable experience.

In 1945, the Labour Party won its first clear election victory and started a radical programme of reform. It set up the Welfare State (see page 249); it nationalised the coal, rail and docks industries; and it repealed the restrictive 1927 Trades Disputes Act. The unions worked closely with this Labour government. During the 1950s, Britain's economy did well, and the unions continued to co-operate with the Conservative governments that ran Britain until 1964.

The union movement itself went from strength to strength.

Growing union membership

In 1960, there were 9.8 million union members. This rose to 11.2 million by 1970 and 12.8 million by 1980. Many of these were women, who made up about 30 per cent of union members by 1976. Union membership was also growing among 'white-collar' (office-based) workers.

SOURCE 23

Trade union membership 1900–1980.

Although total union membership rose, the number of individual unions fell in this period, because smaller unions amalgamated to form large 'super-unions', to which hundreds of thousands of workers belonged.

New 'public sector' unions

Nationalisation and the growth of the Welfare State since the war had vastly increased the number of people employed directly by the government. Two of the largest unions during this period were new ones for these 'public-sector' workers: COHSE (Confederation of Health Service Employees) and NUPE (National Union of Public Employees) were both formed in 1964.

Increasing union influence

As unions became more powerful, they were able to negotiate special terms in the workplace, such as the CLOSED SHOP, which meant that only members of a given union could work in a particular factory or production line. The unions argued convincingly that this made for better industrial relations, as the employers had only one union to deal with on behalf of all the workers. However, it also gave immense power to the unions if a dispute were to occur.

With their increased power, unions were now an accepted part of the political life of Britain. No-one was surprised, for example, that trade unions were represented on the government's two main bodies for setting economic policy: the National Economic Development Council (Neddy), set up in 1962, and the National Incomes Commission (Nicky), formed in 1961. Union leaders were regarded as important politicians.

Militancy

During the 1950s, the unions had tended to co-operate with government and employers to improve their members' situation. In the 1960s, co-operation was increasingly replaced by militancy. (Militant means warlike or aggressive.)

For example, in earlier decades a strike had been seen as a measure of last resort – to be undertaken when all negotiation had failed. During the 1960s, it was increasingly seen as the first weapon. Even workers who previously would not have dreamed of striking, such as nurses and bank clerks, went on strike. More worrying still was a trend towards unofficial 'lightning' strikes, in which local officials suddenly called their members out on strike, without the approval of their union and without any advance warning, over what sometimes seemed to be quite trivial disputes. Source 24 shows how the number of strikes rose. In 1970, over 10 million working days were lost through strike action, which became known as 'the British disease'.

The reasons behind the rise in strikes were complex, as you will see, but one core problem was inflation. Britain's economic growth led to rising prices, which in turn fuelled wage demands: workers (quite reasonably) expected their wages to rise more quickly than prices. Lightning strikes were the quickest way to achieve a pay rise. In a high inflation climate employers could cover the extra wage costs by raising their prices. However, raised prices fuelled further wage demands, and so it went on, in a vicious circle of inflation.

Most people agreed that inflation was a bad thing. But union leaders could not stop inflation, nor could successive Labour and Conservative governments. Increasingly, governments were also powerless in their dealings with the unions. They could not work with the unions, but nor could they curb their power, although as you will see from the timeline on pages 296–97 it was not for want of trying.

---

1 Draw a flow diagram to show the factors which led to the unions growing increasingly powerful.

SOURCE **24**

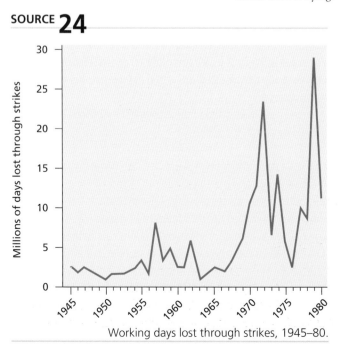

Working days lost through strikes, 1945–80.

SOURCE **25**

Inflation in the 1970s.

SOURCE 26

Mini wages won't buy mini cars

Food Up! Fares Up! Rent Up! What about wages?

Slogans from striking car workers' banners, 1977.

SOURCE 27

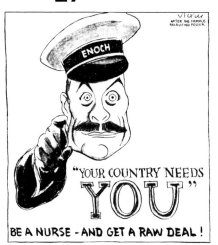

A cartoonist in the 1960s shows nurses' discontent with government policy. The caricature is of Enoch Powell, then Minister of Health.

SOURCE 28

Bank clerks on a picket line in 1967.

ACTIVITY

You are the British correspondent for a European newspaper in the 1970s. Choose one of Sources 26–28. Write a 100-word report to go with it, explaining what Britain's industrial relations are like.

Government action on the unions, 1964–79

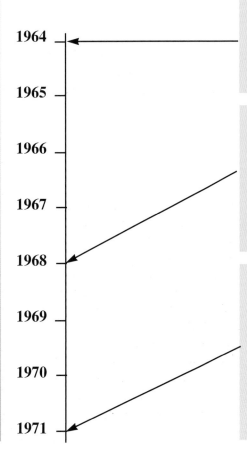

1964
1965
1966
1967
1968
1969
1970
1971

The Prices and Income Act

Labour won the general election of 1964. Harold Wilson quickly passed the Prices and Incomes Act. The idea was that all wage and price rises had to be approved by a National Board for Prices. In practice, the idea was unworkable.

'In Place of Strife'

In 1968, the Labour Employment Minister, Barbara Castle, wrote a paper called *In Place of Strife*. She suggested ballots before strikes and a 28-day cooling-off period before industrial action was taken. Her aim was to stop the unofficial strikes and lightning strikes which stopped production without notice.

The TUC rejected the idea and pressurised Wilson into scrapping it by threatening to withdraw the unions' financial support from Labour.

The Industrial Relations Act

In 1971, a new Conservative government was elected under Edward Heath. It was determined to tackle union power, and passed the 1971 Industrial Relations Act. This Act outlawed the closed shop and made ballots before strikes compulsory. Finally, the Act set up an Industrial Relations Court to judge cases where unions were supposed to have broken an agreement.

The Act was challenged by unions, who saw it as a restriction of their freedom to negotiate. Some employers also criticised it. Heath's relationship with the unions continued to be stormy.

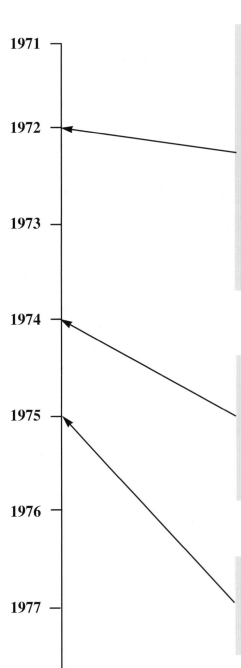

1971

1972

1973

1974

1975

1976

1977

1978

1979

The three-day week

In January 1972, a national coal strike began. Trying to follow Heath's policy of trying to keep wages and inflation down, the National Coal Board offered the miners an eight per cent pay rise. The miners wanted double this.

The miners' strike was solid. By using 'flying pickets' (men who moved from one site to another), they prevented the movement of coal to power stations. Bad weather helped the miners' cause, and soon the generation of electricity was being disrupted. To make matters worse, the country was also facing oil shortages, because of disputes in the Middle East. To conserve supplies, all industry in Britain was limited to three days of energy per week. There were regular power cuts. For ordinary people, this meant spending every other night in houses lit by candlelight and without television, kettles or any electric appliance.

After six weeks, the miners won a complete victory. They squeezed over £116 million pounds from their employers, and the average miner's earnings rose between 17 and 24 per cent.

The Social Contract

The miners' victory was a disaster for Edward Heath and the Conservative government. In 1974 he called and lost a general election, and was replaced by a Labour government under Harold Wilson.

Wilson made an agreement with the unions called the Social Contract. The new government scrapped the Industrial Relations Act and increased pensions and child allowances. In return, the TUC tried to keep wage demands down. It was not a success.

ACAS

Wilson also set up ACAS, the Advisory and Conciliation Service, to help resolve industrial disputes by negotiation, and so prevent strikes. It was quite successful: in 1975 alone, it helped to resolve 2,500 disputes. However, it did not succeed in holding down wages.

The 'winter of discontent'

The Labour government was now as concerned as the Conservatives before it by what seemed to be irresponsible demands by certain unions. Increasing prices and wage demands were forming a vicious circle, each leading to the other, and together they were profoundly damaging Britain's economy. Unemployment was rising.

A new Labour Prime Minister, James Callaghan, took over in 1976. By this time, the government was in serious financial trouble and had to cut back on public spending. This brought it into conflict with the unions, particularly the public-sector unions. In 1978 and 1979, Callaghan was faced with strikes by teachers, health workers and local government workers, and there was also the prospect of a new pay demand from the miners. This was known as the 'winter of discontent', and it forced Callaghan to call another election. Most of the electorate, and many trade unionists, were fed up with Labour policies on unions and wanted a government which would control the extremists. The Conservatives had a new leader, Margaret Thatcher, who promised to do exactly that, and they won the election.

1 Mark each of the events mentioned in the headings in the text above on your own copy of Source 24.

2 Which of the events or developments during the period 1964–79 would you regard as successes for the government, and which as failures?

1 What is the message of Source 29?

2 What were the main differences between Labour and Conservative policies on the unions during this period?

SOURCE 29

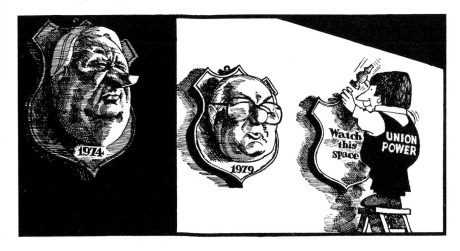

A cartoon from the *Observer*, 6 May 1979. *The Observer* was not as anti-union as much of the press was at the time. The first two trophy heads are Edward Heath and James Callaghan.

SOURCE 30

Industry after industry is swamped by the swelling waters of strikes and violence, with Britain's export trade especially affected. Union leaders are rejected by their men, who turn instead to the nearest agitator.

From the *Spectator*, 27 October 1964.

FOCUS TASK

WHAT FACTORS CONTRIBUTED TO MILITANCY IN THE 1960S AND 1970S?

1 Copy the memo headings in the cartoon below into your book. List the factors which caused militancy under the appropriate heading. Some factors may appear twice.

2 Write a 250-word essay explaining why trade unions became more militant in this period. Use the headings in the diagram as topics for paragraphs.

Were the shop stewards to blame for increased militancy?

Shop stewards were the union representative in a workplace. Often they were elected by fellow workers. Shop stewards held great influence within their own place of work, and many people at the time blamed them for increased militancy (see Source 30). They were the people who called local, unofficial strikes without notice.

Critics of trade unions saw shop stewards as dangerous radicals trying to stir up trouble. Their supporters saw them as the eyes and ears of the union movement, able to spot instantly when an employer was breaking a workplace agreement or trying to undermine wages.

For example, to protect their members' jobs, many unions had negotiated strict rules about 'demarcation', or who could do what work. They did not want an employer trying to save money by paying an unskilled worker to do a job that really needed years of training. When these demarcation rules were broken, the shop steward was the one to take action. Sometimes, whole factories were called out on strike because a worker was asked by management to do something that was not officially part of his or her job. If we look back over union history, we can see that shop stewards acted in this way because employers had generally tended to undercut the job security of workers. At the same time, however, these restrictive practices frustrated employers.

Shop stewards received a very bad press, particularly from the anti-union newspapers, and incidents were exaggerated both by newspapers and by films of the time. However, there is no doubting the power of the shop stewards. They were particularly influential in large industries, especially the natonalised industries. In the 1970s, one of the most famous (or infamous) was 'Red Robbo', a shop steward at British Leyland, the government-owned car manufacturer. This ordinary shop-floor worker was often featured on the daily news for his latest action. He was criticised by newspapers, which carried stories of his negotiations on the length of 'toilet breaks', or accused him of rigging votes at union meetings. It is certainly true that he had the power to call his workers out on strike at a moment's notice, quickly bringing the entire works to a standstill.

It seemed to many critics that shop stewards rather than employers controlled the workplace, and that the unions were blocking industrial progress. Employers were hemmed in by the unions' restrictive practices such as the closed shop and demarcation.

Why has the role of trade unions changed since 1979?

In the 1990s, trade unions play a much less prominent part in British life than they did in 1979. The Labour Party is tied far less closely to the TUC. The TUC itself is more moderate, and the influence of the more militant unions has been greatly reduced. The National Union of Mineworkers is a fraction of its size in 1979. In fact, the membership of trade unions as a whole may have fallen by as much as five million between 1979 and 1993. The proportion of workers who belong to unions has also fallen, from over 50 per cent in 1979 to a little over 30 per cent in 1995. What has led to this decline? Let us examine three factors.

Factor 1: Anti-union legislation since 1979

Shortly before the election of 1979, the Conservative leader, Margaret Thatcher, made it clear that she intended to tackle the unions if elected (see Source 31).

One of the new government's first moves was to introduce the Employment Act of 1980. It concentrated on the aspects of trade union activity which the public disliked most. Flying pickets were banned and closed shop agreements were restricted. The government also made money available for secret ballots, rather than voting by show of hands; it believed that this would give more influence to moderate unionists. A further Act of 1982 said that unions could be fined heavily for unlawful strikes. The Act also increased penalties for secondary picketing and gave compensation to workers who lost their jobs because they refused to join unions.

Despite this legislation, the Thatcher government suffered some early setbacks in its battle against the unions. In 1981, it was forced to continue to pay subsidies to Welsh coal. It also had to continue subsidies to British Rail because of a strike by ASLEF, the train drivers' union. On the other hand, the government completely excluded the unions from any role in economic planning. Early setbacks also strengthened Margaret Thatcher's resolve to 'beat' the unions.

A strike by the printers' union, the NGA, in December 1983 was defeated. The printers had been blocking the introduction of new technology, which would make many of them redundant, but after a short, bitter struggle the NGA was defeated, and the union was heavily fined. By 1984, the government felt strong enough to pass a Trade Union Act: unions now had to hold a secret ballot before any strikes. This was a further attempt to destroy the power of militant activists. Ballots also had to be held to confirm that members wanted to pay money into a political fund (which went to the Labour Party). Trade union officials had to be elected every five years.

Factor 2: The miners' strike

The greatest and most decisive battle with the unions was fought against Arthur Scargill's National Union of Mineworkers (NUM) in 1984–85. This began when the National Coal Board Chairman, Ian MacGregor, announced that many coal mines would have to close to make the industry profitable. It was a long and bitter struggle, but the NUM had met its match. The winter was mild, which reduced demand for coal, and in any case coal was no longer a key industry. Scargill had little support from other unions, and was criticised by the media, not least because he refused to hold a strike ballot which was now a legal requirement under the Trade Union Act.

The tactics which had worked so well for the miners in 1972 failed this time. Many miners in Nottinghamshire and Leicestershire refused to strike, and thousands of police were needed to protect them from other miners trying to prevent them from working. The police set up special intelligence services to monitor and intercept the flying pickets. Coal was imported from many different countries.

The government was determined to win, at any cost. In fact, the estimated cost was around

SOURCE 31

You see, what some unions are doing is ridiculous. It's absurd. One of the things which has knocked the country very badly is its record for unofficial strikes. Wherever I go abroad, they say the same thing, 'Stop all those strikes and we'll buy your goods'.

From a speech by Margaret Thatcher in 1979.

SOURCE 32

In no other country in Europe have unions had to face such hostility from their government ... In recent years the trade union's collective voice has either been silenced or gone unheeded over a wide area of government policy making.

An extract from *The Future of Trade Unions* by Robert Taylor, 1994.

SOURCE 33

If nothing else, the dispute did one thing for us all. It demonstrated that the power of the union movement ... is above neither that of government or of the law. It is as recent as 1979 that a government (for the second time in a decade) was brought down, effectively because of opposition to it. The miners' strike of 1984–5 showed us that it is possible to resist a determined effort to bring about the downfall of a government by the mere flexing of industrial muscle.

A description of the significance of the miners' strike by Ian MacGregor.

£8 billion, but Mrs Thatcher believed this money was well spent, as did the National Coal Board Chairman, Ian MacGregor.

Membership of the NUM fell to 60,000 by the end of 1989. In fact, the power of the entire union movement had been broken by the government, and for the most part this had public support.

Factor 3: Economic change since 1979

Some historians believe that changing economic conditions have played an even more important role in reducing the power and influence of the unions. When the Conservatives came to power in 1979, one of their priorities was to reduce inflation. This was achieved through strict economic controls and cuts in government spending, which in turn increased unemployment to record levels.

Britain's economy has changed during the 1980s and 1990s, and so has the workforce. A House of Commons investigation concluded that trade unions have not adapted well to the new conditions. High levels of unemployment always affect unions, and unionists have argued that many employers still remain hostile to trade unions. Many jobs now involve flexible working arrangements, such as job sharing and part-time work, much of which is carried out by women, who are less inclined to join unions. They tend to see unions as irrelevant to their interests and needs, and as predominantly 'male' organisations.

Although unions have retained their strength in the PUBLIC SECTOR, this sector is now much less important because the major publicly owned industries have been privatised. In the PRIVATE SECTOR, where there have been increasing numbers of no-strike agreements, unions have become much weaker. All of these factors have diminished the core role of the trade union, which is to represent workers.

SOURCE 34

[In 1982] … what was really neutralising the power of the unions was the growing economic crisis and resultant unemployment. The number of strikes fell dramatically … Union membership had fallen … The TUC itself, and especially Len Murray, repeatedly threw its influence … against militancy and against challenging the government through industrial action.

From *The People's Peace* by Kenneth Morgan.

SOURCE 36

Britain's trade unions face a serious challenge arising from the sharp decline in the level of membership and in the extent to which unions can still exercise their traditional core function of collective bargaining …

… trade unions need to make more effort to adapt to the needs of workers in the private sector …

The new flexibility in the workforce is an inevitable development … but we note that unions have not been successful in appealing to this new workforce …

The Committee welcomes the recognition among the major trade unions that the interests of their members are closely linked to the performance of the enterprise …

Some conclusions of the House of Commons Employment Committee Report, 1994.

SOURCE 35

Trade union membership

Government policy: *cutting inflation, reducing public spending, forcing local government to cut spending. This increases unemployment.*

Changing workforce: *increasing number of women workers, many part time or job sharing, who do not see unions as relevant or welcoming to them.*

Working practices: *increasingly, industries require workers to be flexible, making the role of a union representing one type of worker less relevant.*

Investment: *government has worked hard to get overseas companies to build factories in the UK. They insist on single union agreements, demand flexible working practices and use new technology.*

A summary of economic changes in the 1980s and 1990s and their impact on unions.

FOCUS TASK

WHY HAVE UNIONS BECOME LESS POWERFUL SINCE 1979?

You have been commissioned to write a report for a major Korean company. The company is thinking of building a number of factories and showrooms in Britain, but is concerned about the reputation of British trade unions. The local MP has told the company that unions are not as powerful as they were in the 1970s.

Your task is to explain how and why unions are no longer as powerful as they were. Divide your report into four sections:

- **The ways in which anti-union legislation since 1979 has limited union power**
- **The ways in which the miners' strike of 1984–85 limited union power**
- **The ways in which economic conditions have limited union power**
- **Your conclusions: which of these two factors has been more important, and why**

SECTION 6

An age of progress?

11 Medicine, surgery and health 1750–1990

11.1 How good was medical knowledge and understanding in the second half of the eighteenth century?

FOCUS

Like many other areas of scientific and technological development, medicine and surgery made rapid progress in the nineteenth and twentieth centuries. New drugs, techniques and methods of organisation helped to improve Britain's health.

11.1 looks at medicine before 1800.

- You will examine the state of medical knowledge at that time.
- You will look at improvements such as vaccination.

11.2 covers the nineteenth century.

- You will investigate the work of scientists such as Pasteur and the impact of their work.
- You will study advances in surgery and the effects of improvements made in hospitals.

11.3 looks at changes that have occurred during the twentieth century.

- You will study improvements in drugs and the impact of diet and vaccination on public health.
- You will investigate why the NHS was set up and evaluate its effectiveness.

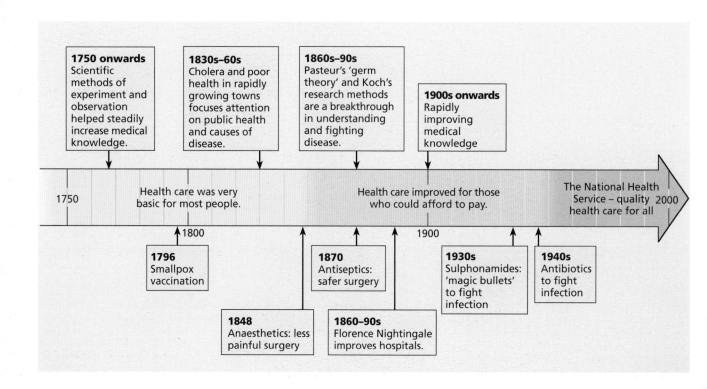

1750 onwards Scientific methods of experiment and observation helped steadily increase medical knowledge.

1830s–60s Cholera and poor health in rapidly growing towns focuses attention on public health and causes of disease.

1860s–90s Pasteur's 'germ theory' and Koch's research methods are a breakthrough in understanding and fighting disease.

1900s onwards Rapidly improving medical knowledge

1750

Health care was very basic for most people.

Health care improved for those who could afford to pay.

The National Health Service – quality health care for all   2000

1800

1796 Smallpox vaccination

1870 Antiseptics: safer surgery

1900

1930s Sulphonamides: 'magic bullets' to fight infection

1940s Antibiotics to fight infection

1848 Anaesthetics: less painful surgery

1860–90s Florence Nightingale improves hospitals.

Medicine in 1750

Medicine in the eighteenth century was primitive by today's standards. Infectious diseases, particularly smallpox – a disease which has been wiped out in Britain today – were killers on a huge scale. In 1796, it was estimated that an outbreak of smallpox killed one in five of the population.

There were no effective anaesthetics or antiseptics. Under surgery, patients often died from shock, blood poisoning or other infections.

Infant mortality was appalling. Many children died before reaching two years of age.

The medical profession

Medicine was practised by physicians and surgeons, while apothecaries mixed and made drugs. There was a good deal of rivalry between these groups, and each was prevented from trespassing on the work of the others. Surgeons operated on the outside of the body (injuries), and physicians treated the inside (diseases). Physicians gained their knowledge from books rather than from experience with patients. Training for all of these branches of medicine was extremely variable.

Treatments

Nobody, including doctors, understood the causes of diseases. It was widely believed that diseases were caused by impurities in the blood or by bad fluids or poisons in the system. Doctors clung to the 2,000-year-old belief that the body contained different 'humours', which needed to be brought back into balance. Treatments were based on these assumptions, and often involved letting blood or giving drugs to cause vomiting (purging).

SOURCE 1

1 What treatments are shown by Sources 1 and 2?

2 Sources 1 and 2 are clearly exaggerated views of events. How can you tell this?

3 Despite this, are they still useful to an historian?

SOURCE 2

An illustration from 1793 by Thomas Rowlandson, supposedly showing an operation.

'The quack doctor', an illustration from 1814 criticising some of the medical treatments of the time.

Were medical knowledge and treatment improving?

By the end of the eighteenth century, some important changes were being made. A new generation of doctors began to improve medical understanding. These men used scientific methods to observe and record what they saw.

The Monros and Scottish medicine

In the seventeenth century, the leading scholars of medicine worked in the universities of northern Europe, but during the eighteenth century the balance began to change, and Scotland became increasingly important as a centre of medical excellence.

In the 1720s, a father, son and grandson, all called Alexander Monro, taught at the University of Edinburgh. Their students would attend lectures from early morning until late at night, and studied chemistry, anatomy, midwifery and many other disciplines. Training at Edinburgh was particularly good because the university medical school had its own infirmary, where people were treated for real illnesses. Many eighteenth-century doctors qualified without ever seeing a patient! One Edinburgh pupil, William Cullen, went on to found the Glasgow Medical School, where one of his innovations was to teach in English rather than Latin.

In 1793, another Scot, Matthew Baillie, published a magnificently illustrated work called *Morbid Anatomy*, which helped surgeons and doctors. In 1795, Dr Gordon of Aberdeen showed through careful and painstaking research that puerperal fever, a form of blood poisoning which killed many women after childbirth, 'seized only women who were delivered by a practitioner or nurse who had previously attended patients affected with the disease'. He admitted that he himself must have unwittingly passed on the fatal infection to many women.

Military medicine

For a 60-year period beginning in the mid-eighteenth century, the British army and navy faced a series of major wars. Military medicine was an important area for testing and developing new ideas.

The army surgeon John Pringle noticed how certain diseases seemed to be connected with climate, time of year and conditions. His ideas were taken up by the navy, including the famous naval explorer Captain Cook, who was an enthusiastic supporter of Pringle's views. Although his sailors grumbled, they were forced to wash themselves and their clothes frequently, scrub the decks on a regular basis, and clear away refuse and rubbish. During a three-year voyage (1772–75), only one of Cook's men died from sickness. Pringle also persuaded the army to clean up barracks and tackle the problem of damp and filth.

Another Scottish surgeon, James Lind, shared Pringle's views. Lind began his career as a surgeon's mate in the navy. Once he qualified as a doctor, he became surgeon at the naval hospital at Haslar. His essays on sailors' health helped the fight against typhus in the navy. Lind also discovered that eating fresh fruits could prevent or cure scurvy.

Both Pringle and Lind used their experience to work out successful ways of fighting disease. Even so, they did not fully understand what caused it or how it worked on the body.

William Hunter

In 1770, William Hunter set up a school of anatomy in Great Windmill Street in London. He taught many students, including Matthew Bailie (see above). He also collected specimens – bones and preserved organs and tissues – vital for students' understanding of the body.

One of Hunter's achievements was to establish obstetrics (the care of women in childbirth) as a branch of medicine in its own right. William Hunter and his partner William Smellie set up new ways of training doctors and midwives in obstetrics. The death rate among mothers and newborns in London fell noticeably.

SOURCE 3

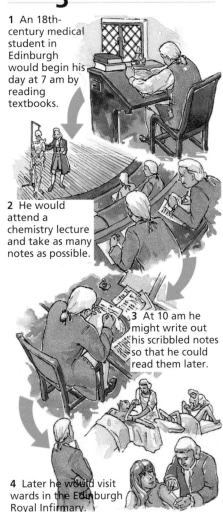

1 An 18th-century medical student in Edinburgh would begin his day at 7 am by reading textbooks.

2 He would attend a chemistry lecture and take as many notes as possible.

3 At 10 am he might write out his scribbled notes so that he could read them later.

4 Later he would visit wards in the Edinburgh Royal Infirmary.

The Edinburgh University School of Medicine training method.

SOURCE 4

The medical pioneer John Hunter, 1728–93.

John Hunter

William's brother John was even more famous. He made important discoveries about how to treat tendon injuries, inflammation, digestive problems and countless other disorders. He studied human and animal anatomy and put together a collection of over 13,000 specimens, which was bought by the government after his death. Hunter rose to become surgeon at St George's Hospital in 1768, chief army surgeon in 1790 and surgeon to the King from 1776.

As well as being a highly skilful surgeon, he was also important for his use of scientific methods. He dissected animals and noted how disease had affected organs or limbs. He also studied the blood supply and experimented on the antlers of deer in Richmond Park. From these experiments he improved the treatment of aneurysms (swollen arteries), which until then had been dangerous and usually unsuccessful.

Richard Mead

In 1720, Mead published *A Short Discourse Concerning Pestilential Contagion and the Methods to be Used to Prevent It*. Even at this early date, Mead was recommending measures such as quarantine, demolishing infected houses, cleaning the streets and improving sanitation. Yet almost 150 years later people were still resisting these ideas.

Alternative theories

In the 1760s, John Brown of Edinburgh came up with the theory that diseases were caused by either too much or too little stimulation. Brown's remedy for such diseases was to prescribe alcohol as a stimulant or opiates as sedatives. His ideas were widely adopted. Today we can recognise that using drink and drugs as a remedy for all ills was rather dangerous. In fact, Brown himself was probably killed by abuse of these substances. His ideas were known as the Brunonian Theory.

Another theorist was the German Samuel Hahnemann, who is credited with the invention of homeopathy. Hahnemann spent many long hours in the laboratory, carefully observing diseases and their causes. His detailed research enabled him to work out that some substances, especially extracts of plants, seemed to be connected with particular diseases and illnesses. As a result of his observations, Hahnemann believed that giving tiny doses of substances which caused the symptoms of diseases would help the body to fight off disease. Hahnemann had some notable successes with his ideas, but opinions were deeply divided about Hahnemann's theory; indeed, homeopathy is still a subject that divides doctors today. Some regard it as a scientific method, others as bogus and unscientific.

Medical historians also find it difficult to judge the effectiveness of Brown's and Hahnemann's theories. They had some success, but many people believe that this was because they rejected purging and bleeding, which actually weakened patients.

Was medical care the same for all classes?

The answer to this question is a resounding no. Even the imperfect skills of doctors such as those on pages 303–05 were available only to the better-off. There was no National Health Service or health insurance, and doctors' fees were notoriously expensive. The cartoonist George Cruikshank (Source 5), for example, had little respect for doctors and often criticised the conditions in which poor people lived.

These criticisms were not entirely fair. As we have seen, James Lind and John Pringle did excellent work promoting the health of the ordinary men in the armed forces. The prison reformer John Howard gained help and advice from Pringle on fighting typhus in Britain's prisons and for his book *The State of the Prisons in England and Wales*, which was published in 1771.

In 1795, Manchester doctors formed the Manchester Board of Health, which tried to persuade local authorities to do more about cleaning the areas where the poor lived. A number of charitable hospitals offered free or low-cost medical treatment. From the 1740s onwards, there were dispensaries which handed out free medicines to the poor.

On the whole, however, these were the exceptions. For most poor people, health care was limited and basic.

Apothecaries

Many of the poor would visit apothecaries. They mixed and dispensed drugs. However, poor people would also go to them to have illnesses diagnosed, as there was no extra charge for this. As with doctors, apothecaries varied in their honesty and skill. There were undoubtedly bad apothecaries, but at the other end of the scale the apothecary William Allen was an extremely able scientist; he became the first president of the Pharmaceutical Society. In 1792, he took over the long-established Bevan's apothecary shop in Old Plough Court. This developed into a large business, Allen and Hanbury's, which prospered until 1958, when it merged with the pharmaceutical giant Glaxo.

SOURCE 5

A Cruikshank cartoon from the 1830s entitled 'Cholera Pie'.

1 What point is the cartoonist making in Source 5?

SOURCE 6

William Allen's membership certificate of the Pharmaceutical Society. Round the top of the illustration are the herbs and plants which the apothecary used. At the bottom are the apothecary's tools and methods. The figures are Avicenna and Galen, two of the most famous doctors in history.

SOURCE 7

I hope I shall always endeavour to vend good drugs and genuine medicines and I intend to be properly paid for them … I would rather decline having my products brought into an improper comparison with those traders in medicine whose only maxim seems to be to sell things cheap.

Written by JG Bevan, whose business was taken over by William Allen.

SOURCE **8**

She had been out all day in the fields gathering wild herbs and medicines, for in addition to her invaluable qualities as a sick nurse and her worldly occupation as a washer woman, she added considerable knowledge of hedge and field simples [cures].

A description of Alice Wilson from *Mary Barton* by Elizabeth Gaskell, 1848.

Wise women

Many poor people did not even visit the apothecary. Even in the mid-nineteenth century, people in the countryside still consulted local wise women. Such women grew healing herbs, which they made into cures using recipes handed down from one generation to the next. Most people also had their own family remedies.

People went to wise women and used herbal medicines for several reasons. Doctors were too expensive, and in any case many people did not trust them: their success rates were certainly not always encouraging. When free services were provided by local parishes, poor people were sometimes too ashamed to use them.

Hospitals

Today we think of hospitals as places in which to get well. In the 1700s they were places where you went to die. The worst nightmare for many people was to end up in hospital. The wealthy avoided hospitals at all costs. Statistically, patients who were operated on at home had a much better chance of surviving than those who were treated in hospital. Hospitals were notorious as places where patients picked up worse illnesses than those with which they went in. There was no segregation of patients, which meant that a patient with a broken limb, one with a highly infectious fever and a woman in labour might all be found in the same ward. Because nobody yet knew about bacteria, infection was a common problem, and might actually be transmitted by the doctor. Without doubt, the worst of the hospitals were the parish workhouse hospitals. Little or no specialised care was available in workhouses, and the sick and mentally ill were simply left to die.

In the late eighteenth century, nursing was widely regarded as a disreputable profession. Most nurses were untrained and unqualified, and an alarming number were drunkards or even prostitutes. There were exceptions, and able nurses could be found, but they worked mainly in the better hospitals which were run by charities or the Church. Private nurses were also employed by wealthy families in their homes to care for invalids. You will investigate hospitals and nursing in more detail on page 320.

SOURCE **9**

Filth was everywhere. The patients wore the same clothes for seven weeks. Some patients slept two to a bed. Bedding was washed and changed once a month. Food was at starvation level. Alcoholic drink was brought into the hospital quite freely. All the windows were kept shut and as the ward was very crowded, the smell was most unpleasant.

A visitor's description of a hospital in around 1800.

FOCUS TASK

WAS MEDICAL CARE THE SAME FOR ALL CLASSES?

The year is 1810. The leading doctors of a large industrial town are planning to form a Board of Health, following Manchester's example in 1795. They have asked you to carry out a survey of medical treatment available to all classes and report back to them.

   Use the evidence and information on pages 306–07 to report back. Your report should mention:

- **recent developments in medical knowledge.**
- **treatment available to the poor.**
- **variations in the quality of hospitals.**
- **nursing.**

You may also wish to make some recommendations to the Board.

How important was Jenner's work in the fight against smallpox?

A smallpox victim who has survived the disease examines the scars on his face. This engraving was made in the 1820s. The presence of a servant and a doctor suggests that the patient is not poor.

> **1 Why was smallpox such a terrifying disease?**

In the eighteenth century, smallpox was one of the most dreaded diseases. It killed and maimed many people, including the rich – even a queen of England died from it. But, as in most aspects of health, the poor were worst affected by smallpox. One doctor has estimated that smallpox killed 40,000 people every year in the period 1750–1800, a total of 200,000 victims. Once smallpox hit a town or village, it could spread like wildfire. It was passed on by contact with an infected person, and young infants were particularly vulnerable.

Once infected, the victim suffered fever and headaches. After about four days, a rash developed on the face, palms and soles of the feet. In another week, the rash turned into blisters and pustules. The disease was often fatal, but those who survived it could be left blind or deaf, and most of them were scarred with pock marks.

Early treatment: inoculation

Lady Mary Wortley Montagu was the wife of the British Ambassador in Turkey. While she was there, she saw young Turkish children being inoculated against smallpox. This involved inserting pus from a smallpox spot into a small scratch on the child's skin. The result was that the child suffered a minor dose of smallpox and was then immune to the full version of the disease.

Lady Mary brought the method back to England in the 1720s and met with approval from the Royal College of Physicians. Unfortunately, inoculation was not a complete success. In some areas, it seemed to spread the disease more quickly. To combat this, doctors set up 'inoculation stables'. Children were herded into these stables, often in very poor conditions. They were given the mild version of the disease and quarantined until the infectious period was over. If the treatment was successful, the children were then immune to smallpox, but it was extremely risky. The danger of contracting full smallpox was very real, and many children suffered the blinding or crippling effects of smallpox as a result of inoculation. Edward Jenner, the man who conquered smallpox, was himself inoculated as a child, and as a result suffered from a hearing problem throughout his life. Although inoculation could be effective, it is likely that it helped to keep smallpox alive in Britain even after Jenner developed vaccination.

Edward Jenner and vaccination

Edward Jenner was born in Berkeley, Gloucestershire, in 1749. As a boy, he studied nature keenly, and at the age of 13 he became an apprentice to the surgeon Daniel Ludlow in Sodbury. During his apprenticeship, he became all too familiar with smallpox, as he was called on to perform inoculations. He also observed a strange phenomenon: inoculation did not have any effect on certain people, such as milkmaids, who had previously had a mild disease called cowpox (which was caught from cows). This fact was known to many ordinary country people and to some doctors, but was dismissed as unscientific and superstitious nonsense.

Jenner ended his apprenticeship at the age of 20, and then became a student and friend of John Hunter. You have already seen (on page 305) that Hunter's success was based on his careful scientific observations and experiments. Jenner was heavily influenced by Hunter's methods and ideas. In 1773, he returned to Berkeley as a village doctor, but he did not lose interest in his studies or in smallpox, which he continued to research. He came to the conclusion that inoculation with cowpox pus rather than smallpox pus would be just as effective and much less dangerous. By 1796, he felt confident enough to try out his ideas, and thanks to his scientific training and methods historians have a full account of his thinking and the steps he took.

> **2 If you were an eighteenth-century parent would you have had your child inoculated? Explain your answer.**

ACTIVITY

Draw a diagram for Jenner's report explaining how to perform a vaccination.

SOURCE 11

Jenner's drawing of the milkmaid Sarah Nelmes's arm.

His source for the cowpox pus was Sarah Nelmes, a milkmaid suffering from the disease. He took some pus from a sore on Sarah's hand. On 14 May 1796, he used that pus to give an eight-year-old boy, James Phipps, a dose of cowpox. After allowing the cowpox to pass its course, Jenner then carried out the usual smallpox inoculation on James on 1 July. The boy showed no sign of developing the disease at all. Jenner had discovered a safe method of inoculating against smallpox. He called it vaccination, after the Latin for cow, *vacca*.

After more tests, he wrote up his ideas: he was sure they worked, although in fact he had no idea how. What we know now is that the cowpox virus is similar to smallpox. The cowpox virus made the body manufacture antibodies, its defences against disease. These defences also worked against smallpox.

Like other medical pioneers, Jenner met with great opposition. Dr William Woodville of the Smallpox Hospital in London was a bitter critic of vaccination. Other doctors claimed that the vaccine did not work, while stories were also circulated that cowpox itself could be fatal. Jenner had to pay for his work to be published, as no journal would take it.

SOURCE 12

Brickbats and hostile weapons of every sort are flying thick around me ... I am beset on all sides by snarling fellows.

Jenner's comment on his opponents.

3 What point is the cartoonist making in Source 13?

SOURCE 13

The Cow-Pock – or – the Wonderful Effects of the New Inoculation! – Vide. the Publications of ye Anti-Vaccine Society.

A late eighteenth-century cartoon by James Gillray.

Once Jenner's work was published, most doctors accepted his findings. Rather than patenting his ideas to make money from them, he made his information available to all. Parliament granted him £10,000 in 1802 in recognition of his work and £20,000 at a later date. However, Jenner spent the last 20 years of his life quietly in Berkeley.

The impact of his discovery was felt everywhere. Once the poor were sure about vaccination, they flocked to physicians to have it carried out. By 1801, vaccination had spread all over the world. A smallpox vaccination kit was a standard part of all doctors' equipment. In 1853, the British government made vaccination compulsory, although this order was not strictly enforced.

Smallpox was not entirely conquered. There was a serious outbreak of smallpox in London in 1871, and after that date the government strictly enforced compulsory vaccination. Even so, Jenner's name was widely revered. One story tells that during the French wars Napoleon held two colleagues of Jenner in Geneva. Napolean refused to release them at first, but when Jenner wrote to him he agreed at once!

SOURCE 14

A doctor in the East End of London carrying out vaccinations on the poor.

SOURCE 15

New Discovery Respecting Inoculation

Inoculation, which has been found so highly beneficial in preserving the human species from the ravages of SMALL POX, has been recently very much improved. The custom of communicating the infection by taking it from the patients who laboured under it is now beginning to be abandoned by a great number of Surgeons in the metropolis. The Cow Pox has been found to supply the infection in a most favourable way to those who are inoculated. It is taken from the nipples of the cows, and the communication of it to the patient is uniformly attended with the happiest effects.

From *The Times*, November 1798.

FOCUS TASK

DID MEDICINE AND SURGERY ADVANCE BETWEEN 1700 AND 1800?

Look back at this section and write a 'school report' on the medical profession during this period. You should report on progress made in:

- understanding disease.
- treating disease.
- surgery.
- access to medical care for all.

For each area give the profession a grade A–E and a comment.

FOCUS TASK

HOW IMPORTANT WAS EDWARD JENNER'S WORK?

The year is 1979. The World Health Organisation has just announced that the smallpox virus is officially extinct. To celebrate this good news, produce a tribute to Edward Jenner and his contribution to the elimination of the disease. You should mention:

- why smallpox was so feared in the 1700s.
- Jenner's training.
- the treatment of smallpox before Jenner.
- how Jenner developed vaccination.
- how his ideas spread.

You should present your work as either an obituary tribute or a wallchart for young pupils.

Why did medicine and surgery advance in the nineteenth century?

The problem of disease

1 Draw a timeline from 1822 to 1905. Label the area above the line Pasteur, and below the line Koch. As you read pages 309–11 note details about their work on to the timeline.

2 When was the real breakthrough in the fight against disease? Explain why you would choose that date.

Despite the victory over smallpox, other diseases were if anything becoming more of a problem during the nineteenth century, particularly for those living in Britain's filthy towns and cities (see page 192). Edwin Chadwick's research revealed that the average age at death of a Liverpool labourer was 17 years – half that of a labourer in rural Rutland. Over the next eight pages, you are going to investigate how different doctors and scientists played their part in conquering the problems of disease.

What caused disease?

In the early nineteenth century, people still did not know that germs spread disease. However, common sense and observation of patterns of disease made doctors and scientists increasingly sure that disease had something to do with dirt. The dominant theory was that disease spread by means of 'miasma', or bad smells. This theory was close enough to the truth to help a little in the fight against disease. When epidemics of cholera hit towns, filth was cleared away, removing many germs – although, as you saw on page 200, they were sometimes disastrously reintroduced through the water supply!

Important steps forward were taken by a London doctor, John Snow, who proved that cholera did not spread through bad air but through polluted water (see page 202). However, neither Snow nor any other doctors at the time could explain how polluted water causes disease. It was in this area that the French scientist Louis Pasteur and the German Robert Koch made vital contributions.

Louis Pasteur

Since the development of an improved microscope in the early nineteenth century, many scientists had become interested in the study of micro-organisms. Louis Pasteur was among them. His experiments, using microscopes to examine fermenting liquids and other materials, showed that micro-organisms were everywhere: in food, in drink, even in the air, although significantly they were rarer in mountain air and more common in towns. They were particularly numerous in decaying matter. Pasteur was particularly interested in this link between micro-organisms and decay.

As a leading scientist, he was asked to advise the French wine industry on how to prevent fermenting grapes going rotten. Pasteur investigated the fermentation process. He formed a theory that one type of micro-organism was causing the fermentation to stop or go bad. Pasteur demonstrated that heating the liquid to about 60 degrees centigrade and then sealing the container to keep out this harmful micro-organism solved the problem. This process became known as pasteurisation and is used throughout the food industry today, especially for milk.

In the 1860s, Pasteur responded to a similar appeal from the French silk industry. Silkworms were being decimated by a disease called pebrine. Pasteur showed that micro-organisms in diseased eggs were the cause of the spreading infection. By isolating healthy eggs and breeding from them, silk merchants were able to preserve the industry.

Germ theory

Pasteur published his germ theory in 1861. This suggested that disease was caused when bacteria or germs entered the body and grew inside it – just as when a fermentation goes bad.

PROFILE

Louis Pasteur

★ Born at Dole in France in 1822.
★ Went to university in Paris.
★ Published his germ theory in 1861.
★ Became Professor of Chemistry at the Sorbonne University in 1867.
★ His special expertise was in decay and rotting materials and the processes which cause decay.
★ He had a rather unfriendly rivalry with Koch throughout the 1870s and 1880s.
★ In 1888, the Pasteur Institute was founded for the treatment and study of rabies.
★ Died in 1895.

Pasteur's ideas were criticised. New scientific ideas are always slow to spread, even today, because scientists naturally ask for more proof. People found it difficult to believe that something so tiny it was visible only under a microscope could kill a human being. However, he was not discouraged, and continued his research. By the mid 1860s, certain doctors, such as Joseph Lister (see page 316), were acting on Pasteur's findings to make surgery safer.

Other scientists began to work hard to prove or disprove Pasteur's ideas. They took samples of blood or tissue from diseased people and animals and looked for micro-organisms which might be to blame. However, any sample contained many different micro-organisms, and they did not know which was the active one. It was impossible to say for certain that germs cause disease until one germ that caused a particular disease had been identified.

Robert Koch

One disease on which scientists had been working hard was anthrax, and suspicion was settling on one particular germ. At this point in the story, the German doctor Robert Koch became the lead player. Koch devised a method which proved beyond any reasonable doubt that this microbe did cause anthrax. These are the steps he took.

He began by taking organs from infected sheep. From these he extracted the anthrax bacterium, which he then grew. He then injected a mouse with it, and the mouse developed anthrax and died. He took infected matter from that mouse, found the same bacterium, isolated it, grew it and injected it into another mouse. It too contracted the disease. He repeated this in 20 generations of mice. At the end of the process, he still had the same bacterium.

Using the same method, the micro-organisms which caused many common killer diseases could be quickly identified. Koch himself discovered the cause of tuberculosis in 1882. The following year, he was able to isolate the organism responsible for cholera. He also trained others in his techniques, such as Paul Ehrlich, who developed a treatment against diphtheria in 1885. By 1900, a host of disease-causing bacteria were isolated. These included leprosy, typhoid, malaria, pneumonia, tetanus, plague and dysentery.

Finding cures

Pasteur saw himself as a rival of Koch rather than a colleague. Germany and France had only recently been at war, and were still enemies. Pasteur was impressed by Koch's methods, but also felt driven to go one better: to find cures for these diseases.

In 1879, Pasteur had a stroke of luck. During his research into chicken cholera, a solution containing the responsible bacterium was left open to the air. It was then accidentally given to some chickens. The results were totally unexpected. Exposure to the air had weakened the solution, and instead of killing the chickens it made them immune. Pasteur called this a vaccine (in deference to Jenner), even though it had nothing to do with cows. Vaccination became the term for giving a weak form of a disease and letting the body's own defences fight it.

This was the beginning of a period of concentrated work on trying to fight deadly diseases. In 1881, Pasteur felt confident enough to announce a vaccine against anthrax. He held a public experiment, open to the press and of course his critics, using sheep infected with anthrax. He vaccinated half of a flock of sheep, then exposed them all to anthrax. He predicted which sheep would live and which would die with perfect accuracy. His anthrax vaccine worked.

In 1885, Pasteur produced a treatment for another deadly disease, rabies. He discovered that rabies attacked the nervous system. Using the spinal column of infected animals, he produced a serum (blood carrying a weak version of the disease) with which he could treat rabies victims.

Pasteur's contributions were vital in the war against disease because, unlike Jenner, he knew exactly why his treatments worked. He was fortunate in that he was working at the same time as other scientists, particularly Robert Koch. It was Koch's isolation of anthrax that enabled Pasteur to create his vaccine. On the other hand, Koch made much use of Pasteur's ideas, as did the pioneering surgeon Joseph Lister (see pages 316–18).

The significance of Pasteur is not that he had all the answers but that he prompted doctors to ask the right questions and think along the right lines. Pasteur gave doctors the tools to fight disease on a mass scale.

Improving techniques

Robert Koch not only made a huge contribution to finding the causes of disease, he also went on to have a major influence on the development of the first cures.

Koch's second major contribution to the fight against disease was to show how to isolate germs and grow them in a laboratory rather than in a living body. There were several advantages to be gained from this. For example, in order to transport the cowpox vaccine to Argentina, the medical officers had to vaccinate children every 10 days in order to keep the virus alive for the length of the voyage! Koch developed a solid medium for growing 'pure cultures' of micro-organisms. Pasteur and others were still using liquids to grow their cultures.

Once he had perfected this process Koch took it a stage further by developing dyes to stain bacteria. This made them easily visible under the microscope, and it also made it easier for drugs effectively to identify and attack the organisms. We will return to this on page 328.

Why did surgery improve in the nineteenth century?

Surgery in the eighteenth and early nineteenth centuries was very primitive. It was excruciatingly painful, because there were no anaesthetics. Surgery was also risky, because of the very high proportion of patients who died from infection after the operation. Almost the only kind of surgery with any prospect of success was amputation, which was especially common in the army and navy, where limbs were often mangled in battle and smaller wounds became infected or gangrenous. By the nineteenth century, more delicate surgery was possible, thanks to the careful research of John Hunter (see page 305). However, the problem was that surgeons could not really use Hunter's findings unless they could control pain and prevent infection.

Controlling pain: anaesthetics

Surgeons in the early nineteenth century must have had nerves of steel, and their patients must have been desperate. Speed was the most important factor. A good surgeon would amputate a limb in about a minute and tie up the arteries in another minute, so that the patient did not bleed to death. Anything more complicated was impossible, as the patient writhed in agony. Some surgeons gave patients opiates or alcohol, but they had little effect. Even Sir Astley Cooper, one of the most successful early nineteenth-century surgeons, hated the speed and brutality of surgery and wished that he could perform more delicate operations (see Source 2).

1 Read Source 2. Why was Cooper ashamed of his profession?

SOURCE 1

An amputation being performed in the eighteenth century.

SOURCE 2

In cases of operation he would show that its performance, although too often considered by the public as the highest point in surgery, was regarded by the profession as an opprobrium [shame] to the science, being a want of skill in the knowledge and application of efficient remedies for the cure of the disease …

From a biography of Sir Astley Cooper, 1843.

SOURCE 3

[After inhaling ether from a handkerchief] … I speedily lost consciousness and in seven or eight minutes awoke in possession of the greatest discovery that had ever been revealed to humanity.

William Thomas Morton describes his discovery of the effects of ether, 30 September 1846.

SOURCE 4

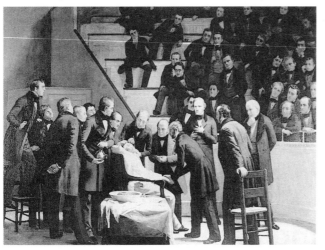

Morton (on the left with his ether) looks on as surgeons remove a neck tumour from a woman he has anaesthetised.

SOURCE 5

[The patient is anaesthetised using ether and therefore does not have to be held down.] He [Liston] then takes from his long, narrow case one of the straight amputating knives of his own invention. It is evidently a favourite instrument, for on the handle are little notches showing the number of times he had used it before. His house-surgeon, Ransome, puts the saw and the artery forceps on to the chair close by, then threads a wisp of well-waxed hemp ligatures through his own buttonhole … The porters are waiting just outside, and the patient is carried in on a stretcher and laid on the table … Liston stands by, trying the edge of his knife against his thumb nail, and the tension increases … Ransome holds the limb. 'Now, gentlemen, time me,' says Liston to the students. The huge left hand grasps the thigh, a thrust of the long straight knife, two or three rapid sawing movements and the upper flap [of skin] is made. Half a dozen strokes and Ransome places the limb in the sawdust. 'Twenty-eight seconds!' says William Squires. The femoral artery is tied with two stout ligatures, a strip of wet lint placed between the flaps and the stump raised.

An observer's description of one of Liston's operations.

It was a long and difficult struggle to improve pain control for patients. In 1799, Sir Humphrey Davy carried out some experiments with the gas nitrous oxide. When used on animals it made them excited. Soon he discovered that it made him laugh, and he invited friends to 'laughing gas' parties. Davy soon realised that his discovery could have serious applications, in controlling pain for surgical patients.

Another technique was hypnosis, which was used with some success in India. The surgeons John Elliotson and James Esdaile actually carried out painless surgery on patients under hypnosis. However, critics of Elliotson, including some leading figures in the medical profession, refused to accept his views. He was accused of being a charlatan and was forced to resign. It was not the first or the last time that a medical pioneer was dismissed by the critics, despite the existence of strong evidence to support his case.

In around 1815, Humphrey Davy's assistant, Michael Faraday, discovered that ether was even more effective as an anaesthetic than nitrous oxide. However, neither Davy nor Faraday was a doctor, and they were therefore unable to conduct any kind of trials or experiments which would convince the medical profession. Nitrous oxide and ether were relegated to use as 'recreational drugs'. Senior doctors found it very difficult to accept that it was possible to carry out surgery without pain, and this probably discouraged even the more adventurous surgeons from experimenting with the new drugs.

In the end, it was medical men not in Britain but in the USA who began to accept the idea of anaesthetics. In 1842, an American surgeon, CW Long, removed a tumour using ether as an anaesthetic. However, even his friends ridiculed him when he told them about the operation, so he kept the development quiet. An American dentist, Horace Wells, used laughing gas when removing teeth after watching a demonstration of the gas at a lecture. In 1846, William Thomas Morton, another American dentist, experimented on himself with ether (Source 3).

Morton was successful in convincing the surgeons at the Massachusetts General Hospital of the value of ether. He acted as anaesthetist while a surgeon removed a tumour from a patient's neck (see Source 4).

As a result, a British doctor finally took an interest in the use of anaesthetics. Dr Robert Liston (1794–1847) had an established reputation as a brilliant surgeon who could amputate a limb in less than a minute. In 1846, he used ether as an anaesthetic. The amputation took only 28 seconds! What was more, the fortunate patient felt nothing at all.

SOURCE 6

Rejoice … Yesterday I amputated a thigh and removed both sides of the great toe nail without the patients being aware of what I was doing.

Written by Liston on 22 December 1846.

James Simpson

James Young Simpson was Professor of Midwifery in Edinburgh. He began investigating the possibilities of using anaesthetics in childbirth. He tried ether, but it had unpleasant side effects on the eyes and throat. His experiments were extremely hazardous, as they consisted mainly of inhaling various chemicals himself. He and several other doctors tried out chloroform in 1847, as described in Source 7.

SOURCE 7

It occurred to Dr Simpson to try a material which he had set aside … a small bottle of chloroform. It was searched for and recovered from beneath a heap of waste paper …

Immediately hilarity seized the party – they became bright-eyed, very happy … a moment more then all was quiet – and then crash. On awakening, Dr Simpson's first perception was … 'This is far stronger and better than ether.'

Professor James Miller, a colleague of Simpson, describes the chloroform trial in 1847.

Simpson was not as reckless with his patients, but he was so convinced by chloroform that within days he was using it to ease the pains of childbirth. Simpson also proved the connection between pain and clinical shock (a sudden failure of the circulation or drop in blood pressure), which was the cause of death of so many surgery patients.

Simpson faced bitter opposition: in fact, it is probably true to say that his success in overcoming this opposition was as important a contribution to anaesthetics as his use of chloroform itself.

Critics argued that chloroform caused higher death rates for mothers and children. It was true that chloroform was a powerful chemical, and there had been deaths from chloroform poisoning. However, Simpson kept careful records which showed that it did not increase the risks of childbirth. Another of his opponents' arguments was that the Bible indicated that childbirth should be painful. Simpson showed that the Bible did not actually say this, and also pointed out that when God created Eve from one of Adam's ribs, he put Adam to sleep before he took the rib.

By clever arguments and force of personality, Simpson established chloroform as the standard general anaesthetic for the next 50 years. By 1853, Simpson's case was generally accepted; the events of Source 9 probably played a major part.

SOURCE 9

The Queen had chloroform [given] to her during her last confinement [the birth of Prince Leopold]. It acted admirably. Her Majesty was greatly pleased with the effect, and she certainly has had a better recovery. I know this information will please you, and I have little doubt that it will lead to a more general use of chloroform in the midwifery practice …

From a letter to James Simpson.

Local anaesthetics

Important progress was also made with local anaesthetics. In 1853, Alexander Wood invented a glass syringe with a hollow needle attached, which solved the problem of how to anaesthetise one area. The next question was which was the best drug. Several doctors tried cocaine: the American surgeon WS Halstead discovered that it was most effective when injected into the nerve trunks of the spinal column. However, many doctors who experimented on themselves discovered with tragic consequences that cocaine was addictive. In 1904, a much safer drug called novocaine was developed.

SOURCE 8

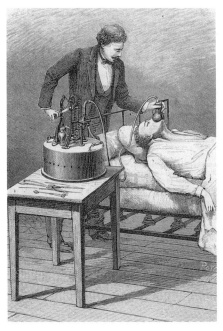

Using chloroform in the later nineteenth century. The job of anaesthetist required great skill: too little and the patient suffered, too much and there was the risk of an overdose.

1 **Why did Simpson face so much opposition?**

2 **How did he overcome the opposition?**

Fighting infection: antiseptics

Whatever advances were made in anaesthetics, one problem of surgery was still inescapable in the mid nineteenth century: the patients tended to die, especially if operated on in hospitals. One in five patients died after amputations. However, of those operated on at home or in doctors' private surgeries, only five out of 46 died.

Today, with the benefit of hindsight, we can look back and see the reasons for these disastrous figures. The wounds became infected. At that time, however, infection, or sepsis, was simply not understood. There was even a school of thought which believed in the appearance of 'laudable pus' as the first stage of recovery. Some surgeons left wounds open to form scabs, because if a healthy scab did form the patient was usually safe. Others believed in sealing wounds, to stop air getting in, which could be disastrous if the wound was already infected. One of the best surgeons of the time was James Syme, who left the ends of ligatures hanging out of wounds to drain pus and infection into a dressing. This was the most successful method of preventing infection, but it was far from perfect.

In fact, it was the doctors who were the main cause of infection. In the operating theatre, surgeons wore their oldest coats. These were not changed for six months and became stiff with blood and pus. The threads used to tied up the wounds from surgery were attached to the surgeon's coat while he worked.

SOURCE 10

I remember the house-surgeon with his threaded needles dangling from the front of his coat, the silken threads sweeping the well-worn cloth which had grown old in the presence of sepsis [blood poisoning]. One of our surgeons lectured on anatomy in an old frock coat. I see it now, faded with age, stained with blood and spotted with pus.

Written by a colleague of the pioneering surgeon Joseph Lister.

This was not the only danger the patients faced. Births and operations were often carried out with the help of students, who had sometimes come to the operating theatre directly from dissecting corpses. Often, the surgeon had not even washed his hands since a previous operation. The worst culprit was the surgeon's probe. This was used to examine wounds and demonstrate features to students. At best, it was given a wipe or wash from one examination to the next.

Joseph Lister

Joseph Lister was deeply concerned about the high mortality rate of patients (see Source 11). As Professor of Surgery at Glasgow University, he had seen the number of operations rise because of anaesthetics, but with no greater success in preventing infection.

In 1865, when Lister came across the work of Louis Pasteur, he realised that infection was caused by germs entering the wound. For the next few years, Lister experimented tirelessly to perfect his methods of antiseptic surgery. He began by using a fine spray of carbolic acid as an antiseptic to try to kill germs in the atmosphere. At first it burnt the patients, so he had to adjust the strength of the acid. He soon gave up the spray when he realised that it was the surgeon's hands and clothes, the instruments and dressings which mattered, and instead these were washed in carbolic. Lister also introduced sterile catgut ligatures. These sealed wounds and arteries without infection and, better still, were simply absorbed by the body. Lister's results were impressive and were soon being copied elsewhere (see Source 13). Pasteur himself joined the struggle to educate surgeons about avoiding infection (see Source 14).

PROFILE

Joseph Lister

★ Born 1827 in Essex.
★ His father was a scientist who studied microscopic organisms.
★ He graduated in medicine from London University in 1852.
★ In 1855 he became house surgeon to James Syme, a leading Scottish surgeon, and married his daughter in 1856.
★ He became Professor of Surgery at Edinburgh University, and later at King's College, London.
★ He was President of the Royal Society from 1895 to 1900.
★ He died in 1912.

SOURCE 11

[Patients were suffering] … in a way that was sickening and often heart rending, so as to make me feel it a questionable privilege to be connected with the institution [the university].

By Joseph Lister.

SOURCE 12

Years	Fractures treated	Recovered	Died
1864–66	34	19	15
1867–70	40	34	6

Figures for Lister's treatment of compound fractures (fractures which pierced the skin).

SOURCE 13

The use of carbolic acid in the treatment of wounds and compound fractures has created quite a revolution in the surgical practice at the Dowlais Iron Works: for during the last 12 months I have used it extensively in the treatment of the varied injuries that are of constant occurrence, and I think I may say in every instance with marked success. Formerly, in severe cases of compound fracture, amputation was the rule; latterly it has been the exception.

A letter from the doctor at the Dowlais Iron Works in the medical journal the *Lancet*, 29 August 1868.

SOURCE 14

This water, this sponge, this lint with which you wash or cover wounds, deposit germs which have the power of multiplying rapidly … If I had the honour of being a surgeon, not only would I use perfectly clean instruments, but having cleansed my hands with the greatest care, and subjected them to a rapid flaming … I would use only lint, bandages and sponges previously exposed to a temperature of 130 degrees to 150 degrees centigrade.

From a lecture by Pasteur in 1870.

SOURCE 15

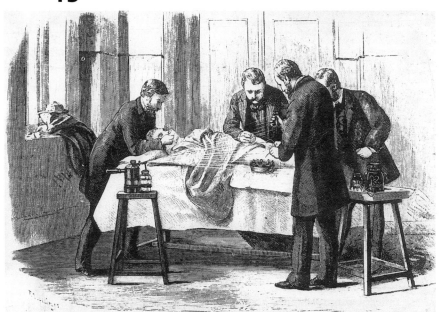

A drawing of an operation in 1870. A carbolic spray is in use.

ACTIVITY

Explain to someone who knows nothing about nineteenth-century surgery what is happening in Source 15. You could do this by writing notes around your own copy of the picture.

Opposition to Lister

Yet again, a medical pioneer had to fight hard to get his theories accepted. When Lister published his ideas in the *Lancet* in 1867, he faced opposition and criticism. James Simpson, the pioneer of chloroform, was one of Lister's bitterest critics. Lister's continuing alterations to his methods were seen as signs of failure rather than as attempts to improve. A greater problem was that Lister's techniques were not put into practice properly, and as a result were branded as failures. When Lister visited the USA in the 1870s, he found surgeons still wearing coats stiff with blood. In the 1880s, they were still using wooden-handled tools, and wounds were dabbed again and again with sponges, increasing the chances of infection.

It was not until the early 1900s that antiseptic surgery was fully accepted. One important factor was a successful appendix operation in sterile conditions on King Edward VII; previously, this operation had been extremely dangerous, with a low success rate. By this time, surgeons had developed aseptic surgery, using rubber gloves, instruments sterilised with steam, face masks and gowns to prevent germs from entering the operating theatre. New industrial technology meant it was possible to manufacture steel implements, which could be boiled and sterilised easily. Students and observers watched from behind glass panels. The sad truth was, however, that Lister's methods had to travel to Germany and America before they were fully accepted back in Britain.

It is difficult to overestimate the combined contribution of Lister and Pasteur to making surgery safer (see Source 16). Modern medicine owes a great deal to their perseverance and talent, and to their determination to stand up to critics. Equally, we must not be too harsh on the critics. The concept of micro-organisms must have been a very difficult one to accept. Doctors had learned to be wary of 'quacks' who continually claimed to have found miracle cures. They also did not want to believe that they themselves caused the infections which killed their patients. In addition, many doctors failed when they tried out the new ideas.

SOURCE 16

To think of Pasteur is to think also of Lister. It is 48 years since Lister in March 1865 first used carbolic acid to destroy the 'germs of putrefaction' in a wound. In his first paper on the subject, published in 1867, comes the famous tribute of his gratitude to Pasteur: 'We find that a flood of light has been thrown upon this most important subject by the philosophic researches of M Pasteur.' All his life, he said again and again, that he had got his inspiration from Pasteur; that he had been on a wrong track till there came that flood of light.

An extract from an article written as a tribute to Pasteur in *The Times*, 1913.

1 Which of Lister's methods do you think was the most significant improvement? Explain your choice.

2 How did Pasteur's work influence Lister's?

FOCUS TASK

WHY DID SOME PEOPLE OPPOSE NEW IDEAS IN SURGERY?

SOURCE 17

The opponents of Pasteur and Lister were not all of them, nor most of them, stupid. It is only the younger men, born after 1865, who call them stupid and blind and jealous, one and all, as if 1865 could have foreseen 1913. The venture of faith in 'the germ theory', the subjection of all experience to be judged by a chemist in Paris and a surgeon in Glasgow, the positive evidence of good results obtained without carbolic acid, the imperfection of Lister's earlier method, the aggressive zeal of some of his followers, the bewildering conflict of statistics, and, above all, the want of more knowledge – here are some of the elements of the great controversy.

Extract from an article written as a tribute to Pasteur in *The Times* in 1913.

1 Read Source 17 carefully. What explanations does it give for the opposition that Lister and Pasteur faced?

2 What evidence on pages 311–18 supports the points made in Source 17?

3 Do you think that Source 17 is a useful source for an historian looking at critics of Pasteur and Lister? Explain your answer.

Other advances

By the early twentieth century, surgery was certainly safer and more effective. Apart from anaesthetics and antiseptics, there were some other important developments. Bleeding and haemorrhaging were addressed by specialist clamps. Another problem was clinical shock, which was common in surgery and more common still on battlefields. By the late 1800s, it was clear that a major cause of shock was a drop in blood pressure, which could be treated by blood transfusions. The earliest transfusion was carried out in 1829, but it was fraught with problems. It was only when the Austrian Karl Landsteiner discovered that there were four blood groups that transfusions became safe.

We have seen that dealing with fractures and broken bones was a regular part of a doctor's work. In 1895, the German Wilhelm Konrad Rontgen discovered X-rays. The early X-ray pictures were primitive but still effective. The use of X-rays helped in the proper setting of broken bones: before this there had always been an element of guesswork involved. However, there was a disadvantage of this development, in that some of the early pioneers were badly affected by radiation poisoning from the X-rays.

SOURCE 18

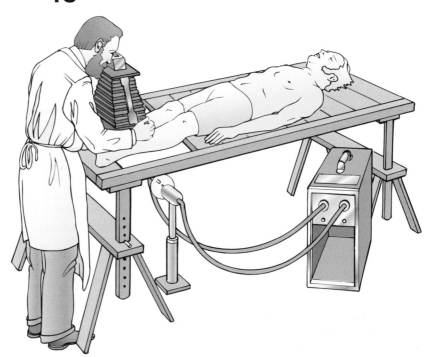

An artist's impression of an early X-ray machine.

ACTIVITY

Look at Source 1 on page 303. It shows an operation in the late eighteenth century. Write a description of the operation and its aftermath from the patient's point of view.

Then imagine the same operation is being performed 107 years later, in 1900. Write another description from the patient's point of view. Emphasise how the developments you have studied on pages 311–19 would change the experience of surgery for the patient.

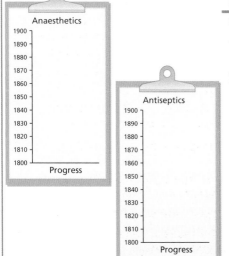

FOCUS TASK

WHAT CAUSED THE ADVANCES IN SURGERY IN THE NINETEENTH CENTURY?

1 Copy the charts on the left. Use the information on pages 311–19 to complete them.

2 The year is 1902. The new King Edward VII has just recovered from his appendix operation, and is soon to take part in his official coronation. Under the title 'Why the King nearly didn't make it', write an article for a national newspaper explaining how the operation which saved the King was the coming together of 100 years of hard work and ingenuity. Mention:

- pain relief – problems and solutions.
- infection – problems and solutions.
- opposition – problems and solutions.

Remember to use pictures, eyewitness accounts or diagrams to keep your readers interested.

How did hospitals improve in the nineteenth century?

Many of the improvements in surgery described in the previous section took place in hospitals. Despite this, it took a long time for hospitals to lose their bad reputation. Florence Nightingale, who led the campaign to clean up hospitals and improve nursing care, called them 'gateways to death'. In 1861, she calculated that 90 per cent of patients in London hospitals died. The best hospitals were voluntary or charity hospitals, often set up to treat specific illnesses. The hospitals run by religious orders were also relatively healthy places. However, many hospitals were little more than places people went to die. The worst of all were workhouse hospitals.

The poor quality of nursing care in hospitals was one of the main problems. Some nurses were simply paupers from the workhouse who were really only cleaners. They had no nursing training, and either ignored the patients or treated them badly.

Sources 19–24 are some descriptions of hospitals and nursing care at this time. However, you should bear in mind that all of these were written by people who were campaigning for reform. You have come across many examples of nineteenth-century reformers overstating problems to support their case. While these descriptions are certainly backed up by evidence from the time, there were also many other nurses, even untrained ones, who were doing a much better job than this.

SOURCE 19

The nurses did not as a rule wash patients, they could never wash their feet and it was with great difficulty and only in great haste that they could have a drop of water just to dab their hands and face. The beds on which the patients lay were dirty. It was common practice to put a new patient into the same sheets used by the last.

Florence Nightingale describing the nursing care in many hospitals.

SOURCE 20

[The sick were] … lying on plank beds with chaff mattresses about three inches thick between their weary bodies and the hard uneven planks … Some idiots and imbeciles share the wards with these patients. The infants occupy a dark stone paved room, bare of furniture, with no rug for the babies to crawl or lie upon and no responsible persons to see to their feeding and cleanliness.

A report from the *British Medical Journal* describing a workhouse hospital in 1890.

SOURCE 21

All drunk without exception, sisters and all, and there are but two nurses whom the surgeon can trust to give the patients their medicine.

A London doctor describes hospital nurses in about 1855.

SOURCE 22

The sick lay on wretched beds, fit only for able-bodied tramps, and were nursed mainly by old pauper women of the lowest possible class … I visited an enormous workhouse in a provincial town where there were nearly 500 sick and infirm patients. The Matron told me she had been lately appointed to the post … 'I never nursed anybody, I can assure you, except my 'usband, before I came here. It was misfortune brought me to this'.

Frances Cobbe, a social worker and feminist, describing a workhouse hospital in 1889.

SOURCE 23

An early nineteenth-century cartoon showing the typical nurse. She is unconscious from alcohol.

SOURCE 24

At present nursing is the last resort of female adversity. Slatternly widows, runaway wives, servants out of place, women bankrupt of fame and fortune, from whatever cause fall back upon hospital nursing. When on rare occasion a respectable young woman takes to it from choice, her friends most likely repudiate her.

Written by the Medical Officer of Health for Glasgow in 1865.

1 What impression do Sources 25 and 26 give you of Florence Nightingale's work?

2 How far do you trust what these sources tell you about her work? Explain your answer carefully.

3 Draw up a chart to summarise the work of Nightingale in the Crimea. Your chart should have two columns, one listing the problems and one the action taken to solve each one.

SOURCE 26

…as her slender form glides quietly along each corridor, every poor fellow's face softens with gratitude at the sight of her. When all the medical officers have retired for the night and silence and darkness have settled down upon those miles of prostrate sick, she may be observed alone, with a little lamp in her hand, making her solitary rounds.

A contemporary report from *The Times*, which sponsored Florence Nightingale's work in the Crimea.

Improvements – the work of Florence Nightingale

The campaign to improve both hospitals and nursing is bound up with the career of Florence Nightingale. Despite the opposition of her family, she trained as a nurse, and by 1854 was working in the Middlesex Hospital.

In that year, the government was facing a barrage of criticism for its handling of a war being fought by British troops in the Crimea, part of Russia. *The Times* featured regular reports on military mismanagement, but also revealed the shocking state of the military hospital at Scutari in Turkey. Florence Nightingale wrote to Sidney Herbert, Minister of War Supplies, an old family friend, volunteering to help. By coincidence, her letter crossed in the post with a letter from Herbert asking her to do just that. With government money and 38 of the best nurses she could find, she set out for Scutari.

When she arrived, she found nightmare conditions in the hospital. There were 1,700 patients in the hospital, but for each casualty of battle, there were 10 typhoid and cholera victims. Soldiers watched as their comrades were operated on in front of them and died under the surgeon's knife. The patients were too weak to digest the food given to them. Filth and vermin (insects and rats) were everywhere. There were not enough beds or medical supplies. There were not even basins, soap and towels, or even knives and forks.

Florence Nightingale faced opposition from the army doctors, who resented her interference. However, she also had some powerful supporters: Sidney Herbert (who had asked her to go) and Dr Andrew Smith, head of the Army Medical Department (who made sure she received the supplies she needed). She also had money, the support of *The Times* and, through it, the support of the public.

Her greatest asset, however, was her own personality. She was determined and energetic, and did not worry whom she upset if she achieved what she thought was right.

Over the next months, she obtained soap and water and made the patients wash themselves or be washed. She set up a new laundry and found new clothing for them. She upset the Turkish Customs authorities by forcing them to let all manner of supplies into the country, and also persuaded the army quartermasters to provide food and medicines. She made sure that the wards were cleaned, and separated out patients suffering from different complaints to prevent the spread of disease.

The results of her work were extraordinary. After six months, only 100 patients were still bed-ridden in the hospital. The death rate at the hospital, which had been running at 42 per cent when she arrived, was just over two per cent six months later.

Sources 25 and 26 date from the Crimean War (1854–56).

SOURCE 25

A ward at Scutari in Turkey, after Florence Nightingale's reforms. Nightingale is in the centre looking at plans. Her supporters made drawings like this to promote her work.

The Nightingale School of Nursing

Florence Nightingale became a national heroine in England. She spent the next four years back in Britain, campaigning to reform army medical services. However, in Scutari she had already established the main principles of running a hospital successfully. In 1859, she published her ideas in *Notes for Nursing* (see Source 27), which sold 15,000 copies in the first month.

The Times established a Nightingale Fund, which, in 1860, she spent on a school for nurses at St Thomas's Hospital, where they would be trained to run hospitals according to her principles.

SOURCE 27

To the experienced eye of a carefully observing nurse, the daily, I had almost said hourly, changes which take place in patients, and which changes rarely come under the cognisance of the periodical medical visitor, afford a still more important class of data, from which to judge of the general adaptation of a hospital for the reception and treatment of sick. One insensibly allied together restlessness, languor, feverishness and general malaise, with closeness of wards, defective ventilation, defective structure, bad architectural and administrative arrangements, until it is impossible to resist the conviction that the sick are suffering from something quite other than the disease inscribed on their bed ticket. The inquiry arises in the mind, what can be the cause?

The defects are four:
1 The agglomeration of a large number of sick under the same roof.
2 Deficiency of space.
3 Deficiency of ventilation.
4 Deficiency of light.

The buildings themselves should avoid the following:
1 Defective means of natural ventilation and warming.
2 Defective height of wards.
3 Excessive width of wards between opposite windows.
4 Having more than two rows of beds between the opposite windows.
5 Arranging the beds along the dead walls.
6 Having windows only on one side, or having a closed corridor connecting the wards.
7 Absorbent materials for walls and ceilings.
8 Defective water closets.
9 Defective ward furniture.
10 Defective accommodation for nurses and discipline.
11 Defective kitchens.
12 Defective laundries.
13 Selection of bad sites and bad local climates.
14 Erecting hospitals in towns.
15 Defective sewerage.
16 Construction without free circulation of external air.

Florence Nightingale's principles of hospital management.

1 Draw up a chart with two columns. In the first column list the problems described in Source 27. In the second column explain *why* they should be avoided.

As well as advising on the construction of hospitals, she also set out the principles of good nursing. Nurses were trained to be as clean as possible, to change dressings and to be proper assistants to doctors and surgeons.

Nightingale nurses were a separate but important new branch of the medical profession. Instead of being simply minders or cleaners, they were a central part of the process of treatment. Nightingale's principles were first taken up in the voluntary hospitals, but by the mid 1860s they were spreading. You can read about one example in the case study opposite.

ACTIVITY

Write a letter for Florence Nightingale to send to people who donated money to the Nightingale Fund, explaining how the money has been spent and how this will help improve hospital care.

Case study: The Liverpool Royal Infirmary

The city of Liverpool provides us with a good example of Florence Nightingale's contribution to improving hospitals.

A city of contrasts

The merchants of the city made huge profits from trade with India and China. Today the magnificent river front, with the Liver Building and other famous landmarks, is well known even to people who have never been to the city. These impressive buildings and the giant nineteenth-century Anglican cathedral all testify to the wealth and success of the city. It also gave Britain mighty politicians such as William Gladstone, and its businesses were household names such as Tate and Lyle (sugar), Crawfords (biscuits) and Holts (furnishing).

Yet Liverpool was a prime example of a Victorian city with two sides. Liverpool had the highest proportion of people who lived in cellars (see page 186), and according to Chadwick's 1842 report Liverpool labourers were the shortest lived in the country. Even in the later nineteenth century, conditions were still desperate for the city's poor.

SOURCE **28**

Liverpool in 1830.

Liverpool infirmary

The city's first infirmary had been built in 1745 in Lime Street (where the main train station is today). It was soon unable to cope with the problems that came with Liverpool's growth, and in 1823 a second infirmary was opened. However, this too was soon inadequate, as Liverpool continued to grow at an amazing rate (see page 9). The health problems of a big city could not be dealt with by this infirmary and a motley collection of Poor Law or workhouse hospitals. William Rathbone, a middle-class Liverpool businessmen, saw the need for an entirely new hospital, with adequate facilities, and staff who were familiar with the latest developments.

Rathbone's interest in health care was stimulated by a visit to the Poor Law hospital, which appalled him. In 1865, he gave £1,200 for 24 Nightingale nurses to be employed there. Unfortunately, the matron, Agnes Jones, who was appointed by Nightingale, died of typhus and overwork after two years. Nevertheless, in that short time she dramatically improved the care and running of the hospital. She also opened a training school for nurses, and these trained nurses spread the Nightingale principles further.

District nursing

Rathbone also realised that adequate care in the home could prevent many people from ever needing to enter the workhouse or its hospital. He therefore set up his own system of district nurses in Liverpool in 1860. District nurses were to care for the poor in their own homes, dealing with problems which did not need hospital treatment.

SOURCE **29**

The people whom I have had to do with are most of them so ignorant that they do not know how to take care of themselves, or even prepare the common necessaries of life. I find by suitable advice that there is very great improvement in many houses as to cleanliness, particularly in the bedding, and more air, and in cooking in a common way …

Example No 1 – Man with wife and six children. Symptoms of consumption; was too weak to work; and the whole family really were starving. I lent them a few shillings (since repaid), procured the woman a little needlework, supplied warm clothing, flannels and nourishment. The man is now apparently quite well …

The report of the Liverpool Training School and Home for Nurses, 1860, written by Nurse Robinson, the first Liverpool district nurse.

The second infirmary under pressure

Before 1870, there were no resident medical staff at the infirmary. In some wards, patients were simply locked in at night while the staff went home. By 1870, however, the city council, which ran the infirmary, recognised the need for resident staff; their first appointment was Frank Paul. Source 30 is his description of his early years. There were many problems, but it is also clear that new ideas and practices were making their way through.

SOURCE 30

[Various forms of infection] were rampant. One in three of [patients in certain operations] died, though done by good men. Edward Bickersteth, the senior surgeon, was quite an exceptional man with a large practice. He was a personal friend of Lord Lister and was the first man I saw who dressed properly for an operation. The usual custom was still to use a dirty frock coat. Reginald Harrison and W Mitchell Banks were the younger surgeons, the latter being appointed full surgeon in 1877. On the medical side, Turnbull and Waters were good men, but rather the type of the previous generation. The junior physician, Glynn, was the outstanding man, keen in every branch of medicine and an excellent pathologist. Rushton Parker was pathologist, but I shared a fair amount of work with him and did 3000 post-mortems before I gave up this work. Apart from ward work and some clerical duties, I gave anaesthetics, usually ether. There was no special anaesthetist at the time and Henry Briggs was appointed the first chloroformist in 1884.

Frank Paul's description of his first years at Liverpool Infirmary.

The new infirmary

Despite improvements, the old infirmary simply could not cope. With donations from William Rathbone, a fund was started to build a new infirmary. Florence Nightingale's interest in the project helped to win public support for it, and Rathbone led an energetic fundraising campaign, persuading the middle classes of Liverpool to help fund the cost. When the city built its new Royal Liverpool Infirmary in 1887, Florence Nightingale was consulted regularly and provided much sensible advice.

SOURCE 31

In accordance with the request made at the meeting ..., I have shown my rough sketch plans to Miss Florence Nightingale ... [She] ... was kind enough to grant me interviews and to freely criticise my plans ...

I found Miss Nightingale was very strong in her opinion that the wards should be higher (particularly in the surgical wards) than I had shown them.

The wards have been arranged in three blocks, running north and south, with a main corridor down the centre east and west. These blocks are about 100 feet apart, and the wards are divided with respect to the number of beds, as far as possible, in accordance with the report drawn up by the Honorary Physicians and Surgeons. They are arranged on the first and second floors of the building.

Every ward has a sister's room and a scullery looking into it. It has also a room for patients' clothing, which is intended to be lined with glazed tiles, and to be surrounded by shelves for the clothes. Besides this, in connection with each two wards, a doctor's room has been provided, and on the first floor looking into Brownlow Street, a sisters' sitting room.

There are two staircases in the hospital opening into the central corridor, and midway between the southern wards. In each case, in the well of the staircase is placed a lift for patients.

Opposite the western staircase, on the ground floor, is an operating theatre, with preparation rooms on either side of it; and (approached from the first floor corridor) a separate entrance for students to the upper part of their gallery. This theatre will hold 127 students (the space for each student being 19 inches wide), and is lighted from the roof.

Alfred Waterhouse, one of the top nineteenth-century architects, describing his plans for the new infirmary to the Mayor of Liverpool in 1886.

ACTIVITY

Draw your own plan of the Liverpool Infirmary described in Source 31. Annotate it to show how the Nightingale principles in Source 27 have influenced the design.

The building work was not completed until 1889, but the first patients were being treated in one part of the hospital by 1887. The Infirmary had taken much hard work and had cost £180,000. However, the city now had a hospital to be envied.

Conclusion

Many other cities and towns also built their own fine new hospitals at the end of the nineteenth century, and a large number of these are still in use today.

From the 1850s onwards, hospitals specialising in particular branches of care began to appear. Hospitals for infectious diseases were built, usually in isolated locations. Other hospitals specialised in infections of the ears, nose and throat. However, many doctors were unsure about the value of these specialist hospitals, and by 1900 the profession was still divided.

What was certain was that the basic standard of hospital care had risen enormously by the end of the nineteenth century. The wealthier classes, who could afford to have a choice, were more prepared to go into hospital for treatment. In addition, nursing was now a respectable career, with real prospects. There were 68,000 trained nurses in 1900.

FOCUS TASK

1   List the different factors which made it possible for Liverpool to build the Royal Liverpool Infirmary.

2   Which of these factors do you regard as most important? Explain your choice.

FOCUS TASK

HOW FAR DID HOSPITALS IMPROVE DURING THE NINETEENTH CENTURY?

Use the information and sources on pages 320–25 to label your own copy of the drawings below.

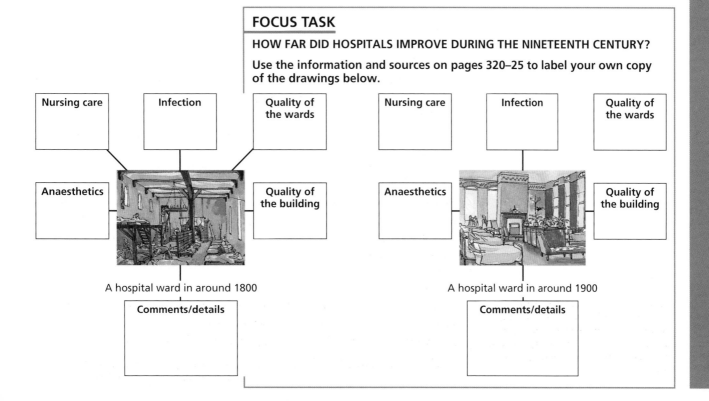

| Nursing care | Infection | Quality of the wards |
| Anaesthetics | | Quality of the building |

A hospital ward in around 1800

Comments/details

| Nursing care | Infection | Quality of the wards |
| Anaesthetics | | Quality of the building |

A hospital ward in around 1900

Comments/details

11.3 *Why has health improved in the twentieth century?*

How healthy were ordinary people in 1900?

As you have seen in 11.2, some important advances were made in terms of the health of ordinary people in the nineteenth century. By 1900, the poor were mainly safe from smallpox. The numbers of deaths caused by tuberculosis and whooping cough had been reduced. In Chapter 8, you read about the attempts to improve housing and sanitation with important measures such as the 1875 Public Health Act.

By using the accurate census materials of the nineteenth century, historians have been able to show that between 1851 and 1901 the annual death rate fell from 22 to 17 per thousand. Average life expectancy for men reached a high of 45.5 years; the figure for women was 49 years.

There was a darker side to this picture, however. Although general life expectancy increased, infant mortality was still high at 163 deaths per thousand in 1899. The miserable poverty, squalor and ill health described by Charles Booth and Seebohm Rowntree (see pages 229–30) certainly did not disappear as the new century began.

What was more, although certain diseases could be prevented, doctors were still powerless in many cases to cure disease once it did strike. There was also the fact that too many ordinary people still could not afford to see a doctor. Although much progress had been made, there was a long way to go.

Why did health improve in the early twentieth century?

The advances in health made during the nineteenth century continued into the twentieth century. Medical historians dispute the details, but a number of factors were certainly important.

Social factors

Housing improved and wages increased. Birth control reduced the number of children born to a family, which resulted in healthier children and mothers. In the early twentieth century, the Liberal governments introduced old-age pensions, National Insurance, school meals and school medical services (see page 233).

Preventing killer diseases

Using Koch's and Pasteur's methods, vaccines were developed to prevent tuberculosis in 1906 and diphtheria in 1913. Improvements in sewage disposal, water supplies and housing helped enormously in the fight against killer diseases such as tuberculosis. Other measures were taken. For example, one of the main sources of tuberculosis was fresh cow's milk. In 1922, the Ministry of Health ordered all milk to be pasteurised.

Diet and vitamins

Sir Frederick Gowland Hopkins found that diseases such as scurvy and rickets (which made children bow-legged) were caused by lack of vitamins. This discovery enabled the government to give better advice on diet. By the 1930s, the average family was spending more money on fruit than on bread. In 1924, the pharmaceutical company Glaxo began manufacturing cod liver oil as a remedy for Vitamin D deficiency. The general health of the nation as a whole was improving.

SOURCE 1

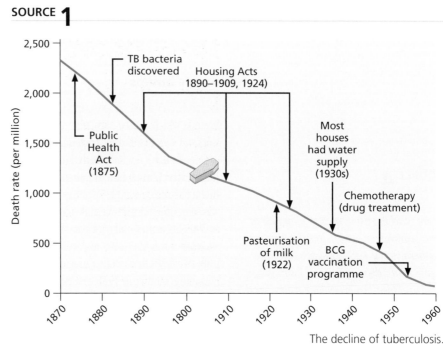

The decline of tuberculosis.

1 **List the factors which contributed to better health. Give them a mark on a scale of 1–5. Compare your marks with a partner.**

SOURCE 2

A full front-page advertisement for Glaxo baby milk in the *Daily Mail*, 1908.

SOURCE 3

· · · · **the nicest way of giving Halibut Liver Oil**

HALIBORANGE
The Vitamin Food . Tonic is invaluable for

building up weakly children and helping the growth of the healthy child.
It assists to 'pull-up' the adult when 'run-down' and builds up strength and stamina.
'HALIBORANGE' is a new preparation which combines Halibut Liver Oil with the juice of ripe, fresh oranges.

It contains the three vitamins:—
Vitamin A (Body-building; anti-germ).
Vitamin C (Fruit juice factor, anti-scurvy).
Vitamin D (Bone-forming. prevents rickets).

HALIBORANGE — the New Vitamin Nutrient that Tastes Just Like Fresh Oranges

Children seldom like taking Cod Liver Oil and even their elders revolt at the pungent 'fishy' taste. Although Cod Liver Oil is good, Halibut Liver Oil is BETTER. They both contain Vitamins A & D. But best of all is 'Haliborange' because it contains Vitamin C as well as Vitamins A & D. Children love its fresh 'fruity' taste and adults find that taking Halibut Liver Oil now becomes a pleasure. Mothers will not have to coax reluctant children to take their daily dose as an aid to growth and perfect health.

— there's Health in every spoonful

HALIBORANGE
Get a bottle from your Chemist to-day.
2/6 & 4/6
ALLEN & HANBURYS LTD., 37 Lombard St., E.C.3.

GIVE HALIBUT LIVER OIL THE 'HALIBORANGE' WAY

An advertisement for Haliborange, 1934.

From prevention to cure

Most of these improvements helped in preventing disease. However, once diseases such as blood poisoning, tuberculosis and influenza were contracted there was still not much that doctors could do to help patients. The next great advance for the medical profession was in the curing of diseases once they had been caught.

Magic bullets

Robert Koch's research (see page 312) had enabled scientists to isolate and experiment on the bacteria which caused particular diseases. Clearly, the next major development would be to work out how to kill these bacteria.

One of Koch's research team, Paul Ehrlich, studied the bacterium that caused syphilis. Koch had showed Ehrlich how to stain bacteria with coloured dyes. Ehrlich believed it was possible that a chemical might be identified which would not only stain bacteria but also kill them. He was searching for what he called a 'magic bullet'. Ehrlich had to proceed by trial and error, but in 1905 his team finally discovered a dye which would both stain and kill syphilis bacteria. However, it was also toxic, and would harm or kill the patient, so it could not be used. It was not until the 1930s that another magic bullet was discovered: this one could be used to treat blood poisoning. Finally, in 1931, researchers in France isolated the ingredient in the magic bullet dyes which actually attacked the bacteria. It was called sulphonamide.

One reason why research on magic bullets took so long was the disruption caused by the First World War. However, in some ways, the war and its aftermath accelerated the pace and intensity of medical developments. As the war ended, influenza, or 'Spanish flu', swept across Europe. The population was weakened by war and rationing, and in less than a year more people were killed by influenza than had died in four years of fighting. Influenza and pneumonia continued to be fatal, especially for children and the poor, until the 1930s. In 1933, the pharmaceutical company May and Baker developed two sulphonamide drugs which were extremely effective against these two diseases.

SOURCE 4

We used to call two or three times a day or more, and there was a chap sitting up in bed, panting for breath, looking blue, temperature of 105, you gave him these things and I'd say, 'Give him four of these now and then two every four hours,' and you'd call the next morning carrying your death certificates with you and you'd have a chap sitting up in bed … and he was a good colour … he wasn't panting for breath.

A doctor of the 1930s, interviewed 50 years later, describes the impact of new drugs on a pneumonia case.

SOURCE 5

Maternal mortality, 1910–90.

SOURCE 6

	1928	1929	1930	1931	1932	1933
Liverpool	94	97	82	94	91	98
St Helens	98	114	80	88	89	119
Bath	47	48	48	39	40	52
Oxford	38	64	41	44	61	32

A health survey from the 1930s, showing infant deaths per 1,000.

Antibiotics

The disadvantage of sulphonamides was that they attacked and killed only specific diseases. What was needed was a drug that treated a range of diseases.

The real breakthrough was made by Alexander Fleming, who had witnessed the misery caused by infection during the First World War. In 1928, he discovered that a bacterial mould, which he called penicillin, acted as an antibiotic (it killed other micro-organisms). In fact, Fleming was not the first man to investigate this mould. The scientist John Sanderson first noted its properties in the early 1800s. Joseph Lister also experimented with it, but he did not pursue any serious investigations or research into the mould. It was Fleming who first observed its effects on other organisms and wrote up his research. Unfortunately, progress was slow. Fleming's discovery did not shake the medical world because he was unable to grow a pure culture. This meant that he could never make the antibiotic in large quantities.

In the late 1930s, two scientists at Oxford University, Howard Florey and Ernst Chain, tried to solve this problem. They gathered together a team of researchers and, just as the Second World War began in September 1939, gained funding from the government for their research. After intensive efforts, they succeeded in freeze-drying the culture. They then carried out successful experiments on mice. Eight mice were injected with deadly microbes. Four were also given penicillin and four were not. One day later, the mice treated with penicillin were still alive, but the others were not.

The next step was to attempt a human trial, but it was 1941 before they had enough penicillin to do this. A policeman was dying from a terrible infection which was spreading over his body. The team gave him penicillin, and the drug clearly had a powerful effect on the infection. Unfortunately, they were simply not able to make enough of the drug to save the patient. Despite this, it was clear that penicillin was a powerful antibiotic. The timing of this work was excellent, because Britain was now at war: penicillin was to be a life-saving weapon against infection on the battlefield.

It was now vital to find a way to make penicillin in large quantities. Boots and Glaxo both made valiant efforts to mass produce the drug, but it was difficult, particularly with the constant threat of German bombing. Soon, manufacture was transferred to the USA, and the American government made $80 million available to four pharmaceutical companies to solve the problem. By 1942, penicillin was in mass production. However, it was only after the war ended that penicillin became available to civilian patients. This was a great leap forward for medicine. Doctors were now able to cure infectious diseases, and even patients who had contracted blood poisoning during surgery could be effectively treated.

ACTIVITY

1 Write your own 10-word definitions of sulphonamides and antibiotics.

2 What similarities are there between the sequence of events that led to the discovery of sulphonamides, and that which led to the discovery of antibiotics?

3 Which do you regard as the most important development? Explain your choice.

SOURCE 7

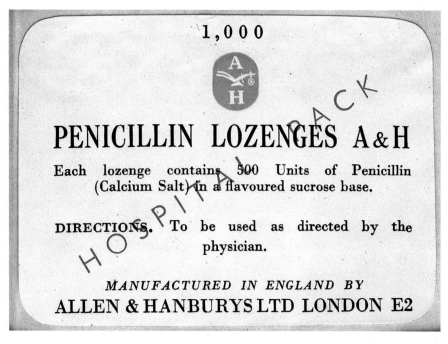

1,000

PENICILLIN LOZENGES A&H

Each lozenge contains 500 Units of Penicillin (Calcium Salt) in a flavoured sucrose base.

DIRECTIONS. To be used as directed by the physician.

MANUFACTURED IN ENGLAND BY
ALLEN & HANBURYS LTD LONDON E2

By the 1950s penicillin was mass produced and widely available. This pack of 1,000 doses cost the enormous sum of £24 in the 1940s. Mass production brought the price down to 40 pence.

FOCUS TASK

WHAT FACTORS LED TO THE DEVELOPMENT OF ANTIBIOTICS?

Write a report of about 200–250 words using the title: *The Story of Antibiotics.*

Your aim is to explain why and how these new drugs developed. In your report mention:

• the successes and limitations of prevention.
• the importance of war.
• the work of scientists.
• the contribution of large companies.

Other antibiotics

The fight against disease continued. In the USA, Selman Walksman discovered that antibiotics could be found in soils. He studied and categorised thousands of different organisms. In doing so, he discovered an organism which could be made into streptomycin, the first antibiotic to be effective against tuberculosis. However, the disease began to develop immunity to the antibiotic. To solve this problem, doctors in the late 1940s gave patients different combinations of chemical drugs, a process which became known as chemotherapy.

Did health care need improving in the 1930s?

The average family: health improving

If we look at Britain as a whole and take average figures, the health of the nation gradually improved during the 1930s. Average wages rose between the wars, and the average family was spending more money on fruit and fresh produce and less on bread. This was a sign of a healthier diet and of greater prosperity: bread was a survival food, whereas fruit was a luxury food. One in three families even managed a week's holiday every year.

Another factor was that the average number of children in a family fell from three to two in the 1930s. This meant extra spending money, healthier children and healthier mothers.

Housing also improved, and overcrowding decreased. Between the wars, around three million private houses and one million council houses were built. Housing Acts made sure that the new housing was of a decent quality, but market forces were just as important. More prosperous people wanted semi-detached houses, and they took out mortgages to buy them. Local authorities continued to connect houses to water and sewage systems, and by the late 1930s most houses in towns were connected. Even the poorer houses, with no hot water taps or baths, did have a scullery where water could be heated on a stove to boil water for washing clothes.

SOURCE 8

Healthy food supplements from the 1930s.

Poor families: less improvement

The picture was not entirely rosy, however. For the poorest of the poor and the unemployed, little had changed since the nineteenth century. A survey on Tyneside in 1933 showed that children from poor working-class families were far more vulnerable to diseases such as pneumonia and rickets than middle-class children. In 1935, Seebohm Rowntree found that by the standards of 1899 primary poverty in York (see Chapter 9) had fallen by a third. Yet when he used a higher standard, based on what was felt to be a satisfactory diet in the 1930s (rather than the 1890s), he was disappointed. He found that one in three working class people was unable to afford a proper diet. So, while much had improved on average, it was still a fact that some 16 per cent of the males called up to fight in 1939 were unfit for military service.

Health care for the poor

The poor still tended to avoid doctors. They would keep a few remedies at home, and for a more serious problem they would visit the pharmacist. In some ways, health care seemed not to have changed since the eighteenth century, when the poor used to consult the apothecary. It was not quite that bad, of course. The typical medical cupboard at home contained aspirin, bismuth and chlorodine (for stomach upsets), Syrup of Squills (for coughs and colds) and iodine (an antiseptic). However, if a serious illness came along people still had to ask themselves whether they could afford a doctor.

A disorganised service

Health care was also terribly disorganised. Services were patchy. For example, wealthy and fashionable Kensington had plenty of doctors, while the slums and industrial cities suffered from desperate shortages. Hospitals were generally funded by voluntary or charitable donations. This inevitably meant huge variations in funding and quality in different parts of the country. Most working men paid health insurance and were entitled to treatment by a so-called 'panel doctor', but their wives and families were not covered. Many families paid money into 'sick clubs', or took out private health insurance for wife and children. However, this did not include dental work or treatment by an optician.

---

1 How does your medicine store at home compare with the one described in the text?

2 Read Source 9 carefully. Explain whether you think the doctor was being fair.

3 Can we use Source 9 on its own for finding out about the state of health care in the 1930s?

Source 9 tells us a great deal about the problem of illness for the poor in Britain before the Second World War. These people continued to suffer from poor housing and a bad diet, which in turn made them vulnerable to disease.

SOURCE 9

My mother used to sit in a misery of embarrassment on the edge of a chair in the consulting room on the rare and desperate days when one of us had to be taken to the doctor – opening and shutting her purse, waiting for the right moment to extract the careful, unspareable half crown. She never knew whether to just slide it across the desk, which she said might make the doctor feel like a waiter, or to actually put it in his hand and make him feel as if he worked in a shop. Sometimes we dropped the money and that was the least dignified of all, especially if the fat doctor let my mother pick it up. And sometimes he would shout at my mother for not having come before, like the time we had to wait for my sister's sore throat to turn unmistakably into diphtheria before she was pushed off in a pram to his surgery: 'Good God, woman, why didn't you bring this child days ago?'

A newspaper article from 1964 in which the writer remembers health care in the 1930s.

SOURCE 10

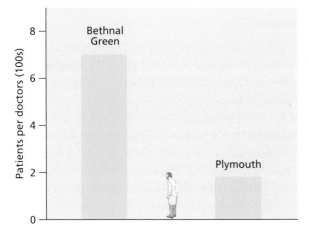

The proportion of patients to doctors in Plymouth, Devon (a mainly middle-class area), and Bethnal Green, London (mainly working class), in 1938.

SOURCE 11

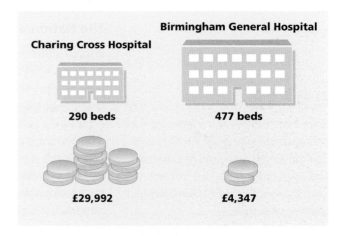

Donations made to hospitals in different areas in 1938.

SOURCE 12

[The old arrangements] …. cover only 22 million; the rest of the population have to pay whenever they desire the services of a doctor; the National Health Insurance Scheme does not provide for the self-employed nor the families or dependants … A person ought not to be financially deterred from seeking medical assistance at the earliest possible stage by the financial anxieties of doctor's bills …

Our hospital organisation has grown up with no plan; it is unevenly distributed over the country … In the older industrial districts of Britain hospital facilities are inadequate. Many hospitals are very much too small to provide general hospital treatment … It is intended that there shall be no limitations on the kind of assistance given – by general practitioners, specialists, hospitals, eye treatment, dental treatment, hearing facilities …

Furthermore – I want to be quite frank with the House – I believe it is repugnant to a civilised community for hospitals to have to rely upon private charity … I have always felt a shudder of repulsion when I see nurses and sisters who ought to be at their work, going about the streets collecting money for the hospitals.

Failings of the health-care system described by Aneurin Bevan when he introduced plans for the new National Health Service to Parliament.

4 Explain why hospital provision varied so much.

Why was the National Health Service introduced in 1948?

Effects of the Second World War

The Second World War had a major effect on attitudes. To begin with, there was the need to treat large numbers of civilian casualties from German bombing raids. This gave many people access to health care which they had never had before. There was a general feeling of unity within the nation, and also a sense that when war ended a new era would begin. Also, during the war, the state controlled almost every aspect of people's lives, and so the idea of the government looking after citizens' health did not seem strange.

The war also brought the situation of the poor to the public's notice. For example, research showed that rationing actually improved poor people's diet! As a result of evacuation, many middle-class people gained their first real insight into the squalor and poverty suffered by some British citizens. Many evacuees were in a wretched physical state, and infested with fleas or head lice – problems that had largely been dealt with among country children by the schools medical service. Skin complaints such as ringworm or scabies, which were the result of bad diet or hygiene, were also common.

1 List the ways in which the Second World War changed attitudes to health.

The National Health Service

Plans for the future of post-war Britain were set out in 1943 in the Beveridge Report, whose author was a civil servant, William Beveridge (see page 247). He identified the principal problems which British society faced, one of which was disease. The report laid the foundations of what came to be known as the Welfare State.

The Labour government elected in 1945 set in motion an extensive programme of welfare measures, including a National Health Service. The Minister for Health, Aneurin Bevan, was given the task of introducing the Health Service. He faced bitter opposition from the doctors and from the Conservative Party. Doctors resented losing their independence and becoming government employees. They thought their incomes would drop. Conservative opponents particularly criticised the cost of the NHS. However, after two years of struggle, compromise and preparation, the National Health Service opened its doors on 5 July 1948.

Hospitals were nationalised and organised into regional groups or health authorities. Doctors in hospitals received salaries, and all treatment to patients was free. General practitioners, dentists and opticians received fees according to the number of patients on their register, not according to the treatment given, and again the treatment was free to the patient. Finally, local authorities were paid to provide vaccination, maternity care, district nurses, health visitors and ambulances.

SOURCE 13

Your doctor will give you a prescription for any medicines and drugs you may need. You can get these free from any chemist who takes part in the scheme. In some country areas the doctor himself may dispense medicines.

From a Ministry of Health information leaflet, 1947.

2 What impression do you get from Source 14 of Bevan's personality?

SOURCE 14

The organising of a good medical hospital service for all Great Britain ought to be something which would inspire all doctors. They were approaching it in circumstances of great difficulty, because the war had destroyed many hospitals, and there was a danger of a depletion of nursing staffs. He was informed that wards were closing down all over the country because of lack of nursing staffs, and they would have to pull together to attract to the nursing profession many more nurses.

He said that he thought the housing problem would be solved in five years with the provision of many happy homes. He did not share the depressing attitude of some political speakers about some of Britain's problems. He felt distinctly optimistic. He was convinced that a nation which had achieved so much in the last six years was not going to fail to solve those problems which were immediately ahead of us.

A report of a speech by Bevan in 1945.

FOCUS TASK

WHY WAS THE NATIONAL HEALTH SERVICE INTRODUCED IN 1948?

1 Look back at pages 330–32. In pairs or groups, list all the factors which you think were reasons for the introduction of the NHS.

2 For each factor explain:

   a) How it contributed to the setting up of the NHS.
   b) How it is connected to any other factors on your list.

How successful has the NHS been?

SOURCE 15

The day is here. For years the reformers of all parties have tried to safeguard the aged, the poor and the sick. Much has been done – much more than in any other country. But always you wanted greater protection against misfortune. You wanted the state to accept larger responsibility for the individual citizen who served it faithfully. You wanted Social Security, from this day hence, you have it.

From the *Daily Mirror*, 5 July 1948.

SOURCE 16

A *Punch* cartoon, 'A Santa Claus Service', 22 December 1948.

SOURCE 17

'Dentist says if there are any more of you thinking of fitting one another up with NHS teeth for Christmas presents you've had it.'

A humorous comment by the cartoonist Giles on the enormous take-up of NHS benefits in 1948 (detail).

SOURCE 18

I was an apprentice in 1948. I spent some time at the School of Pharmacy and some at the shop. When I came in to the shop at the end of the first day of the National Health Service, there had been 50 prescriptions. In those days that was amazing. Before then the highest ever had been about 20. People seemed to go mad. I knew lots of people who got two sets of false teeth. Why did you need two sets one day when you had none the day before? I heard stories about people taking sheets of surgical gauze and using them as net curtains!

Frank Walsh, a Liverpool pharmacist, describes the early days of the NHS.

ACTIVITY

It is the first day of the National Health Service. Use Sources 15–18 to write:

a) **100 words criticising the NHS in 1948.**

b) **100 words praising the NHS in 1948.**

Massive demand

One way to measure the success of the NHS was the amount of health care it provided. The demand for health care under the new NHS exceeded all predictions. Obviously, in some cases, people were just trying to get something for nothing. However, what the huge demand really proved was how badly the nation's health had been neglected in the past.

As soon as the NHS started the number of patients on doctors' registers rose to 30 million. The NHS budgeted for £1 million of work for opticians, but within a year it had a bill of £32 million for 5.25 million pairs of spectacles and other work. In 1947, doctors gave out seven million prescriptions per month. In 1951, that figure rose to 19 million prescriptions per month. Local clinics reported that many of the women who came in had lost all or half of their teeth.

For the first time, the poor gained access to doctors and a range of treatments previously beyond their means. They also had the tremendous psychological boost of not having to worry about illness or injury. However, it was not only the poor who benefited. Bevan had said that he wanted the NHS to treat everyone. Certainly, the middle classes made full use of the NHS rather than continuing to pay for medical care. Over 95 per cent of doctors joined the NHS, and there were only 6,000 private beds in British hospitals out of a total of 240,000.

New treatments for all

From the 1950s onwards, the scale and the quality of the treatment provided by the NHS improved. Between 1948 and 1973, the number of doctors doubled. Anaesthetics became more sophisticated, allowing longer and more complex operations. Spectacular transplant surgery was carried out (see page 336). New technology enabled scans to be made of the brain and internal organs. Today, lasers are used in eye surgery and to destroy tumours.

The more everyday work of the NHS improved the lives of millions of people, with hip replacement operations, emergency treatment for accident victims and fertility treatment for childless couples, for example. Programmes of vaccination protected children from whooping cough, measles, tuberculosis and diphtheria. Even cosmetic surgery became available on the NHS in some cases. Advances in the care of the mentally ill have been huge.

The NHS has played an important part in prevention as well as cure. In the mid 1960s, governments began to invest in health education. There were campaigns to warn people about the dangers of smoking and to encourage them to take more exercise. The government has also tried to get people to drink less alcohol and to eat a more healthy diet.

These seemed to have had rather mixed success. In general, the majority of the population is healthier and lives longer. On the other hand, the Black Report in 1980 reported that there were still inequalities. The poorest people suffered more from low birth weight, cancer, heart disease and chest problems. They also made less use of dental services, immunisation, and cancer screening. According tio the report, their health had got worse since the 1960s.

Does this mean that the NHS has been a failure? It is important to see matters in perspective. In a way, the NHS can never succeed. As medicine improves, so the quality and range of services it offers increase, and expectations rise.

The NHS has produced vast improvements in the nation's health. Women in particular have benefited. Before the war, few women were entitled to the services of doctors under insurance schemes. Today, women are four times more likely to use a doctor than men, and their life expectancy is 78. These are improvements which would have been unthinkable with a system of private health insurance or health savings plans. In fact, studies have shown that the NHS treats people more cheaply than countries which operate other systems.

SOURCE 19

MORE MONEY · MORE FUN · IF YOU DON'T SMOKE!

An anti-smoking poster published by the government's Health Education Council.

FOCUS TASK

HOW BENEFICIAL HAS THE NHS BEEN?

Work in pairs or small groups.
   The aims in setting up the NHS were:

- **To make health care accessible for all**
- **To provide the same levels and quality of care in all areas**
- **To reorganise and equip hospitals properly.**

Use pages 333–34 to find some examples of these aims being met.

Health improvements in the twentieth century

As the twenty-first century approaches, we can look back at some important achievements in terms of public health. Housing, sanitation and diet are all greatly improved since 1900. Fewer children die at birth, and the children who are born are heavier and healthier. They are also far less vulnerable to diseases such as measles, tuberculosis and whooping cough. Doctors can treat an enormous range of diseases with chemical drugs which are thoroughly researched and tested. Doctors also have access to X-rays, ultrasound scans and other technology, which enable them to treat some conditions without surgery.

Defeat of the old killer diseases

In the 1990s, the dreaded killers of 100 years ago are virtually unknown. Smallpox is extinct. Tuberculosis was defeated by a vaccine known as BCG. Widespread BCG vaccination began in Britain in 1950, and it is probably fair to say that this is one of the greatest success stories of preventative medicine. A vaccine for diphtheria was available in Britain in 1920, but it was 1940 before a national programme of immunisation was introduced. The anti-tetanus vaccine came into common use during the Second World War. You may well have had an anti-tetanus booster injection if you have been bitten by a dog or other animal. There are similar stories to be told for other diseases, such as typhoid, whooping cough and measles, as you can see from Source 20.

In the late 1940s, an outbreak of polio hit Britain, leaving many thousands of children paralysed. There was no cure for this illness, but in 1955 an American, Dr Jonas Salk, developed a polio vaccine. Since 1957, a nationwide programme of immunisation against polio has virtually wiped out the disease in the UK.

Improved living standards and lifestyles

Improved health in Britain is also a result of environmental factors. For most British people, housing has improved dramatically since the Second World War. Many local authorities completed the work begun by German bombs in demolishing slums, and rehoused whole communities. New estates of council houses were built: the estates were spacious and open, with shops and facilities nearby, and the houses themselves had gardens. Above all, the new accommodation was supplied with running water and proper sanitation. In 1946, the New Towns Act created towns such as Stevenage, Basildon and many others. With the 1947 Town and Country Planning Act, the government planned for 300,000 new houses per year.

Other factors contributed to greater health. Wartime rationing had improved the diet of many British citizens, but as prosperity returned after the war people could choose from a wide range of fruit and vegetables. Technology and the Trading Standards Office made sure that food was always of a high quality. Fashions changed, and people wore modern fabrics which were simple to keep clean. Washing machines and detergents made cleanliness easy and fashionable.

But...

There have been failures, however. Some of the less successful rehousing schemes put people into badly designed high-rise flats. Unemployment, which can be associated with poor health, remains high in many areas. There are fewer smokers in Britain today, but smoking-related diseases still kill thousands each year. The numbers of people with alcohol-related problems continue to rise steadily. Stress-related illnesses consume a large proportion of Britain's health and welfare budget, and drug abuse is now a major health issue.

SOURCE 20

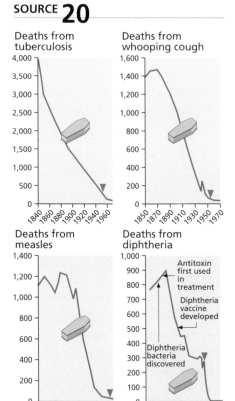

Deaths from tuberculosis

Deaths from whooping cough

Deaths from measles

Deaths from diphtheria

Antitoxin first used in treatment

Diphtheria vaccine developed

Diphtheria bacteria discovered

▼ Immunisation campaign begun

The decline of major killer diseases. The figures shown are death rates per million children.

---

1 **Does Source 20 suggest that immunisation was an important element in the decline of each disease?**

SOURCE 21

In order of importance, the major contributions to improvements in health in England and Wales were from limitation of family size (a behavioural change), increase in food supplies and a healthier physical environment (environmental influences) and specific preventative and therapeutic measures.

From *The Role of Medicine*, by T McKeown, 1976.

Diseases and treatments today

We are still a long way from conquering disease in the 1990s. At the beginning of this part of the chapter, you saw how by 1900 killer diseases were being fought in two ways: by prevention and by cure. To a large extent, this is still true of the present day.

Cancer

One of the largest killers is cancer in all its forms. Cancer is caused by the rapid spread of rogue cells which affect an organ or some other part of the body. Although there is no cure for cancer, as there is for other diseases, great advances have been made. For women, scans and tests provide important early warning of cervical and breast cancer. Many cancers can be treated successfully if they are dealt with early.

Surgery is highly effective in removing cancerous growths, although it does not always stop cancer recurring. In recent years, chemotherapy treatments have become more effective, but they have serious side effects on the patient. Radiotherapy and lasers have also been used to treat cancer, and the pharmaceutical companies continue to pour money into research. Cancer can be prevented through improved diet or changed behaviour (particularly giving up smoking).

AIDS

AIDS stands for Acquired Immune Deficiency Syndrome. The virus itself cannot kill, but it attacks the body's immune system, weakening the sufferer so much that he or she could be killed by a cold or similar infection.

There is no cure as yet, but AIDS can be avoided because it is spread mainly through sexual activity and by drug users sharing needles.

A vast amount of money has been spent on research into AIDS by pharmaceutical companies. It seems that important progress has been made, and doctors are already able to slow the progress of the HIV virus, which causes AIDS.

Historians may look back on AIDS in the late twentieth century and see it as the Black Death of its time, or it may appear simply as a minor downturn in the general improvement of public health. It is too early for us to say.

Arthritis and rheumatism

These are particularly common amongst elderly people. In some cases, diet can play an important part in prevention and cure. For example, some people find their pain is relieved if they avoid certain acidic food and drinks. Some drugs, such as Opren, have had some success in relieving rheumatism, but the side effects have been unacceptable. Again, progress is being made, but arthritis continues to be a painful and sometimes crippling disease.

Kidney disease

Failure of the kidneys or other vital internal organs is fatal without treatment. However, great advances have been made in the treatment of these illnesses. Kidney disease patients can be kept alive by dialysis, which has been made considerably more efficient by improved technology.

The only long-term solution is a kidney transplant. The success of transplant operations improves each year, but any transplant is a difficult and risky operation. Only in this sense have we 'cured' the problem of kidney failure.

Heart disease

In the 1990s, heart disease and circulatory disease are the largest killers of men and women in Britain. Much heart disease is preventable by an improved diet and more exercise, and an important cause is smoking. This has caused some controversy, as doctors have tried to refuse treatment to smokers who refuse to give up smoking. Treatments for heart disease now include bypass surgery or the fitting of an electronic pacemaker, which regulates the heart. Like kidneys, hearts can also be transplanted. The first successful transplant was on Louis Washkansky in 1967 (see Source 22). Washkansky lived for only 18 days, but in the 1990s transplant patients have a 75 per cent chance of survival. A continuing problem is the matching of organ donors to patients, because the body rejects organs which are not compatible with it.

ACTIVITY

A Draw up a 'healthy living' poster for people in your area, explaining how they might avoid the diseases and illnesses on this page.

B Would your advice have also been relevant at the beginning of the twentieth century? Explain your answer.

Hard decisions

The expense and nature of many new treatments has begun to raise moral and ethical questions for doctors, as described in Source 22.

SOURCE 22

The tragic, though not unforeseeable death of Mr Washkansky [the first heart transplant patient] in the Groote Schuur Hospital, Cape Town, brings to a close an episode which throughout has raised more anxiety than enthusiasm.

Material problems are easy to solve. It is their moral and ethical implications that reveal the defects in human nature. Particularly is this the case in medical matters.

In isolation, transplantation of a human heart raises no moral or ethical problems, but no such operation can ever be viewed in isolation. If carried out, it inevitably raises a host of direct and indirect problems, such as the dividing line between life and death, euthanasia and the cost of life; a fascinating, if devastating triad which should give lifetime employment to every moral philosopher and theologian in Christendom.

If all potential candidates up to age 54 were treated on intermittent dialysis, about £30 million per annum of direct costs and over 10,000 staff might be tied up in treating 23,000 patients. The indirect cost of treating these patients, particularly the unsuitable ones, defy computation.

From *The Times*, December 1967.

> **1 What do you think is the most serious problem facing health care today?**

This moral dilemma is becoming more and more complex. For example, modern technology can keep people in a coma alive for years: when, if ever, should the machines be switched off? Another question has arisen over terminally ill people in pain. Should the doctor, if asked, be able to give them a lethal injection? Genetic research has raised the possibility of altering babies while still in the mother's womb. As medicine becomes more powerful, this sort of problem will become more common.

Alternative medicine

In the 1980s, people began to pay more attention to 'alternative' forms of medicine. Many of these were ancient practices which had been kept alive by a few practitioners, usually in the face of hostility from the established medical profession. Acupuncture and reflexology, for example, date back thousands of years. For physical pains, chiropractors and osteopaths are increasingly in demand, and have become more 'respectable'. Homeopathy and herbal medicines are also accepted by some doctors, particularly since some patients seem to react badly to today's synthetic drugs.

It is only in recent years that these alternative medicines have begun to be widely used. Organisations such as the British School of Osteopathy and the London Homeopathic Hospital train practitioners properly in the use of their techniques.

FOCUS TASK

WHY ARE BRITISH PEOPLE HEALTHIER TODAY THAN IN 1900?

1 Look back at your work in this part of the chapter and list as many factors as you can find that have contributed to Britain's health.

2 Now decide which five factors were the most important. Write:

    a) a paragraph to explain your five chosen factors.
    b) another paragraph to explain why you have rejected the other factors.

12 The changing role of women in British society since Victorian times

12.1 Women in Victorian society

FOCUS

In Victorian Britain, women were second-class citizens. They could not vote and had far fewer legal rights than men. However, change was coming. Better education, well-organised campaigning and two world wars have dramatically changed the position of women in the late twentieth century.

In 12.1 of this chapter you will investigate:

- attitudes to women in Victorian times.
- the opportunities for education and employment that became available to women in the nineteenth century.

In 12.2 you will see:

- how and why these attitudes changed in the late nineteenth and early twentieth centuries.
- how women won the vote.

In 12.3 you will look at the effects of the two world wars on women in Britain.

In 12.4 you will examine how far women have managed to achieve equality in the late twentieth century.

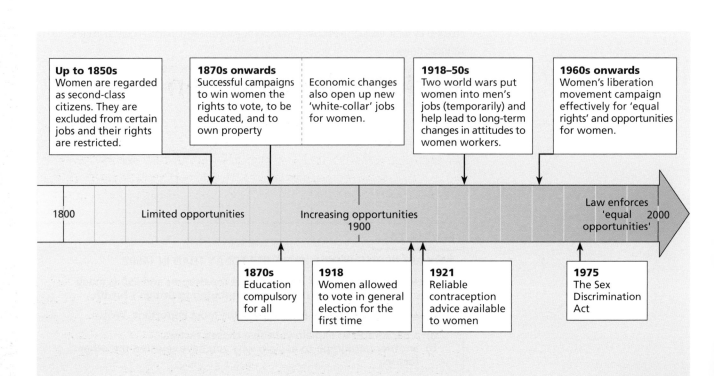

Diversity

Imagine a visiting speaker comes to your school to talk to you. The speaker's first comment is: 'I know what you all think, because you all come from this school.' Would you feel annoyed at being lumped together with all the other pupils in your school? The historian must be careful not to do this with women's history. Women make up about half of society, and cannot be treated as one group. After all, historians do not generalise about how men thought about a particular issue. We must remember that in Britain there were rich and poor women, urban and rural women, old and young women, healthy and unhealthy women. There were women living in workhouses and others living in mansions. There were women who worked in the mines, women who ran shops, and many women who stayed at home. In this chapter we will be looking particularly at the lives of middle-class and working-class women.

What are your views on equality between the sexes in Britain today? For example, do boys get more attention in class? Do girls get better marks for coursework than boys? Perhaps you have not given the issue much thought. In the middle of the nineteenth century, very few men had really considered the issue of women's rights.

The status of women in Victorian society was not high. In terms of legal rights, women seemed to be equal with children, criminals and lunatics! If a woman was married, her husband owned her property as well as his own. An important campaigner for women's rights, Millicent Fawcett, pointed out how ridiculous this law was when she had her purse stolen. When the thief was caught, he was charged with stealing the property of Mrs Fawcett's husband, Henry Fawcett.

The justification for this state of affairs was that men were said to be the decision makers, who carried the responsibility of supporting a family, whereas women were weak and needed to be protected. Women's role was as carers, and as keepers of the home.

What do you think about this argument? Think back to your work in earlier chapters of this book. Did the farmers' wives in Chapter 1 have no responsibility? What about the female textile workers in the cotton mills of Lancashire which you read about in Chapter 2? Do you think that the women coal workers would have had much time for this argument? Look back at the experiences of the women described in those chapters before you decide how they might have thought.

Middle-class women

One of the big changes caused by the industrial revolution was the growth of the middle class. The massive wealth created by the growth of Britain's economy was not shared equally around society. The middle class – a broad group, ranging from traders, shopkeepers and business owners to professionals such as lawyers and doctors – grew in size and became much richer. These people could afford to buy their own homes and pay for their children to be educated.

The middle-class wife

The middle classes also had a different idea from many working-class families about the role of women. Because hard work and manual labour was what working-class women did, the middle classes saw it as inferior. In the middle-class family, the man saw it as his responsibility to earn enough money so that his wife did not have to work. The man went out to work, while the woman ran the home. The middle-class woman's role was to support her husband: her own wishes, desires and ambitions came second to his needs and those of her family.

This middle-class ideal was reinforced by literature, art and the Church. The ideal wife was described as 'the angel in the house'. Artists invariably showed her supporting her husband or adoring her children. Although women were encouraged to attend church regularly, the Church reinforced the view of the woman as the subordinate partner in marriage. In the marriage service in the Book of Common Prayer, each partner had to promise 'to love, comfort and honour' the other. However, only the woman had 'to obey and serve'. As for sex, it was supposed to be an ordeal to be endured rather than something that women should enjoy. The ideal married woman should be respectable and delicate and demure.

SOURCE 1

'Dorothea, my love, this is not the first occasion, but it were well that it should be the last, on which you have assumed a judgement on subjects beyond your scope. Into the question how far conduct, especially on the matter of alliances, constitutes a forfeiture of family claims, I do not now enter. Suffice it, that you are not here qualified to discriminate. What I now wish you to understand is, that I accept no revision, still less dictation within that range of affairs which I have deliberated upon as distinctly and properly mine. It is not for you to interfere between me and Mr Ladislaw, and still less to encourage communications from him to you which constitute a criticism on my procedure.

In the novel *Middlemarch*, by George Eliot, written in 1872, a husband tells his wife not to interfere in a family dispute.

Many middle-class women did not even have to do housework. Their husbands were wealthy enough for them to employ servants from the working classes (just as the very richest families did). Increasingly, the role of the middle-class woman consisted of managing her servants in order to maintain a respectable and comfortable home. Women's magazines concentrated on giving advice to women about the efficient management of the household.

With the job of housework being done by working-class servants, middle-class women were encouraged to spend their time in good works or 'ladylike' hobbies, such as doing beautiful but impractical needlework. By the 1860s, a large part of Victorian girls' education consisted of social and artistic skills. The main aim of a young woman was to 'catch' a suitable husband. Women were thought to be either too delicate to work, or perhaps too empty-headed, as Source 4 suggests.

Women's fashions were luxurious, ornate and impractical, making any kind of physical activity difficult. Ladies wore their long hair in elaborate styles, and caring for it was very time-consuming. In a wealthy household, ladies would be expected to change their dresses several times a day, with different outfits for the morning, for walks, for the afternoon and for dinner.

SOURCE 2

The younger lady was in the lovely bloom and springtime of womanhood; at that age, when, if ever angels be for God's good purposes enthroned in mortal forms, they may be, without impiety, supposed to abide in such as hers.

She was not past 17. Cast in so slight and exquisite a mould; so mild and gentle; so pure and beautiful; that earth seemed not her element, nor its rough creatures her fit companions.

A description of a character, Rose Maylie, in *Oliver Twist* by Charles Dickens. Although he was a campaigner for social reform, Dickens had little time for the women's movement.

SOURCE 3

A Victorian middle-class mother poses for the camera with her daughters. Note the elaborate dresses.

1 **Write your own 20–word definition of the term 'angel in the house'.**

2 **Choose one source which you think best illustrates the middle-class ideal for women. Explain your choice.**

The unmarried middle-class woman

The above description applies only to the middle-class woman who was able to marry. However, in the nineteenth century there were fewer middle-class men than women, and many middle-class women therefore never found a husband. This put a great strain upon them, and many felt themselves to be failures. There were also very few options for paid employment. Often, unmarried women became seamstresses, but this was poorly paid and insecure work. A preferred option was to be a governess, but this too had its drawbacks: it was an extremely demanding and stressful job, and again the pay was usually low.

3 What point is the cartoonist making in Source 4?

4 How would you reply to someone who had this attitude today?

SOURCE 4

A mid-nineteenth-century cartoon.

Middle-class feminists

Some women freely accepted this life of leisure, free of housework, without the need to work, and playing a supporting role to men. Others, however, felt bored, frustrated or trapped and wanted a more meaningful life.

The sisters Elizabeth and Millicent Garrett, along with Emily Davies, were among the most determined campaigners for women's rights. It is said that Emily Davies remarked to Elizabeth Garrett, 'Well, Elizabeth, it's quite clear what has to be done. I must devote myself to securing higher education, while you open the medical profession to women. After these things are done, we must see about getting the vote.'

SOURCE 5

A lady … must not work for profit, or engage in any occupation that money can command … Ladies, [excluded] from the dairy, the confectionery, the store-room, the still-room, the poultry yard, the kitchen garden, and the orchard, have hardly yet found themselves a sphere equally useful and important … to which to apply their too abundant leisure … Life is too often divested of any real and important purpose.

An entry in Margaretta Grey's diary in 1853. Margaretta Grey was the aunt of the early feminist reformer Josephine Butler.

SOURCE 6

Women are supposed to be very calm generally: but women feel just as men feel; they need exercise for their faculties, and a field for their efforts as much as their brothers do; they suffer from too rigid a constraint, too absolute a stagnation, precisely as men suffer; and it is narrow minded in their more privileged fellow creatures to say that they ought to confine themselves to making puddings and knitting stockings, to playing the piano and embroidering bags.

An extract from *Jane Eyre*, by Charlotte Bronte, written in 1847.

5 Compare Sources 5, 6 and 7. How does each woman feel about the situation she is describing?

6 What might the authors of Sources 5–7 say to the cartoonist of Source 4?

SOURCE 7

Oh weary days, oh evenings that never seemed to end – for how many years have I watched the drawing room clock and thought that it would never reach 10! I know nothing, but the petty grinding tyranny of a good English family. Yet I love them and what am I that their life is not good enough for me? Why cannot I be satisfied with the life that satisfies so many people?

Florence Nightingale describing her boring life as a young middle-class woman in 1851.

There were role models for the early feminists to look up to. As early as 1792, Mary Wollstonecraft published *A Vindication of the Rights of Woman*. Novelists such as Charlotte Bronte showed that women were able to take a public role in some respects at least. Elizabeth Fry was the principal force in improving the dreadful state of Britain's prisons in the first half of the nineteenth century. Mary Carpenter campaigned on behalf of children who ended up in gaol, and set up special reforming schools for young criminals. However, these women were exceptions to the rule, and indeed, many of them, including Elizabeth Fry, disapproved of the idea of women's rights, as did Queen Victoria, the most powerful woman in Britain (see Source 8).

SOURCE 8

The Queen is most anxious to enlist everyone who can speak or write to join in checking this mad, wicked folly of women's rights with its attendant horrors, on which her poor, feeble sex is bent, forgetting every sense of womanly feeling and propriety … It is a subject that makes the Queen so furious that she cannot contain herself. God created men and women different – then let them remain each in their own position.

Extract from an 1870 document criticising Lady Amberley, a former lady-in-waiting of the Queen; Lady Amberley had spoken in favour of suffrage.

Working-class women

The lives of working-class women were usually very different from those of middle-class women. Although in industrial Britain most working-class women carried the main responsibility for looking after the home and family, many also had a paid job. About a third of working-class women *had* to work because they were unmarried or widowed or their husbands had left them. Most others chose to work because their husbands' wages were too low to support a family. Much of the work they did was poorly paid and based at home, and included washing, sewing or box making. The privileged few had well-paid jobs in a factory or an office.

1 Who seems to be working the hardest in Source 9?

2 Why do you think the man is not helping the woman?

SOURCE 10

Who is the fitter to have the vote, the woman who is the real head of the house – or the drunken husband?

An early comment on women's rights.

3 Do Sources 9 and 10 give a similar impression of the role of women in working-class households?

SOURCE 9

An illustration of a typical working-class home in around 1850.

The maid of all work

A common job for younger, unmarried, working-class women was in domestic service. The homes of the very rich usually had a large number of servants. Less well-off middle-class households had a maid of all work, or sometimes a maid of all work and a cook.

The maid of all work did all the housework. It was an extremely hard life, and it is not surprising that many girls preferred factory work to domestic service. The maid of all work had virtually no social life, because she was 'on call' at all hours of the day and evening. Often, her employers could only just afford a servant, which meant that her wages and accommodation were usually very poor. The constant round of shopping, cleaning, cooking and clearing up was exhausting and extremely stressful, as Sources 11 and 12 show. Servants were often badly treated and even physically beaten.

SOURCE 11

I open'd the shutters and lit the kitchen fire – shook my sooty things in the dusthole and emptied the soot there, swept and dusted the rooms and the hall, laid the cloth and got breakfast – cleaned two pairs of boots – made the beds and emptied the slops, cleared and washed the breakfast things up – cleaned the silver – cleaned the knives and got dinner ready – cleared away, cleaned the kitchen – unpacked a hamper – took two chickens to Mrs Brewer's and brought a message back – made a tart and picked and gutted two ducks and roasted them – cleaned the steps and floor on my knees, polished the boot scraper at the front of the house – cleaned the pavement outside the house on my knees – had tea – cleared away – washed up – cleaned the pantry on my knees and scour'd the tables – scrubb'd the flags round the house and clean'd the window sills – got tea at nine for the master and Mrs Warwick – cleaned the privy and passage and scullery floor on my knees – washed the door and cleaned the sink down – put the supper ready.

Hannah Cullwick was employed as a maid of all work in London. This is her diary entry for 14 July 1860.

SOURCE 12

The doctor says that, on the female side of lunatic asylums, the largest class, but one, are the maids of all work (the other being governesses). The causes are obvious enough: want of sufficient sleep from late and early hours, continual fatigue and hurry, and, even more than these, anxiety about the future from the smallness of the wages. She has no prospect but to work till she drops, having from that moment no other prospect than the workhouse. With this thought chafing at her heart, and her brain confused by her rising at five, after going to bed at an hour or two past midnight, she may easily pass into the asylum some years before she need otherwise have entered the workhouse.

An extract from an article on female industry by a feminist writer, Harriet Martineau, 1859.

4 **Why did girls avoid domestic service if they could?**

5 **Many working-class parents were keen for their daughters to take jobs as servants. Why do you think this was?**

SOURCE 13

WHAT WILL BECOME OF THE SERVANT-GALS?

Charming Lady (showing her house to benevolent old gentleman),
'THAT'S WHERE THE HOUSEMAID SLEEPS.'
Benevolent Old Gentleman. 'DEAR ME, YOU DON'T SAY SO! ISN'T IT VERY DAMP? I SEE THE WATER GLISTENING ON THE WALLS.'
Charming Lady. 'OH, IT'S NOT TOO DAMP FOR A SERVANT!'

A *Punch* cartoon from the later nineteenth century, commenting on the treatment of servants.

SOURCE 14

The young working-girl of today prefers to become a Board School Mistress, a post office clerk, a typewritress, a shop-girl, or a worker in a factory – anything rather than enter domestic service.

A Mrs Peel commenting that it was difficult to find domestic servants in 1902.

SOURCE 15

Women colliery workers, 1874.

1 **Source 16 describes a long and tiring day for a working mother. Why do you think she wanted to continue doing her job even though she got so tired?**

ACTIVITY

Imagine a conversation between a young Florence Nightingale (Source 7) and the woman in Source 16 about why each one envied the other. What would they say about each other's lives? What would they say about the men in their families?

Women in industry

Many people assume that factory work was common among working-class women. In fact, far fewer women worked in factories than as domestic servants. Young girls might prefer factory work to domestic service, but the jobs were not available. The Factory and Mines Acts of the 1830s and 1840s further reduced their opportunities to work in industry.

Factory work was highly sought-after because it was well paid and women valued the independence it gave them. Many women actually opposed the laws which reduced their working hours in the 1840s, although the laws were supposed to protect them. In the 1850s, mine inspectors found women still working underground, despite the ban on women workers (see page 123). Some were disguised as men. Women also continued to do heavy manual work above ground (see Source 15).

SOURCE 16

I get up around 5 a.m., lay the fire, clean the grate, make the tea and wake my husband. I organise the children and take them to a baby-minder on my way to work, where I arrive with my husband at 6 a.m. After a 10-hour day in the factory, I come home, light the fire to heat the bath water, collect the children and fetch the pies for tea. If it's pay day, I go shopping for the week's food and pay the rent man, the union man and the death insurance man. My next job is to blacklead and polish the grate in the living room before it gets too hot. Then I go upstairs to make the beds. After I've done that, it's time to clean the flags and bath the children. Then I prepare my husband's supper and the breakfast for the morning. Sometimes I fall asleep over my evening meal.

A Lancashire cotton worker's description of her day in 1892.

The sweated labourer

For the majority of women, the main employment option was to take in work at home, washing, ironing or sewing, or to work in a local SWEATSHOP, sewing or making objects such as brushes, boxes or candles.

SOURCE 17

2 **Do you think Source 17 is a realistic portrayal of a sweatshop? Explain your answer.**

Dressmaking in a sweatshop in the 1870s.

SOURCE 18

On entering their house, the air becomes thick with millions of hairs which float in it … Two prematurely aged women whose hair is hidden under a thick coating of fluff are sitting on low stools.

A description of a visit to a fur puller's house, 1890. Fur pullers skinned rabbits.

Political campaigners

Working-class women played an important part in the Chartist movement (see pages 266–69). In fact, they were sometimes the most RADICAL participants at Chartist gatherings. In one incident, at Llandiloes in Wales, women led a riot which resulted in the freeing of several prisoners from police cells. Women also wrote articles in Feargus O'Connor's Chartist newspaper, the *Northern Star*.

> **FOCUS TASK**
>
> **THE DIFFERENT LIVES OF VICTORIAN WOMEN**
>
> **Work in groups to create a short scene about domestic life in either a working-class household or a middle-class household in the nineteenth century. You can improvise your performance, or write a script. The scene should use as much of the evidence on pages 338–45 as possible.**

How was women's work changed by industrialisation?

As you have seen in Chapters 2–6, industrialisation dramatically changed the whole concept of work. In farming communities and the domestic system, there was no real division between work and home. People did not 'go to work' as they do today, because their work was in or around the home. In the same way, there was no sharp divide between jobs done by women. Industrialisation changed all this. When people had to 'go out' to work, work and home became separate parts of people's lives.

This change greatly affected the role of women. The best jobs in the thriving new industries were taken by men. Women tended to be left with the jobs that men did not want or which could still be done at home. Such jobs were usually poorly paid, of low status and insecure. A good example of this process was domestic service. At the beginning of the nineteenth century, roughly equal numbers of men and women were servants. However, with industrialisation men could generally earn more in industry. As a result, by the end of the century domestic service was seen as a female job (see Source 19).

SOURCE 19

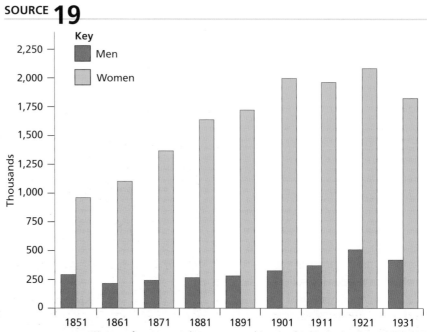

Figures for men and women working in domestic service, 1851–1931. This data comes from census returns. Questions about occupation were only added to the census in 1851.

New opportunities for women

Towards the end of the nineteenth century, new job opportunities opened up for middle-class and working-class girls.

Shop work

The building of the railways and Britain's increasing prosperity changed shopping in several ways. The grocer was no longer a skilled tradesman, blending teas and smoking hams. He now sold commodities ordered by catalogue, and he needed help in the shop. On a much larger scale, department stores were established in Britain's major towns, and these stores too needed assistants. Around half a million new jobs were created in chain stores between 1875 and 1907. Similarly, the rapid expansion of the postal service created new counter jobs in a network of local post offices.

Hours were long (sometimes 80–90 hours per week) and pay was poor, but shop work offered some free time and independence for younger girls. It was far preferable to domestic service.

Office work

For better-educated women, the horizons broadened even further. As technology improved and businesses grew, new opportunities opened up for women who were literate and could operate the new technology such as typewriters and telephones. As the Post Office's role expanded to take in the telephone service and the distribution of old-age pensions, the need for clerks grew. By 1914, the Post Office employed 90 per cent of the government's female workforce. Private companies needed people to deal with the increasing amount of paperwork and administration created by modern business methods, and these jobs were often taken by women with shorthand and typing skills. It is interesting that the growth in women's employment was closely paralleled by the rising sales of Remington typewriters!

The growing importance of women in this area must be seen in perspective, however (see Source 21). Men still held the skilled and responsible posts, which involved keeping business or public records in good order. The new technology brought lower-status jobs. It was these which became more open to women.

Teaching

The position of schoolteacher was seen as particularly respectable, and opportunities in this profession also grew rapidly. You will see on pages 348–49 how schooling for girls expanded during the period 1850–1900. In 1870, the government passed an Education Act which doubled the number of elementary school pupils, and most of the new teachers who met the increasing demand were women. Many of the young ladies who might once have become governesses now turned their ambitions in the direction of school teaching instead. There was no doubt that a career in teaching was less stressful and confining than one as a governess. By 1900, around 75 per cent of teachers were women.

Again, we must be careful to see these changes in context. If women teachers married, they had to resign. A headmistress was paid only the same as a male teacher in his first job. There were no women inspectors.

SOURCE 20

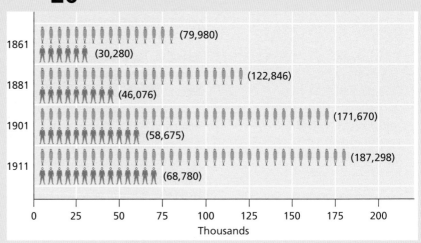

Numbers of men and women working as teachers, 1861–1911.

SOURCE 21

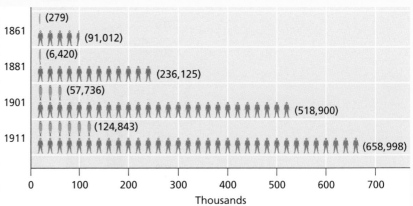

Numbers of men and women working as clerks, 1861–1911.

Nursing

You can read in Chapter 11 about how Florence Nightingale transformed the role and status of the nurse in the second half of the nineteenth century. By the 1880s, there were many new hospitals, and they were staffed by trained nurses. By 1900, around 60,000 nurses were working in British hospitals, and nursing became almost exclusively a woman's job. However, as in other areas, nurses had to resign once they were married.

SOURCE 22

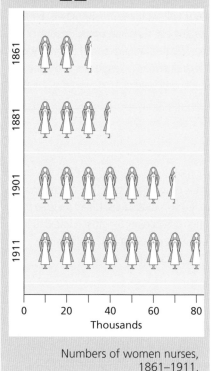

Numbers of women nurses, 1861–1911.

Limited progress

While these advances were important, we must be aware of their limitations as well. Men were paid more than women for doing the same work. Very few women were able to rise through the ranks and gain promotion as men could. Only in entirely female areas, such as the teaching of typing, could women get ahead. Banks would not appoint women cashiers, as they felt customers would be concerned about the safety of their money.

What is more, all the opportunities were for single women. Once they married, female clerks were expected to resign and stay at home. It was a similar story with shop work and, to a lesser extent, in the factories. Once working-class women married, they usually took in home work such as laundry or ironing.

The effects of legislation

Many women worked long hours for poor pay in other trades, such as the metal and pottery industries. You read in Chapter 4 about the Factory Acts, and how they controlled hours and conditions in the textile mills; you have also looked at the Mines Acts in Chapter 5. In some respects, these Acts did improve working conditions for women. However, recent historians have pointed out that the campaigners for these bills seemed to be motivated as much by a desire to keep women at home as to improve their working conditions! As a result of the Acts, the number of women in heavy industry fell, but the number working in other trades rose. Since only mines and factories were covered by these laws, one could argue that they made working conditions for women worse, because they drove them into industries which were unregulated.

SOURCE 23

[When you cough] … if you have worked in the reds, it [matter from the lungs] will come up red. If you have worked in the blues, it will come up blue. If you have worked in the blacks, it will come up black … and the yellow too.

A report of a Parliamentary Committee on lead poisoning in the metal industry, 1893–94.

SOURCE 24

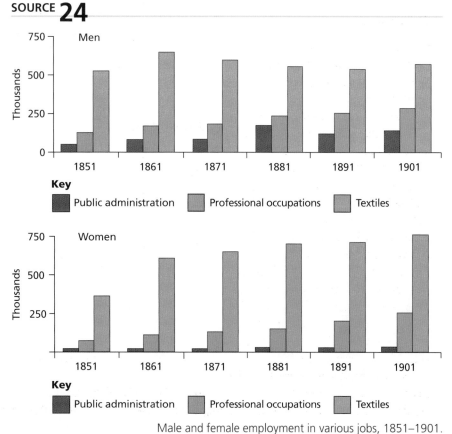

Male and female employment in various jobs, 1851–1901.

SOURCE 25

Girls are told that Latin is not a feminine requirement, mathematics is only fit for boys and she must devote herself to ladylike accomplishments ... nothing is more common than to hear the difference in the future destiny of boys and girls assigned as a reason for a difference in the character and extent of their education, but I cannot find that any part of the training given in ladies' schools educates them for a domestic life or prepares them for womanly duties. The reason why modern languages, which are especially useful in business, should be considered particularly appropriate for women, who spend most of their time in the home, is still one of the unsolved mysteries of the English educational system.

Comments made by the Schools Inquiry Commission (the Taunton Commission), 1864.

SOURCE 26

In the girls' department [of the school] ... everywhere we are met by tokens of penury [poverty] and bad conditions at home. Children are pointed out to us as stunted in growth, with faces old beyond their years, burdened out of school with the whole charge of the wretched little home. 'Never no time to play,' as one of them explains ... Even the youngest of these girls, we find, has often to wash and dress and feed the baby, cook the father's dinner when the mother is at work, and 'clean up' the single room in which the family live.

A government inspector's report from 1870.

SOURCE 27

Girls at Cheltenham Ladies' College surveying and making maps.

How was women's education improved in Victorian Britain?

Each of the new jobs mentioned on pages 346–47 depended on education. Shop assistants needed to be able to count and add; clerks had to be skilled readers and writers; nurses and teachers had to be widely educated.

In early Victorian Britain, education for both girls and boys was patchy and disorganised. Working-class children might receive some basic education at either Sunday School or dame school, or, if they worked in a cotton mill, at a mill school (this was compulsory after the 1833 Factory Act). However, the vast majority of working-class children had no education at all.

Middle-class parents did educate their daughters, but often very differently from their sons. Middle-class boys were educated at school, daughters usually at home by governesses. Boys were taught a broad curriculum to prepare them for a working life. Girls had a much narrower curriculum, geared towards the pursuit of a husband. Middle-class girls would learn etiquette, dancing and crafts such as needlework. They usually studied foreign languages and some literature, but 'important' subjects such as mathematics and geography were seen as suitable only for boys (see Source 25).

The Royal Commissions

This situation began to alter in the 1850s and 1860s. A key figure in bringing about this change was Emily Davies, who led campaigns for reform in the education of girls. The campaigners convinced the government to set up a series of three Royal Commissions. Under pressure from Davies, the Taunton Commission paid special attention to schooling for girls. It found that there were very few secondary schools for girls – in 1868 there were only 12 in the whole country – and even when there was education for girls, it was of poor quality.

Elementary education

In 1870, the government made it compulsory for all local authorities to set up enough schools to provide elementary education for all children up to the age of 10 in their area. This was extended to 11 and then 12 in the 1890s. The authority could make school attendance compulsory, and some did. However, they faced problems in enforcing this, particularly in the case of girls (see Source 26). The first schools were not free: the parents paid a few pence each week. The children were often kept away from school when their parents needed them to help with work. In 1880, elementary school attendance was made compulsory, and in 1891 schooling was made free. In 1893, the leaving age was fixed at 11.

Secondary and higher education

Some middle-class women campaigners had their eyes set on a higher prize than women becoming teachers or nurses. They wanted to enter the professions, including law and medicine. Access to such jobs was entirely dependent on obtaining secondary and higher education.

By the middle of the nineteenth century, the variable quality of governesses was causing concern. In 1848, professors from King's College, London, founded Queen's College to educate governesses. Two students from Queen's went on to make important contributions to schooling for girls. In 1853, Frances Buss transformed her private school into the North London Collegiate School for Ladies. In 1858, Dorothea Beale became headmistress of Cheltenham Ladies' College. Both taught subjects such as maths, science and geography, which were generally frowned upon for girls. They also used the latest teaching methods and eagerly entered their girls for public examinations. Miss Beale recorded in her diaries the opposition to her views of many fathers, who felt that girls' schooling did not require such vigour.

Nevertheless, the example of these two pioneers inspired other women. Maria Grey founded the Girls' Public Day School Trust, which was funded by business sponsors and share certificates. It began with three schools in Chelsea, Notting Hill and Croydon, but by the 1890s it ran 40 schools and taught 7,000 pupils. Maria Grey also began to try other new ideas: for example, the Trust's school in Croydon opened a kindergarten. She also set up the National Union for Promoting Higher Education of Women in 1872, and in 1878 established the first teacher training college for women.

The universities

The campaigns for secondary and higher education were closely linked. Emily Davies succeeded in persuading Cambridge, Durham and Oxford Universities to allow women to sit their examinations from the mid 1860s onwards, although women still could not be students or receive degrees. In 1869, Davies opened a girls' college at Hitchin, which in 1873 became Girton College, the first women's college at Cambridge.

Other institutions went a step further and accepted women on equal terms with men: the University of London in 1878, Victoria University (which later became the Universities of Liverpool, Manchester and Leeds) in 1880, and Durham University in 1895. However, it was a long and difficult struggle, and was nowhere near complete even by 1900. Davies was fighting a deeply ingrained prejudice against competent, well-educated and independent-minded women. Oxford did not give equality to women students until 1947. At Cambridge, male students organised demonstrations against the admission of women to the University. Their banner hung over a Cambridge square read, 'Get you to Newnham [College], Beatrice; here's no place for you maids'.

1 **Read Source 28. With a partner, list all the different arguments used to suggest that educating women is a mistake.**

SOURCE 28

The Woman of the Future! She'll be deeply read, that's certain,
With all the education gained at Newnham or at Girton;
She'll puzzle men in Algebra with horrible quadratics,
Dynamics, and the mysteries of higher mathematics;
Or, if she turns to classic tomes, a literary roamer,
She'll give you bits of HORACE, or sonorous lines from HOMER.

You'll take a maiden in to dine, and find, with consternation,
She scorns the light frivolities of modern conversation;
And not for her the latest bit of fashionable chatter,
Her pretty head is well-nigh full of more important matter;
You talk of Drama or Burlesque, theatric themes pursuing,
She only thinks of what the Dons at Oxford may be doing.

The Woman of the Future may be very learned-looking,
But dare we ask if she'll know aught of housekeeping or cooking;
She'll read far more, and that is well, than empty-headed beauties,
But has she studied with it all a woman's chiefest duties?
We [know] she'll ne'er acknowledge, till her heated brain grows cooler,
That Woman, not the Irishman, should be the true home-ruler.

O pedants of these later days, why go on undiscerning,
To overload a woman's brain and cram our girls with learning?
You'll make a woman half a man, the souls of parents vexing,
To find that all the gentle sex this process is unsexing.
Leave one or two nice girls before the sex your system smothers,
Or what on earth will poor men do for sweethearts, wives and mothers?

A poem from *Punch*, 1884.

Elizabeth Garrett Anderson

★ Born 1836 in London, brought up in Suffolk.
★ At the age of 24 she studied medicine, but found it difficult to qualify because of opposition from doctors.
★ In 1865 she passed the Apothecaries Hall examination (a medical qualification).
★ In 1870 she became a physician at the East London Hospital and gained an official medical degree from the University of Paris.
★ She was a member of the London School Board.
★ Like her sister Millicent Fawcett she was a feminist and became England's first woman mayor in 1908.
★ She died in 1917.

1 What reasons did people have for not educating girls in the same way as boys?

2 Which of Sources 25–29 is most useful for finding out about opposition to education for women?

3 What reasons did women campaigners have for wanting better education for girls and women?

How did women gain access to medical schools?

There were no officially recognised women doctors in Britain before 1866. One of the most dramatic battles for access to higher education was over medical training. This campaign was spearheaded by Elizabeth Garrett (later Anderson) and Sophia Jex-Blake. In 1859, Garrett began her campaign to be allowed to train as a doctor. To begin with, she became a nurse at the Middlesex Hospital, where she was also allowed to attend lectures. However, the male students protested against her presence in the lecture theatre and asked for her to be banned.

SOURCE 29

I must decline to give you instructions in anatomy … the entrance of ladies into dissecting rooms and anatomical theatres is undesirable in every respect … it is not necessary that fair ladies should be brought in contact with such foul scenes …

A letter to Elizabeth Garrett from a surgeon in 1863.

Garrett persevered, managing to pass her medical exams in 1866, but she was not allowed to practise as a doctor. Even so, her example inspired others. In 1876, campaigners succeeded in persuading MPs to pass a law opening up all medical qualifications to women. In the same year, Jex-Blake and six others passed their medical exams. However, the battle was not yet over. Garrett had to take the Royal College of Apothecaries to court to have her qualification recognised before she was allowed to register as a doctor, and for another five years the Royal College of Surgeons continued to forbid women to train alongside men.

In 1874, Jex-Blake and Garrett founded the London School of Medicine for Women, specifically to train women doctors. By the time Garrett retired as head in 1902, it had 200 students, and there were 355 practising women doctors.

FOCUS TASK

HOW DID EDUCATION FOR WOMEN IMPROVE IN THE SECOND HALF OF THE NINETEENTH CENTURY?

1 Look back over pages 348–50 and draw a timeline of the developments in education for girls and women over the period 1850–1900.

2 Now write two paragraphs explaining:
   a) what education for women was like in 1850.
   b) what improvements were made between 1850 and 1900.

3 List the reformers mentioned on pages 348–50. Beside each one note her main achievement.

4 Which reformer's achievements do you think were most significant? Explain your choice.

Did women achieve greater equality in marriage?

Caroline Norton was a popular novelist (one of the acceptable jobs for middle-class women in the early nineteenth century). She was married with three sons, but the marriage was a deeply unhappy one. Her husband, George Norton, was a violent and jealous man. In 1836, after nine years of marriage, they separated, and George accused Caroline of having an affair with Lord Melbourne, the Prime Minister. The case was thrown out, but Caroline, far from being a winner, was left with nothing. She was unable to obtain a divorce, because although husbands could divorce wives it was virtually impossible for wives to divorce husbands. Furthermore, she had lost the right to see her children, and her husband continued to try to take possession of the money she earned from writing.

Caroline Norton was not a feminist (as the campaigners for women's rights were called). However, she campaigned vigorously against the laws which left her powerless as a married woman. She had many factors in her favour. In her youth she had been a leading light in fashionable society, and as a result she had powerful friends. She was very beautiful and intelligent, and as a bestselling writer was well equipped to write letters and pamphlets pointing out the injustice of the laws as they stood.

SOURCE 30

A married woman in England has no legal existence: her being is absorbed in that of her husband. Years of separation or desertion cannot alter this position … She has no professions … her property is his property … An English wife has no rights even to her clothes or ornaments; her husband may take them and sell them if he pleases, even though they may be the gifts of relatives or friends, or bought before marriage. An English wife cannot make a will … the law gives what she has to him, and no will she could make would be valid … An English wife cannot legally claim her own earnings. Whether wages for manual labour, or payment for intellectual exertion, whether she weed potatoes, or keep a school, her salary is the husband's.

A letter from Caroline Norton to the Queen, 1855.

ACTIVITY

Write a letter from Queen Victoria in response to Source 30. You will need to look back at Source 8, but remember also that the Queen knew Caroline Norton.

4 Write a headline to summarise the measures in each of the Acts as they might have appeared in:

a) a feminist newspaper.
b) an anti-feminist newspaper.

5 Explain how each Act would have helped Caroline Norton.

6 Do you think these Acts gave women equality with men within marriage? Explain your answer.

7 It was more difficult to pass the Property Acts than the other Acts. Why do you think this was?

8 Would you regard the changes to the legal position of women as evidence of a changing attitude to women, or as a reluctant response to women's protests? Explain your choice.

Custody of Infants Act, 1839

Norton soon found that she was not alone. Many women and some men supported her case. The first major step had come in 1839 with the Custody of Infants Act. Mothers gained legal custody of children under seven years and access to children over that age (so long as the woman had not been found guilty of adultery).

Matrimonial Causes Act, 1857

Another campaigner, Barbara Leigh Smith (later Bodichon) published a pamphlet in 1857 explaining the position of women under the law in simple English that everyone could understand. Her work and that of other campaigners led to the passing of the Matrimonial Causes Act of 1857. This Act meant that divorces could be obtained through a new Court of Divorce rather than only by an expensive private Act of Parliament. Also, women who had been deserted by their husbands now gained the same rights to own or bequeath property as single women.

It was an important step, but the main result of the Act was to make it easier for men to divorce their wives for adultery. Unlike men, who could divorce their wives purely on the grounds of adultery, women had to prove that husbands had been cruel or committed an offence. The divorce rate began to rise steadily, but men were still far more free than women to end an unsuccessful marriage.

Married Women's Property Acts, 1870 and 1882

The next important improvement in women's rights came in 1870. The Married Women's Property Act gave married women the right to own property and to keep their earnings from work. However, there were several loopholes. Married women's property was not entirely under their own control until the second Married Women's Property Act of 1882. There was much opposition to these measures in Parliament, and it took 18 attempts to get the two Married Women's Property Acts passed.

Guardianship of Infants Act and Married Women's Act, 1886

Parliament passed two more important Acts in 1886. By the Guardianship of Infants Act, the mother now became the legal guardian of the children in a family if the father died. As a result of the Married Women's Act, a husband who deserted his wife had to pay maintenance. In 1891, a court passed a judgement that a man could not force his wife to live with him.

What about the vote?

The advances in work, education and legal rights in this period were real and significant. Women, particularly middle-class women, had gained important rights over their property and new opportunities for education. New jobs and careers were available.

However, one should not overstate the progress made. Women were still very much the inferior partners in marriages. They were barred from most professions. They could not even vote. For many campaigners, this was the most basic injustice of all. To them, it seemed that gaining the right to vote would be a key to many other changes. Yet the evidence of the nineteenth century was that every advance involved an intense struggle. With an all-male Parliament elected by an all-male electorate, women were going to have to fight to move closer to the centre of politics.

You will examine the struggle to win the vote for women in Part 2 of this chapter.

SOURCE 31

"WOMAN'S WRONGS."

Brutal husband: 'Ah! You'd better go snivellin' to the House of Commons, you had! Much they're likely to do for yer! Read that!'

A cartoon published in *Punch* in 1874.

FOCUS TASK

FACTORS FOR CHANGE

1   Write a paragraph to explain how each of the following factors affected the role and status of women. You should include both positive and negative effects.

   • Government action.
   • Education.
   • The Church.
   • New technology.
   • Changes in industry.

2   You might think other factors were also important. If so, add them to the list and write a paragraph to explain how they affected the role and status of women.

---

1   Look at Source 31. Is the cartoonist sympathetic to or opposed to women's fight for legal rights? Explain your answer.

FOCUS TASK

THE STATUS OF WOMEN IN VICTORIAN SOCIETY

1   Work in groups. One half of your group should prepare a display of sources and comment with the title *Women 1850–1900: All Change*. The other half should prepare a display of sources and comment entitled *Women 1850–1900: Business as Usual*.

2   Compare the two displays, and then write your own balanced report, weighing up the evidence. You may wish to organise it under headings such as the following:

   • Education.
   • Work.
   • Standing in society.
   • Middle-class women.
   • Working-class women.

12.2 *Why did some women get the vote in 1918?*

SOURCE 1

Why should women be left out when the Bill makes it possible for some paupers and lunatics to be given the vote? We are always talking about political revolutions but we do not take notice of the fact that there has been a silent domestic revolution taking place around us.

Written by John Stuart Mill in 1866, when Parliament was discussing a Bill to give the vote to working-class men. Mill was a radical political thinker and writer.

> 2 What do you think Mill means by a 'silent domestic revolution' in Source 1?
>
> 3 Does this tie in with the impression of the role of women you have gained from the last 14 pages?

By 1900, women campaigners had secured wider opportunities for women in education, and had also made important changes to their legal position. However, they had not achieved one of their major objectives: women's SUFFRAGE, the right to vote in general elections. Women had been campaigning for this since the 1850s, along with some influential male supporters.

The case for women's suffrage

In 1897, organisations such as the Female Political Union and the Manchester Women's Suffrage Committee joined together to form the National Union of Women's Suffrage Societies (NUWSS). These campaigners pointed out that the FRANCHISE had been extended for men in 1832, 1867 and 1884. They were particularly upset about the 1884 Act, because the men enfranchised by it were generally less well off and much less well educated than the suffragists.

It is important to stress that these early campaigners were mainly middle-class women. They did not demand the vote for all women; they simply felt that women should have equal access to the franchise. In other words, just as men qualified to vote by means of their wealth or property, women who owned property should qualify too. They could point out that women made up over half the population; because of this surplus of women, more and more of them had to earn their own living instead of marrying. (In 1871, two-thirds of all women aged 20–24 were single.) If they owned property or earned money, they paid tax as men did. The suffragist campaign emphasised the responsibilities carried by most women, as shown in Source 2. It was a well-organised movement, concentrating on powerful, simple arguments.

SOURCE 2

A postcard published by the women's suffrage movement.

SOURCE 3

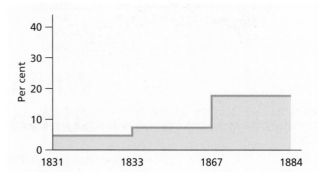

The percentage of the adult population (male and female) who could vote, 1831–84.

SOURCE 4

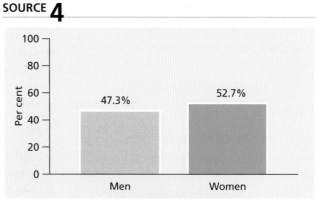

The adult population (over the age of 21) in 1911.

B. 60.

National Union of Women's Suffrage Societies,
14, GT. SMITH STREET, WESTMINSTER, LONDON, S.W.
LAW-ABIDING.   NON-PARTY.

President:—Mrs. HENRY FAWCETT, LL.D.
Colours—Red, White and Green.

Anti-Suffrage Arguments.

Anti-Suffragists say that the "The Voter, in giving a vote, pledges himself to uphold the consequences of his vote at all costs" and that "women are physically incapable of making this pledge."

What does this Mean?

When the issue at a General Election is PEACE or WAR, and a man votes for WAR, does he himself have to fight?

No!!

The men who fight are seldom qualified to vote, and the men who vote are never compelled to fight.

What is the Voters part in War?

He is called upon to PAY THE BILL.

Are Women Physically incapable of this?

Apparently **NOT**.

They are forced to pay in equal proportions with the men who alone have made the decision. Surely this is not fair! Since men and women are equally involved in the consequences, should not men and women equally have power to decide?

"But some matters discussed in the House of Commons concern men more than women."

True, but just as many concern women more than men.

Is not the Housing Problem a woman's question since

"Woman's Place is the Home?"

Are not EDUCATION, a Pure Milk Supply, and a Children's Charter questions for women, since

"The Woman's Business is to look after the Baby?"

Is not the Taxation of Food a woman's question since women are

"The Housekeepers of the Nation?"

Women claim **votes**, not because they are, or want to be, LIKE MEN, but because they are **Different**, and have somewhat different interests and different views. They want the vote as a tool, with which to do **not Men's Work**, but **Women's Work**, which men have left undone, or are trying unsuccessfully to do.

LET THE WOMEN HELP!

"Two Heads are Better than one!!"

Published by the NATIONAL UNION OF WOMEN'S SUFFRAGE SOCIETIES, 14, Great Smith Street, S.W.; and Printed by THE TEMPLAR PRINTING WORKS, 168, Edmund Street, Birmingham.

A handbill published by the NUWSS.

Who opposed women's suffrage?

The opposition to reform was extremely strong, however. You can see from Source 6 how Queen Victoria felt about women's suffrage. The evidence is that many women shared the Queen's views. Even a prominent woman such as Florence Nightingale felt that there were more important issues. The Liberal leader William Gladstone had fought bitterly against the 1857 Matrimonial Causes Act and continued to oppose extensions of women's rights.

When John Stuart Mill suggested female suffrage in 1867, he was confronted with a range of arguments against the measure. For example, women were said to be too emotional and impulsive to be trusted with the vote. The mental strain of making the decision would be too great for some women. Women should be protected from the harsh and sometimes grubby world of politics.

SOURCE 6

With the vote, woman would become the most hateful, heartless and disgusting of human beings. Where would be the protection which man was intended to give the weaker sex?

A comment by Queen Victoria.

SOURCE 7

The women who wish [for the vote] form but a very small proportion of those whose opinions they say they represent.

From an article in the *Englishman's Domestic Magazine*, 1870.

SOURCE 8

Women strongly protest against the proposed parliamentary franchise to women, distasteful to the great majority of women and mischievous to themselves and the state.

An extract from *Appeal Against Female Suffrage*, a document published in 1889 and signed by 104 women.

SOURCE 9

... that women should have the suffrage I think no one can be more deeply convinced than I ... But it will be years before you obtain the suffrage for women. And in the meantime there are evils which press much more hardly on women than the want of suffrage ...

Written by Florence Nightingale in 1867.

---

1 **List the different reasons for opposing women's suffrage given in Sources 6–11.**

2 **Why would opponents of women's suffrage be particularly pleased to see Sources 6 and 11?**

3 **How could Source 11 be used by both supporters and opponents of women's suffrage?**

4 **From pages 353–55 choose what you regard as the most effective piece of propaganda for or against women's suffrage. Explain your choice.**

SOURCE 10

No man of sense has any blind prejudice against female voting in the abstract ... If it were proved that the sex really desired to be represented by the maiden and widow householders who belong to it, or asked for a still larger enfranchisement, the case of Mr Mill would be much strengthened ... But ever since the world was created, the great mass of women has been of weaker mental power than men and with an instinctive tendency to submit themselves to the control of the stronger sex. Their destiny is marriage, their chief function is maternity.

A leading article from *The Times* in 1867, written in response to John Stuart Mill's comments in Source 1.

SOURCE 11

I take the view that giving the vote to capable citizens, be they many, is an addition to the strengths of the state. This strength of the state is in a representative system of government.

I do not wish to trespass on the delicacy, the purity and the refinement of woman's nature by giving her the vote.

Two statements made in 1880 by William Gladstone, leader of the Liberal Party.

Why did Parliament not give women the vote before 1900?

By 1900, the suffragists had the majority of MPs on their side (in other words, more than half of MPs said that they wanted to give women the vote). However, there was a rather curious political situation in Parliament with regard to women's suffrage. Many backbench Liberal MPs were supporters of votes for women, but the Liberal leaders were opposed to it. This was because only better-off, property-owning women would get the vote, and they feared these women would vote Conservative. On the other hand, some Conservative leaders were quite interested in women's suffrage, because they liked the prospect of more Conservative voters, but they held back from taking action because Conservative backbench MPs were completely opposed.

ACTIVITY

Write a letter from a campaigner for women's suffrage to Parliament, suggesting ways out of the political stalemate and reasons for working hard to find a solution.

FOCUS TASK

VOTES FOR WOMEN: FOR AND AGAINST

Work in pairs. Use the information and sources in this section to produce two campaign pamphlets or posters.

One should argue for giving women the vote, responding to the arguments in Sources 6–11. Here are some arguments you could use:

- **Women making up the majority of the population.**
- **There were many single women who were well educated or ran businesses; they were just as productive members of society as men were.**
- **Women taxpayers.**

The other pamphlet should argue that this would be unwise, using the ideas in Sources 6–11 and the following:

- **The government's lack of interest.**
- **The corrupting influence of the vote; women were seen as pure and good, and it was believed that exposing them to the big wide world might 'damage' them.**
- **Other more pressing issues.**

---

5 **In 1900, which of the following do you think was the most significant barrier facing the suffragists in the fight to win the vote?**

- **The fact that the issue was not considered important enough.**
- **Men's low opinion of women's minds.**
- **The state of the political parties in Parliament.**

Were the suffragettes more important than the suffragists in the campaign for the vote?

The suffragists

The early campaigners for the vote were known as suffragists, and as you have seen they were mainly (though not all) middle-class women. They had achieved some success, gaining the support of many Liberal MPs and some Conservative leaders, and the new but rather small Labour Party. When John Stuart Mill had suggested giving votes to women in 1867, 73 MPs had supported the motion.

The suffragists' campaign was extremely effective in terms of bringing the issue to people's attention. After so many MPs voted in favour of women's suffrage in 1867, large numbers of local women's suffrage societies were formed. By the time they came together in 1897 to form the National Union of Women's Suffrage Societies, there were over 500 local branches. By 1902, the campaign had gained the support of working-class women as well. In 1901–1902, Eva Gore-Booth gathered the signatures of 67,000 textile workers in northern England for a petition to Parliament.

The leader of the movement was Millicent Fawcett, sister of the medical campaigner Elizabeth Garrett Anderson (see page 350). Her husband Henry was a Liberal MP, who clashed several times with the Liberal leader Gladstone over this issue. Millicent Fawcett believed in constitutional campaigning. For example, she argued her case with MPs, presented petitions and organised meetings. She felt that it was crucial to keep the issue in the public eye: this campaign, along with other changes going on, would achieve the vote. She talked of the suffragist movement as being like a glacier, slow but unstoppable.

SOURCE 12

Women's suffrage will not come, when it does come, as an isolated phenomenon; it will come as a necessary corollary [side effect] of other changes which have been gradually and steadily modifying during the century the social history of our country. It will be a political change ... based upon social, educational and economic changes which have already taken place.

Written by Millicent Fawcett in 1886.

The suffragists issued leaflets, collected signatures on petitions and held meetings. They met leading politicians and argued their case. At every election, they questioned the candidates on their attitudes to women's suffrage. However, they had no real success, even though sympathetic MPs introduced private bills to Parliament proposing to give women the vote in every year of the 1870s except 1874. In the 1880s and in 1897, there seemed to be a real chance of success, as a majority of MPs supported the measure, but Parliament ran out of time to discuss the reform. The problem was that no party was prepared to adopt women's suffrage as a policy. In all, the issue of votes for women was raised in Parliament 15 times before 1900, and 15 times women were refused the vote.

1 What 'other changes' is Mrs Fawcett referring to in Source 12?

SOURCE 13

THE ANTI-SUFFRAGE SOCIETY AS PROPHET

THE ASS – 'Woe and desolation! Behold a woman-enfranchised England, prostrate beneath her descending foes!'

A

WOMAN SUFFRAGE

Mʳˢ BULL – 'We should get on better, John, if I rode a horse of my own'.

B

SHE. IT IS TIME I GOT OUT OF THIS PLACE. WHERE SHALL I FIND THE KEY?

CONVICTS AND LUNATICS HAVE NO VOTE FOR PARLIAMENT

Should all Women be classed with these?

C

Three suffragist cartoons.
The first cartoon is attacking the Anti-Suffrage Society (ASS) who had predicted giving women the vote would leave Britain vulnerable to attack. 'Das Vaterland' refers to Germany.

> 2 How would each of the cartoons in Source 13 help the suffragist cause?
>
> 3 Which is most effective, in your opinion? Explain your choice.

The suffragettes

The lack of success frustrated many suffragists. As a result, in 1903, Mrs Emmeline Pankhurst founded a new campaigning organisation, the Women's Social and Political Union. Mrs Pankhurst felt that the movement had to become more radical and militant if it was to succeed. The *Daily Mail* called these new radicals 'suffragettes', and they soon made the headlines.

The suffragettes disrupted political meetings and harassed ministers. The Liberal Prime Minister, Asquith, who was firmly opposed to women's suffrage, came in for particularly heavy abuse, but, as Source 14 shows, other members of the Cabinet were not safe.

SOURCE 14

Last night the Liberals held a meeting in Manchester. Sir Edward Grey, the Foreign Secretary, was to speak. Miss Christabel Pankhurst [daughter of Emmeline] got up from her chair and shouted, 'Will you give votes to women?' Sir Edward replied, 'This is a party matter which I am not prepared to discuss.' Miss Pankhurst was then forcibly ejected from the meeting.

From *The Times*, 4 October 1905.

The relationship between the suffragists and the suffragettes was difficult. Rivalry between the two groups did not help the cause, and Christabel Pankhurst called for the two wings of the movement to join forces. However, Millicent Fawcett was not prepared to link up with the suffragettes. She could understand their frustrations, but she was concerned that their more violent methods might be counter-productive.

SOURCE 15

If Mrs Fawcett and Mother [Emmeline Pankhurst] had stood together at the door of the House of Commons, it might have opened. The Prime Minister could not easily have fought both wings of the Women's Movement.

Christabel Pankhurst writing in 1959.

1 Read Source 16 carefully. What point are the writers making?

SOURCE 16

Hampstead Women's Social and Political Union,
178, FINCHLEY ROAD, N.W.

WINDOW BREAKING
AND
INCITEMENT
TO
MUTINY.

For Breaking Windows as a Political protest, Women are now in H.M. Gaols serving sentences of **Four and Six months imprisonment.**

For Inciting Soldiers to Disobey Orders, a much more serious crime, known to the law as a felony, and punishable by penal servitude, the Publishers of the " Syndicalist," were sentenced to nine months hard labour, and the Printers of the paper to six months hard labour.

The Government under the pressure of men with votes reduced this sentence on the Publishers to **Six months imprisonment without hard labour.**

and the sentence on the Printers to
One month without hard labour.

IS THIS JUSTICE TO VOTELESS WOMEN ?

A suffragette handbill.

2 Do you regard Source 19 as effective propaganda? Explain your answer.

3 Why might a suffragette be more annoyed by Source 19 than Source 18?

Direct action

Despite the disapproval of the suffragists, the suffragette campaign intensified and became more vocal. In 1908, the suffragette Edith New began making speeches in Downing Street; to stop the police moving her on, she chained herself to the railings. In the same year an enormous rally was held in Hyde Park. In October, the Pankhursts and 'General' Flora Drummond were sent to prison for inciting a crowd to 'rush' the House of Commons. The reaction of the public was mixed: some were bemused by this behaviour, while others were alarmed. Millicent Fawcett also watched developments with concern. The suffragettes, for their part, claimed they were being singled out for unfair treatment (see Source 16).

SOURCE 17

Militancy is abhorred by me, and the majority of suffragists. None of the great triumphs of the women's movement … have been won by physical force: they have been triumphs of moral and spiritual force. But militancy has been brought into existence by the blind blundering of politicians … If men had been treated by the House of Commons as women have been treated, there would have been bloody reprisals all over the country.

I don't feel it is the right thing, and yet the spectacle of so much self-sacrifice moves people who would otherwise sit still and do nothing … I am told that the reporters who actually see what takes place in the street are impressed; but they are not allowed to report things as they happened … Nothing is reported except what can be turned into ridicule.

Millicent Fawcett on the events of 1908.

Opposition

The suffrage campaigners had always faced opposition, but as their activities increased, so did the campaign of their opponents.

SOURCE 18

A poster advertising an anti-suffrage demonstration.

SOURCE 19

An anti-suffragette poster, typical of the sort of attitude suffragettes faced.

SOURCE 20

A suffragette postcard from 1913.

Hunger strikes

In prison, the suffragettes continued to protest, by going on hunger strike. The government responded by ordering the force feeding of protesters. The WPSU made the most of this, with posters such as Source 21, but it was hardly necessary. Force feeding was brutal and degrading, and it won a good deal of public sympathy for the suffragettes (see Source 21).

In 1913, the government passed a new Act which allowed hunger strikers to leave prison, recover a little and then return to finish their sentence. Campaigners called this the Cat and Mouse Act (see Source 20).

SOURCE 21

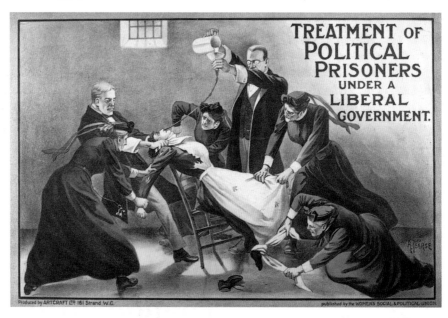

A suffragette poster from 1909, protesting about force feeding.

Increasing militancy

In 1911, Prime Minister Asquith announced that he planned to introduce votes for all men, and that an extra clause about women's votes could be tacked on to the Bill. The suffragettes were furious, because they wanted a proper Suffrage Bill dealing only with women. The attitude of the government was that there were other issues that were much more pressing and urgent than a separate Bill on votes for women.

The campaign became much more violent. Suffragettes smashed windows, set fire to letter boxes and damaged cricket pitches and golf courses. Bombs were placed in warehouses, and telephone wires were cut. Art galleries closed after suffragettes slashed valuable paintings.

SOURCE 22

Police arresting a suffragette who has chained herself to the railings of Buckingham Palace, May 1914.

ACTIVITY

Work in groups.

You are organising a museum exhibition about the campaign for women's suffrage. You must make a split panel – one half giving a flavour of the suffragist campaign, and the other half showing that of the suffragettes. Include a picture and an extract from a written source, and your comparison of the aims, message and methods of the two groups.

SOURCE 24

The woman rushed from the rails as the horses swept round Tattenham Corner. She did not interfere with the racing but she nearly killed the jockey as well as herself and she brought down a valuable horse. A deed of this kind is unlikely to increase the popularity of the women's cause.

From *The Times*, June 1913.

SOURCE 25

Haven't the suffragettes the sense to see that the very worst kind of campaigning for the vote is to try to intimidate or blackmail a man into giving them what he would otherwise gladly give?

A comment by Lloyd George, 1913.

1 **Choose what you regard as the most effective piece of propaganda for or against women's suffrage and explain your choice.**

2 **What do you regard as the greatest achievement and the greatest failure of the suffragettes?**

3 **Do you think that their achievements outweigh their failures or the other way round? Explain your choice.**

4 **Some people say that 'all publicity is good publicity'. Would the Pankhursts agree with this statement? Would Millicent Fawcett agree?**

FOCUS TASK

'The impact of the suffragettes was more spectacular, but the work of the suffragists was more effective.' Do you agree with this statement? Explain your answer in paragraphs, covering:

- **evidence which shows that the suffragists were effective.**
- **evidence which shows the limits of their success.**
- **evidence of the impact of the suffragettes.**
- **evidence showing how the suffragettes actually damaged the cause of women's rights.**
- **your own conclusion.**

Emily Davison

The most highly publicised act came when a militant suffragette, Emily Davison, was killed trying to disrupt the Derby in 1913. There is still disagreement among historians about Davison's intentions. For many years, historians assumed that she had deliberately committed suicide, hoping to advance the cause of women's suffrage by giving the movement a martyr. However, more recent evidence seems to suggest that she was merely planning to disrupt the race. Her aim was to force the King's horse to stop and then pin a suffragette banner to its bridle. It was reported that in the preceding weeks she had been practising stopping horses on a lane near her home in Morpeth. Whatever her intention, she misjudged the speed and power of a racehorse in full flight. She was knocked down by the King's horse and her skull was fractured (see Source 24).

The role of the suffragettes

There is little doubt that the suffragettes' increasing violence alienated support for the women's cause. In 1912, Asquith's measure to give votes to some women was rejected by MPs. By 1913, many suffragettes were in prison, and the Pankhursts were co-ordinating the campaign from Paris. The suffragettes had certainly raised the profile of the issue, but they had also damaged their own cause, because they gave their opponents a reason for rejecting women's suffrage. If MPs gave in to violence on this matter, then what hope would they have when the Irish protested violently for HOME RULE, or the dockers or mine workers rioted for higher wages? What was more disturbing, the suffragettes had even lost the goodwill of many of their leading supporters (see Source 25). From 1911 onwards, each time the issue was raised in Parliament there was a bigger majority against women's suffrage.

Did the First World War change attitudes to women's suffrage?

Many historians believe that some voting rights for women might have been gained in 1912, but that the opportunity was wrecked by the suffragettes. In 1918, a section of the female population was given the vote in the Representation of the People Act. What made this possible?

As soon as the war broke out in 1914, both the suffragists and the suffragettes suspended their campaign for the vote. The suffragists, with their formidable publicity machine, worked to persuade the men of Britain to join the army. Meanwhile, Mrs Pankhurst staged a huge demonstration demanding that women be allowed to work in MUNITIONS factories.

As the war took its terrible toll on the male population, more and more women stepped in to fill the gaps. A kind of revolution was taking place. Women gained access to a whole range of jobs which had previously been the preserve of men. They worked as bus conductors, postal workers and farm labourers, and delivered coal. They also surprised the male population by succeeding both in heavy work and in skilled jobs at engineering workshops. Above all, it was women's vital contribution to the munitions industry which stood out in people's minds.

SOURCE 26

	Women 1914	Women 1918	Women replacing men
Metals	*170,000*	*594,000*	*195,000*
Chemicals	*40,000*	*104,000*	*35,000*
Food and drink	*196,000*	*235,000*	*60,000*
Timber	*44,000*	*79,000*	*23,000*
Transport	*18,000*	*117,000*	*42,000*
Government	*2,000*	*225,000*	*197,000*

Women at work 1914–18.

SOURCE 27

Women at work in an engineering workshop.

SOURCE 28

[The work women were doing] … is not of the repetitive type, demanding little or no manipulative ability … it taxes the intelligence of the operatives to a high degree. Yet the work turned out has reached a high pitch of excellence.

From the trade journal *The Engineer*, 20 August 1915.

5 **Why might the changes described in Sources 26–29 be surprising for men in 1916?**

6 **Why would women be less surprised by these changes?**

SOURCE 29

Time was when I thought that men alone maintained the State. Now I know that men alone never could have maintained it, and that henceforth the modern State must be dependent on men and women alike …

From an article by JL Garvin in the *Observer*, 1916.

SOURCE 30

Some years ago I used the expression 'Let the women work out their own salvation'. Well, sir, they have worked it out during the war. How could we have carried on the war without them?

Wherever we turn we see them doing work which three years ago we would have regarded as being exclusively 'men's work'. When the war is over the question will then arise about women's labour and their function in the new order of things. I would find it impossible to withhold from women the power and the right of making their voices directly heard.

From a speech by ex-Prime Minister Asquith in 1917.

SOURCE 31

The front cover of *Votes for Women* magazine, November 1915. The government had talked of creating a 'land fit for heroes' when the soldiers returned.

In 1916, the government began to consider changes to Britain's electoral system. Until then, citizens living outside Britain were not allowed to vote in elections. This was clearly unfair to soldiers who were serving abroad. They wanted to change the voting system to allow the 'hero' soldiers to vote. The campaigners jumped at this chance (see Source 31). Women had shown themselves to be capable and responsible under the strains of war, and by 1916 were even serving in the armed forces. There was no backlash against the women's movement now.

SOURCE 32

Former opponents are now declaring themselves on our side, or at any rate withdrawing their opposition. The change of tone in the press is most marked … The view has been widely expressed in a great variety of the organs of public opinion that the continued exclusion of women from representation will … be an impossibility after the war.

Millicent Fawcett writing in the magazine *Common Cause*, 1916.

SOURCE 33

The history of the women's movement for the last 50 years is the gradual removal of intolerable grievances. Sometimes the pace was fairly rapid; sometimes it was very slow; but it was always constant, and always in one direction. I have sometimes compared it … to the movement of a glacier. But like a glacier it was ceaseless and irresistible. You could not see it move, but if you compared it with a stationary object … you had proof positive that it had moved.

Written by Millicent Fawcett in 1918.

SOURCE 34

I'm against the extension of the franchise to women. I shall always be against the extension of the franchise to women … It was in the year 1918, after the war, that the disaster took place. Had it not been for the war, in my judgement we should have continued successfully to resist this measure for an indefinite period of time.

Lord Birkenhead, speaking just before all women gained the vote in 1928.

1 **What do Sources 33–35 agree about?**

2 **What do they disagree about?**

The Representation of the People Act finally became law early in 1918. The House of Commons passed the new measure by a majority of seven to one. The Bill was given a rougher ride in the Lords, but even so was passed by 63 votes. As a result of the Act, all males aged over 21 gained the right to vote. Women who were over the age of 30, and those over 21 who were householders or married to householders – a total of about nine million women – also gained the vote.

As you can see, the old fears about women having the vote had not entirely disappeared. Although all men now had the vote, MPs were prepared to support votes only for older married women, or women who owned property and were therefore more trustworthy. One leading historian has pointed out that the young, single, working-class women who did most of the war work were the ones who did not gain the vote. MPs were reluctant to enfranchise this new group, whose ideas might be a little too radical.

Women could now also stand for Parliament, and in 1919 Nancy Astor became the first woman MP to take her seat in the Commons. (In fact, the first woman MP to be elected was Countess Markiewicz, but as an Irish nationalist she refused to sit at Westminster.)

Full voting rights for women were not granted until 1928. Even so, for Millicent Fawcett, the 1918 Act was the fulfilment of a lifetime's work. On the other hand, attitudes such as those of Lord Birkenhead in Source 34 had not gone away.

FOCUS TASK

DID THE WAR CHANGE ATTITUDES TO WOMEN'S SUFFRAGE?

Read the following statements:

- **War completely changed attitudes to women's suffrage.**
- **Women's war work did not change attitudes but it did make it impossible for opponents to criticise the idea of women's suffrage.**
- **Men benefited most from the 1918 Act, but the government felt it could not ignore women entirely.**

1 **Read through pages 360–62. Decide what evidence supports each statement.**

2 *Either:*
Choose one statement you agree with and set out in detail why you agree with it.
Or
Make up your own statement about women's suffrage and support it with evidence from the last three pages.

FOCUS TASK

Source 35 is an extract from the obituary of Millicent Fawcett from the *Guardian* newspaper, 6 August 1929.

SOURCE 35

There were three stages in the emancipation of women. The first was the long campaign of propaganda and organisation at the centre of which, patient, unwearying and always hopeful, stood Dame Millicent Fawcett. The second was the campaign of the militants. The third was war.

Had there been no militancy and no war, the emancipation would have come, although more slowly. But without the faithful preparation of the ground over many years by Dame Millicent Fawcett and her colleagues, neither militancy nor the war could have produced the crop.

From the *Guardian* obituary of Millicent Fawcett.

In small groups, discuss the following question: In your opinion, did women gain the vote in 1918 because of four years of war work or 50 years of campaigning?
Agree on an answer which all of your group can accept. You may have to compromise.

12.3 *How did two world wars change the role and status of women?*

War is often an agent of change. One change that was caused, or perhaps accelerated, by the First World War was the fact that women were given the vote. You are now going to study another example: the influence of two world wars on work opportunities for women.

SOURCE 1

A recruitment march for the WAAC.

SOURCE 2

I suddenly saw my job [in domestic service] as a useless one – doing things for lazy people that they could quite well do for themselves … There was talk of 'jobs of national importance' for women as well as men.

Winifred Griffiths talks in an interview about her feelings during the First World War.

3 Some union leaders were labelled unpatriotic for opposing the employment of women workers during the First World War. Do you think it was a fair criticism?

How far did the First World War change women's work?

From an early stage in the First World War, British industry began to suffer a desperate shortage of labour. By early 1916, Britain had up to two million workers fewer than were necessary to keep the country going.

In office-based businesses, the absence of men did not pose a particular problem. Women were soon employed in place of male office clerks who joined up, and by the end of the war half a million women had replaced men in office jobs. Government departments employed a further 200,000 female clerks.

In industry, however, it was a different story, at least to start with. Employers were very reluctant to take on women to fill men's jobs. They thought women would not learn the necessary skills, and also feared trouble from the unions. In fact, the unions did resist the employment of women workers, fearing that women would be paid less and that this would be a threat to men's wages. Most unions did not even accept female members.

By 1916, the shortage of engineering workers was desperate, especially as more and more munitions and supplies, and increasing numbers of men, were needed at the front. For practical reasons, employers were persuaded to take on women workers. The government set an example to private industry by employing women almost exclusively in its own munitions factories. By the end of the war, almost 800,000 women had taken up work in engineering industries. The evidence soon showed that even with very little training they were as skilled as men.

Similarly, women became farm workers, grave diggers, road layers, welders, steel workers and bus drivers. In 1918, the first women's army unit (the Women's Army Auxiliary Corps, or WAAC) was founded, although members were never involved in front-line fighting.

Women workers came from many different backgrounds. Some married women took on their husband's jobs, but it was mostly unmarried women who took jobs in factories. The situation caused by the war was particularly popular amongst women who had been in domestic service. The government called on middle-class families to do without their servants; with higher wages and preferable conditions in factories, many servants did not need much persuading.

What happened after the war?

Many women, especially working-class women, enjoyed the experience of war work. They escaped the restrictions of their homes, supported themselves financially, gained confidence and improved their social life. When interviewed soon after the war, 2,500 out of 3,000 women said they wanted to keep their jobs.

Of course, the number of jobs in the munitions industries declined once war ended, but in fact the other opportunities were lost as well. Women were expected to return to their low-paid jobs in domestic service, or to give up working altogether. People assumed that every woman could rely on a wage-earning man, and that any woman who went on working was doing so out of selfishness.

SOURCE 3

Women still have not brought themselves to realise that factory work, with the money paid for it, will not be possible again. Women who left domestic service to enter the factory are now required to return to their pots and pans.

From the *Southampton Times*, 1919.

> 1 **What do you regard as the most significant change of attitude towards women during the First World War?**

SOURCE 4

They [women] appear more alert, more critical of the conditions under which they work, more ready to make a stand against injustice than their pre-war selves or their prototypes. They have a keener appetite for experience and pleasure and a tendency quite new to their class to protest against wrongs even before they become intolerable.

The magazine *New Statesman* describing the effect of wartime employment on women in 1917.

SOURCE 5

I thought of stacks of dirty dishes to tackle after tea, of furniture that was once polished every week, and now only got done when I had the time. I wondered if people would ever get back to the old ways. I cannot see women who have done worthwhile things settling to trivial ways.

From a housewife's diary in 1942.

> 2 **Compare Source 5 with Source 2. How are these two accounts similar?**
>
> 3 **How are they useful in comparing the experiences of women during the two world wars?**

For many women, however, it was not that simple. They needed the money. The war had killed almost a million people, mostly men between the ages of 18 and 40. Inevitably, in that age group, many women would never find a husband: with three women to every two men, one woman in three had to be self-supporting. The war had also made many women poorer. In 1918, prices were double what they had been in 1914, while average wages had risen far less. Women who had lived on small allowances or fixed incomes could do so no more.

These facts were ignored. Women who had been praised as heroines were now seen as 'blacklegs', keeping men out of jobs. Employers were urged to turn them out. Trade unions were particularly strident in their criticism of women workers. The vast majority of women did leave their jobs. Some did so willingly, but others had no choice, particularly when severe unemployment hit Britain after the war (see page 240). By 1920, there were fewer working women than there had been before the war.

The evidence so far would suggest that the war did not bring about great changes. However, there is other evidence. Some women workers – especially clerks – did stay on, largely because men did not particularly want their jobs. The First World War marked a decisive end to the era of the male clerk: the female shorthand typist took his place. The war also caused a steady decline in domestic service. After the war many had to go back to service as there was nothing else available, but young women who had enjoyed the independence and high wages of wartime work were, not surprisingly, reluctant to do this.

A government inquiry was set up specifically to investigate the shortage of domestic servants. It estimated the shortage at 400,000, and produced a report which recommended changes to domestic service, including fixed mealtimes, days off, paid holidays, a changed uniform, better food and the introduction of appliances to help with some household chores. The government shelved the report, but in any case it might have had little effect. The decline of domestic service was never reversed. As early as 1931 domestic work had disappeared as an occupational section in its own right, being included under 'personal work'. Perhaps this decline would have happened without the war, but it would certainly not have been so rapid.

How far did the Second World War change women's work?

The Second World War required a larger war effort than the First. Although British military casualties were lower, civilian casualties were far higher. Every part of society was mobilised, children were evacuated and rationing was in place from the start.

In industry and commerce, problems were similar to those experienced during the First World War, except that the government was better prepared. From the outset, it was in almost complete control of the economy. The Labour Minister, Ernest Bevin, was able to keep unions, workers and employers happy and committed to the war effort.

By the summer of 1941, over half of the working population was employed by the government or on government schemes. It was not enough, however, and in late 1941 women were conscripted. This meant they had to register for war work at a labour exchange. Unless they were ill, or pregnant, or had small children, they were then sent to work in industry or the auxiliary forces. Some women were reported as working 80–90 hours per week on plane assembly lines. There were 7.5 million women working in 1939, out of a total population of 40 million. Of these, 260,000 women were working in the munitions industry in 1944. Millions became involved in the war effort in other ways, as air-raid wardens, fire officers, evacuation officers or hosts and so on. The war also brought large numbers of women into the armed services, some of whom served overseas.

The novelty of women working in men's jobs wore off much more quickly than during the First World War, because they were doing so in such large numbers. Women workers were taken

SOURCE 6

A wartime advertisement for Mrs Peek's puddings.

SOURCE 9

Manufacture/repair of cars, aircraft	Key
	☐ 1938
	☐ 1944

Local government, fire service

Chemicals, explosives

Farming

Banking, insurance

National government service

Per cent

0 10 20 30 40 50 60 70

The proportion of workers in various occupations who were women, 1938 and 1944.

4 Look at Source 8. Why might the government be both encouraged and discouraged by this protest?

for granted as a fact of life. Eight times as many women took on war work in the Second World War as in the First. For example, during the First World War the Women's Land Army took on 33,000 women as rural labourers; by 1943, it employed around 200,000.

As far as industry was concerned, the unions welcomed women workers much more willingly than during the First World War. In engineering, where opposition to women workers had previously been so strong, the Amalgamated Engineers' Union accepted women as members for the first time. The unions negotiated on women's behalf, although they resisted women being promoted to responsible jobs and were still troubled about women undercutting men's pay. Indeed, in the Rolls Royce armaments factories, women received 25 per cent less than men for the same work; they even received less compensation for war injuries. The TUC successfully lobbied for equal compensation for women and men with workplace injuries (see Source 7).

SOURCE 7

A woman's life is at least as valuable as a man's and her physical and mental well being are just as important. We do not accept that injured women and girls should receive lower wages than men and boys at government retraining centres.

A statement by the General Council of the TUC.

Employers, too, were more flexible than during the First World War. Women who had to juggle family and work commitments were allowed shift work and job shares. Nurseries were provided by the government and employers for married workers with babies. This was a major innovation, considering that before the war women had surrendered their right to work simply by getting married.

SOURCE 8

Women in 1942 protest about a shortage of nurseries in London at a time when government propaganda was urging everyone to 'do their bit'.

SOURCE 10

A woman making hand grenades in 1942.

SOURCE 11

Q: Women have taken on many new jobs during the war. Can you see a day when they might take on your job?
A: There is no likelihood of that.
Q: Can you tell us why you think that?
A: She might have to read bad news!

A summary of an interview with a BBC radio newsreader in 1943.

1 **Suggest reasons why the scene in Source 12 would not have occurred during the First World War.**

SOURCE 12

Women of the ATS (Auxiliary Territorial Service) on duty as anti-aircraft observers.

2 **Does Source 13 tell us more about the changing role of women or the attitudes of American soldiers? Explain your answer with reference to the source.**

3 **'The same work but more of it.' Is this a fair summary of the difference between women's war work in the First World War and their work in the Second World War?**

SOURCE 13

British women officers often give orders to men. The men obey smartly and know it is no shame. For British women have proved themselves in this war. They have stuck to their posts near burning ammunition dumps, delivered messages on foot after their motorcycles have been blasted from under them. They have pulled aviators from burning planes ... There isn't a single record of any British woman in uniformed service quitting her post, or failing in her duty under fire. When you see a girl in uniform with a bit of ribbon on her tunic, remember she didn't get it for knitting more socks than anyone else in Ipswich.

A War Department booklet for American soldiers coming to Britain in 1942.

SOURCE 14

The attitude of the housewife to gainful employment outside the home is not and should not be the same as that of a single woman. She has other duties … in the next 30 years housewives and mothers have vital work to do in ensuring the adequate continuance of the British race and of British ideals in the world.

A comment by William Beveridge in 1943.

SOURCE 15

WE NEED THE WOMEN BACK AT WORK AGAIN

Help to make the goods we want

Join your friends at work

Put more money in your bag

GO, PHONE OR WRITE TO YOUR NEAREST MINISTRY OF LABOUR OFFICE

A government poster issued soon after the war.

4 Do you think Sources 16 and 17 are aimed at the same people? Explain your answer with reference to the sources.

5 How were the problems of the textile industry after the Second World War similar to the problems of domestic service after the First World War?

6 Look carefully at the measures taken by the government after the Second World War. Was the emphasis on full-time or part-time work?

7 List the different strategies and methods used by the government to persuade women to stay in work after the war. Does this suggest that attitudes to women changed?

What happened after the war?

When the civil servant William Beveridge surveyed the likely future of Britain in 1943 (see page 247), one area on which he expressed views was the position of women (see Source 14).

It seemed that the experience of 1918 might be repeated when the Second World War ended. However, in 1945 the situation was rather different from that of 1918. The task of rebuilding after the war required a huge labour force, which even the returning soldiers could not fill. The government speeded up demobilisation of soldiers, and took in many homeless Europeans. However, there was only one real answer, and that was to keep women in the workforce, and even to try to recruit more. The Labour Minister George Isaacs said that, 'in the battle for recovery there are still many front-line jobs for women to do'.

Older married women responded quickly to the government's campaign. Their children tended to be at school, and so they were more free to take up part-time jobs. They generally worked in light industry (such as electrical appliances) or shops, or for local authorities. In 1947, 18 per cent of married women were working, as compared with 10 per cent in the 1930s.

Younger married women were more reluctant to work. The war had not changed deeply ingrained attitudes, and most women still saw their primary role as having children and raising a family. Women's magazines of this period were almost exclusively preoccupied with the image of women as housewives, bringing up children, cooking, washing and looking after the family. After the war, there was a boom in marriages, and women with young families were very unwilling to take jobs.

In response, the government persuaded employers to offer special incentives to attract women back to work. Part-time and shift work helped women cope with the demands of jobs and families. Laundries were installed at places of work. Shops were encouraged to deliver groceries to factories, which eased women's anxieties about not being able to queue for rations (food rationing continued for eight years after the war). The government allocated building materials to nurseries, and asked education authorities to keep schools open late and during holidays to look after the children of working mothers. Women with young children were encouraged to leave their children with relatives or babysitters.

SOURCE 16

★ **MOTHER OF SIX**

FINDS TIME TO HELP

THE EXPORT DRIVE

M RS. KATE VICKERS, of Chaddesden, Derby, shows the fine spirit in which many British women are tackling the shortage of textile workers. Almost 27 years ago, before her marriage, she was employed by British Celanese ; now, although she has a husband and a large family to look after, she is working there again on five evenings a week from six to ten.

Five of her children are still at home, two working and three at school—the youngest is only 5—but Mrs. Vickers finds that she can manage all the shopping and housework during the day and work a shift every night. The family has rallied round wonderfully to help her.

Mrs. Vickers thinks that many more married women with families would welcome evening work. "Mothers of families can't go out to work in the day-time," she says, "but an evening shift gives us the chance to do something to help the country pull through."

An advertisement issued by the government.

Despite the government's campaigns, the textile industry faced a particular problem. It was important that textile production increased, because exports of cloth brought much-needed

SOURCE 17

An attempt to recruit workers into the Yorkshire mills. At this time, tinned pineapples and salmon were real luxuries.

1 **The war gave many women an experience of satisfying and worthwhile work and of financial independence. How might this affect other aspects of their lives?**

money into the country. However, it was extremely difficult to convince women to work in the textile industries. During the war, many textile workers had been moved to more modern, cleaner jobs, with higher pay. Not surprisingly, they did not want to return.

How much real change occurred?

Overall, the war changed employment patterns for women quite radically. The old attitude that working women were a problem had been replaced by the idea, on the part of the government at least, that they were an asset. By 1948, seven million women had some kind of paid work, and the figure continued to rise steadily. By 1957, 29 per cent of married women were part of the workforce. Some things, however, changed very little. In particular, women were still paid less than men: on average they received half of what men earned.

Changes in fashion

The demands of work triggered important changes in women's fashions. During the First World War, cloth and dressmaking materials were in short supply, and the heavy, elaborate layers of undergarments and frills which women had worn before the war were seen as wasteful and impractical. Elaborate hairstyles took up too much time for busy workers and women who now had no maids to help them. Simple hairstyles, plainer clothes and shorter skirts became the norm. Some women even took to wearing trousers, a trend unheard-of before the war.

A similar situation occurred during the Second World War. English designers came up with the 'austerity' look, which used far less material than pre-war fashions. Women could still look stylish, but they were helping to conserve resources.

SOURCE 18

A photograph of Queen Alexandra, 1905. Her dresses had a 15-inch waist.

SOURCE 19

1920s fashion.

SOURCE 20

'Austerity' outfits from the Second World War, by one of Britain's top dress designers. These designs used cheap fabrics (and less of them).

2 Study Sources 18–20 and the other pictures of women on pages 353–66. Write a paragraph explaining:

- how fashions changed from 1900 to 1950.
- why they changed.
- how these changes reflect wider changes in the role of women.

3 Do you think changes in fashion are useful evidence in looking at the changing role of women? Explain your answer carefully.

4 Find examples of each of the following from both wars:

- Women gaining confidence through their work.
- Patronising attitudes towards women.
- Changing attitudes towards women.

FOCUS TASK

ATTITUDES TO WOMEN AND THE FAMILY

A Although during the two world wars women took on new roles, the basic attitudes to women and the family went unchanged.

B The war changed attitudes to women and the family once and for all.

Work in pairs.

1 One of you look for evidence to support statement A. The other look for evidence to support statement B. You can use pages 363–68 but you could also use other resources and your own oral history research.

2 Compile your evidence as a poster.

3 Put your two posters together with an explanation as to why it is possible to find such conflicting evidence on this topic.

FOCUS TASK

WOMEN'S EMPLOYMENT IN TWO WORLD WARS

1 Look at the following statements. Some apply to the First World War only, some to the Second World War only, some to both wars and some to neither war. Write them out and mark them with the correct abbreviation: WW1, WW2, Both, Neither.

> Women took over 'men's jobs' in engineering, farming and munitions.

> Women were treated very much as temporary and second-class workers.

> Women were treated as equals to men.

> Most of the women who joined the workforce were unmarried.

> Married and unmarried women joined the workforce.

> After the war, women were expected to leave their wartime jobs and return to their traditional roles.

> After the war, there was high unemployment, which meant women had very few work options.

> After the war, there was a shortage of workers, which meant that some of the new opportunities opened up to women by the war continued.

> Unions resisted the idea of women workers.

2 Use the statements to help you structure a report comparing employment during the two wars. You should include a paragraph on each of the following topics:

- Describe the similarities between women's employment during the two wars.
- Describe the differences.
- Choose one difference between the two and explain why that difference arose.
- Reach your own conclusion as to which war had the greatest impact on women's employment. Make sure you explain your reasons.

12.4 *Have women won equality with men in the twentieth century?*

It will be clear to you from pages 363–69 that the two world wars had opened up new opportunities for women to work. Women were still not 'equal' partners in the workplace, by any means, but by the 1950s women's employment was seen in a different light from one hundred years earlier.

However, this change was not just the result of two world wars. Other factors were at work to increase opportunities for women and to change attitudes to women and the family. You are now going to investigate some of these other factors.

1. Reliable and affordable contraception

In Victorian times there was no reliable method of contraception available. What options there were were very expensive. Furthermore, spreading information about contraception was illegal. Annie Besant and Charles Bradlaugh's book *The Law of Population*, which contained contraceptive advice, was a best-seller, selling 35,000 copies in 1877, the year it was published – but the authors were arrested for obscenity. Victorian men (and some women) feared that making contraceptive advice available would encourage immorality and independence among women.

Because the Victorian woman had virtually no control over conception, she spent a good deal of her life pregnant. Motherhood kept women in the home most of the time and severely restricted their opportunities.

SOURCE 1

In the last century it was clearly understood that one of the most effective ways of keeping a woman in her place – inside the home – was to make sure she didn't know how to stop getting pregnant ... The women of the first women's movement, at the end of the last century, saw the right to choose motherhood as one of the most important conditions for women's emancipation, just as it is now in the modern women's movement.

From For Ourselves, by Anja Meulenbelt, 1981.

Early in the twentieth century more reliable and affordable contraceptive methods were developed. Male contraception in the form of the sheath became widely available in 1914, and for women, diaphragm caps were available from 1919.

However, attitudes were just as important as methods: contraception was still a delicate issue, so many people were ignorant of the options available. The work of Dr Marie Stopes in educating women about contraception was to change many lives. In 1918, Dr Stopes published two books, *Married Love* and *Wise Parenthood*. These books contained a great deal of sensible advice about family planning, and helped hugely in fighting ignorance and in bringing the subject of sex and birth control into the open.

Although some people disapproved, Dr Stopes received thousands of letters of thanks from women of all classes. In 1921, she opened a birth control clinic in north London, and in 1930 she joined other campaigners to form the National Birth Control Council, which became the Family Planning Association. By 1939, this organisation had more than 60 clinics and birth control was becoming more widely accepted. With the school leaving age set at 14, children were dependent on their parents for longer than in the past. Smaller families made good economic sense, and they also improved the mother's quality of life.

The 1950s saw the introduction of the contraceptive pill. This was the most important development since Dr Stopes began her work. It was an easy and highly effective method of birth control.

PROFILE
Marie Stopes

★ Born 1880 in Surrey.
★ Studied at university in London and Munich.
★ Became the first female lecturer at Manchester University, and later lectured in Tokyo.
★ She was a leading palaeontologist and biologist.
★ She was interested in women's suffrage and rights.
★ She was alarmed at the lack of family planning she saw around her. Her concerns increased after her own marital breakdown.
★ With her second husband (the aircraft manufacturer Humphrey Verdon Roe) she set up the first birth control clinic in 1921.
★ She wrote over 70 books, many about marriage and family planning.
★ She died in 1958.

1 Is Source 1 exaggerated in any way?

2 Would you regard the author of Source 2 as a feminist? Explain your answer.

3 How could Marie Stopes's critics respond to Source 2?

4 Explain the link between contraception and quality of life.

SOURCE 2

I belong to the working class and know only too well how bitterly the working classes need the help Dr Marie Stopes is giving … I thank God every day I visited the clinic when I did. I think it is wicked as well as ridiculous to … call the poor mothers who go there victims – very willing victims and very grateful too. I only wish I had become one sooner. I think us poor mothers was more of a victim by suffering the strain of constant childbearing year after year … we get broken in health, have sickly babies and too often have to go to work to make ends meet … our poor husbands have to suffer for it. You nag at them and they pay toll at the nearest public house.

A letter to Marie Stopes in 1923.

5 The historian AJP Taylor has called Marie Stopes 'one of the great benefactors of the age'.

  a) What do you think he meant?

  b) Do you agree with his view?

In 1967 Parliament made abortion legal. In the early 1970s some schools and youth services began to teach sex education.

Contraception could not change society's attitudes towards women, but it did vastly increase the range of options open to women.

2. Longer lives

In the twentieth century life expectancy for women has increased greatly. In 1870 life expectancy for women was around 45 years. Today it is around 76 years. Contraception has played a part in this improvement – women's health often suffered greatly from the demands of childcare.

However, other factors have had an even greater influence.

Childbirth itself is safer. In the nineteenth century one in five mothers died in childbirth. Beginning with the invention of sulphonamides in the 1920s, the medical improvements described on pages 311–37 have reduced this to one mother in 60,000.

Women's health has particularly benefited from the introduction of the National Health Service and the Welfare State described on pages 332 and 249. Both reforms placed a great emphasis on the needs of women.

Longer lives, coupled with the freedom to plan the child-bearing part of their lives more effectively, have brought about striking changes in the life cycle of women, as you can see from Source 3. At the beginning of this century, a typical working-class mother devoted some 15 years of her adult life to producing and nursing her children. She would expect to be occupied with raising her large family until she was nearing the end of her active life. Today, by the time a woman approaches 40, her children are often nearing adulthood themselves, yet she herself can expect to live for up to another 40 years. She may be ready to start a new career.

SOURCE 3

Born 1970   Leave school Age 18

Born 1870   Leave school Age 12

Married Age 22

Married Age 26

End of child bearing and looking after small children Age 32

End of child bearing and looking after small children Age 42

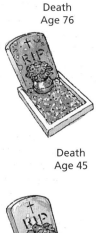
Death Age 76

Death Age 45

A comparison of the typical life cycles of women born in 1870 and 1970. These are based on the averages for the population as a whole.

FOCUS TASK

HOW HAS ACCESSIBLE CONTRACEPTION CHANGED WOMEN'S ROLE AND STATUS?

'Effective and accessible contraception has made women healthier and wealthier.'

What evidence is there to support this statement?

SOURCE 4

A photograph of washing day in Scotland at around the turn of the century.

SOURCE 5

£25 (plus £6.5.0. tax) Hire Purchase available

An advertisement for Hoover washing machines from the *Radio Times* in 1950.

3. Domestic technology

After the Second World War, the lives of many women were improved immensely by new technology. The government built thousands of new houses and improved existing ones as part of the post-war social reforms. By the 1960s, most people lived in homes with gas, electricity and piped water. As a result, back-breaking jobs such as bringing in the coal became less of a feature of women's lives.

Much more importantly, electricity in the home meant that women had access to a range of so-called 'labour-saving devices' which revolutionised housework. Refrigerators kept food fresh, reducing the need for shopping trips. Today, freezers enable people to stock up with food for weeks, or even months. Vacuum cleaners also made household cleaning easier and quicker.

The washing machine removed the back-breaking toil of the weekly wash. In the 1970s, these machines became increasingly sophisticated, spinning and drying as well as washing. Other important technological developments included dishwashers, pre-packaged food and microwave ovens.

The theory was that such 'labour-saving' devices freed women to pursue their careers outside the home. However, it is important to remember that many of these devices were available only to middle-class women. Some feminists have also argued that these devices were not, in reality, labour-saving. For example, washing machines did not save time spent on washing, because washing is now done more often. Most importantly, the assumption remained that it was women who would use these devices, because it was their job to clean the house. Consider how many advertisements for irons, cookers or washing machines you have seen which are aimed at men! The best-selling author Shirley Conran (Source 6) devoted a whole book to how a modern woman could juggle the demands of family, home, career and leisure.

SOURCE 6

No one should waste her life on the treadmill of housework. So decide how much you're prepared to do and when. Four hours a day? One day a week? None? (A high aim, I feel, but good luck to you.) Decide how much mechanical help you want, how much it will cost, and how you're going to get the money to pay for it. Don't use that help to raise your housewifely standards. Use it to get more free time to get out and enjoy yourself. Remember that the whole point of housework is to keep the place functioning efficiently as a cheerful background for living – so live!

Shirley Conran, *Superwoman*, 1975.

1 Why was the change from the washing day in Source 4 to that in Source 5 significant for women?

2 Explain whether you think this was a change for the better.

3 Do you think domestic technology really helped

   a) increase work opportunities for women?

   b) change attitudes to women?

'The glass ceiling'

While the changes on pages 370–72 increased women's opportunities to work, they did not guarantee equality. In the 1950s and 1960s, eight out of ten women were secretaries, factory or shop workers. A large number worked part-time, and women earned less than men for the same work.

SOURCE 7

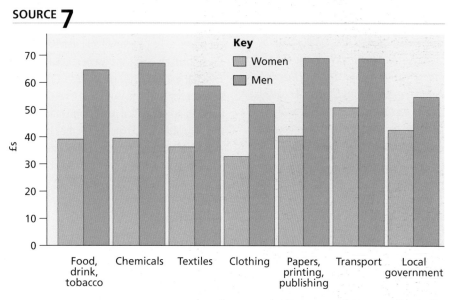

Average weekly earnings for full-time manual workers, 1976.

A report by the National Council for Civil Liberties (Source 8) highlighted the fact that women had made very little headway in terms of achieving top jobs. There were important exceptions: Evelyn Sharp was a senior civil servant in the Housing Department; Grace Wyndham Goldie was a senior figure in the BBC; Barbara Castle, a Labour MP, was a Cabinet Minister in the government from 1964 to 1976. Other women became prominent in business and in politics, but they were the exceptions rather than the rule.

In 1979, Britain's first woman Prime Minister, Margaret Thatcher, was elected. However, she was relatively uninterested in women's rights, and there were still very few women MPs.

SOURCE 8

Law: 103 women practising barristers out of a total of 2073 … Just over 400 women were practising solicitors out of a total of 20,250.
Accountants: 11,000 chartered accountants, 82 of them women.
BBC: When the survey was made, women held six of the 150 'top' jobs in the BBC.
Journalism: About 2000 women among the 18,000 members of the National Union of Journalists. There has never been a woman editor of a daily newspaper and even among the magazines which cater especially for women the majority of editors have been male.
Medicine: 17 per cent of those on the Medical Register were women … Taking all medical students in all schools, just under 24 per cent were women and about 400 qualified each year …
Dentists: 1446 women out of 16,279 on the Register.
Architects: About 700 women were working as architects, against 16,300 men.
Civil Service: In the Civil Service as a whole there were 189 women in the Administrative class out of a total of 2482; in the Foreign Service there were 23 out of 750. In the Executive class there were 358 women in the grades of Senior Executive Officer and above, out of a total of 4326, and 598 out of 19,003 of equivalent level in the Professional, Scientific and Upper Technical classes …
Finance and Commerce: Of 40,574 members of the Institute of Directors, only 850 were women.

From a report on discrimination against women, by the National Council for Civil Liberties, 1964.

SOURCE 9

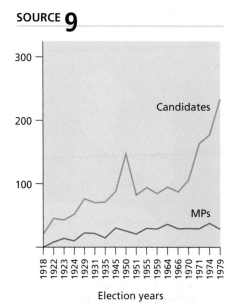

Women candidates and MPs, 1918–79.

SOURCE 10

It seemed clear that emancipation had failed; the number of women in Parliament had settled at a low level; the number of professional women had stabilised as a tiny minority; the pattern of female employment had emerged as underpaid, menial and supportive. The cage door had been opened and the canary had refused to fly out. The conclusion was that the cage door ought never to have been opened because canaries are made for captivity; the suggestion of an alternative had only confused and saddened them.

The feminist Germaine Greer writing about the women's movement before 1970.

SOURCE 11

The highest value is placed on jobs like designing goods, writing adverts or books, and helping companies to think up new ideas. British trade depends on new ideas and men are no better at thinking up these than women.

From *The Female Eunuch*, by Germaine Greer, 1970.

---

1 **How do these figures about boys and girls taking particular subjects compare with the situation in your own school?**

2 **Do you think there is more or less sex discrimination in your school than in other areas of society? Explain your answer.**

These findings provided powerful evidence that equal work opportunities for women were still a long way off. People began to talk about a 'glass ceiling': women could progress in their careers to a certain extent, but then they hit subtle or hidden prejudice which denied them further promotion.

Attitudes

There was clear evidence that men's attitudes towards women were not changing. Women continued to be patronised and treated as second-class citizens. In 1967, a female journalist for the *Guardian* newspaper went into a furniture store to buy a bed on hire purchase. She was told that she had to bring her husband along to act as a guarantor on the deal. When she asked whether her husband would have needed a guarantor, the answer was no. In 1975, the feminist Anne Sharpley pointed out that no other political leader in history had their looks analysed as much as Margaret Thatcher. On the news, reports of major conferences would mention the colour of her outfit, whereas nobody discussed the clothes worn by the male leaders.

A more sinister trend was the increasing amount of domestic violence and other violence against women reported to the police.

Education

By the 1960s, it also seemed that little progress had been made in terms of equality for women in education. Girls did as well as boys in the new General Certificates of Education at Ordinary (O) Level, but far fewer stayed on to Advanced (A) Level. In 1962, men outnumbered women by three to one at British universities.

In schools, it seemed that the culture of women's place being in the home remained extremely strong. In boys' schools, the curriculum offered business and practical subjects, whereas girls' schools focused on arts, languages and domestic subjects. The situation seemed to have changed little by the 1970s. In 1972, 97 per cent of entries for domestic subjects were from girls and 99 per cent of entries for technical drawing were from boys. In 1982, a Certificate of Secondary Education Housecraft examination paper seemed to reinforce the role of woman as the home maker (see Source 12).

SOURCE 12

Your brother and his friend are arriving home for breakfast after walking all night on a sponsored walk. Iron his shirt that you have previously washed, and press a pair of trousers ready for him to change into. Cook and serve a substantial breakfast for them including toast.

From a 1982 CSE Practical Housecraft paper.

SOURCE 13

---

3 **How did the election of Margaret Thatcher as Britain's first woman Prime Minister both help and hinder the work of campaigners for women's rights?**

4 **Do Sources 7–13 present similar pictures of the status of women?**

A cartoon published in the *Guardian* in 1981.

Women's liberation

It was this question of attitudes to women which was the main focus of the women's liberation movement, which developed in the late 1960s and early 1970s.

Local women's groups were started all over the country. Inspired by writers like Germaine Greer (Sources 10 and 11), ordinary women joined together to question what they saw as traditional male assumptions: that the woman would be the home maker, leave work when she married, and give up her independence on the birth of children.

Such groups made many women feel part of a new movement. The groups talked about 'consciousness raising', which meant making members aware of how widespread discrimination against women was. It also meant making women more aware of their own ideas about themselves and the role of women. It meant developing women's awareness of their own skills and their own rights so they could seize opportunities which were offered to them. By 1969 most major British towns had women's liberation groups. They came together at a national conference in 1970 to plan an overall programme of action for the women's liberation movement. They agreed four 'demands':

1 Equal pay
2 Equal education and opportunity
3 Twenty-four hour nurseries
4 Free contraception and abortion on demand.

This launched the women's liberation movement on the national scene. Over the next two decades its leaders campaigned against discrimination in work and civil rights. They had a major impact on public opinion. The publishing house Virago commissioned and published feminist writing. There were also many feminist magazines, such as *Shrew* and *Spare Rib*. There were marches and public demonstrations. One of the most famous gestures of protest was the burning of bras (seen as a symbol of male domination). Sources 14–18 are other examples of the movement's methods and messages.

ACTIVITY

Sources 14–18 are to be left in a time capsule which aims to show people of the future what the women's liberation movement was about, and the methods it used.

Write an explanation to go with each source.

SOURCE 14

WOMEN MAKE
POLICY
NOT
COFFEE

A feminist car sticker from the 1970s.

SOURCE 15

A crucifix carrying 'the symbols of male oppression of women'.

SOURCE 16

A march calling for equal opportunities legislation in the early 1970s.

SOURCE 17

A street theatre event, protesting about the way marriage restricts women.

SOURCE 18

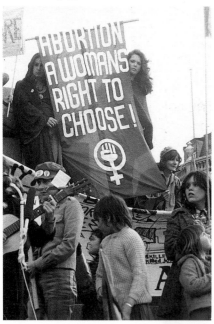

A 1970s abortion demonstration. The logo on the banner was widely adopted as a symbol of the women's liberation movement.

SOURCE 19

One mistake made by Women's Lib, it seems, has been to show open contempt for 'sisters' who actually like to stay at home … Many busy housewives find their lives a good deal more varied than their husbands' working day. And they enjoy cooking, needlework and other pursuits derided by the feminists. Women's Lib may also have erred in ignoring the fact that men, too, often have boring and unfulfilling jobs. Anthropologist Sheila K Johnson notes that 'feminists, when they lobby for greater access to male occupations, always seem to cast their argument in terms of highly visible, satisfying careers such as those of doctors, lawyers, university professors or journalists. They never stop to consider that for every one such job there are at least 10 which consist of working on an assembly line, driving a truck or bus, or clerking in a store.'

An extract from an article in *Punch* magazine, 1973.

1 **How would a member of the women's liberation movement respond to Source 19?**

SOURCE 20

SOURCE **20**

Anita Roddick's Body Shop showed that women could be hugely successful in business.

> **2** Was the Sex Discrimination Act the end of the battle for women's rights, or the end of a phase in that battle? Explain your answer.

Have women achieved equality?

In 1969, the government passed the Equal Pay Act, which meant women had to be paid the same wages for doing the same work as men. This law met enormous opposition from trade unions and employers and was difficult to enforce. In 1975, Parliament passed the Sex Discrimination Act. In theory, this was a great step forward, making it illegal to discriminate in any way solely on the grounds of gender. However, in practical terms it has taken over 20 years of continuing hard work to change attitudes. Women now have more secure employment and benefits such as maternity leave. It is also possible for women to fight injustices such as sexual harassment at work, but this does not mean it is easy to do. Discrimination, like any other form of bullying, can be very hard to prove.

The Victorian woman would be astounded by the freedom, opportunity and independence enjoyed by the women of today. On the other hand, she would be able to see that women still face the dilemma of balancing the demands of homes, children and careers, while most men are not restrained in this way. As Sources 21 and 22 show, great progress has been made but few would say 'equality' has yet been achieved.

SOURCE 21

The Employment Protection Act (1975) gave mothers who had been with their employers for at least two years the right to their former employment (not the same job) after childbirth, to return within 29 weeks following the birth, together with a small amount of paid leave (18 weeks at 90 per cent of earnings). The Act required women to return to full-time employment … [Today] only mothers are assumed to require such leave: fathers are not considered to have a role to play.

From *Money, Marriage and Motherhood*, by Julian Brannen, 1992. This publication was commissioned by the European Union.

SOURCE 22

… by the end of the 1980s, while a larger and larger proportion of the female population was in employment, it was seldom employment at a high level of command, and often not of a permanent kind. In 1987, 3,430,000 part-time women workers fell below the Council of Europe's 'decency threshold' for pay. Under a female prime minister in 1989, Britain was still very much a man's world.

From *The People's Peace, British History 1945–1990* by Kenneth Morgan.

ACTIVITY

A producer of radio programmes for GCSE History has commissioned you to write a short play about women's rights.

The opening scene should include a women's rights campaigner reading Sources 21 and 22 and feeling frustrated and despairing. Suddenly she is aware of a presence. She has been visited by the ghost of Millicent Fawcett.

Write a script for a conversation between these two. Begin with the two sources and how each woman would view them. Think about progress in relative terms.

FOCUS TASK

WHAT FACTORS HAVE CHANGED WOMEN'S ROLE IN SOCIETY SINCE 1950?

1 Copy the diagram right into your book.

2 On the axes, draw line graphs which show the position of women in 1950 compared with 1990. Draw lines to represent progress in:

- work.
- education.
- housework.
- family life.
- political life.
- attitudes to women.

You might want to draw more lines, or split these lines into two. Your teacher can give you a worksheet to help you.

3 Working with a partner, decide where you would put men on your graph.

4 Write a two-minute presentation on the theme: Are women equal to men in today's society?

Your presentation should make clear whether you feel women are equal to men, not equal or only partially equal.

You should use at least six pieces of evidence or examples. At least one example should come from your personal experience.

Glossary

alloy　a mixture of metals. Steel is an alloy made by mixing iron with other materials to make it harder, stronger and more flexible than pure iron

aristocracy　a privileged class of people, usually landowners

bacteria　micro-organisms that cause disease

closed shop　a factory in which a contract is made between a trade union and the employer whereby only members of the union can be employed

coalition　an alliance between parties, especially in order to form a government

copyholder　similar to a **freeholder**, except that copyholders did not hold their own documents of ownership; their rights were recorded in a copy of the Great Roll in Parliament

enclosure　the process of taking open fields and dividing them into enclosed plots which were farmed by one person. The numbers of enclosures increased in the eighteenth century

entrepreneur　the owner of a business who attempts to make profits by using initiative and taking risks

franchise　the right to vote; see also **suffrage**

freeholder　farmer who owned his own land and held his own documents of ownership, known as title deeds

friendly society　an association of workers who paid monthly contributions in return for sickness pay and a 'decent funeral'

gentry　part of the **aristocracy**, just below the nobility

home rule　self-government

laissez faire　a policy of non-interference by government or other authorities, literally 'leaving things alone to sort themselves out'

Luddite　originally a textile worker opposed to mechanisation who took part in riots and machine breaking. The term is used today to refer to anyone who does not like the latest technology

miasma　smells from decomposing material which, in the nineteenth century, were believed to cause disease

mission　a group of people from a religious group, especially a Christian church, sent to a place to do religious and social work

missionary　a member of a religious **mission**

munitions　military equipment and stores

nationalisation　the process of putting industries under government control and ownership

National Insurance　state insurance introduced by the Liberal government in 1911. Based on weekly contributions from employees and employers, the insurance provided payments for the unemployed and the sick, and paid for the medical care of insured workers

navvy　short for 'navigator'; referring to labourer involved in building the canals, and later the railways

Nonconformist　a member of a Protestant denomination that does not conform to the views of the established church, such as the Church of England

outdoor relief　a system of looking after the poor by giving them food, clothing and medical care in their own homes rather than sending them to a workhouse

parish　the main division of local government until the nineteenth century. It was an area, usually an entire village, served by a single church

pauper　a very poor person who was unable to feed or clothe him- or herself and so had to rely on the local **parish** or charity

pauper apprentice　an orphan who worked in a mill or factory. In return for board and lodging apprentices signed an agreement which meant that they were bound to the mill until they became adults. Many were badly treated, working long hours for low pay

permissive　not compulsory (referring to an Act of Parliament)

philanthropy　performing actions for charity or for the good of others

picket　to protest outside a factory or other place of employment during a strike in order to dissuade employees from entering

poverty line　the level below which people are too poor to afford the necessities of life, such as food and clothing

private sector　those industries and services which are owned and run by private companies and individuals (see **public sector**)

provenance　information about an historical source, such as its date or authorship

public sector　those industries and services which are owned and run by the government and financed from taxes (see **private sector**)

puddling　the process of stirring molten iron while it cooks so that impurities are brought to the surface and burned off. The process was developed by Henry Cort in 1784

radical　a person who favours extreme changes in political, social or economic conditions or to existing institutions

smallholders　**tenant farmers** who rented a few strips of land on which to work, rather than having their own farm

socialist　person who believes that the community as a whole should own businesses, rather than individuals

squatters　the poorest people in the countryside in the eighteenth century. They lived on the common land, sometimes working as casual labourers

staple industries　industries providing the main part of a country's production or trade – in early twentieth-century Britain these were coal, iron and steel, shipbuilding and textiles

subsidy　financial aid given by the government, for example to industry or for reasons of public welfare

suffrage　the right to vote in elections

sweatshop　a workshop where employees work long hours under bad conditions for low wages

tenant farmer　a farmer who rented his land from a landowner, usually a member of the **aristocracy** or **gentry**

welfare　financial and other help given to people in need

Welfare State　the range of measures introduced by the Labour government between 1945 and 1951 in which the government took the main responsibility for providing for the social and economic security of the entire population

yeomen　the largest **freeholders**; farmers who owned land worth more than 40 shillings a year

Index

Numbers in brackets refer to the source on that page. Numbers in bold type indicate that information on that topic is to be found both in the text and in the sources on that page.